EMPIRE FIRST:

Churchill's War Against D-Day

GRAEME BOWMAN

First published 2023
001

Published by DNA of Dissent.

ISBN: 978-1-9196440-2-8

This book is dedicated to the men and women who gave their lives so that I might enjoy freedom, particularly:

SERJEANT ALBERT DARROCH,
DCM 6.2.15 - 29.12.41

and to my three uncles

TOMMY BOWMAN

BILL BOWMAN

RICHARD BOWMAN

who did not return from the fighting unscathed.

Thank you, Mum - for every single day.

PRAISE FOR EMPIRE FIRST

Dr. Bowman has done the daring thing, criticising Britain's iconic wartime leader... Churchill is shown here in his real colours as an old-fashioned imperialist and an incompetent strategist.... a lively read with a strong central argument.
Prof. Richard Overy

This is a fine new analysis of the role Winston Churchill actually played in World War II that differs in important ways from substantial portions of existing accounts and beliefs.
Gerhard L. Weinberg, William Rand Kenan Jr. Professor of History Emeritus, University of North Carolina.

I greatly enjoyed Empire First. It is well-researched, clear, fluent... a convincing indictment of the Churchill myth. A book with immense appeal for both specialist and lay readers. It was very satisfying to read such a book on a major subject.
Prof. Sir Tom Devine

Graeme Bowman takes on British icon Winston Churchill and radically re-interprets his legacy, specifically his WWII leadership, when his focus was less on the struggle against fascism in Europe and more on preserving Britain's Empire. Bowman's big, brawling book deserves a wide audience because it presents an essential corrective to the ill-informed triumphalism that produced Brexit. He has mapped out the theatre of war in the Mediterranean and Far East with a thoroughness I've encountered nowhere else.
Prof. Willy Maley

Rips a new aperture in WWII historiography... the best and most original book of the last twenty years.
Don MacColl

*A thumpingly good read from a sound c***! I laughed aloud several times while reading Empire First - a real achievement for a history book! Comprehensive, fearless and very readable, it sparked a real interest in history for me.*
Gary Morton

An informative and revealing account of a major subject.
Prof. Priya Gopal

Empire First is hugely enjoyable. Accessible and knowing, it encourages all serious students of Churchill's leadership during WWII to 'think again'. This is the book I've been waiting for.
Kenny Paton

There's never been a book like this - it's history, but not as we know it! Graeme Bowman manages the almost impossible task of presenting detailed, complex history in an engaging and accessible way. The scope of the book is hugely impressive. Most writers tackle World War II through a narrow European focus but Bowman examines the key events of this period through a much wider lens, challenging the conventional view of Churchill as the great hero who saved the world from Nazism. If you thought you knew all there was to know about Churchill's priorities and preoccupations, this book will make you think again.
Dini Power

Empire First is a fantastic achievement and a great read! I thoroughly enjoyed it. As someone with a fairly limited knowledge of the two world wars, I really appreciate gaining insight into these epic events and Churchill's role in them. The extensive research that underpins this book has been fashioned into a hugely readable and engaging text.
Michael Darroch

A hugely enjoyable book that belies its historical content, a real page-turner which tells the truth about Churchill's wartime priorities - a message which must be heard above the post-Brexit turmoil. Can't recommend this book highly enough.
Gordon Robb

This is a great book. I particularly enjoyed the fact that it doesn't just focus on D-Day but goes right back to the start of Churchill's life to explain why certain things happened. I also enjoyed the tremendous detail the author goes into on each point.
Kiernan Lo

It starts with Zappa, ends with Brando and compares Churchill to Captain Mainwaring… what more could you ask of a book?
Claire Adams

Graeme Bowman explores in extensive detail the chasm between the self-promoting Churchill we've been taught to revere and the bumbling Churchill whose human frailties threatened Allied victory.
Nancy Brown

Bowman's research and dry wit combine to produce a much-needed revision of Churchill's concerns and motivations, leading us into the grim underbelly of a foreign policy in which imperial obsession trumped anti-fascist resistance. Compelling reading and a welcome alternative to the conventional hagiography.
Joshua McDermott

Graeme Bowman re-tells the Churchill story based on fact - and its **not** *what you expect. A real page-turner and a totally fresh take.*
Angus McIntosh

Empire First is a great piece of work - a triumph of data assembly, archive presentation and argumentation.
Jim Doran

Empire First completely recalibrates our nation's moral compass … Bowman's book helpfully illuminates Churchill's imperial obsession which - at times - jeopardised victory over fascism and the safety of Britain's armed forces.
Graham Wilson

Excellent book. Very persuasive and impeccably well researched. Well done!
Peter Strachan

Most historians pull their punches on Churchill and WWII… NOT GRAEME BOWMAN!! This book is a game-changer!
Paul Taggart

An enlightening exposé of the true motives of our national hero. Not quite the staunch anti-fascist of popular imagination.
David Carr

You know the old saying 'don't judge a book by its cover'? Well, Graeme Bowman's scholarly and eminently readable volume on Churchill grabs that maxim by the scruff of the neck and shakes it to death. Dr. Bowman's work crackles with academic research and attention to detail. He charts his course methodically and leaves no stone unturned. His use of archives is reassuringly comprehensive… Bowman is right up there with E.P. Thompson and Eric Hobsbawm in terms of clarity and vigour. A challenging book for anyone with a closed mind, but I give it 10/10.

James Treacy

Graeme Bowman's view of Churchill emphasises the man's character and prejudices - not the myth. Bowman demonstrates time and again how many of Churchill's successes were attributable to others and how - had Churchill had his way - the war would have been extended and the Empire lost… Bowman's book encourages you to make informed choices about our leaders and avoid being hoodwinked by reckless adventurers. I commend it to you.

Philip Hutchison

Churchill's continued deification is one aspect of WWII that's well worth re-visiting and - over 450 pages - Bowman proves comprehensively what a menace he was to Britain's efficient conduct of the war... Bowman makes carefully researched points and arrives at conclusions that are well put and corroborated by evidence. By evidence. *As a corrective to the Disneyfied version of WWII, this is an important work.*

Simon Matthews

A ruthless, evidence-based demolition of Churchill's competence and integrity as a strategist. Greatest Ever Briton… my arse!

Paul Shields, Rebel City

Empire First totally transformed my view of WWII.

Ryan Doran

Don't trash Churchill statues… BUY BOWMAN'S BOOK!!

James Charkow

[Overlord] has been forced upon us by the Russians and by the United States military authorities.

Churchill to Sir Alexander Cadogan,
19th April 1944

All our war experience present and past goes to prove the importance to us of controlling this [Mediterranean] sea, for when we have temporarily lost control we have suffered, and have then found it necessary to take drastic steps to regain that control.

Military Sub-Committee Report,
December 1942

Had we had our way... there can be little doubt that the invasion of France would not have been done in 1944.

General John Kennedy, Assistant
Chief of the Imperial General Staff

Progress demands deviation from the norm.

Zappa

CONTENTS

MAPS

ACKNOWLEDGEMENTS

I'd like to thank every friend and family member who read drafts of *Empire First* or simply asked *"How's the book getting on?"* - your faith and interest kept me going through tough times and is massively appreciated.

I'd also like to thank Professor Gerhard Weinberg who read an early draft of *Empire First* simply because I asked him to. His kindness, generosity and willingness to share thoughts and ideas embody the best academic ideals - I'm forever in his debt.

I'd also like to thank the hugely talented Claire Adams for her fantastic work on realising my book jacket with humour, patience and exemplary skill. Send more work her way at claire_a@mail.com. Noemi Zillmann also did a brilliant job converting Empire First into an ebook available at www.empirefirst.org.

Big thanks also to John, Steve, Paul, Glen, Sid, Malcolm, Vivienne and Jamie who made the world a better place by renouncing mediocrity.

I'd also like to thank library staff everywhere and all who support their work - the world generally becomes a better place whenever a book is borrowed, opened or read.

PREFACE

During the war, American strategists believed that British statesmen prioritised defence of their Mediterranean oil and empire interests over efforts to defeat Hitler. US Secretary of War Henry Stimson argued that the British were *"straining every nerve to lay a foundation throughout the Mediterranean area for their own Empire after the war is over."* Admiral King (US Navy Chief) informed newsmen that *"Churchill's main interest was to preserve the British Empire and that cooperating with the United States to win the war took lower priority."* Admiral Leahy (Roosevelt's Chief of Staff) perceived a *"British desire to control the Mediterranean regardless of how the war may end."* Even Dwight Eisenhower - the living embodiment of Anglo-American cooperation - insisted that *"Britishers instinctively approach every military problem from the viewpoint of the Empire."*

Senior British soldiers confirmed these suspicions. General John Kennedy - War Office Director of Military Operations and Assistant Chief of the Imperial General Staff - conceded that *"had we had our way... there can be little doubt that the invasion of France would not have been done in 1944."* General Frederick Morgan - author of the Overlord draft plan - observed that *"the British authorities proceeded to make every possible step to impede progress in NW Europe by diverting their forces... to other theatres"* and that *"until the invasion of NW Europe was actually demonstrated to be successful... [the Prime Minister] had the conviction it could not succeed."*

Most British historians downplay Churchill's vehement opposition to D-Day, either dismissing it entirely or insisting that he blocked the operation in 1942 and 1943 only to secure success under more favourable conditions in 1944. Bollocks! Churchill opposed Overlord in 1944 as much as he had in 1942-43 and to understand why, we must return to 1875 when the great man was a bawling, lusty babe and Britain acquired an interest in Suez...

Congratulate/excoriate the author via:
graeme@empirefirst.org

Buy more books (print and ebooks) via
www.empirefirst.org

CHAPTER ONE: JOLLY LITTLE WARS AGAINST BARBAROUS PEOPLES, 1874-1901

When you learn to think of a race as inferior beings, it is difficult to get rid of that way of thinking. When I was a subaltern, the Indian did not seem to me equal to the white man.

Churchill to his doctor, Lord Moran, 1952

Whatever happens, we have got
The Maxim gun and they have not.

Hilaire Belloc

I

There are no pictures of Churchill with his father, Lord Randolph.

His mother Jennie's alleged and confirmed lovers included:

Count Karl Kinsky
Viscount Falmouth
William Bourke Cockran
Lord Dunraven
HRH, Prince of Wales
Major Caryl Ramsden
Henry Cust
Marquis de Breteuil
Colonel John Brabazon
John Delacour
Lord Wolverton
Lord Astor
George Cornwallis-West
(married, 1900)
Count Herbert von Bismarck
Thomas Trafford
Baron Hirsch
Norman Forbes-Robertson
Hugh Warrender
Thomas Kincaid-Smith
Paul Bourget
Francis Marion Crawford
Viscount D'Abernon
Lord Rossmore
Sir Charles Dilke
King Milan of Serbia
Montagu Porch
(married, 1918)[1]

On taking office in 1940, Churchill arranged for a picture of his nanny - Mrs. Everest - to be displayed in his Downing Street study.

From the above, it's clear that Churchill enjoyed the dysfunctional upbringing characteristic of his generation and class. At prep school, he was flogged until blood was drawn and only Mrs. Everest's intervention secured his transfer to a more sympathetic regime. His four years at

[1] An active social life implies no moral failing, other than perhaps being too busy to spend time with one's children - Churchill constantly, and unsuccessfully, craved his mother's attention.

Harrow were marked by loutish behaviour and academic mediocrity within a staunchly imperialist atmosphere.

Regarded by his father as too dim for law, Churchill was steered towards the army but outraged Lord Randolph by opting for the more expensive and easier to enter cavalry over the infantry. Gaining admission to Sandhurst at his third attempt, Churchill proved to be an enthusiastic and enterprising cadet, graduating eighth out of 150 in December 1894. Shortly after his father's death in January 1895, Second Lieutenant Churchill was gazetted into the Queen's Own 4th Hussars and reported for duty at Aldershot.

The late Victorian army offered its junior officers an idyll of indolence and indulgence punctuated by intense bursts of soldiering. Britain had abjured major conflict since the Crimean débâcle and the Army functioned largely as a 'police force', enforcing colonial control over the unwilling. Officers enjoyed eleven weeks leave each winter so - in November 1895 - Churchill sailed for Cuba to observe Spanish efforts to crush a popular rising. From the outset, Churchill combined soldiering with journalism in an attempt to fatten his wallet, enhance his profile and build a platform for a political career. Long before the term became popular, Churchill was an 'embedded journalist', reporting on army operations - usually favourably - but with a uniquely Churchillian twist and the implication that - had he been in charge - things would have gone just a little bit better. Churchill stayed in Cuba for less than three weeks, producing five articles for the *Daily Graphic* at five guineas apiece. In Cuba, he came under fire for the first time and developed the penchant for cigars and siestas so irksome to his wartime generals and advisers.

Returning to Britain in January, Churchill was horrified to learn that his regiment was bound for India and he embarked on a vigorous campaign to dodge his duty. India, at the time, was largely quiescent, an imperial backwater resting between spasms of revolt and offering few opportunities for self-promotion. Unfortunately, his efforts proved in vain and on 4th October 1896, Lieutenant Churchill landed in India - and fell flat on his face. Transferring from ship to shore, he lost his footing on the quayside - damaging his shoulder - and thereafter, played polo with his shoulder strapped to his side and charged into battle firing a Mauser instead of brandishing a sabre.

Despite his unfortunate landing, Churchill enjoyed a life of pampered ease at the Hussars' garrison in Bengaluru (Bangalore) in southern India. He shared a bungalow with two other officers who maintained a staff of nineteen butlers, dressing boys, gardeners and laundry maids plus grooms for each individual horse. Churchill's day started with a servant gently lathering his face for a shave while another brewed *chai* in the pantry. Officers and other ranks paraded at 6am sharp but - for officers at least - the working day was over by 10:30am, leaving them free to enjoy a chukka of polo, play cards or swap banter in the mess. When Kipling lamented the crushing weight of *The White Man's Burden*, he probably wasn't thinking of a junior officer's life in Bengaluru. Churchill was more honest in his assessment of the luxury he enjoyed: *"if you liked to be waited on and relieved of home worries, India... was perfection... princes could live no better than we."*

Churchill adored being waited on and was unfamiliar with domestic duties but Bengaluru's torpor grated against his dynamic personality. He craved action and, if none was available, was liable to create his own. Convinced that he would die prematurely like his father, he embarked on a furious burst of self-directed reading to eliminate gaps in his knowledge. While other officers pickled their livers with chota-pegs, Churchill consumed Gibbon's *Decline and Fall of the Roman Empire*, devoured Macaulay's *History of England* and savoured Smith's *Wealth of Nations*, plus works by Plato, Schopenhauer and Darwin. Kipling, Wells and Haggard were read for enjoyment while a series of Annual Registers from the 1870s provided familiarity with modern politics. Churchill also enjoyed William Winwood Reade's *The Martyrdom of Man* and, as he later commended this work to others, it offers insight into his nascent worldview. Reade argued that the age of nation states had been replaced by an era of empires in which colonial conquest was essential for survival. European civilisation was superior to all others so, paradoxically, colonisation by European powers emancipated 'lower' civilisations from error and ignorance. War and suffering were essential engines of progress (hence the title), while Reade despised the *"sickly school of politicians who declare that all countries belong to their inhabitants, and that to take them is a crime,"* a charter which, if applied to the homes of individual readers, would have provoked paroxysms of disgusted outrage. White supremacy, colonial conquest, the inevitability of war, contempt for indigenous rights - it's hard to find a better capsule summary of Churchill's adult views. In 1897, the tribes of the Swat Valley rebelled against British 'emancipation' and provided Churchill with an opportunity to test Reade's theories. Gaining one month's leave from his regiment, he travelled north to join the Malakand Field Force as a correspondent for the *Daily Telegraph* and *Allahabad Pioneer* under the redoubtable Sir Bindon Blood.

The mountainous border between Afghanistan and Pakistan - the North West Frontier in the days of the Raj[2] - has been a cockpit of conflict between indigenous peoples and interventionist powers for centuries. The indigenous peoples have generally wanted to live their lives in their own way whilst imperial powers such as Britain, America and the Soviet Union have sought to impose their will on the region for economic or ideological purposes. During the Raj, the fiercely independent Pashtun tribes (Afridis, Mohmands, Shinwaris) blocked British expansion to the north and west while also inhibiting Russian penetration of British India. In effect, they served as a double-edged sword and in the summer of 1897, the blade was turned against Britain when Pashtun tribes attacked British bases at Chakdara and the Malakand Pass. Churchill had met Blood at his aunt's house and extracted a promise that - should he ever return to India for serious soldiering - he would employ Churchill on his staff. In August 1897, Churchill redeemed this promise and travelled north to join Blood's force. No opportunity to promote the Churchill brand was to be missed.

Blood's force was a punitive expedition and skirmishing in the region was brutal and bloody. The Pashtuns declined open combat so Blood's force resorted to scorched earth tactics in an effort to break their will. As Churchill recorded,

> *with fire and sword in vengeance... we proceeded systematically, village by village, and we destroyed the houses, filled up the wells, blew down the towers, cut down the great shady trees, burned the crops and broke the reservoirs in punitive devastation.*

Both sides routinely slaughtered prisoners and, on one occasion, Churchill observed British Sikh soldiers tossing a prisoner into an incinerator to burn him alive. Churchill labelled the Pashtuns *"little savages,"* describing them as

> *among the most miserable and brutal creatures of the earth. Their intelligence only enables them to be more cruel, more dangerous, more destructive than wild beasts... Their habits are filthy; their morals cannot be alluded to.*

Reade and Churchill had both partially digested Darwin and mangled it into a credo justifying white supremacy and ethnic cleansing. It was Churchill's belief that

---

[2] Raj means 'rule' in Hindi and covers the period 1858-1947 when India was under Crown control.

> *in proportion as these valleys are purged from the pernicious vermin that infest them, so will the happiness of humanity be increased, and the progress of mankind accelerated.*

Promoting human happiness through ethnic cleansing is an unusual concept but paradox rarely perturbed Churchill. Similarly, the possibility that such actions might punish non-combatants more severely than warriors and, in the long run, amplify Pashtun hostility towards British rule did not deter him.

By early October it was all over - the tribes were subdued, British authority restored and the valley pacified. Churchill returned to Bengaluru to start work on his first book - *The Story of the Malakand Field Force* - which proved to be a best-seller, winning Churchill an audience with Prime Minister Salisbury and a letter of praise from HRH Prince of Wales. Churchill was on his way and - bored by Bengaluru's stultifying inertia - looked around for further opportunities to wield pen and sword in the service of Empire and the Churchill name. Fortunately for him, the 1890s was a busy period of empire-building and Africa provided fertile soil for his adventuring.

Like Pakistan and Afghanistan, Sudan has endured intermittent European intervention in its affairs. Egypt's southern neighbour, it governs Egypt's water supply, controls access to southern Suez and borders the Red Sea, a vital waterway for a maritime power such as Britain. Under the Mahdi ('Guided One'), Sudan had expelled its Anglo-Egyptian overlords in the early 1880s and the revived Islamic state sought to expand its influence into neighbouring territories. Crushing Sudan's Mahdist regime would not only secure Egypt and Suez, it would thwart Britain's rivals and fulfil Cecil Rhodes' dream of connecting Cairo to the Cape through an unbroken arc of British-controlled territory. Imperial logic demanded the subjugation of Sudan and General Kitchener - Commander of the Egyptian Army - patiently constructed a railway between Wadi Halfa (on the Egypt-Sudan border) and Atbara (200 miles north of Khartoum) to underpin British conquest of the region. A Sudanese force was defeated outside Atbara in April 1898 and - by late summer - Kitchener was poised to capture Khartoum and crush Sudanese resistance.

A great imperial triumph was in the offing and Churchill was desperate to lend a hand. The only problem was that Kitchener despised unprincipled mountebanks such as Churchill who exploited British empire-building for personal gain. Undeterred by such trivialities, Churchill secured a secondment to the 21st Lancers - a British regiment outwith Kitchener's control - and joined the Anglo-Egyptian army on the plains north of Omdurman in time for the decisive encounter on 2nd September.

Omdurman was an imperial triumph and an epic of industrial slaughter. The Sudanese force outnumbered Kitchener's army 2:1 but whereas the Mahdist army was equipped with spears and single-shot rifles, Kitchener's force was supported by modern artillery, Maxim guns, Lee Enfield rifles and gunboats firing from the Nile. Kitchener ranged his force with the Nile at its back, firing at the Mahdi's tomb to provoke a rash response. The Sudanese obliged with a frontal assault and, within five hours of battle commencing, had sustained a 50% casualty rate (25,000 killed or wounded) while Anglo-Egyptian losses numbered 429. Omdurman also gave Churchill an opportunity to participate in the British Army's last cavalry charge when - towards the end of the encounter - three hundred Lancers slammed into a body of Sudanese infantry and sustained 70 dead or wounded; Churchill was extremely fortunate to emerge unscathed. After the battle, wounded Sudanese soldiers were slaughtered in their thousands by the victorious Anglo-Egyptians, prompting Churchill to complain to his mother that *"the victory at Omdurman was disgraced by the inhuman slaughter of the wounded and… Kitchener was responsible for this."*[3] The Mahdi's tomb was razed to the ground, his bones tossed into the Nile and his skull buried at Wadi Halfa.

Britain and Churchill profited greatly from the Sudanese conquest. His *Morning Post* articles excited great interest and his book of the campaign - *The River War* - enjoyed healthy sales. However, his occasional criticism of Kitchener's conduct attracted attention and sparked a hostile reaction from his superiors. Victorian society was intensely deferential and it was deemed unseemly for junior officers to critique their superiors. Piqued by Churchill's brash insubordination, the War Office issued an edict banning officers from moonlighting as journalists and ordered them to focus on military matters while leaving the reporting to journalists.

Churchill therefore had to choose between soldiering and journalism but the decision wasn't difficult. His writing was generating three times his soldier's salary and he'd served his four-year commission. The army had fulfilled its purpose and he'd no intention of languishing under the command of individuals less gifted than himself. After returning to India for one final polo tournament, he resigned his

---

[3] As the wounded troops were unlikely to receive medical attention, a swift end might have been preferable to a lingering death.

commission in May 1899. Churchill left India in 1899 but - as events would prove - India never really left him.

Churchill was now a name journalist. He was well-connected and had a sparkling reputation as a scintillating military author. However, as a freelancer, he required a constant stream of conflict to generate new material for his books and, once again, Africa obliged when the Second Boer War erupted in October 1899.

By the late nineteenth century, Boers, Britons and Africans - Zulu, Xhosa, Ndebele and others - had been contesting control of southern Africa for 250 years. The Dutch had settled Cape Town and British interest in the region increased as trade with India expanded. Cape Colony on Africa's southernmost tip was annexed in 1814 and Durban settled in 1824. The Boers chafed under British rule - particularly resenting the 1834 ban on slavery - and in the 1830s, several thousand *voortrekkers* headed north-east across the Drakensberg Mountains to establish independent republics in Natal, Transvaal and the Orange Free State. British interest followed - Natal was annexed in 1843 - but the fate of the Boer republics was sealed after diamonds were discovered in Kimberley in 1867 and a huge reef of easily accessible gold uncovered in the Transvaal in 1886. Thousands of non-Boer *uitlanders* poured into the region and Britain demanded they receive full voting rights to consolidate its control. The Boers declined and attacked British settlements in Kimberley, Mahikeng (Mafeking) and Ladysmith in a desperate bid to retain their freedom. Two hundred thousand Boers[4] now faced the full might of the British Empire - surely this war would be no more than the minor *'wrench'* predicted by Churchill?

The war unfolded in three phases. In phase one (Oct 1899 - Feb 1900), the Boers besieged Ladysmith, Kimberley and Mahikeng and humiliated imperial troops at Colenso, Magersfontein and Spion Kop. In phase two (Feb - July 1900), imperial troop numbers increased until they enjoyed a 7:1 superiority and the sieges were lifted. The Boer Republics were invaded and Pretoria captured in June 1900. In phase three (Aug 1900 - May 1902), the Boers employed guerrilla tactics against isolated British telegraph stations and storage depots and Britain, led by Kitchener from November 1900, employed scorched earth tactics similar to those used on the North West Frontier - farms were burned, animals slaughtered and wells poisoned while 100,000 Boer non-combatants (mainly women and children) were

---

[4] This represents the total Boer population of Transvaal and the Orange Free State. Approximately 60,000 Boer farmer-soldiers took up arms against Britain's Empire.

herded into captivity as hostages. The Boer conflict introduced two new phrases to the English language. The highly mobile Boer soldiers were organised into local units known as 'commandos' which provided the term for highly trained raiding forces. At the same time, 100,000 Boer women and children were corralled into 'concentration camps' which, although not intended for slaughter, contributed to the death of 28,000 Boer and 14,000 Black African detainees through a combination of disease, poor sanitation and starvation. Images from British concentration camps at Bloemfontein, Port Elizabeth and Norvalspont evoke the more familiar horrors of Belsen and Auschwitz.

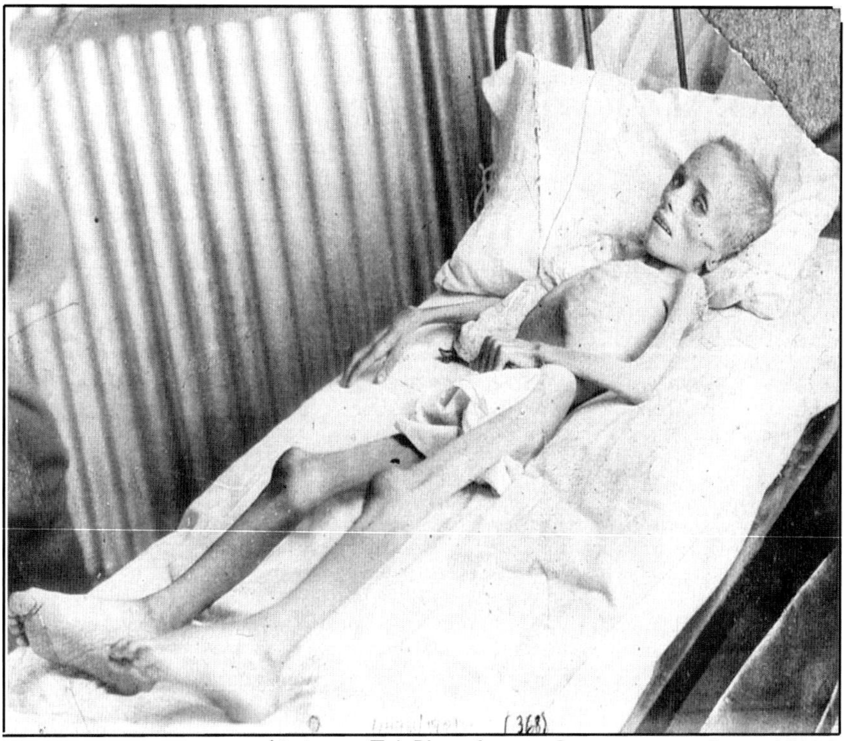

Lizzie van Zyl, Bloemfontein Concentration Camp, 1901.[5]

By May 1902, the camps, scorched earth tactics and overwhelming numbers had done their work. The Boers conceded and the whole of South Africa, its fertile land and mineral resources, came under British control. After the Treaty was signed, Kitchener insisted on

[5] Lizzie van Zyl was a seven year old detainee at Bloemfontein concentration camp who was placed on reduced rations when her father refused to surrender. She died of typhoid fever in May 1901. (Tony Maxwell, *Searching for the Queen's Cowboys* (2010), pp.59-60; Elsabé Brits, *Emily Hobhouse: Feminist, Pacifist, Traitor?* (2018), p.68). This image is identified as being in the public domain in its country of origin and other territories where the copyright term is deemed to be the author's life plus 70 years or less.

shaking hands with each Boer signatory while murmuring *"we are all good friends now,"* a pious platitude from a man who'd wrecked the Boer economy and created the concentration camps.

Such was the backdrop against which Churchill's fourth imperial foray unfolded. Commissioned once more to write for the *Morning Post*, he landed in South Africa in October 1899, basing himself in Estcourt in Natal and making regular trips into the surrounding countryside to gather information for his articles. On the evening of 14th November, he accepted an invitation to travel by armoured train to Frere and Chieveley, a decision which profoundly impacted on his career, though not initially in the manner intended.

The armoured train embodied Britain's military posture in the War's early stages - huge and immensely powerful but also predictable and inflexible. The journey to Frere and Chieveley passed off without incident but as the train returned to Estcourt, it was ambushed by Boers and partly derailed. The British commander was concussed so Churchill - a non-combatant - assumed control, issuing orders, supervising clearance of the line and transferring the wounded from the carriages to the engine and tender. At the last moment, he jumped off the engine to round up more stragglers and the train shunted off, leaving him to be captured by Boer horsemen.

Churchill was livid. Despite firing on his ambushers and issuing orders to troops, he demanded his freedom as a non-combatant but the Boers knew they had a minor celebrity on their hands and had no intention of releasing him. On 17th November, Churchill was transferred to an improvised POW camp at Pretoria's State Model School.

Churchill's life now assumes the contours of a *Boy's Own* yarn fused with elements of Flashman. Arriving at camp, he insisted on joining an escape plan devised by Captain Haldane - the British commander on the train - and Sergeant Major Brockie. All three planned to escape by scaling an iron fence next to a latrine in a poorly lit section of the camp. Their first attempt on 11th December was foiled when a sentry appeared unexpectedly and the three men returned on 12th December to try again but were once more deterred by a sentry's presence. At this point, Brockie and Haldane withdrew - planning to return in an hour - while Churchill remained in the latrine, but when Brockie and Haldane returned, they found Churchill crouching on the other side of the fence, claiming he couldn't re-enter. The return of the sentry prevented Brockie and Haldane from joining him so the two captives watched Churchill scurry off to freedom, knowing full well that Boer security would be tightened following his escape.

Churchill's behaviour on 12th December has excited controversy. Was he motivated by impetuosity or calculation? Did he simply display more daring than his comrades or should all three have escaped together as planned? When the story surfaced in later years, Churchill employed libel law and his full political clout to suppress criticism of his actions, even attempting to browbeat Haldane into exonerating him. In his diary, Haldane attributed Churchill's actions to impetuosity and this probably explains his behaviour. What is clear however is that Churchill failed to display *"the self-control, the discipline, the cooperation [and] the esprit de corps"* which his Harrow headmaster had drummed into his pupils - impetuosity and a disregard for the interests of others would remain key Churchill qualities.

After escaping from the camp, Churchill wandered for three days before knocking on the door of an English colliery manager, John Howard, who was only too happy to help. Howard concealed Churchill on his premises for several days before arranging for the fugitive to travel east by train to Mozambique, concealed in bales of wool.

Churchill's arrival in Maputo on 21st December caused a sensation. The war was going badly for Britain and the plucky young aristocrat's escape was just the sort of derring-do needed to knock bad news off the front page. At the age of 25, Churchill became a household name and the subject of music hall songs. Over the next six months, he and his mother assiduously cultivated his celebrity through speeches, newspaper articles and judiciously placed word of mouth.

Churchill had already contested Oldham for the Tories before sailing to South Africa and with a General Election looming, was swiftly re-adopted as a candidate. The War was a key election issue and Churchill was a *bona fide* war hero. Campaigning on a platform of 'Tory Democracy', jingoistic imperialism and support for Kitchener's farm-burning, Churchill came second but this was enough in a two-member constituency. On 1st October 1900, Churchill commenced his relationship with Parliament which - with only a two-year gap - would endure for six decades. Through a blend of industry, application and brazen self-promotion, the ambitious young man had transmuted the base metal of a dirty colonial war and ignominious capture into the burnished gold of a long-desired political career.

II

Churchill's rise coincided with an aggressive phase of British imperialism. Britain was the world's leading economy in the later nineteenth century and translated this potency into geopolitical dominance. Sudan and South Africa were 'emancipated' in 1899 and 1902, and large tracts of southern Africa (present-day Malawi, Zimbabwe, Botswana, Zambia and Lesotho) joined the fold around the same time. Egypt became a *de facto* protectorate after Sir Garnet Wolseley's army smashed an Egyptian force at Tel-el-Kebir, and British Somaliland accepted British 'protection' after 1888. In central Africa, Uganda appreciated the benefits of British civilisation after 1894, while the Gold Coast (Ghana) and Nigeria became protectorates in 1896 and 1901. Kenya joined the Empire as the East Africa Protectorate in 1895.[6]

Britain was equally active in Asia and the Pacific. New Guinea was acquired in 1884 and Brunei followed in 1888. Despite his vigorous opposition to Britain's invasion of Egypt, Lord Randolph Churchill annexed Upper Burma (Myanmar) during his brief period at the India Office, suggesting that the apple rarely falls far from the tree - consistency was never a conspicuous Churchill quality. The world's leading sea-power also scooped up a series of small but strategically vital Pacific Islands, including Fiji (1874), the Cook Islands (1888) and Tonga (1889). By liberating these countries from the tedious burden of running their own affairs, Britain saw itself as a global 'welfare state', a vast charitable enterprise dispensing peace and justice to the unenlightened. British politicians reconciled this pleasing image with Boer War concentration camps and Swat Valley farm-burnings through a form of 'moral dyslexia' which allowed them to emphasise the positive features of British rule while ignoring its blatant barbarism.

The century between Waterloo and Sarajevo witnessed a tremendous irruption by Europe into Asia and Africa and, as Europe's most powerful economy, Britain was the most successful intruder. Between 1860 and 1914, Britain's imperial population jumped from 174 million to 400 million and - by the latter date - covered one quarter of the globe. Given the relatively small Anglo-Irish population - 42m in 1900 - this expansion certainly represented a considerable application of effort and industry.

---

[6] Of course, it's merely coincidence that gangsters and criminal syndicates often run 'protection' rackets.

Despite these nineteenth-century acquisitions, India remained the 'jewel in the crown' and, in the days of the Raj, comprised present-day India plus Pakistan, Bangladesh, Sri Lanka and (until 1937) Myanmar and Aden, a vast sub-continent containing 300m people in 1900. Controlling India justified British claims to greatness and conferred an aura of invincibility. If a small island nation such as Britain could control a vast territory such as India, surely this reflected divine favour and inherent racial superiority? Controlling India allowed British politicians to strut and preen on the world stage and conferred other more tangible benefits.

Firstly, India was a treasure trove systematically looted by Britain over the course of two centuries. The East India Company gained the right to collect revenues in Bengal, Bihar and Odisha (Orissa) in 1765 and started stripping these provinces of their wealth - Bengal's revenue totalled £4m at that time of which the East India Company retained £1.65m, and men such as Robert Clive and Warren Hastings returned home with vast fortunes.

The looting continued into the nineteenth century. India was occupied and had to pay all the costs associated with its occupation including 'home charges' such as maintaining the Indian Army, government contracts fulfilled in Britain, India Office administrative costs and pensions for retired officials. Forty percent of India's budget went on the Army alone,[7] and India also had to pay for Indian troops stationed abroad on British service - India therefore paid for its own occupation while subsidising the colonisation of other countries.

India was also a huge market for British goods. In the 1890s, India absorbed a full twenty per cent of British industrial output, an arrangement which kept British workers in jobs and its factories in profit. The trading relationship was also rigged in Britain's favour - the rupee was tied to silver (which became increasingly plentiful as the century wore on) while sterling was tied to gold (which remained relatively scarce), ensuring that Indian goods became progressively cheaper. In simple terms, India exported raw materials - such as cotton - to Britain and imported blouses and bloomers in return.

India also provided the Empire with huge resources of cheap labour. Between 1830 and 1916, more than one million Indians were transported overseas to work as indentured servants in locations such

---

[7] British troop numbers increased after 1857 and - by 1901 - the Indian Army comprised 143,000 Indian troops and 66,000 British troops (David Omissi, *The Sepoy and the Raj: The Indian Army, 1860-1940* (1998), p.133).

as Mauritius and Trinidad. Indentured servitude is a form of free market slavery in which the servant contracts to work for the employer at a fixed rate for a fixed term (usually five years). The servant is free at the end of the contract and receives a wage but must meet his living costs from his wage. Indentured servitude always favours the employer as the relationship in unequal at the outset, and the system continued until 1917 when 16,000 workers were still contracting.

Grinding poverty, hunger and unemployment drove many Indians into the Indian Army. Indian troops were first deployed outside of India to capture Manila in 1762 and the practice increased after the 1858 Mutiny (or Rebellion) when the Raj thought it wise to send large numbers of Indian troops overseas. Between 1838 and 1920, Indian troops served overseas on nineteen separate occasions, and more than one million Indians served the Empire during 1914-18, mainly in the Middle East. Given that India paid all the costs associated with these deployments, Lord Salisbury's description of India *"as an English barrack in the oriental seas from which we may draw any number of troops without paying for them"* is apposite.

India conferred huge benefits on Britain in the form of money, manpower, markets and materials which explains why India - 4,500 miles distant from Britain - was at the heart of the imperial project. According to Indian Viceroy Lord Curzon,

> *as long as we rule India, we are the greatest power in the world. If we lose it, we shall straightaway drop to a third rate power.*

Churchill echoed Curzon's assessment. When he felt that the Government of India Bill[8] was threatening British control, he warned that

> *our continued existence as a great power is at stake. The loss of India would mark and consummate the downfall of the British Empire. That great organism would pass at a stroke out of life into history. From such a catastrophe there could be no recovery.*

There can be no blunter assessment of India's vital importance to Britain. India made Britain great and so - *ipso facto* - Britain must

[8] see Chapter 6.

control India. This credo shaped British policy and guided British policy-makers for six decades prior to World War Two, producing some questionable strategic choices during that conflict.

However, India lies 4,500 miles distant from London as the crow flies and 10,500 miles distant via the Cape of Good Hope. In an era reliant on sea transport and postal communications, this vast distance compromised British authority over India, a fact demonstrated by the slow response to the 1857 Mutiny[9] when some British detachments required four months to travel to India to quell the disturbance. Remoteness hampered British rule over India, and anything which brought Britain and India closer together carried the greatest implications for the Empire. The opening of the Suez Canal in 1869 represents a critical juncture in world history. Whereas the Queen's Bays needed four months to sail from Canterbury to Kolkata via the Cape in 1857, Churchill required only 23 days to sail from Southampton to Mumbai via Suez in 1896. British politicians had opposed the Canal while it was under construction[10] but, as soon as it opened, desperately sought to gain control.

Map 1: Suez - imperial fulcrum

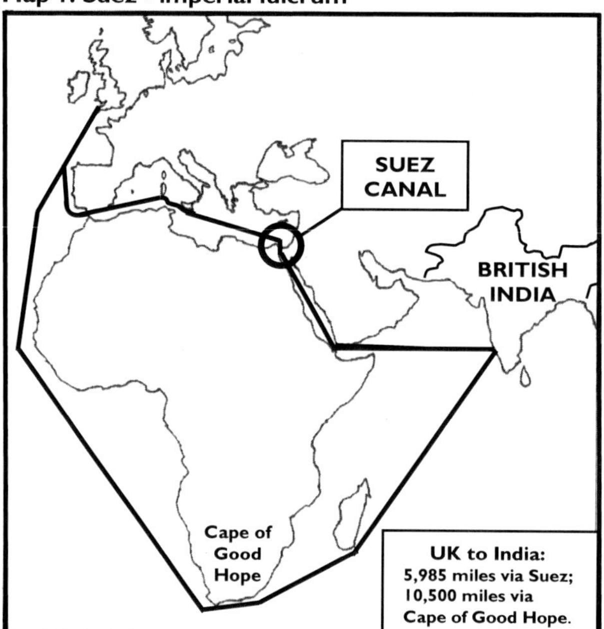

---

[9] Britain characterised the events of 1857-58 as a 'mutiny' while many Indians view these events as part of India's struggle to regain its sovereignty.

[10] Britain suspected that construction of the Canal would carry great implications for its eastern Empire and resented that it was built under French auspices.

The only problem was that Suez flowed through the territory of another state (Egypt) which was under the control of a rival empire (Ottoman Turkey) and the Suez Canal Company was French. This affronted the world's leading power - the fastest route to its greatest possession was controlled by Johnny Foreigner who might, at any moment, block the Canal and force Britain back onto the slower and more hazardous Cape route. Imperial logic demanded British control of Suez.

Fate, finance and the vagaries of great power politics now intervened in Britain's favour. In the mid-1870s, Egypt's Khedive (Viceroy) was deep in debt but couldn't secure a Turkish loan because Turkey itself was on the verge of bankruptcy. His 44% stake in the Suez Canal Company formed one of his few realisable assets and France was reluctant to buy these shares because it required British support to restrain Germany in Europe.[11] Without major competition, Britain therefore purchased the Khedive's shares for the modest sum of £4m in November 1875, twelve months after Churchill entered the world. In Parliament, Disraeli described the purchase as a political speculation

> *calculated to strengthen the Empire… [the people of England] want the Empire to be maintained, to be strengthened… because they think we are obtaining a great hold and interest in this important portion of Africa - because they believe it secures to us a highway to our Indian Empire and our other dependencies, the people of England have from the first recognised the propriety and the wisdom of [this] step.*

Disraeli's Lord Chancellor summarised the symbiosis between Suez and Empire by confirming that

> *it is now the Canal and India; there is no such thing now to us as India alone. India is any number of ciphers; but the Canal is the unit that makes these ciphers valuable.*

Five months later - in March 1876 - Queen Victoria proclaimed herself Empress of India. Britain had been acting imperially for centuries and Victoria wanted the title largely because King Wilhelm I of Prussia had recently elevated himself to Kaiser but the timing of Victoria's elevation - directly after the Canal shares' acquisition - illustrates the synergy between Canal, India and Empire. Britain was now officially an

---

[11] Germany (as Prussia) had defeated France in the 1870-71 Franco-Prussian War and tension between the two countries was running high in 1875-76.

'Empire' and four of Victoria's descendants carried the title 'King-Emperor' until India regained its sovereignty in 1947.

Having acquired an interest in Suez, Britain moved quickly to safeguard its investment. Britain and Turkey had a joint interest in excluding Russia from the Mediterranean, so Britain supported Turkey in the peace conference following the 1877-78 Russo-Turkish War and gained Cyprus as a thank you. Cyprus lacks deep water facilities but is only 230 miles north of Egypt and offers a handy place to store troops to respond to crises throughout the region. Britain maintains Sovereign Base Areas on Cyprus to this day at Akrotiri and Dhekelia.

The value of Cyprus became apparent when Egyptian nationalists attempted to reduce British, French and Turkish control over their country. Egypt was part of Turkey's Ottoman Empire and Turks dominated Egyptian society while Britain and France controlled the country's political and economic development. In 1879, they forced Turkey to depose Khedive Ismail (who'd sold his shares to Britain) and replace him with his more pliant son Tawfiq, who promptly announced plans to reduce the size of his army and exclude Egyptians from the officer class. This sparked a revolt led by Colonel Ahmed Arabi who proposed to introduce a draft constitution, a representative assembly and full equality for Egyptians. This assertion of independence alarmed Britain which had only recently acquired an interest in Egypt and feared a nationalist takeover. In a grim foretelling of later events, British ships bombarded Alexandria and landed a force at Port Said with the goal of seizing Cairo. Sir Garnet Wolseley's British army smashed Arabi's force at Tel-el-Kebir on 13th September 1882 and occupied Cairo on the 15th. In the aftermath of invasion, Tawfiq was restored but it was clear where real power lay. Egypt remained within the Ottoman Empire - Britain had no wish to offend its anti-Russian ally - but it became a *de facto* British protectorate, backed up by a British occupying force and British control of Egyptian debts, and the 1888 Treaty of Constantinople compelled Tawfiq to govern in line with the British Consul General's advice. In the aftermath, Britain developed Alexandria as a major naval base to dominate the eastern Mediterranean and guard northern Suez and, by 1890, three-quarters of all ships navigating the Canal were British.

Domination of Egypt, Canal shares, possession of Cyprus, Alexandria's development - all these events reinforced British control over Suez but the Canal was only one link in a chain joining Britain to its eastern Empire. Suez linked the Mediterranean with the Red Sea but both these waters flow into larger oceans (the Atlantic and Indian) through narrow channels at either end - Gibraltar in the west and Bab-el-Mandeb in the east - and Britain had to control **all** these areas to fully exploit its domination of Suez. Britain had to control the entire Med-Red Zone (the Mediterranean-Red Sea basin) if its ships were to enjoy

Map 2: British Mediterranean and Middle East interests

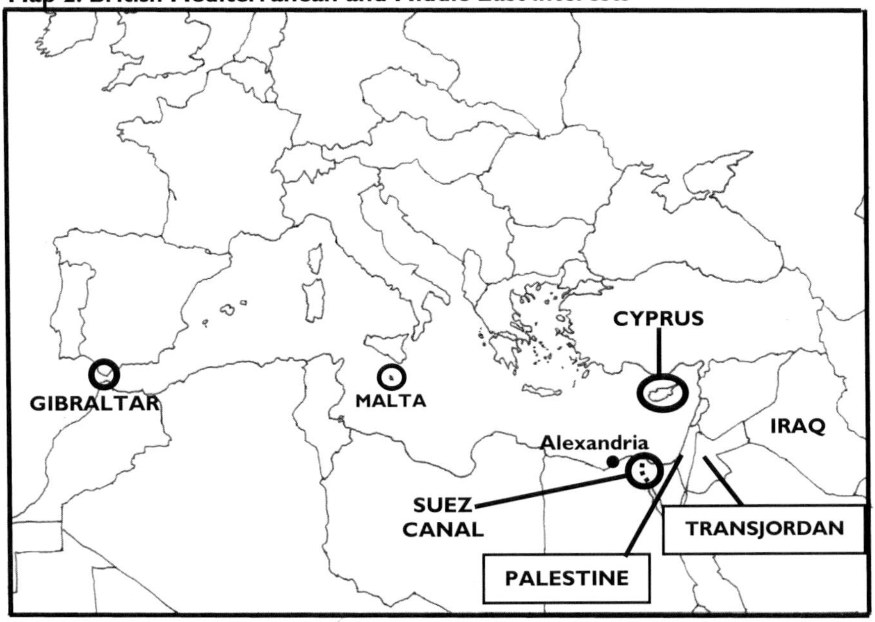

unrestricted access to India and in realising this goal, Britain was aided by a legacy of imperial acquisition, naval supremacy and a programme of vigorous land-grabbing before 1914.

Parliament passed the Naval Defence Act in 1889 which committed Britain to the 'two-power standard', allocating £21.5m to build seventy ships over a five-year period. Under this Act, the Royal Navy was to match the next two largest navies combined and the 1893 Spencer Programme funded the construction of 7 battleships, 30 cruisers and 82 destroyers. By such means, Britain hoped to retain full and unambiguous control over the world's oceans but merely instigated an arms race which fuelled the cataclysm of 1914-18.

Britain also operated the world's largest merchant fleet - half the global total - but naval and merchant ships need friendly fuel depots, refitting yards and ports to provision them so - in the later nineteenth century - Britain developed a series of bases between Gibraltar and Bab-el-Mandeb to ensure safe and speedy passage to India.

- Gibraltar was acquired from Spain in 1704 and progressively fortified to enable Britain to control the flow of traffic between the Atlantic and western Mediterranean. Gibraltar remains a British overseas territory to this day.

Map 3: British interests, Horn of Africa and Middle East

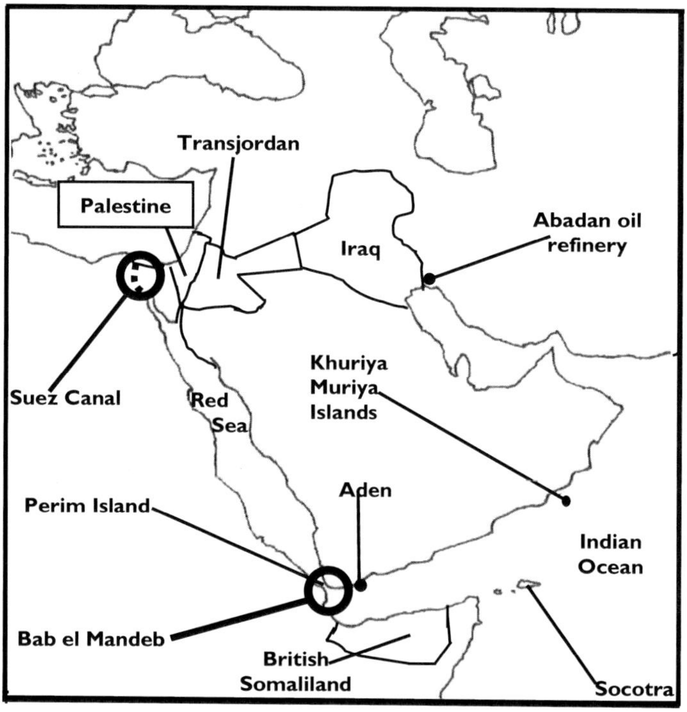

- Britain gained Malta from France in 1814, developing it as a base for its Mediterranean fleet.

- Britain acquired Sudan - to protect Egypt and southern Suez - following Omdurman and leased the port of Aden on the Yemeni coast from a local sheikh. Aden was developed into a major re-fuelling station which allowed Britain to control the Indian Ocean and govern passage through Bab-el-Mandeb where the gap between Africa and Arabia shrinks to eighteen miles. Britain's grip on the region was consolidated through the acquisition of Perim Island - in the middle of Bab-el-Mandeb - in 1857 and the Khuriya Muriya islands off the Omani coast in 1868. British Somaliland was acquired in 1888 to provide Aden with fresh food and became known as 'Aden's butcher shop'.[12]

---

[12] In response to reported German interest, the British Government also concluded a protectorate treaty with the Sultan of Qishn and Socotra in 1886, obliging him to inform HM Government of any foreign power(s) wishing to develop facilities on Socotra. (R. J. Gavin, *Aden Under British Rule, 1839-1967* (1975), p.198).

Aden, Malta, Gibraltar, Alex, Cyprus all recall an era in which Britannia waived the rules. These bases and garrisons were acquired for one predominant reason - to facilitate the safe and swift passage of British ships between Europe, India and the Far East, particularly Singapore and Malaya. Controlling the Med-Red Zone obsessed British policy-makers for sixty years prior to World War Two, a policy objective which permeated their DNA and seeped into their bones. When these statesmen glanced at a world map, the territory between Gibraltar and Bab-el-Mandeb glowed in brilliant flaming red. Dominating the Mediterranean basin was the principal obsession of British policy makers for six decades prior to 1939 and this over-riding priority shaped the consciousness of imperial soldiers and statesmen - such as Churchill - who matured during this era. When fresh threats emerged from new quarters in the 1930s and 1940s, they proved extremely reluctant to jettison this Mediterranean obsession, even when new Allies and new circumstances demanded fresh priorities.

III

Britain's Empire reflected its economic supremacy. Britain dominated the nineteenth century global economy, enabling Britain to build the world's biggest navy, maintain multiple armies in the field, equip them with advanced weaponry and ferry in reinforcements as required. A powerful synergy operated between Empire and economy but, over time, this relationship vitiated the foundations of imperial power and political power and economic supremacy increasingly transferred to Germany and America. A few choice facts illustrate the corrosive interplay between imperial expansion and economic decline:

Firstly, Britain's Empire was much larger than those of its rivals. In 1909, Britain's Empire covered 12.7 million square miles - one quarter of the earth's surface - making it three times larger than the French Empire and ten times larger than that of Germany. At its peak, 458 million people enjoyed *'pax Britannica'* while only 113 million lived under French rule.

British foreign investments also overshadowed those of its rivals. In 1914, British overseas investments totalled £4.1bn while France invested £1.9bn, Germany £1.2bn and America £700m.

In the later nineteenth century, British overseas investment increasingly migrated towards imperial destinations. In 1854, Britain had £260m invested abroad, 55% in Europe and 5% in the Empire.

Sixty years later, this ratio was reversed with 46% of a much larger sum (£4.1 billion) invested in the Empire and only 5% in Europe. The Empire - the Dominions in particular - had become the prime focus for British overseas investment and 80% of all City of London capital issues in 1913 were for foreign ventures.

While billions were pouring into Canada, Australia, South Africa and India, British domestic industry was starved of investment. Between 1870-1913, Germany and America invested 12% of their respective GNP in domestic projects while Britain invested 7%. During this same period, 21.7% of American GNP was invested in domestic capital formation, while Germany invested 12.8% and Britain 8.7% (two-fifths of the American total). The impact of such disparities was telling. Between 1870 and 1913, German industrial efficiency increased by 2.6% per annum, American productivity grew by 1.5% while British performance stumbled along at 0.6%. By 1914, German and American firms were out-performing British businesses, expelling them from markets they'd dominated for decades and capturing market share. The profits generated were re-invested in further efficiency improvements which, in turn, increased market share and reduced profits for British businesses. This bleak trend of Britain as economic laggard originated in the later nineteenth century as the Empire neared its peak. As M.W. Kirby noted, *"no country before or since [1870-1913] ... invested as high a proportion of its resources abroad over such a sustained period."* In 1913, 9% of British GNP was invested overseas as Britain's financial houses boosted the fortunes of Melbourne, Toronto and Durban while businesses in Glasgow, Liverpool and Manchester stagnated. British banks and businesses failed to invest in the large-scale capital-intensive industries - motor vehicles, chemicals, electrical engineering - which would dominate the twentieth century and, as a result, Britain increasingly lost its ability to pay its way in the world, relying heavily on American munificence during World War Two.

In 1900, such dismal prospects lay in the future. As Churchill embarked on his glittering political career, everything in the imperial garden seemed rosy. Britain had the world's largest navy and the world's mightiest empire. It produced 33% of world manufacturing exports and invisible earnings generated £200 million per annum. Even as the Empire undermined the economy, it offered illusory protection from the troubles which lay ahead. India remained a vast dumping ground for British manufacturing and foreign investments generated 8.5% of British GDP. Like *latrodectus mactans,*[13] the Empire slowly smothered its prey in silk before devouring it.

---

[13] The black widow spider.

The only clearly visible fly in the ointment was the series of military reverses Britain suffered at the hands of sixty thousand Boer farmers. How could two miniscule republics defy the will of the world's mightiest Empire? Was Britain nothing more than a 'paper tiger'? The humiliations at Spion Kop, Colenso and Magersfontein reverberated throughout Britain's political and military establishment demanding answer and resolution.

IV

The Army Churchill joined in 1895 was rooted in the seventeenth century Restoration. The zeal and competence of Cromwell's New Model Army had terrified the ruling elite so, on regaining the throne, the Stuarts neutered the Army's ability to challenge its authority. Starting in 1681, officers were forced to purchase commissions from the Crown, a practice which favoured wealth and status over talent, with the added advantage of excluding undesirable elements (i.e. capable men of humble origin) from the officer corps, ensuring its domination by the gentry. Such men considered it honourable to serve the Crown in the style of their forefathers and enjoyed the prestige conferred by military rank. Independently wealthy, they eschewed such notions as 'working for a living' and - a further benefit to the Crown - happily funded their own living expenses (i.e. mess bills, uniforms, horses etc). Nineteenth-century officers' salaries were never more than an honorarium, a nominal thank you for services rendered and a huge gulf separated officers' salaries from their requirements as 'gentlemen'. When Churchill joined the 4th Hussars in 1895, the £500 gap between his 'gentleman's living expenses' and his officer's salary came out of Churchill family funds - a skilled craftsman of the time earned around £100 per year so one can appreciate how such a system restricted recruitment to a rather shallow and uninspiring gene pool.

This mode of recruitment perpetuated conservatism, amateurism, snobbery and hostility to innovation. Officers enjoyed generous leave entitlements - approximately four or five months per year - and promotion was on the basis of seniority, perpetuating the notion of 'Buggins' turn' which has blighted Britain for decades. Regiments reserved the right to veto candidates they considered unsuitable, further restricting recruitment to a narrow and unrepresentative caste. Training outside of the Engineers and Artillery was patchy and irregular and anyone interested in modernisation was branded a dangerous radical. Regiments resembled small families, reflecting the feudal values of the society from which they sprang, while individual officers preferred country pursuits - huntin', ridin' and fishin' - over more subversive activities such as readin' or thinkin'.[14] James Mill once described Britain's Empire as a *"vast system of outdoor relief for the upper classes"* and the same might be said of Britain's pre-1914 army.

Even when the system was reformed - purchasing commissions was banned in 1871 - the essential elements of the old system persisted. Salaries remained an honorarium rather than a living wage, officers paid their own living expenses and regiments reserved the right to blackball 'blackguards and bounders'. Promotion reflected length of service and three impeccably establishment figures attest to the mediocrity of British officer recruits before 1914.

Bernard Montgomery entered Sandhurst in 1907 and became Britain's best-known soldier of World War Two. A bishop's son, Monty was alarmed to discover that a gap would separate his salary from his living costs and felt that such a system discouraged talent, noting in his *Memoirs* that *"in those days the Army did not attract the best brains in the country."* Montgomery passed the Sandhurst entrance exams with ease and was

> *astonished to find later that a large number of my fellow cadets had found it necessary to leave school early and go to a crammer in order to ensure success in the competitive entrance examination.*

Monty joined the Warwickshires - an unfashionable county regiment - and served for five years in India to reconcile his expenses with his income.

Lt. Gen. Brian Horrocks commanded XIII Corps in North Africa and was described by Eisenhower as *"the outstanding British general under Montgomery."* Horrocks entered Sandhurst in 1912 and describes his peer group thus:

> *Up [until my graduation] my life had been typical of that led by many young men with average or slightly below average intelligence who entered the British Army in those days. I was a games addict, did as little work as possible and seemed all set for a normal, somewhat humdrum, military career.*

Horrocks proved to be an able and imaginative soldier but how many

---

[14] Churchill, of course, bucked this trend.

of his peers *"with average or slightly below average intelligence"* performed with comparable skill?

Churchill entered Sandhurst in 1893 at the third attempt with the aid of a crammer. In *My Early Life*, he compared the crammer's teaching methods to a *"renowned system of intensive poultry-farming,"* observing that instruction was so heavily focused on exam success that *"no one who was not a congenital idiot could avoid passing thence [from the crammer] into the army."*

Two of the above comments are humorous and somewhat self-deprecating but the tenor is clear - British officer recruits in the years before 1914 were, with some notable exceptions, not particularly bright. This is important because the officer-cadets of 1900-1914 would be the generals of 1939-45 and if they were mediocre, Britain's armies would perform poorly against more professional opponents and this is exactly what happened. Britain's armies were trounced by the Wehrmacht during 1940-42 and their performance thereafter was not exceptional. Further reasons for this are considered later but Churchill and his advisers certainly considered poor leadership a contributory factor. Writing after the Singapore surrender, Lt. Gen. Henry Pownall asserted that

> *our [career officers] regard [war] as an upsetting, rather exhausting and distinctly dangerous interlude in the happier, more comfortable and more desirable days of peace-soldiering... We need... a tougher army... an army which is regarded by the people as an honourable profession to which only the best can gain admittance ... where the competition is in efficiency, not in games or pipe-blowing and band concerts... Training must be harder, exercises must not be timed to suit meal-times.*

Pownall was no maverick. He served as Wavell and Mountbatten's Chief of Staff but even he was forced to concede that many of his peers were unsuited to modern technological warfare. Britain's disastrous performance in the War's opening years shattered Churchill's belief in the prowess of Britain's Army and informed his profound aversion to Overlord - he doubted the British Army's ability to defeat German forces in a decisive encounter.

Britain's military malaise affected the body as much as the head. Alarmed by early Boer victories, thousands of young men rallied to the cause during 1899-1902 only to be rejected as physically unfit - throughout the country, 30% of young men volunteering for Army service during 1899-1902 were rejected on medical grounds, a figure which rose to six in ten in large cities such as Manchester and Liverpool. At this point, Britain was 'the greatest Empire the world had ever seen' so the physical incapacity of so many young Britons raised serious questions about poverty and wealth distribution. While the Boer War recruitment scandal was unfolding, researchers such as Charles Booth and Seebohm Rowntree were identifying the root causes of urban poverty. In his 1901 classic *Poverty, A Study Of Town Life*, Rowntree discovered that a full 10% of York's population lived with hunger and malnutrition on a daily basis as their income - no matter how efficiently expended - was simply insufficient to maintain basic physical health. A further 18% fluttered so close to poverty that spending a single farthing on an indulgence such as a newspaper or a tram ride pushed them below the poverty line. Rowntree's criteria for attaining 'basic physical health' were extremely frugal so it's likely that an even higher proportion of York's population lived in dire poverty, but it's worth noting that the 28% Rowntree identified as living in 'primary' or 'secondary' poverty tallies almost exactly with the 30% of young men rejected for military service - their defective vision, rickets and tuberculosis rooted in malnutrition suffered since birth.

Rowntree was not alone in highlighting the scandal of poverty and inequality. Trades unions and socialists organised around these issues and a host of activists, researchers and writers investigated the subject. Millionaire ship owner Charles Booth investigated poverty in London's East End throughout the 1890s and discovered that one-third of the city's population lived in what he termed 'abject poverty', while the American author Jack London spent three months in the East End slums and workhouses, writing up his experiences in *The People of the Abyss*. Where Booth and Rowntree were objective, London railed against poverty in powerful, evocative language.

> *The greater number of [English folk] are vilely housed, do not have enough fuel to keep warm, and are insufficiently clothed. A constant number never have any houses at all.... Many are to be found, winter and summer, shivering on the streets in their rags. They have good times and bad. In good times, most of them manage to get enough to eat, in bad times they die of starvation... there are forty million of the English folk, and 939 out of every thousand of them die in poverty, while a constant army of eight million struggles on the ragged edge of starvation.*

The coincidental publication of such works with the Boer War recruitment scandal triggered a crisis of confidence in Edwardian society. If Britain was the world's greatest Empire, why were so many of its young people malnourished? If so many young Britons were unfit to shoulder a rifle for the Army, how could Britain hope to retain its overseas possessions? And if young Britons were so physically stunted, what price 'white racial superiority'?

These questions - and Germany's emergence as a rival - agitated Edwardian society, precipitating a split within its ruling class between those (mainly Liberals) who demanded a constructive response to sustain British supremacy and others (mainly Tories) who advocated tried and tested methods. The issue polarised Edwardian society and anyone wishing to get on had to have an opinion, there was no scope for fence-sitting. Winston Churchill was not, by nature, a fence-sitter and was desperately keen to get on. While he'd previously shown little interest in working people - except as servants - he cared deeply about the Empire and appreciated the connection between the two, noting - after reading Rowntree's work - that there was *"little glory in an Empire which can rule the waves... [but] is unable to flush its sewers."* Churchill's maiden speech coincided with the publication of Rowntree's groundbreaking work and for the next thirteen years, he and his colleagues wrestled with a major dilemma - how to project imperial power abroad while promoting social welfare at home? Chapter Two examines this debate on 'National Efficiency'.

CHAPTER TWO: WEARY TITAN, 1901-14

We are not a young people with an innocent record and a scanty inheritance. We have engrossed to ourselves... an altogether disproportionate share of the wealth and traffic of the world. We have got all we want in territory... and our claim to be left in the unmolested enjoyment of vast and splendid possessions, mainly acquired by violence, largely maintained by force, often seems less reasonable to others than to us.

Winston Churchill, Cabinet paper, January 1914

We do require your assistance in the administration of the vast empire which is yours as well as ours. The Weary Titan staggers under the too vast orb of its fate. We have borne the burden for many years... it is time that our children should assist us to support it.

Joseph Chamberlain, Colonial Secretary, 1902

Churchill's imperial obsession warped and distorted Allied military strategy during 1940-44 and informed his earliest political pronouncements.

I

Churchill's very first public speech - at Bath in July 1897 - championed imperialism and challenged its critics. After enjoining labour and capital to work together (i.e. urging workers to support a system which starved them), Churchill concluded with a clarion call to defend and extend Britain's 'civilising mission'.

There are not wanting those who say in this Jubilee year our Empire has reached the height of its glory and power and that now we shall begin to decline.... Do not believe these croakers but give the lie to their dismal croaking by showing by our actions that the vigour and vitality of our race is unimpaired and that our determination is to uphold the Empire that we have inherited from our fathers... [We] shall continue to pursue that course marked out for us by an all-wise hand and carry out our mission of bearing peace, civilisation and good government to the uttermost ends of the earth.

The contrast between Churchill's noble sentiments and the slaughter at Omdurman or horror of Bloemfontein requires little emphasis. Imperial enthusiasm informed a December 1897 letter to his mother.

> *I shall devote my life to the preservation of this great empire and to trying to maintain the progress of the English people.*

Churchill reaffirmed his commitment at critical moments in his career. Assuming leadership of the Tory Party in October 1940, he reassured MPs that

> *at all times… I have always faithfully served two public causes which, I think, stand supreme - the maintenance of the enduring greatness of Britain and her Empire, and the historical continuity of our island life.*

He famously endorsed the Empire directly after El Alamein by declaring that

> *we mean to hold our own. I have not become the King's First Minister in order to preside over the liquidation of the British Empire. For that task, if ever it were prescribed, someone else would have to be found.*

In making these comments, Churchill was defying Roosevelt as much as Hitler. Over the preceding three months, the President's personal emissary - Wendell Willkie - had been touring China, Russia and the Middle East advocating indigenous rights and Churchill felt moved to offer a swift rebuttal. In expressing such sentiment, he was merely reminding Roosevelt of their Placentia Bay conference which had exempted Britain's colonies from the provisions of the Atlantic Charter.[15]

America's vice-consul in Marrakech - Kenneth Whittemore Pendar - heard a similar story following the Casablanca Conference. Settling down to paint the Atlas Mountains at sunset - his only painting of the war - Churchill offered to swap Morocco for India and include Gandhi in the deal as *"he is very cheap to keep now as he is on hunger strike."* Churchill continued,

> *there are always earnest spinsters in Pennsylvania, Utah, Edinburgh or Dublin persistently writing letters and… giving*

---

[15] Covered in Chapter 11.

their advice to the British Government, urging that India be given back to the Indians and South Africa back to the Zulu or Boers, but as long as I am called by his Majesty the King to be his First Minister, I shall not assist at the dismemberment of the British Empire.

These remarks illustrate Churchill's determination to defend Britain's Empire to the death. Holding such views, it was therefore essential to retain control over the Empire's highly sensitive chokepoint - the eastern Mediterranean - at all times, even in the midst of a life or death struggle with Nazi Germany.

II

Churchill's Empire operated within an evolving geopolitical context and later nineteenth and early twentieth century developments did not favour Britain. In 1860, Britain ruled an Empire of 174 million people and was commercially and economically dominant. By 1914, the Empire had swollen to 400 million people but British economic power was in decline, largely supplanted by German and American vigour. In 1880, Britain produced 23% of world manufacturing output while America generated 15% and Germany 8.5%. By 1913, Britain's share had slumped to 13.6% while America's portion had risen to 32% and Germany's to 15%. In 1913, America produced 485,000 motor vehicles while Britain built 34,000, one-fifth manufactured by an American company (Ford) operating in Britain. Britain was still extremely affluent but its mid-nineteenth-century hegemony was evaporating and the gulf between imperial commitment and military-industrial muscle was growing. Throughout much of the nineteenth century, Britain had - wherever possible - shunned entanglements with other powers, preferring to project its power onto Africa and Asia through its well-equipped navy and modern army supported by colonial levies. However, as the gap between imperial reach and economic grasp widened, Britain was forced to accommodate other states within a system of alliances which contributed to the convulsion of 1914.

America sits next to the Caribbean and shares a border with Canada. American military-industrial power was growing in the later nineteenth century and it possessed the power to challenge Britain in the western hemisphere. Starting in the 1890s, Britain curried favour with America to minimise its North American and Caribbean commitments and avoid a war it could not win. Britain supported America in its 1898 conflict with Spain and America reciprocated during the Boer War.

The 1901 Hay-Pauncefote Treaty recognised America's right to build and fortify a canal through Panama in defiance of the earlier Clayton-Bulwer Treaty.[16] In the 1903 Alaskan boundary dispute, the British representative sided with his American colleagues against the two Canadian representatives, ensuring that the final boundary favoured America. This abasement had achieved such success by 1908 that the Foreign Office confidently discounted all possibility of war with the United States and Britain withdrew most of its forces from Canada and the Caribbean, leaving America to dominate Latin America and the Pacific.

France had been Britain's great military and economic rival since the Middle Ages, and relations between the two had soured following Britain's solo occupation of Egypt. The 1898 Fashoda Incident[17] demonstrated the ability of colonial disputes to generate Anglo-French friction, but if Britain and France reached agreement in Africa, this would not only reduce tensions in that region but the new friendship would offset growing German power in Europe. France had lost two provinces (Alsace-Lorraine) to Germany in the 1870-71 Franco-Prussian War and welcomed the new arrangement. The Entente Cordiale of 1904 - which heightened European tensions - was entirely colonial in character. Britain recognised French 'rights' over Morocco while France recognised British 'rights' over Egypt, and France renounced its claims to western Newfoundland, being compensated with West African territory. Although far short of a military alliance, the Entente drew Britain and France closer together as European animosities intensified. Secret Army staff talks were convened in December 1905 and, by 1908, the broad outlines of Britain's subsequent deployment in Europe - the British Expeditionary Force (BEF) operating on the left flank of the French Army - had been agreed. In 1910, Georges Clemenceau and Sir John French - France's future war leader and Britain's future BEF commander - toured the Belgian frontier and naval understandings followed the Army talks. The road to hell was paved with the very best colonial intentions.

Russia had long been Britain's great rival in the eastern Mediterranean, Middle East and India and its hostility was neutralised through a judicious blend of carrot and stick. Russia was allied to France after 1892 and the combined Franco-Russian Far East fleet out-

---

[16] The 1850 Clayton-Bulwer Treaty confirmed that neither Britain nor America could unilaterally build a canal through Nicaragua to link the Pacific and the Atlantic. The 1901 Treaty acknowledged America's right to act without reference to Britain in Panama.

[17] Britain wanted to develop a north-south axis in Africa while France hoped to develop an east-west axis; the two axes intersected in Fashoda (now Kodok in present day South Sudan) and France backed down following a stand-off in 1898.

gunned its British counterpart so, in 1902, Britain concluded a five-year Treaty of Alliance with Japan, Russia's rival in Korea and Manchuria. The Alliance committed Britain and Japan to support each other in the event of war against any two powers and, following Japan's victory in the 1904-5 Russo-Japanese War, the Alliance was renewed with assistance to be offered if either party was challenged by a single power. Japan agreed to assist Britain if Russia menaced the Raj, while Britain turned a blind eye to Japanese depredations in Korea and Manchuria where it had no direct interests.

As Russia and France were allies, a more conciliatory approach was required closer to home. Britain and Russia had long contested control over Iran (Persia) but the 1907 Anglo-Russian Entente resolved these difficulties by dividing the country into three sections - a Russian-dominated northern zone, a neutral central sector and Britain's south-eastern coastal corner. Similar arrangements eliminated Axis influence from Iran in 1941.

By 1907, diplomacy and negotiation had reduced Britain's overseas commitments to a more manageable level, but while Britain sought positive understandings with Russia, France, Japan and America, friction mounted with Germany which contributed to the impending conflagration.

Germany did not exist as a unitary state until 1871 but its ascent thereafter was swift. In 1890, Germany produced half the iron and steel of Great Britain but, in 1913, it produced twice as much. As German industrial strength developed, it desired all the attributes of a 'Great Power' and - commencing in 1898 - started developing its *Kaiserliche Marine* into a formidable weapon. Germany's decision to build battleships rather than cruisers - which are more suited to defending commerce and overseas colonies - was perceived as a direct threat to British national security. Battleships of the pre-1914 era were extremely coal-hungry and required access to friendly ports and coaling stations around the world and this partly explains Britain's acquisition of overseas bases. Germany however had relatively few overseas colonies and so - through a mixture of circumstance and design - Germany's growing battleship fleet was largely based in the North Sea and North Atlantic, compromising British home security. Germany's Naval Laws were designed to discomfit Britain, and Britain - committed to preserving the 'two power' naval standard - interpreted them in a hostile light. The 1900 Naval Law committed Germany to developing a fleet of 38 battleships by 1917 and provoked a hostile British response. Commenting on German naval growth in

1902, First Lord of the Admiralty Selborne warned Cabinet colleagues that

> *the more the composition of the new German fleet is examined, the clearer it becomes that it is designed for a possible conflict with the British fleet. It cannot be designed for the purpose of playing a leading part in a future war between Germany and France and Russia.*

German Naval Laws - and British determination to retain dominance - triggered a self-defeating arms race which magnified tension. In 1906, Britain unveiled *HMS Dreadnought*, a ship so revolutionary in its 'all big gun' armament and steam turbine propulsion that it gave its name to a new class of battleship. Germany's Third Naval Law of 1906 mandated the construction of six large cruisers, while the Fourth Naval Law (1908) endorsed the building of four battleships per year over the next three years and two per year during 1911-17. In that same year, Prime Minister Asquith reiterated British commitment to the 'two power standard' and - after much controversy - committed the country to laying down eight new dreadnoughts during 1909/10. Germany started widening the Kiel Canal in 1909 - to speed the passage of ships between the Baltic and North Sea - and passed a Fifth Naval Law in 1912. In March 1912, First Lord of the Admiralty Winston Churchill abandoned the 'two power standard' but promised that Britain would retain a 60% superiority over Germany and build two new battleships for every German warship completed. As dreadnoughts cost more than £2m apiece, it was a ruinous competition which diverted money away from social welfare programmes and contributed to political instability. Attempts to introduce 'naval building holidays' in 1912 and 1913 failed as Germany's charge for undertaking such a holiday - British neutrality in any European war - was considered too high a price to pay.

By 1910, the battle lines of the First World War had been drawn. Britain was linked to France and Russia through the Triple Entente, had good relations with America and was allied to Japan. Germany was associated with Italy and Austria-Hungary through the Triple Alliance and was cultivating good relations with Turkey to constrict Britain's Mediterranean chokepoint. The combustible elements were all in place when Princip's bullet ignited the pyre on 28th June 1914.

III

Churchill entered the Commons a young man in a hurry, convinced he would die prematurely like his father and - coupled with his ebullient personality - quickly sparked controversy. In 1901, War Secretary Brodrick introduced proposals to increase defence spending by £5m and expand Britain's army from one to three corps, supported by three corps of reserve militia and volunteers. Churchill's strategic concepts had been informed by his Indian reading and he argued that Britain should remain aloof from world affairs, *"isolated if you like... a mighty Navy must keep the seas. The Army may be reduced to a training depot for India with one corps for petty expeditions."* He condemned Brodrick's plans and assured the House that the reforms

> *will not make us secure and that if we went to war with any great power his three army corps would scarcely serve as a vanguard. If we are hated, they will not make us loved. If we are in danger, they will not make us safe... The only weapon with which we can expect to cope with great nations is the Navy... and surely to adopt the double policy of equal effort both on Army and Navy... is to combine the disadvantages and dangers of all courses without the advantages or security of any.*

Churchill endorsed the 'Blue Water' approach, a strategic conceit which held that British power was best projected by a mighty navy backed up by a small modern army (plus colonial levies) restricted to imperial policing. His support for *"retrenchment and economy"* was disingenuous as he didn't fully endorse defence cutbacks but merely wished to ensure that *"the first and main principle which should animate British statecraft... [is] the promotion of a steady transfer of expenditure from military to marine."* His early enthusiasm for naval spending notwithstanding, Churchill reversed his position on naval budgets in 1909 only for his enthusiasm to be re-kindled on gaining the Admiralty in 1911; like most politicians, Churchill wanted his Departments to enjoy massive budgets and his zigzags on this issue were worthy of one of the navy's impressive new dreadnoughts.

The row over Brodrick's proposed reforms coincided with the great 'Free Trade vs. Tariffs' controversy of the early twentieth century. Since 1895, Britain had been governed by a Conservative-Liberal Unionist coalition but the coalition unravelled after 1903 when Liberal Unionist leader Joseph Chamberlain resigned as Colonial Secretary and embarked on a campaign for 'imperial preference' (i.e. tariff protection for British and Empire goods). The Liberal opposition endorsed Free Trade and a minority of Conservatives supported Chamberlain while Prime Minister Balfour tried to steer a middle course. Churchill favoured Free Trade - it was the glue which bound the Empire together - and this - plus the prospect of the Liberals forming the next government and introducing a programme of social reform - drew him towards the opposition. In October 1903 he wrote, *"I am an English Liberal. I hate the Tory Party, their men, their words & their methods,"* and many Tories reciprocated with venom. As his attacks on the opponents of Free Trade intensified, his estrangement from his party grew. His constituency organisation disowned him in December 1903 and, when he rose to address the House in March 1904, Balfour and eighty Conservative MPs stood up and walked out. Returning to Parliament after Whitsun, Churchill crossed the floor and sat next to Lloyd George, a move which provoked profound Tory enmity and would haunt him for years to come. In December 1905, Balfour resigned as Prime Minister and was replaced by Liberal leader Henry Campbell-Bannerman who offered the outspoken young backbencher the post of Colonial Under-Secretary. The Liberals won a landslide victory in January 1906 and Churchill was now a junior minister in a government with a massive mandate for social reform.

The years before 1914 were politically turbulent. The Lords rejected Lloyd George's 'People's Budget' in 1909, triggering a constitutional crisis which required two elections and passage of the 1911 Parliament Act to provide resolution. Ireland lurched towards civil war and Britain was engulfed by industrial conflict as unions agitated to improve their members' conditions. Labour gained 42 seats in the January 1910 election and the Suffragettes sustained a campaign of civil disobedience to convert the rhetoric of 'parliamentary democracy' into tangible reality.

The era was fulfilling for Churchill personally and professionally. He married Clementine Hozier in 1908, a marriage which produced five children,[18] a degree of stability and a good deal of solid - if often unheeded - advice. The affection in their personal correspondence is touching. Churchill established himself as a 'big beast' in British politics and became a leading member of Asquith's cabinet after 1908.

As Colonial Under-Secretary (1905-1908), Churchill defended his Department's policies in the Commons while Colonial Secretary Lord Elgin rested in the upper chamber. During this period, the Liberal Government gerrymandered the Boer Republics' voting systems to try to install pro-British majorities and, after condemning indentured Chinese labour in South African mines in opposition, allowed it to

[18] Four Churchill children - Diana, Randolph, Sarah and Mary - reached adulthood but Marigold (b.1918) died of septicaemia in 1921.

continue until the Boers proscribed it. Churchill also supported the 1906 Trades Disputes Act which granted immunities to trades unions.

Churchill was an ardent liberal reformer throughout 1906-10. As part of the Liberal Government, he supported a range of reforms to remedy capitalism's worst excesses and 'improve the British breed'. The Liberal Government introduced free school meals, old age pensions and medical testing for children. As President of the Board of Trade, Churchill oversaw passage of the 1908 Mines Act - which reduced the miners' working day to eight hours - and the 1909 Trade Boards Act - which set minimum wages in sweated industries - while the 1909 Labour Exchanges Act created forerunners of the Job Centre. Churchill's enthusiasm for social reform compromised his earlier passion for a well-funded Navy. In autumn 1908, First Lord of the Admiralty McKenna brought forward naval estimates of £32.3m and recommended construction of six new dreadnoughts. Churchill and Lloyd George argued for four and expressed concern that naval spending would divert money from social programmes. The 'four versus six' controversy escalated into the 1909 Naval Estimates crisis which saw Churchill on the side of the 'lambs' and 'economists'[19] urging naval retrenchment and economy. The impasse was resolved by a compromise which committed Britain to building four dreadnoughts in 1909-10 and another four if required later. First Lord of the Admiralty Churchill reversed his position five years later, introducing naval estimates of £50.7m and threatening resignation if they were rejected. Churchill could argue any political or military position with gusto and his pre-1914 'mental flexibility' presaged later inconsistencies on a range of issues.

Churchill became Home Secretary in February 1910 and continued his programme of social reform. The 1911 National Insurance Act introduced elementary forms of unemployment and sickness benefit, while humanitarian reforms softened the brutality of Britain's prison system. However, following the January 1910 election - when the Liberals lost their majority and depended on Irish and Labour Party support to continue - a more authoritarian personality emerged. A convinced eugenicist, Churchill urged the sterilisation of adults with enduring mental illness[20] and learning disabilities to purify the gene pool, advising Asquith that

---

[19] The 'lambs' supported the League of Liberals Against Aggression and Militarism and the economists favoured naval economies - they didn't necessarily possess great economic expertise.
[20] Ironic given Churchill's own struggles with intermittent mania and depression.

> *The unnatural and increasingly rapid growth of the feeble minded and insane classes, coupled... with a steady restriction among all the thrifty, energetic and superior stocks constitutes a national and race danger which it is impossible to exaggerate... I feel that the source from which the stream of madness is fed should be cut off and sealed up before another year has passed.*

He equivocated over votes for women. He'd supported the notion in 1904 but reversed his position after the Suffragettes engaged in civil disobedience. Throughout his career, Churchill happily dispensed largesse as an act of charity but was reluctant to do so when reform was demanded as a right. Had the electoral arithmetic favoured the Liberals, his position might have been different. At the time, Britain operated a 'householder' franchise and enfranchising a large number of female householders would have increased the Tory vote at a time when the Liberals were vulnerable. Of course, the notion of universally enfranchising all British males and females did not occur to members of Britain's ruling elite before 1918. As Home Secretary, Churchill authorised the army to support the police in a series of industrial disputes and unarmed strikers were killed in clashes. His presence at the Sydney Street Siege of January 1911 reinforced his reputation as a rash adventurer, as did his involvement in the 1914 Antwerp Siege when he commanded a British detachment in the field.[21] The whiff of cordite and crackle of gunfire attracted Churchill throughout his career and he had to be dissuaded from observing the Normandy landings on D-Day.[22]

Tensions between Britain, France and Germany escalated in 1911 when Germany despatched a gunboat to Agadir in Morocco, territory claimed by France. So alarmed was Asquith by the prospect of war that he invited the Army's Director of Military Operations (General Sir Henry Wilson) and the First Sea Lord (Admiral Sir Arthur Wilson) to present their plans for continental deployment to the Committee of Imperial Defence. General Wilson offered a masterly exposition of the Army's plans to station the British Expeditionary Force (BEF) to the left of the French Army while Admiral Wilson presented an *"opaque and rambling"* overview of ill-formed plans to land troops on Germany's northern coast which, in the interests of security, existed only in his head. Alarmed by this poor showing and convinced that McKenna had lost control of his Department, Asquith looked round

---

[21] see Chapter 3.

[22] He eventually visited the Normandy beachhead on 12th June.

for a replacement and his eye alighted on a 36 year old former cavalry lieutenant. In October 1911, Winston Churchill gained control of the world's mightiest war weapon.

IV

Churchill's three and a half years at the Admiralty were characterised by a tremendous reforming zeal which consolidated long-term trends and introduced numerous innovations. Convinced that German sea power threatened British security, Churchill renounced his former opposition to naval expenditure and campaigned for massive increases. In 1913, he introduced naval estimates of £50.7m and threatened resignation if they were rejected, precipitating a second Estimates Crisis and another classic fudge - expenditure was to increase by 5.6% over the original 1913-14 estimates but would be reduced the following year. The outbreak of war ensured that these cuts were never implemented.

Naval spending increased significantly - from £32.2m in 1909/10 to £44.4m by 1913/14 - and the Navy's budget share increased. In 1904/5, the defence budget was split 51/49 in favour of the Army but by 1913/14, the Navy received 61% of the overall spend. Churchill's aspiration to promote *"a steady transfer of expenditure from military to marine"* had been realised. For a country with global commitments such as Britain, this represented a rational distribution of resources but the consequence was a small, under-funded army unsuited to continental operations. In August 1914, Germany deployed 1.7 million men on the western front, France deployed 1.65 million and Britain deployed 125,000, ensuring that British forces played no major role in defending Paris. The persistence of the 'Blue Water' strategy into the 1930s had even more baleful consequences - in 1939, Britain again went to war with a small, under-funded army and suffered a string of humiliations.

Anglo-French naval cooperation increased under Churchill's leadership. The Triple Alliance linked Germany to Italy and Austria-Hungary and both states had become significant Mediterranean powers by 1914. The Italian navy laid down sixteen battleships (ten dreadnoughts) between 1898 and 1915, while the Austro-Hungarians laid down ten battleships (four dreadnoughts) in the same period. The Mediterranean ranked second only to British home waters in strategic significance and the growth of Italian and Austro-Hungarian power generated concern in London. Britain would be unable to counter Germany's threat in the North Sea if it diverted resources to neuter the Italian and Austro-Hungarian challenge, so the solution lay in an

Anglo-French partnership to maximise their respective strengths. France - with its major naval base at Toulon - assumed responsibility for the Mediterranean while Britain looked after the Channel, North Sea and French Atlantic coast. In the years immediately before 1914, Britain relaxed its direct and rather neurotic control over the Mediterranean, entrusting this task to its French ally. On the eve of war, Britain had twenty dreadnoughts and two semi-dreadnoughts stationed in home waters but only six battleships and three battlecruisers in the Mediterranean and the post of Commander-in-Chief, Mediterranean Fleet was suspended in August 1914. This arrangement was only temporary and the post was reactivated in July 1917 in an effort to nullify Germany's u-boat threat.

Overall, Churchill constituted a dynamic reforming presence at the Admiralty and his most far-reaching decision came in 1912 when he ordered the Navy's warships to convert from coal to oil. The advantages of liquid fuel had been known for some time[23] but the Agadir scare finally prompted Churchill to take the plunge. As he later explained,

> *to commit the navy irrevocably to oil was indeed to take arms against a sea of troubles. If we overcame the difficulties and surmounted the risks, we should be able to raise the whole power and efficiency of the navy to a definitely higher level; better ships, better crews, higher economies, more intense forms of war power - in a word, mastery itself was the prize of the venture.*

The Anglo-Persian Oil Company (APOC) had discovered oil in south-western Iran in 1908 and constructed a huge refinery at Abadan to process this resource. At Churchill's prompting, the Government acquired a 51% stake in APOC, guaranteeing APOC a steady market and securing the Navy's oil supplies.

This oil had to be transported to Britain by sea and the Med-Red Zone offered the most direct route, so Churchill's 1912 decision carried the most profound implications for Britain's strategic posture. Before 1912, Britain had used Suez and the Med-Red Zone to communicate with its eastern Empire and dominate India. After 1912, this was also the artery through which the lifeblood of the Navy - and therefore of the Empire - flowed and the region's importance to Britain increased

[23] Oil burns more efficiently, it is quicker and easier to load, produces faster and more manoeuvrable ships, enables ships to spend less time in port and requires fewer sailors. It also contributes to a cleaner and healthier workplace.

exponentially. Britain was now wedded to Suez and, as the UK economy and merchant fleet increasingly switched to oil, it became a *de facto* adjunct of Britain's home economy. As the Ottoman Empire crumbled to dust in 1917-18, Britain scavenged on the remains, acquiring new commitments it could ill afford to sustain.

CHAPTER THREE: THE PREPARATIONS HAVE A HIDEOUS FASCINATION FOR ME, 1914-18

I think a curse should rest on me - because I love this war. I know it's smashing and shattering the lives of thousands every moment - and yet - I can't help it - I enjoy every second of it.

Winston Churchill to Violet Asquith,
22nd February 1915

I am absolutely unable to remain with W.C. (HE'S A REAL DANGER!) ... W.C. MUST go at all costs! AT ONCE... W.C. is leading them all straight to ruin... A very great national disaster is very near in the Dardanelles... W.C. is a bigger danger than the Germans.

Admiral Fisher to Andrew Bonar Law,
17th May 1915

Franz Ferdinand's assassination triggered ten years of simmering hostility into open conflict. Dreading a war on two fronts, Germany sought to eliminate France by driving through Belgium before Russia could mobilise its forces and almost won Paris by the end of August. Repulsed on the Marne, the two sides initiated a 'race to the sea', desperately trying to outflank each other but merely forming two lines of trenches linking Pfetterhouse on the Swiss border to Nieuwpoort in Belgium. Equal in numbers and employing technology which favoured defence over attack (barbed wire, machine guns, artillery), the protagonists settled down to four years of grotesque carnage in which thousands of lives were routinely squandered for a few miles of shell-pocked wasteland. The mobile part of the western war was over by Christmas 1914 and both sides engaged in grinding attritional strife while strategists in London, Paris and Berlin sought ever more imaginative means of breaking the deadlock. In this pursuit, none was more industrious than the former cavalry lieutenant who fancied himself the heir to Alexander the Great and Napoleon Bonaparte.

I

The eve of war found Churchill feverish and excited, a mood he guiltily confessed to his wife six days before hostilities commenced.

Everything trends towards catastrophe and collapse. I am interested, geared-up and happy. Is it not horrible to be built like that? The preparations have a hideous fascination for me. I pray to God to forgive me for such fearful moods of levity.

Despite having risen no higher than lieutenant in the regular army, Churchill was supremely confident in his war-making abilities, an assessment he shared with Clemmie in 1909.

> *These military men very often fail altogether to see the simple truths underlying the relationship of all armed forces... I would greatly love to have some practice in the handling of large forces. I have much confidence in my judgement in things... but on nothing do I seem to feel the truth more than in tactical combinations... I am sure I have the root of the matter in me.*

Five years later, Churchill's disdain for military convention had hardened into outright contempt. Over dinner with Asquith in October 1914, he advised the Prime Minister that *"a political career was nothing to him in comparison with military glory,"* and Asquith relayed the tenor of Churchill's comments to his confidante, Venetia Stanley.

> *His mouth waters at the sight and thought of Kitchener's new armies. Are these 'glittering commands' to be entrusted to 'dug-out trash', bred on the obsolete tactics of twenty-five years ago - 'mediocrities who have led a sheltered life mouldering in military routine'.*

Churchill despised the mediocrities who had frustrated his early career and now, as First Lord of the Admiralty, was determined to display the true extent of his genius and earn the nation's grateful homage. In reality, a large gulf separated Churchill's skills from his assessment of those skills and - within a year - he would be deposed from the Admiralty and plunged into a pit of despair.

II

The War started badly for the Royal Navy. When the conflict commenced, two German cruisers - *Goeben* and *Breslau* - were trapped in the Mediterranean but managed to evade the entire Anglo-French fleet and reach the safety of Turkish waters. Churchill's operational meddling assisted this escape. On 30th July, he instructed Admiral Milne, Commander of the Mediterranean Fleet, to avoid *"action against superior forces, except in combination with the French"* but failed to clarify what constituted *"superior forces."* Consequently, when four cruisers under Admiral Ernest Troubridge encountered the fugitives off the west coast of Greece, they were allowed to escape on the grounds that the *Goeben's* eleven-inch guns outclassed the British ships' nine-inch guns and constituted a *"superior force"*.

The *Goeben-Breslau* escape profoundly affected world history and the course of the war. Germany presented the ships to Turkey, which helped precipitate Turkish belligerence. On 29th October, *Goeben* and *Breslau*[24] bombarded Russia's Black Sea ports, initiating conflict in the Caucasus. Turkish control of the Dardanelles prevented Russia from exporting its grain surplus; grain prices collapsed inside Russia and peasants refused to sell their food to the cities, fuelling the disaffection which would overwhelm the Romanovs in spring 1917. The Bolshevik Government concluded an armistice with Germany which allowed the Germans to transfer troops to the west and launch a major offensive which threatened to over-run Allied positions in spring 1918. Such were the unwonted consequences of Churchill's operational meddling. Troubridge was court martialled for failing to engage the enemy in November but was acquitted on the grounds of imprecise instructions. However, the ignominy he suffered affected the course of a second engagement later in the year.

Churchill was desperate to grapple with the German fleet and on 21st September, declared that if the Imperial Navy would not come out and fight *"they will be dug out like rats in a hole."* The following day, one German submarine sank three British cruisers off the Dutch coast with the loss of 1,460 lives. Churchill can be exonerated for his role in this disaster for, on 18th September, he had ordered these cruisers to be withdrawn as *"the risk to such ships is not justified by any services they can render."* However, the Chief of the Naval War Staff countermanded this order, arguing that no other ships were available to replace the 'Live Bait Squadron' on blockade duty. The dead included many untrained reservists and cadets from Dartmouth Naval College.

Churchill's emotional volatility further eroded his political credibility. On 2nd October, General Kitchener and Foreign Secretary Grey sent him to Antwerp to report on the city's efforts to resist the German siege. Churchill's mission was largely intelligence-gathering but, just as he'd taken control of the armoured train in South Africa, he couldn't resist the temptation to assume responsibility for directing Antwerp's defences and organising resistance to the Germans. Churchill's actions may have helped save Calais, Boulogne and Dunkirk but the message sent to his Cabinet colleagues on 5th October prompted only derision.

> *If it is thought by HM Government that I can be of service here, I am willing to resign my office and undertake command*

[24] *Goeben* and *Breslau* were renamed *Yavuz Sultan Selim* and *Midilli* when they passed into Turkish service. However, they remained under German command with German sailors wearing Ottoman uniforms.

of relieving and defensive forces assigned to Antwerp… provided that I am given necessary military rank and authority, and full powers of a commander of a detached force in the field. I feel it my duty to offer my services because I am sure this arrangement will afford the best prospects of a victorious result

Churchill's colleagues responded with *"roars of incredulous laughter"* and denied his request.

On 1st November, two cruisers of Sir Christopher Cradock's South Atlantic Squadron were sunk by Admiral von Spee's East Asia Squadron off the Chile coast and the shadow of *Goeben-Breslau* loomed large. Cradock's ships were outgunned by von Spee's battlecruisers but Cradock knew that Troubridge was facing court martial for failing to engage superior enemy forces and wished to avoid a similar fate. Cradock therefore ordered his cruisers into a battle they couldn't win and Britain suffered its first naval defeat for more than a century. Churchill was distracted by machinations to re-install his old friend Jackie Fisher at the Admiralty and unable to provide the guidance that may have averted tragedy. The Royal Navy gained revenge in the Battle of the Falkland Islands five weeks later but the damage had been done.

Finally, German ships emerged from their 'rat-hole' to shell Scarborough, Whitby and Hartlepool on 16th December, killing 137, injuring 592 and shattering the belief that Britons could sleep soundly in their beds, protected by an all-powerful Navy.

Churchill's reputation - and the Navy's prestige - had taken a bit of a battering and then, in late December, Russia's Commander-in-Chief, Grand Duke Michael, asked his Anglo-French allies to launch an operation in the eastern Mediterranean to relieve pressure on his Caucasus front. The operation that was devised was designed to remove Turkey from the war, assist Russia and reinforce British influence in a strategically sensitive theatre. The action was to occur within the vicinity of a rocky peninsula known to the Turks as Gelibolu but known throughout the world as Gallipoli.

III

In declaring war on Turkey, Britain was breaking with decades of diplomacy in which the Ottomans had denied Russia access to the Mediterranean and Middle East. However, Turkey's alignment with the

Central Powers and Britain's growing friendship with Russia demanded a dramatic *volte-face*. A successful war with Turkey would, it was hoped, not only diminish the Central Powers and assist Russia, it also held out the prospect of enhancing British influence in a strategically sensitive region and open up a promising new front in southern Europe. Lloyd George - a leading figure in Asquith's cabinet and future Prime Minister - was a major exponent of this indirect strategy which he hoped would 'knock the props from under Germany' and - by defeating its weaker allies - create *"the prospect of a triumph which would have a determining effect on the fate of the struggle."* Lloyd George's 1914-18 Eastern strategy directly anticipated Churchill's 1940-44 Mediterranean strategy.

Churchill was equally enthusiastic about the peripheral strategy in World War One, proposing to Prime Minister Asquith on 29th December that

> *it is quite possible that neither side will have the strength to penetrate the other's line in the Western theatre... [and] the question arises, how ought we to apply our growing military power? Are there not other alternatives than sending our armies to chew barbed wire in Flanders... if it is impossible or unduly costly to pierce the German lines on existing fronts, ought we not... to engage him on new frontiers and enable the Russians to do so too?*

Like most of Churchill's stratagems, the Dardanelles naval operation was intended to offer great returns for minimal outlay against a secondary opponent in a peripheral theatre. In Churchill's original plan, an Anglo-French Fleet would push through the Dardanelles into the Sea of Marmara where it would bombard Constantinople (Istanbul) and drive Turkey from the war. Troops were not required and the ships deployed would be older vessels unsuited to North Sea operations. Having conceived his idea, Churchill was stunned by its strategic brilliance.

The Navy's senior admirals were less enthusiastic but - overwhelmed by the First Lord's blustering enthusiasm - failed to convey the true extent of their misgivings. Admiral Scott, the Navy's chief gunnery expert, believed the Navy had been set *"an impossible task"* and when Third Lord Admiral Jackson attempted to discuss the subject, his views were *"not welcomed and had no effect."* Even First Lord Fisher - no shrinking violet - was forced to complain that *"[Churchill] always out-argues me."*

Consequently, when Churchill unfolded his plans to the War Council on 13th January, he presented a false bill of goods which magnified the prospects of success and downplayed potential pitfalls. Fisher remained silent throughout the meeting, unwilling to contradict his chief before his Cabinet colleagues.

The Dardanelles is 28 miles long and, at its narrowest point, three-quarters of a mile wide. Its hillsides bristled with Turkish gun emplacements and its waters were heavily mined. The Navy was being forced to operate in a tight arena with little room for manoeuvre where its ships would be immensely vulnerable. The naval operation commenced on 18th March and, within a few hours, three battleships had been sunk and three further vessels severely damaged. It was a great Turkish victory and Allied naval operations were immediately cancelled.

The War Council then did a curious thing. Having advertised its interest in the region, it decided to land troops on Gallipoli to assist future naval operations but it took six weeks to assemble the 70,000 men required for the operation, giving the Turks plenty of time to ready a warm welcome. Consequently, when Allied troops landed at dawn on 25th April, the Turks were entrenched in positions overlooking the landing beaches and Allied losses were horrendous. By early May, 20,000 Allied casualties had been sustained and those who survived were plagued by disease, heat, flies, thirst and constant Turkish sniping. Gallipoli was supposed to present an alternative to 'chewing barbed wire in Flanders' but merely transposed the horrors of the Western Front to the eastern Mediterranean. By the time Allied forces evacuated the peninsula in January 1916, 250,000 men had been killed or wounded for zero gain.

Gallipoli coincided with the May 1915 'Shell Crisis' in which *The Times* revealed that ammunition shortages were significantly hampering the war effort. Asquith had assured the public there were no problems so *The Times* revelations undermined his waning credibility. He could only survive by inviting senior Tories to form a coalition government; the Tories were keen but looked at Asquith's cabinet and saw a turncoat First Lord who'd 'ratted' on the Party. Admiral Fisher's resignation on 15th May - citing the impossibility of working with Churchill - wounded the First Lord. The Tories would only enter the coalition if the garrulous renegade was humbled and so, in the 25th May Cabinet reshuffle, Churchill was compelled to swap the prestige of the Admiralty for the Ruritanian delights of Chancellor of the Duchy of Lancaster. From having directed the world's mightiest navy, Churchill was now responsible for managing the King's investment portfolio and appointing county magistrates. For the greatest military genius of the age, it was a bitter pill to swallow.

IV

Clementine Churchill poignantly summarised her husband's agony five decades later.

> *The Dardanelles haunted him for the rest of his life. He always believed in it. When he left the Admiralty, he thought he was finished... I thought he would never get over the Dardanelles. I thought he would die of grief.*

Churchill depicted his predicament in characteristically vivid terms.

> *Like a sea-beast fished up from the depths or a diver too suddenly hoisted, my veins threatened to burst from the fall in pressure... at a moment when every fibre of my being was inflamed to action, I was forced to remain a spectator of the tragedy, placed cruelly in a front seat.*

Churchill remained in the War Council (now renamed the Dardanelles Committee) but played no part in shaping strategy. The only thing that made life tolerable was his discovery of painting as a pastime. After initial experiments with a child's paint box, he switched to oils and was immediately hooked, producing five hundred paintings over the next forty years and hosting two pseudonymous exhibitions. Churchill summed up the importance of painting when he noted that *"if it weren't for painting, I couldn't live. I couldn't bear the strain of things"*. It was perhaps the only activity that fully absorbed his attention without requiring conversation.

Churchill served at the Duchy for six months, hoping that a change in circumstance might revive his career. However, when Asquith excluded him from the War Committee in November 1915, he reluctantly accepted that his exile would be lengthy. Churchill resigned on the day that Asquith formed the War Committee and searched for an army commission. He hoped to be a Major General in charge of a Corps but had to be content as a Lieutenant Colonel commanding a battalion. After a short period training with the Grenadier Guards, Churchill was posted to 6th Battalion of the Royal Scots Fusiliers in a quiet part of the line in Ploegsteert, Belgium. His brother officers initially resented his presence but his energy, industry and concern for the enlisted men quickly won them over. In later years, a brother officer described Churchill's time with the Fusiliers in glowing terms:

> *I am firmly convinced that no more popular officer ever commanded troops. As a soldier he was hard-working, persevering and thorough... He was out to work at tiresome but indispensable detail and to make his unit efficient in the very highest possible degree... We came to realise... his transcendent ability... and much more, he became our friend.*

Soldiering provided Churchill with the tonic he needed. It offered an outlet for his energies and he enjoyed the occasional danger of coming under fire. His life at the front was made pleasant by the portable bath and boiler he'd brought with him and the gourmet delights Clemmie regularly shipped over from London.

However, Churchill had been bored by soldiering in India and quickly came to resent the routine duties of a battalion commander. His letters home were full of requests for political gossip and pleas to Clemmie to keep his name in front of prominent politicians and newspaper editors. As leave and circumstance permitted, he returned to the Commons to deliver speeches but his bizarre March 1916 suggestion that Admiral Fisher - whose resignation had torpedoed his career - should return to the Admiralty found few admirers.

Churchill's 6th Battalion merged with 7th Battalion in May and - as 7th Battalion was commanded by a regular officer - there was no place for Churchill in the amalgamated unit. He now had a respectable reason to renounce soldiering and seized it with alacrity. He left the frontline on 7th May, having spent just over three months at the sharp end of the war.

The next twelve months were spent in a concerted effort to revive his reputation and his prospects were enhanced when Lloyd George replaced Asquith as Prime Minister in December 1916. Lloyd George had a high regard for Churchill's energy and Churchill had supported him in the Marconi Shares Scandal[25] so a political debt was owed.

A Commission of Enquiry into the Dardanelles was established in June 1916 and delivered its interim report the following March. Although Churchill was criticised for stifling Admiralty opposition to his naval venture, he was no longer seen as the fiasco's sole author and gained partial rehabilitation. Churchill sparkled in a May 1917 debate on the future of the war and re-established his reputation as a political

---

[25] In 1912, Lloyd George and several other ministers had purchased shares in the American Marconi Company shortly before the British Marconi Company won a major government contract, provoking claims of insider trading. Churchill volubly supported Lloyd George.

heavyweight. If the war situation deteriorated, Churchill might provide a focus for opposition so, acting in the spirit of Lyndon Johnson's celebrated maxim,[26] Lloyd George appointed Churchill Munitions Minister in July 1917 over the vocal opposition of many Tories. Still exiled from the War Cabinet it was - nevertheless - an astonishing political comeback.

V

Churchill proved to be an efficient and energetic Munitions Minister. The Ministry had been formed in response to the 1915 Shell Crisis and its original incumbents had improvised solutions to pressing problems. Churchill's great contribution was to convert the Department into a mainstream Ministry by forming a Munitions Council to coordinate policy and by reducing fifty divisions to ten. As a major employer, much of Churchill's time was taken up with labour issues and he employed both carrot and stick to achieve his ends. The 'leaving certificate' - which prevented munitions workers from moving between employers - was abolished and he authorised a 12% bonus for skilled workers on time rates. At the same time, engineering workers in Coventry who threatened to go on strike were told that their immunity from conscription would be withdrawn, a move which quickly restored harmony. The Department's smooth running allowed Churchill to spend considerable time in France, ostensibly discussing munitions issues but - in reality - to indulge his deep-seated desire for proximity to combat.

Although barred from the War Cabinet, Churchill twice attempted to influence war strategy during 1917/18 and these contributions illuminate his later preoccupations.

When Churchill delivered his major Commons speech in May 1917, the War was going badly. The Tsarist regime had just collapsed and the French Army was on the verge of mutiny following the disastrous Nivelle Offensive. America had joined the Allies but its troops wouldn't arrive in large numbers until spring 1918. Britain was scarred by the Somme offensive - in which 57,470 had fallen on the first day - and the ruling Saxe-Coburg-Gotha dynasty had changed its name to 'Windsor' to deflect rising anti-German sentiment. Unsurprisingly, Churchill recommended postponing major offensive operations until American forces landed in Europe. As he put it,

---

[26] When an aide enquired about Johnson's reluctance to dismiss J. Edgar Hoover from the FBI, the President replied: *"If you've got a skunk around, it's better to have him inside the tent pissing out, than outside the tent pissing in."*

> *we ought not to squander the remaining armies of France and Britain in precipitate offensives before the American power begins to be felt on the battlefields... Let the House implore the Prime Minister to use [his] authority... to prevent the French and British High Commands from dragging each other into fresh bloody and disastrous adventures. Master the u-boat attack. Bring over the American millions. And meanwhile maintain an active defensive on the Western Front... to train, increase and perfect our armies ... for a decisive effort in a later year.*

The situation was even worse in March 1918 when Churchill drafted his 'Munitions Programme, 1919' memorandum - Russia had been forced from the war and Churchill counselled even greater delay and postponement.

> *Until the arrival of the Americans in force, that is to say, during the whole of this year [1918], we are not in a position, without running a desperate risk, to seek a general battle; but next year, in 1919, we may again be unmistakably superior in strength. It will then be right to fight a battle... to seek a military decision for which, the whole strength of the armies is employed - every man, every gun, every resource.*

By March 1918, Churchill had been Munitions Minister for seven months and was used to number-crunching. In his second paper, he called for a different kind of warfare based on tanks and aircraft (as opposed to artillery and infantry) and urged a fifty per cent increase in the use of air power, a four-fold increase in the deployment of tanks and a nine-fold increase in the use of gas. Churchill always believed in air power and his March 1918 memo contained the seeds of an especially malevolent bloom by declaring that

> *if either side possessed the power to drop, not five tons, but five hundred tons of bombs each night on the cities and manufacturing establishments of its opponent, the result would be decisive.*

By 1942, his enthusiasm for air operations had mushroomed into the Area Bombing Strategy which employed one-third of Britain's war industry to pulverise German cities without producing any great result. Churchill neatly merged his two principal themes by declaring that

> *there are only two ways of winning the war and they both*

> *begin with an A. One is aeroplanes and the other is America… everything else is swept away.*

Postponing decisive engagement with Germany, reliance on American power, enthusiasm for strategic bombing and a preference for peripheral operations against supposedly weaker opponents - the key elements of Churchill's 1940-44 strategy are all evident in his 1914-18 thinking. Britain and Churchill remained wedded to the 'blue water school' with its emphasis on shunning major continental commitments in favour of nibbling away at secondary enemies in peripheral – but imperially sensitive - theatres.

Germany's spring 1918 offensive denied the Allies the luxury of waiting till 1919 but, paradoxically, the collapse of this offensive finally led to victory. While Germany's *Kaiserschlacht* prevented Lloyd George from following Churchill's advice in the west, he displayed an enthusiasm for peripheral operations in the east which perfectly anticipated Churchill's Mediterranean obsession in World War Two.

VI

Britain's 1914-18 war with Turkey had multiple motivations. It was designed to assist the Russians and provide a fluid alternative to *"chewing barbed wire in Flanders."* It also provided Britain with an opportunity to extend its influence into the Med-Red Zone and Britain moved quickly to consolidate its authority in areas it already dominated. Cyprus - effectively British since 1878 - was annexed on 5th November and a formal protectorate was established over Egypt on 18th December. The Canal was closed to enemy shipping and Prime Minister Asquith identified dismemberment of the Ottoman Empire as a British war aim on 9th November.

Britain's struggle against Turkey also contained an ideological element for the Turkish Sultan - acting as Caliph of Islam - had declared *Jihad* (Holy War) against the Triple Entente on 11th November and - if this call was heeded in India (with its large Muslim population) - it would destabilise British rule in the sub-continent. A successful war against Turkey would, it was hoped, damage the Caliph's credibility and discourage dissent within the Raj and this is why Indian Army troops landed at Shatt al-Arab (in southern Iraq) as early as 6th November, one day after Britain declared war on Turkey. Basra was captured on 22nd November and the Anglo-Indian force pushed up the Tigris River, reaching Al-Mada'in - 25 miles south of Baghdad - on 23rd November. However, the imperial force was badly over-stretched and retreated to Al-Kut (Kut-al-Amara) where it was besieged and forced to surrender in April 1916. Thereafter, London took control of the Mesopotamian campaign but the motives remained the same - expel the Turks, extend British influence and discourage dissent in India.

Map 4: Key Eastern Mediterranean/Middle East locations

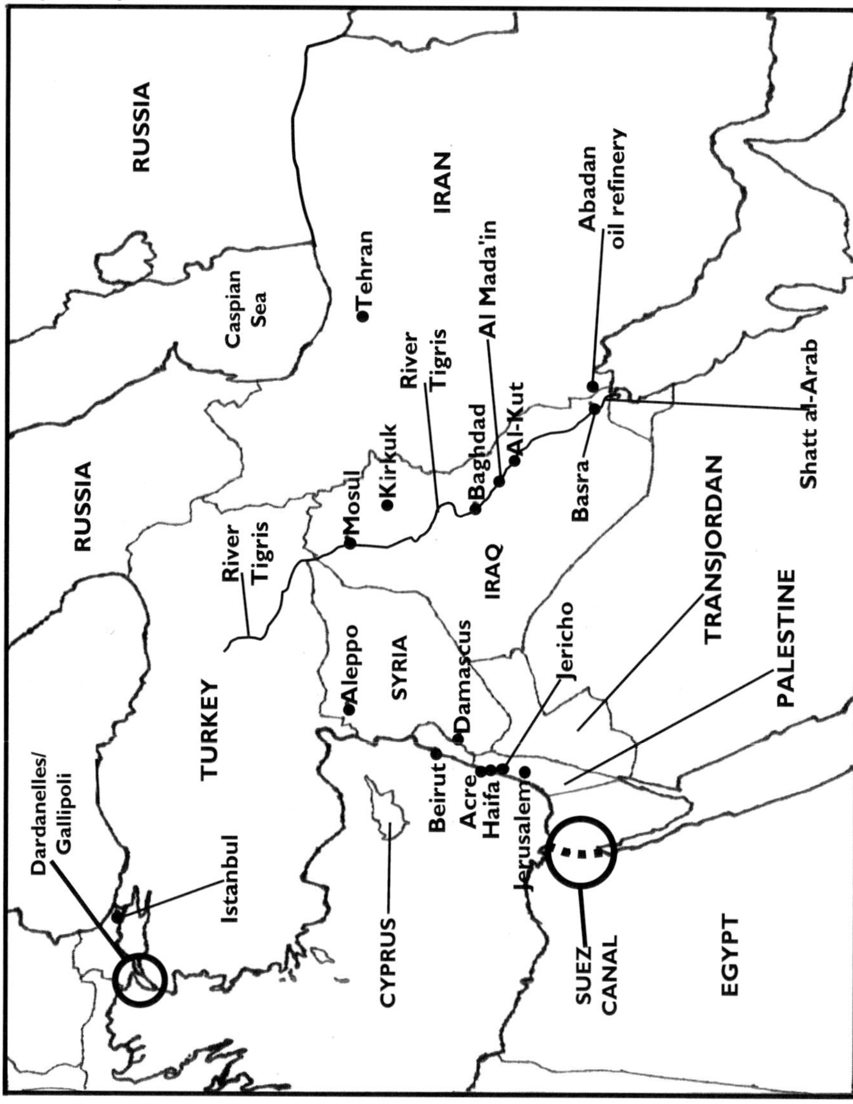

The Mesopotamian Campaign served a further purpose for - following the Navy's switch from coal to oil - Britain and its Empire depended heavily on Middle Eastern oil supplies. Iran was a major oil producer after 1908 and Iraq was thought to contain huge untapped reserves, so extending British control over Iraq would not only protect the southern Iranian oilfields but would also bring Iraqi oil under British control. War Cabinet Secretary Sir Maurice Hankey clarified the strategic importance of Middle Eastern oil in August 1918 by informing Foreign Secretary Arthur Balfour that

> *oil in the next war will occupy the place of coal in the present war, or at least a parallel place to coal. The only big supply that we can get under British control is the Persian [Iranian] and Mesopotamian [Iraqi] supply... control over these supplies becomes a first class British war aim.*

Balfour echoed Hankey's views, advising a meeting of Dominion Prime Ministers that "*I do not care under what system we keep the oil... but I am quite clear it is all-important for us that this oil should be available.*" In his July 1918 memorandum on 'The Petroleum Situation in the British Empire', Admiral Edmond Slade - the Navy's oil expert - urged the British government to

> *encourage and assist British companies to obtain control of as many oil-producing areas in foreign countries as possible, with the stipulation... that the oil produced should only be sold to or through British oil-distributing companies. These oil-producing areas could be developed to assist in providing our requirements in times of peace whilst our own resources in British territory can be conserved to war.*

Britain employed some fancy footwork to secure its Middle Eastern goals. In a flurry of correspondence with Hussein bin Ali (Sharif of Mecca), Britain's High Commissioner in Egypt - Sir Henry McMahon - promised the Arabs statehood and independence after the war if they rebelled against the Turks. At the same time, Britain and France signed the secret Sykes-Picot Agreement in which they agreed to carve up the Ottoman Empire and replace the Turks as the region's colonial masters. This May 1916 Agreement granted France control over south-eastern Turkey, northern Iraq, Syria and Lebanon while Britain was to gain southern Iraq, Jordan, Haifa and Acre, with Palestine placed under international administration and the Arabs simply swapping one set of colonial masters for another.

However, the November 1917 Balfour Declaration undercut both the McMahon-Hussein Correspondence and the Sykes-Picot Agreement by confirming British support for "*the establishment in Palestine of a national home for the Jewish people*." Britain's motive in issuing this Declaration was simple. If Britain sponsored a Jewish home in Palestine populated by westernised Jews, this home (or state) and its grateful inhabitants would be indebted to Britain and seek protection from its sponsor. Such a state would further protect Suez and allow Britain to project its power into the region. Zionist leader Chaim Weizmann summarised the situation by noting that

> *should Palestine fall within the British sphere of influence, and should Britain encourage Jewish settlement there... they would develop the country, bring back civilisation to it and form a very effective guard for the Suez Canal.*

Herbert Samuel - the first non-Christianised Jew to serve in a British Cabinet - made a similar point in spring 1915 by declaring that

> *the solution of the problem of Palestine which would be much the most welcome to the leaders and supporters of the Zionist movement throughout the world would be the annexation of the country to the British Empire.*[27]

Britain therefore supported the creation of a Jewish home (or state) on the northern flank of Suez to protect this vital waterway and project its power into the region. This concern was real as Germany and Turkey had attacked eastern Suez through Sinai in January 1915 and came close to capturing it, and British planners never considered the possibility that forming such a state might inflame Arab opinion and turn it against the west. The seeds of Israel - and several decades of Arab-Israeli conflict - were sown in 1917 when Britain declared its support for a Jewish home in Palestine to reinforce control over Suez. In 1956, Britain, France and Israel again tried to consolidate British control over this vital waterway at the expense of Arab interests.

Britain therefore had multiple reasons for wishing to supplant the Turks in the Middle East - to secure its oil supply, reinforce control over Suez and discourage Islamic dissent in India. The 1917 Bolshevik Revolution added a new motive - the determination to exclude communist influence from the region.

The demands of the Western Front - and the chastening influence of Gallipoli - discouraged Britain from investing major resources in the Middle East until 1917 but, in the last two years of the war, British

---

[27] Churchill concurred, noting in 1908 that *"the establishment of a strong, free Jewish state astride the bridge between Europe and Africa, flanking the land roads to the East, would not only be an immense advantage to the British Empire, but a notable step towards the harmonious disposition of the world among its peoples."* (Hyam, *Understanding the British Empire*, p.324. Books fully cited in the Bibliography feature in abbreviated form in the footnotes).

imperial forces and their Arab allies advanced against the war-weary Turks. In the Levant Campaign, Gaza and Jerusalem were occupied in late 1917 and Jericho fell in February 1918. There was a lull in the fighting in mid-1918 when resources were transferred to the Western Front but the advance resumed in the autumn. Haifa was captured in September 1918, Damascus and Beirut fell in early October and Allied forces entered Aleppo in northern Syria in late October.

Similar progress was recorded in Mesopotamia. Al-Kut was recaptured in February 1917, Baghdad was occupied in March and Kirkuk fell in October 1918. On 14th November, **two weeks after** Britain had concluded an armistice with Turkey, British-imperial forces surged forward to occupy Mosul in northern Iraq - the region was believed to be oil-rich and Britain had no intention of sharing this precious asset with France. British boots on the ground trumped paper agreements and Britain's unilateral action in seizing Mosul and northern Iraq generated considerable friction with France during 1918/19.

The Central Powers were on the verge of collapse by autumn 1918. Bulgaria sued for peace on 29th September and Austria-Hungary - crumbling into its component parts - concluded an armistice on 3rd November. The Turks signed the Armistice of Mudros on 30th October and - symbolising British determination to dominate the region - the armistice was signed on board a British ship by a British admiral with his French opposite number *"reduced to 'almost battering on the door of the conference room' to get in."* The guns of the western front fell silent on 11th November and the victorious Allies now faced the perils and pitfalls of peace.

CHAPTER FOUR: THE OLD WORLD IS A GOOD ENOUGH PLACE FOR ME, 1919-24

Winston Churchill: *What is the use of being War Secretary if there is no war?*

Andrew Bonar Law: *If we thought there was going to be a war, we wouldn't appoint you War Secretary.*

Lord Beaverbrook records a conversation between Churchill and Bonar Law, December 1918

Churchill's career fluctuated wildly during World War One, from the apogee of the Admiralty to the disappointment of the Duchy of Lancaster, followed by eighteen months in the wilderness before resurrection as Munitions Minister. His post-war career reflected a similarly erratic trajectory. After proving himself at Munitions, Churchill was appointed Secretary for War and Air in January 1919 and spent two years in that post before assuming the Colonial Office in February 1921. However, Churchill lost his seat in the November 1922 election and spent two years in exile before returning as Chancellor in Stanley Baldwin's Government. Whatever else it embodies, Churchill's career reflects tremendous resilience and tenacity.

I

Four years of industrial slaughter transformed the world in which Churchill and his Empire operated. Two of Britain's imperial rivals were - at least temporarily - removed from the scene. Germany lost its Kaiser, its colonies and its High Seas Fleet. Under Versailles, the German Army was reduced to 100,000 men and it was to have no air force and no submarines. Clause 231 of the Treaty held the Central Powers responsible for wartime damage and demanded £6.6bn in reparations.

Russia's two revolutions in 1917 were followed by four years of foreign intervention, civil war and famine which prostrated the country. Lenin prioritised survival and consolidation and, over time, 'socialism in one country' replaced 'export the revolution'.

The Habsburg Empire crumbled into multiple successor states (Austria, Hungary, Yugoslavia, Czechoslovakia) while the Ottoman Empire was reduced to its Anatolian rump through the loss of its North African and Middle Eastern territories. Disillusioned by old world cynicism and venality, America withdrew into splendid isolation while retaining a watchful eye on the Pacific.

As a result, Britain was the leading - indeed only - post-war superpower. Potential rivals had been removed by defeat, necessity or choice and Britain could wallow in the prestige of victory, its glorious Empire intact. Indeed, Britain's Empire **expanded** as a result of the war as it seized Tanganyika (mainland Tanzania) and portions of Cameroon and Togo from Germany to forge an arc of territory joining Cairo to the Cape. Turkey yielded Palestine and Iraq, while Britain's dominions also profited from victory - South Africa gained Namibia, Australia acquired New Guinea and Samoa went to New Zealand. Britain's imperial zenith is usually portrayed as a Victorian achievement but it was during the grim grey interwar era - the years of the Depression, hunger marches and General Strike - that Britain's Empire assumed its greatest size.

However, all was far from well below the surface. Foreign competitors and indigenous producers had penetrated Britain's overseas markets and British exports regained only 80% of their pre-war level. Britain owed America £1.365bn and the national debt soared from £650m to £7.435bn - these debts alone would require massive retrenchment to attain the classical ideal of 'balancing the budget'. Wall Street and the dollar increasingly replaced London and sterling in international finance and in 1919, Britain left the Gold Standard in the hope that a flexible exchange rate would promote economic revival. Unfortunately, sterling plummeted against the dollar, sparking a clamour for a return to gold which, once implemented, would prove disastrous.

Britain had no enemies and was under pressure to reduce spending so, in August 1919, the Cabinet - with Churchill's wholehearted support - endorsed the Ten Year Rule stating that

> *it should be assumed, for framing revised estimates, that the British Empire will not be engaged in any great war during the next ten years, and that no Expeditionary Force is required for this purpose.*

This principle prompted massive defence cuts throughout the 1920s. Defence spending slumped from £692m in 1919/20 to £115m by 1924/25 and remained at that level for the rest of the decade. The Army was more severely affected than the other services. In 1920/21, the Army had received 62% of the defence budget, the Navy 30% and the RAF 8%. In 1925/26, the Army received 37% while the Navy gained 50% and the RAF 13%. These ratios remained largely static for the rest of the decade, the RAF share increasing slightly at the Army's expense. Once the great emergency was over, Britain reverted to its old 'Blue Water' preference - a mighty Navy and a small army to police the Empire and maintain order at home, with the RAF providing what was euphemistically known as 'air policing'.[28]

As British military muscle atrophied, America challenged its naval supremacy. Asquith had committed Britain to the 'two power standard' as recently as 1908 but America initiated a massive naval construction programme in 1916 which - if fully implemented - would transfer ascendancy across the Atlantic. The 1916 Naval Expansion Act committed America to building ten battleships, six battlecruisers, fifty destroyers and sixty-seven submarines over a three-year period to create *"incomparably, the greatest Navy in the world,"* and President Wilson articulated America's grand ambition when he urged his confidant Colonel House: *"Let us build a navy bigger than hers [Great Britain] and do what we please."*

America's naval ambition created a crisis for cash-strapped Britain which could either surrender its naval supremacy - unpalatable for a nation raised on the traditions of Nelson and Hood - or engage in a building war which would recreate the pre-war tensions that had existed with Germany. Lloyd George outlined Britain's dilemma to the Committee of Imperial Defence in December 1920.

> *If the Committee were to decide now that Great Britain must enter into competition with the United States in naval shipbuilding, it would be the biggest decision they had taken since 1914... There would follow precisely the same tension as had resulted from our naval competition with Germany. The two countries would begin to scowl and to snarl at each other; newspapers on both sides would stir up public feeling... The first result of this would be that America would insist upon her debt being paid in full... we should be up against the greatest resources of the world.*

A third option was to reach an 'accommodation' with America but if America was to renounce its naval ambitions, what could Britain offer in return? Britain was allied to Japan in 1920 and America attributed Japan's cocky assertiveness in the Pacific to this alliance. If Britain renounced its friendship with Japan, perhaps America might do a deal over naval construction?

---

[28] Section III offers an example of 'air policing'.

And so it transpired. At the November 1921 - February 1922 Washington Naval Conference, Britain abandoned its Japanese alliance and replaced it with a vague Four Power Treaty in which Britain, France, Japan and America agreed to respect each other's Pacific interests and resolve any disputes through mediation. The *quid pro quo* came with the February 1922 Washington Naval Treaty in which Britain, America and Japan agreed to a 5:5:3 ratio in capital ships and a ten-year moratorium on capital ship construction. Subsidiary sections of the Treaty regulated French and Italian naval strength and battleships could not exceed 35,000 tons.

The Washington Treaty represented triumph and disaster for Britain. On the one hand, it avoided a costly naval building war and guaranteed parity - not inferiority - with the United States, but whereas America was a hemispheric power with interests in the Pacific and Atlantic and Japan was a regional Pacific power, Britain was a global power with interests on virtually every ocean and continent. Accepting the constraints of the Washington Treaty meant that if Britain faced major threats in the Atlantic or Mediterranean, as it would in the 1930s, it would lack the resources to confront a third enemy in the Pacific and this is exactly what happened - the seeds of Appeasement were sown in 1922 when Britain buckled before America's rising naval strength.

The Washington Naval Treaty was the first occasion in 250 years in which Britain had modified its foreign policy to accommodate a stronger power. Britain appeased America over the Washington Naval Treaty - just as it had done over the Alaskan border dispute - and the battle-lines of World War Two were being drawn. Britain was assuming the role of America's lackey while Japan - freed from the restraints of friendship with Britain - could embark on the aggressive adventurism which would culminate in the conquest of Singapore, Hong Kong, Malaya and Burma (Myanmar), territories it had once pledged to protect.

II

Britain ruthlessly crushed colonial dissent while yielding to America. One million Indian troops had served Britain during World War One and both the Muslim League and Indian National Congress felt that this contribution merited recognition, but Britain's response was contradictory and inconsistent. The 1919 Government of India Act granted Indians a measure of control over 'soft' departments within the provincial and central legislatures (e.g. agriculture, education, public works) while authority over all the 'hard' controlling departments (finance, revenue, home affairs) remained with the Raj.[29] At the same time, Britain passed the Rowlatt Act, extending wartime security measures into peacetime and giving the Raj the right to arrest without warrant, detain without trial, try without juries and curtail press freedom. The repression of Rowlatt and the begrudging Government of India Act sparked a storm of protest throughout India, particularly in the Punjab where Britain responded by imposing martial law and banning meetings attended by more than five people.

On 13th April 1919, fifteen thousand people gathered in Amritsar's Jallianwala Bagh walled garden to celebrate Vaisakhi - a major Sikh festival - and listen to speeches denouncing the Raj. In the late afternoon, a troop of Ghurkha and Baluchi soldiers commanded by General Reginald Dyer arrived and - without warning - started firing into the crowd. After fifteen minutes, 1650 rounds of ammunition had been expended and between 379 and 1,000 people were dead, many having suffocated when they jumped down a well to try to escape the shooting. When asked why he hadn't ordered the crowd to disperse, Dyer explained that he *"could have dispersed the crowd without firing but they would have come back again and laughed and I would have made, what I consider, a fool of myself."* Dyer's concern for his 'dignity' obviously trumped any Indian's right to life.

Shock waves reverberated throughout the Empire. In the Commons, Churchill denounced the slaughter as standing *"without precedent or parallel in the modern history of the British Empire... an extraordinary event, a monstrous event, an event which stands in singular and sinister isolation."* Dyer was invalided out of the army in 1920 and the Indian National Congress embraced *swaraj* (independence). Indian unrest was quelled by the end of 1922 using the ferocity of the Rowlatt Act but notice had been served - the Raj was living on borrowed time.

Ireland also challenged British supremacy after the war. The Easter Rising had been crushed in 1916 but Sinn Fein won 70% of Irish seats in the December 1918 election and established a Dáil (Assembly) in Dublin to demand independence. The Irish people had expressed their preferences through the ballot box but Britain refused to acknowledge the result and established two paramilitary *freikorps* to support the Royal Irish Constabulary (RIC) and suppress dissent. Ex-soldiers were recruited into the 'Black and Tans'[30] and paid ten shillings a day for the *"rough and dangerous task"* of suppressing Irish nationalism, while ex-

---

[29] Scotland endures a similar system under Devolution.

[30] So called because their uniforms were a motley blend of army khaki and RIC dark green.

officers joined the RIC Auxiliary Division (Auxies) and received £1 per day to round up suspected IRA activists on the basis of intelligence tip-offs. By autumn 1920, two thousand Auxies and 9,500 Tans were operating in Ireland.

The presence of British-paid mercenaries inflamed the situation, provoking an upsurge in violence. In September 1920, the IRA killed a senior RIC constable in Balbriggan, a small town twenty miles north of Dublin and in retaliation, the Black and Tans torched twenty houses, ransacked an English-owned hosiery factory and murdered two IRA suspects. On 21st November, the IRA executed two Auxies and twelve British intelligence officers in Dublin and, in retaliation, Auxie units fired into a crowd at a Gaelic football match in Croke Park, killing twelve. After the IRA killed seventeen Auxies in an ambush at Kilmichael, Auxie and Tan units rampaged through Cork, setting fire to buildings and causing £3m worth of damage.

By mid-1921, Britain faced two choices: it could continue to suppress Ireland's independence movement through violence and earn international opprobrium or it could strike a deal with pragmatic Republican elements to retain a foothold on the island. Britain opted for the latter and the December 1921 Anglo-Irish Treaty partitioned Ireland along ethnic and sectarian lines. Britain retained six northern counties - home to a large loyalist community and Ireland's heavy industry - while 26 southern counties, where resistance to British rule was strongest, were recognised as the Irish Free State. The Free State remained within the Empire as a Dominion and Dáil members were forced to swear allegiance to the crown; Britain also retained control over three deep water ports (Cobh, Castletownbere and Lough Swilly) to protect its Atlantic trade. A Civil War erupted between supporters and opponents of the 1921 Treaty and Britain provided the Free State with aircraft, armoured cars and machine guns to crush proponents of a fully united Ireland.

By 1922, the citizens of Britain's oldest colony had gained a significant - though partial - victory over the Empire while, at the same time, people in Britain's newer possessions were also contesting imperial control.

III

Put simply, Britain played the Arabs for chumps during WWI, inciting rebellion against the Turks with promises of post-war freedom while, at the same time, cynically plotting to carve up the region with France.

The chickens came home to roost in 1919 when Syrian and Egyptian delegates arrived at the Paris Peace Conference to demand the independence they'd been promised but - as Britain and France had gone to war to defend their Empires - they were never going to relinquish their new acquisitions to Arab nationalists. Britain gained Palestine and Iraq as League of Nations mandates while France acquired Syria and Lebanon, and France renounced Mosul - in northern Iraq - in return for British support for a punitive settlement against Germany. The April 1920 San Remo Conference confirmed these arrangements.

The Arab world exploded in fury at this betrayal. Faisal - son of the Sharif of Mecca - declared himself sovereign of Syria while Iraq erupted in armed insurrection and Egypt was convulsed by demonstrations and strikes. Britain suppressed the unrest through a blend of guile and violence, the settlement in each area reflecting the local balance of power and Britain's ability to enforce its will.

Egypt had been a British protectorate since 1914 but was never formally incorporated into the Empire so, following mass protests in 1919 and 1922, Britain formalised its relationship with Egypt by issuing a unilateral Declaration of Independence which recognised Egypt as a sovereign state while *"absolutely reserv[ing]"* four key points *"to the discretion of His Majesty's Government"*: (i) the security of the communications of the British Empire in Egypt (ii) the defence of Egypt against foreign aggression (iii) the protection of foreign interests in Egypt, and (iv) Sudan (which controlled Egypt's water supply). The Declaration gave Egypt some control over its domestic and internal affairs while Britain retained authority over the things that really mattered - the Suez Canal and the right to re-enter the country in time of war. Britain's High Commissioner - Lord Lloyd of Dolobran - characterised the new arrangement by noting that

> *to tell a country she is independent while you keep an army of occupation is not only a contradiction in terms but a fraud.*

The partial and unsatisfactory nature of the 1922 settlement would demand further revisions in the future.

Iraq exploded in fury following the San Remo Conference and by July 1920, 130,000 Shias, Sunnis and Kurds were in arms against British rule and Ayatollah al-Shirazi issued a *fatwa* declaring that service in the British administration violated Islamic law.

The Iraq rebellion created problems for War Secretary Churchill who was under great pressure to cut costs but - fortunately for him - the RAF was also searching for a job to justify its independent existence. Air power had recently crushed a Somali rising - Leo Amery dubbed it *"the cheapest war in history"* - so Churchill opted to use air power to quell the rising and cut costs in a primitive version of 'shock and awe'. Throughout 1920, the RAF flew 4,000 hours of combat missions, dropping 97 tons of bombs and firing 184,000 rounds of ammunition to kill between 6,000-9,000 Iraqis; RAF losses totalled eleven aircraft and sixteen servicemen killed or wounded. Wing Commander J.A. Chamier described the harsh reality of 'air policing' by noting that

> *the Air force must, if called upon to administer punishment, do it with all its might and in the proper manner. One objective must be selected - preferably the most inaccessible village of the most prominent tribe which it is desired to punish. All available aircraft must be collected... The attack with bombs and machine guns must be relentless and unremitting and carried on continuously by day and night, on houses, inhabitants, crops and cattle... This sounds brutal I know but it must be made brutal to start with. The threat alone in the future will prove efficacious if the lesson is once properly learnt.*

45 Squadron's Commanding Officer offered a similarly bleak account of 'air policing'.

> *The Arabs and Kurds... now know what real bombing means, in casualties and damage; they now know that within forty-five minutes a full-sized village can be practically wiped out and a third of its inhabitants killed or injured by four or five machines which offer them no real target, no opportunity for glory as warriors, no effective means of escape.*

The identity of this second officer is significant for it was none other than Arthur 'Bomber' Harris who would later direct RAF bombing against Germany.[31] The theoretical aim of area bombing was to 'de-house' Germany's urban workforce but it was basically Iraqi air

---

[31] Harris served in Iraq during 1922-24 and his memoirs offer the following account of air policing: *"When a tribe started open revolt we gave warning to all its most important villages, by loudspeaker from low-flying aircraft and by dropping messages, that air action would be taken after 48 hours. Then, if the rebellion continued, we destroyed the villages and by air patrols kept the insurgents away from their homes for as long as necessary until they decided to give up... It was, of course, a far less costly method of controlling rebellion than by military action and the casualties on both sides were infinitely less than they would have been in the pitched battles on*

operations on a much larger scale using modern technology. Seventeen years before the Condor Legion obliterated Guernica, the RAF pioneered terror bombing and employed the same tactic to uphold imperial control in Yemen, Afghanistan, Kuwait and Transjordan. It was essentially a hi-tech version of the old-fashioned torching of Swat Valley farms.

Britain also installed a puppet to govern Iraq on its behalf and the man chosen for the job was Faisal, third son of the Sharif of Mecca and – briefly - King of Syria. Faisal had fought with T.E. Lawrence against the Turks and Lawrence assured Churchill - Colonial Secretary after February 1921- that Faisal would prove an excellent British proxy. In 1921, British High Commissioner Sir Percy Cox rigged a plebiscite to demonstrate widespread support for Faisal and on 23rd August, Faisal was crowned King in a ceremony stage-managed by Britain and modelled on British ritual. Faisal attempted to govern Iraq in the interests of its people but he was an artificial king in an artificial country without an indigenous powerbase who relied on British support to retain power. In 1922 he signed a twenty year treaty confirming that he would accept British advice on all matters affecting British interests and on fiscal policy as long as Iraq retained a balance of payments deficit with Britain. British inspectors worked in eighteen Iraqi government departments with Iraq covering half their salaries. A renewed treaty in 1930 provided for *"full and frank consultations between the two countries in all matters of foreign policy"* and Britain gained the right to move troops across the country and develop air bases at Basra and Habbaniya.

Terror bombing and puppet rulers saved British taxpayers' money as the cost of garrisoning Iraq plummeted from £32m in 1921 to £0.5m by 1930 and, by the latter date, hardly any British ground troops remained in the country. Britain's mission in Iraq was fully vindicated in 1927 when a huge oil gusher was discovered at Baba Gurgur (near Kirkuk) and the Turkish Petroleum Company started extracting the country's oil wealth for its British shareholders.

Britain gained Palestine at the same time as it acquired Iraq and it was here that it sought to build a Jewish national home to consolidate its control over Suez. Churchill outlined Britain's aspirations for the region by writing that

> *if... there should be created in our lifetime by the banks of*

---

the ground." (Harris, *Bomber Offensive,* pp.22-23). Readers can decide which account seems most plausible.

the Jordan a Jewish state under the protection of the British Crown… an event will have occurred in the history of the world which would from every point of view be beneficial and would be especially in harmony with the truest interests of the British Empire

Palestine's first High Commissioner was Herbert Samuel, the same Cabinet member who had supported the creation of a Jewish home in Palestine to advance British interests in 1914.

Map 5: Middle East Mandates and Mosul-Haifa Pipeline

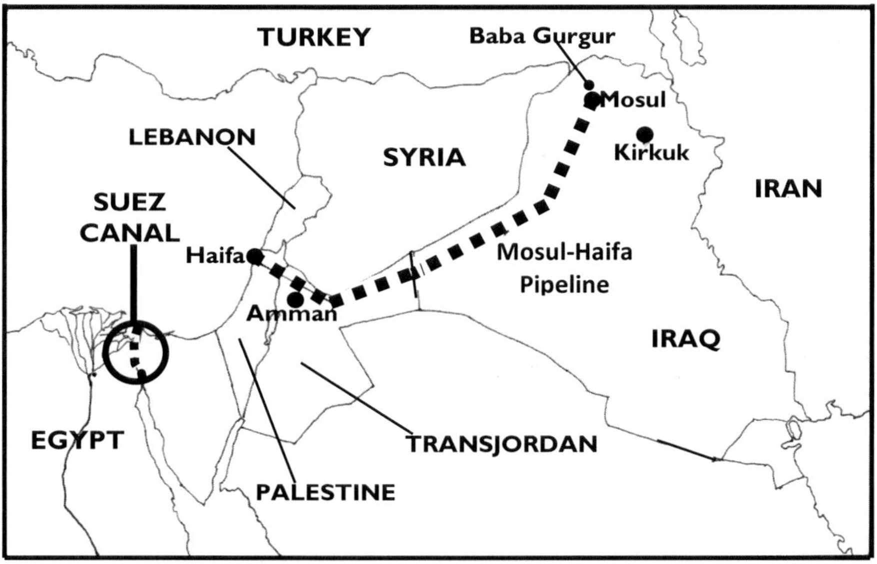

Nevertheless, independent Arab action forced Britain to modify its plans for the Mandate. Faisal's brother Abdullah had established himself in territory south of Syria and to the east of the River Jordan (Transjordan) during 1920/21 and he threatened to invade Syria to install an Arab government. Britain hoped to avoid friction with France and so - as Abdullah had already established himself in Transjordan - Britain offered to recognise him as Emir on condition that he abandoned his plans to invade Syria. Abdullah proved to be as pragmatic as his brother in his dealings with Britain which recognised him as Emir of Transjordan, hiving off the eastern portion of the Mandate - containing 77% of its territory - as his new kingdom. Like his brother, Abdullah ruled Transjordan on Britain's behalf and remained dependent on British subsidies while British advisers managed the statelet's defence, foreign policy and finance. The RAF base at Marka - just outside Amman - consolidated British control of the region and defended Jordan against Wahhabi incursions from the south.

Britain and France redrew the Middle East map during 1918-24 with five British- and French-controlled client states replacing the old Ottoman Empire. Britain secured its control over Suez from a nominally independent Egypt, and Palestine and Transjordan provided extra security to the north and east. Britain gained control over Iraqi oil and the combination of Palestine, Transjordan and Iraq created a 'land bridge' linking the Mediterranean to the Persian Gulf and offering an alternative route to India. The Mosul-Haifa pipeline started pumping oil from northern Iraq to the Mediterranean port of Haifa in 1935 and - even though the oil travelled through three different states on its 585-mile journey to the sea - it remained within British-controlled territory at all times, vividly illustrating Britain's rationale for dismembering the Ottoman Empire and establishing itself as the region's new master.

IV

Churchill could derive great satisfaction from his achievements of 1919-22. He'd overseen the demobilisation of Britain's conscript army and had helped negotiate an end to Ireland's War of Independence. As Secretary for War and Air, he'd devised a cost-effective means of suppressing colonial dissent and advocated the use of mustard gas[32] against Iraqi civilians. He'd nominated Faisal to rule Iraq as a British proxy and installed his brother Abdullah as Transjordan's Emir. In September 1922, he'd also taken advantage of Clementine's confinement with their fifth child to purchase Chartwell, the Kentish manor house that would be his family home for the rest of his life.

And then - when all seemed to be going well - Churchill lost his seat in the November 1922 Election. He'd been diagnosed with appendicitis on 17th October so could only campaign for four days but the Tories were deeply unpopular in Scotland and he'd been largely absent from his constituency. He trailed in third behind Labour and Temperance candidates and, after the vote, quipped that he found himself *"without an office, without a seat, without a party and without an appendix."*

Churchill's political world was changing dramatically. The 1918

---

[32] Churchill sent the following note to Air Marshal Trenchard on 29th August 1920: *"I think you should certainly proceed with the experimental work on gas bombs,* ***especially mustard gas*** *[emphasis added], which would inflict punishment on recalcitrant natives without inflicting grave injury upon them."* (Gilbert, *Winston S. Churchill,* Vol. IV, Companion, p.1190). Some writers disingenuously claim that Churchill only wished to employ a lachrymatory 'tear gas' against Iraqi civilians. However, Britain's long-term plan for the region was to reduce ground forces to a bare minimum and tear gas - employed mainly for crowd control - would have been ineffective in such a context. Mustard gas more effectively demonstrated imperial might and majesty.

Representation of the People Act almost tripled the size of the electorate,[33] greatly aiding the Labour Party. In 1923, the party won more seats and a bigger share of the vote than the Asquith and Lloyd George Liberals combined and - in 1924 -Ramsay MacDonald formed the first minority Labour government.

Churchill was horrified. He detested socialism - even Labour's cautious reformism - and looked for ways to block its progress. The Liberal Party was hopelessly divided and seemed unlikely to form a government or furnish Churchill with a vehicle for his ambitions. In his view, the Tories offered the only credible opposition to Labour and so, after 1922, Churchill moved steadily to the right as he attempted to re-join his old party. The December 1923 election was his last as a Liberal, losing Leicester West to Labour by 4,000 votes. In March 1924, he fought a by-election in the Abbey Division of Westminster as an Independent Anti-Socialist and came within 43 votes of defeating the official Tory candidate. By this stage, Baldwin was Tory Party leader and whereas Bonar Law had regarded Churchill as having an *"entirely unbalanced mind,"* Baldwin was more emollient. Seeking to prevent one final link-up between Churchill and Lloyd George, he felt it safer to have Churchill inside the party as a dynamic nuisance than outside as a potential threat. When Churchill contested Epping as a Constitutional Anti-Socialist in October 1924, there was no Conservative candidate and he romped home with a 10,000 majority. With only a minor name change - Epping changed to Woodford in 1945 - this would remain his Parliamentary home for the next four decades.

Having re-admitted Churchill to the Tory fold, Baldwin now had to find him a job and - on 5th November - stunned his new colleague by offering him the post of Chancellor. Churchill was astonished to be offered such a plum position but quickly regained his composure and graciously accepted - it was a post his father had held for five months and he still had Randolph's old robes, carefully preserved in camphor and tissue paper. A Churchill would once more direct the nation's finances.

---

[33] From 7.7m to 21m as men gained the vote at 21. Women had to wait till they were 30.

CHAPTER FIVE: THE ECONOMIC CONSEQUENCES OF MR CHURCHILL, 1924-29

I wish they were admirals or generals, I can speak their own language, and I can sink them if necessary. But after a while, when I am talking to bankers and economists, they begin to talk Persian; and then they sink me instead; and I think this a great misfortune for this country.

Churchill outlines his economic ignorance
to his Private Secretary, Bob Boothby

The true defence of our country, owing to scientific development, is now no longer the Channel ... but upon the Rhine.

Foreign Secretary Austen Chamberlain
addressing the 1926 Imperial Conference

The Great War's worst wounds were starting to heal by 1925. American money flowed into Europe under the Dawes Plan and Germany was peaceful and prosperous. The 1925 Locarno Treaties guaranteed the French, German and Belgian borders and fifteen leading powers renounced war as a means of resolving disputes in 1928. In that same year, Britain's government permanently endorsed the Ten Year Rule, discounting the possibility of war for at least another decade. Europe appeared to be entering a new age of peace and prosperity - what could possibly go wrong?

I

British imperial power declined as its economic and industrial muscle atrophied. By 1914, Germany and America had assumed leadership in industries which would dominate the twentieth century - electrical engineering, chemicals, motor vehicles - while Britain's older industries - coal, iron and steel, textiles, shipbuilding - failed to keep pace while the First World War exacerbated British problems. The 1919 National Debt was eleven times larger than it had been in 1913 and Britain had sold many of its assets to pay for the War. While British businesses were producing bullets, shells and guns, foreign and indigenous competitors penetrated their overseas markets and post-war sales slumped. Cotton exports declined by half between 1913-22 while - at the same time - Japanese and Indian power looms increased by 66%. If these trends continued, Britain would be ruined by mounting unemployment, rising poverty and a collapse of imperial authority. By the mid-'twenties, Britain faced a stark choice between re-inventing itself as a dynamic, innovative economy or continuing down a path towards stagnation, under-investment and declining productivity. The country needed a genius, an economic visionary who could chart a path to prosperity, but what it got was Winston Churchill, a Chancellor who - by his own admission - couldn't even understand his own officials. Churchill was offered the Treasury because Baldwin's first choice - Neville Chamberlain - preferred Health, and he was determined to prove himself a good Conservative to the backbenchers who viewed him as a renegade who'd ratted on the Party in 1904, ditched the Liberals in 1924 and who might jump ship again if it suited his interests. For once, Churchill felt rather insecure and proposed to silence his critics by embracing unimpeachable orthodoxy.

The biggest issue facing him on entering Number Eleven was the timing of Britain's return to the Gold Standard. The world's leading currencies had all been gold-backed before 1914 but this system had been suspended on the outbreak of war as governments funded their war efforts with paper money. Gold, however, was regarded as synonymous with rising prosperity and it was assumed that all right-thinking nations would revert to gold once the crisis passed. The United States returned to gold in June 1919 and only extreme post-war fluctuations prevented an equally rapid return by sterling. By December 1922, sterling was trading at $4.61 so a return to gold at the pre-war $4.86 rate seemed feasible. The chorus of convention - conducted by Bank of England Governor Montagu Norman - argued that such a move would be good for business and send a strong message to the upstart dollar.

Other voices - such as John Maynard Keynes - argued that sterling was overvalued by 10% and that a return to gold at the pre-War rate would prove disastrous - exports would become more expensive, sales would slump and employers would be forced to cut wages to remain competitive, a point argued with force and clarity in *The Economic Consequences of Mr Churchill* in which he warned that the Chancellor

> *was just asking for trouble... the working classes ... are faced with a depression in their standard of life... and, therefore, they are justified in defending themselves... They are bound to resist as long as they can; and it must be war, until those who are economically weakest are beaten to the ground.*

Churchill discounted Keynes' warnings and returned Britain to the Gold

Standard at $4.86 in April 1925, quickly vindicating Keynes' concerns. A coal subsidy averted industrial unrest in 1925 but when the subsidy expired in April 1926 and the miners refused to accept a pay cut, the mine-owners locked them out to starve them into submission - the 1926 General Strike therefore began with a bosses' lockout rather than union militancy. The Trades Union Congress (TUC) offered the miners their modest support and for nine days, Britain was convulsed by its first ever General Strike, precipitated mainly by long-term under-investment and Churchill's inane policies. Having initiated unrest through his disastrous economics, Churchill lambasted the strikers from the pages of the *British Gazette*, denouncing them as militants hell-bent on subverting Britain's constitution. The TUC was unprepared for major confrontation and folded after nine days but the miners held out until October when hunger forced them back on the employers' terms, beaten by an economic policy which *"favoured the special interests of finance at the expense of the special interests of production."*[34]

The miners were only the first and best-known victims of Churchill's orthodoxy. Unemployment remained at 8.5% for the rest of the decade (higher than France, Germany and the United States) and reached 20% in areas reliant on older export industries. A pall of gloom descended over Britain's economy as high interest rates choked off investment and a strong pound sucked in imports. Shipbuilders, cotton spinners, miners and steelworkers all suffered as a result of Churchill's ineptitude but so too did the men of Britain's armed forces.

II

For someone with a reputation as a re-armer, Churchill's record is decidedly patchy. He had opposed dreadnought construction in 1908 and, as Secretary for War and Air, supported the Ten Year Rule which was used to slash defence spending after the War. As Chancellor, Churchill's antipathy to defence spending was even more pronounced. The table below summarises British defence spending during the 1920s and some salient facts merit attention:

---

[34] Churchill used this phrase in a 29th January note before finally opting to embrace Gold. Churchill was fully aware that such a move would benefit finance more than industry and questioned the wisdom of such a move before yielding to irresistible orthodoxy (D. E. Moggridge, *British Monetary Policy 1924-1931: The Norman Conquest of $4.86* (1972), p.65; Ponting, *Churchill*, p.295).

Table I: British Defence Expenditure, 1920-1930 (£m)

	Army spend (% share)	Navy spend (% share)	RAF spend (% share)	Total Budget
1920/21	181.5 (62)	88.5 (30)	22.3 (8)	292.2
1921/22	95.1 (50)	80.8 (43)	13.6 (7)	189.4
1922/23	45.4 (41)	56.2 (51)	9.4 (8)	110.0
1923/24	43.6 (41)	52.6 (50)	9.6 (9)	105.8
1924/25	44.8 (39)	55.6 (49)	14.3 (12)	114.7
1925/26	44.3 (37)	59.7 (50)	15.5 (13)	119.4
1926/27	43.6 (38)	57.6 (49)	15.5 (13)	116.7
1927/28	44.2 (38)	58.1 (50)	15.2 (12)	117.4
1928/29	40.5 (36)	56.9 (50)	16.1 (14)	113.5
1929/30	40.5 (36)	55.8 (49)	16.8 (15)	113.0

- during Churchill's five years as Chancellor, total defence spending declined by 5.5% (from £119.4m to £113m). In some years, he even under-spent Ramsay MacDonald.

- during this period, the Army's budget shrank by 8.5% (£44.25m - £40.5m) while the Navy's budget declined by 6.5% (£59.7m - £55.75m).

- RAF spending increased by 8% from its modest base of £15.5m in 1925/26.

- throughout Churchill's period as Chancellor, the Admiralty received approximately half of the defence budget, while the Army received 37% (50% in 1921) and the RAF between 13-14%.

Churchill's hostility to defence expenditure had multiple roots. Firstly, the international scene supported reduced expenditure. The 1925 Locarno Treaties ushered in a new era of reconciliation and Germany was prosperous and disarmed. America was comfortably isolationist, the Soviet Union was absorbed in its New Economic Policy and Japan's worst depredations had not yet commenced. The British Empire faced no immediate threat and so, if fiscal parsimony was required to balance the books, the late 'twenties offered the ideal time to wield the axe.

Economic orthodoxy further inspired Churchillian austerity. All Conservative Chancellors aspired to a balanced budget and as Britain still carried huge war debts (£7.45bn), further retrenchment was judged necessary. In his April 1925 budget, Churchill cut income tax by 11% (from 4s.6d (22½p) to 4s. (20p)) to stimulate enterprise but high interest rates and an overvalued pound choked investment, so this strategy merely served to reduce government revenues during a recession, leaving even less for public spending. The service chiefs fully appreciated the link between defence cuts and tax cuts as First Sea Lord Beatty acidly observed to his wife.

> *That extraordinary fellow Winston has gone mad... and no sacrifice is too great to achieve what in his short-sightedness is the panacea for all evils, to take one shilling off the Income Tax. Nobody outside a lunatic asylum expects a shilling off the Income Tax.... As we, the Admiralty, are the principal spending Department, he attacks us with virulence and now proclaims that a Navy is a quite unnecessary luxury.*

Whatever funds were available should be diverted towards social programmes to thwart Labour, as Churchill explained to Stanley Baldwin.

> *To accept these armaments increases [proposed by the Navy] is to sterilise and paralyse the whole policy of the government. There will be nothing for the taxpayer and nothing for social reform... there is nothing for it - if we accept the armament policy - but to put out of our mind all idea of reduction of taxation and practically all plans of social reform... such a policy will not only bring the government into ruin but might well affect the safety of the state... I cannot conceive any course more certain to result in a Socialist victory.*

Economic orthodoxy, overvalued sterling, tax cuts, a desire to thwart Labour, economic recession, high levels of national debt and the absence of threat - all these forces drove Churchill into conflict with the three service departments, particularly the Navy.

The Treasury-Admiralty clash of 1925-29 was motivated by differing perceptions of Japan's rising threat. Churchill was adamant that no such threat existed nor would it emerge in the foreseeable future and, in 1924, asked Prime Minister Baldwin:

> *Why should there be a war with Japan? I do not believe there is the slightest chance of it* ***in our lifetime*** *[emphasis added]. The Japanese are our allies*[35]*... Japan is at the other end of the world. She cannot menace our vital security in any way.*

---

[35] The Anglo-Japanese Alliance had lapsed in 1921-22 so Churchill is simply wrong here.

When the Admiralty submitted its 1925/26 service estimates, Churchill demanded they

> *recast all their plans and scales and standards on the basis that no naval war against a first class navy is likely to take place* ***in the next twenty years*** *[emphasis added].*

While Churchill discounted the Japanese threat, the Navy was more alarmed, pointing to Japan's new generation of 10,000-ton cruisers equipped with 8-inch guns. In Beatty's opinion,

> *an eight-inch [gun] ship is in a position to crush a 7.5-inch ship without laying itself open to be crushed in return… the advent of the eight-inch gun ship has made not only the 6" ship but also the 7.5" gunships out of date.*

As most British cruisers carried only 5.5-inch or 6-inch guns, Beatty's concerns were fully justified. In 1924/25, the Admiralty estimated that it required a fleet of seventy modern cruisers to protect imperial trade and support the Navy's battleships and - as 32 of the existing fleet of 56 cruisers were due to be scrapped by 1936 - the Navy needed 46 new cruisers by 1936 to meet minimum requirements. Treasury officials pointed out that the Admiralty's estimates for 1925/26 were £10m higher than those of the previous year and warned they would rise to £80m by 1927-28 if left unchecked.

Contrasting aspirations set Churchill and the Admiralty on a collision course and both sides mobilised support. The Admiralty roused backing among Tory backbenchers who favoured a strong Navy while Churchill invited Foreign Secretary Austen Chamberlain to rule out *"a war with Japan… in the next 10, 15 or 20 years."* Chamberlain duly obliged, restating his support for the Ten Year Rule in the Committee of Imperial Defence (CID) by arguing that *"aggressive action by Japan against the British Empire… within the next ten years is not a contingency to be seriously apprehended".* After initial skirmishes, the Navy submitted estimates of £62.5m, Churchill offered £60m and the entire Admiralty Board threatened resignation if its demands were rejected, a curious inversion of the 1913 crisis when Churchill had threatened resignation if his own Admiralty estimates were spurned. Churchill referred the matter to the Prime Minister and in July 1925, Baldwin ruled that the Navy should have four new cruisers during 1925/26 but that construction should be delayed till as late as possible to maximise savings, and three more cruisers were to be built during 1926/27. It was a tactical victory for the Navy and Churchill responded by delaying construction of the Singapore naval base and slashing the Navy's fuel oil reserve. The Navy was forced to accept a truncated Singapore scheme (£7.75m instead of £11m) and when the base finally opened in February 1938 (fifteen years after construction commenced), building was still underway.

After a short truce, Navy-Treasury hostilities resumed in autumn 1927 and the Great Re-Armer was much better prepared. In July 1928, he convinced the Committee of Imperial Defence (CID) to endorse a more permanent version of the Ten Year Rule whereby *"it should be assumed for the purposes of framing the estimates of the fighting services that, at any given date, there will be no major war for ten years"* and having gained this support, used it to slash Admiralty spending during his last two years in office. The Naval Programme Committee - chaired by his friend, Lord Birkenhead - ruled that the Navy could only have three new cruisers during 1927-29 (rather than six) and the Navy's 1928/29 estimates were reduced by £1m to £57.3m. By the time Churchill left office, Navy spending had been pruned to £55.8m, almost £4m less than it had received in 1925. Churchill had triumphed in his titanic struggle with the Navy but would the Navy win its impending contest with Japan (and Germany and Italy) which Churchill entirely discounted?

RAF spending increased slightly during the late 'twenties - it offered imperial 'policing' on the cheap - but it was still desperately under-funded. In 1923, Prime Minister Baldwin ruled that Britain needed a 52 squadron Home Defence Force (HDF) by 1930 to protect it from attack but in 1927 - with the heady scent of Locarno in the air - this completion date was delayed to 1936, and in 1929 it was further postponed to 1938. Indeed, at no point prior to 1939 did Britain possess an HDF equal in size to the one advocated in 1923 when air power was in its infancy. If Hitler's aggressive adventuring in the late 1930s was motivated by perceptions of British weakness, all those responsible for this under-preparation - including Churchill - must shoulder the blame for Appeasement and the war which followed.

The army also faced cuts during 1924-29 but - before examining its fate - some context is essential.

The seven Locarno Treaties of 1925 promised harmony and reconciliation but the text demands scrutiny. The most significant issue concerns the contrast between the treaties governing Germany's western borders (with France and Belgium) and those regulating its eastern frontiers (with Czechoslovakia and Poland). Under Locarno, the western borders set at Versailles were regarded as sacrosanct - guaranteed by Britain and Italy - while the eastern frontiers with Czecho

-slovakia and Poland were viewed as temporary and transient, subject to revision through 'arbitration'. Britain and France also differed markedly in their attitudes towards Europe's 'successor states'. France hoped to construct strong alliances with the eastern powers to contain Germany and exclude Bolshevism while Britain was largely indifferent to their fate, viewing them as 'far away countries containing people of whom we know nothing' and - having no strategic interests in the area - was happy to see them chopped and re-shaped as long as overt violence was avoided. Foreign Secretary Austen Chamberlain's description of the Polish Corridor as something *"for which no British Government ever will and ever can risk the bones of a British grenadier"* epitomised British attitudes towards the region and Hitler skilfully exploited Anglo-French differences over eastern Europe to secure his eastern goals before focusing on the west. In the end, Austen Chamberlain's half-brother Neville was forced to risk much more than *"the bones of a British grenadier"* in a belated effort to rescue a successor state - Poland - of so little consequence to his sibling.

Locarno also committed Britain to assist France or Belgium if either state was attacked by Germany and, to do so, Britain needed a large army capable of continental operations. However, the Locarno Treaties were concluded at a time when the Army's continental capacity was being eroded by budget cuts and cabinet instructions. In 1922, the Cabinet informed the Army that its two principal functions were imperial policing and maintaining order at home, and the Army's budget was progressively reduced, from £95.1m in 1921/22 (50% of the total) to £40.5m (35% of total) by 1929. Britain's army also contracted during this period, from 3.5m in November 1918 to 370,000 by 1920 and 200,000 by the end of the decade, with half of this force overseas on imperial duties. Through Locarno, Britain's politicians were committing Britain's soldiers to an obligation they couldn't possibly keep and which directly contradicted both the Ten Year Rule and the Cabinet's 1922 instructions. The Chiefs of Staff highlighted these contradictions in their 1926 Imperial Defence Review which advised that *"so far as commitments on the continent are concerned, the Services can only take note of them."* This view was reiterated in 1930 when they confirmed that

> *this country is in a less favourable position to fulfil the Locarno guarantees than it was, without any written guarantee, to come to the assistance of France and Belgium in 1914.*

Such views raised no concerns in the balmy, quiescent days of the 'twenties but as global tensions mounted in the 1930s and Britain made no great effort to increase its continental capability, the discrepancy between commitments and resources prompted disaster.

While the Locarno Treaties were being signed, Britain's vulnerability to foreign attack also increased. Until 1914, Britain was safe from continental assault as long as hostile forces remained on the far side of the Channel, but this changed with the first Zeppelin raids of 1915 and - as air power grew increasingly deadly with each passing year - Britain's vulnerability also increased, particularly with so much wealth and power concentrated in London. The obvious solution lay in ensuring that London and other large cities remained beyond the range of hostile bombers and - for most of the 1920s and 1930s - this meant restricting hostile air forces to the east bank of the Rhine so that - with their limited range - they couldn't reach Britain. This is what Chamberlain was referring to in 1926 when he advised that *"the true defence of our country, owing to scientific development, is now no longer the Channel ... but upon the Rhine"* and the General Staff made the same point.

> *The true strategic frontier of Great Britain is the Rhine: her security depends entirely upon the present frontiers of France, Belgium and Holland being maintained and remaining in friendly hands... Any line of policy which permitted Germany ... first to swallow up France and then to deal with Great Britain would be fatal strategically.*

This awareness demanded a large British Army capable of continental operations - and a solid working relationship with France - but no such army or French alliance emerged in the 1920s or 1930s and by the time war erupted in 1939, the British Expeditionary Force (BEF) was similar in size to the token force available for European operations in 1914 - just four divisions. Instead, Britain placed heavy reliance on France holding the line as Britain rearmed - as it had in 1914 - and the folly of this position was brutally exposed in 1940 when Hitler swept western Allied forces aside before blitzing Britain. To identify a clear threat yet take no action to remedy it is tantamount to criminal negligence.

III

Churchill's tenure of Number Eleven must therefore be judged a failure. His economic orthodoxy - the over-valued pound, tax cuts, emphasis on balanced budgets - stifled recovery and condemned millions to poverty and unemployment. Having exacerbated unemployment through his rebarbative policies, he then tried to blame it on the *"growing up [of] a habit of qualifying for unemployment relief"* and advocated abolition of the dole to discourage this alleged dependency. He knew his policies were failing by 1927/28 but instead of changing them, blamed his advisers for luring him into unsuccessful stratagems. In September 1945, he finally confided to his doctor, Lord Moran, that *"the biggest blunder of my life was the return to the Gold Standard"* so - by his own admission - Churchill failed as Chancellor.

His attempts at prophecy were equally ineffective. In 1924/25, he confidently predicted that no war with Japan would occur *"in our lifetime"* and that *"no naval war against a first class navy is likely to take place in the next twenty years."* In 1924, he reassured Baldwin that an attempted Japanese invasion of Australia would *"never happen in any period... which we or our children need foresee"* but Japan bombed Northern Australia in 1942, a mere eighteen years after these Nostradamian utterances. By every standard, the Navy's predictions proved more accurate and it is unfortunate that a bumptious and blasé Chancellor over-ruled their counsels.

Churchill's defence cuts also stunted British military capability. During his tenure as Chancellor, Churchill blithely predicted that his defence cuts would have no deleterious long term effect on British defence capability and that Britain could always *"build war ships faster than anyone else in the world, and much faster than the Japanese, consequently it has always paid us to lay back as long as possible and then go one better in design."* He also informed Sir Douglas Hogg that *"it is certainly stupid deliberately to make weapons which will be out-matched."* In Churchill's topsy-turvy view of the world, abstaining from building up sizeable stocks of armaments over an extended period was desirable as it would ensure that Britain never went to war with large stocks of obsolete weapons. The possibility that depleting one's defences might encourage other powers to hasty or precipitate action didn't trouble him until the 1930s when other politicians had to clean up his mess, and several defence analysts and Whitehall insiders argue that Britain's difficulties with the dictators in the 1930s were, in large part, a product of defence cuts in the 1920s and early 1930s. Surveying Britain's warship-building industry in the 1930s, historian Paul Kennedy noted that

> *the long years of virtually no construction, the lack of incentive for technological innovation, the unwillingness to invest capital in what had been regarded as unprofitable fields and, above all, that steady cancerous decay of the country's industrial sinews, were ... [by the mid-1930s] showing their fruit. The*

drastic reduction in the shipbuilding industry... was the chief cause of the delays in the Admiralty's rearmament schemes.

M.M. Postan - official historian of British war production during 1939-45 - offers a similar view of Britain's aircraft industry.

The aircraft firms, including the principal engine firms, found themselves in a position of chronic penury and sometimes on the very verge of bankruptcy, [their diet of orders] though just sufficient to keep the bulk of the firms alive, was too meagre to enable them to keep pace with the aircraft industry abroad... and to acquire the equipment and technique for quantity production.

Finally, Permanent Secretary to the Treasury and key Churchill ally Sir Warren Fisher summarised the impact of Baldwin's 1924-29 government on British defence readiness by declaring that

we converted ourselves to military impotence. To have disarmed so drastically in the two or three years after the war was not unnatural though possibly not wise. But the government of 1924 to 1929 had no excuse for further reducing our armed forces to a skeleton, as by then it was known that the Weimar Republic was in process of reconstructing a disguised army on a truly formidable scale. The British government's tragic action formed unfortunately a model for subsequent governments.

If one accepts these views then one must reject Churchill's fanciful notion that - following a long period of retrenchment - British defence capability could be reactivated as easily as switching on an electric light. Holding such a view reflects a marked misunderstanding of the complexity of military-industrial production, the long period of research and development required to produce quality weapons, the impossibility of retaining skilled staff and plant when orders are low, and the benefits to be gained through economies of scale based on consistent orders. As indicated earlier, Churchill did not really grasp economics so its perhaps not surprising that he held such defective views or simply refused to consider the long-term consequences of his actions. In 1929, Britain controlled the world's largest Empire but its defence capability was comparable to that of a medium-sized power without extensive overseas commitments. Nazi aggression and Appeasement flourished in this toxic soil.

* * * * * * * * * * * * * * * * *

Britain initiated a bold experiment with democracy in May 1929 by staging a General Election in which men and women could vote equally at 21 - a new day had dawned in British politics. The Tories campaigned on 'Safety First' but - with the economy languishing - many voters opted for the novelty of Labour. The Labour Party won more seats but gained fewer votes than the Tories so Ramsay MacDonald formed a second minority government with Liberal backing. Churchill anticipated another short-lived administration and an opportunity to demonstrate his skills in opposition but then Wall Street crashed and the world plunged into Depression. Most politicians emphasised economic issues over the next 5-6 years but Churchill saw other dangers. The Raj was under attack and he was determined to rescue it - for the next six years, Churchill was hell-bent on excluding Indians from Indian government.

CHAPTER SIX: A SEDITIOUS MIDDLE TEMPLE LAWYER POSING AS A FAKIR, 1930- 36

The loss of India will be the death-blow of the British Empire, and every one of our foreign rivals is waiting to see that hideous signal hoisted.

Churchill addressing a Junior Imperial League rally, Chingford 22nd April 1931

He is really not quite normal on the subject of India.

Indian Secretary Leo Amery describes Churchill's views on the sub-continent

This short but crucial chapter considers Churchill, India and the vital significance of Suez to Empire. Churchill's Indian obsession - coupled with his determination to retain control over Middle Eastern oil - prompted him to prioritise the Mediterranean over other theatres during World War Two. British domination of India and the Middle East demanded British control of the Mediterranean, and this coupling compelled Churchill and his generals to oppose operations which would have diverted resources elsewhere. Although Allied strategy was officially resolved at Tehran, Churchill and his generals continued to advocate operations which could only undermine Overlord.

I

Churchill said relatively little about India before 1929 as its status within the Empire was unquestioned. He had fought on the North West Frontier in 1897 and condemned the Amritsar atrocity. His friend, Lord Birkenhead, was Indian Secretary 1924-28, so Churchill had little cause for concern but this changed abruptly in 1929 when Indian Viceroy[36] Lord Irwin announced a series of Round Table Conferences to discuss India's constitutional future and suggested that *"the natural issue of India's constitutional progress.... is the attainment of Dominion status."*

This innocuous remark induced paroxysms of Churchillian rage and animated his political energies over the next six years. India was the cornerstone of the Empire, while gaining Dominion status would allow India to secede from the Empire. Within two weeks of Irwin's announcement, Churchill thundered from the pages of the *Daily Mail* that it was

[36] The Viceroy was the Governor-General of India, governing the sub-continent on the King-Emperor's behalf and responsible to HM Government in London.

> *the duty of public men and of political parties to make it plain without delay that the extension of Dominion Status to India is not practicable at the present time and that any attempt to secure it will encounter the earnest resistance of the British nation... the idea that Home Rule for India or Dominion Status or full responsible government for India can emerge from anything that is now being done or inquired into is not only fantastic itself, but criminally mischievous in its effects.*

When Stanley Baldwin indicated that a future Conservative government would implement the Round Table recommendations, Churchill resigned from the Shadow Cabinet and retired to the backbenches. When Gandhi visited Irwin at the Viceregal palace, Churchill vituperated with gusto.

> *It is alarming and also nauseating to see Mr. Gandhi, a seditious middle temple lawyer, now posing as a fakir of a type well known in the east, striding half-naked up the steps of the viceregal palace... to parley on equal terms with the representative of the King-Emperor.*

Opposition to Indian reform drove Churchill's career for six years between 1929 and 1935. He renounced his front bench status and became titular head to 50-60 diehards who shared his regressive views. He compromised his career for a deeply held principle and is, at least, to be congratulated for his consistency. Churchill's career was wrecked by India during 1929-35 and a similar obsession with India and the Mediterranean almost weakened the anti-Nazi alliance at a critical moment. The same unwavering obsession drove Churchill in both cases, and his hostility to Indian independence derived from multiple sources.

Firstly, his testimony to the 1936-37 Peel Commission on Palestine reveals an unabashed white supremacist who believed that strong powers could take whatever they wanted from weaker states without compunction. When Lord Peel invited him to consider how Palestinians might feel on being evicted from land they had occupied for centuries, Churchill responded that he did

> *not agree that the dog in a manger has the final right to the manger even though he may have lain there for a very long time. I do not admit that right. I do not admit for instance, that a great wrong has been done to the Red Indians of America or the black people of Australia. I do not admit that a*

wrong has been done to these people by the fact that a stronger race, a higher-grade race, a more worldly wise race... has come in and taken their place.

The message was clear - 'stronger, higher-grade' races (such as Britain) could take whatever they wanted from 'weaker, lower-grade' races (such as India) without compunction. In its own way, Churchill's vision is as bleak and misanthropic as Hitler's.

Map 6: India under the Raj

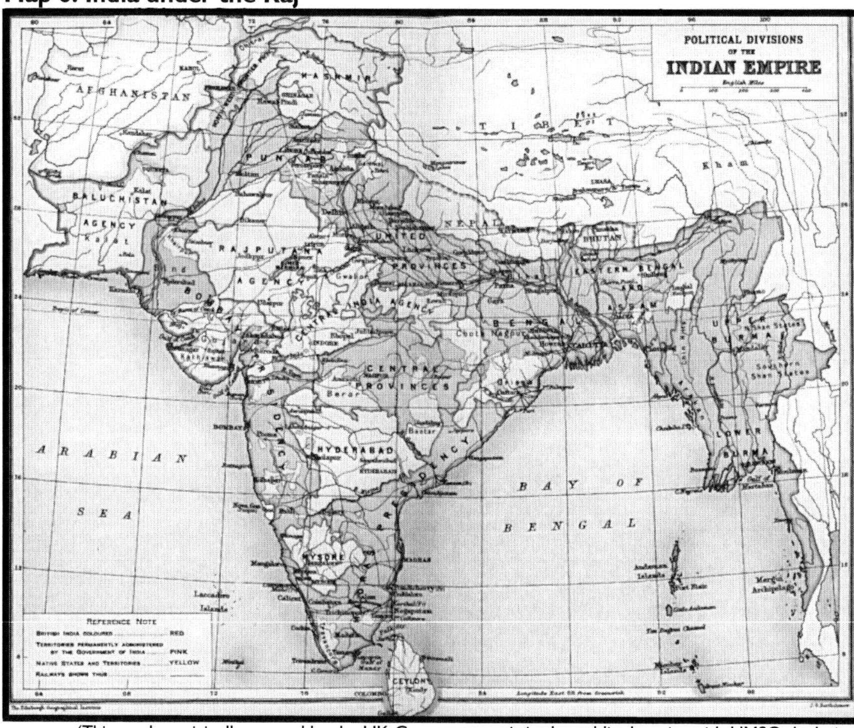

(This work - originally created by the UK Government - is in the public domain, with HMSO declaring that the expiry of Crown Copyright applies worldwide. Source: *Imperial Gazetteer of India,* 1909.)

Churchill testified to the Commission *in camera* - which may explain his unusual candour - but his imperial enthusiasm was usually justified on less overtly racist grounds. Inspired by Winwood Reade, he argued that India benefited from its subjugation. In his November 1929 *Daily Mail* article, he presented a vision of selfless British officials working tirelessly on India's behalf.

The rescue of India from ages of barbarism, tyranny, and intestine war, and its slow but ceaseless forward march to civilisation constitute... the finest achievements of our history. The work has been done in four or five generations by the

> *willing sacrifices of the best of our race. War has been banished from India; her frontiers have been defended against invasion… famine had been gripped and controlled… Justice has been given... Science, healing or creative, has been harnessed to the service of this immense and, by themselves, helpless population. And by the new streams of health and life and tranquillity which it has been our mission to bring to India, the number of its people has grown… by scores of millions.*[37]

Removing this benign influence would plunge India into primordial chaos.

> *If that authority is injured or destroyed, the whole efficiency of the services, defensive, administrative, medical, hygienic, judicial; railway, irrigation, public works and famine prevention, upon which the Indian masses depend for their… progress, will perish with it. India will fall back quite rapidly through the centuries into the barbarism and privations of the Middle Ages… To let the Indian people fall, as they would, to the level of China, would be a desertion of duty on the part of Great Britain.*

Violence would engulf the sub-continent without the *"appeasing sceptre"* of British rule.

> *If you took the antagonisms of France and Germany, and the antagonisms of Catholics and Protestants, and compounded them and multiplied them ten-fold, you would not equal the division which separates these two races [Hindus and Moslems]... Were we to wash our hands of all responsibility and divest ourselves of all our powers… ferocious civil wars would speedily break out between the Moslems and Hindus. No one who knows India will dispute this.*[38]

India's elite - who paid lip service to western ideals - would then exploit India's masses.

---

[37] Churchill's glowing testimonial is rebutted by research revealing that 61% of all Indians and 78% of all Bengalis were either 'poorly nourished' or 'very badly nourished' in the 1930s (Mukerjee, *Churchill's Secret War*, p.79).

[38] Churchill offered a different view of community relations in January 1940 when he informed Cabinet colleagues that *"he did not share the anxiety to encourage and promote unity between the Hindu and the Moslem communities. Such unity... if it were to be brought about, the immediate result would be that the united communities would join in showing us the door. He regarded the Hindu-Moslem feud as the bulwark of British rule in India."* (Rafiq Zakaria, *The Man Who Divided India* (2009), p.87).

> *The Indian congress and other elements in this agitation represent neither the numbers, the strength nor the virtue of the Indian people. They merely represent those Indians who have acquired a veneer of western civilisation, and have read all those books about democracy which Europe is now beginning increasingly to discard... it would be altogether wrong to entrust the welfare of the great masses to the Indian political classes. That would not be 'India for the Indians'; that would only be India for some Indians, and would only be India for a very few Indians.*

India, in Churchill's view, lacked the sophistication to sustain a modern nation state.

> *There are 450,000 villages in India, and only 11,000 odd have been able to evolve the simple organisation of a village council. Yet it is out of these people... that we are to try and lay the foundation of... a united state of India - a vast structure of 40 or 50 nations woven together, the size of Europe and practically the population of Europe. You are to try to build the kind of organisation which Europe struggles after... upon these humble primitives who are unable in 450,000 villages even to produce the simple organisation of four or five people sitting in a hut in order to discuss their common affairs.*

Abandoning India would destroy Britain's economy, particularly the Lancashire textile mills.

> *The great enterprises and business institutions which we have founded in India, are all in succession to be swept away. As for the hundreds of millions of loans which we have advanced to create the railways and irrigation services and public works of India... all this is in jeopardy... At the very centre of this struggle will be the trade of Lancashire. The new Indian Parliaments will attack British trade by a dozen means. They will give their contracts to foreign nations out of spite to us. They will harass British firms trading in India in a score of ways. The cotton trade, upon the existence of which Lancashire wage earners and employers depend, will... become a mere pawn in a struggle for more power.*

And finally, Britain needed Indian manpower to maintain its dominant position in the world as twentieth century liberalism was

> *superseded... by the establishment of dictatorships real or veiled in almost every country... We are entering a period when the struggle for self-preservation is going to present itself with great intenseness to thickly populated industrial countries. It is unsound reasoning therefore to suppose that England alone among the nations will be willing to part with her control over a great dependency like India. The Dutch will not do it; the French will not do it; the Italians will not do it... England is now beginning a new period of struggle and fighting for its life, and the crux of it will be not only the retention of India but a much stronger assertion of commercial rights.*

Churchill's hostility to Indian self-rule absorbed his political energies for six years while the Round Table Conferences convened (1930-1932) and the Government of India Bill wound its way through Parliament (February-August 1935). However, the content of the 1935 Act makes it difficult to understand why Churchill invested so much energy in this folly. The Act was framed by imperial policy-makers to perpetuate India's subordinate status within the Empire and detach moderates - willing to collaborate with the Raj - from activists demanding *swaraj*. Diarchy was reinforced at the centre and the Viceroy retained control over Indian finance, defence, foreign affairs and the Army. The central legislature could only consider finance bills approved by the Viceroy, and the Viceroy made key appointments to India's Reserve Bank and Railway Board. India could evolve into a federal state if fifty per cent of the provinces endorsed such a move but - as Westminster correctly anticipated - the maharajahs and nabobs blocked such a move when the Act was passed. The reforms increased the electorate from 3% to 14%, and provincial Governors were empowered to assume direct control over the provinces if they felt that such action was required. They could also repudiate bills proposed by the legislatures which encroached on their areas of 'special responsibility'.

The 1935 Act was in line with initiatives in other areas - Egypt, Iraq, Transjordan - in which the illusion of authority in non-essential areas was devolved to indigenous groups while finance, foreign affairs and imperial communications continued under imperial control. It's surprising that an experienced politician such as Churchill failed to grasp the Act's true purpose and his inflexible opposition eroded the capital he'd accumulated as Chancellor, while his dire warnings about India's future undermined his credibility over Germany. Churchill sabotaged his own career between 1930-36 and only the crisis of 1939-40 propelled him back to the front rank.

II

India was only one piece of the imperial jigsaw. British control over India demanded control over Suez and the following comments illustrate the region's vital significance to imperial statesmen,[39] contradicting Andrew Roberts' bizarre notion that *"control of the Mediterranean had not really been a British policy objective since Nelson's day."*[40] On the contrary, controlling the Mediterranean was the prime objective of British policy-makers for six decades prior to 1940, as the following statements reveal.

William Massey (New Zealand PM, 1912-25) had migrated to New Zealand from Ireland and was well-placed to appreciate the crucial importance of Suez to imperial communications. At the 1921 Imperial Conference, Massey dubbed Egypt

> *the British Empire highway from the very heart of the Empire... to India, to Australia, to the whole of the Far East... [I don't know] ... of any country so important to Empire as Egypt with the exception of Britain itself. Even Australia and New Zealand might be parted with and the Empire would go on, but I do not think you could run the Empire without keeping control of the main artery.*

In a December 1929 Commons debate on Anglo-Egyptian relations, Shadow Foreign Secretary Austen Chamberlain observed that

> *the relationship between Egypt and ourselves [is]... the result of the geographical position occupied by Egypt as one of the high roads and arteries of imperial communications. It is to that fact that the [1882] intervention in Egypt originated. It is to that fact that the occupation of Egypt by British forces is due, and it is... to protect those interests that British Forces have continued in Cairo, Alexandria and elsewhere, as our guarantee for the security of those vital interests.*

Anthony Eden, a rising Tory star, also contributed to the debate. A humble backbencher at the time, Eden would serve Churchill and Chamberlain as Foreign Secretary and was Prime Minister during 1955-57. His opinions therefore demand attention and, in the debate, he dubbed Suez *"a link in our chain of imperial defence"* before insisting that

---

[39] Chapter 24 reveals considerable consistency in imperial thinking over a quarter of a century.

[40] This comment appears on p.359 of *Masters and Commanders* (2008).

> *if the Suez Canal is our back door to the east, it is the front door to Europe of Australia, New Zealand and India... it is, in fact, the swing-door of the British Empire, which has got to keep continually revolving if our communications are to be what they should... I am not content, and none of us should be content, to leave the protection of a vital artery, the jugular vein of the British Empire, to the good will of the people of Egypt.*

Labour politicians espoused similar views. Writing to the High Commissioner in Cairo in 1924, Ramsay MacDonald insisted that

> *it is no less true to-day than in 1922 that the security of the communications of the British Empire in Egypt remain a vital British interest and that absolute certainty that the Suez Canal will remain open in peace as well as in war for the free passage of British ships is the foundation on which the entire defensive strategy of the British Empire rests... No British Government... can divest itself wholly of its interest in guarding such a vital link in British communications.*

When Egyptian Prime Minister Saad Zaghloul suggested that Egyptian troops might guard the Canal, MacDonald retorted *"that the whole of the British imperial strategy turned upon the safety of the Suez Canal and the British government must be in a position to protect it."*

In 1938, Sir Maurice Hankey - Secretary to the Committee of Imperial Defence for twenty-six years - declared that

> *the keeping open of the Suez Canal for the passage of the British fleet to the Far East is a strategical interest of vast importance to the whole of the British Empire east of Suez. It is no exaggeration to say that the security of our position in India, of Australia and New Zealand, of the rich colonies and protectorates of Malaya and Ceylon and elsewhere in the Indian and southern Pacific oceans, to say nothing of a vast trade turn on the ability of our fleet to reach the pivotal naval base of Singapore with reasonable speed, and this in turn depends on the secure passage of the Suez Canal.*

No sharper exposition of the Canal's vital importance is possible. In fact, Suez had actually gained in importance by the time these remarks were delivered. By 1938, Britain was being threatened by Germany (in Europe), by Italy (in the Mediterranean) and Japan (in the Far East), with Italy replacing Japan as Britain's principal enemy after Germany. Three convinced Mediterraneanists - Earl Stanhope and Admirals Backhouse and Cunningham - arrived at the Admiralty in autumn 1938 and the Chiefs of Staff noted that

> *the first commitment of our land forces, after the security of the United Kingdom, should be the security of Egypt and of our interests in the Middle East.*

In March 1939, future Prime Minister Churchill drafted a *'Memorandum on Sea-Power'* in which he argued that the Mediterranean should be *"England's first battlefield"* while maintaining a defensive posture against Germany. Italy was therefore not only replacing Japan as a focus for British strategy, it was also supplanting Germany as the first focus for offensive action in the event of war. Long before Churchill's strategic struggles with Stalin and Roosevelt, the Mediterranean Strategy had become deeply embedded within British thinking and Chapter Seven considers the manner in which this occurred and its long-term implications.

CHAPTER SEVEN: A VERY RICH AND VERY VULNERABLE EMPIRE, 1936-39

We are in the remarkable position of not wanting to quarrel with anybody because we have got most of the world already, or the best part of it, and we only want to keep what we have got and prevent others from taking it away from us.

Admiral Chatfield to Sir Warren Fisher, 4th June 1934

It is beyond the resources of this country to make proper provision in peace for the defence of the British Empire against three major powers in three different theatres of war.

Sir Thomas Inskip, 8th February 1938

While Churchill was busy denying democracy to India, the peace he'd confidently predicted evaporated under the impact of the Great Depression and Wall Street Crash. Japan seized Manchuria in 1931 and menaced Shanghai, home to 75% of British Chinese investments. Hitler became Chancellor in 1933 and set about dismantling German democracy and the institutions of Versailles. Italy joined the feeding frenzy in 1935, violating Abyssinia (Ethiopia) to start constructing a new 'Roman Empire' in Africa. The emergence of three predatory powers presented Britain and its Empire with profound problems for, so vast were Britain's domains, that any attempt by Germany, Italy or Japan to forge their own *imperiums* would almost certainly provoke conflict with Britain somewhere in the world. However, as a result of long term decline, the United Kingdom lacked the resources to confront three enemies simultaneously in three different theatres and Britain's story in the 1930s is that of an ailing giant, struggling vainly to fulfil virtually limitless obligations with strictly finite resources - such a strategy could postpone war but could never avert it.

I

Britain's economic decline continued throughout the 1930s. Unemployment reached 17% in 1932 and - with the exception of 1935 - Britain recorded significant Balance of Payments deficits throughout the decade. A Conservative-dominated National Government emerged in 1931 to address the crisis and employed the most orthodox methods; even as late as 1938, with rearmament underway, unemployment remained at 10% and was even higher in traditional manufacturing areas. The Government reduced public spending in an effort to balance the books and provoked a mutiny amongst Atlantic Fleet sailors. Neville Chamberlain - Chancellor of the Exchequer 1931-37 and Prime Minister 1937- 40 - viewed economic stability as the *"fourth arm in defence, alongside the three Defence Services, without which purely military effort would be of no avail"* and would do nothing to jeopardise Britain's modest recovery after abandoning the Gold Standard in 1931. When the Cabinet repudiated the Ten Year Rule in 1932, it also warned that this *"must not be taken to justify an expanding expenditure by the Defence Services without reference to the very serious financial and economic situation."* British rearmament remained slow and cautious till the end of the decade, severely limiting the country's foreign policy options. The tables below summarise British defence spending throughout this turbulent decade.

Table 1 British Defence Expenditure, 1928/29 - 1939/40 (£m)

Year	Total Budget
1928/29	113.5
1929/30	113.0
1930/31	110.6
1931/32	107.3
1932/33	103.0
1933/34	107.9
1934/35	113.9
1935/36	136.9
1936/37	186.0
1937/38	262.2
1938/39	382.5
1939/40	719.0

Table 1 summarises British defence spending in the 1930s. Defence spending had stabilised around £115m per annum by the late 1920s and was reduced even further during the worst years of the Depression, recovering its pre-Depression level only in 1934/35. Defence spending accelerated following re-election of the National Government in November 1935 and in response to the deteriorating world situation - Germany introduced conscription in 1935 and remilitarised the Rhineland in 1936, while Italy attacked Ethiopia in October 1935.

Table 2 depicts each service's share of the annual budget. As in the 1920s, the government declined to deploy large scale land forces in

Europe - it hoped that France and Belgium would hold the line against Germany - and Army spending fell from 36.3% of the total in 1930/31 to 29.7% by 1937/38. In 1938, Britain could field only three divisions (two infantry, one armoured) which explains its muted response to the Anschluss and Sudetenland Crisis. Army spending - as a proportion of the total - increased only after 1938/39 when the government introduced conscription and doubled the size of the Territorial Army following Hitler's absorption of Czechoslovakia.

Table 2 British Defence Expenditure, 1929/30 - 1939/40 (£m)

	Army spend (% share)	**Navy spend (% share)**	**RAF spend (% share)**	**Total Budget**
1929/30	40.5 (36.0)	55.8 (49.0)	16.8 (15.0)	113.0
1930/31	40.2 (36.3)	52.6 (47.6)	17.8 (16.1)	110.6
1931/32	38.5 (35.9)	51.1 (47.6)	17.7 (16.5)	107.3
1932/33	35.9 (34.9)	50.0 (48.5)	17.1 (16.6)	103.0
1933/34	37.6 (34.8)	53.5 (49.6)	16.8 (15.6)	107.9
1934/35	39.7 (34.9)	56.6 (49.7)	17.6 (15.4)	113.9
1935/36	44.6 (32.6)	64.8 (47.3)	27.5 (20.1)	136.9
1936/37	54.8 (29.5)	81.1 (43.6)	50.1 (26.9)	186.0
1937/38	77.9 (29.7)	102.0 (38.9)	82.3 (31.4)	262.2
1938/39	121.4 (31.7)	127.3 (33.3)	133.8 (35.0)	382.5
1939/40	242.4 (33.7)	181.8 (25.3)	294.8 (41.0)	719.0

While the Army's budget share declined steadily throughout the 1930s, RAF spending increased dramatically from 15% in 1929/30 to 41% in 1939/40 and - by 1938/39 - its budget share exceeded both the Army and the Navy's. This reflected Stanley Baldwin's fear that *"the bomber will always get through"* and for most of the 1930s, the government sought to shield Britain from aerial assault through the doctrine of 'mutually assured destruction' and by developing its own fearsome strike capability.[41] Fighters were prioritised as a form of defence after 1938, mainly because they were cheaper to build. The Spitfires and Hurricanes that saved Britain in 1940 were the product of chance and parsimony rather than any clear strategic vision.

Table 3 compares British and German arms spending in the years following Hitler's accession. Both countries spent roughly the same amount during 1933-34 but German spending was two or three times greater by the middle of the decade. British spending increased

[41] Chapter 25 assesses Britain's 'fearsome strike capability' in the war's early years.

dramatically following Hitler's annexation of the Czechoslovak rump, but so too did German spending to maintain its overall lead. If one adds Japanese and Italian armaments into the equation, one can readily appreciate Britain's dilemma.

Table 3 Comparative Defence Expenditure (% GNP)

Year	Britain	Germany
1933	3.0	1.9
1934	3.0	4.1
1935	2.0	6.0
1936	5.0	10.8
1937	7.0	11.7
1938	8.0	17.2
1939	22.0	30.0

Other forces underpinned appeasement. The British public rejected war as an instrument of policy and - as Britain had recently embraced democracy - such sentiment could not be ignored. Eleven and a half million Britons supported the Peace Ballot in 1934/35, endorsing disarmament and condemning the sale of arms for profit. As noted earlier, rapid rearmament occurred only after the National Government was re-elected and in February 1936, it authorised a defence budget to govern arms spending over the next six years. British voters wanted their leaders to resolve foreign difficulties without war and it was only after Hitler revealed his true colours in spring 1939 that Britain and its people willingly countenanced the introduction of conscription, the inauguration of staff talks with France and formation of a Ministry of Supply to co-ordinate military spending and production.

Britain also lacked allies with whom it could form durable coalitions. France was even more traumatised by 1914-18 than Britain and Italy joined the enemy camp after 1936. America was isolationist and Russia was a pariah state, hated for its communism and despised for its purges and presumed military weakness. The Empire was a 'paper tiger', a drain on resources rather than a source of strength. While Britain was spending 5-6% of its national income on defence in the mid-1930s, Australia devoted 1% and New Zealand 0.8%, yet Britain was expected to defend these territories against aggressors. At the 1937 Imperial Conference, South Africa advised that it would remain neutral in any future European conflict and Canada pursued an increasingly independent foreign policy, prompting Michael Howard to compare the Empire to *"a brontosaurus with huge, vulnerable limbs which the central nervous system had little capacity to protect, direct or control."* Britain's highly dispersed thalassocracy[42] and the multiplicity of challenges it faced induced paralysis, preventing Britain from meeting the dictators' challenge. If British resources were deployed in Europe to counter a German threat, Japan and Italy could threaten the Mediterranean and Far East, and if Britain prioritised the Mediterranean and the Far East, Hitler could menace Europe. Multiple papers summarised the strategic dilemma throughout the 1930s. For example, in November 1935, the Chiefs of Staff warned that

> *we cannot foresee the time when our defence forces will be strong enough to safeguard our territory, trade and vital interests against Germany, Italy and Japan simultaneously. We cannot therefore exaggerate the importance, from the point of view of Imperial defence, of any political or international action that can be taken to reduce the number of our potential enemies or to gain the support of potential allies.*

In April 1939, the Chiefs of Staff again warned of

> *a situation in which we, allied to France, would be engaged in a war with Germany and Italy simultaneously and when Japan would also be a potential enemy... The British Empire and France would thus be threatened at home, in the Mediterranean and in the Far East... and it would be hard to choose a worse geographical combination of enemies.*

These were the harsh realities confronting Britain and, given the resources at their disposal and their unimaginative, austerity-driven mindset, it is difficult to condemn the architects of appeasement for their inadequate efforts. Responsibility for the conflict lies with those who sponsored the violence, rather than those who sought to prevent it, however ineffective their methods.

II

Churchill, of course, was cut from radically different cloth and prescribed different remedies for Britain's ills. Austerity's great champion now advocated militant rearmament, one of many policy somersaults flawlessly executed over the course of a lengthy career.

Churchill was marginalised for much of the 1930s as a result of his extreme views on India and ill-judged intervention in the Abdication

---

[42] Maritime empire.

Crisis[43] and his credibility revived only after Munich and the destruction of Czechoslovakia. Within six months, he was back at the Admiralty and his strategic views from spring 1939 illuminate his later preferences.

Churchill outlined his strategic ideals in his 27th March 'Memorandum on Sea-Power, 1939' and in speeches and newspaper articles from the same period. In these musings, Churchill proposed a radical overhaul of Britain's defence strategy to reflect the new circumstances it faced. Italy had emerged as a potential enemy and Churchill's remedy was simple - should Italy prove hostile, *"England's [sic] first battlefield is the Mediterranean. All hopes for sealing up the ends must be discarded in favour of decisive victory there."* He made the same point in his 16th March Naval Estimates speech by declaring that *"for Britain in time of war, the command of the Mediterranean must be the prime objective."* Churchill articulated this view in spring 1939 and remained wedded to it for the next five years despite changing circumstance. Churchill held Italy's fighting ability in some contempt, anticipating swift, decisive victories in his preferred theatre.

> *Our forces alone should be sufficient to drive the Italian ships from the sea and secure complete command of the Mediterranean, certainly within two months [of war commencing], possibly sooner... British domination of the Mediterranean will inflict inevitable injuries upon Italy which may be fatal to her power of continuing the war. All her troops in Libya and Abyssinia [Ethiopia] will be... cut flowers in a vase. The French and our own people in Egypt could be reinforced to any extent desired, while theirs will be overweighted if not starved.*

Long before his strategic conflicts with Roosevelt and Stalin, Churchill viewed Italy as a liability and argued that success against Italy would discomfit Germany. Writing for the *New York Herald Tribune* in April 1939, he acknowledged that

> *there is a school of British strategists who would hold that in a world struggle with Nazidom it would be a positive advantage to have Italy as an enemy. In this long, vulnerable peninsula with its lack of raw materials they observe a theatre in which important victories could be gained... Germany would have to carry Italy as she carried Austria in the late war. German munitions and supplies would have to be poured southward...*

---

[43] Churchill supported Edward VIII.

> *German troops, above all German aviation, would become involved in the defence of Italy and so far as possible of Italy's overseas ventures.*

His 'Memorandum on Sea Power' declared that:

> *a series of swift and striking victories in this [Mediterranean] theatre, which might be obtainable in the early weeks of the war, would have a most healthy and helpful bearing upon the main struggle with Germany. Nothing should stand between us and these results.*

As always, the Empire influenced Churchill's priorities:

> *Not to hold the Mediterranean would be to expose Egypt and the Canal, as well as the French possessions, to invasion by Italian troops with German leadership. We cannot tolerate this on any account.*

Such a strategy could only be pursued if Japan was removed from the picture, and Churchill invited the reader to

> *consider how vain is the menace that Japan will send a fleet and army to conquer Singapore. It is as far from Japan as Southampton from New York. Over these two thousand miles of salt water, Japan would have to send the bulk of her fleet, escort at least sixty thousand men in transports... and begin a siege which would end only in disaster if the Japanese sea-communications were cut at any stage. One can take it as quite certain that Japan would not run such a risk. They are an extremely sensible people.*

The Japanese were also extremely shrewd - in 1941/42, they charged overland through Malaya to capture Singapore, bypassing the risks so eloquently described by Churchill.

Senior British politicians and statesmen endorsed Churchill's enthusiasms and analyses. Copies of his Memorandum were sent to Chamberlain and Foreign Secretary Halifax, and Halifax forwarded a copy to the Washington Embassy. Chamberlain met and discussed the paper with Churchill, and Halifax noted: *"I find my thoughts going very much with yours."* Britain's senior soldiers and sailors were even more forceful in their enthusiasm for Mediterranean action. General Ironside - Inspector General of Overseas Forces - identified Italy as the Axis weak link and advocated decisive action.

> *We must attack... and we must attack where we can have the greatest effect. Italy is the Achilles heel of the Berlin-Rome Axis and we must concentrate on knocking her out... Egypt, Palestine and Turkey are the centre of the world and the centre of the British Empire. It is from here that we can prepare our offensive.*

Britain's Middle East commander, General Wavell, concurred:

> *The next war, as I see it, will be won or lost in the Mediterranean; and the longer it takes us to secure effective control of the Mediterranean, the harder will be the winning of the war.*

Admiral Cunningham, Commander-in-Chief of the Mediterranean Fleet after June 1939, also endorsed an Italy/Mediterranean first strategy on the grounds that

> *the surrender of the Italian Army in Libya coupled with attacks on the Italian coast in places where material damage can be done would certainly have a great moral effect and might well cause the Italians to lose heart.*

After Italy conquered Albania in early April, Britain guaranteed Greece (on 13th April) and Turkey (12th May) and, by so doing, gave warning that it would fight to defend its Mediterranean interests. The French endorsed this Mediterranean emphasis and in staff talks in March-April, agreed that

> *the objective would be to secure their interests in the Mediterranean and Middle East, and to knock Italy out of the war as soon as possible. This would entail offensive naval action from the outset.*

However, the whole picture changed dramatically in June-July following the Tianjin Incident when, for several weeks, it looked as if Britain and Japan might go to war.[44] The entire Mediterranean strategy was premised on Japan being distracted by war with China and tensions with the Soviet Union, but renewed friction with Japan invalidated the whole Mediterranean enterprise. If Britain lost ships fighting Italy in the Mediterranean, it couldn't despatch its fleet to the East to counter

---

[44] Japanese forces blockaded foreign concessions in Tianjin during June-August 1939 after Chinese nationalists assassinated a collaborator and sought refuge within the British concession. Britain resolved the crisis on 20th August by surrendering four Chinese nationalists to the Japanese.

Japan or nullify the Nazi menace in the North Sea. Yet again, it was the old story of too many enemies and not enough resources, as First Sea Lord Dudley Pound lamented on 18th July.

> *If there is any doubt as to the attitude of Japan and the USA, we cannot, with our present strength, afford to risk the loss of these ships [deployed in the Mediterranean], as not only would this serious reduction in our capital ship strength afford every inducement to Japan to come in against us, but if she did so we should have insufficient ships to send to the Far East even if we abandoned the eastern Mediterranean.*

Once more, imperial overstretch, paucity of resources and the absence of allies paralysed British initiative. After a few months in which fighting spirit and a determination to remove Italy from the picture had predominated, Britain lapsed once more into inertia and appeasement. During July and August, Chamberlain looked for new ways to purchase Italian neutrality through territorial concessions and - in its last meeting before the war - the Committee of Imperial Defence repudiated the whole Mediterranean/Italy First strategy by stating that British interests would be best served by prolonging Italian neutrality and urged politicians to prioritise this goal.

By August, all talk about Italy and the Mediterranean was rendered redundant by the Nazi-Soviet Non-Aggression Pact. Germany attacked Poland on 1st September and, to Hitler's great surprise, Britain honoured its 31st March Polish guarantee by declaring war on Germany. In 1925, Foreign Secretary Austen Chamberlain had dismissed the Polish corridor as something *"for which no British Government ever will and ever can risk the bones of a British grenadier,"* but his half-brother Neville went to war on that very pretext. Churchill returned to his old post at the Admiralty, Italy remained neutral and the Mediterranean strategy was placed in abeyance, only to be revived when Churchill became Prime Minister when it proved to be a remarkably durable precept.

CHAPTER EIGHT: WINSTON'S BACK... AND SCREWING UP AGAIN, September 1939 - May 1940

> *Early misfortunes in war cannot be avoided by pacific democracies, since it is not in the character of a pacific democracy or its chosen leaders to believe in war before it happens and prepare for it.*
>
> Sir William Beveridge, June 1940

> *The British have planned this campaign on the lines of a punitive expedition against the Zulus, but unhappily we and the British are in the position of the Zulus, armed with bows and arrows against the onslaught of scientific warfare.*
>
> French officers describe the Norwegian campaign, April 1940

Given the disasters lying in wait, Britain and France approached the war with remarkable equanimity. They had little desire for conflict - and had worked hard to avoid it - but now that struggle was forced upon them they shared a common belief in the certainty of Allied victory. Britain and France jointly controlled Empires containing 600m people spread across one-third of the globe while Germany's 1939 population stood at 80m. Once these vast resources were fully mobilised, there was little doubt they would crush the Nazi state and this explains Anglo-French passivity in 1939/40 - they preferred to wait until their superior resources were fully mobilised before engaging Germany on optimal terms. All they needed was for Germany to play the same game.

I

Allied reluctance to fight in 1939/40 reflected a further fallacy. As a result of its rapid rearmament, Germany was believed to be on the verge of collapse. Given Germany's later resilience under aerial assault, holding such a view in 1940 seems ludicrous but this delusion enjoyed widespread currency among Allied leaders. On 10th September, Neville Chamberlain informed his sister that *"what I hope for is not a military victory... but a collapse of the German home front,"* and in October he assured her that

> *my policy continues to be the same. Hold on tight. Keep up the economic pressure, push on with munitions production and military preparations with the utmost energy, take no offensive until Hitler begins it. I reckon that if we are allowed*

> *to carry on this policy we shall have won the war by the spring.*

Churchill shared this view. In March 1939, he informed the Commons that Germany was

> *at full extension in armament production, groaning and straining in that tremendous effort... All labour, skilled and unskilled, is employed to the utmost. The park railings and even iron crosses in the graveyards are being melted down for scrap.*

Six months later, he informed cabinet colleagues that Germany was short "*of certain vital materials... [and] after a few months weaknesses would begin to show in the German military machine.*"

With Germany supposedly on the brink of collapse, it made no sense to rush into war but to wait until the Nazi state unravelled of its own accord. And so the planes that flew over Germany in the winter of 1939/40 carried nothing more deadly than leaflets, the BEF slowly took up its position to the north-west of the French army and the French Saarland 'offensive' was cancelled after only nine days. In the 'through the looking glass' thinking which dominated the 'Twilight War', each day's delay in provoking combat brought Germany closer to ruin and gave the Allied powers more time to mobilise their own resources. On 4th April, Chamberlain crowed that Hitler had "*missed the bus*" but - five days later - Hitler revealed which European leader had lost contact with reality.

While Britain and France shunned direct combat with Germany, they devised plans to attack various neutral states who, in their opinion, were aiding and abetting the Nazis. From the outset, the Allies looked to engage secondary opponents in peripheral theatres as alternatives to fighting Germany.

II

Although Hitler and Stalin were, on the surface, antagonists, it was the August 1939 Non-Aggression Pact that had facilitated Germany's invasion of Poland. Poland could receive direct assistance only from Russia and Hitler had to nullify this option before implementing 'Case White'. This was achieved on 23rd August and, one week later, German forces inaugurated World War Two by bombarding Wieluń and Westerplatte. Russia secured its reward on 17th September by attacking Poland from the rear, regaining territory lost to the Poles in 1919-21.

Nazi-Soviet cooperation extended beyond the destruction of small, inconveniently located states. Two Nazi-Soviet Trade Agreements signed in 1940 and 1941 facilitated 1.1 billion Reichsmarks of trade between Germany and Russia in the twenty-two months before Barbarossa. Russia supplied Germany with oil, grain and metals while Germany provided manufactured goods, machinery and military hardware, and it was this trade that thwarted feeble British attempts at blockade and disappointed Allied hopes for an early German collapse. As a result of this trade - and the fresh resources acquired through conquest - German economic power expanded during 1940/41 and, even then, was still not fully mobilised.

The Soviet Union remained neutral after Britain and France declared war on Germany but its commercial partnership with Germany - and its aggressive action against Poland and Finland[45] - rendered it, in Allied eyes, a *de facto* German ally. If the Soviet economy could be weakened, it would both destabilise a detested Communist regime and destroy Russia's trade with Germany. And so, while RAF bombers carried nothing more lethal than leaflets on their flights over Germany, Britain and France devised plans to attack the Soviet Union, such was their passion for peripheral action.

Allied plans focused on bombing Baku, the heart of Russia's Caucasian oil industry. At the time, Baku produced three-quarters of Soviet oil, so destroying this capacity would cripple the Soviet economy and sabotage exports to Germany. A February 1940 French assessment stated that

> *dependence on oil supplies from the Caucasus is the fundamental weakness of [the] Russian economy... More than 90% of oil extraction and 80% of refinement was located in the Caucasus (primarily Baku). Therefore, interruption of oil supplies on any large scale would have far-reaching consequences and could even result in the collapse of all the military, industrial and agricultural systems of Russia.*

Apart from its flagrant illegality, the idea of attacking Baku - an Anglo-French version of Pearl Harbor - had much to commend it. The ground around the refining plant was sodden with oil and would

[45] Russia attacked Finland on 30th November 1939 hoping to gain a slice of territory to protect Leningrad (St. Petersburg).

provide a highly flammable target while Baku - and subsidiary targets in Batumi and Grozny - were within easy reach of Allied air bases in Syria and Iraq. The plans were proposed by the French and developed by Air Commodore John Slessor in spring 1940 as Operation Pike. RAF reconnaissance planes over-flew Baku on 30th March and photographed Batumi on 5th April, and tests were conducted on means of igniting oil tanks at Woolwich Arsenal. Four squadrons of Bristol Blenheim Mark IV bombers were earmarked to carry out the raid and Slessor estimated that the RAF could destroy Baku in 5-12 weeks acting alone or 1-3 weeks with French support. To implement this plan, France constructed new airfields in northern Syria which were to be operational by mid-May.

One can only speculate on what might have happened had this lunacy prevailed. Would Russia have joined Germany in a war against Britain and France? Would Hitler have seized a golden opportunity to attack Russia a year ahead of schedule? Would Allied aircraft have been swatted from the sky or - given the ineffectuality of early RAF raids on Germany - would these attacks have been nothing more than annoying pinpricks? We shall never know for on 9th April, Hitler invaded Norway and Denmark and, on 10th May, unleashed his blitzkrieg on the west. Allied leaders had more pressing issues to deal with and the First Lord of the Admiralty gained a golden opportunity to demonstrate his military genius.

III

Allied strategy in the early months of the war sought to postpone conflict with Germany until Britain and France were fully mobilised. There was also a commendable desire to hold back from initiating a conflict that might prove more deadly than 1914-18 and a forlorn hope that diplomacy might yet resolve the crisis. Allied strategy emphasised economic offence and military defence, and the RAF didn't attack a German land-based target until 19th March when a force of Whitleys and Hampdens bombed the Luftwaffe seaplane base on Sylt, Germany's northernmost island.

Churchill - recalled to the Admiralty on 1st September - abhorred such inaction and yearned to make Germany 'bleed and burn', informing Admiral Pound on 5th December that

> *an absolute defensive is for weaker forces. If we go on indefinitely like this we shall simply be worried & worn down, while making huge demands upon the national resources… I*

> *c[ould]d never be responsible for a naval strategy wh[ich] excluded the offensive principle.*

Unfortunately, his preferred opponent - Italy - had remained neutral and Japan was embroiled in China, so Churchill would have to satisfy his thirst for action through operations against Germany - or its partners - which fell short of a major shooting war.

Churchill devised multiple schemes to harass Germany in the war's opening months. Operation Catherine was a plan to send a self-supporting fleet of warships into the Baltic to menace Germany's coastal trade and - by means never fully explained - lure Russia into the Allied orbit. However, this scheme would have provided the Luftwaffe with nothing more than convenient target practice and was discarded in the face of Admiral's Pound's dogged opposition. Operation Royal Marine proposed to disrupt German river traffic by flooding the Rhine with mines but the French objected as they dreaded German reprisals on their own industrial centres. In March 1940, Churchill proposed sending a submarine fleet into the Black Sea on the grounds that *"two or three submarines would not only interrupt the Russian oil traffic in that sea, but would also have a terrifying moral effect on Russia,"* but the Turks blocked naval vessels passing through their waters.

The one constant that dominated Allied thinking in the early months of the war was the desire to interdict German access to Swedish iron ore. If this could be achieved, Germany's war-making capacity would be gravely weakened and the Allies would have scored a major advantage. Most Swedish ore is mined in the north of the country and shipped south via Luleå in the Bothnian Gulf. However, Luleå is ice-bound for five months each year and so, in the winter, the ore is transferred to Narvik in northern Norway before being shipped south to German ports via Norway's extensive coastline.

In mid-September, Churchill proposed mining Norway's territorial waters to force the ore-carrying ships into international waters where the Royal Navy could intercept them. Churchill advocated such action on the grounds that

> *an adequate supply of Swedish iron ore is vital to Germany, and the interception… of these Narvik supplies during the winter months, i.e. from October to the end of April, will greatly reduce her power of resistance… If Germany can be cut from all Swedish ore supplies from now onwards till the*

> *end of 1940, a blow will have been struck at her war-making capacity equal to a first-class victory in the field or from the air… It might indeed be immediately decisive.*

Churchill cared nothing for Norway's territorial integrity, arguing that

> *small nations must not tie our hands when we are fighting for their rights and freedom. The letter of the law must not in supreme emergency obstruct those who are charged with its protection and enforcement.*

However, his Cabinet colleagues displayed greater concern for international law and shelved Churchill's plans for several months.

Map 7: Key Norwegian locations

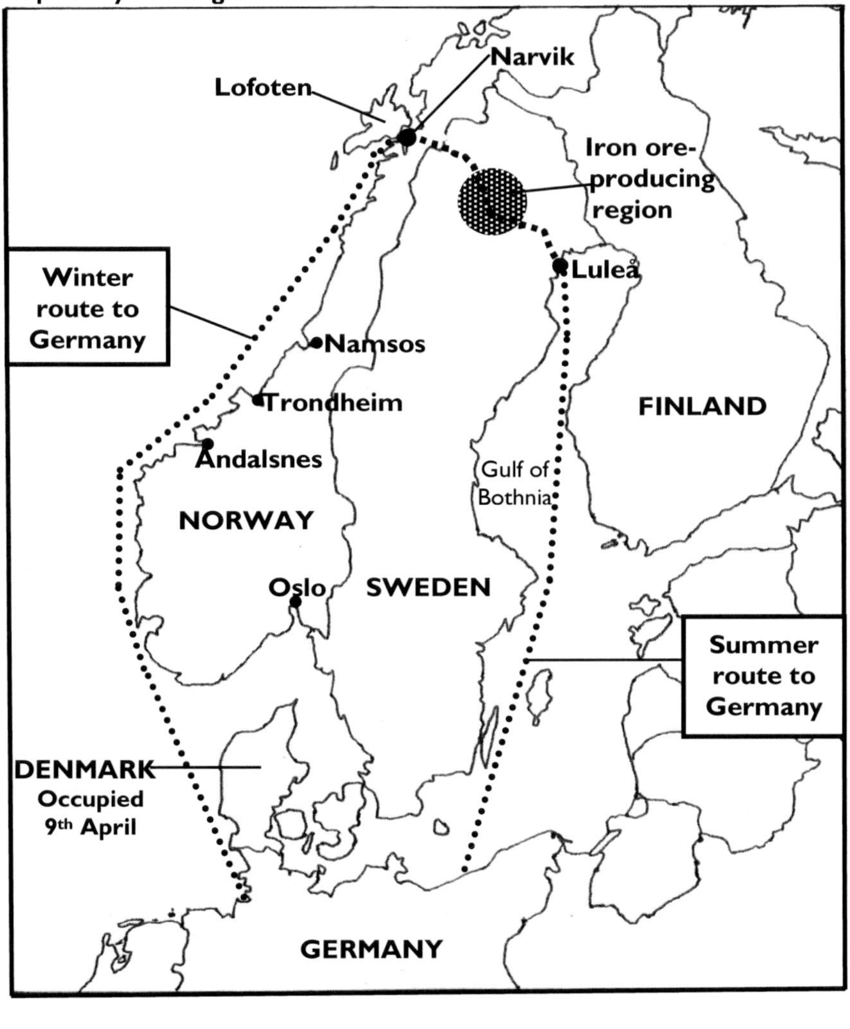

The Soviet invasion of Finland on 30th November offered an alternative means of blocking German iron ore supplies. If Finland accepted Allied military assistance - transported via Norway and Sweden - this would discomfit Russia and give the Allies a military presence in Scandinavia from which they could dominate the ore-fields and deny German access. On 5th February, the Allied Supreme War Council agreed to provide Finland with three or four divisions to fight against Russia on the understanding that Finland would request assistance by 5th March and Allied troops would start landing in Narvik from 20th March onwards. However, Finland sued for peace on 12th March, forcing the Allies back onto their original plan of mining Norwegian waters. On 28th March, the Supreme War Council agreed to implement this plan on 5th April and an Allied Expeditionary Force would sail for Norway as soon as Germany responded. The Allied Expeditionary Force would seize key Norwegian ports and secure Allied control of Scandinavia. However, by early April, Operation Wilfred (the plan to mine Norwegian waters) had become entangled with Operation Royal Marine (mining the Rhine) and France raised fresh objections to Royal Marine. Wilfred was therefore postponed to 8th April and this minor delay created grave difficulties for on 9th April, Germany seized the initiative by attacking Denmark and Norway, quickly establishing a presence in key Norwegian cities. His earlier bluster notwithstanding, it was Chamberlain - not Hitler - who had 'missed the bus'.

Germany's invasion of Norway magnified the scale and complexity of the Allied task. Instead of occupying Norway in the face of minimal opposition, the Allies would now have to dislodge a well-organised German force from a foreign state while operating without air cover at a distance of eight hundred miles. Such an operation demanded strong leadership and exemplary army-navy cooperation but these attributes were sadly lacking and Churchill bears a heavy responsibility for nurturing chaos. Churchill's contribution to the Norway fiasco assumed three principal forms.

Firstly, when German ships were spotted en route to Norway, he wrongly assumed they constituted a purely naval force aimed at breaking into the Atlantic and the British fleet set off in hot pursuit. Troops were disembarked from Royal Navy warships and, once the mistake was discovered, the Allied fleet had to return to port, re-embark the troops and set sail for Norway, granting the Germans a considerable time advantage. When Allied troops finally landed in Norway on 14th April, German forces had already been present for five days.

Despite the chaos of army operations, the Royal Navy performed well in Norway and sank eight enemy destroyers in Narvik Fjord on 13th April.[46] Churchill wrongly presumed the port to be under Allied control and ordered the convoy sailing for Narvik to split in two, with one half proceeding to Trondheim and the other half to Narvik. *The Ironside Diaries* describe Churchill's role in this fiasco.

> *At 2am on the morning of 14 April, Mr. Churchill... came to Ironside's room at the War Office. 'Tiny, we are going to the wrong place. We should go for Trondheim... The Navy will make a direct attack on it and I want a small force of good troops... to follow up the naval attack'.... Ironside protested that he had no troops available for Trondheim until Narvik had been taken. Mr. Churchill then insisted that the rear half of the Narvik convoy... should be directed to Namsos [to attack Trondheim from the north]. Ironside again protested that... Mr. Churchill at least should know how impractical such a diversion would be. If half the Narvik force were removed, the Narvik operation would be ruined. The troops and their equipment had been loaded and the administration organised for a single operation, and everything would be upset if half the convoy was dispatched. It would be better, said Ironside, to abandon Narvik altogether, or at most, to invest it. He was overruled.*

Clive Ponting describes the chaos resulting from Churchill's intervention.

> *The troops which landed at Namsos... only had maps for Narvik and all their vehicles, some of their ammunition and their commander were still sailing to their original destination... when they landed at Namsos they would have to advance for eighty miles over one road with no air cover. The troops landing further south at Åndalsnes... only had maps of Namsos.*

By splitting the Allied force in two, Churchill ensured that neither force could achieve its goal, and Ponting estimates that Churchill changed his mind about Allied objectives fourteen times over a three-week period, creating considerable confusion.

The British command structure was poorly organised and riven by

---

[46] The Navy's success owed much to luck. The Germans were using torpedoes armed with magnetic detonators designed to explode under a ship's keel to inflict maximum damage. However, the detonation system proved faulty and many torpedoes failed to explode - RN losses would have been catastrophic otherwise.

petty inter-service disputes, and while this mess pre-dates Churchill's arrival at the Admiralty, he aggravated matters by replacing Admiral Evans - who had planned the Norway operation with General Mackesy - with Admiral Boyle on 10th April, and Boyle and Mackesy never met before leaving for Norway on separate ships. Boyle never got a chance to view Mackesy's written instructions from the Chief of the Imperial General Staff and these instructions were not made available to the Chiefs of Staff or Military Coordination Committee. Churchill also failed to give Admiral Boyle a clear written brief and General Ismay - Churchill's future Chief of Staff - describes the administrative confusion thus:

> *The Chief of the Naval Staff and the Chief of the Imperial General Staff acted with sturdy independence. They appointed their respective commanders without consultations with each other; and worse still, they gave directives to those commanders without harmonising them. Thereafter they continued to issue separate orders to them. Thus was confusion worse confounded.*

Facing such obstacles, the Norway expedition was doomed to failure and Allied forces started withdrawing after only three weeks. Allied troops lacked air cover, anti-aircraft guns, adequate transport, cold weather equipment and relevant maps. German forces controlled the country by late April and King Haakon and his government fled to Britain on 7th June. Allied forces occupied Narvik at the end of May but were forced to withdraw on 8th June as - with the rest of the country under German control - they couldn't be supplied. Norway finally surrendered on 10th June, two months after the invasion commenced.

Norway fell because the Allies dithered for several months and allowed Germany to seize the initiative but once the operation commenced, Churchill's mismanagement aggravated an already challenging situation. He attempted to micro-manage an operation at a distance of 1,300 miles and was relieved as Chairman of the Military Coordination Committee on 16th April when the service chiefs refused to work with him. Three senior figures describe Churchill's working methods during this period. According to Neville Chamberlain, Churchill's

> *methods of work are most wearing to others. He goes to bed after lunch for a couple of hours… and holds conferences up to 1 in the morning at which he goes into every detail… officers and officials … are sent for and kept up until they are dropping with fatigue and service ministers are worn out in*

> *arguing with him... [He has] smashed the machine [the Military Coordination Committee] we had so carefully built up to ensure that all projects should be thought out or examined by a planning staff drawn from all services... he does enjoy planning a campaign... and he believes so earnestly in all his own ideas... that he puts intenser pressure on his staff than he realises... [the] result is that they are bullied into a sulky silence - a most dangerous position in a war.*

Admiral John Godfrey, Director of Naval Intelligence, describes Churchill's working methods in a manner that recalls his behaviour before Gallipoli.

> *To get his own way he used every device and brought the whole battery of his ingenious, tireless and highly political mind to bear on the point at issue. His battery of weapons included persuasion, real or simulated anger, mockery, vituperation, tantrums, ridicule, derision, abuse and tears, which he would aim at anyone who opposed him or expressed a view contrary to the one he had already formed, sometimes on quite trivial questions.*

General Ironside described Churchill as

> *like a child in many ways. He tires of a thing, and then wants to hear no more of it. He was mad to divert the brigade from Narvik to Namsos... now he is bored with the Namsos operation and is all for Narvik again. It is most extraordinary how mercurial he is.*

Lest these assessments sound harsh, Churchill later accepted considerable responsibility for the Norway débâcle. Writing to General Ismay in 1946, he conceded that *"I certainly bore an exceptional measure of responsibility for the brief and disastrous Norwegian campaign - if campaign it can be called."*[47] Despite this, Norway provided his passport to Downing Street.

IV

By the end of April, Churchill's credibility in Whitehall and among the service chiefs was at a low ebb but this didn't reflect his standing in the country. He had made several highly effective radio and public

[47] In an unpublished draft of his memoirs, he also wrote *"it was a marvel - I really do not know how - I survived and maintained my position in public esteem while all the blame was thrown on poor Mr. Chamberlain."* (Bell, *Churchill and the Dardanelles,* p.343).

pronouncements and was viewed as a man of action who would defy Hitler. In contrast, Chamberlain was seen as the man who had been duped by the dictators, neglected his country's defences and had presided over a first class disaster. He had to go.

During the Commons debate on Norway on 7th and 8th May, several heavyweights lined up to condemn him. Sir Roger Keyes spoke for the *"officers and men of the fighting, sea-going Navy who are very unhappy"* and repeated Nelson's claim that the boldest measures are also the safest. Lloyd George demanded Chamberlain's resignation and Leo Amery echoed Cromwell's advice to the Rump Parliament by declaring

> *you have sat too long for any good you have been doing lately... Depart, I say; and let us have done with you. In the name of God, go!*

And then on 8th May, Chamberlain reminded the Commons that he had *"friends in the House,"* transforming a debate on the conduct of the Norway campaign into a vote on his management of the war. When the votes were counted, the Government majority had slumped to 81 and it was clear that a National Government was needed. Labour refused to serve under Chamberlain, so the Prime Minister called the two principal contenders - Halifax and Churchill - to his office to discuss the succession. Chamberlain asked Churchill if he knew of any reason why Halifax - a peer - could not serve as PM but, according to legend, Churchill remained stonily silent, forcing Halifax - who knew his limitations - to concede that his position as a peer made it impossible for him to serve as Prime Minister. With Halifax out of the running, Chamberlain recommended Churchill as his replacement, and when Churchill finally became Prime Minister in the early evening of Friday 10th May, he felt that he was

> *walking with destiny, and that all my past life had been but a preparation for this hour and for this trial... I thought I knew a good deal about it all, I was sure I should not fail.*

The man who'd bungled Norway and been sacked as Chair of the Military Coordination Committee was now charged with leading Britain through its most desperate hours. He would need all the assistance destiny could provide for - earlier that day - Germany had unleashed *blitzkrieg* on the west.

CHAPTER NINE: THE GREATEST ADVENTURER OF MODERN POLITICAL HISTORY, May - September 1940

The good clean tradition of English politics... had been sold to the greatest adventurer of modern political history... a half breed American, whose main support was that of inefficient but talkative people.

R.A. Butler on Churchill becoming Prime Minister, 10th May 1940

We have no continental army which can defeat the German military power.

Churchill to Beaverbrook, 8th July 1940

June 1940 shattered the foundations on which British strategy rested. France - in Lord Halifax's words - was *"the one firm rock on which everybody had been willing to build for the last two years,"* a defensive bulwark that would - it was assumed - protect north-western Europe, safeguard the Channel and confine Germany to the eastern Rhine. Britain and France would dominate the Mediterranean, jointly defend their vast Empires and at a propitious moment, mobilise their resources to crush Hitler. All this vanished in six short weeks as German forces rampaged across north-western Europe, forcing France to surrender. From having been one half of a hegemonic partnership, Britain was now a vulnerable little island off the coast of a continent dominated by a seemingly unstoppable enemy. The BEF was expelled from Europe and - while Britain lost an ally - it gained a new Italian adversary determined to provoke conflict in the Mediterranean. Churchill and the British people faced a military and political disaster of the first magnitude and their response to this crisis would determine British hopes of survival and shape world history. Could Britain and its new P.M. rise to the challenge?

I

Churchill nominated a National Government to mobilise Britain for war. Labour politicians Clement Attlee and Arthur Greenwood comprised two-fifths of his first War Cabinet and Labour figures occupied other senior posts - Ernie Bevin (Minister of Labour), Hugh Dalton (Minister of Economic Warfare), A.V. Alexander (Admiralty) and Herbert Morrison (Home Secretary). Archie Sinclair (Air Secretary) and Viscount Simon (Lord Chancellor) represented the Liberals while continuity with the old régime was maintained by retaining Neville Chamberlain (Lord President) and Lord Halifax

(Foreign Secretary) in the War Cabinet. As Rab Butler's comment indicates, Churchill was not universally popular and retaining Chamberlain in the Cabinet would deflect the harshest criticism. It is to the credit of both men - and a reflection of the crisis threatening Britain - that they did not allow past differences to sully their working relationship and Chamberlain remained a faithful and diligent War Cabinet member until he retired on 30th September.[48]

Churchill appointed himself Minister of Defence on becoming Prime Minister to gain direction of the war effort, and two new bodies were formed to assist in this work. The military wing of the Cabinet Secretariat evolved into the Office of the Minister of Defence (headed by General Ismay) and the Military Coordination Committee - which Churchill considered too ponderous - was transformed into the Defence Committee,[49] which he chaired. Churchill's role as Minister of Defence entitled him to attend meetings of the Chiefs of Staff (COS) Committee - where the professional heads of the three armed services met - and over time, it was this body - Churchill plus COS - that determined strategy. The three service ministers became *"little more than superior civil servants"* and even the War Cabinet became little more than a 'rubber stamp', endorsing decisions made by Churchill and COS. Senior officials fully appreciated the revolutionary impact of these changes. According to General Ismay,

> *the Prime Minister himself... exercised a personal, direct, ubiquitous and continuous supervision, not only over the formulation of military policy at every stage, but also over the general conduct of military operations... For the first time in their history, the Chiefs of Staff were in direct and continuous contact with the Head of the Government, and were able to act as a combined Battle Headquarters - 'a superchief of a War Staff in Commission'.*

The formation of the Defence Committee and Office of the Minister of Defence plus Churchill's attendance at COS Committee provided Britain with the machinery it needed to fight a modern global war. However, as Churchill eventually became Britain's supreme political and military warlord, he would carry direct personal responsibility for Britain's successes **and** its failures throughout the conflict - there

[48] Chamberlain resigned from the War Cabinet on 30th September and died of bowel cancer on 9th November (Sheila Lawlor, *Churchill and the Politics of War, 1940-1941* (1995), pp.109-110; Keith Laybourn (ed), *British Political Leaders: A Biographical Dictionary* (2001), p.72).

[49] The Defence Committee initially comprised the Prime Minister/Minister of Defence, the three service chiefs and the three service ministers. Senior cabinet members (Eden, Attlee etc) were added later (Blake and Louis (eds), *Churchill*, p.329).

could be no hiding place for a man who'd appointed himself *"supreme director of the war on the military side."*

Churchill's greatest achievement in 1940 was keeping Britain in the fight but - on occasion - his expression of this desire was more nuanced than bullish. One illustration of this can be found in his management of five War Cabinet meetings at the end of May which met to discuss Lord Halifax's suggestion that - with France collapsing and the BEF in full retreat - it was a judicious moment to enquire into Hitler's terms for ending the war. Halifax wasn't proposing capitulation; he simply wished to clarify Britain's options at a critical moment. Halifax believed that better terms could be obtained with France still fighting than might be available later and he hoped to employ Mussolini as a conduit to Hitler. The military situation was uniformly bleak - the Dunkirk evacuation commenced on 27th May - and Halifax believed that Britain couldn't fight on alone.

Churchill opposed these proposals but - given his political vulnerability - couldn't reject Halifax's suggestions outright, adopting instead a Fabian strategy of delay in the hope that - like Mr. Micawber - something might turn up. Churchill was not opposed to ending the war through negotiation but declined to do so in 1940 when the terms offered to Britain would be extremely unfavourable, reducing the country to the status of Germany's satellite. Consequently, when Halifax suggested seeking terms on 26th May, Churchill suggested it would be better to wait

> *until we saw how much of the Army we could re-embark from France. The operation might be a great failure. On the other hand, our troops might well fight magnificently, and we might save a considerable portion of the force.*

Churchill and his Labour colleagues also suggested holding out till the end of the year in the hope that Germany's economy might crumble and when Halifax asked Churchill directly if he would consider terms if *"matters vital to the independence of this country were unaffected,"* Churchill replied that he

> *would be thankful to get out of our present difficulties on such terms, provided we retained the essentials and the elements of our vital strength, even at the cost of some cession of territory.*

In his diary that night, Chamberlain recorded Churchill's alleged willingness to use Malta, Gibraltar and some African colonies as bargaining chips in any negotiations to end the war, though he also noted Churchill's conviction that *"the only safe way [to escape the current crisis] was to convince Hitler that he couldn't beat us."*

On 27th May, Halifax again asked Churchill if he was willing to consider terms, to which Churchill replied that he

> *would not join France in asking for terms; but if he were told what the terms offered were, he would be prepared to consider them.*

In the final meeting on 28th May, Churchill again advocated delay on the grounds that *"nations which go down fighting rise again but those which surrender tamely are finished"* and declared that Britain

> *should get no worse terms [from Hitler] if we went on fighting, even if we were beaten, than were open to us now... A time might come when we felt that we had to put an end to the struggle, but the terms would not then be more mortal than those offered to us now.*

If these comments undercut the legend of belligerent bulldog defiance, we should consider the stresses and strains under which the Prime Minister was operating, the rapidly changing and entirely bleak military picture and his own political vulnerability. When Halifax threatened resignation on 27th May, Churchill spent time walking his sensitive colleague around the Number Ten garden, urging him to remain in post to preserve unity. Germany's unconditional surrender would not be confirmed as an Allied war aim until January 1943 and - in expressing willingness to end the war through negotiation - Churchill was merely acting within accepted convention in which wars were settled through negotiation and compromise rather than total destruction of an opponent's state power. Churchill did not rule out ending the war through negotiation - with a non-Hitler government - but he opposed such moves in summer 1940 when Britain's bargaining power was extremely weak and the outcome of the fighting uncertain.

Belgium's surrender on 28th May removed the question of seeking terms from the War Cabinet's agenda. The loss of such a key ally - Belgium's army had been covering the BEF's retreat - convinced the War Cabinet that any terms offered by Hitler at that point would be too severe to be worth considering and - during a break in the meeting - Halifax and Chamberlain adjourned to draft a note explaining this point to the French Government. During that same break, Churchill met with thirty non-Cabinet ministers to advise them of recent developments. Freed from the need for discretion, Churchill unleashed some rousing oratory, no doubt gaining some much-needed psychological relief. According to Hugh Dalton, Churchill declared that

> *I have thought carefully in these last days whether it was part of my duty to consider entering into negotiations with That Man. But it was idle to think that, if we tried to make peace now, we should get better terms than if we fought it out. The Germans would demand our fleet… our naval bases, and much else. We should become a slave state… under Mosley or some such person. And where should we be at the end of all that... I am convinced… that every man of you would rise up and tear me down from my place if I were for one moment to contemplate parley or surrender. If this long island story of ours is to end at last, let it end only when each one of us lies choking in his own blood upon the ground.*

The ministers heartily endorsed the PM's defiance and he returned to the War Cabinet to inform his senior colleagues that the junior ministers

> *had not expressed alarm at the position in France, but had expressed the greatest satisfaction when he had told them there was no chance of our giving up the struggle. He did not remember having ever heard before a gathering of persons occupying high places in political life express themselves so emphatically.*

The issue of seeking terms disappeared from the War Cabinet agenda until mid-June when it re-appeared as an independent Foreign Office initiative and - when Churchill learned of the move - he quashed it immediately and transferred Halifax to Washington following Lord Lothian's death in December 1940. Churchill had thwarted his colleague through cunctation and in the long run, his gambler's instinct proved a surer guide to strategy than his colleague's cold logic. Something did indeed turn up - Hitler attacked Russia in June 1941 and declared war on America six months later - but until that point, Churchill could offer the British people little more than blood, toil, tears and sweat. And a deal of hope.

II

Britain not only lost an ally in June 1940, it gained an enemy when Italy joined the war on 10th June, confirming the Mediterranean as a vital battleground. As in 1914-18, Britain and France had hoped to jointly dominate this theatre but the loss of the French Navy forced Britain to consider dividing its resources between the Atlantic and the Mediterranean. Germany was about to gain the French Atlantic ports and Britain relied on its transatlantic trade for survival, and relocating the fleet from Alexandria (in the eastern Mediterranean) to Gibraltar would provide a safer harbour and fast access to both waters.

Map 8: Gibraltar and Alexandria

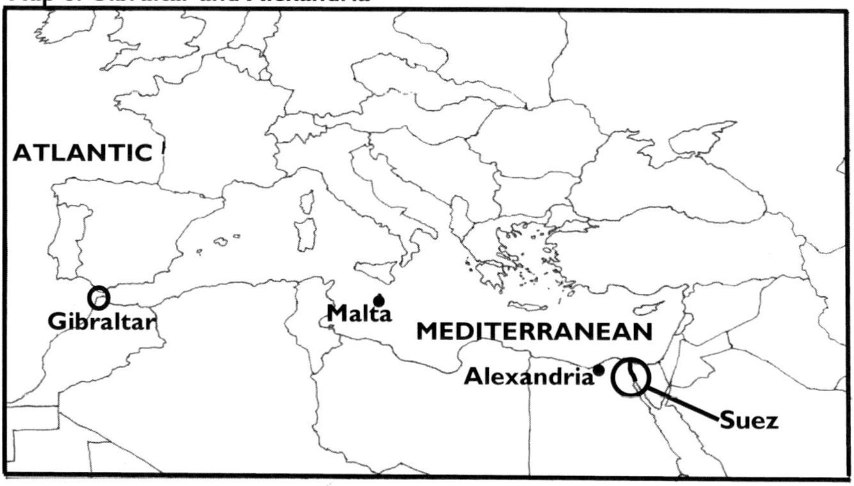

However, the implications of this move - proposed by First Sea Lord Dudley Pound - were so great that the Joint Planning Sub-Committee was invited to consider the matter and its 17th June report decisively rejected Pound's proposal. While appreciating the Admiral's logic, abandoning Alexandria

> *would be interpreted throughout the Middle East as a sign of weakness ... [and] a military withdrawal from the Middle East... would lose us our position in south east Europe, in Palestine and Transjordan and throughout the Arab World. It would complicate our position in India and would increase the temptation to which Japan was subject to attack our Far Eastern possessions.*

Long term imperial considerations coloured the Planner's perceptions.

> *Withdrawal of the fleet might, under present conditions, be regarded in the East as the first stage in the abandonment of our Imperial position. Even if we recovered that position later as the result of a victory in Europe, the blow to our prestige might not be easily forgotten*

With COS locked in stalemate, Churchill - as Minister of Defence - was invited to adjudicate and on 23rd June, he vetoed Pound's proposal - the fleet would remain at Alexandria to contest the Mediterranean. In spring 1939, Churchill had argued that *"for Britain in time of war, the command of the Mediterranean must be the prime objective"* and now that Mussolini had renounced his feeble 'non-belligerence', Churchill was free to concentrate on the Mediterranean and smash the weaker Axis partner. Not only would the Fleet remain at Alexandria but half of Britain's tank force (154 vehicles) and much of its depleted arsenal[50] were despatched to Egypt in August to ward off an anticipated Italian attack.[51] With the Battle of Britain hanging in the balance, this was a risky - not to say reckless - move. Fighter Command air bases were under heavy attack and pilot attrition was rising - if the Luftwaffe gained control of England's skies, invasion would surely follow and Britain would need every tank, bullet and gun despatched by Churchill to Egypt to satisfy his craving for combat in imperially sensitive theatres. As the PM observed on 8th July, *"we have no continental army which can defeat the German military power,"* so fighting Italy was the next best option.

At this point, fortune smiled on Britain. German planes accidentally bombed London on 24th August, the RAF attacked Berlin on the 25th and on 7th September, Göring diverted his bombers from Fighter Command's air bases towards Britain's major cities. Fighter Command revived and on 17th September, Hitler cancelled Operation Sea Lion (the proposed invasion) 'until further notice'[52] - Britain was safe for the next six months thanks to the Channel's wintry volatility. Britain had survived the gravest threat to its security for centuries but was now locked into an African and Mediterranean theatre which would become a British - and Allied - prison for the next four years, and Britain's ebullient Prime Minister was not entirely displeased.

---

[50] Britain sent a full tank brigade to Egypt - 50 infantry tanks, 52 cruiser tanks and 52 light tanks. Additional resources included 48 field guns, 48 anti-tank guns, 250 anti-tank rifles, 20 anti-aircraft guns, 500 Bren guns, 50,000 anti-tank mines plus ammunition, spare parts and radio kit. As the BEF had left much of its equipment behind in France, this represented an extremely risky investment (Lewin, *Churchill As Warlord*, p.55; Churchill, *The Second World War*, Vol. II, pp.371-372 and pp.378-379).

[51] Mussolini invaded British Somaliland on 3rd August and had 250,000 troops based in Libya (against Wavell's 90,000 throughout the entire Middle East). With France *hors de combat*, Italy no longer had to worry about French intervention via Tunisia. (MacGregor Knox, *Hitler's Italian Allies: Royal Armed Forces, Fascist Regime, and the War of 1940-43* (2000), p.101; Zabecki (ed), *World War II in Europe,* p.1605).

[52] On that day, Britain intercepted German messages ordering the dismantling of equipment used to load troop-carrying aircraft, suggesting that invasion was no longer imminent (Richard M. Ketchum, *The Borrowed Years, 1938-41: America on the Way to War* (1991), p.504).

CHAPTER TEN: THE BALKAN CHIMERA, September 1940 - June 1941

The Cabinet is deplorable - dumb men most of whom disagree with Winston but none of whom dare to say so... Winston is a dictator; he cannot be over-ruled, and his colleagues fear him.

Australian P.M. Robert Menzies describes Churchill's political arrangements, April 1941

The loss of Egypt and the Middle East would be a disaster of the first magnitude to Great Britain, second only to a successful invasion and final conquest [of Britain itself]... the life and honour of Great Britain depends upon the successful defence of Egypt.

Winston Churchill, 28th April 1941

Churchill's investment of resources in the Mediterranean in 1940 warped and distorted Allied strategies for defeating Hitler but, in the winter of 1940/41, provided the *matériel* for a series of stunning victories over Italy's African Army. Then, with total victory within its grasp, the Desert Army was broken up and three of its most experienced divisions despatched to Greece on a fool's errand, enabling Rommel to re-establish an Axis presence in Africa. The decision to divert forces to Greece in 1941 stands as one of the most calamitous ever authored by a British Prime Minister, carrying grave consequences and locking the Allies into the Mediterranean for three sterile years.

I

On 13th September, Italy's Tenth Army advanced into Egypt with the verve and panache of the French Army's earlier Saarland 'offensive'. They progressed sixty miles in four days and stopped outside Sidi Barrani. The Italian commander (Graziani) cited lack of water and supplies as his reason for halting but he was profoundly pessimistic about the venture, advising Count Ciano (Italy's Foreign Minister) that Italy was moving *"towards a defeat which, in the desert, must inevitably develop into a rapid and total disaster."* His troops lacked trucks and his tanks were little more than armoured cars so, instead of advancing towards British-imperial positions at Mersa Matruh, he built a series of camps around Sidi Barrani and disaggregated his army into smaller units capable of being defeated in detail.

The Empire reinforced as Italy rested. The 154 tanks sanctioned by Churchill arrived on 24th September and 126,000 extra men landed in the Middle East between August and December. Wavell and his field commander General O'Connor trained during October and November for an early December offensive.

Map 9: Operation Compass

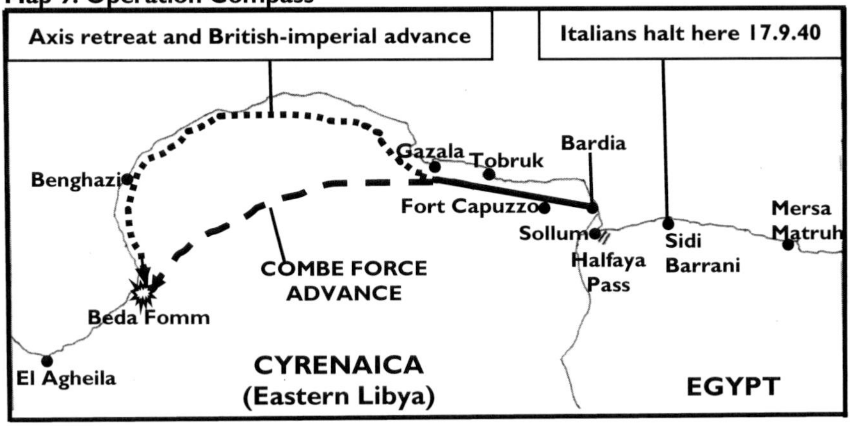

Operation Compass launched on 9th December as a five-day raid against the Sidi Barrani camps but its resounding success - 38,000 prisoners captured in three days - led to it being rolled out as a major offensive over the next two months. Halfaya - the pass which governs movement between Egypt and Libya - was captured on 15th December and Fort Capuzzo (an Italian base inside Libya) fell on 18th December. O'Connor's army of 36,000 men advanced along the coast, seizing Bardia on 5th January and Tobruk on the 22nd. Graziani evacuated Cyrenaica (eastern Libya) on 31st January and Combe Force - an improvised flying column - raced across the desert to intercept him at Beda Fomm. The Italian force was crushed between Combe Force, the Australian 6th Division and 7th Armoured Division and routed over the course of two days, yielding 25,000 further prisoners. O'Connor wired back to Wavell *"Fox killed in the open"* and Wavell informed London that

> *the extent of Italian defeat at Benghazi seems to me to make it possible that Tripoli [five hundred miles further west] might yield to small force if despatched without delay.*

Complete and total victory lay within the Desert Army's grasp but it received orders to halt on 12th February and ready its three best divisions for deployment to Greece. On that same day, Rommel landed in Tripoli - quickly followed by the first Afrika Korps units - and the opportunity to swiftly erase the Axis from Africa was lost.

II

British involvement in Greece reflected its long-standing desire to dominate the eastern Mediterranean and protect the northern approaches to Suez. Greece and its myriad islands project into the middle of the region and could sustain air bases from which Turkey, Italy, North Africa and the Balkans could be dominated. Turkey - Greece's eastern neighbour - offers vital access to the Middle East, the oilfields of Iraq and an alternative route to Suez, and Britain wanted to protect Greece, both as an end in itself and to prevent its use as a stepping stone to Turkey and the British Middle East.

Britain had guaranteed Greece in April 1939 and when Italy attacked on 28th October 1940, Churchill immediately informed the Greek Prime Minister that *"we will give you all the help in our power. We will fight a common foe and share a united victory."* However, Greece declined Britain's offer of ground forces as it felt capable of dealing with Italy on its own and wished to avoid antagonising Germany. In mid-November, the Greeks launched a successful counter-offensive which, within six weeks, had occupied southern Albania and pinned down 500,000 Italian soldiers.

The situation changed dramatically in early 1941 when sizeable German forces entered Romania[53] - which had joined the Axis on 23rd November - and as Bulgaria grew increasingly pro-German. The prospect of German intervention alarmed the Greeks and Churchill, who *"dreaded"*[54] the appearance of German forces in the region. Greece requested British assistance on 8th February, and Foreign Secretary Eden and General Dill (Chief of the Imperial General Staff since May 1940) were despatched to Athens to clarify the terms of British support on 22nd-23rd February. This sequence of events led to the cancelling of Wavell's Libyan advance on 12th February,[55] four days after Greece requested assistance.

---

[53] German forces first entered Romania in September 1940 and 370,000 troops were based there by spring 1941. The further entry of German forces into Romania in October 1940 inspired Mussolini's 28th October assault on Greece (Craig Stockings and Eleanor Hancock, *Swastika over the Acropolis: Re-interpreting the Nazi Invasion of Greece in World War II* (2013), p.37).

[54] In Volume Two of *The Second World War*, Churchill explained that *"by running a few special convoys [in the Mediterranean] we might... provoke a trial of strength with the Italian fleet. I hoped that this might happen.... before the appearance, which I already dreaded, of the Germans in this theatre."* (Churchill, *The Second World War*, Vol. II, p.391).

[55] The Defence Committee decided on 11th February that Wavell should abandon any serious effort towards Tripoli and prioritise Greece and Turkey and he received these orders on 12th February (Raugh, *Wavell in the Middle East,* p.120).

The debate over Hellenic intervention resolved into two basic options. COS, CIGS, General John Kennedy (Director of Military Operations), Leo Amery and Sir Alexander Cadogan all favoured a continuing advance on Tripoli to capture Libya and expel the Axis from Africa. They felt that stripping the Desert Force of its best divisions would squander this opportunity and that any support given to Greece would be too small to be meaningful. Kennedy summarised this view on 16th February by recommending that O'Connor's force should

> *push on to Tripoli before the opportunity to do so has disappeared. If we do not deprive the Italians of this last base in Africa it is certain that the Germans will build up forces there… With regard to Greece… it may be possible to form a political front in the Balkans. But a political front is of no use unless it can be backed up by an effective military front. It is impossible to form an effective military front because the Balkan nations are so ill-equipped and we have not sufficient forces to spare to do it ourselves. Nothing we can do can make the Greek business a sound military proposition.*

Churchill rejected this advice, arguing that Britain was obliged to honour its guarantee to Greece lest it *"be said that in spite of our guarantees we had allowed one more small ally to be swallowed up."* Churchill also nurtured fantasies of a 'Balkan Front' which - in his view - could defend the Balkans and provide a base for offensive operations against the Axis in southern Europe. Churchill described the Greek request for military assistance as the moment

> *when the irrevocable decision must be taken whether or not to send the Army of the Nile to Greece. This grave step was required not only to help Greece in her peril… but to form against the impending German attack a Balkan Front comprising Yugoslavia, Greece and Turkey… It was not what we could send ourselves that could decide the Balkan issue. Our limited hope was to stir and organise united action. If* ***at the wave of our wand*** *[emphasis added] Yugoslavia, Greece and Turkey would all act together, it seemed to us that Hitler might either let the Balkans off for the time being or become so heavily engaged with our combined forces as to create a major front in that theatre… It was our aim to animate and combine Yugoslavia, Greece and Turkey.*

Churchill defended his decision after the war in conversation with Bob Boothby, his former Private Secretary.

> *They said that I was wrong to go to Greece in 1940 [sic]. But I did not do it simply to save the Greeks… I wanted to form a Balkan Front. I wanted Yugoslavia and I hoped for Turkey. That, with Greece, would have given us fifty divisions. A nut for the Germans to crack.*

In Churchill's over-active mind, Britain had merely to 'wave its wand'(!) and despatch three divisions to Greece to summon up a durable 'Balkan Front' of fifty battle-ready divisions. The naïveté behind such thinking is breathtaking, completely ignoring local political realities and the Balkan states' complicated histories. Greece and Turkey had fought a bitter territorial war - characterised by 'ethnic cleansing' - during 1919-22 and were unlikely military partners. Yugoslavia was divided between pro-British Serbs and pro-Axis Croats and Slovenes and shared a border with the Reich following the Anschluss; it had to be careful not to offend Germany and even joined the Axis for two days in March 1941.[56] Turkey rejected all British overtures to form a constructive military/diplomatic partnership throughout the war and signed a Non-Aggression Pact with Bulgaria on 17th February, indicating a desire for neutrality in any coming conflict. In championing a 'Balkan Front', Churchill was reviving the flawed dreams of the First World War 'easterners' - Lloyd George *et al* - who hoped that an offensive in south-eastern Europe would 'knock the props from under Germany' and create *"the prospect of a triumph which would have a determining effect on the fate of the struggle."* Churchill also believed that the September/October 1918 Salonika campaign - which removed Bulgaria from the war - contributed materially to German capitulation, and his enthusiasm for a Balkan venture in 1941 may have reflected a desire to lay the Gallipoli ghost to rest by sponsoring a successful operation in that same theatre. Unfortunately, in seeking to inspire a Balkan Front in 1941, Churchill was fashioning bricks from straw; the Front had no basis in reality and remained wishful thinking on his part, a 'glittering phrase' that captivated his mind for several weeks before precipitating disaster.

---

[56] Under pressure from Germany, Prince Paul's Regency Government adhered to the Tripartite Pact (i.e. the Axis) on 25th March 1941. However, two days later a group of pro-western air force officers instigated a coup and placed 17-year-old King Peter II on the throne. The new government immediately repudiated the Tripartite Pact and Germany invaded Yugoslavia on 6th April in direct retaliation (Gregor J. Kranjc, *To Walk with the Devil: Slovene Collaboration and Axis Occupation, 1941-1945* (2013), p.49; J. Eichenberg and J. Newman (eds), *The Great War and Veterans' Internationalism* (2013), pp.97-98).

Map 10: Greece, Crete and North Africa

Greek hesitancy and internal British discussion ensured that the debate over intervention rumbled on into early February but, following two Defence Committee meetings on 10th and 11th February, Wavell was ordered to

> *make yourself secure at Benghazi and concentrate all available forces in the Delta in preparation for a movement to Europe... Our first thoughts must be for our ally Greece... if Greece is trampled down or forced to make a separate peace with Italy... effect on Turkey will be very bad... we should... offer the Greeks the... fighting portion of the army which has hitherto defended Egypt and make every plan for sending and reinforcing it to the limit with men and material.*

Following this, Eden and Dill travelled to Athens and Belgrade to try to drum up support for the Front and to finalise British preparations for supporting Greece. Bulgaria joined the Axis on 1st March and British-imperial forces started deploying to Greece on 5th March. By early April, 58,000 troops had been moved to Greece - leaving Libya defenceless - and Germany launched its twin assault on Greece and Yugoslavia on 6th April. The wisdom of Greek intervention and the viability of the Balkan Front now faced the supreme test.

The fact that Yugoslavia was subdued within eleven days and Greece in slightly more than three weeks - and Turkey's steadfast neutrality throughout - suggests that Churchill's hopes for a dynamic Balkan Front were sadly misplaced. German forces simply by-passed Greek positions on the Metaxas Line and British-imperial positions further south and, once these positions were outflanked, it was merely a matter of mopping up Allied forces as they fled south in chaos. Germany controlled Greece by the end of April and the Royal Navy was forced to evacuate 51,000 men from southern Greece at the end of the month, while a further 16,000 were killed, wounded or captured. The Expeditionary Force also abandoned 8,000 trucks, 200 planes and 100 tanks that could have been better employed in Africa. Following the Greek catastrophe, Crete fell after a week-long airborne assault in late May and, once more, the Navy had to rescue Britain's Army, plucking 18,000 men to safety while 14,000 others were killed, wounded or captured. And as British-imperial power crumbled in Greece, Rommel flexed his muscles in Libya.

III

Hitler only became involved in the Mediterranean to spare his Axis partner's blushes and to secure his southern flank but the deployment of German forces in North Africa prolonged the war and extended the life of his bestial Reich.

Erwin Rommel and 5th Light Division landed in Libya in February 1941 - coincidentally with Wavell's advance halting - to fulfil a defensive role and shore up Italy's crumbling position. However, Rommel quickly exploited British-imperial weakness in the region by launching an offensive at the end of March which - by late April - had re-taken all of Libya (apart from Tobruk) and captured Sollum and Halfaya. In just over four weeks, O'Connor and Wavell's work had been undone by an Axis force of one German and two Italian divisions - equivalent to the British-imperial force despatched to Greece.

Rommel needed to control Tobruk to advance further into Egypt and the Empire needed Tobruk to harass Rommel's rear and block his supplies so - during May and June - the desert war resolved into a struggle to gain mastery of this vital seaport and the strategic pass at Halfaya. Rommel launched attack after attack on Tobruk but was repulsed by General Leslie Morshead and the men of 9th Australian Division. On 15th May, Wavell launched Operation Brevity in an effort to capture Halfaya, but while the attack enjoyed some initial success - capturing the Pass on the first day - Axis forces had regained control by the end of the month.

Churchill's defective decision-making had precipitated a crisis in Libya, but he demanded a desert victory and rushed 295 tanks and 53 fighters to Wavell to provide the punch needed to dislodge Rommel. The convoy arrived on 12th May and Churchill demanded immediate action, ordering Wavell to launch Operation Battleaxe within the month. Wavell requested time to prepare his tanks and crews for desert warfare but was overruled and - against his better judgment - initiated Battleaxe on 15th June.

Battleaxe reveals British military amateurism at its worst. Loose radio talk gave the Germans advance warning of the assault and Rommel deployed his forces accordingly. His panzers, mines and 88mm guns shattered more than one hundred British tanks while the Axis lost fewer than twenty-five. After three days of hard fighting, Sollum and Halfaya remained under Axis control and Tobruk was still under siege. Churchill looked for a scapegoat and blamed Wavell. On 21st June, he was ordered to swap places with General Claude Auchinleck (Commander-in-Chief, India) while Auchinleck gained Wavell's North African command, a poor reward for a general who had presented Churchill with such dazzling victories only four months earlier but who had never enjoyed full Prime Ministerial favour.[57]

The desert war descended into stalemate following Battleaxe. Auchinleck couldn't organise a follow-up offensive until the losses of June were made good and British possession of Tobruk prevented Rommel from advancing into Egypt. Hitler attacked Russia on 22nd June and the Afrika Korps was starved of supplies and equipment until early 1942.

---

[57] Churchill's dislike of Wavell originated in the August 1940 evacuation of British Somaliland. Churchill felt that the low British casualty rate indicated a lack of martial ardour with Wavell responding that *"a big butcher's bill was not necessarily evidence of good tactics,"* a remark which infuriated Churchill. Wavell was taciturn (where Churchill was loquacious) and he did not deliver the military victories Churchill craved although, given the circumstances, it is difficult to hold him directly responsible for British military failure in the war's early years (Jackson, *British Empire and the Second World War*, p.211).

Map 11: Operation Battleaxe locations

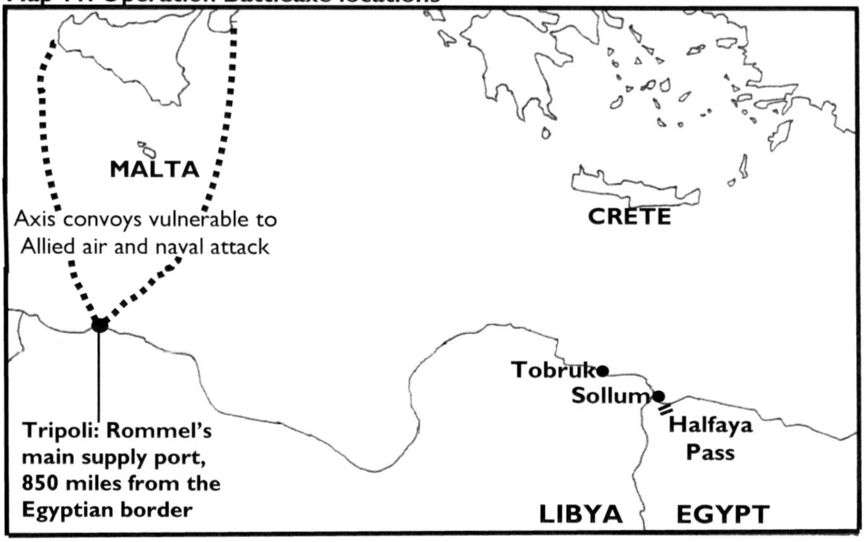

IV

Churchill's direction of Britain's war effort in spring 1941 was calamitous. He squandered a golden opportunity to evict the Axis from Africa and ensured that fighting in this theatre dragged on until 1943. Expeditions to Greece and Crete ended in disaster and the Axis regained Libya and part of Egypt. The 'Balkan Front' failed to materialise and Battleaxe was blunted at Halfaya. Such were the consequences of Churchill's military meddling.

Churchill also exhibited confusion over Britain's strategic purpose. In August 1940 - as the Battle of Britain neared climax - he despatched half of Britain's tank force to Egypt but no sooner had Egypt been secured than Greece and the Balkans gained prominence in his mind. On 11th January, he informed Wavell that the

> *destruction of Greece [through German attack] would eclipse victories you have gained in Libya and might affect decisively Turkish attitude, especially if we had shown ourselves callous of fate of allies.*

On 12th February, he again instructed Wavell that Britain's

> *major effort must now be to aid Greece and/or Turkey. This rules out any serious effort against Tripoli... if [the Greeks] have a good plan it would be worth our while to back it with all our strength and fight the Germans in Greece, hoping thereby to draw in both Turks and Yugoslavs.*

Yet while Churchill was actively championing military intervention in Greece, he presented an entirely different picture to Harry Hopkins - President Roosevelt's personal envoy - who visited London in January 1941 to assess British political-military resolve. Keen to coax America into the conflict, Churchill extended every courtesy to Hopkins - even accommodating him in Downing Street - and granted him privileged access to his thinking. On 10th January, Hopkins informed Washington that:

> *[Churchill] thinks Greece is lost - although he is now reinforcing the Greeks - and weakening his African Army... and is now preparing for the attack which must bring its inevitable result. He knows this will be a blow to British prestige and is obviously considering ways and means of preparing the British public for it.*[58]

Hopkins' comments illuminate Churchill's chaotic thought processes. On the one hand, he was assuring senior British colleagues that Greek military support represented a sound investment of resources while, on the other, was conceding to the President's envoy that support for Greece was futile. The prospect of seizing Libya and ending the desert war in 1941 was therefore squandered for an operation Churchill considered pointless, while the 30,000 men lost in Greece and Crete were sacrificed to no good effect.[59] The degree of mental agility required to reconcile such contrasting propositions is truly remarkable.

And yet, as soon as Greece was lost, Egypt regained its supremacy in Churchill's mind, as his 28th April COS directive indicates.

> *The loss of Egypt and the Middle East would be a disaster of the first magnitude to Great Britain, second only to a successful invasion and final conquest [of Britain itself]... It is to be impressed on all ranks... that the life and honour of Great Britain depends upon the successful defence of Egypt...*

---

[58] Hopkins goes on to say that Churchill *"realizes [Britain's defeat in Greece] will have a profound and disappointing effect in America as well"* - an intriguing comment given suggestions by some historians that Churchill squandered resources in Greece in order to impress America and secure passage of the Lend-Lease Bill (introduced into Congress on 10th January). Hopkins also states Churchill's belief that *"this debacle in Greece will be overcome in part by what he considers to be the sure defeat of the Italians in Africa"* - a strange hope given his decision to strip the Desert Army of everything it needed to defeat the Italians (Sherwood, *White House Papers of Harry Hopkins,* Vol. I, p.240).

[59] Heavy German losses on Crete discouraged Hitler from using paratroopers in other operations, probably saving Malta.

> *not only must Egypt be defended, but the Germans must be beaten and thrown out of Cyrenaica.*

Churchill's defective decision-making had placed Egypt in grave jeopardy, and for Egypt to regain its strategic primacy so soon after Greece and Turkey had occupied that position reflects extreme fickleness. With British military planning plagued by chronic indecision at the top,[60] it's hardly surprising that Britain's armies performed so poorly in the early years of the war.

Churchill also employed his political prestige - greatly enhanced by the Battle of Britain - and his overbearing personality to impose his will on colleagues even when they considered his vision defective. Memoirs and diary entries from spring 1941 reveal growing disquiet over Churchill's management style and the conviction that one man was directing the Empire's entire war effort. Churchill had imposed his will on colleagues in the run-up to Gallipoli and during the Norway fiasco, and a similar tendency emerged in spring 1941. Lord Hankey - Cabinet Secretary and Secretary to the Committee of Imperial Defence for quarter of a century - described Churchill's management of political and military affairs as

> *a complete dictatorship. The War Cabinet and the War Committee on military matters consist of a long monologue by one man. The others are just 'yes men'. The Chiefs of Staff, worn out by incessant late night meetings of the Defence Committee, are reduced almost to the position of 'Joint Planners'.*

General John Kennedy described a similar situation.

> *Criticism of Churchill was bitter and general, and it was said that all was not well with the machinery for the military control of the war... no clear-cut military appreciations were being laid before the War Cabinet... military opinions were being distorted and coloured by the formal advocacy of the Prime Minister... that he was not only advocate, but witness, prosecutor and judge. He was also criticized for sending personal directives to the commanders-in-chief without professional advice, and for exhausting the Chiefs of Staff to the point of danger.*

Even loyalists such as John Colville, Churchill's Assistant Private Secretary, detected worrying trends, confiding in his diary that

---

[60] Already evidenced in the Norway shambles.

> *the P.M. does not help the Government machine to run smoothly and his inconsiderate treatment of the service departments would cause trouble were it not for the great personal loyalty of the Service Ministers... He supplies drive and initiative but he often meddles where he would better leave things alone and the operational side of the war might profit if he gave it a respite and turned to... labour and production.*

If one adds the already cited views of Robert Menzies - who attended War Cabinet meetings during March and April - Churchill's dictatorial behaviour is confirmed and he therefore carries great personal responsibility for Britain's abject military failures throughout this period. His decision to support Greece in 1941 prolonged the desert war until 1943 and one can only speculate on what might have been achieved had the resources wasted in North Africa during 1941-43 been used elsewhere. The Battle of the Atlantic might have been won in 1942. Singapore, Malaya and Burma might have been saved. British-imperial units could have fought alongside Soviet forces in the Caucasus or perhaps an Italian Mediterranean island might have been captured, precipitating *Il Duce's* early fall from grace. Most tantalising of all, the conclusion of the desert war in 1941 might have cleared the path for Overlord in 1943 and a speedier end to the war. An early Channel crossing carried its own hazards but also held the possibility of ending the war in 1944 with the attendant saving of lives on Europe's battlefields, in Germany's ruined cities and in the death camps. All this was cast away when three crack divisions were diverted to Greece in 1941, and Churchill accepted responsibility for this colossal blunder in his post-war memoirs:

> *I take full responsibility for the eventual decision [to support Greece], because I am sure I could have stopped it all if I had been convinced.*

CHAPTER ELEVEN: MR. PRESIDENT, I BELIEVE YOU ARE TRYING TO DO AWAY WITH THE BRITISH EMPIRE, June - December 1941

> **Roosevelt:** *After the war, one of the preconditions of any lasting peace will have to be the greatest possible freedom of trade.*
>
> **Churchill:** *England does not propose... to lose its favoured position among the British dominions... There can be no tampering with the Empire's economic arrangements... They're the foundation of our greatness.*
>
> Roosevelt and Churchill discuss economics
> at Placentia Bay, August 1941

Operation Barbarossa transformed the scope and scale of the global conflict. In the early hours of 22nd June, four million Axis troops armed with four thousand tanks and five thousand aircraft hurled themselves against a Red Army of five million men equipped with twenty thousand tanks and fifteen thousand aircraft. This was war on a colossal scale, dwarfing the desert conflict in which 120,000 Axis troops battled 600,000 British-imperial forces. In 1940, Britain had considered bombing Russia and allying itself with Finland but Hitler's insatiable bloodlust forged a bond between the world's leading Empire and the workers' utopia. On the other side of the Atlantic, Roosevelt watched and waited, pondering the circumstances that might inspire American intervention.

I

Churchill detested socialism. He loathed every '-ism' that threatened his class interests and - in Lloyd George's cabinet - was the leading advocate of military intervention to 'strangle the babe of Bolshevism in its cradle'. Only a combination of war weariness, fiscal restraint and working class support for the new Soviet state thwarted his desire to crush an ideology that was

> *not a policy; it is a disease. It is not a creed; it is a pestilence ... it is violently contagious; it throws people into a frenzy of excitement; it spreads with extraordinary rapidity.*

Despite such enmity, Churchill responded pragmatically to Barbarossa, knowing that Britain was safe while Hitler was busy in Russia and, as he cheerfully informed his Private Secretary, *"if Hitler invaded hell, I would make at least a favourable reference to the devil in the House of Commons."* On 22nd June 1941, Churchill advised the British people that

> *any man or State who fights against Nazism will have our aid... we shall give whatever help we can to Russia and to the Russian people. We shall appeal to all our friends and Allies... to take the same course... We have offered the Government of Soviet Russia any technical or economic assistance which is in our power and is likely to be of service to them.*

Despite such noble sentiment, British aid to Russia over the next eighteen months was more moral than material. Britain itself was rearming and had little *matériel* to spare and if Russia was going to collapse in a matter of months - as Churchill and many of his advisers feared - why donate supplies to its likely conqueror? Others found it difficult to forget Russia's cooperation with Germany over the preceding twenty-one months, and Allied assistance to Russia only became significant after America entered the war and the Red Army stopped the Wehrmacht in its tracks. Unable to materially assist Russia, Churchill promised that Britain would

> *bomb Germany by day as well as by night in ever-increasing measure, casting upon them month by month a heavier discharge of bombs and making the German people taste and gulp each month a sharper dose of the miseries they have showered upon mankind.*

However, British bombing raids on Germany had preceded Barbarossa and offered the only means by which Britain could strike at Germany without risking a ground offensive.[61] Stalin submitted his first request for a Second Front within a week of Britain and Russia concluding their 12th July Mutual Assistance Treaty and - in his reply - Churchill listed the reasons against such an operation, including the presence of

> *forty [German] divisions in France alone, and the whole coast has been fortified with German diligence for more than a year... This is one mass of fortifications, with scores of heavy guns commanding the sea approaches, many of which can fire right across the Straits. There is less than five hours of darkness, and even then the whole area is illuminated by*

---

[61] Chapter 25 considers Britain's bombing offensive against Germany.

> *searchlights. To attempt a landing in force would be to encounter a bloody repulse, and petty raids would only lead to fiascos, doing far more harm than good.*

Stalin would become familiar with these excuses over the next two and a half years until finally, in December 1943, combined Soviet-American pressure forced Churchill to commit to an operation he actively opposed. However, while the Prime Minister ruled out operations in north-western Europe to aid Russia, he was only too happy to cooperate in a region where Allied strategy and British Oil and Empire interests neatly converged.

II

Britain needed little encouragement to become involved in the Middle East. The 1908 discovery of oil in Iran had led to the construction of a massive British-controlled refinery at Abadan to furnish fuel for the Royal Navy. When Turkey sided with Germany in 1914, Britain identified *'dismemberment'* of the Ottoman Empire as a key war aim and consolidated its grip on Iraq during 1917-19. The Greek fiasco was undertaken to safeguard British Oil and Empire interests, and British puppets governed Iraq and Transjordan. Egypt had been granted nominal independence in 1922 but the 1936 Anglo-Egyptian Treaty - signed following Mussolini's brutal invasion of Abyssinia (Ethiopia) - gave Britain the right to maintain a sizeable military presence in the Canal Zone and enter Egypt in time of war.

The region's geopolitical significance expanded exponentially following Barbarossa. Every combatant craved oil and if German forces penetrated Russia's southern defences, they could irrupt into the Middle East via the back door to seize the region's oil reserves and threaten Suez. Similarly, if Rommel penetrated British defences in North Africa, he could drive north through the Levant to link up with German forces advancing from the west to seize the Caucasus. Geopolitical and strategic considerations demanded British domination of the Great Persian Plateau to defend its imperial domain and those of its ally.

Intervention in Iraq was required after Rashid Ali and his Golden Square clique toppled Prince Abdallah's regency in April 1941.[62] Ali's National Defence Government was openly pro-Axis and besieged the

[62] Prince Abdallah served as Regent for King Faisal II who had succeeded his father as a three year-old in 1939.

RAF base at Habbaniya (near Baghdad), declaring its intention to breach the 1930 Anglo-Iraq Treaty which gave Britain the right to transport troops across the region. Rashid Ali's coup threatened British access to oil and served as a beacon for disaffected Arab nationalists everywhere - the virus had to be quarantined before spreading.

An invasion force was cobbled together from Indian Army units, troops en route to Malaya and detachments from Palestine. Indian Army units occupied Basra in mid-April and a flying column set off to relieve Habbaniya on 11th May, while aircraft from RAF Habbaniya bombed Iraqi targets in early May. Fallujah was occupied on 21st May and Rashid Ali's government collapsed eight days later. By early June, Prince Abdallah was back on the throne and a friendly government re-installed. The virus had been contained and Auchinleck was offered Middle East Command partly as a result of his decisive intervention.

Map 12: Allied Intervention in Iraq, Iran and the Levant

Rashid Ali had received German and Italian support through Vichy-controlled Syria, so operations in Iraq quickly inspired British-imperial intervention in Syria and Lebanon. An invasion force entered Syria (from Iraq) and Lebanon (from Palestine) on 8th June, and the presence of Free French troops in the force encouraged Britain to believe the Vichy garrison would defect en masse. Damascus fell on 21st June, Beirut was occupied on 12th July and the whole area came under Free French control on 14th July. Four months later, the Free French administration recognised Syria and Lebanon as independent states.

Iran remained studiously neutral throughout these disturbances but the presence of several hundred German and Italian nationals in the country provided a pretext for an Anglo-Soviet occupation on 25th August. Britain and Russia had partitioned Iran in 1907-08[63] and the 1941 occupation followed this precedent with Russia controlling the north and Britain dominating the south. Reza Shah was forced to abdicate in favour of his son Mohammad Reza Pahlavi and in January 1942, Britain, Russia and Iran concluded a Treaty of Alliance against Germany. Britain and America funnelled aid to Russia through the 'Persian Corridor' while Churchill, Roosevelt and Stalin gathered in Tehran for Eureka in November 1943.

By autumn 1941, Britain had been evicted from Norway, France, Belgium and Greece but had consolidated its grip on Iran, Iraq, Syria and Lebanon. It was against this backdrop of minor key success that Churchill set off to confer with Roosevelt in Newfoundland.

III

As a politician, Churchill set great store by personal relationships and in the eighteen months between the fall of France and Pearl Harbor, no-one was courted more assiduously than Franklin D. Roosevelt. Churchill's task was challenging for he had to convince Roosevelt of Britain's pressing need for support without appearing weak or desperate - such an impression would choke off American aid entirely and it's a credit to Churchill's diplomatic skills that he managed to extract several concessions from Roosevelt in such trying circumstances.

At the same time, Churchill's entreaties created difficulties for Roosevelt for while he recognised that a vibrant and resolute Empire constituted America's first line of defence, he had to contend with isolationist sentiment at home and had no desire to prop up a decaying *imperium*. Consequently, America used the aid offered to Britain prior to Pearl Harbor to advance its own interests. In September 1940, America exchanged fifty obsolete destroyers for the right to build bases on ninety-nine year leases on British territories throughout the western hemisphere (e.g. Jamaica, Trinidad, Newfoundland). Similarly, the March 1941 Lend Lease Act was formally titled 'An Act to Promote the Better Defence of the United States' and was sold to the American people on the principle of lending a hose to a neighbour

[63] See Chapter Two

whose house had caught fire.[64] Churchill dubbed Lend Lease *"the most unsordid act in the history of any nation"* but assistance was provided on a deferred payment basis and Britain remained in hock to the United States until December 2006.

Consequently, when Roosevelt and Churchill met at Placentia Bay in Newfoundland[65] between 9th - 12th August, their behaviour resembled a mating ritual between two rather cautious and tentative lovers thrown together by circumstance and somewhat suspicious of each other's motives. Britain required American support but, at the same time, America could not allow Britain to go under. Roosevelt yearned for the dissolution of Britain's Empire while Churchill was committed to its preservation. And all the time, the clock was ticking, nudging the two leaders towards compromise before the conference concluded.

Churchill set off for the meeting with high hopes, advising the Queen before departing that *"I do not think our friend would have asked me to go so far for what must be a meeting of world-wide notice, unless he had in mind some further forward step."* However, if Churchill anticipated an American expression of belligerence or an early declaration of war, he would be disappointed for Roosevelt's motives in calling the meeting were political and diplomatic rather than military. He wanted to articulate a series of war aims to animate allies and neutrals around the world and prepare America for possible entry into the war. He also wanted to ensure Britain didn't exploit the upheaval to expand its Empire - as it had done in the First World War - and wanted a public declaration confirming this.

Churchill was pathologically hostile to discussing war aims (other than *"victory at all costs… victory however long and hard the road may be"*) and travelled three thousand miles to meet the President at a time when Britain was experiencing grave difficulties in North Africa and the Atlantic. To discover that he was expected to discuss theoretical war aims with the Chief Executive of a state not yet at war must have been extremely galling but - such was Britain's need for assistance - he had no choice but to knuckle down and indulge the President's preferences. If hypothetical discussions about the post-war world were necessary to cement the union between Britain and America, Churchill would prove an ardent suitor.

Given the largely theoretical nature of the discussions and the time

---

[64] The Congressional Bill was also numbered '1776' to confirm that Lend-Lease was intended to promote American interests (Benjamin D. Rhodes, *United States Foreign Policy in the Interwar Period, 1918-1941* (2001), p.175).

[65] A base ceded to America under the 'destroyers for bases' deal.

limits on the meeting, the negotiations proceeded in a largely amicable manner but British and American interests clashed in two specific areas and Churchill had to execute some fancy footwork to safeguard British imperial interests against Rooseveltian idealism.

Article Four of what became known as the Atlantic Charter addressed the issue of free trade and British and American views diverged sharply. Roosevelt viewed protectionism as an impediment to American economic interests while Britain and the Dominions had signed the 1932 Ottawa Agreements endorsing tariffs and imperial preference. Churchill had been an enthusiastic free trader in his younger days but could brook no interference in the Empire's economic arrangements, sparking the conflict alluded to in the introductory epigraph. To resolve the issue - and defend the Empire - Churchill reminded the President that the Dominions had not empowered him to speak on their behalf but - if the President wished - he would canvass their views. However, it might take a full week for the Dominions to offer a response and Roosevelt didn't have a week to spare. To reach agreement on this issue, he therefore allowed Churchill to insert a caveat into Article Four which largely nullified its impact on the Empire. The final draft of Article Four committed Britain and America to

> *endeavour, with due respect for their existing obligations, to further the enjoyment by all States, great or small, victor or vanquished, of access, on equal terms, to the trade and to the raw materials of the world which are needed for their economic prosperity.*

The phrase *"with due respect for their existing obligations"* exempted the Empire from the Article's main thrust.

Article Three of the Charter addressed the right to self-determination and reflected another thorny topic. Anglo-America had to endorse self determination to distinguish it from the Axis but an unqualified endorsement of self-determination would threaten Britain's Empire which was entirely based on denying self determination to subject peoples. Again, Churchill inserted an innocuous phrase into the Article to completely invalidate its ethos. The final wording of Article Three committed Britain and America to

> *respect the right of all peoples to choose the form of government under which they will live, and they wish to see sovereign rights and self-government restored to those who have been forcibly deprived of them.*

Churchill inserted the phrase concerning the restoration of sovereign rights and self government *"to those who had been forcibly deprived of them"* to exempt the Empire from this Article. Adopting a narrowly legalistic view, Churchill could argue that many British Empire territories possessed no 'sovereign rights' at the time of their subjugation so could not expect to have such rights restored in the future. It was a neat, if rather cynical, trick which gutted the thrust of the article with reference to Britain's Empire, and all doubt on the matter was resolved when Churchill informed Parliament on 9th September that

> *the Joint Declaration does not qualify in any way the various statements of policy which have been made… about the developments of constitutional government in India, Burma, and other parts of the British Empire... At the Atlantic meeting we have had in mind, primarily, the restoration of the sovereignty, self-government, and natural life of the States and nations of Europe now under the Nazi yoke... that is quite a separate problem from progressive evolution of self-governing institutions in the regions and peoples which owe allegiance to the British Crown.*

In other words, sovereignty and self-determination were the preserve of white Europeans violated by Hitler and had no relevance at all for Africans or Asians violated by Britain's Empire. It was an extremely narrow and self-serving conception of sovereignty which restricted fundamental human rights by ethnicity and geography and reveals the chicanery Churchill would employ to defend his Empire. The young subaltern who had devoured Winwood Reade and the maverick politician who had opposed the Government of India Bill were alive and well in the mature war leader.

The main business of the conference was concluded by Monday 11th August and the two leaders set off for home on the 12th.[66] The Joint Declaration was published on 14th August and quickly became known as the Atlantic Charter, informing the January 1942 United Nations Declaration. It generated predictable howls of derision in Berlin, Rome and Tokyo and strong support in parts of the world which valued freedom.

---

[66] The Conference also introduced Field Marshal Dill to General George Marshall. As Chief of the Joint Staff Mission in Washington, Dill - promoted to Field Marshal in November 1941 - formed an excellent working relationship with Marshall which greatly assisted Allied victory.

IV

Stalemate reigned in the desert as Churchill and Roosevelt squabbled over semantics. The Axis held Sollum and Halfaya but - starved of resources - Rommel could not break through at Tobruk. In contrast, Auchinleck's army was steadily reinforced throughout the summer and by August, he had 600,000 men under his command and his tank strength - including the Tobruk garrison - stood at 748 vehicles against Rommel's 390. In September, the Western Desert Force was reconstituted as Eighth Army - comprised of XIII (infantry) and XXX (armoured) Corps - and placed under General Alan Cunningham who had performed well in Abyssinia (Ethiopia) but who was exhausted and had no experience of commanding desert armour. From London, Churchill pressed for an early offensive but Cunningham and Auchinleck held out for an operation in November when both troops and equipment would be ready.

Operation Crusader launched on 18th November in an effort to draw Axis armour into a decisive battle around Gabr Saleh - south of Tobruk - where it could be destroyed by superior British force. Unfortunately, Rommel was preoccupied with Tobruk in mid-November and initially declined to respond to XXX Corps' forward thrust. Without an enemy to fight, British armour was dispersed in operations around Sidi Rezegh, Bir El Gubi and Gabr Saleh and when General Crüwell moved south to investigate, XXX Corps was dangerously divided. A fierce battle raged around Gabr Saleh-Sidi Rezegh on 22-23 November with both sides experiencing heavy losses, particularly the British-imperial force. On 24th November, Rommel stunned his adversary by driving east into Egypt, hoping to catch his opponent off-guard and forcing a retreat. His tactic nearly worked - Cunningham requested permission to withdraw on 25th November and, sensing a lack of offensive spirit in his subordinate, Auchinleck dismissed him and assumed direct command of 8th Army.[67] Auchinleck guessed that Rommel's move was a gamble that would soon run out of supplies and his intuition proved correct. On 7th December, Rommel ordered a retreat back to the Gazala Line - west of Tobruk - and Tobruk itself was relieved on 10th December. Buoyed by the presence of additional forces in their number, Eighth Army broke through the Gazala Line in mid-December and by 6th January, Rommel was back at El Agheila from where he'd launched his offensive eight months earlier.

---

[67] General Neil Ritchie replaced Cunningham as Eighth Army Commander on 26th November but Auchinleck directed the force's movements during this critical period.

Crusader relieved Tobruk and expelled Rommel from Cyrenaica so it must be considered a success but it was a costly one as Auchinleck's tank losses prevented him from exploiting his initial triumph by excluding Rommel from Libya altogether. In January, he learned that promised reinforcements were being sent to Malaya in a futile effort to stem Japan's assault on Singapore. The hollowness of Britain's victory was exposed in late January when, bolstered by fresh supplies, Rommel launched a new offensive that pushed his opponents all the way back to El Alamein, only sixty miles from Alexandria.

Map 13: Operation Crusader

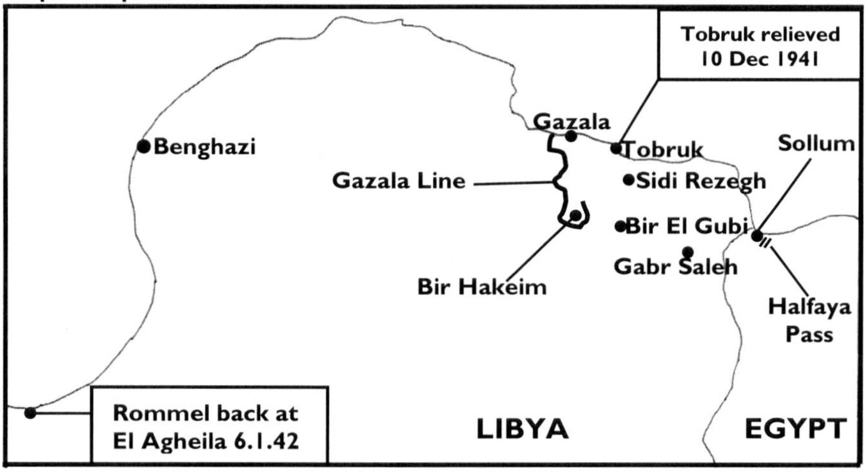

V

The global conflict intensified on 7th December when Japan savaged the American Fleet at Pearl Harbor and launched an all-out attack on British and Dutch possessions throughout south-east Asia. Britain declared war on Japan on 8th December and Germany and Italy supported their Axis partner by declaring war on the United States on 11th December. Axis belligerence therefore accomplished what eighteen months of Churchillian wooing had failed to achieve by drawing America into the war. Britain and America were now partners in a worldwide struggle against fascism - but what sort of Allies would they be and what sort of war would they fight?

CHAPTER TWELVE: THE LEAST HARMFUL DIVERSION, December 1941 - July 1942

It was… a blessing that Japan attacked the United States and thus brought America... into the war. Greater good fortune has rarely happened to the British Empire.

Churchill surveys the benefits of Pearl Harbor from the vantage point of 1943

The U.S. has been seeking to establish a prompt offensive to ultimately destroy Hitler in Europe and in the meanwhile to keep Russia in the war. The UK, while professing the same purpose, is equally if not more insistent upon a present attempt to preserve its empire in the Middle East.

U.S. Secretary of War Henry Stimson to President Roosevelt, 15th July 1942

America was ill-prepared for war in 1941. Its army was small[68] and deficient in weapons, munitions and transport. America's military establishment lacked a unified command structure, President Roosevelt and Army Chief of Staff General Marshall met only sporadically, and the country was still reeling from Pearl Harbor. Consequently, many of the decisions confirmed by Arcadia - the first Anglo-American conference with both states as full combatants – were tentative and subject to revision.

I

Churchill attended Arcadia (22nd December - 14th January) to confirm American adherence to the 'Germany First' strategy agreed in secret Anglo-American staff talks held in spring 1941. Germany was the only Axis power with the potential to overwhelm a major Allied state - Britain or the Soviet Union - and its destruction was considered essential before nullifying lesser threats such as Italy or Japan. America had confirmed 'Germany First' in its May 1941 Rainbow-5 War Plan but - following Pearl Harbor - Churchill was worried lest America prioritise the Pacific over Europe.

His fears proved groundless for Arcadia's principal strategy document confirmed Germany as *"the predominant member of the Axis Powers"* and the Atlantic and European area as *"the decisive theatre."* Pearl Harbor notwithstanding,

---

[68] With 190,000 men in 1939, America's Army was nineteenth largest in the world, smaller than Portugal's but bigger than Bulgaria's.

> *Germany is still the prime enemy and her defeat is the key to victory. Once Germany is defeated, the collapse of Italy and the defeat of Japan must follow. In our considered opinion... it should be a cardinal principle of A-B [American-British] strategy that only the minimum of force necessary for the safeguarding of vital interests in other theatres should be diverted from operations against Germany.*

Arcadia envisaged Germany's slow encirclement in a ring encompassing Arkhangelsk, the Black Sea, Anatolia, the northern Mediterranean and Europe's western seaboard and its depletion through a prolonged campaign of *"air bombardment, blockade, subversive activities, and propaganda."* No land offensives were planned for 1942 but in 1943

> *the way may be clear for a return to the Continent, via the Scandinavian Peninsula, across the Mediterranean, from Turkey into the Balkans, or by simultaneous landings in several of the occupied countries of Northwestern Europe.*

Arcadia confirmed one offensive operation - Operation Gymnast - a plan for Allied landings in North West Africa to wrest Morocco, and possibly Algeria, from Vichy, a strategy with great appeal to the new Allies. For Roosevelt, it offered the prospect of early involvement by American forces in the Atlantic theatre and - if the landings proved successful - an opportunity to solidify support behind 'Germany First' through low-risk victories. Gaining bases on the Atlantic coast would help Allied operations against the u-boats and Churchill - as ever - endorsed any strategy likely to enhance Britain's Mediterranean influence. In 'The Atlantic Front' - a strategy paper drafted en route to Arcadia - Churchill identified his preferred strategy for 1942 as

> *the occupation and control by Great Britain and the United States of the whole of the North and West African possessions of France, and the further control by Britain of the whole North African shore from Tunis to Egypt, thus giving... free passage through the Mediterranean to the Levant and the Suez Canal.*

Suez and the Mediterranean, as always, dominated Churchill's thinking.

Arcadia's other major decisions were primarily administrative. The British Chiefs of Staff (COS) and American Joint Chiefs of Staff (JCS) formed a unified body - the Combined Chiefs of Staff (CCS) - to coordinate Allied strategy and decision-making. CCS would provide

Churchill and Roosevelt with professional military advice at their summit meetings and - at all other times - oversee the implementation of Allied strategy. CCS did not eliminate inter-Allied rivalry but provided a forum in which contrasting views could be thrashed out and constructively resolved. The Axis Powers possessed nothing similar and CCS proved invaluable in harnessing superior Allied military strength. For security and political reasons, CCS sat in Washington and Field Marshal John Dill[69] - Chief of the British Joint Staff Mission - represented British interests, nurturing a strong bond with General Marshall.

The American-British-Dutch-Australian Command (ABDACOM) was formed on 28th December to coordinate Allied resistance to Japanese aggression in Southeast Asia and the Southern Pacific. ABDACOM attempted to fuse together the land, sea and air forces of all Allied powers with interests in the region under the command of General Archibald Wavell. However, Japan was already dominant by the time ABDACOM formed and its short, unhappy life was terminated on 25th February, ten days after Singapore's surrender. However, the principle of unified Allied command over multinational land, sea and air forces would be revived later in the war to greater effect.

Overall, Churchill could feel content with Arcadia. America had confirmed 'Germany First', Gymnast offered the pleasing prospect of landings in French North Africa and the Conference's general strategy - Germany's slow, inexorable strangulation - was fundamentally British in origin. However, by the time Churchill returned to the UK on 16th January, events had invalidated many of Arcadia's principal resolutions.

II

Arcadia rested on the assumption that Anglo-American control of the Philippines and Singapore would exclude Japan from the south-west Pacific and enable the Allies to prioritise 'Germany First'. However, the loss of Force Z[70] and devastation of Pearl Harbor changed everything as Japan exploited its temporary air and naval superiority to

---

[69] General Sir Alan Brooke replaced Dill - who had a poor relationship with Churchill - as Chief of the Imperial General Staff (CIGS) on 1st December 1941, and Dill became Chief of the British Joint Staff Mission. Brooke's appointment was announced in early December, effective from 25th December when Dill 'retired' at 60. Dill led the British Joint Staff Mission in Washington until his death in November 1944 (David G. Chandler and Ian Frederick (eds), *The Oxford History of the British Army* (1994), p.310).

[70] Force Z comprised the battleship HMS *Prince of Wales*, the battle-cruiser HMS *Repulse* and several destroyers and was despatched to Malaya in November 1941 to deter Japanese aggression in the region. The two capital ships arrived on 2nd December and were sunk eight

capture the Philippines, occupy the Dutch East Indies (Java, Sumatra, Timor etc) and seize Singapore and Malaya following a ten-week campaign. In December 1924, the Chartwell Oracle had prophesied that a Japanese invasion of Australia would *"never happen in any period... which we or our children need foresee"* but Japan bombed Darwin in Australia's Northern Territory on 19th February 1942 - killing 243 people - and suddenly the 'Yellow Peril' seemed very close indeed.

Japan's success and Britain's collapse transformed Australia's relationship with the 'mother country'. Australia had always looked to Britain for protection but with Britain collapsing on all fronts and prioritising other theatres - Burma, the Mediterranean - over Australia, the Dominion now turned to America for security, a point PM John Curtin[71] clarified in his 1942 New Year Message.

> *The Australian Government... regards the Pacific struggle as primarily one in which the United States and Australia must have the fullest say in the direction of the Democracies' fighting plan. Without any inhibitions of any kind, I make it clear that Australia looks to America, free of any pangs as to our traditional links or kinship with the United Kingdom. We... shall exert all our energies towards the shaping of a plan, with the United States as its keystone.*

Before 1941, America had no defence commitments in the south-west Pacific but it was now being tasked with defending a major British dominion and assume responsibility for holding the south-west Pacific. An American convoy bound for Pearl Harbor was re-routed to Australia in early December and - on 5th January - America formed the United States Army Forces in Australia (USAFIA) Command to coordinate its responsibilities in the region. In mid-January, Brigadier Dwight Eisenhower - Deputy Chief of the War Plans Division - scraped together enough ships and weapons to transport 21,000 American troops to Australia to animate the new Command. America was ill-prepared for war but was now stepping up to the plate and accepting major responsibilities in the Pacific - how would this impact on its other commitments?

---

days later with the loss of 840 officers and men (Tom Womack, *The Allied Defense of the Malay Barrier, 1941-1942* (2016), pp. 83-88). HMS *Indomitable*, a modern aircraft carrier, should have accompanied Force Z but it was damaged off Jamaica and sailed to Norfolk, Virginia for repairs.

[71] After a short interlude, John Curtin replaced Robert Menzies as Australia's PM on 7th October, 1941.

III

Japan's triumphs in early 1942 forced a major re-think in American strategy. 'Germany First' rested on the assumption that *"only the minimum of force necessary for the safeguarding of vital interests in other theatres should be diverted from operations against Germany"* but America now faced an unexpected challenge in the south-west Pacific. With its limited resources, it could fight Japan in the Pacific **or** engage Germany in Europe but it couldn't do both.[72] At Marshall's prompting, Eisenhower - War Plans Division Chief after 16th February - reviewed America's defence commitments throughout February and March to maximise the deployment of scarce American resources and resolve a dispute between the Army and Air Force (who prioritised Europe) and the Navy (which favoured a Pacific thrust).

Eisenhower's number one priority was to maintain Russia as an active combatant. In 1942, Russia was absorbing three-quarters of Germany's military strength and - as long as Russia kept fighting - Europe's liberation remained a realistic prospect. However, if Russia withdrew from the war - through defeat or a negotiated peace - Hitler would dominate Europe from the Urals to the Atlantic and would be difficult to dislodge. Throughout 1942/43, Marshall and Eisenhower desperately wanted to keep Russia actively engaged, and operations against Germany in Europe offered the best means of achieving this end, both by drawing German forces away from the east and by demonstrating clear Allied support for Russia. In a late February memo, Eisenhower identified Russia's retention in the war as *'necessary'* while defending Australia against Japanese occupation was merely *'desirable'* and this sort of thinking propelled Marshall and Eisenhower towards early engagement in Europe. Eisenhower clarified his thinking on 22nd January by declaring that

> *we've got to go to Europe and fight - and we've got to quit wasting resources all over the world - and still worse - wasting time If we're to keep Russia in, save the Middle East, India and Burma, we've got to begin slugging with air at West Europe; to be followed by a land attack as soon as possible.*

Eisenhower's completed Review presented three options to his bosses. America could:

---

[72] Operation Gymnast, the plan for Allied landings in North West Africa, was the first victim of these new realities. It was quietly shelved as Japan rampaged through the South Pacific and was not revived until June 1942 (Coakley and Leighton, *Global Logistics and Strategy,* p.353).

(i) focus on the Pacific at the expense of executing a vigorous offensive against Germany; or

(ii) concentrate on Europe and Germany while accepting the possibility that the South West Pacific may be lost; or

(iii) maintain a minimum defensive position in the South Pacific while building up forces in the United Kingdom for an offensive at the earliest practicable time.

The Joint Chiefs endorsed Option Three - a compromise between Options One and Two - on 16th March and instructed Eisenhower to clarify the specific means by which America would carry the war to Germany. In devising their strategy, Eisenhower and his colleagues sought to (i) use scarce resources effectively (ii) fulfil multiple goals within one broad overarching strategy, and (iii) end the European war quickly to allow America to concentrate on the Pacific.

These considerations all pointed towards a massive build-up of Anglo-American force in Britain during 1942 to prepare for a decisive assault on north-western Europe in 1943. Such a strategy would protect Britain against invasion, and ferrying troops and resources across the Atlantic would demand nullification of the u-boat menace which would also benefit Allied merchant shipping. The passage from America to Britain - and thence to France - offered the fastest and most direct route to Europe and would use scarce shipping resources efficiently. British-based bombers could soften up German defences prior to attack while British-based fighters would provide air cover for any assault. The presence of large Anglo-American forces in Britain during 1942 would compel Germany to withdraw troops from Russia while the landing itself would demand a massive redeployment of German forces to the west, forcing Germany to fight on two fronts. The proposed landing grounds were sufficiently near to Germany's Ruhr heartland to provoke a major response and - once German armed forces had been defeated - the Allies could drive rapidly across the North European Plain to occupy the Ruhr and force a surrender. Britain also possessed supply, communications and transport networks capable of sustaining major cross-Channel operations and American troops would enjoy a congenial billet before the invasion.

The build-up of American forces in Britain prior to invasion was codenamed BOLERO and - by spring 1943 - it was assumed that one million American troops and sixty-nine air combat groups would be based in Britain ready for action. The northern French landings scheduled for 1943 were codenamed ROUNDUP and it was anticipated that thirty American and eighteen British divisions would participate in a landing by 1st April 1943 with the capture of Antwerp as its main goal. If Germany or the Soviet Union showed any sign of collapse, five Allied divisions - three and a half British, one and a half American - would land in France in autumn 1942 to exploit this opportunity and/or aid the Russians. This operation was codenamed SLEDGEHAMMER and would only launch under these circumstances - it was an emergency operation to be undertaken only in the event of German disintegration or Soviet collapse. Most of the Sledgehammer troops would be British, giving Britain a veto over this operation and indeed over all other cross-Channel operations which could only proceed from UK ports with enthusiastic British support. During the course of 1942 and 1943, Britain exercised this veto to divert Allied resources into operations it considered more congenial to its long term oil and Empire interests.

Roosevelt, Marshall and Stimson approved BOLERO-ROUNDUP-SLEDGEHAMMER (BRS) on 1st April and - aware that it represented a major departure from Arcadia's encirclement strategy - Roosevelt ordered Marshall and Harry Hopkins (his confidant and key civilian adviser) to travel to London to sell their proposals to the British, a journey which would prove instructive for both men.

IV

Bolero-Roundup-Sledgehammer (BRS) presented a distinctly American approach to global war. With the exception of Pearl Harbor and the Philippines, America was unfamiliar with military defeat and had avoided mass casualties in 1917-18. American planners had boundless faith in the economy's ability to furnish the resources required for victory and - unlike their British counterparts - didn't have to worry about upholding a vast global Empire.

Britain's experience could not have been more different. The United Kingdom had traditionally favoured a 'Blue Water' strategy which shunned continental commitments in favour of peripheral operations, and the French landing grounds were redolent of the Somme and more recent humiliations. British troops had been bested by German forces in virtually every encounter during 1940-42 and Britain itself had been heavily blitzed during 1940-41, while Churchill's determination to maintain Britain's widely dispersed Empire didn't sit well with the more pressing need to win the war. Moreover, by 1940 Britain had experienced two decades of military austerity, a process which General Frederick Morgan - author of the draft Overlord plan -

believed had stunted his colleagues' ambitions. According to Morgan, the

> *Americans knew at first hand of the immense power and resources that the United States could throw into the battle. We British had... to overcome the effects of a lifetime of niggling, cheeseparing, parsimony and making do such as had characterised the service of most of us during the past quarter of a century. We had been brought up to advocate the answer that was least costly. An answer that cost nothing but appeared good enough had always been a winner.*[73]

Boldness and audacity do not flourish in environments characterised by niggling, cheeseparing and decline - timidity, caution and a desire to avoid decisive engagements thrive in such soil, and the chasm separating British and American strategy was evident in a series of strategy papers drafted by Churchill, COS and the Joint Planning Staff between March 1941 and March 1942.

Whereas American planning anticipated a decisive encounter with unbroken German forces, British strategists shied away from such an encounter. According to Churchill,

> *there can be no question of an advance in force against the German armies on the mainland of Europe... [circumstances] make it impossible for the Army, except in resisting invasion, to play a primary role in the defeat of the enemy.*

The Joint Planners shared this gloomy sentiment, even allowing for American intervention.

> *Nowhere on the continent... could we subsequently prevent the existing German Army and Air Force concentrating quickly in a strength we could not resist.... We cannot hope, therefore, even with full American help, to defeat the existing German Army in the field and so to open the road to Germany and victory.*

---

[73] Brigadier C.J.C. Molony endorsed this view in his official history of the Sicilian Campaign: "*The British were accustomed to make war on a shoe-string, and therefore to strategic improvisation, following where Fortune led... The Americans on the other hand, confident in their almost unlimited resources, believed in marching to their strategic goal by... inexorable steps. Their strategic goal in the European theatre was to reach the heart of Germany in the shortest possible time in overwhelming strength.*" (Molony, *The Mediterranean and Middle East,* Vol. 5, pp. 845-846).

United States planners hoped to return to France in spring 1943, but British planners could only envisage a return to the continent in the remote future after Germany had been reduced by prolonged bombing, blockade and subversion and the continent was ablaze with insurrection comparable to *"the anarchy of Ireland in 1920 or Palestine in 1936."* According to the Joint Planners, *"the attack from within is the basic conception,"* and Churchill maintained that *"the uprising of the local population... will supply the corpus of the liberating offensive."* British forces would only return to the continent to support mass uprisings by local resistance groups, so only a small invasion force would be required. Churchill estimated that *"an amphibious striking force of 8 or 10 divisions, mostly armoured, is the utmost that need be envisaged in the west,"* while COS *"[did] not foresee vast armies of infantry as in 1914-18."* British troops wouldn't perform the same function as in 1914-18 so would not employ 1914-18 tactics. In this new struggle

> *there would be no methodical advance from one linear objective to another. The only line to be secured is the boundary of the theatre of operations which enemy reinforcements must be prevented from crossing.*

As always, British thinking was dominated by the need to defend Egypt and the Middle East. According to COS,

> *the loss of our position in the Middle East would have disastrous effects... A German occupation of Egypt would result in the loss of essential installations and vast accumulations of military material... Our withdrawal from the Middle East would have a very grave effect not only on neutral opinion... but also throughout the whole Moslem world.*

Britain's own survival was linked to ongoing control of the Middle East.

> *If, after the collapse of [Egypt], we were unable to maintain our control of the outer ring, namely the Red Sea and the Persian Gulf, or to secure the oil of Iran (Persia), even our power of defence might be vitally affected.*

According to the Joint Planners, *"the loss of Egypt would be a disaster of the first magnitude. No sacrifice is too great in order to avoid it."*

Apart from a shared desire to free Europe from Nazi control, British and American planning had nothing in common. American planners anticipated a decisive encounter with German forces in 1943, whereas British planners could only envisage a return to the continent after Germany had been shattered by prolonged bombing and blockade and the continent was ablaze with insurrection. Even then, *"the local population... [would] supply the corpus of the liberating offensive"* with Allied forces restricted to a supporting role. The timing and location of such risings could not be predicted, nor was much said about the means by which British planners could prepare for multiple landings in places unknown at unpredictable times. American planning could perhaps be faulted for a certain naïve enthusiasm in its desire to get to grips with the enemy but British 'plans' offered nothing more than a recipe for inertia, inaction and prolonged German supremacy. Defeating Germany was never going to be easy but British planners were remarkably reluctant to modify their plans to reflect new circumstances, such as Russia and America joining the Allied cause. Their thinking was trapped in a period when a weak and unprepared Britain faced Germany alone and could expect help from no quarter.[74]

Marshall and his party landed in London on 8th April to evangelise for Bolero-Roundup-Sledgehammer (BRS) and - given the vast gulf separating British and American thinking - it's surprising that, at first, Churchill appeared to endorse Marshall's proposals.

V

Marshall, Harry Hopkins and Colonel Albert Wedemeyer - a senior American planning officer - landed in London on 8th April and spent nine days pitching their proposals to Churchill and Brooke at Chequers and Downing Street and at formal meetings of the War Cabinet, Defence Committee and Chiefs of Staff. While Brooke and his advisers remained sceptical about key elements of the BRS package - notably Sledgehammer in September 1942 - Churchill enthusiastically endorsed the American proposals. On 12th April, he cabled Roosevelt that he was

> *in entire agreement in principle with all you propose... I thought the proposals made for an interim operation... [in 1942] met the difficulties in an absolutely sound manner. If... we can carry this whole plan through successfully, it will be one of the grand events in all the history of the war.*

---

[74] Of course, Britain never faced Germany alone. It was supported by its vast, slow to mobilise Empire so the myth of 'plucky little Britain' facing Germany alone is entirely fictive.

Two days later, he again enthused over Marshall's plans, declaring that

> *he had no hesitation in cordially adopting the plan. The conception underlying it accorded with the classic principles of war - namely, concentration against the main enemy.*

He also solemnly informed Marshall and Hopkins that

> *our two nations are resolved to march forward into Europe together in a noble brotherhood of arms, in a great crusade for the liberation of the tormented peoples.*

However, Churchill had enthusiastically endorsed the Atlantic Charter *in principle* before nullifying its application *in practice* through caveats, qualifications and post-conference repudiations, and thus it was with Bolero-Roundup-Sledgehammer. At the same meeting in which he *"cordially adopted the plan,"* Churchill inserted one major caveat that would free Britain from its commitment to a Channel assault. While trumpeting his desire to march into Europe with America *"in a noble brotherhood of arms,"* he also advised that

> *it was essential to carry on the defence of India and the Middle East. We could not possibly face the loss of an army of 600,000 men [in the Middle East] and the whole manpower of India... This meant that we could not entirely lay aside everything in furtherance of the main object proposed by General Marshall.*

In mid-April, Japan presented the leading threat to British control of India and the Middle East. Japan had bombed Sri Lanka on 5th and 9th April and was in the process of driving Britain out of Burma and advancing to the gates of India. If Japan gained control of the Indian Ocean, it could threaten Iran and Iraq via the Arabian Gulf or possibly even Egypt and Suez via the Red Sea. Marshall assured Churchill that America would never allow Japan to gain control of the Indian Ocean and left London believing the British had endorsed his plan. However, within seven weeks, a more familiar adversary would emerge to threaten British control of the Middle East and allow Churchill to renege on commitments so freely given in London.[75]

---

[75] Describing Marshall's visit to London, General Ismay later recorded that *"our American friends went happily homeward under the mistaken impression that we had committed ourselves to both Roundup and Sledgehammer."* He later conceded that *"I think we should have come clean, much cleaner than we did, and said. 'We are frankly horrified because of what we have been through in our lifetime... We, who survived [WWI] had got that into our minds: 'Never again'. We are not*

VI

Britain's position in North Africa crumbled following Auchinleck's costly Crusader victory. Rommel launched a new offensive on 21st January which, by early February, had pushed Eighth Army 250 miles back to a defensive position forty miles west of Tobruk - the Gazala Line. As both sides prepared for a new offensive, Rommel struck first with a feint to the north end of the Line on 26th May while his main force bypassed the Line's southern end on the 27th. By 28th May, Rommel's tanks had inserted themselves between the rear of the British line and Tobruk to the east.

Map 14: Rommel's spring 1942 offensive

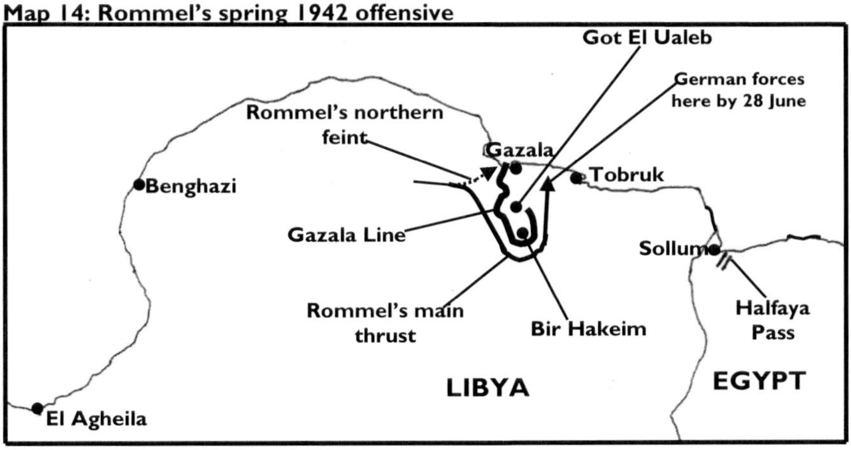

On that same day, Churchill sent two telegrams to Roosevelt expressing grave doubts over Sledgehammer and urging a revival of Gymnast. In the first telegram, he updated Roosevelt on his recent conversations with Foreign Minister Molotov in which he'd raised serious concerns over Sledgehammer on the grounds of insufficient landing craft, America's minimal contribution and the operation's limited capacity to draw troops away from the east. Churchill also warned Molotov - and Roosevelt - that

> *it would not further either the Russian cause or that of the Allies... if, for the sake of action at any price, we embarked on some operation which ended in disaster and gave the enemy an opportunity for glorification at our discomfiture.*

---

going into this [invading Europe] until it is a cast-iron certainty." Candour and honesty would not have served British interests at this stage in the war. (Ismay, *Memoirs*, p.250; Roberts, *Masters and Commanders*, p.158).

His second telegram advised Roosevelt that Combined Operations Chief Louis Mountbatten[76] would shortly visit Washington to *"explain to you the difficulties of 1942,"* while Churchill also indicated that the battle around Gazala *"may be the biggest encounter we have ever fought,"* ending with the earnest recommendation that *"we must never let Gymnast pass from our minds. All other preparations [i.e. Bolero and Roundup] would help if need be towards that."* Having once committed to Marshall's BRS package, he was now sturdily retreating from it.

British-imperial forces suffered further setbacks in early June. Rommel overwhelmed the Got el Ualeb defensive 'box' on 1st June and beat off a strong British counter-attack the following week. He then turned his attention to the southern end of the line, capturing Bir Hakeim on 10th June.

While Rommel was besieging Bir Hakeim, Mountbatten arrived in Washington to champion Gymnast in place of Roundup. Mountbatten dined with Roosevelt and Hopkins on 9th June, informing the President that the Allies lacked the landing craft to support a successful operation in September 1942 and that a small scale assault would only sustain heavy losses without aiding Russia. Roosevelt was perturbed by this information, expressing concern about American troops standing idle in Britain *"on the off-chance of Roundup being on in the spring of 1943"* and stressing the need for American troops to be in action somewhere in the Atlantic theatre during 1942. It was in this context that Gymnast re-surfaced, with Roosevelt advising Mountbatten that he'd been greatly impressed by Churchill's reminder of this operation in his 28th May telegram. The conversation then considered means by which American forces could intervene in Africa, either by supporting British units in Libya or by landing in French North West Africa.

Mountbatten saw Churchill immediately on his return, updating him on the President's revived interest in Gymnast and his need for swift American engagement somewhere within the Atlantic theatre. This was all Churchill needed to hear - he immediately cabled Roosevelt

[76] Churchill established Combined Operations Headquarters in July 1940 to coordinate raids on German-held territory with Admiral Keyes as its first director until his replacement by Lord Louis Mountbatten in October 1941. Mountbatten's appointment entitled him to a seat on the COS Committee although Brooke, as Chief of the Imperial General Staff, questioned his suitability for such a role. (T. A. Heathcote, *British Admirals of the Fleet: 1734-1995* (2002), p.147; Robin Neillands, *The Dieppe Raid: The Story of the Disastrous 1942 Expedition* (2005), p.35; Robin Brodhurst, *Churchill's Anchor: The Biography of Admiral Sir Dudley Pound* (2000), p.213; Peter Neville, *Britain in Vietnam: Prelude to Disaster, 1945-46* (2007), p.69; D'Este, *Bitter Victory*, p.47).

that *"in view of the impossibility of dealing by correspondence with all the many difficult points outstanding, I feel it is my duty to come to see you"* and proposed 18th June for their next meeting.

Map 15: Rommel advances, June 1942

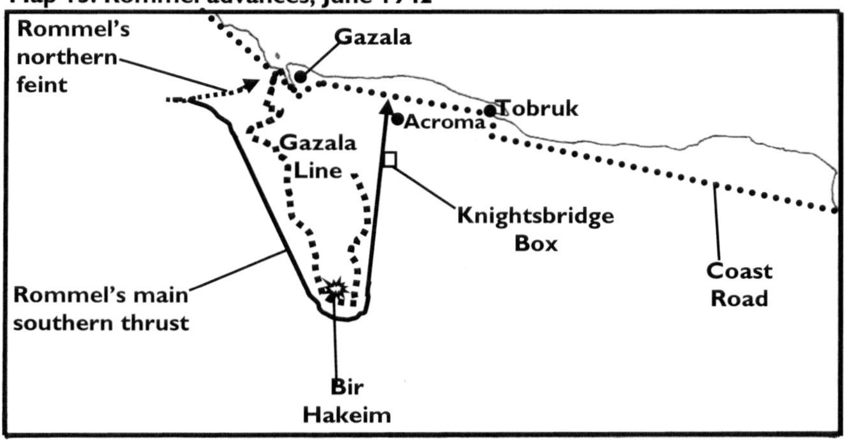

Britain's fortunes in the desert declined further even before Churchill arrived. After subduing Bir Hakeim, Rommel captured the Knightsbridge box at the north end of the Gazala Line on 13th June and threatened to cut off the coast road, trapping all British-imperial forces to the west of Acroma. General Ritchie[77] responded by ordering a hasty withdrawal into Egypt - the 'Gazala Gallop' - and at this point, Tobruk should have been abandoned as its defences had been badly eroded since 1941 and the Navy - fully occupied in the Mediterranean - couldn't re-supply it. Auchinleck had proposed such a move in Operational Instructions transmitted to London in January and neither Churchill nor Brooke had objected but Churchill's own position was threatened by June 1942 and Tobruk was more than just a port in Libya - it was a symbol of British defiance in the face of Axis aggression and on 14th June, Auchinleck was ordered to hold Tobruk in defiance of all military logic, a decision with momentous consequences both for the 33,000 men trapped in the town and Allied military planning.

VII

Churchill, Ismay and Brooke landed in Washington on 18th June and

---

[77] General Neil Ritchie had been appointed 8th Army commander following General Alan Cunningham's dismissal on 25th November 1941, a surprising choice given his lack of desert fighting experience (Peter Willett, *Armoured Horseman: With the Bays and Eight Army in North Africa and Italy* (2015), p.65; Mitcham, *Rommel's Desert War*, p.35).

divided into two parties. Brooke and Ismay remained in Washington to confer with the Joint Chiefs, while Churchill met the President at his Hyde Park retreat for more intimate conversations. Over the next two days, the two sets of discussions diverged sharply, setting the scene for a potentially explosive confrontation when the soldiers and statesmen re-convened in Washington on 21st June.

Despite their differences of opinion over Sledgehammer, Brooke and Marshall found common ground in their shared distaste for Gymnast and joint support for large-scale European operations in 1943. During the meeting, Brooke and Marshall agreed that Gymnast "*would seriously curtail reinforcement in the Middle East with possibly disastrous consequences in that theatre,*" slow up Bolero and "*tend to disperse further our available resources and weaken our effort.*" The Combined Chiefs' conference ended by noting that "*(a) Gymnast should not be undertaken under the existing situation, and (b) that the United States and Great Britain should adhere firmly to the basic decision to push Bolero with all possible speed and energy*" - Marshall and Brooke unambiguously supported a French landing in 1943 at this point.

While Brooke and Marshall were combining against Gymnast in Washington, Churchill and Roosevelt were exploring different options at Hyde Park. Hyde Park was a private Roosevelt home so these conversations were not recorded, but Churchill outlined his views in a 20th June memo to the President. After stating that Sledgehammer "*was certain to lead to disaster*" and that British strategists had not "*been able to make a plan for September 1942 which had any chance of success,*" he rhetorically asked "*can we afford to stand idle in the Atlantic theatre during the whole of 1942?*" He went on to answer his own question by affirming that the Allies should prepare

> *within the general structure of Bolero some other operation by which we may gain positions of advantage and also directly or indirectly to take some of the weight off Russia. It is in this setting and on this background that the operation Gymnast should be studied.*

Churchill and Roosevelt were therefore moving towards Gymnast for 1942 while Brooke and Marshall were uniting against it and the stage was set for an explosive confrontation when the two parties reconvened in Washington. However, directly after lunch on 21st June, Churchill received what he later described as "*one of the heaviest blows... [of] the war.*" An aide entered the Oval Office bearing news that Tobruk had surrendered earlier that day with the loss of 25,000 men,[78] two thousand vehicles and seven thousand tons of fuel and supplies. Churchill was devastated, declaring later that *"defeat is one thing; disgrace is another"* and the President tactfully enquired, *"What can we do to help?"* After some discussion, America agreed to give Britain the first 300 Sherman tanks poised to roll off the production lines, plus one hundred 105cm self-propelled guns to prop up Britain's crumbling position in the desert.

Tobruk was more than just a staging post in Britain's long, slow imperial decline - the surrender of this garrison also shattered Brooke and Marshall's freshly-forged opposition to Gymnast and their support for cross-Channel operations in 1943. In his conversations with Marshall in April, Churchill had indicated that he could only support Bolero-Roundup-Sledgehammer if Britain's position in the Middle East was secure and Tobruk's loss indicated that it was not. Roosevelt received a copy of the Combined Chiefs' recent discussion for his records but Churchill never even received a draft - Tobruk's surrender confirmed its redundancy. Once the full impact of Tobruk's surrender had been digested, the conversation turned to means of addressing this new crisis and a heated debate was only averted when General Ismay (Churchill's Chief of Staff) drafted a memo synthesising the views of all present. It was at this point that prospects for a Channel crossing in 1943 receded into the distant future. While Ismay's Memorandum opened by confirming that *"operations in Western Europe in 1942 would, if successful, yield greater political strategic gains than operations in any other theatre,"* he quickly torpedoed Bolero-Roundup-Sledgehammer by stating that

> *if a sound and sensible plan can be contrived [for operations in Western Europe in 1942], we should not hesitate to give effect to it. If on the other hand detailed examination shows that despite all efforts success is improbable, we must be ready with an alternative.*

Point Three identified the alternative.

> *Provided that political conditions are favourable, the best alternative in 1942 is operation GYMNAST. Accordingly the plans for this operation should be completed in all details as soon as possible. The forces to be employed in GYMNAST*

---

[78] Churchill learned later that 33,000 men had been captured.

would in the main be found from BOLERO units which had not yet left the United States.

Tobruk's June 1942 surrender therefore killed off plans for a Channel crossing in 1943 and replaced it with North West African operations. Political conditions were favourable as both Roosevelt and Churchill supported such operations and Britain exercised a veto over whether or not a Channel assault could proceed. Put simply, Tobruk killed off a Second Front in Europe to support Russia, replacing it with a sham 'Second Front' in North Africa to prop up Britain's chaotic position in the desert. Over time, this decision carried the gravest implications for Allied strategy but - in the summer of 1942 - everything had to be dropped to shore up Britain's crumbling Empire in Africa.

VIII

Eighth Army's position disintegrated after Churchill left Washington on 25th June. Axis forces captured Sollum, Halfaya and Sidi Barrani on the same day and 21st Panzer Division shattered 29th Indian Infantry Brigade at Fuka on 28th June. On 27th June, Mussolini left for Libya with the white horse he hoped to ride in triumph through Cairo's streets. Auchinleck sacked Ritchie on 25th June and assumed direct command of Eighth Army. Auchinleck had observed Rommel's penchant for outflanking manoeuvres in earlier battles and looked for a place where the terrain would deny the panzer General that opportunity, eventually settling on a sleepy little railway town sixty miles west of Alexandria and forty miles north of the Qattara Depression, a vast salt marsh of soft sand and lake beds impassable for armour. If Auchinleck arranged his forces between El Alamein and Qattara, Rommel would be forced into a head-on assault which the less imaginative but numerically superior Eighth Army might win. Both sides faced great challenges in the desert drama. Hitler launched his second great Russian offensive on 28th June and, with the Royal Navy commanding the Mediterranean, Rommel knew he would be on short supplies for some time. He therefore needed a quick victory before Auchinleck gained full access to rising Anglo-American industrial output. Eighth Army's position was equally desperate. If Rommel broke through at El Alamein, he could drive through the Middle East to seize Iranian and Iraqi oil supplies and converge with German forces pushing down from southern Russia or possibly even link up with Japanese forces advancing from the east. Rommel had to be stopped at El Alamein before Britain's Empire was bisected. The First Battle of El Alamein began on 1st July, with civil servants burning so many secret papers in Cairo that it became known as 'Ash

Wednesday'. To others, the jittery anxiety of early July was simply 'The Flap'.

Map 16: Alamein and Qattara Depression

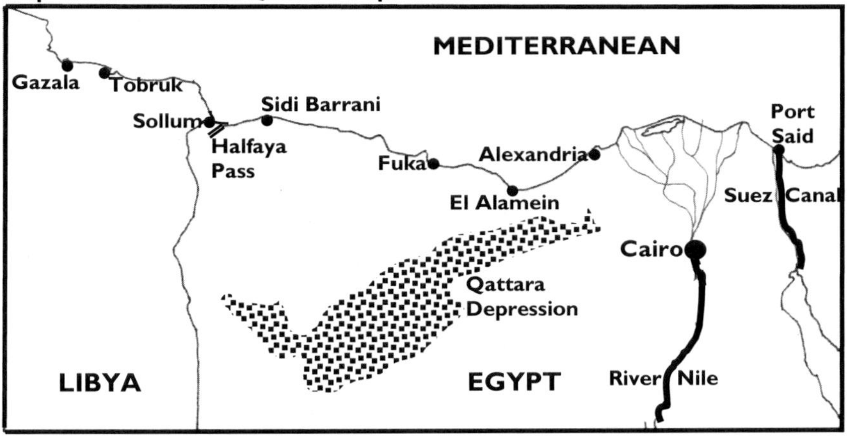

Having defeated Marshall in Washington and with their desert position so tenuous, British opposition to Sledgehammer - which the United States had only ever envisaged as a last ditch operation to save Russia - intensified. On 2nd July, COS advised the War Cabinet that *"if we were free agents we could not recommend that the operation should be mounted"* and on 7th July, the War Cabinet voted unanimously against proceeding with Sledgehammer. Churchill relayed this information to Roosevelt in a telegram which began:

> *No responsible British General, Admiral or Air Marshal is prepared to recommend Sledgehammer as a practicable operation in 1942... premature action in 1942 while probably ending in disaster would decisively injure the prospect of well organised large scale action in 1943.*

Having repudiated Sledgehammer for 1942, Churchill nudged the President towards Gymnast, skilfully insinuating that it had been his idea all along.

> *I am sure myself that Gymnast is by far the best chance for effective relief to the Russian front in 1942. This has all along been in harmony with your ideas. In fact it is your commanding idea. Here is the true second front of 1942... Here is the safest and most fruitful stroke that can be delivered this autumn.*

Formal British repudiation of Sledgehammer enraged the Joint Chiefs in Washington who now experienced either a sincere Damascene conversion to Pacific operations or who hoped to bluff the British back to their earlier cross-Channel commitment. On 10th July, they informed Roosevelt that Gymnast

> *will definitely curtail if not make impossible the execution of 'Bolero-Roundup' in the spring of 1943. We are strongly of the opinion that 'Gymnast' would be both indecisive and a heavy drain on our resources, and that if we undertake it, we would nowhere be acting decisively against the enemy.*

Marshall and his colleagues therefore advised that

> *if the United States is to engage in any other operation than forceful, unswerving adherence to full BOLERO plans, we are definitely of the opinion that we should turn to the Pacific and strike decisively against Japan; in other words assume a defensive attitude against Germany, except for air operations, and use all available means in the Pacific.*

Roosevelt called Marshall's bluff by asking to see detailed plans for a Pacific offensive, and Marshall and Stimson were summoned to the White House for meetings in which the President asserted his full authority as Commander-in-Chief, advising both men that there would be no switch to the Pacific in 1942 and that America would not abandon Britain in Europe.[79] American troops were to be in action somewhere in the Atlantic theatre during 1942 and Marshall was to travel to London immediately to agree joint operations with the British. Moreover, to prevent any unhelpful 'drift', Marshall was to reach agreement with Churchill and COS on joint operations within one week of arriving.

Marshall's second visit to London (18th- 25th July) must have been galling for the straight-backed General. Roosevelt and Churchill were both enthusiasts for Gymnast, and if the President accepted that Gymnast ruled out Roundup for 1943 - as Marshall insisted it would - he didn't seem unduly perturbed. The British held a veto over Sledgehammer and if they exercised this power, Marshall would be forced to support operations he considered wasteful and unproductive. His one attempt to lure the British back to cross-

[79] Allied naval victories in the Coral Sea (in May) and Midway (June) terminated further Japanese advances in the Pacific, so Roosevelt was on sure ground when he ordered Marshall and Stimson to prioritise the Atlantic theatre.

Channel operations - by pitching Sledgehammer as a permanent lodgement in France from which larger 1943 operations could be launched - was rejected out of hand and by 22nd July, the discussions were locked in stalemate. Marshall cabled the President for instructions and Roosevelt responded by identifying five operations that were acceptable to him. They included:

(i) a British-American operation against French North Africa (either Algeria or Morocco or both);

(ii) an entirely American operation against French Morocco

(iii) combined operations against northern Norway (JUPITER);

(iv) the reinforcement of Egypt;

(v) the reinforcement of Iran.

All five operations would - in Marshall's view - undermine Roundup for 1943 but he was under pressure to endorse one major undertaking so he selected the activity he considered *"the least harmful diversion"* - Allied operations in French North Africa - writing this up in a document (CCS 94) for presentation to his British counterparts.[80] In CCS 94, Marshall accepted that Sledgehammer was no longer a 'scheduled operation' for 1942 but he sought to delay a definitive commitment to Gymnast by proposing that the final decision on the operation should be delayed until 15th September to monitor unfolding events in Russia. If Russia was still actively engaged by 15th September, Marshall would have gained an extra seven weeks to proselytise for Roundup and counsel against Gymnast, but if Russia was close to collapse by mid-September - ruling out cross-Channel operations for 1943 - Marshall was prepared to countenance Gymnast for late November on the grounds that it was the next best option. To ensure that everyone fully appreciated the gravity of the situation, Marshall warned that

> ***a commitment to this [North West African] operation renders Roundup in all probability impracticable of successful execution in 1943*** *and therefore that we have definitely accepted* ***a defensive, encircling line of action for the continental European theatre,*** *except as to air operations and blockade [emphasis added].*

---

[80] Eisenhower dubbed 22nd July - when Torch decisively defeated Roundup - *"the blackest day in history."*

With some minor modifications, COS endorsed CCS 94 but when it was transmitted to Roosevelt on 25th July, he simply ignored Marshall's stalling tactics and interpreted Gymnast as an agreed operation, insisting that it be implemented by 30th October to reap maximum political advantage in the 3rd November US mid-term elections. In the final analysis, cross-Channel operations for 1942 - and almost certainly for 1943 - were torpedoed by a President keen to extract maximum political advantage for himself and his party from America's first ground operations against German-Italian forces in the Atlantic theatre. As Churchill had long campaigned for North West African operations as the definitive Allied venture for 1942, he was not about to carp at the President's motive, noting in his memoirs that

> *all was therefore agreed and settled in accordance with my long-conceived ideas… This was a great joy to me, especially as it came in what seemed to be the darkest hour. At every point except one [Operation Jupiter] the plans I cherished were adopted.*

The long-term consequences of this decision are considered later but, by early August, the Allies were irrevocably committed to North West Africa and Marshall's carefully constructed Bolero-Roundup-Sledgehammer plan was in tatters. Two days after Roosevelt finally opted for Gymnast (re-named **Torch** by Churchill), the First Battle of El Alamein petered out in an inconclusive stalemate, denying Rommel his decisive breakthrough and - with Britain and America committed to North West African operations in the autumn - the tide of battle in this theatre swung remorselessly in the Allies' favour.

IX

Allied strategy therefore revolved by a full 360 degrees in the seven months between Arcadia (December 1941) and First Alamein (July 1942). At Arcadia, the Allies had endorsed North West African operations and Germany's slow, cautious encirclement but - in April and May - they embraced cross-Channel operations and a decisive encounter with German forces in Europe. Then in late July, the Allies reverted to North West African operations and *"a defensive, encircling line of action for the continental European theatre."*

British military incompetence played a major role in dictating this zigzag. Had Eighth Army been more successful in its encounters with Rommel in the first half of 1942, there would have been less need for a 'second front' in North Africa, and resources could have been built up in Britain for a Channel crossing in 1943. Poor leadership, unimaginative tactics, organisational rigidity and inferior equipment - particularly in armour - confined the Allies to extended desert operations.

Roosevelt's political priorities also pushed the Allies towards North West Africa. Having committed to Germany First, he needed American troops to be in action somewhere in the Atlantic theatre during 1942 and was agnostic regarding location. Gymnast was the only operation Churchill would countenance and Sledgehammer - described by General Marshall as *"a sacrifice in the common good"* - held little appeal for a President seeking easy victories to impress his voters.

Churchill's long-term obsession with the Mediterranean and his desire to avoid decisive engagement with German forces also detained the Allies in Africa during 1942. In March 1939 he'd declared that *"for Britain in time of war, the command of the Mediterranean must be the prime objective"* and in August 1940, had despatched half of Britain's tank force to Egypt when Britain itself faced the prospect of invasion. His December 1941 strategy paper 'The Atlantic Front' identified Allied control of North and North West Africa as 1942's supreme objective and so, in pressing for Gymnast/Torch over Sledgehammer, he was simply remaining true to his deep-rooted Mediterranean obsessions and enthusiasm for minor operations against secondary opponents. Churchill also believed that Britain had *"no continental army which can defeat the German military power"* and his 1941 strategy papers also shied away from decisive engagement with German forces. Far better to remain in Africa where the Allies faced no more than three German and six Italian divisions - plus indeterminate Vichy forces - whereas in France they would encounter at least twenty-five well-equipped Wehrmacht divisions. Throughout 1942, Churchill had counselled against Sledgehammer on the grounds that it would jeopardise Roundup for 1943 but the possibility that Torch might also preclude Roundup for 1943 didn't appear to trouble him. Churchill's motives for such inconsistent and highly selective thinking are considered in subsequent chapters.

CHAPTER THIRTEEN: CARRYING ICE TO THE NORTH POLE, August 1942

A man who was not prepared to take risks could not win a war. Why were [the British] so afraid of the Germans?
Stalin to Churchill, 12th August 1942

There is one thing I would like to make absolutely clear. We are determined to fight for Egypt and the Nile Valley as if it were the soil of England itself.
Churchill to the Cairo Press Corps,
22nd August 1942

George Marshall wasn't the only individual with a strong interest in opening a Second Front in Europe. With Axis forces operating deep inside Russia, it was a matter of some concern to First Secretary Josef Stalin who had despatched Foreign Minister Molotov to London and Washington in May-June 1942 to secure a firm Anglo-American commitment to a cross-Channel assault. Churchill had been guarded and negative but Roosevelt - who believed that Britain was committed to Bolero-Roundup-Sledgehammer at that point - was more forthcoming and approved a joint communiqué confirming that Russia and America had reached *"full understanding ... with regard to the urgent tasks of creating a second front in Europe in 1942."* The confirmation of Torch on 25th July undermined this commitment and Churchill offered to carry the news to Stalin in person, a task he compared to *"carrying a large lump of ice to the North Pole."* However, before enduring Stalin's icy disdain, Churchill and Brooke visited Egypt to remedy Britain's difficulties in the desert.

I

As Prime Minister and Minister of Defence, Churchill took a keen interest in senior appointments, though not always to great effect. On his insistence, Admiral Boyle - an old friend - replaced Admiral Evans as Naval Commander of the Norway expedition two days before launch, contributing greatly to operational chaos and precluding effective Army-Navy cooperation. Wavell was removed after Battleaxe and Auchinleck - who had been given a full year to deliver a desert victory - was also to be dismissed.[81]

---

[81] He also supported Mountbatten's elevation to Combined Operations Adviser in October 1941. Mountbatten was photogenic and well-connected but - as the August 1942 Dieppe Raid revealed – not suited to command operations which risked men's lives.

Auchinleck's removal coincided with the detachment of Iran and Iraq from Middle East Command to form a separate Iran-Iraq Command. The post was offered to Auchinleck - who declined - so it went to General Henry Maitland Wilson, while the remainder of the Middle East (Egypt, the Levant, Sudan, Somaliland, Aden) was placed under General Harold Alexander who had just completed the British Army's longest ever retreat, six hundred miles across Burma pursued by a relentless Japanese enemy.

Auchinleck's departure created a command vacancy in Eighth Army and the post was originally offered to Churchill's choice, General William Gott. However, Gott was killed two days after accepting the appointment,[82] clearing the way for Brooke's candidate, General Bernard Montgomery, thus initiating one of Britain's most celebrated and contentious senior military careers.

Satisfied with his desert revisions, Churchill embarked for Moscow in the company of American envoy Averell Harriman, while Brooke, Wavell and other diplomatic and military advisers travelled in a separate aircraft. However, the Liberator carrying Brooke, Wavell *et al* developed engine trouble shortly after leaving Tehran, ensuring that Churchill met Stalin for the first time on Wednesday 12th August without his usual retinue of diplomats and generals to restrain his impetuosity.

II

Churchill met Stalin for the first time at 7pm on 12th August and - aware that nothing could be gained by delaying the delivery of bad news - informed him at the outset that there would be no Second Front during 1942. Stalin believed that the Americans had promised such an operation and with German forces pouring into the Caucasus (the centre of Soviet oil production), his frustration can be readily appreciated. However, this first meeting remained largely free of rancour and recrimination. As the official records note, Stalin looked 'glum' and the mood was sombre but the Soviet leader stoically accepted that if Britain and America *"could not make a landing in France this year, he was not entitled to demand it or insist upon it, but he was bound to say that he did not agree with Mr. Churchill's arguments."*

Having discharged his most difficult task, Churchill then informed Stalin that the operation for 1942 had - in large part - been cancelled to

[82] Gott was killed on 7th August when German fighters attacked the plane carrying him to meet Churchill in Cairo (Zabecki (ed), *World War II in Europe,* p.325).

ensure the success of a larger venture in 1943, and he described Allied plans for this project in detail. One million men would land in 48 divisions (27 American, 21 British) with almost half of these divisions being armoured.[83] This force would land in the Scheldt, Gironde or Loire estuaries (or on the French coast directly opposite England) and Churchill repeatedly assured Stalin that the 1942 operation had been cancelled to pave the way for a bigger venture in 1943. When Stalin questioned the difficulties involved in launching such an undertaking, Churchill conceded that *"it would indeed be difficult to land a million men, but that we should have to persevere and try."*

Churchill was therefore committing the Allies to a full Roundup in 1943 even though senior British and American planners had informed him that such a commitment was out of the question. Such an acknowledgement had been written into the document committing Britain and America to Torch on 24th July (CCS 94) and British planners had drawn the same conclusion after Brooke commissioned them to investigate the matter earlier in the month. The Chiefs discussed the Joint Planners report on 16th July, agreeing that *"Super-Gymnast [i.e. Torch]... must be regarded* ***as an alternative*** *[emphasis added] and not as a supplement to Roundup."* The issue was explored again during a War Cabinet meeting on 24th July when Churchill confidently asserted that *"it did not... follow that Torch would necessarily be regarded as an alternative to Roundup. We had sufficient forces to make it possible for planning to proceed concurrently for both operations,"* but Brooke corrected this view, stating that

> *there was complete unanimity between the British and United States Chiefs of Staff on the matters covered by [CCS 94]. Both the British and United States Chiefs of Staff believed that it was unlikely that Roundup would be carried out in 1943, and that... Operation Torch therefore had the field.*

As Prime Minister and Minister of Defence, Churchill was entitled to discard professional military advice but only on the basis of superior evidence and argument. By the time he met Stalin in mid-August, no such re-assessment of Torch-Roundup had been undertaken, so when Churchill was committing Britain and America to cross-Channel operations in 1943 - fuelling Stalin's expectations of such an assault - he was doing so on the basis of his own highly subjective intuition

---

[83] Eight months earlier, Churchill had rejected major Allied operations in north-western Europe, insisting that *"the local population... [would] supply the corpus of the liberating offensive"* and a *"striking force of 8 or 10 divisions... is the utmost that need be envisaged in the west."* Like all politicians, Churchill's relationship with truth was fairly flexible

rather than any careful analysis. Churchill accepted that Torch might delay Roundup but he believed it could still proceed later in the year, and his rationale for offering such a firm commitment merits investigation. He certainly saw himself as a master strategist, more prescient than his professional advisers, and he may have simply believed that the strength of his convictions out-weighed any professional advice. Having disappointed Stalin over 1942, he may also have wished to forestall an explosion of Soviet anger by promising a big event for 1943 which would also encourage Soviet forces to continue fighting. Whatever his motives, Churchill's judgment proved faulty and his Chiefs' views were vindicated. No cross-Channel assault was launched in 1943 - partly because Churchill later opposed all such operations - but his rash promises - delivered in the absence of Brooke and Wavell - certainly fuelled Stalin's hopes for such an operation and, when it failed to materialise, provoked the worst crisis in Anglo-American-Soviet relations of the war.[84] Such were the consequences of Churchill's rash and unsustainable promises to Stalin in August 1942.

Having committed Britain and America to cross-Channel operations in 1943, Churchill also committed the western Allies to significant operations in southern Europe through his method of explaining Torch to Stalin. Sketching a crocodile to illuminate matters, Churchill explained that Britain and America proposed *"to attack the soft belly of the crocodile [southern Europe] as we attacked its hard snout [northern France]."* Churchill was therefore committing the western Allies to major operations in both southern and north-western Europe without giving any thought to the logistical, manpower or shipping resources required to support such operations. Indeed, over the next two years - until June 1944 - the western Allies lacked the capacity to sustain major operations in both northern and southern Europe and were continually forced to choose between the two and - on every occasion when confronted with such a choice - Churchill favoured the 'soft underbelly' over the 'hard snout', completely invalidating his promises to Stalin.

Churchill's naïve depiction of southern Europe as the Axis 'soft underbelly' is also questionable for while Italy is blessed with a balmy summer climate, its peninsular terrain is dominated by a rugged mountain range (the Apennines) characterised by steep hillsides, narrow passes, plunging ravines and fast-flowing rivers. As such, it is infinitely more suited to defence than attack - and defence by a

---

[84] In July/August 1943, Stalin replaced his pro-western ambassadors in London and Washington (Maisky and Litvinov) with hardline Kremlin *apparatchiks* (Gusev and Gromyko).

relatively small army against a much larger force - particularly in winter when snow, mud, rain and ice complicate matters. Once Hitler decided to contest Italy - as he did following Italy's armistice - it could never be depicted as a theatre of 'easy victories' and Churchill's insistence on portraying Italy as a land of great opportunity - and his determination to commit Allied resources to this theatre long after its sterility had been revealed - merits comment. As noted earlier, he continually espoused peripheral operations in marginal theatres against secondary opponents, an impulse which found expression at Gallipoli in 1915, in Norway, Libya and Egypt in 1940 and Greece in spring 1941. In March 1939, he'd described Italy as a *"long, vulnerable peninsula... in which important victories could be gained"* and he continued to espouse this view long after it was shown to be false. As noted earlier, Churchill was in no hurry for a decisive encounter with unbroken German forces, and Italy - because of its terrain - could never sustain large-scale engagements on the scale of Kursk, Stalingrad or Normandy. At its peak, Germany had 29 divisions based in Italy (against 195 in the Soviet Union), so Italy could never be classed as a primary theatre, and even if the Allies gained the whole peninsula, the physical barrier of the Alps would deny easy access into Germany. Outright Allied victory in Italy would yield little in terms of forcing Germany from the war. Finally, Italy's position in the middle of the Mediterranean - straddling Britain's highway to India and the Far East - explains Churchill's persistent obsession with operations in this theatre even when they contributed nothing to weakening Germany. In spring 1939, he had declared that *"for Britain in time of war, the command of the Mediterranean must be the prime objective"* and he clung to this view long after the strategic considerations supporting such analyses had evaporated and the accession of Russia and America to the Allied cause justified more aggressive strategies.

Churchill's first session with Stalin concluded at 11pm on Wednesday 12th August. He'd undertaken a long and arduous journey for a man in his late 'sixties and delivered unwelcome news to the Soviet leader without suffering any major backlash. Indeed, he believed he had established warm and friendly relations with Stalin, but the depth and durability of these relations would be tested to the limit at their next meeting.

III

The second meeting opened at 11pm on 13th August when Stalin presented Churchill and Harriman with a note castigating western failure to open a Second Front. In Stalin's view, such an omission *"inflict[ed] a mortal blow to the whole of Soviet public opinion… [and] complicates the situation of the Red Army at the front and prejudices the plan of the Soviet Command."* In Stalin's view, 1942 was a propitious time to launch a Second Front *"inasmuch as almost all the [best] forces of the German army… have been withdrawn to the Eastern front, leaving in Europe an inconsiderable amount of forces and these of inferior quality."* Stalin's rebuke set the scene for two hours of bitter wrangling in which Stalin accused the British of being

> *afraid of fighting. You should not think the Germans are supermen. You will have to fight sooner or later. You cannot win a war without fighting.*

These comments echoed Churchill's own bleak assessment of British military prowess[85] but it must have been galling to hear a foreign leader express such views. Wisely, Churchill declined to respond, noting merely that he pardoned *"that remark only on account of the bravery of the Russian troops."* Throughout this second meeting, Stalin made the case for a Second Front, Churchill assured him that Britain and America had *"made up our minds upon the course to be pursued and that reproaches were in vain"* and the session ended in stalemate. Stalin could not force the western Allies to launch a Second Front and Churchill stoically endured the Soviet leader's reproaches.

The mood did not improve at a formal dinner in the Kremlin the following night - the Russians were in full fig while Churchill sported his 'siren suit' - and the British Prime Minister was all for leaving on the 15th without repairing his breach with Stalin or contributing to a joint communiqué until Sir Archibald Clark Kerr[86] pointed out that only Hitler would benefit from such a rift. Churchill considered this argument and agreed to meet Stalin at 7pm.

By this stage, the two leaders had gained some personal familiarity and - with no substantive issues to discuss - this meeting passed off without acrimony. After an hour or so, Stalin invited Churchill to his private apartment for drinks and the two leaders stayed up to 2:30am drinking, snacking and teasing Molotov who joined later. Churchill hinted at the major raid planned for Dieppe on 19th August and Stalin observed that *"the fact that he and Churchill had met and got to know each other and had prepared the ground for future agreements, had great significance. He was inclined to look at the matter more optimistically."* Shortly before Churchill departed, the two leaders agreed a joint

---

[85] Considered in detail in Chapter 28.

[86] British Ambassador to the Soviet Union.

communiqué stressing their determination *"to carry on with all their power and energy until the complete destruction of Hitlerism... has been achieved"* and reaffirming *"the existence of the close friendship and understanding between the Soviet Union, Great Britain and the United States of America."* The crisis had passed. The Alliance had survived Stalin's frustration with western refusal to open a Second Front and Churchill and Stalin had established a tolerable working relationship. Churchill departed Moscow at 5:30am and - after a brief stop in Tehran - returned to Egypt on 17th August to assess his new desert commanders.

IV

Churchill spent six days in Egypt inspecting Montgomery's forward positions, visiting troops in the field and conferring with generals and diplomats. Montgomery and Alexander had taken up their posts while Churchill was in Moscow and he craved reassurance that imperial defence was in safe hands. Detecting a new mood of optimism in Eighth Army, he informed Cabinet colleagues that "*we were heading for disaster under the former regime... [but]... a complete change of atmosphere has taken place... The highest alacrity and activity prevails. Positions are everywhere being strengthened, and extended forces are being sorted out and regrouped in solid units.*" Despite this expression of faith, Churchill authorised additional measures to defend Cairo and the Canal just in case Eighth Army buckled at Alamein - the security of the Empire was at stake and nothing could be left to chance.

On 30th August, Rommel launched his third and final offensive to seize the Nile Valley before the balance of forces tipped irrevocably against him. The Allies dominated the Mediterranean and used this power to deny Rommel the fuel, ammunition and reinforcements he needed to sustain large scale offensive action. At the same time - courtesy of the 'arsenal of democracy' and steadily rising British output - Eighth Army had acquired an overwhelming preponderance in troops, tanks, guns and planes. With Germany fully committed to Russia, the Axis had to break through decisively in the summer of 1942 or lose the opportunity forever.

The Battle of Alam Halfa raged for five days in early September but effectively ended on 2nd September when Rommel ordered his fuel- and ammunition-starved panzers to withdraw. Montgomery fought an entirely defensive battle around this decisive ridge, allowing Rommel's tanks to come onto his well-entrenched artillery positions and ordering his tanks to fight in static hull-down positions where they benefited from the terrain's natural protection. Even when Rommel's force withdrew, Montgomery declined to give chase - he was preparing a meticulous set-piece battle for late October and nothing would deflect him from that purpose.

Map 17: Alam Halfa and El Alamein

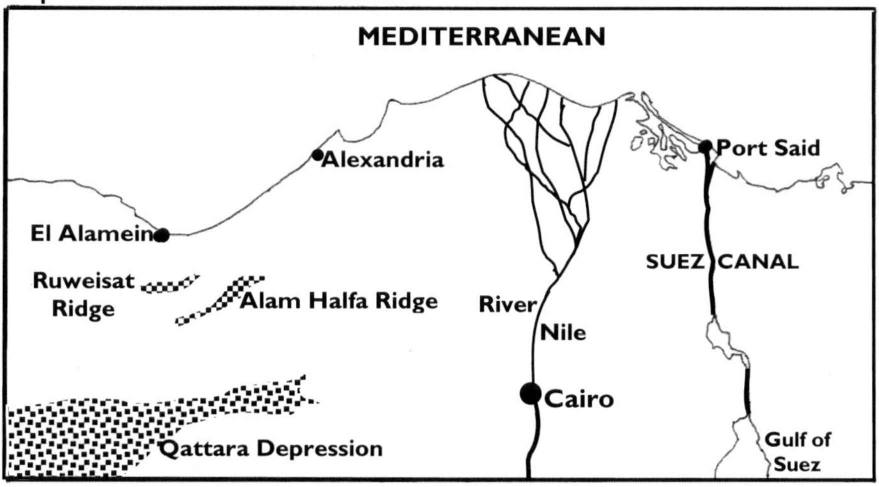

CHAPTER FOURTEEN: THE END OF THE BEGINNING, September - December 1942

Let me... make this clear in case there should be any mistake about it... We mean to hold our own. I have not become the King's First Minister in order to preside over the liquidation of the British Empire. For that task, if ever it were prescribed, someone else would have to be found.

Churchill after Torch and Alamein, 10th November 1942

I think the best way to describe our [Tunisian] operations... is that they have violated every recognised principle of war, are in conflict with all operational and logistic methods laid down in text-books, and will be condemned, in their entirety, by all Leavenworth and War College classes for the next twenty-five years.

General Eisenhower to General Handy, 7th December 1942

Allied and Axis forces were in balance by September 1942. Japan controlled vast swathes of Asia and the Pacific but defeat at Midway - and the loss of four aircraft carriers - blunted its reckless aggression. In Russia, German armies stormed into the Caucasus in August and September only to become trapped in Stalingrad's hellish *kessel*. In Africa, Rommel's forces remained within Egypt but were held at Alam Halfa while Eighth Army accumulated an overwhelming preponderance in men and *matériel*. With the two sides evenly matched, operations conducted in the final quarter of 1942 would determine the final outcome of the great global struggle.

I

General Bernard Montgomery enjoyed the full fruits of Allied logistical superiority by October 1942. He held a 2:1 advantage in troops, tanks and artillery, the Desert Air Force controlled the skies, he had unlimited fuel and - thanks to Ultra - even knew what his opponent was thinking. Rommel, in contrast, was reduced to five hundred tanks (many of them thinly armoured Italian 'self-propelled coffins'), half his fighting force consisted of poorly-trained and badly-equipped Italians and - thanks to Allied domination of the central Mediterranean - his fuel and ammunition supplies were low. Without fuel, Rommel could not manoeuvre to exploit an opponent's errors, forcing him to shelter behind a vast defensive minefield stretching from the Mediterranean to the Qattara Depression and christened '*der teufelsgarten*' (devil's garden). To break his opponent's will and deliver the victory Churchill craved, Montgomery would have to bludgeon his way through the *teufelsgarten* to Rommel's rear - there could be no outflanking manoeuvre.

Map 18: Second Battle of El Alamein

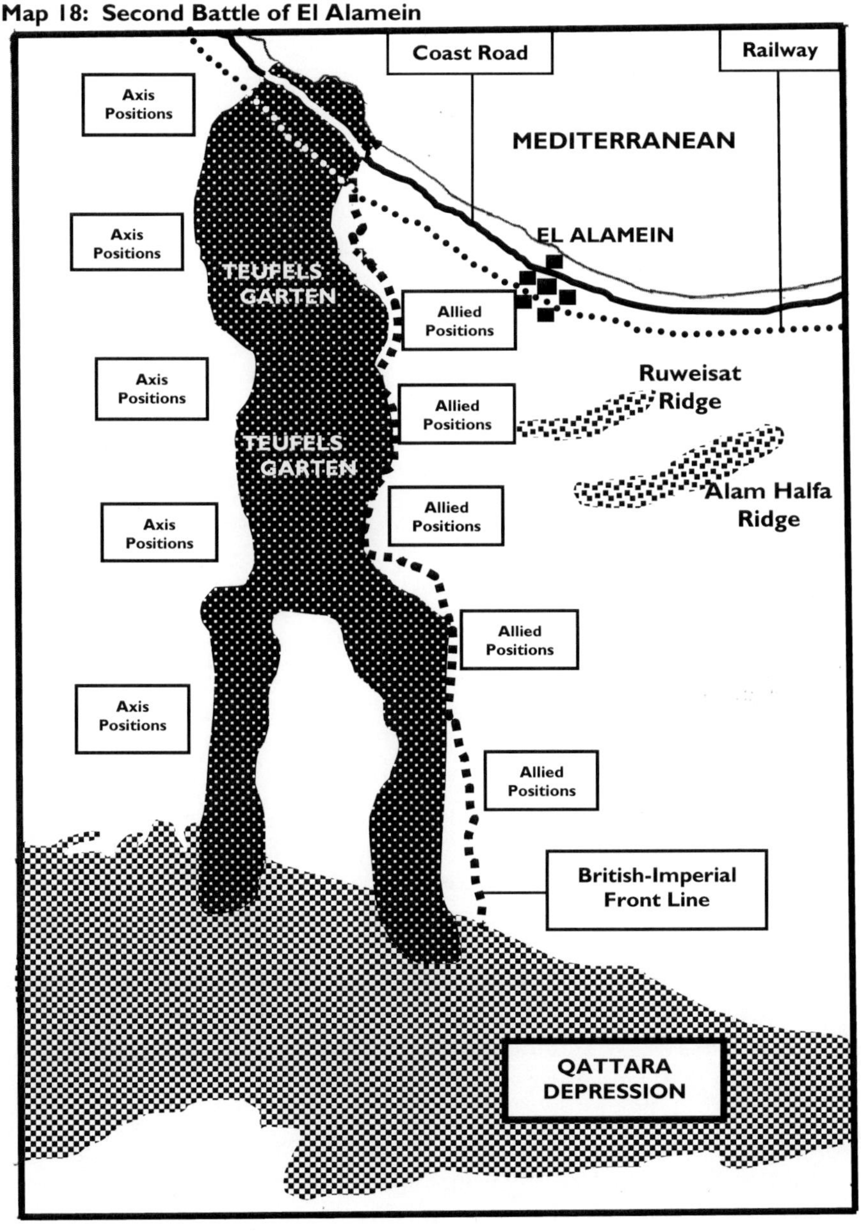

Act One of the Second Battle of El Alamein - Operation Lightfoot - commenced at 9:40pm on Friday 23rd October with a massive bombardment of Axis positions. The infantry advanced - their tread too light to trip the millions of anti-tank mines spread before them - followed by sappers charged with clearing paths for Montgomery's armour. Unfortunately, the *teufelsgarten's* depth and complexity had been under-estimated and the engineers cleared paths only wide enough for tanks to advance in single file, offering the Axis gunners easy targets. Montgomery had hoped to break through Rommel's defences by Day Two but was still embroiled in a vicious dogfight by Day Six and panic reigned in London where Churchill knew his Prime Ministerial career depended on the outcome of Monty's desert struggle. General Brooke - Chief of the Imperial General Staff - was summoned to the Prime Minister's office on 29th October where Churchill unleashed a

> *flow of abuse of Monty. What was my Monty doing now, allowing the battle to peter out...? [Montgomery] had done nothing now for the last three days, and now he was withdrawing troops from the front. Why had he told us he would be through in seven days if all he intended to do was to fight a half hearted battle? Had we not got a single general who could even win one single battle?*

Fortunately for Brooke and the entire Allied cause, Montgomery had sufficient resources to launch a second offensive when Lightfoot's failure became apparent, and Act Two of the desert drama - Operation Supercharge - launched at 1am on 2nd November. By 3rd November, Rommel was down to thirty operational tanks - Montgomery still had 550 - and he requested permission to withdraw only to receive strict instructions to stand fast. By 4th November, Rommel's position was untenable and he signalled a general retreat, countermanding Hitler's directive. With some pride, General Alexander informed Churchill that

> *Eighth Army has inflicted a severe defeat on the German and Italian forces under Rommel's command. The enemy's front has broken, and British armoured formations in strength have passed through and are operating in the enemy's rear areas.*

Rommel withdrew to Mersa Matruh, then Sidi Barrani and on 11th November, passed out of Egypt into Libya, never to return. The great seesaw struggle was finally over and Rommel's battered remnants - 70,000 strong - embarked on a trek across Libya that took them to the relative safety of southern Tunisia's Mareth Line by late January.

Map 19: Rommel's Retreat, Nov 1942- Jan 1943

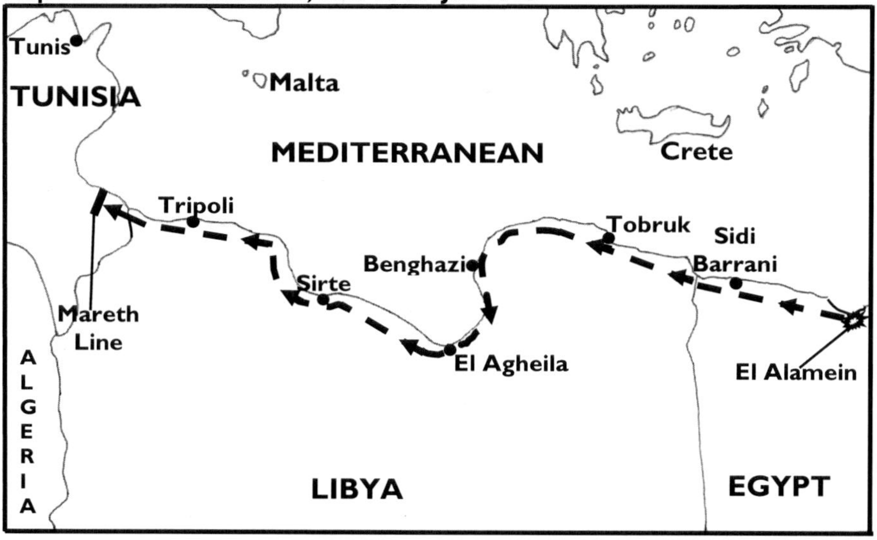

Three days before Rommel abandoned Egypt, Allied troops landed in French North Africa under Operation Torch. Torch was the product of an extended 'transatlantic essay contest' between British and American planners and the final operation reflected strategic compromise. With a well-developed supply infrastructure and long-standing interests in the region, the British were extremely bullish about North African operations - more so than about landing in France. They favoured landings well inside the Mediterranean - to the east of Gibraltar - to insure against any failure at El Alamein and also deny the Axis a bridgehead in Tunisia. They pushed for landings in central and eastern Algeria, as close to Tunisia as possible.

The Americans in contrast had no Mediterranean interests, no supply infrastructure and were markedly less enthusiastic about operations in the theatre. They favoured landings on Morocco's Atlantic coast - to guard against a German or Spanish seizure of Gibraltar - and in western Algeria, beyond the range of Axis air units operating from Sicily.

The resulting operation combined American caution with British optimism. A landing at Casablanca - on Morocco's Atlantic coast - would secure a supply base free from Axis interference while landings in Oran (western Algeria) and Algiers (central Algeria) gave the Allies a fighting chance of pressing on to Tunisia before Germany could respond. However, four hundred miles of sub-standard road and poorly maintained single track railway separated Algiers from Tunis (Tunisia's main port) while Axis reinforcements were only ninety miles away in Sicily. The Allies would require a large measure of luck and Axis lethargy to complete their mission and purge North Africa of malign influence by the end of the year.

Map 20: Operation Torch

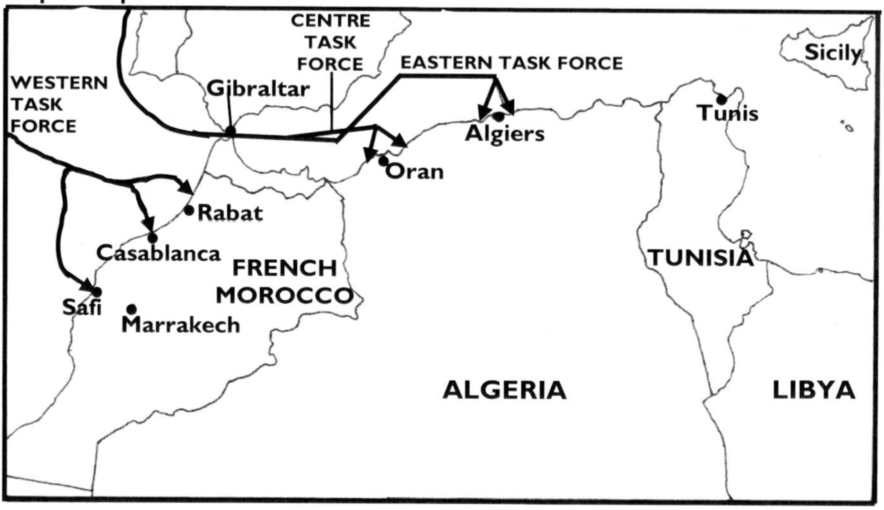

The Allies enjoyed remarkable good fortune when Admiral Darlan - Vichy Commander-in-Chief - was discovered in Algiers on 8th November visiting his polio-stricken son. Darlan was an odious collaborator who had served as Petain's Prime Minister but, sensing a change, he now offered the Allies a seductive proposition - accept him as High Commissioner of French North Africa and he would order Vichy forces in the region to stop fighting. In his first ever combat command, General Dwight Eisenhower could not resist such a tempting offer that would both minimise Allied casualties and give General Anderson's Eastern Task Force a chance of capturing Tunis before Germany could respond. He accepted Darlan's offer and Vichy resistance ceased on 10th November, enabling Blade Force and 11th Infantry Brigade from Anderson's Task Force to drive towards Tunis as fast as the inferior road system, single track railway and severe transport shortages allowed.[87]

Hitler responded swiftly to Darlan's defection. German troops occupied the rump of France - ending Vichy's nominal 'independence' - and flooded into Tunisia. By the end of November, 7,000 Axis troops were based in Tunisia, to be joined - by the end of the year - by a further 60,000 and a battalion of Tiger tanks. Hitler had opted to contest Tunisia, a decision with grave implications for Allied planning.

---

[87] The Allies anticipated strongly opposed landings in north-west Africa so their landing craft were packed with troops and assault weapons rather than trucks or transport.

II

As these dramatic events unfolded, Churchill and his advisers plotted the next stages of the conflict, the Prime Minister his usual 'catherine wheel' of buzzing manic energy and mutually exclusive fancies. In mid-September he again advocated an old favourite - a landing in northern Norway to nullify the *Kriegsmarine* threat to Arctic convoys (Operation Jupiter). Churchill had discussed this idea with Stalin in Moscow and felt that

> *there were the strongest reasons... for seizing northern Norway thus joining hands with our powerful Russian ally and enabling us to send munitions and help to her... We could not contemplate a period of inactivity between Torch in late 1942 and Round-up in late 1943.*

Having advocated Jupiter as an operation that could be implemented <u>between</u> Torch and Roundup, Churchill contradicted himself the next day (16th September) by noting *"that if Jupiter as well as Torch should get going there could be no Roundup till 1944."* Churchill had promised Stalin Roundup in 1943 during their August meeting and now, barely one month later, was willing to sacrifice Roundup and the Second Front for an operation that could offer only marginal assistance and require only three British divisions, perfectly illustrating the PM's woolly-minded thinking and penchant for peripheral operations in secondary theatres. The operation's impracticality - northern Norway being beyond the range of British-based fighters - never troubled Churchill and he repeatedly advocated Jupiter throughout the war, even as late as February 1944 when Overlord should have merited full and undivided attention.

While Churchill supported Jupiter, he was a staunch Mediterraneanist at heart and - one month after endorsing Jupiter - he advocated the Mediterranean as the principal focus for Allied operations in 1943. Such a focus would demand the swift expulsion of the Axis from Africa and if this materialised, Churchill anticipated a time when the Allies could *"attack the under-belly of the Axis at whatever may be the softest point, i.e. Sicily, Southern Italy or perhaps Sardinia; or again, if circumstances warrant... the French Riviera or... the Balkans"*. On 24th October, Churchill confidently predicted that *"however [events] may turn out... our war from now on till the summer of 1943 will be waged in the Mediterranean theatre"* and - as cross-Channel operations are only feasible during the summer months - Churchill's advocacy of Mediterranean operations throughout the summer of 1943 would completely preclude Roundup for that year.

By November however, Churchill had abandoned his Norwegian and Mediterranean passions and was once more a committed Roundup enthusiast. In mid-November, he warned COS that failure to commit to Roundup in 1943 might result in the United States switching its resources to the Pacific and - on 18th November - reminded his advisers that

> *Torch is no substitute for Roundup.... My own position is that I am still aiming at a Roundup retarded till August. I cannot give this up without a massive presentation of facts and figures which prove physical impossibility.*

On 29th November, he repudiated a COS strategy paper on the grounds that it represented

> *a practical abandonment of any resolute effort to form a second front in 1943. I certainly think we should make all plans to attack the French coasts either in the Channel or in the Bay of Biscay, and that July 1943 should be fixed as the target date. Judging from the conditions on the Russian Front, it does not look as if Hitler will be able to bring back any large force from the east to the west.*

Sixth Army's recent encirclement at Stalingrad undoubtedly explains Churchill's enthusiasm for Roundup at this point.

However, while Churchill temporarily endorsed cross-Channel operations for 1943, his advisers remained resolutely opposed, regurgitating arguments from 1941 when Britain was bereft of major allies. COS outlined its preferences in a 30th October 'American British Strategy Report' which - without advancing any evidence to support its claims - asserted that

> *sufficient experience has already been gained to show that it will not be tactically possible to establish and maintain a large army in France until German military power had been undermined. An unsuccessful invasion resulting in a large allied defeat would be a disaster.*

As before, COS could only contemplate returning to France after German power had been smashed by a lengthy campaign of bombing, blockade and subversion and on 22nd October, General Brooke estimated that a further eighteen months might be required to weaken German resistance to the point where Channel operations became feasible. Hostile to Roundup, COS proposed that

> *the successful conclusion of Torch will open up wide opportunities for tightening the ring around Germany... It may afford us the opportunity to occupy Sardinia and Sicily which would complete the opening up of the Western and Central Mediterranean. In short, it should be possible to turn the Mediterranean as a whole, and Italy in particular, into an immense liability for Germany.*

Churchill and others had advocated turning Italy into a 'liability' for Germany in spring 1939 and COS seemed reluctant to acknowledge the tremendous advantages Britain had gained by acquiring Russia and America as allies and the opportunities this created for more aggressive action. Instead, they remained mired in the 1940/41 mindset when Britain - and its Empire - 'stood alone' and Germany was all-powerful. Rejecting Roundup, COS argued that

> *our main amphibious operations in 1943 should be conducted in the Mediterranean with the object of stretching the enemy forces to the greatest possible extent. Small raids on the N.W. coast of Europe must be undertaken with increasing frequency... [but] British resources for amphibious warfare are insufficient... to provide for a full-scale cross-Channel combined operation in 1943 at the same time as sustaining our amphibious campaign abroad.*

When Oliver Harvey - Eden's Private Secretary - learned of the COS strategy, he observed:

> *The Chiefs of Staff... wish to do nothing till 1944 except carry out a few raids and give arms to Russia to carry on the fight. The Russian Army having played the allotted role of killing Germans, our Chiefs of Staff think by 1944 they could stage a general onslaught on the exhausted animal.*

It is difficult to dispute such a damning assessment.

While COS opposed Roundup on theoretical grounds, other more practical considerations undermined the operation. The longevity of Axis resistance in Tunisia certainly compromised Allied planning for 1943. In January 1943, the 70,000 Axis troops already in Tunisia were joined by Rommel's 70,000 arriving from the east, and an additional 110,000 despatched via Sicily, giving 250,000 in total. Blade Force and 11th Infantry Brigade came within twenty miles of Tunis in mid-December before encountering resolute opposition and - at that point - the heavens opened and Tunisia's rainy season commenced, churning the road network into a quagmire and delaying further campaigning for six weeks. When the weather improved in late January, the Axis attacked, capturing Faïd Pass from the French and inflicting humiliating reversals on the Americans at Kasserine and Sidi Bouzid. Churchill's naively optimistic predictions for 1943 were all premised on a swift Allied victory and - when this failed to materialise - Allied plans had to be completely recast.

Map 21: Tunisia

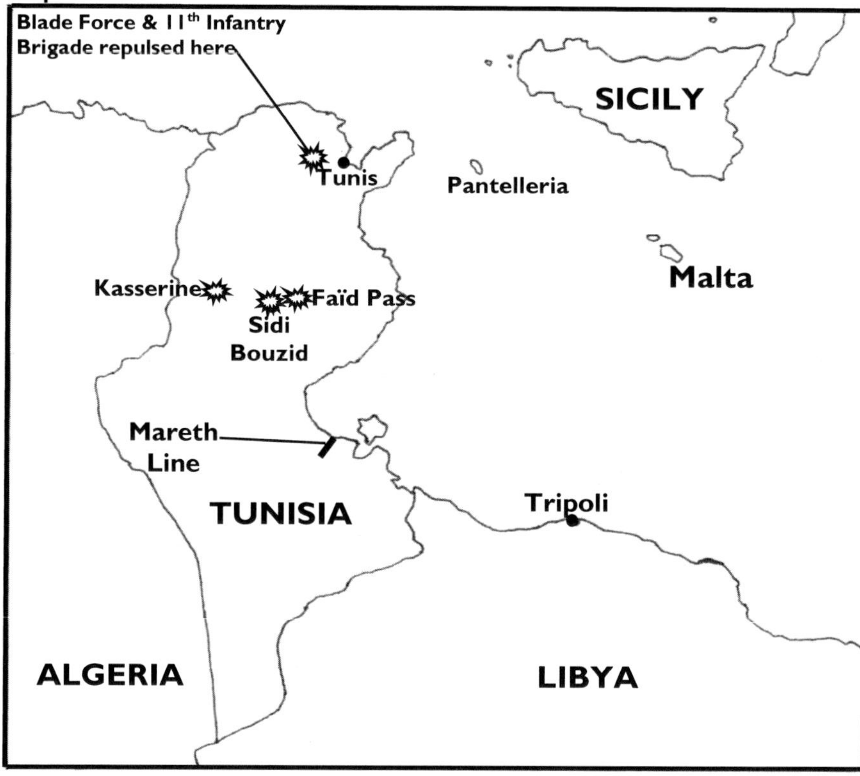

Tunisia also absorbed large numbers of troops originally destined for Britain and Roundup. The original Bolero plans had anticipated 500,000 American troops based in Britain by the end of 1942, with a further 500,000 arriving in spring 1943 to provide the manpower for Roundup's anticipated 28-30 US divisions. However, by early December 1942, only 170,000 American forces were based in the UK - one third of the anticipated total - and at this point, ground troops in the Mediterranean (128,000) actually outnumbered those in the UK (123,000).[88] American planners were equally gloomy about the future, estimating in December that

[88] The other 47,000 were non-combatant support personnel.

> *even if movements to North Africa were stopped in January 1943 convoy restrictions would permit no more than half a million Americans to be assembled in the United Kingdom and made ready to cross the Channel by July - about eight divisions with supporting troops.*

Roundup plans were premised on the participation of 28-30 US divisions and one million men but US planners were now estimating a force of 8 divisions and half a million men in the UK by July 1943, far fewer than was required. Under such circumstances, Roundup became impossible.

Nor was the Mediterranean the only theatre diverting resources from Bolero-Roundup. Britain and America were both - in principle - committed to 'Germany First' but evolving politico-military circumstance replaced it with a de facto 'Japan First' strategy as more and more US troops were diverted to the Pacific. This was both a response to developments in that theatre and General Marshall's response to COS opposition to Channel operations. By late 1942, America's army had grown to five million men and neither Marshall nor Roosevelt could countenance large numbers of US troops standing idle in Britain in anticipation of an operation that never launched. Roosevelt clarified this point to Mountbatten when they met in Washington in June and Marshall made a similar point later in the year when he warned that he

> *would send no more American forces to the United Kingdom over and above the minimum needed for the defence of this island, until such time as the Combined Chiefs of Staff approved an offensive operation… which did not depend upon a crack in German morale.*

The message was clear - British opposition to Roundup would undermine Bolero which, in turn, would starve Roundup of essential resources, rendering it impossible to launch. In late July, when Roosevelt and Churchill had endorsed Torch as the prime Allied operation for 1942, Marshall warned that this decision would render "*Round-up in all probability impracticable of successful execution in 1943*" and commit the Allies to *"a defensive encircling line of action for the continental European theatre [in 1943]"* and the significantly reduced Bolero build-up by the end of 1942 was the direct consequence of this trend, something which neither Churchill nor Roosevelt were keen to accept.

If America's rapidly expanding army was not to be employed in Europe, where should it be deployed? Admiral King (US Navy Chief), General MacArthur and large sections of the American public clamoured for action in the Pacific against Japan and events in mid-1942 reinforced this tendency. In June, Japanese and Korean construction workers started building a bomber base on the southern Solomon Island of Guadalcanal which - if it became operational - would disrupt American communications with Australia, project Japanese power into the South West Pacific and undermine America's entire strategy for the theatre. In response to this threat, America initiated its first Pacific offensive on 7th August when it undertook to expel Japanese forces from Guadalcanal. Operation Watchtower was conceived as a limited offensive but ferocious Japanese resistance ensured that it dragged on until February 1943 and - because of the distances involved - consumed large quantities of shipping and other resources that might otherwise have been sent to Europe.

Map 22: Guadalcanal

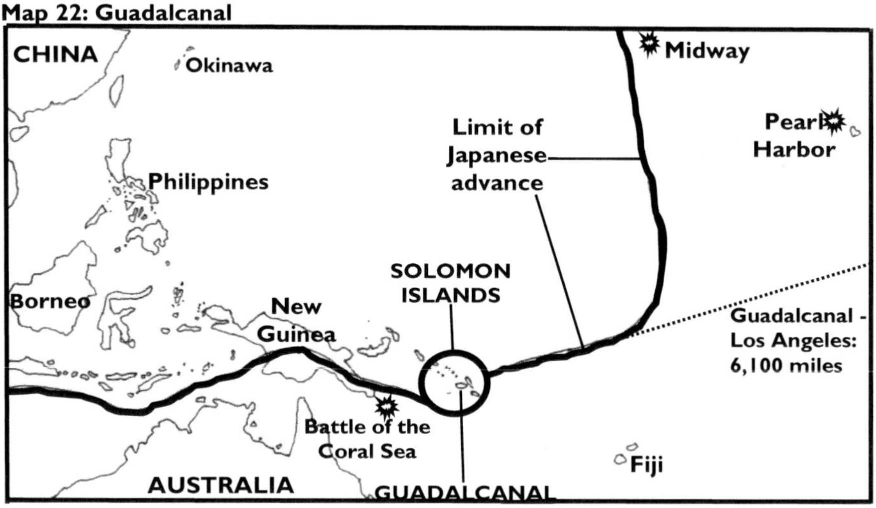

As a result of Guadalcanal and other Pacific commitments, by the end of 1942 more American troops were fighting the Japanese in the Pacific (464,000) than were confronting Germans and Italians in the Mediterranean and UK combined (378,00). This further undermined the Bolero build-up and in Prof. David Reynolds' words, by January 1943, *"the 'Germany First' principle was being honoured more in the breach than in the observance."*

III

The collapse of Bolero, his advisers' opposition and the lengthy Tunisian campaign finally convinced Churchill to drop Roundup as a

1943 operation. On 18th November, he'd declared he'd only renounce Roundup following *"a massive presentation of facts and figures which prove physical impossibility"* and COS provided this evidence on 13th December by estimating that by summer 1943, Britain and America could furnish no more than twenty-five divisions to cross the Channel (instead of the planned 48) and that this force would face forty well-equipped German divisions. These discrepancies raised severe doubts about Roundup and Churchill finally surrendered on 16th December with a suddenness that General Brooke considered worthy of recording.

> *At 6pm we had a COS meeting with PM... all about policy for 1943. As the paper we put in went straight against Winston, who was pressing for a western front in France, whilst we pressed for amphibious operations in the Mediterranean. I feared the worst!! However, meeting went well... and I succeeded in swinging him round. I think he is now fairly safe, but I still have the Americans to convince first, and then Stalin.*

Churchill's abrupt capitulation so impressed General John Kennedy - Director of Military Operations - that he later

> *could not help wondering whether he [Churchill] had been arguing against the Chiefs of Staff partly to be sure that our calculations had been thoroughly worked out, and partly so that he might be well primed with all the points of the controversy for his discussions with the President.*

If Kennedy's assessment is correct, Churchill's support for Roundup was no more than a ploy to help him challenge the operation in subsequent conversations with the Americans. However, Churchill was a man of pronounced - if rather fickle - passions and it is not implausible that his short-lived support for Roundup in November 1942 when Sixth Army was trapped in Stalingrad was genuine.

Following Churchill's Damascene conversion, British strategy was articulated in a 3rd January *'American-British Strategy in 1943'* paper which outlined British opposition to Roundup, arguing that the Allies lacked the resources required to guarantee its success, that a premature operation would fail disastrously and that the build-up for Roundup would deprive Russia of effective support for 7-8 months. As an alternative, COS proposed operations in the Mediterranean to remove Italy from the war and - a Churchill *idée fixe* - draw Turkey into the conflict. In a list of seven priorities, a Channel crossing was seventh, the first three priorities being (i) defeating the U-boat menace (ii) initiating a major bomber offensive against Germany, and (iii) *"exploiting our position in the Mediterranean."*

While COS curtailed its New Year celebrations to outline the British position, the US Joint Chiefs renounced Boxing Day to articulate their views in a paper titled *'Basic Strategic Concept for 1943'* and the gulf separating the strategies could not have been greater. Hostile to Mediterranean operations, the United States wished to *"insure that the primary effort of the United Nations is directed against Germany rather than against her satellite states,"* a focus that would be achieved by developing *"an integrated air offensive on the largest practicable scale against German production and resources... [and by]... building up as rapidly as possible adequate balanced forces in the United Kingdom in preparation of a land offensive against Germany in 1943."* While the Joint Chiefs could accept a bomber offensive against Italy to sap its will to resist, they only wished to *"consolidate and hold [North Africa] with the forces adequate for its security"* after it had been cleared, and *"transfer any excess forces to the U.K. for employment there as part of the build-up for the invasion of Western Europe in 1943."*

A chasm separated the two strategies. COS favoured Mediterranean operations as an alternative to cross-Channel operations while the Americans wished to close down the Mediterranean and divert Allied resources towards the war against Germany in north-west Europe as quickly as possible.

By the time these views were articulated, Churchill and Roosevelt had committed their staffs to a convocation in Casablanca. With the two sides holding such divergent views, Symbol was bound to be lively, a conference that carried the greatest implications for both Anglo-American strategy and western Allied relations with Russia.

CHAPTER FIFTEEN: WE CAME, WE LISTENED, WE WERE CONQUERED, 14th January - 12th May 1943

They swarmed down upon us like locusts with a plentiful supply of planners and various other assistants with prepared plans... From a worm's eye viewpoint it was apparent that we were confronted by generations and generations of experience in committee work, in diplomacy and in rationalising points of view. They had us on the defensive practically all the time.

Brig. Gen. Albert Wedemeyer,
United States War Plans Division

If I had written down before I came what I hoped that the conclusions would be, I could never have written anything so sweeping, so comprehensive, and so favourable to our ideas.

Colonel Ian Jacob, Military Assistant
Secretary to the War Cabinet

Symbol (14th - 24th January) was the first of four major Allied military conferences convened during 1943. Churchill had proposed the meeting in November 1942 when hopes for a swift North African victory were high but - by the time the meeting convened in January - Allied forces were bogged down in the morass of a Tunisian winter. Hopes for an early victory had vanished but the Allies still had to plan their next move. The British favoured ongoing operations in the Mediterranean - leaping onto Sicily or Sardinia from North Africa - while the Americans wanted to close down the Mediterranean as quickly as possible. As with 1943's other major conferences (Trident, Quadrant, Eureka), Symbol was characterised by haggling, wrangling, horse-trading and - ultimately – a consensus reflecting the protagonists' balance of power and influence.

I

Britain held all the aces in this first encounter. Most combat-ready troops in Europe were Mediterranean-based and the majority British-imperial by a ratio of around 3:1.[89] If Churchill and COS wished to deploy them in fruitless Mediterranean operations, Marshall and Roosevelt could not prevent this. Moreover, returning these troops to

---

[89] To illustrate this, six US infantry divisions were fighting in North Africa in December 1942 while only one was based in Britain. The bulk of Britain's best fighting units had already been deployed to the Mediterranean while most of those in the UK were training or forming up (Matloff and Snell, *Strategic Planning for Coalition Warfare, 1941-42*, p.354; Matloff, *Strategic Planning for Coalition Warfare, 1943-44*, p.394).

England while Allied shipping was under intense pressure would prove problematic.[90] Churchill's decision to invest heavily in North Africa after August 1940 generated a logic and momentum of its own which compromised Allied planning processes. Long before the term 'mission creep' was coined, Churchill and his generals fully appreciated its meaning and value.

The British were also better prepared. The War Cabinet's Military Assistant Secretary - Colonel Jacob - reconnoitred Casablanca in late December and the bulk of the British delegation sailed down to Casablanca in early January on HMS *Bulolo*, a liner converted to serve as a headquarters ship, giving COS access to a *"floating file cabinet... complete with technical details on all possible aspects of any proposed operation."* Churchill and his generals had discussed strategy at length during 1942 and were united behind a Mediterranean strategy, divided only over Sicily or Sardinia as their next target. That aside, Britain's politico-military leadership spoke with one voice.

The Americans, in contrast, were deeply divided between Marshall (who favoured cross-Channel operations), Admiral King (who demanded a doubling of resources for the Pacific) and Air Force General 'Hap' Arnold (who didn't mind if his B-17s bombed the Reich from Lincolnshire or southern Italy), while the President's views remained opaque. Roosevelt and his Chiefs met only once - on 7th January - to coordinate strategy for the conference when Marshall was forced to concede that the Joint Chiefs were divided over the question of cross-Channel operations and that *"there was not a united front on that subject, particularly among the planners."* Brigadier Albert Wedemeyer - one of only two senior American planners to attend Symbol - described American preparations thus:

> *We had gone to Casablanca without an agreed or clearly defined position among the American Army and Navy representatives. Nor did President Roosevelt bring mature leadership to our own Joint Chiefs of Staff. While permitting them freedom to state their personal views, he seldom gave them any specific knowledge of his own plans and policies... We had no assurance that the President would support our choice of concentration, and, on the military level, we were without agreement among ourselves as to how to convince the British of the danger of frittering away our combined resources on indecisive, limited operations.*

---

[90] Chapter 26 considers the Battle of the Atlantic.

However, British dependence on American money, munitions and *matériel* restricted Churchill's ability to exploit this weakness, while any overt opposition to carrying the fight to Hitler would simply propel America towards the Pacific - a prospect Britain dreaded and which Marshall had already threatened. Consequently, Britain had to temper any temptation to exploit its tactical advantage with the need to keep America committed to 'Germany First' (even as Britain advocated 'Italy First') and by the deference paupers must display towards their benefactors. Roundup could only launch from England with British backing, while Britain needed American resources to remain at war, a constellation of circumstance that inclined the negotiators towards conciliation and compromise. Dwight Eisenhower identified the maturity and pragmatism that - in the final analysis - underpinned Allied relations when he informed a colleague that

> *I am not so incredibly naive that I do not realize that Britishers instinctively approach every military problem from the viewpoint of the Empire, just as we approach them from the viewpoint of American interests. But one of the constant sources of danger to us in this war is the temptation to regard as our first enemy the partner that must work with us in defeating the real enemy.*

And thus it was during the first half of Symbol, the two sides firing warning shots across each other's bows to ensure that any subsequent climb-down would be interpreted as evidence of wisdom and maturity rather than weakness. Marshall extolled the virtue of cross-Channel operations, King demanded more resources for the Pacific and Brooke denounced King's thinking as 'unscientific', while arguing that any force sent to France in 1943 would be repulsed by a German army twice its size. Brooke - known to his subordinates as 'Colonel Shrapnel' - was a forceful negotiator but he was also highly strung and - over lunch on 18th January - he informed Dill that he was close to despair. Dill assured Brooke that he was closer to agreement than he suspected and urged the Combined Chiefs to find common ground, otherwise Churchill and Roosevelt would become involved, and *"you know as well as I do what a mess they would make of it."*

While Brooke emoted to Dill, Air Vice Marshal John Slessor was up on the hotel roof, penning a compromise to break the deadlock. 'Pug' Ismay had crafted a compromise to enable the Allies to move forward following Tobruk, and Slessor performed a similar function at Casablanca. His contribution lay in devising a formula that reconciled the competing demands of Europe and the Pacific while leaving both parties feeling that their interests were being served. In Slessor's words,

> *operations in the Pacific and Far East shall continue with the forces allocated, with the object of maintaining pressure on Japan, retaining the initiative and attaining a position of readiness for the full-scale offensive against Japan by the United Nations as soon as Germany is defeated. These operations must be kept within such limits as will not, in the opinions of the Combined Chiefs of Staff, prejudice the capacity of the United Nations to take any opportunity that may present itself for the decisive defeat of Germany in 1943.*

Slessor's draft was handed to Air Marshal Portal who passed it to Brooke and - after Dill had squared things with Marshall - it was presented to the Americans at the start of the afternoon session. Slessor recalled the tense few moments at the start of the session as Marshall and King scrutinised his formula.

> *I can still see Marshall and King poring over it, exchanging a few words in undertones, Marshall making some notes on it in pencil.*

After what seemed like an eternity, Marshall signalled his assent and was delegated to present the breakthrough to Churchill and Roosevelt at a plenary session. The Prime Minister and President endorsed the settlement and the Combined Chiefs were now free to develop the implications inherent in Slessor's formula over the next five days. While CCS 170/2 'Final Report of the Combined Chiefs of Staff to the President and the Prime Minister' (23rd January) embodies the Conference's final views, the nub and essence of Casablanca is contained in the document drafted directly after this 18th January breakthrough - CCS 155/1 'Conduct of the War in 1943'.

CCS 155/1 identified six main elements of Anglo-American strategy. Point One confirmed that *"the defeat of the U-boat must remain a first charge on the resources of the United Nations"* and, given the destruction being wrought by Dönitz's u-boats at this time, the need to eradicate the submarine menace was certainly pressing.[91] An island nation, Britain relies on the security of its sea-lanes for survival and Europe could only be liberated if the required men and *matériel* could be shipped across the Atlantic to their southern English jumping-off points

---

[91] see Chapter 26.

without major loss. Europe's liberation demanded the elimination of Dönitz's sea-wolves.

Point Two confirmed that *"Soviet forces must be sustained by the greatest volume of supplies that can be transported... without prohibitive cost in shipping,"* but Casablanca's true essence is contained in Points 3, 4 and 6.[92]

Point Three blandly recapitulated the 'Germany First' strategy by stating that *"operations in the European theatre will be conducted with the object of defeating Germany in 1943 with the maximum forces that can be brought to bear upon her."* However, having identified Germany's defeat as the principal Allied objective for 1943, Point 4(a) confirmed that *"the main lines of offensive action"* will be *"in the Mediterranean [through] the occupation of Sicily."* In other words, Germany was to be defeated in 1943 but the action intended to achieve this would be directed against Italy in the Mediterranean, a commitment which neatly encapsulates Britain's strategic victory at Symbol and embodies a long-standing Churchillian enthusiasm. Point Four justified the occupation of Sicily on the grounds that it would (i) secure Allied lines of communication through the Mediterranean, (ii) divert German resources from Russia, and (iii) intensify pressure on Italy.

Having committed the Allies to defeating Germany via the Mediterranean in 1943, Point 4(b) underlined the primacy of the *mare internum* by declaring that the Allies should *"create a situation in which Turkey can be enlisted as an ally,"* reflecting another Churchillian obsession. He had diverted resources from Europe to Turkey in his disastrous Gallipoli campaign and had tried to recruit Turkey to his phantom 'Balkan Front' in spring 1941. Now, in 1943, Britain was trying to cultivate Turkey as an ally both on account of its strategic position in the eastern Mediterranean/Middle East and by virtue of its capacity to thwart Russian ambitions in this sensitive arena. Churchill spent an inordinate amount of time trying to draw Turkey into the conflict during 1941-44, travelling to Adana to meet President Inönü directly after Casablanca but the Turks - who lacked the resources to mount serious offensive operations - feared the Russians as much as the Germans and remained neutral until their belligerency served no useful purpose.[93] Churchill, however, was determined to draw Turkey

---

[92] Point 5 reiterated the need to balance the forces allocated to Europe and the Mediterranean with those allocated to the Pacific and Far East.

[93] Turkey finally declared war on Germany on 23rd February 1945 to gain entry to the nascent United Nations (Kemal H. Karpat, *Turkey's Politics: The Transition To A Multi-Party System* (1959), p.140).

into the conflict and initiated his disastrous Dodecanese Campaign in September 1943 in pursuit of this end (covered in Chapter 19).

Having confirmed the primacy of the Mediterranean for 1943, Point Four then considered offensive operations that could be directed against Germany from the United Kingdom in that year. Point 4(c) urged *"the heaviest possible bomber offensive against the German war effort"* while Point 4(d) envisaged *"such limited offensive operations [against Germany] as may be practicable with the amphibious forces available."* Britain had been drained of resources capable of sustaining offensive operations against Germany, so Point 4(d) merely committed the Allies to nuisance actions against German-occupied territory, hit and run raids which irritated Germany without weakening its grip on the continent. Britain had committed to strategic area bombing in February 1942 and the inclusion of Point 4(c) in CCS 155/1 merely committed America to the same sterile tactic.

Having emphasised the importance of the submarine war, the Mediterranean, strategic bombing and nuisance raids as means of defeating Germany in 1943, Point 4(e) finally endorsed cross-Channel operations but in terms so anodyne and ambiguous as to render their inclusion virtually meaningless. Point 4(e) advocated *"the assembly of the strongest possible force (subject to (a) and (b) above and paragraph 6 below) in constant readiness to re-enter the Continent as soon as German resistance is weakened to the required extent,"* a watery and vapid formula neatly encapsulating Britain's strategic triumph. The forces required to re-enter the continent could only be assembled as long as their gathering didn't compromise more significant Mediterranean and Far Eastern operations [described below]. In other words, cross-Channel operations came second to the prime Allied Mediterranean objective for 1943. Secondly, these forces could only be deployed on the continent after *"German resistance... [had been] weakened to the required extent,"* embodying Churchill and Brooke's fervent conviction that Europe could only be invaded **after** Germany had been brought to the point of collapse and which rejected American willingness to take the field against unbroken German forces. The phrase *"to the required extent"* also provided generous wiggle room for anyone opposed to cross-Channel operations to delay the venture almost indefinitely. Reading this point, one can readily appreciate Colonel Jacob's gleeful assertion that British ideas *"prevailed throughout"* Symbol.

Having comprehensively defeated their American allies in the first half of CCS 155/1, part two offered token concessions to salve the raw taste of defeat and pacify Admiral King. Point 6(c)(i) committed Britain to *"the recapture of Burma (Anakim) beginning in 1943"* while point 6(c)(ii) endorsed offensive operations against the Marshall and Caroline Islands after Rabaul (a major Japanese base in eastern New Britain) had been neutralised. Along with Churchill and Brooke, King was a major victor at Casablanca as his determination to initiate offensive operations against Japan in the Pacific was sustained and - as a Navy man - he could readily appreciate the shipping gains to be made by opening up the Mediterranean to convoys.[94] Anakim would help China by opening up the Burma Road to United States supplies and - by strengthening China - would draw Japanese forces away from the Pacific.

Taken as a whole, CCS 155/1 and Symbol must be regarded as strategic triumphs for Britain. Cross-Channel operations had been ruled out for 1943 (though lip service was paid to the ideal) while the primary emphasis was placed on the Mediterranean, with the Pacific a secondary theatre. Amphibious assault forces can only cross the Channel with confidence during May - September and so, for Roundup to proceed in 1943, Axis forces would have to be expelled from Africa and Sicily by early spring and in the end, the Axis remained in North Africa till mid-May and Sicily was not cleared until mid-August. Under such conditions, Roundup could never proceed in 1943, a fact Britain and America conceded after the conference. One can only conclude that the idea of crossing the Channel in 1943 was included as a sop to Marshall - who remained the operation's foremost advocate - and Stalin, who had been promised a Channel assault for 1943 by Churchill. The western allies' reneging on the Second Front for a second year in a row sparked a major rift in Anglo-American-Soviet relations at a crucial moment, resulting in the replacement of two western-oriented ambassadors (Maisky in London and Litvinov in Washington) with hard-line *apparatchiks* (Gusev and Gromyko). British caution, timidity and committee work had prevailed and Brooke and his colleagues were delighted by Casablanca's results. The peripheral strategy had triumphed and Italy and the Mediterranean would be the principal targets for 1943. One can readily appreciate Brigadier Wedemeyer's mordant confession that, at Casablanca, the Americans had *"lost our shirts... we came, we listened and we were conquered."*

---

[94] Brooke estimated that the Allies would gain 225 additional merchant ships by opening up the Mediterranean and avoiding the long haul round South Africa (Atkinson, *Army at Dawn,* p.284). However, many of the ships gained were used in Mediterranean operations such as Anzio which, for a time, became the fourth largest port in the world - the shipping 'savings' were therefore squandered in futile Mediterranean operations (see Chapter 21).

II

The elevation of Husky (the invasion of Sicily) over Roundup (the cross-Channel assault) was far from Symbol's only significant outcome. Marshall's efforts to promote cross-Channel operations had been thwarted but several documents acknowledged the need for such an operation and he used this concession to create a body to commence serious operational planning. CCS 169 considered the *"organisation of command, control, planning and training for operations for a re-entry to the continent across the Channel"* and acknowledged the need for a Supreme Commander to direct the operation but *"if this is not feasible, his Chief of Staff or Deputy and a nucleus of the combined staff [should] be appointed immediately to give the necessary impetus and cohesion to planning."* CCS 169 also noted that

> *for some months, a special inter-allied staff drawn from all three services has been... studying the problem and planning for a return to the continent... [and] this special planning staff should be adapted to the new conditions [of 1943] and strengthened by the addition of American personnel. They should work, under the direction of the Supreme Commander (or his deputy), in conjunction with the nucleus of his combined staff in London.*

This led to the appointment of General Frederick Morgan - a British officer - as Chief of Staff, Supreme Allied Commander (COSSAC) in March 1943 with a brief to drive forward cross-Channel planning until such times as a Supreme Commander was appointed. On 23rd April, Morgan was instructed to start planning for *"a full-scale assault against the continent in 1944, as early as possible"* (revealing the hollowness of Symbol's assertion that this operation was feasible in 1943) while maintaining a pretence of operations for 1943 in order to detain German forces in France. Churchill's grand promises to Stalin were now reduced to the level of a ruse, as was his assumption that major North African operations in 1942 would not preclude northern European operations in 1943, vindicating his advisers' hard-headed realism.

Symbol also approved a new Mediterranean command structure. The document that endorsed the invasion of Sicily for *"the period of the favourable July moon"* (CCS 171/2/D) also elevated General Eisenhower to the post of Supreme Allied Commander with General Harold Alexander (in charge of ground forces) as his deputy, Admiral Cunningham as his naval commander and Marshal Tedder in charge of air. British acquiescence in Eisenhower's elevation at a time when most troops in the theatre were British-imperial - and his three British deputies outranked him - appears, on the surface, as a gesture of great solidarity but, as always, Britain was pursuing a hidden agenda. British senior commanders blamed Eisenhower for slow Allied progress in Tunisia and his lacklustre presentation of plans for future Tunisian operations at Symbol only strengthened this view. Brooke - who regarded only Stalin and Douglas MacArthur as his peers - lambasted Eisenhower, claiming in his diary that

> *Eisenhower as a general is hopeless! He submerges himself in politics and neglects his military duties, I am afraid, because he knows little if anything about military matters.*

While Eisenhower's elevation appeared - on the surface - to be a vote of confidence in his ability, Brooke's real agenda was to detach him from day to day direction of military affairs which his British deputies would then exercise. Brooke clarified this by informing his diary that

> *by bringing Alexander over from the Middle East, and appointing him as Deputy to Eisenhower, we were carrying out a move which could not help flattering and pleasing the Americans in so far as we were placing our senior and most experienced commander to function under their commander who had no war experience... and they did not at the time appreciate the underlying intentions. We were pushing Eisenhower up into the… rarefied atmosphere of a Supreme Commander, where he would be free to devote his time to the political and inter-allied problems, whilst we inserted under him one of our own commanders to deal with the military situations and to restore the necessary drive and coordination which had been so seriously lacking.*

Two things thwarted this scheme. Firstly, Eisenhower's steely resolve to play patsy to no-one, and General Marshall's determination that Britain should not dominate the Mediterranean. The two men corresponded on this issue and on 8th February, Eisenhower reassured Marshall that

> *as far as I am concerned no attention will be paid to such observations [that military operations will be directed by my deputies]... I believe that I have grasped your idea and that I will be constantly on my guard to prevent any important military venture depending for its control and direction upon the 'committee' system of command.*

Brooke and his colleagues would neither be the first nor the last to under-estimate the genial Kansan's gritty resolve.

The post-Symbol press conference delivered two further surprises. Firstly, the press corps was treated to the unlikely spectacle of two latter-day Jeanne d'Arcs - Generals Charles De Gaulle and Henri Giraud - shaking hands in an imitation of solidarity. In reality, the two generals detested each other and contested control over Free French forces. In fact, their first touching of hands was so brief it had to be re-staged for the cameras' benefit and - once completed - the two behemoths stalked off in opposite directions, muttering imprecations against each other and those who had forced them into such an unnatural act. Nevertheless, the illusion of metropolitan and colonial French solidarity was fostered to please the public.

Having coordinated this charade, Roosevelt encored with an announcement that the western Allies would accept nothing less than 'complete and unconditional' Axis surrender as the basis for ending hostilities. Churchill later claimed to have been caught off guard by this pronouncement but the two men had discussed the issue on 18th January and Churchill had reported back to his War Cabinet, securing their consent to this hard-line stance. While this declaration may or may not have stiffened Germany's will to fight, it fulfilled three important goals. Firstly, it reassured Stalin that the west would not conclude a separate peace with Hitler which would allow him to fasten his fury on the east. Secondly, the 'unconditional surrender' commitment precluded any further 'Darlan deals' with Quislings or collaborators that had so tarnished the Allied cause. Thirdly, comprehensive defeat of German forces in the field would prevent any repetition of the bogus 'stab in the back' myth exploited by the Nazis during their rise to power. Whatever happened to the Nazi state, bourgeois politicians would not be blamed for its demise.

Their business concluded, the hierarchs went their separate ways but not before Churchill persuaded Roosevelt to visit Marrakech where the two men watched the sun set over the Atlas Mountains. Churchill was so moved by the spectacle that he burst into song and - following Roosevelt's departure - painted his only picture of the war, a scene of Marrakech and the surrounding heights. He also took time to advise his host - US Vice Consul Kenneth Whittemore Pendar - that

> *there are always earnest spinsters in Pennsylvania, Utah, Edinburgh or Dublin persistently writing letters and... giving their advice to the British Government, urging that India be*

> *given back to the Indians and South Africa back to the Zulu or Boers, but as long as I am called by his Majesty the King to be his First Minister, I shall not assist at the dismemberment of the British Empire.*

Having just secured the triumph of his 'Italy First' Mediterranean strategy over America's more direct 'Germany First' approach, the Prime Minister felt fully entitled to such bullish observations.

III

The battle for Tunisia re-ignited as Symbol ended. Montgomery - who had trailed Rommel across North Africa with *"all the bustling confidence of an archdeacon entering a maison clos [brothel]* "[95] - seized Tripoli (Rommel's main supply port) on 23rd January, and the bruised and battered German Italian Panzer Army limped into Tunisia the following week. Rommel hoped to link up with von Arnim's Panzer Army to deal with Anglo-American forces in northern Tunisia before turning south and - on 19th/20th February - inflicted a stunning defeat on American forces at Kasserine. However, von Armin failed to support his superior and Rommel was prevented from exploiting his victory. In early March, the Desert Fox moved south, hoping to repulse Eighth Army before it reached the Mareth Line, a series of defensive positions constructed by France to exclude Italy from Tunisia. Alerted by Ultra, Montgomery stationed large numbers of anti-tank guns around Medenine and cauterised Rommel's already depleted tank force. By this stage, Rommel knew the Tunisian game was up and he flew to the Ukraine to try to persuade Hitler to abandon Africa. Perturbed by Rommel's pessimism, Hitler ordered him on extended sick leave and - after two years of tumultuous defeats and victories, advances and retreats - the Desert Fox was exiled from Africa, never to return.

With Rommel gone, the Allies seized the initiative and Patton's II Corps shattered 10th Panzer Army at El Guettar on 23rd March while Montgomery simultaneously attacked the Mareth Line. When his direct assault failed, Monty shifted his weight onto an outflanking manoeuvre, forcing Axis units to withdraw to avoid encirclement.

By late April, von Arnim's Army Group Africa was merely delaying the inevitable. The force that had once held the Nile within its grasp was now hemmed into a small defensive perimeter around Tunis and Bizerte, outnumbered in tanks, troops and guns and starved of

---

[95] The phrase is Correlli Barnett's and comes from p.287 of *The Desert Generals* (1999).

supplies by Allied command of the air and sea. A coordinated Allied assault was launched on 22nd April and - when Eighth Army units moved north to assist General Anderson's First Army at Tunis - the Allies achieved a decisive breakthrough, capturing Tunis and Bizerte on 7th May. After further mopping up operations in the Cap Bon peninsula - which yielded 267,000 German-Italian prisoners (including von Arnim) - General Alexander sent Churchill the news he'd been craving for three years: *"Sir, it is my duty to report that the Tunisian Campaign is over. All enemy resistance has ceased. We are masters of the North African shores."* In 1939, Churchill had written that *"for Britain in time of war, the command of the Mediterranean must be the prime objective"* and, by ejecting the Axis from Africa, he'd secured the first half of this ambition - he'd spend the rest of the war trying to achieve the second part by winning control of south-eastern Europe.

Map 23: Final Tunisian operations

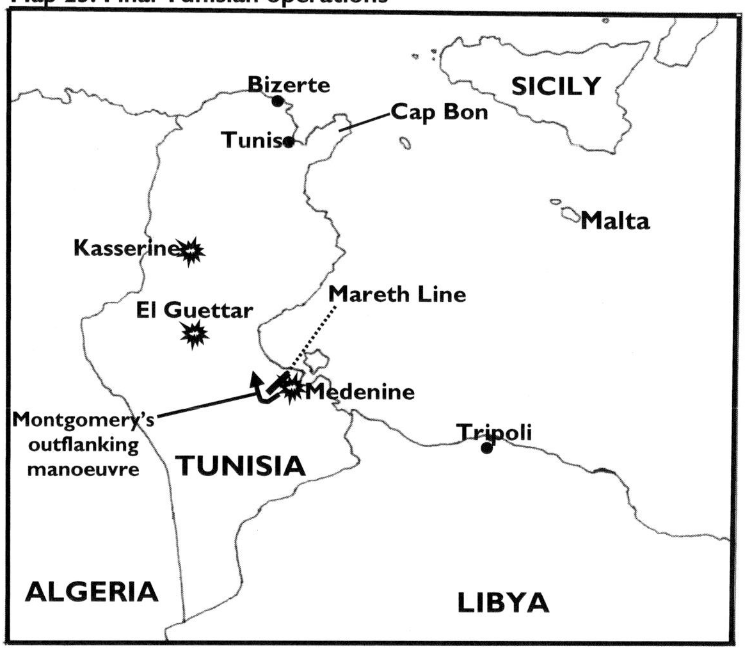

In the final analysis, Casablanca and victory in Tunisia raised almost as many questions as they answered. How would Stalin react to a second successive postponement of the Second Front? Where would the Allies go after Sicily? How would Marshall respond to being outfoxed at Casablanca? Churchill was about to learn the answers to these questions for - on the very day he received Alexander's triumphant telegram - he was in Washington, planning global strategy at Trident.

CHAPTER SIXTEEN: NO MAJOR OPERATIONS UNTIL 1945 OR 1946, 12th May - 3rd June 1943

At this [Trident] meeting… Winston Churchill appeared to some of us to carry his insistent campaign to preserve the British Empire to a point where it might not be in full agreement with the President's fundamental policy to defeat Hitler as quickly as possible.

Admiral Leahy in his memoirs, *I Was There*

In private conversation... Brooke told me that he would be glad to reconsider the cross-Channel project, even to the extent of eliminating that bold concept from accepted Allied strategy... He said that he favoured a policy of applying our naval and air strength toward the blockading of Germany and the destruction of its industry but avoiding great land battles on the main fronts. He held the belief that in ground conflict in a large theatre we would be at a great disadvantage and would suffer tremendous and useless losses. He wanted to open no larger front than one we could sustain in Italy.

General Brooke outlines his strategic vision to General Eisenhower, 29th May 1943

Allied military prospects were robustly healthy when Trident convened in Washington on 12th May. Axis forces in Africa surrendered as the conference opened and the u-boats evacuated the Atlantic as it closed. Sixth Army disintegrated at Stalingrad as the Red Army regained large chunks of territory lost in 1942. Japanese forces withdrew from Guadalcanal in early February and American marines landed on Attu in the Aleutians on 11th May. Over Germany, the Battle of the Ruhr commenced on 5th March with a 450-bomber raid on Essen, followed by devastating attacks on Dortmund, Dusseldorf and Duisburg. The Allies were advancing everywhere and, with so much positive news flooding in, one might reasonably expect Trident to be marked by sweetness and light.

I

The Trident controversies were Casablanca's quarrels with added vigour and vehemence. In Churchill's strategic conception, Italy was the 'soft underbelly,' an easy target and - as vast Allied resources were already deployed in the Mediterranean - it seemed sensible to deploy them against mainland Italy following the capture of Sicily. Invading Italy might topple Mussolini and force Italy from the war, providing airfields from which to aid the Balkan partisans, bomb southern Germany and interdict the Romanian oilfields. An Italian collapse would force Germany to replace Italian garrisons in Greece and the Balkans with German forces and reduce pressure on the Red Army. British intelligence predicted that Hitler would withdraw to the north following an Allied landing, opening up the prospect of huge swathes of enemy territory falling into Allied hands without a struggle, a prospect with immense appeal for Churchill.

Marshall and the Joint Chiefs viewed such prospects with a jaundiced eye, regarding Italy as a 'suction pump' which might drain forces away from a decisive showdown with Germany in north-western Europe. Marshall and Secretary of War Henry Stimson viewed the Mediterranean as a 'prestige theatre' in which *"[the British] are straining every nerve to lay a foundation… for their own empire after the war is over."* Stimson and Marshall had no interest in propping up Britain's Empire; they wanted to conclude the European war as swiftly as possible before turning to the Pacific where American interests were greater. By mid-1943, Marshall also had eighteen months' experience of working with the British and evaluating their promises. In April 1942, Churchill had endorsed Sledgehammer for 1942 and Roundup for 1943 only to renege on this commitment by July. Torch was supposed to clear the Axis from Africa by December 1942 but Allied troops were still embroiled in Tunisia six months later. Churchill had insisted that Torch would not compromise Roundup but by May 1943, Operation Bolero - the movement of troops to Britain to prepare for the Channel crossing - was in disarray; America had nine divisions in North Africa but only two in Britain and thirteen in the Pacific.[96] Marshall had grown weary of British promises of quick and easy victories and - if Roundup was to proceed in 1944 - planning and preparation must commence in summer 1943 without further 'scatterisation' of force.

Marshall was also better placed to advance United States' interests at Trident as American war-planning geared up to reflect the nation's massive industrial potential. The War Department moved to the Pentagon in January 1943, a purpose-built edifice sprawling over 6.24 million square feet and accommodating 30,000 office staff. In spring 1943, the tired and overworked Joint U.S. Strategic Committee was replaced by the Joint War Plans Committee and an independent Joint Strategic Survey Committee which advised the Joint Chiefs on

[96] At the same time, America had 61 divisions in the United States, mostly fully trained. Britain had 19 combat-ready divisions in the UK in May 1943 and 29 divisions based in North Africa and the Mediterranean (mostly combat-ready) (Ponting, *Churchill*, pp.599-600).

combined, grand and global strategy and the relation of military strategy to national policy. Chagrined by his Casablanca humiliation, Marshall instructed his planners to develop proposals to counter every plan the British might present and more than thirty papers were drafted exploring various means of carrying the war to Germany, all championing Channel operations. Brig. Albert Wedemeyer was delighted by these preparations.

> *We decided, in preparing for... Trident to consider every possibility that might be conjured up by our allies. By anticipating their proposals we might be prepared to hold the British within reasonable strategic bounds. We worked day and night, mulling over the advantages and disadvantages of various types of operations in the Mediterranean. Always we sought to assess their likely effect on our one key operation, the cross-Channel blow. We studied Sardinia, Corsica, Spain, Crete, the Dodecanese, the entire southern littoral of Europe, examining once again the terrain, the port facilities, the communications, and the availability of bases, both naval and air.*

Marshall also prepared the Joint Chiefs to present a united front to their British counterparts. Marshall and Leahy[97] would champion Pacific operations - to prevent any isolation of King - and if any member of the team wanted extra time to consider a subject, Leahy would request a postponement by stating *"I am having a study made which bears on this subject which will not be ready until tomorrow."* Marshall and Secretary of War Stimson worked hard to convert Roosevelt to their cause and lure him away from 'pinprick warfare' in the Mediterranean. Stimson was particularly assiduous in this regard, bombarding his Chief with letters and memoranda urging cross-Channel operations over all other options, and Marshall and Stimson were greatly assisted by the electoral timetable. A Presidential election was scheduled for autumn 1944 and a shrewd operator such as Roosevelt knew that the American people were unlikely to unseat their Commander-in-Chief while their sons were engaged in a life or death struggle with Nazi barbarism on the far side of the Atlantic. So - as German power waned and the Presidential election drew nearer -

---

[97] US Army Air Force Chief 'Hap' Arnold was hospitalised with a heart attack between 10th-20th May so Admiral Bill Leahy played a more prominent role in the Trident proceedings. Leahy was appointed Roosevelt's Chief of Staff in July 1942 and served as Chair of the US Joint Chiefs throughout the war (Bill Yenne, *Hap Arnold: Inventing the Air Force* (2013), p.146; Nathan S. Lowrey, *The Chairmanship of the Joint Chiefs of Staff 1949-2016* (2016), p.4; David Alexander, *The Building: A Biography of the Pentagon* (2008), p.53).

Roosevelt's enthusiasm for Roundup increased and, with Roosevelt on board, Marshall and Stimson possessed a decisive asset.

Thus, when the *Queen Mary* docked in Staten Island on 11th May, the stage was set for a highly combustible struggle between two competing strategies. As at Symbol, victory would be enjoyed by whichever side marshalled its resources to greatest effect.

II

The President and Prime Minister outlined their rival philosophies at the outset. For Churchill, "*the first objective was in the Mediterranean. The great prize there was to get Italy out of the war by whatever means might be best.*" Comparing Italy's collapse to Bulgaria's defection from the Central Powers in 1918, Churchill argued that "*the collapse of Italy would cause a chill of loneliness over the German people, and might be the beginning of their doom.*" Italy's neutralisation would encourage Turkey to enter the war, nullify the Italian fleet, create dazzling opportunities in the Balkans and materially aid the Soviet Union. Having outlined the multiple benefits to be gained from invading Italy, Churchill enumerated the hurdles blocking a Channel assault, including "*the problem of landing on the Channel coast... the difficult beaches, with the great rise and fall of the tide, the strength of the enemy's defences, the number of his reserves, and the ease of his communications [which] all made the task one which must not be under-rated.*" Such impediments notwithstanding, Churchill nevertheless assured his hosts that "*H.M. Government earnestly desired to undertake a full-scale invasion of the continent from the United Kingdom as soon as possible. [HM Government] certainly did not disdain the idea if a plan offering reasonable prospects of success could be made.*" Significantly, Churchill declined to set a date for this 'earnestly desired' operation, preferring instead to insert qualifications that could be used later to undermine the scheme.

Roosevelt adopted the opposite tack, affirming that "*he had always shrunk from the thought of putting large armies in Italy [as] this might result in attrition for the United Nations and play into Germany's hand.*" Dismissing Sledgehammer and Roundup for 1943, Roosevelt insisted that

> *if one or other were to be mounted in the spring of 1944, preparations should begin now. Roundup and Sledgehammer have been talked about for two years but as yet none of these operations had been accepted as a concrete plan to be carried out at a certain time. Therefore he wished to emphasize that Sledgehammer or Roundup should be decided upon definitely as an operation for the spring of 1944.*

The difference between British and American thinking was stark. Churchill offered grandiloquent enthusiasm and 'jam tomorrow' while Roosevelt insisted on a clear and unambiguous timetable for liberating Europe from tyranny.

Their presentations completed, the panjandrums withdrew, permitting their proxies to pursue the discussion. Brooke couldn't match Churchill's rhetorical panache but he sturdily advanced Mediterranean operations as essential adjuncts to cross-Channel operations, maintaining that *"if we did not continue operations in the Mediterranean, then no possibility of an attack into France would arise".* Brooke also insisted that Italian operations carried no threat to Roundup.

> *The reduction in BOLERO build-up resulting from the undertaking of operations in the Mediterranean would only be some three to four divisions in 1943 and none in 1944. Operations in the Mediterranean were not an unlimited commitment.*

However, as the Conference progressed, some of Brooke's comments cast doubt on his real commitment to Roundup. For example, while endorsing Roundup in principle, Brooke still argued that

> *only by attacking in the Mediterranean could we achieve immediate results and that* ***this was more valuable than building up for a 1944 ROUNDUP which might not even then be possible*** *[emphasis added].*

Brooke also employed the classic dissemblers' tactic of denouncing operations no-one was advancing. Roosevelt had already ruled out Roundup and Sledgehammer for 1943 but Brooke still felt moved to declare that

> *the seizure of the Brest Peninsula, which was all we could now achieve, would merely lock up 20 divisions.... A lodgment in the Brest Peninsula would not be a decisive blow. There were only some ten to twelve British divisions available in England.*

By denouncing cross-Channel operations for 1943, Brooke was also undermining them for 1944.

And then, during the first major session on 13th May, Brooke delivered a remark that eliminated all doubt over his commitment to

Roundup as an urgent or imminent task. In a debate over whether an assault on France would provide only a bridgehead or prompt a more decisive thrust into enemy territory, Brooke advanced the startling thesis that

> *no major operations would be possible* ***until 1945 or 1946*** *[emphasis added], since it must be remembered that in previous wars there had always been some 80 French Divisions available on our side.*

Brooke's argument was entirely ludicrous, circular and self-defeating. If a deep drive into north-western Europe required the support of 80 French divisions then no such drive could ever be mounted as these divisions would only become available following France's liberation - Catch-22 *par excellence*. Not surprisingly, Brooke omitted this remark from his post-war publications as it vividly demonstrates his profound aversion to Overlord, his willingness to postpone the operation into the dim and distant future and the extent to which the lessons of 1914-18 - rather than current circumstance - informed his thinking. Brooke's remarks also echo the tenor of his conversation with Eisenhower in Algiers on 29th May, subsequently repudiated by Brooke [and discussed later in this chapter]. However, a man who could consider deferring the cross-Channel assault to 1945 or 1946 might also be keen on *"eliminating that bold concept from accepted Allied strategy."*

Responding to Brooke's comments, Marshall drily observed that *"it appeared that Roundup was still regarded as a vague conception"* by the British and enquired if Brooke's remarks indicated that *"the British Chiefs of Staff regarded Mediterranean operations as the key to a successful termination of the European war?"*

III

Sterile, unproductive debate continued over three further days and a weekend 'bonding' session in Williamsburg, where Air Marshal Portal lost his trunks in a swimming pool and Admiral Pound lost his way in a maze. The wrangling peaked on 19th May when the Combined Chiefs met to consider rival proposals for prosecuting the war. General Brooke opened the session by noting that

> *it appeared from the two papers before the Committee that there were certain basic factors on which the US and British Staffs were in agreement. On others there were differences which must be eliminated.*

Marshall went further, maintaining that

> *the British paper throughout was over-pessimistic with regard to the possibilities of cross-Channel operations, particularly in so far as the results of our vast air power and its relation to ground operations. On the other hand, in considering Mediterranean operations, the British paper was very optimistic with regard to the forces required, the Axis reaction and the logistic problem.*

Marshall also rejected key elements of the British analysis, specifically their estimate of the landing craft required for a Channel crossing, the suggestion that Romania's Ploieşti oilfields could only be bombed from Italy and Italian civilian attitudes towards Allied troops following invasion.

Bitterly divided on principles and specifics, further genteel conversation would only entrench these divisions and so - in a move to be repeated at future conferences - the debating chamber was cleared of all support staff to allow the principals to vent their opinions in a full and frank manner in order to clear the air and strike a deal to take to their masters.

The contents of this discussion are unknown - the participants never divulged details - but this cathartic exchange certainly produced the desired result for by the time the Chiefs reconvened in full session at 4:30pm, the basis of a deal had been struck, albeit one which reflected America's improved staff work and burgeoning military-industrial muscle. CCS 237/1 'Resolutions by the Combined Chiefs of Staff (20th May) comprised only three resolutions but this concise document carried the most profound implications for the future conduct of the war.

Resolution A stipulated that *"forces and equipment shall be established in the United Kingdom with the object of mounting an operation with target date 1 May 1944 to secure a lodgment on the Continent from which further offensive operations can be carried out."* Twenty-nine divisions were earmarked for this operation - nine for the initial assault and twenty for the immediate follow-up.[98] Marshall and Roosevelt had finally tied the cross-Channel assault to a specific date and clarified the forces required.

---

[98] Reduced from 48 in the original Bolero-Roundup plan

Resolution B further underscored Marshall's victory by confirming that the Mediterranean Theatre Commander (Eisenhower) would determine future Mediterranean operations, and that forces currently based in the Mediterranean were to be withdrawn to support the Channel assault. Resolution B specifically stated that

> *the Allied Commander in Chief, North Africa, should be instructed to mount such operations in exploitation of HUSKY as are best calculated to eliminate Italy from the war and to contain the maximum number of German forces. Each specific operation will be subject to the approval of the Combined Chiefs of Staff. The Allied Commander in Chief in North Africa may use for his operations all those forces available in the Mediterranean Area except for four American and three British Divisions which will be held in readiness from 1 November onward for withdrawal to take part in operations from the United Kingdom.*

In simple terms, future operations in this theatre were to be decided by an American officer (who also happened to be Marshall's protégé) and - as a further safeguard - the Combined Chiefs had the right to veto his proposals. Italy might well be the target after Sicily but - if Eisenhower deemed it appropriate - it could equally well be Sardinia or a bombing campaign against northern Italy. The redeployment of seven battle-hardened divisions to Britain would provide the Channel assault with a cutting edge and prevent the Mediterranean from developing into Marshall's dreaded 'suction pump'.[99]

Having achieved their breakthrough, the Combined Chiefs spent the next five days fleshing out their decision and considering other aspects of the war (the Asian-Pacific conflict, the u-boat war, rearming French troops in North Africa etc). These tasks completed, they presented the outcome of their discussions to their political masters on 24th May. The paper presented to Churchill and Roosevelt (CCS 242/3) was the product of two weeks' tense and protracted negotiation during which the Chiefs had reached agreement only through a finely calibrated compromise. Any rejection of this paper by the President or Prime Minister would not only invalidate the Chiefs' achievements but would also corrode Anglo-American unity. Much depended on the

---

[99] Resolution C committed the Combined Chiefs to review these commitments in July or August *"in order that the situation may be examined in the light of the result of Husky and the situation in Russia."* It also instructed General F.E. Morgan to prepare an outline plan for the Allied invasion of Europe by 1st August 1943 (Trident Conference, May 1943, Papers and Minutes of Meetings Edited and Published by the Office, US Secretary, Office of the Combined Chiefs of Staff, 1943 (Digitised 2001), pp.122-123).

reception of this document and as Roosevelt sonorously read through it, all was going well until he reached Section IV, Paragraph 2c 'Operations in the Mediterranean to Eliminate Italy from the War', an innocuous paragraph which merely restated the Resolution B formula that the Theatre Commander would determine future Mediterranean operations following Husky's implementation. The paragraph did not identify specific operations but the failure to nominate Italy as the next Allied target inflamed Churchill who

> *hoped that it was not the intention of this paragraph to commit us to carrying out particular operations. For example, he would be very much opposed to any idea of an operation to capture Sardinia as a sequel to HUSKY. This would be an eccentric operation, which would have no influence on the securing of the great prize open to us if we could take the toe and heel of Italy, and gain touch with the insurgents of the Balkan countries.*

Revealing the depth of his Balkan, Turkish and eastern Mediterranean obsessions, Churchill insisted that

> *the prime factor which should be kept in mind was the position in the Balkans, where 34 Axis Divisions were held in play by rebels, who would become much more active if we could gain touch with them through Durazzo [in Albania]... Of course, if Italy went out of the war, then the Italian Divisions would have to withdraw, and Germany would either have to fill the gap, or retire to the Danube. The effect on Turkey would be very important... Operations in the general directions of the Balkans opened up very wide prospects, whereas the capture of Sardinia would merely place in our possession a desirable island.*[100]

Having expressed his concerns, Roosevelt, Marshall, King and Brooke all moved to pacify the fractious Premier, assuring him that the paragraph neither contained a hidden agenda nor confirmed or denied specific operations. Faced with such overwhelming opposition - including from his own CIGS - the Churchillian volcano sputtered and subsided, emitting one final warning puff that *"he should take further time to consider this paragraph, and said that he would propose certain amendments for consideration."*

---

[100] The emphasis on supporting partisan activity also reflected British hopes that German power could be weakened by resistance and subversion by captive peoples, obviating the need for an opposed landing.

In the end, Churchill proposed no further amendments and CCS 242/3 was finally approved as CCS 242/6 'Final Report of the Combined Chiefs to the President and Prime Minister.' However, this would not be the last occasion on which Churchill's Balkan, Turkish and eastern Mediterranean passions provoked dissent.

IV

Despite Churchill and Brooke's best efforts, Trident must be considered an American victory - the invasion of Italy was not confirmed as a follow-up to Husky, Roundup was tied to a precise date (1st May, 1944) and forces were to leave the Mediterranean to prepare for Roundup. The one crumb of comfort Trident afforded Churchill was that the direction of future Mediterranean operations now lay in Eisenhower's gift so, as soon as Trident concluded, Churchill and Brooke resolved to visit Ike in his Algiers HQ to convince him of the need to invade Italy. To ensure that Eisenhower wasn't overwhelmed by Churchillian rhetoric, General Marshall accompanied Brooke and Churchill on this trip and - whenever Churchill raised substantive issues on the flight over - Marshall sidetracked him by soliciting his opinion on a wide range of eccentric subjects unconnected to the war.[101] Ever eager to share his profound insights, Churchill swallowed the bait every time, outsmarted by a superior tactician.

Churchill, Brooke, Marshall and Eisenhower - joined from time to time by Eden, Tedder, Montgomery and Cunningham - met several times in Eisenhower's Algiers HQ between 29th May and 3rd June. Churchill was transparent in his motives for visiting Eisenhower, championing Italian operations and recycling arguments rejected at Trident. Eisenhower may well have succumbed to Churchillian rhetoric had it not been for the presence of Marshall who was determined to discourage any outbreak of 'localitis'.[102] Such was Churchill's zeal to invade Italy that he offered to strip the Middle East of eight British-imperial divisions to support the campaign and cut the British people's already meagre food ration to provide shipping for these divisions. As Churchill put it,

> *it would be hard for me to ask the British people to cut their rations again, but I would gladly do so rather than throw away a campaign which had possibilities of great success.*

---

[101] Topics covered in this manner included the Abdication Crisis, the Hess flight to Scotland and Warren Hastings' Governor-Generalship of India (Eisenhower, *Allies,* pp.299-302).

[102] Marshall's term for the tendency of commanders to always request more resources for their own theatre, regardless of the overall picture.

In other words, Churchill - who was exceptionally well fed and watered throughout the conflict[103] - was willing to deprive the British people of food to maintain Britain's Mediterranean dominance.

Eden attended the 31st May session and startled the Americans by assuring them that Turkey would become more amenable to Allied interests *"when our troops had reached the Balkan area."* Marshall and his colleagues were astounded by Eden's remarks which confirmed their worst fears that Britain wanted to drag the war into the Balkans for purely imperial purposes. Churchill moved to squelch American concerns by *"observ[ing] emphatically that he was not advocating sending an army into the Balkans now or in the near future"* but he would break this undertaking in 1944 by advocating Operation Armpit - a plan to land Allied forces in the northern Adriatic in the hope of entering Austria via the so-called 'Ljubljana Gap'[104] - as an alternative to a landing in southern France (Dragoon).

Marshall said little throughout these discussions, sticking to the Trident formula that post-Husky operations were best planned following Husky's implementation, enabling the Allies to gauge both the Axis response and evaluate conditions in Russia. Blinded by his Italian enthusiasms, Churchill misinterpreted Marshall's silence as tacit support for Mediterranean operations, a notion he only abandoned later with the greatest reluctance.

V

This chapter must conclude by considering the remarks attributed to General Brooke in the chapter's introduction for, if true, they reveal a deeply held - though rarely voiced - antipathy to cross-Channel operations under almost any circumstance. This quote features in Eisenhower's 1948 memoir *Crusade in Europe* and, following the book's publication, Brooke insisted that Eisenhower had misheard, misinterpreted or misremembered him. No third party was present to confirm or deny Eisenhower's account so, in judging the accuracy of his recollection, one must evaluate Brooke's purported remarks within the context of other substantiated evidence. Chapters Twelve

---

[103] His 7th September 1944 dinner menu on the Queen Mary included *"oysters, consommé, turbot, roast turkey, ice with cantaloupe melon, Stilton cheese and a great variety of fruit, petit fours etc; the whole washed down by champagne (Mumm 1929) and a very remarkable Liebfraumilch, followed by some 1870 brandy"* (Gilbert, *Churchill, Vol. VII: Road to Victory,* 1941-45, p.941).

[104] Ljubljana is the capital of present-day Slovenia and the 'gap' refers to a slight break in the Julian and Dinaric Alps (which run parallel to the Dalmatian coast). Operation Armpit was an entirely fanciful scheme, discussed in detail in Chapters 28 and 29.

and Fourteen introduced a range of British strategy documents - authored by Churchill and his Chiefs - which maintained that *"we cannot hope... even with full American help, to defeat the existing German Army in the field"* and *"there can be no question of an advance in force against the German armies on the mainland of Europe."* Convinced that an opposed landing against unbroken German forces would provoke disaster, British strategists maintained that Allied forces could only return to Europe after German power had been broken through prolonged bombing, blockade and subversion, enabling Allied armies to enjoy a stately progress to Berlin during which disorganised enemy forces were merely 'rounded up'.[105]

We also have Brooke's argument at Trident that *"no major operations would be possible until 1945 or 1946"* because eighty French divisions were unavailable to support the Allies. We have also noted how senior British figures appeared to endorse Sledgehammer/Roundup in spring 1942 only to renege on this commitment by July. Taking all this evidence into account, the comments attributed to Brooke by Eisenhower appear to be highly consistent with both the historical record and official British statements.

Subsequent chapters will consider additional evidence on this topic but the final word goes to Dwight Eisenhower who revisited the subject in his final years (1967-69). By this time, Eisenhower was a two-term American President and five-star General of the Army with a reputation for unimpeachable integrity. He had scaled every peak open to him, was not considered a vindictive man and - perhaps more than any other - had forged Anglo-American forces into a war-winning coalition. He had neither the need nor motive to impugn a former colleague and yet, in his final writing on the subject, Eisenhower repeated his 1948 remarks - in sharpened form - indicating that, in his mind at least, he had no doubt over Brooke's comments. The quote below is extracted from Eisenhower's 104-page manuscript on Anglo-American relations[106] and readers can decide if it accurately reflects

---

[105] The first plan for a British (or Allied) return to the continent was developed by British planners in late 1941 and code-named 'Roundup.' It was premised on the notion that German power in Europe might collapse and that Allied forces could cross the Channel to 'round up' any remaining German forces as they advanced into the Franco-German interior. More realistic plans for an opposed cross-Channel assault were developed during 1942-43 but the name 'Roundup' remained until replaced by Overlord in July 1943. The Allies, particularly the British, still hoped for a sudden crumbling of German resistance (as occurred in 1918) and developed plans for a swift return to the continent following such a collapse (codenamed Rankin) (Robert H. Keyserlingk, *Austria in World War II: An Anglo-American Dilemma* (1990), pp.28-29).

[106] Eisenhower hoped to produce a major work on the Anglo-American alliance in his final years but was too frail to complete the task. His son John used his unpublished 104pp manuscript in

Brooke's views. According to Eisenhower, Brooke was convinced that

> *the European fortress, defended by the Axis was, in a practical sense, invulnerable to any attack from the West... [Brooke] went on to explain that the proper role of the Western Allies in the European war was not to commit great land forces to bloody battlefields... We should 'thrust and peck' around the Axis perimeter, always threatening and feinting, but never attempting a major invasion. He had no objection to an attack on lower Italy but he argued that the destruction of Hitler's land forces was the business of the Soviets - while Allied contributions of our air and naval operations would make the Soviet task easier.*

If true, such comments clearly confirm the principal thesis of *Empire First* by demonstrating that Brooke - and Britain's military leadership - resolutely opposed Overlord in any form, and one can only speculate on his willingness to communicate these views privately to Ike and his reluctance to articulate them in a full Allied conference.

****

ROUNDUP BECOMES OVERLORD: In spring 1943, COSSAC developed three plans linked to cross-Channel operations. COCKADE was a deception operation designed to pin German forces to the coast; RANKIN was a plan for Allied forces to quickly re-enter western Europe in the event of a sudden German collapse; and OVERLORD was the planned full-scale assault on north-western Europe scheduled for summer 1944. General Morgan delivered his draft OVERLORD plan on 15th July 1943 and - from that date onwards - OVERLORD describes all Allied cross-Channel assault plans. ROUNDUP describes Channel assault plans before July 1943, OVERLORD is employed thereafter.

---

his own book (*Allies: Pearl Harbor to D-Day*). (Eisenhower, *Allies,* pp. xix-xx; Herbert Mitgang, *Eisenhower Manuscript Used By Son For A Book,* New York Times, 29 May 1982).

CHAPTER SEVENTEEN: GREEKS IN THE AMERICAN EMPIRE, JULY 1943

It is true... that the Americans consider we have led them up the garden path in the Mediterranean - but what a beautiful path it has proved to be. They have picked peaches here, nectarines there. How grateful they should be.

Winston Churchill at a July 1943 COS meeting

We cannot now rationally hope to be able to cross the Channel and come to grips with our German enemy under a British commander. His Prime Minister and his Chief of the Imperial Staff are frankly at variance with such a proposal. The shadows of Passchendaele and Dunkerque still hang too heavily over the imagination of these leaders... they have rendered lip service to the operation [but] their hearts are not in it.

Secretary of War Stimson to President
Roosevelt, 10th August 1943

The fortunes of war swung decisively towards the Allies in July 1943. Hitler's dreams of a grand eastern empire crumbled to dust on the steppes to the north and south of Kursk. Mussolini's pretensions were punctured by Allied successes in Sicily and - by the end of the month - he was a pariah, shunned by both King and colleagues. In that same month, Hamburg's citizens endured the torments of Gomorrah when a man-made firestorm ravaged their city, stealing air from the lungs of the living and immolating their broken remains. Arthur Harris had declared in June 1942 that the Nazis had *"sowed the wind, and now they are going to reap the whirlwind"* and - after July 1943 - this grim prophecy was fulfilled on an almost nightly basis over the Reich.

I

Whilst the Allies and Axis grappled for territorial advantage, Britain and America jostled for dominance within their politico-military marriage of convenience. Both sides had invested heavily in North Africa and their rivalries found eloquent expression within this theatre. In January 1943, Britain endorsed Eisenhower's elevation to supreme status in the hope that - in reality - his British subordinates would run the show but - four months later - Churchill and Brooke travelled to Ike's court in Algiers to try to convert him to 'Italy First'; Eisenhower quickly revealed how wrong they'd been to suppose him a man of straw. Churchill endorsed De Gaulle as the Free French figurehead while Roosevelt backed Giraud. When Roosevelt nominated Robert D. Murphy as his personal representative in North Africa, elevating him to ministerial rank, Churchill responded by appointing Harold MacMillan as Britain's Resident Minister in the Mediterranean, answerable to Number Ten. Britain presumed it had first call on American *largesse* but Roosevelt extended Lend Lease to French North Africa in November 1942 and re-armed eleven French colonial divisions. Britain resented this 'misuse' of scarce shipping and grumbled that such a move would place *"strong pressure on our imports programme"* but Roosevelt intended these divisions to play a key role in liberating France and - by equipping them - hoped to curry favour with the reborn Republic.

Invading Sicily intensified these rivalries. Sicily would be the first Axis territory over-run by the Allies and there would be no friendly domestic government or supportive colonial regime to administer it on their behalf. The Allies would have to exercise direct political and military control and precedents established in Sicily would influence events elsewhere. Britain had ceded influence over North Africa to the United States - to avoid antagonising the French - but Sicily, sitting athwart imperial lines of communication in the centre of the Mediterranean, was an entirely different matter. Britain had dominated this region for six decades and presumed it would do so indefinitely. Eden explained the matter thus to MacMillan:

> *Owing to vital British interests in the Mediterranean, there is something to be said for allowing us prime responsibility in this area [Sicily] and therefore instituting a British administration. We feel there is much force in this point of view.*

However, in the two months since his appointment, MacMillan had developed a strong working relationship with General Eisenhower at Allied Forces HQ (AFHQ) and Ike strongly endorsed a *"policy of joint Anglo-American responsibility and joint conduct of military government... to function under the Allied commander."* Moreover, the suave Etonian, with his patrician pedigree and classical learning, believed the experienced British could easily manipulate the *"great big, vulgar, bustling"* Americans and had no need for direct control as - with their expertise and knowledge - they could *"run AFHQ as the Greek slaves ran the operations of the Emperor Claudius."* He therefore advised Eden that

> *I do not like the terminology... regarding vital British interests in the Mediterranean. This is the old empire stuff that they [the Americans] hate so. We can get what we want without treading on these particular toes... I venture to suggest that your phrase 'instituting British administration' goes too far.*

Churchill exploded on learning of MacMillan's comments, tartly reminding his Resident Minister that

> *it is a great mistake... to be shy about defending… 'vital British interests in the Mediterranean'. I do not like your expression 'old empire stuff' which also seems to argue an apologetic outlook. In my experience... Americans respect Englishmen who do not hesitate to take a firm line about their country's rights and the British Empire.*

Chastened, the urbane classicist repented.

> *I stand corrected. But I only meant that there are fashions and phrases as in costume which it may be politic to follow. You can rely on me to fight hard for the substance of British Imperial interests. I would never surrender anything but the shadow.*

When Churchill learned in March 1943 that Marshall and Stimson might allow Britain to play the leading role in Italy, he intervened directly, informing Roosevelt that

> *in view of the fact that the force commander [Alexander] under the supreme direction of General Eisenhower will be British we should be senior partner in the military administration of enemy occupied territory in that area [Sicily]. Our proposal would be that under the supreme authority of General Eisenhower a British General Officer should be appointed as Military Governor of Husky-land and that he should be assisted by a joint Anglo-American staff. Thus there would be no dualism in the actual executive decisions on the spot.*

Whatever Marshall and Stimson thought - and they tended to prioritise military matters - Roosevelt was unimpressed and responded promptly to the PM's note. While accepting Alexander as Sicily's Military Governor, Roosevelt insisted that *"this military government should be presented to the world as a definitely joint Allied control and that there should be no 'senior partner'."* Moreover, given the close links between many Sicilians and their American brethren, Roosevelt affirmed that the military government should have

> *as much of an American character as possible. This could be accomplished... to some extent by appointing to the offices of the allied military government a large proportion of Americans.*

The same P.M. who had once chastised his Resident Minister for kowtowing to American interests now prostrated himself before the President, hoping

> *that [I] made it perfectly clear that I contemplated 'Husky' as our joint enterprise on terms of perfect equality... and with no question of a 'Senior Partner'... In the executive and administrative sphere there ought not to be two voices but only one voice which will say what you and I have agreed. General Alexander would be directing the military operations under the supreme commander and he would delegate the powers of military governor to a British Officer mutually agreeable to us both... All the above is of course without prejudice to the United States being supreme throughout the whole of French North Africa and my continuing to be your Lieutenant there. I hope I have given satisfaction.*

Within a fortnight of Churchill penning these unctuous phrases, the character of the Allied Military Government for Occupied Territories (AMGOT) was settled. One of MacMillan's old Balliol chums - Lord Rennell - was appointed Chief Civil Affairs Officer under Alexander, but an American - Colonel Julius Holmes - would head the Military Government Section at Eisenhower's Allied Forces HQ. Alexander was Eisenhower's subordinate and having an American in charge of military government affairs at AFHQ would ensure that, in reality, the Americans dominated Sicily's government while maintaining a façade of joint Allied control. MacMillan reassured Churchill that he could control Holmes and *"give full protection to British interests"* but - as time passed - the Americans had less and less need for their British ally except as a fig-leaf to conceal the naked reality of burgeoning American power. Until the end of war, Churchill railed against this new reality.

II

The invasion of Sicily (Husky) was planned by British officers so it's hardly surprising that a British general (Montgomery) was allotted the starring role. The invasion task force - larger than the one that landed in Normandy eleven months later - stormed ashore on either side of Cape Passero on 10th July, Monty to the east (charged with capturing Messina) and Patton's Seventh Army to the west (charged with protecting Monty's left flank as he advanced towards Messina).

Map 24: Operation Husky

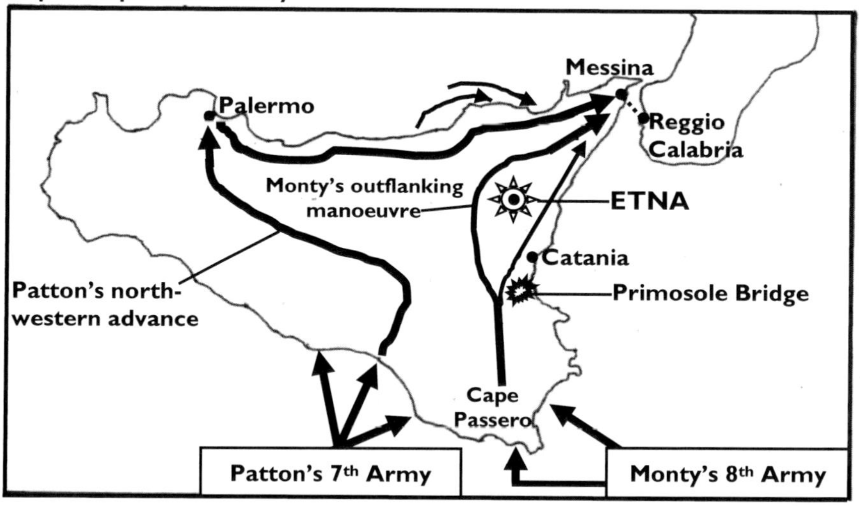

Unfortunately, Monty's paratroopers failed to take the Primosole Bridge on the first attempt and Eighth Army encountered stiff opposition in its attempts to take Catania, a port on Sicily's eastern seaboard. The Germans took up strong defensive positions around Mount Etna and - to counter this - Monty threw his forces in a wide looping arc to Etna's west to outflank his opponents. Without any consultation, he grabbed a road allocated to Patton's US Seventh Army, a move General Omar Bradley described as *"the most arrogant, egotistical, selfish and dangerous move in the whole of combined operations in World War II."* Stripped of its original purpose, Patton's army now moved north and west, acquiring acres of strategically worthless territory while garnering screeds of positive press. Palermo fell on 22nd July and Patton advanced towards Messina along the north coast while Montgomery moved up from the south. Messina fell on 17th August but not before 110,000 Germans and Italians and most of their equipment escaped. The conquest of Sicily was a considerable Allied victory but the slow pace of the campaign (Ike and Monty had hoped it might take a fortnight), the friction between Montgomery and the Americans (presaging later tensions) and the successful Axis evacuation (rescuing troops and supplies for later use against Allied forces) tainted the lustre of this successful operation.

III

The invasion of Sicily profoundly impacted global military affairs. In Russia, it contributed to Hitler's decision to cancel Citadel - his attempt to cauterise the Kursk salient - after just one week. Citadel was Germany's last great thrust in the east and its cancellation gave the Red Army its first warm weather triumph over German forces. Russia now dominated the Eastern Front.

Early successes in Sicily also convinced General Eisenhower to endorse an invasion of Italy following Husky. As Chapter 16 noted, Trident gave Eisenhower the right to determine future Mediterranean operations and - while Churchill clamoured for an early decision on Italy - Eisenhower adopted a cautious 'wait and see' policy. By 17th July, it was clear that Allied forces wouldn't be driven back into the sea so Eisenhower and his advisers approved an attack on Italy's mainland. For Eisenhower, this decision was taken to support Overlord by drawing German forces into the peninsula and by shutting down the theatre as a major focus for operations after the airbases around Foggia had been captured. For Churchill, every step into Italy offered extra opportunities to embroil the Allies within this sterile theatre.

The success of Husky also prompted Mussolini's demise and his replacement by Marshal Pietro Badoglio. The Badoglio government's long-term policy was uncertain but - during July and August - the Marshal protested his devotion to Hitler and the Axis while, at the same time, despatching emissaries to explore Allied peace terms. Hitler, in turn, graciously accepted Badoglio's protestations of loyalty but, at the same time, developed plans to occupy Italy as soon as the Marshal revealed his hand. The situation was pregnant with promise and - for Churchill - the downfall of the 'whipped jackal' offered full vindication of his 'Italy First' obsession.

IV

As these momentous events unfolded, Churchill started retreating from the Trident commitment to withdraw three experienced British divisions from the Mediterranean by 1st November. This commitment had been extracted under pressure but - freed from the need to conceal his feelings from his Allies - Churchill revealed his true preferences to trusted confidants and advisers. On 15th July - two days before Eisenhower committed to Italian operations - Churchill informed General Smuts that he would *in no circumstances allow the powerful British and British-controlled armies in the Mediterranean to stand idle... Not only must we take Rome and march as far north as possible in Italy, but our right hand must give succour to the Balkan patriots... I shall go to all lengths to procure the agreement of our allies. If not, we have ample forces to act by ourselves.*

In other words, Churchill was willing to break the great transatlantic alliance just as it was starting to bear fruit by acting unilaterally in pursuit of his addled Mediterranean-Balkan dream. A 19th July note to COS - just one week after Hitler cancelled Citadel - further clarified his strategic preferences.

I have no doubt myself that the right strategy for 1944 is a) Maximum post "Husky" certainly to the Po, with option to attack westward in the south of France or north-eastward towards Vienna, and meanwhile to procure the expulsion of the enemy from the Balkans and Greece. b) "Jupiter" prepared under the cover of Overlord. I do not believe that 27 Anglo-American divisions are sufficient for Overlord in view of the extraordinary fighting efficiency of the German Army, and the much larger forces they could so easily bring to bear against our troops even if the landing were successfully accomplished.

To clarify any uncertainty, the Po River runs through Italy's far north - three hundred miles north of Rome - and passes through Turin and Piacenza before discharging into the Gulf of Venice. Churchill was therefore advocating a campaign to occupy the entire Italian peninsula and then - after Allied forces had slogged six hundred miles through extremely rugged and easily defensible terrain[107] - was proposing a left turn into southern France or a right wheel into Austria via northern Yugoslavia. These were not minor operations compatible with ambitious cross-Channel operations, they were alternatives to Overlord which could only proceed at Overlord's expense.

His antipathy towards Overlord is further evident in part (b) where he suggests that preparations for cross-Channel operations could serve as a cover or diversion for operations in northern Norway (Jupiter), a lunatic scheme which not even his senior advisers could

[107] Of course, Churchill may have hoped that German forces would simply withdraw to strong defensive positions in northern Italy and yield the bulk of the peninsula to Allied forces without a fight. In this, he would be sorely disappointed [see Chapters 18 and 19].

bring themselves to endorse.[108] Proposing Jupiter as a serious option at a time when the war was finally and irrevocably turning against Germany reveals Churchill's eternal enthusiasm for peripheral operations and his deep-rooted desire to shun decisive engagement with German forces, further revealed by his reference to *"the extraordinary fighting efficiency of the German Army."* His concern that the Germans - with their internal lines of communication - could reinforce a beachhead more rapidly than the Allies is entirely valid but Allied planners and commanders were determined to overcome this difficulty in 1944. And for someone who had supported the dispersal of Allied strength and avoidance of concentration in the United Kingdom to complain that 27 Anglo-American divisions were insufficient to mount a successful cross-Channel assault represents the most brazen hypocrisy. The Americans had initially proposed an assault force of 48 divisions (30 American, 18 British) in 1942/43 and this force was now reduced to 27 divisions, largely because of Churchill's enthusiasm for 'pinprick warfare' and dispersal of force.

A note to COS later that day further illustrates his enthusiasm for Jupiter and his antagonism towards Overlord. In this note he declared that *"the forces available in the United Kingdom 'will not be equal to the task of landing and maintaining themselves on land'."* Consequently, he advocated a revival of Jupiter because *"in my view* ***it is a preferable alternative [to Overlord] and, in all probability, the only one which will be open in the west*** *[emphasis added]."*

Churchill further emphasised his opposition to Overlord in a series of discussions with US War Secretary Henry Stimson during Stimson's visit to Britain in July. Stimson had travelled to Britain to review American troops,

> *but when I reached London, the P.M. virtually took possession of my movements for the first week and I found myself launched in the discussion of subjects and with people which I had not expected. These unexpected subjects were so important that I devoted the bulk of my time to their consideration and altered my trip accordingly.*

Stimson conferred with the two officers charged with planning Overlord (General Morgan and his US deputy, General Barker) and Foreign Secretary Eden but his most substantive discussions were

---

[108] When Brooke asked Churchill why he was so keen on Norwegian operations, Churchill simply stated that *"Hitler had unrolled the map of Europe starting with Norway and he [i.e. Churchill] would start rolling it up again with Norway."* (Chris Mann, *British Policy and Strategy Towards Norway, 1941-45* (2012), p.89).

necessarily with the PM. On 19th July - when Churchill was at his most vehement against Overlord - Stimson updated him on his discussions with Morgan and Barker - who both fully supported Overlord - and a transatlantic phone call to General Marshall in which the Army Chief reiterated his view that cross-Channel operations must take priority over Italian activities. Far from endorsing such views, Churchill

> *at once broke out into a new attack upon ROUNDHAMMER.*[109] *The check received by the British attack at Catania, Sicily, during the last few days had evidently alarmed him. He referred to it and praised the superlative fighting ability of the Germans. He said that if he had fifty thousand men ashore on the French Channel coast, he would not have an easy moment because he would feel that the Germans could rush up sufficient forces to drive them back into the sea. He repeated assertions he had made to me... of having the Channel full of corpses of defeated allies... I directly charged him that he was not in favour of the ROUNDHAMMER operation... On this he said that... if he was C-in-C he would not set up the ROUNDHAMMER operation.*

Churchill expressed his views with such vigour that Stimson believed

> *he was looking so constantly and vigorously for an easy way of ending the war without a trans-channel assault that, if we expected to be ready for a ROUNDHAMMER... early enough in 1944 to avoid the dangers of bad weather, we must be constantly on the lookout against Mediterranean diversions.*

The significance Churchill attached to Catania demands clarification. Catania lies on Sicily's east coast, some forty miles north of Siracusa (where Eighth Army landed) and Montgomery had initiated operations in this region on 13th July when paratroopers were ordered to capture the Primosole Bridge, seven miles south of Catania. However - due to fierce German resistance and initial difficulties in capturing the Bridge - Montgomery's forces didn't actually enter Catania until 5th August, some three weeks after it first became a focus for Eighth Army operations. The Battle of the Catania Plain was certainly a setback but not a reverse on a scale sufficient to threaten Overlord[110] and

---

[109] At this stage, Stimson hadn't started referring to the cross-Channel operation by its new Overlord code name. He still referred to it as a fusion of two earlier operations (Sledgehammer and Roundup) due to force of habit and to confuse potential Axis eavesdroppers.

[110] Eighth Army losses between 10th-21st July stood at 700 killed, 2239 wounded and 877 missing. Total Allied losses during Husky included 5,532 killed, 14,410 wounded and 2,819 missing (Morison, *Sicily-Salerno-Anzio,* p.179; Liddell Hart, *History of the Second World War*, p.562).

Churchill's emphasis on this event - and on *"the superlative fighting ability of the Germans"* - illuminates his thinking and the manner in which he intended to employ Italian operations to undermine Overlord. If the Allies enjoyed major victories in this theatre, Churchill would request additional forces - diverted from Overlord - to exploit and develop such achievements but if they sustained major reverses, he would also request additional forces - again drawn from Overlord - to prevent an Allied collapse. In Churchill's hands, Italy was a double-edged sword he could wield in either direction to hack away at Overlord's green shoots. Unfortunately for the Allies - and in contrast to Churchill's fanciful depiction of Italy as a 'soft underbelly' where Allied soldiers could enjoy peaches and nectarines - Italy would present many more threats to Overlord over the coming months.

V

Alarmed by Churchill's outbursts, Stimson recorded his thoughts on paper to present to Roosevelt on his return to Washington. After flying to Algiers to confer with Eisenhower, he drafted a note in which he characterised Churchill's peripheral strategy as being advanced not

> *as an aid to ROUNDHAMMER but as a substitute to supplant it. It contemplates an invasion from the south - in the direction of the Balkans and Greece or possibly towards southern France.... Such a southern invasion and the ROUNDHAMMER invasion cannot be both maintained. On the contrary, if they are both held in contemplation, they will be in constant interference and will tend to neutralise each other.*

Roosevelt invited Stimson to the White House to discuss these matters and on 10th August, Stimson drafted a further memo warning Roosevelt that

> *we cannot now rationally hope to be able to cross the Channel and come to grips with our German enemy under a British commander. His Prime Minister and his Chief of the Imperial Staff are frankly at variance with such a proposal. The shadows of Passchendaele and Dunkerque still hang too heavily over the imagination of these leaders of his government. Though they have rendered lip service to the operation, their hearts are not in it and it will require more independence, more faith and more vigour than it is reasonable to expect... in any British commander.*

Stimson therefore urged the President

> *that the time has come for you to decide that your government must assume the responsibility of leadership in this great final movement of the European war... We cannot afford to confer again and close with a lip tribute to BOLERO which we have tried twice and failed to carry out. We cannot afford to begin the most dangerous operation of the war under half-hearted leadership which will invite failure or at least disappointing results. Nearly two years ago the British offered us this command. I think that now it should be accepted - if necessary, insisted upon.... I believe that [General Marshall] is the man who most surely can now by his character and skill furnish the military leadership which is necessary to bring our two nations together in confident joint action in this great operation.*

While Stimson and Roosevelt were conferring, Marshall and the Joint Chiefs were also clarifying their views. Roosevelt was scheduled to meet the Chiefs at 2:15pm and he invited Stimson to sit in. Stimson recorded his impressions of the discussion by noting that

> *the President went the whole hog on the subject of ROUNDHAMMER. He was more clear and definite than I have ever seen him since we have been in this war and he took the policy that the American staff have been fighting for fully. He was for going no further into Italy than Rome and then for the purpose of establishing bases. He was for setting up as rapidly as possible a larger force in Great Britain for the purpose of ROUNDHAMMER so that... we should have more soldiers in Britain dedicated to that purpose than the British... He said he wanted to have an American commander and he thought that would make it easier if we had more men in the expedition at the beginning... The military and naval conferees were astonished and delighted at his definiteness.*

By the beginning of August - despite their successes in Sicily and elsewhere - Allied planning was close to crisis. Roosevelt was as supportive of Overlord as Churchill was hostile and - only five days after General Morgan submitted his draft Overlord plan to COS in London - those same British Chiefs issued a 'stand-still' order prohibiting the withdrawal of troops and resources from the Mediterranean theatre until further notice.[111] In other words, Britain

[111] Morgan submitted his draft Overlord plan on 15th July and COS issued its 'stand still' order five days later.

was reneging on a key Trident commitment to withdraw three battle-hardened British-imperial divisions from the Mediterranean to furnish Overlord's cutting edge. Further discussion was required to resolve this *impasse* and - on 17th August 1943 - the great and good of the Allied cause convened in Quebec for Quadrant.

CHAPTER EIGHTEEN: THE SONS OF BELISARIUS, AUGUST- SEPTEMBER 1943

If we once set foot on the Italian mainland we are in for a big commitment… The Americans… do not realise that limited operations in Italy e.g. against Naples are impossible. We must either stop at the Straits of Messina or go the whole hog.

General John Kennedy, 30th August 1943

I was ordered to invade the mainland of Europe without being given adequate resources, and without even being given any object... the High Command in the Mediterranean Theatre of War invaded Italy, and thus embarked on a major campaign on the continent of Europe, without having any clear idea - or plan - as to how they would develop the operations and fight the land battle... The whole affair was haphazard and untidy - in fact typically British.

Monty ponders Allied strategic shortcomings, 26th September 1943

Allied military power was clearly ascendant by August 1943. Axis strength was waning and Kursk reversed Germany's rape of Russia. Allied bombers were pounding Germany, Italy was suing for peace and the u-boats no longer threatened.[112] As of July 1943, the Combined Chiefs of Staff had a draft plan for liberating Europe, developed by General Morgan and his COSSAC colleagues. The Allies possessed a clear outline vision for reducing German power in the west and - in line with Trident - should have vigorously and wholeheartedly pursued this objective. Unfortunately, the British Chiefs remained profoundly pessimistic over any landing in France and were determined to exploit elements of Morgan's draft plan to undermine the fragile momentum building behind Overlord and divert Allied resources into the Mediterranean.

I

Morgan's vision was both prescient and a victim of circumstance. He correctly identified Normandy as the ideal location for a cross-Channel assault and - following the initial lodgement - advocated a thrust into the Cotentin peninsula to secure Cherbourg. Allied successes in summer 1944 owe much to Morgan's original vision.[113]

---

[112] Chapter 26 covers the Battle of the Atlantic.

[113] Chapter 22 examines Overlord's detailed planning.

However, Morgan's proposal was also the victim of circumstance, notably the dispersal of Allied resources and failure to concentrate force in Britain. Bolero had envisaged one million US troops in Britain by summer 1943 but as of July, barely 250,000 had arrived. Roundup had anticipated an assault force of 48 divisions (30 American and 18 British) but Morgan could only muster 26-30 divisions (a 40% reduction in scale) and his landing craft could only carry three divisions in the first assault, followed by two divisions later in the day. Overlord was the key to winning the war in the west but - in its original conception - was a chronically under-resourced operation with a tight margin of error. And after crossing eighty miles of open water, Allied forces would confront well-armed German troops occupying strong defensive positions and enjoying all the advantages of playing at home (albeit somebody else's home). Under such circumstances, Overlord was an extremely risky proposition.

Morgan's plan therefore contained three preconditions which - if fulfilled - would confer a *"reasonable prospect of success."* Firstly, the problem of 'beach maintenance' (i.e. reinforcing and provisioning troops once ashore) had to be resolved but Morgan also advocated:

(i) a major reduction in German fighter strength by May 1944; and
(ii) no more than twelve full-strength first-quality German divisions to be based in France and the Low Countries by May 1944, and Germany to deploy no more than fifteen first-quality divisions in France during Overlord's first two months.

If these conditions were fulfilled, Morgan believed his plan would succeed and he identified several means of realising these goals. For example, German fighter strength could be reduced *"by destruction of sources of supply, infliction of casualties by bringing on air battles, and, immediately prior to the assault, by the disorganisation of GAF [German Air Force] installations and control system[s] in the Caen area."* He also stressed that *"the conditions under which the operation might be successful do not depend solely on the numerical strength of the reserves available to the Germans. The scale of German resistance will depend on such things as the state of the French railways and the strength, quality, and morale of the enemy's front line units."* Morgan viewed his preconditions as challenges to be overcome rather than excuses for delay or justifications for diverting resources to other theatres. In point eight of his plan, Morgan admonished the Chiefs *"to adopt the outlook that Operation Overlord is even now in progress, and to take all possible steps to see that all agencies... are... coordinated in their action... and every possible effort made... to soften German resistance and to speed up our own preparations."*

However, as soon as the British Chiefs received Morgan's plan on 15th July, they pounced on his preconditions in an effort to undermine the project. They had a full month to consider the draft's implications before Quadrant convened on 14th August, and the five-day crossing on the *Queen Mary* offered Churchill and his Chiefs plenty of time to develop proposals to scupper Morgan's scheme.

COS responded to Morgan's plan in a 6th August aide memoire titled *Operations in the European Theatre of War* which - after lauding the impact of the Combined Bomber Offensive - noted that

> *65 per cent of the total German Fighter production, including the whole of their ME109 production, is situated in areas which are much more easily attacked from Northern Italy than from any of our existing bases... [and]... it is therefore clear that the possession of airfields in Northern Italy would be a considerable factor in achieving General Morgan's first condition.*

The Chiefs therefore advocated seizing airbases around Milan and Turin to bomb the Messerschmitt factories of Augsburg and Regensburg and diminish German fighter production.[114] They also highlighted Germany's relatively weak southern air defences and the disruptive impact of the Alps on German radar.

Acquiring airbases around Milan and Turin demanded control of the surrounding Po Valley and the aide memoire further contended that

> *the only way in which the large battle-tried British and American forces in North Africa can remain fully engaged with the enemy, and pave the way for the climax, is by pressing forward to exploit the success achieved against Italy. In doing so, we can ensure the fulfilment of General Morgan's second condition by drawing all Germany's disposable reserves to Northern Italy and by keeping them fighting there throughout the winter [of 1943-44].*

In other words, the Chiefs proposed to assist Overlord not by bolstering the size of the Normandy assault force or by striving to

---

[114] The possibility that the Germans might disperse their fighter production or that Augsburg and Regensburg could be bombed just as easily from central Italy didn't perturb the Chiefs.

influence battlefield conditions in northern France but by conducting major land operations in a theatre more than six hundred miles away. In summary, the Chiefs urged the Allies *"to exploit to the full our success against Italy by advancing with the Milan-Turin area as our objective."*

Map 25: Key 6th August Aide Memoire locations

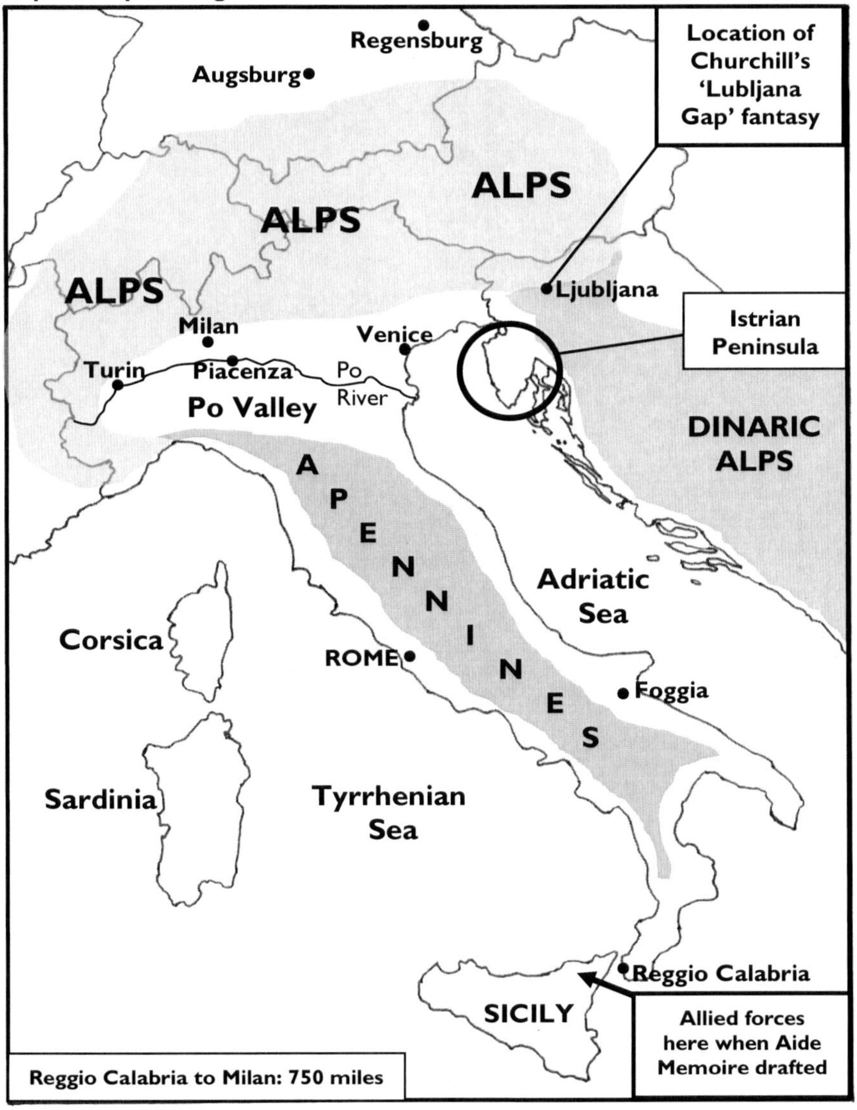

The absurdity of this scenario is self-evident. Italian operations were being proposed to assist Overlord which - at that time - was scheduled for 1st May 1944. To meaningfully assist Overlord, the Allies would therefore have to reach Milan-Turin by January 1944 to have sufficient time to repair any damage left behind by the Germans, adapt the airfields to Allied bomber use, significantly disrupt German fighter production and draw German forces down into Italy. However, the Allies were still struggling in Sicily when the aide memoire was drafted and would not land on the Italian mainland until early September. In short, the Chiefs were proposing a 750 mile advance up the Italian peninsula from Reggio Calabria to Milan in approximately four months, a rate of advance never before achieved against well-motivated and properly-equipped German troops. Three other considerations rendered this scenario highly fanciful.

Firstly, as a theatre of battle, Italy is infinitely more suited to defence than attack. Italian geography is dominated by

> *the central mountainous spine of the Apennines [which] rises above 10,000 feet and has lateral spurs that run east and west toward the coast, between which are deep valleys containing wide rivers flowing rapidly to the sea. The north-south roads are confined to 20-mile-wide strips adjacent to the Adriatic and Tyrrhenian coasts, where the bridges that carry them are dominated by natural strong points.*

The addition of minefields, road-blocks, barbed wire, blown bridges, machine-gun nests and concrete command bunkers would magnify the impenetrability of these barriers.[115]

Secondly, COS proposed to undertake this epic trek during autumn and winter (September to January) when snow, mud, rain, ice and swollen rivers would enhance any natural or man-made obstacles.

Finally, COS appears to have completely discounted the possibility of German resistance, a rather reckless omission. The tenacity of the German soldier - even when outnumbered and inadequately equipped - had been amply demonstrated in Tunisia and Sicily and similar resistance in Italy - aided by advantageous terrain and foul weather - would have reduced forward movement to a crawl. While the Chiefs were drafting these proposals, Hitler was reviewing his options in the light of conflicting advice from his senior commanders. Rommel - commanding Army Group B in the north - recommended a retreat to the northern Apennines to shorten German supply lines and avoid the danger of being outflanked by an amphibious assault. Kesselring, in

[115] Significantly, when General Brooke visited Italy in December 1943, he lamented: *"The terrain defies description. It's like the North-West Frontier; a single destroyed culvert can hold up an army for a day."* (Roberts, *Masters and Commanders*, p.463). Given Brooke's skills as a tactician, it's surprising that he never thought to invest sixpence in a basic Italian geography primer or thought to consult an Italian topography expert before committing major forces to Italy. Perhaps the information gleaned through such enquiries might have proved inconvenient?

charge of southern Italy, counselled a spirited defence south of Rome to exploit the favourable terrain and maintain distance between enemy forces and the Reich. Hitler would determine the practicality of the COS proposals but would wait until after the Allies had landed in Italy and committed major resources to the region before committing to any course of action.

The 6th August aide memoire therefore represents British 'soft underbelly' thinking at its most delusional. For reasons best known to themselves, COS continually perceived Italy as an arena of easy victories and rapid advances, even when bitter experience and mounting casualty figures contradicted this naïveté. One can only conclude that the desire to retain control of the Mediterranean and dodge decisive engagement with German forces blinded them to military and logistical reality. They certainly perceived French and Italian operations by starkly contrasting lights. While the 6th August aide memoire blithely advocated a 750 mile advance up the Italian peninsula in the middle of winter, the Chiefs' 10th August Overlord appreciation highlighted the difficulties Allied troops must face in Normandy in the summer, including "*the handicap under which our newly-landed divisions must suffer when engaging the enemy's divisions which have all along been established on land*" and the "*country south of the Caen beaches [which] is...* ***admirable for delaying actions*** *[emphasis added].*" This assessment also acknowledged the "*recent experience in Sicily [which] shows that if the enemy is resisting fiercely... the advance is bound to be slow.*" In other words, unfavourable terrain and fierce enemy resistance in Italy could be used to oppose operations in Normandy but - in the Chief's topsy turvy view - had no bearing at all on Italian operations! The mental elasticity required to reconcile such inconsistency is astonishing and - if similar eccentricity and bias coloured the COS position at Quadrant - the conference was bound to be stormy.

II

Quadrant was preceded by two days of informal discussion between Churchill and Roosevelt at the latter's Hyde Park home in upstate New York. The Joint Chiefs remained nervous about their boss's susceptibility to Prime Ministerial blather but the favourable military situation and America's growing military-industrial muscle insulated Roosevelt against Churchillian rhetoric more effectively than any admonition from General Marshall. America was on its way to becoming the world's dominant power and no amount of Churchillian hyperbole could counter this.[116] The only issue of substance confirmed at Hyde Park was that an American officer would command Overlord, and Churchill's willingness to concede on this ensured that British officers would exercise command in imperially sensitive theatres where British or imperial troops formed the majority. Mountbatten would lead the newly formed South East Asia Command (dubbed 'Saving England's Asian Colonies' by American wags) while General Maitland Wilson assumed command in the Mediterranean following Eisenhower's departure for Overlord. As Churchill acknowledged on 2nd September, *"it will be a great advantage to us to have our own Commander [in the Mediterranean] and to be able to correspond directly and constantly with him"* and the rationale behind such a remark is obvious.

Quadrant opened at 10:30am on Saturday 14th August with an agreement on meeting times and a review of global strategy but - given the gulf separating British and American positions[117] - differences quickly emerged. General Brooke opened on 15th August by emphasising his deep-rooted support for Overlord ("*the British Chiefs of Staff were in entire agreement that Overlord should constitute the major offensive for 1944*") before throwing up impediments to its implementation. The American insistence on *"over-riding priority"* for Overlord was *"too binding,"* with Brooke arguing that *"sufficient forces must be used in Italy in order to make Overlord a possibility."* Advocating an advance to northern Italy, Brooke insisted that

> *some 20 divisions might be required to hold the neck of Italy which might entail retaining three of the seven divisions earmarked for Overlord. If the Milan-Turin area were taken, then all seven might be required, but a decision should be deferred until it could be seen what forces were required to attain the desired result.*

---

[116] Between Sept 1939-Aug 1945, America provided 78% of Britain's tank transports, 60% of its transport and air-sea rescue aircraft, 47% of its tanks and 38% of its landing craft and ships (Postan, *British War Production,* p.247).

[117] America's Quadrant agenda was summarised in a 9th August document, 'Strategic Concept for the Defeat of the Axis in Europe' (CCS 303). In this paper, the US Chiefs argued that weakness had forced the Allies to pursue an opportunistic strategy in the early years of the war but with the tide now turning in the Allies' favour - they advocated *"the adoption of and adherence to sound strategic plans which envisage decisive military operations conducted at times and places of our choosing - not the enemy's."* To achieve this, the Americans insisted on rigid implementation of the Trident agreement, *"overriding priority"* for Overlord and the withdrawal of seven battle-hardened divisions from the Mediterranean by November 1943. They also supported a southern French landing for summer 1944 to divert German forces from Normandy and gainfully employ American-equipped French colonial divisions based in North Africa (World War Two Inter-Allied Conferences. Quadrant Conference, 1943. Papers and Minutes of Meetings (Joint History Office, Washington DC, 2003), pp.72-83).

Brooke was therefore not only proposing to renege on the Trident commitment to return seven experienced divisions to the UK, but was also suggesting that Overlord could be strengthened by stripping it of essential resources, a quixotic approach from a self-proclaimed master of strategy.

Brooke's comments drew a sharp retort from Admiral King who observed that *"the British Chiefs of Staff had serious doubts as to the possibility of accomplishing Overlord"* but it was General Marshall who deftly dissected the British threat to cross-Channel operations. In his view, *"the essence of the problem was whether or not the required conditions for a successful Overlord could only be made possible by an increase in the strength in the Mediterranean"* and while it would be preferable for the Allies, rather than the Axis, to control Milan and Turin, he insisted that

> *unless a decision were taken to remove the seven divisions from the Mediterranean, and unless overriding priority was given to Overlord... Overlord would become only a subsidiary operation... [and the] whole strategic concept would have to be recast and the United States forces in Britain might well be reduced to the reinforced army corps necessary for an opportunist cross-Channel operation... in which case we should be depending for the defeat of Germany on air bombing alone.*

In such a case, Marshall warned that

> *we were opening a new concept which in his view weakened our chances of an early victory and rendered necessary a re-examination of our basic strategy, with a possible readjustment towards the Pacific.*

Already, by day two of the conference, Marshall was deploying arguments the British simply couldn't countenance (i.e. American disengagement from Europe and re-orientation towards the Pacific) and, as at Trident, 'off the record' discussions were required to resolve this impasse by enabling the principals to voice their opinions and find compromise without losing face. General Brooke's diary offers a flavour of these terse conversations on 16th and 17th August.

> *Our talk was pretty frank. I opened by telling them that the root of the matter was that we were not trusting one another. They doubted our real intentions to put our full hearts into the*

> *cross-Channel operation next spring, and we had not full confidence that they would not in future insist in our carrying out previous agreements irrespective of changed strategic conditions. I then had to go over our whole Mediterranean strategy to prove its objects... and finally I had to produce countless arguments to prove the close relation that exists between cross-Channel and Italian operations.*

However disagreeable the discussions, the Chiefs had to converge on strategy to preserve Allied unity and present a united front to their masters. Churchill and Roosevelt were scheduled to attend a plenary session on 19th August and - if the Chiefs couldn't agree - their civilian bosses would intervene, a prospect which alarmed the commanders.

The compromise document of 17th August (CCS 303/3) was essentially the 9th August American document (CCS 303) with a few token concessions to appease the British. Where the original American paper had insisted on *"over-riding priority"* for Overlord in the allocation of resources, CCS 303/3 noted that *"resources will be distributed and employed with the main object of insuring the success of Overlord."* The American Chiefs' insistence that seven battle-hardened divisions be withdrawn from the Mediterranean to provide Overlord's cutting edge was replaced by a more ambiguous declaration that Mediterranean operations should be conducted with the forces allocated at Trident *"except insofar as these may be varied by decision of the Combined Chiefs of Staff."* As the Joint Chiefs sat on the Combined Chiefs body, the flexibility seemingly conferred by this concession was entirely illusory. Finally, the connection between Italian and French operations so dear to the British was reflected by a commitment to maintain *"unremitting pressure on German forces in Northern Italy, and the creation of the conditions required for Overlord and of a situation favourable for the eventual entry of our forces... into southern France."* CCS 303/3 also advocated a landing in southern France to assist Overlord by drawing German forces away from Normandy and while the British Chiefs initially endorsed this proposal, they later repudiated it.

If CCS 303/3 largely embodies American strategic preferences, this simply reflects the shifting balance of power. Britain needed American money, munitions and *matériel* to continue fighting and this dependency circumscribed British freedom of action. Eureka would further expose the harsh realities of Allied power politics.

Having concocted their compromise, the Chiefs presented it to Churchill and Roosevelt for approval and while Roosevelt rarely offered direct military advice - appreciating his limitations as a strategist - Churchill suffered no such inhibitions and was always willing to enhance any paper with his masterly insights. His comments on 19th August - and at a subsequent session on 23rd August - betray the blend of idiosyncrasy and inconsistency that made him such a challenging master to serve.

Responding to the paper's suggestion that Overlord receive priority in the allocation of resources, Churchill re-emphasised General Morgan's preconditions and stated that Overlord's implementation depended *"on certain conditions being fulfilled regarding relative strengths... [and]... if the German strength [in terms of divisions in France] proved to be considerably greater than this, the plan should be subject to revision by the Combined Chief of Staff."* However, having expressed some caution over Overlord, Churchill then exceeded his Staff by proposing that *"every effort should be made to add at least twenty-five percent strength to the initial [Overlord] assault,"* a suggestion speedily endorsed by Marshall. In all their analyses of Overlord, the British Chiefs had never considered the possibility of expanding the initial assault force and Churchill deserves credit for correcting this omission. Churchill hoped that the additional landing craft required by the larger force could be constructed in the nine months remaining before Overlord.

Turning to Italy, Churchill advised that *"he was not committed to an advance into Northern Italy beyond the Ancona-Pisa Line"* contradicting not only his own Chiefs - who had advocated an advance to Milan-Turin - but his own 19th July strategy paper. From the outset, Churchill opposed landings in southern France, declaring that *"he would be hesitant in putting our good divisions into that area to meet the resistance which might be anticipated, and he doubted therefore if French divisions would be capable of an operation of the kind suggested."* A minor issue at Quadrant, strong British opposition to Anvil (the southern French landing) would sour Anglo-American relations in 1944.

Finally, on 23rd August, Churchill revived his favoured old chestnut - Operation Jupiter, the descent on northern Norway. While *"he did not in any way wish to imply that he was not wholeheartedly in favour of Overlord... he wished to emphasize that its launching was dependent upon certain conditions"* and he felt that the United Nations should *"have a 'second string to their bow' in the form of a prepared plan to undertake Operation Jupiter."* To pacify the Prime Minister, the conference agreed to *"include [in the final report] a paragraph which would provide for continued planning for the launching of Operation Jupiter in the event that*

Overlord should have to be abandoned," a concession unlikely to enhance General Brooke's good humour

Quadrant had been called to reassert Overlord's primacy in British-American strategic thinking and the Final Report to the President and Prime Minister (CCS 319/5) summarised ten days of discussion by confirming Overlord as

> *the primary US-British ground and air effort against the Axis in Europe (Target Date 1 May 1944)... [and]... available resources were to be distributed and employed with the main object of insuring the success of Overlord. Operations in the Mediterranean theatre will be carried out with the forces allotted at Trident except insofar as these may be varied by decision of the Combined Chiefs of Staff.*

Morgan's draft plan was approved and he was *"authorised... to proceed with the detailed planning and with full preparations"* for a cross-Channel assault. British hopes for advancing to Milan-Turin were replaced by a vague commitment to maintain *"unremitting pressure on German forces in Northern Italy, and the creation of the conditions required for Overlord and of a situation favourable for the eventual entry of our forces... into Southern France."* The southern French landing *"to create a diversion in connection with Overlord"* was endorsed and the 20th July COS 'stand-still' order was revoked on 19th August. However, Churchill and COS would continue to agitate against southern French operations throughout the first half of 1944.

Churchill and Brooke expressed some satisfaction over Quadrant but it's difficult to see why. COS had arrived in Quebec with an outlandish proposal to advance 750 miles through rugged Italian terrain in four winter months but left having given their support to a document confirming Overlord as *"the primary US-British ground and air effort against the Axis in Europe"* for 1944, and which relegated Italian operations to secondary status. Marshall knew that Italian operations, once launched, had the capacity to siphon resources away from Overlord and had taken steps to ensure Italy never became the 'suction pump' Churchill and his Chiefs hoped it might become.[118]

---

[118] The British Joint Planning Staff entertained even more fantastic hopes for Italian/Mediterranean operations. In their COS (T) 11 paper they argued that *"the Mediterranean offers us opportunities for action in the coming autumn and winter which may be decisive, and at the least will do far more to prepare the way for a cross-Channel operation in 1944 than we should achieve by attempting to transfer back to the United Kingdom any of the forces now in the Mediterranean theatre. If we take these opportunities, we shall have every chance of breaking the Axis and of bringing the war to a successful conclusion in 1944."* In other

III

As Quadrant drew to a close, Generals Castellano and Zanussi were despatched from Rome to Lisbon and Madrid to ascertain Allied peace terms. The Italians wanted an Allied presence in Italy before Germany consolidated its grip on the peninsula while the Allies wanted Italy out of the war before any landing on the mainland. With the two sides pursuing complementary goals, the Armistice of Cassibile was signed on 3rd September but remained secret until 8th September, shortly before the Allied landing at Salerno (Avalanche). If the Allies could establish a strong presence in Italy before Germany responded, British hopes of reaching Milan by January might yet be fulfilled.

Unfortunately, Hitler had been anticipating Italian treachery for some time and had deployed sixteen divisions throughout the country to ensure it didn't fall easily into enemy hands. German forces secured key locations such as Rome, Florence and Milan once the armistice was announced, and Italian troops were offered the opportunity to serve alongside their former German comrades or face internment in labour camps. The Badoglio government relocated to Brindisi in southern Italy on 9th September and although Italy eventually joined the United Nations, it became just one more country requiring liberation from Nazi control.

Operation Avalanche (the Salerno landing) had been concocted in haste following Mussolini's downfall on 25th July and the operation's near failure reflected this speedy improvisation. Two British divisions (46th and 56th) and one American division (36th) landed at Salerno Bay - thirty-five miles south of Naples - but were spread over a thirty-five mile defensive perimeter and separated from each other by the Sele River. If the Germans - on the bluffs overlooking the bay - advanced down the river to the sea, they could split the Allied force in two and defeat it in detail.

And this almost happened. Kesselring ignored the lesser Allied landings at Reggio di Calabria (3rd September) and Taranto (9th September) and concentrated Tenth Army against the Salerno beachhead. By 14th September, the Allied position was so precarious that General Clark - the Allied commander - was contemplating withdrawal, a move carrying grave implications for Allied morale and

---

words, the Joint Planners felt that a concentration on Italy and the Mediterranean during 1943/44 might actually end the war in 1944 without requiring a cross-Channel assault! (Michael Howard, *History of the Second World War, Grand Strategy*, Vol. IV, 1942- 1943, p.419).

strategy. In the end, Clark was saved by massive naval and aerial bombardments of the German positions and by airborne forces landing directly on the beachhead. By 16th September, Germany's Tenth Army was considering withdrawal and on that same day, foot patrols from 36th Division inside the perimeter linked up with advance units of Monty's Eighth Army - pushing up from Reggio Calabria - to secure the beachhead. German forces withdrew in good order on 18th September, Naples was liberated on 1st October and by 6th October, Allied forces controlled all of Italy south of the Volturno and Biferno Rivers. Hopes of advancing to the Po Valley by January 1944 now seemed eminently feasible.

Map 26: Operation Avalanche and the Volturno-Biferno Line

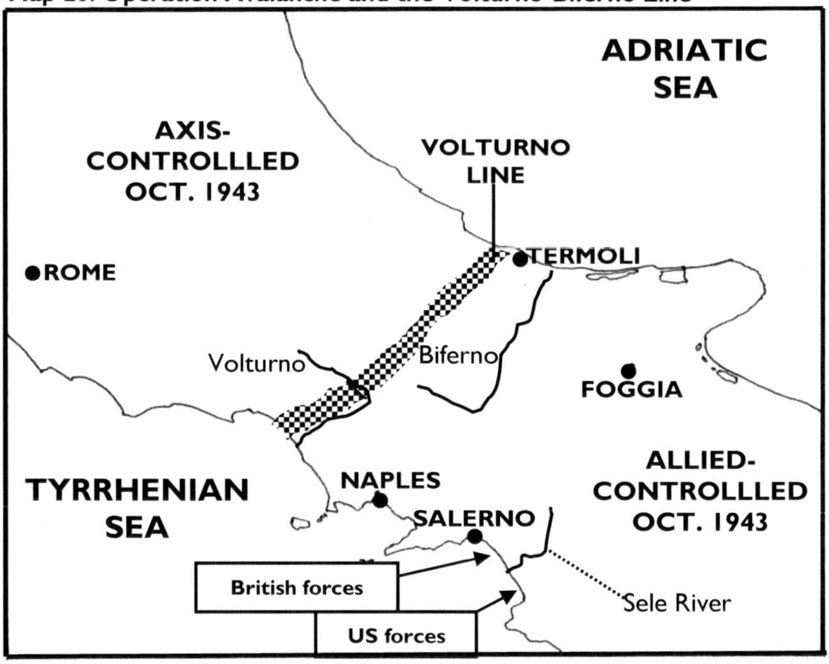

Unfortunately, German resistance now stiffened as Hitler increasingly endorsed Kesselring's plans and his own rebarbative instinct to contest every inch of Italy[119]. During September - when the Germans declined to contest southern Italy - the Allies had advanced more than three hundred miles in just over a month but, coming up against the

---

[119] Hitler issued orders - on 4th October and 6th November - committing German forces to defend the Bernhardt Line south of Monte Cassino. Kesselring's triumph was complete on 21st November when Rommel was transferred out of Italy - to command German forces in France - and Kesselring assumed command of the entire Italian peninsula (Richard Raiber, *Anatomy of Perjury: Field Marshal Albert Kesselring, Via Rasella, and the Ginny Mission* (2008), p.38; Peter Caddick-Adams, *Monte Cassino: Ten Armies in Hell* (2012), p.17).

four defensive positions of the Winter Line,[120] Allied progress stuttered to a halt and gained barely forty miles in the three months between October 1943 and January 1944. By mid-January, the Allied advance was blocked by the vertical massif of Monte Cassino and the Gustav Line and remained stalled for four further months until Rome - only eighty miles away - finally fell on 4th June, two days before D-Day.[121] Milan and Turin remained under German control until April 1945 and the 'soft underbelly' of Churchillian fantasy proved to be - in Mark Clark's words - an extremely 'tough old gut'.

Map 27: German Winter Line Positions

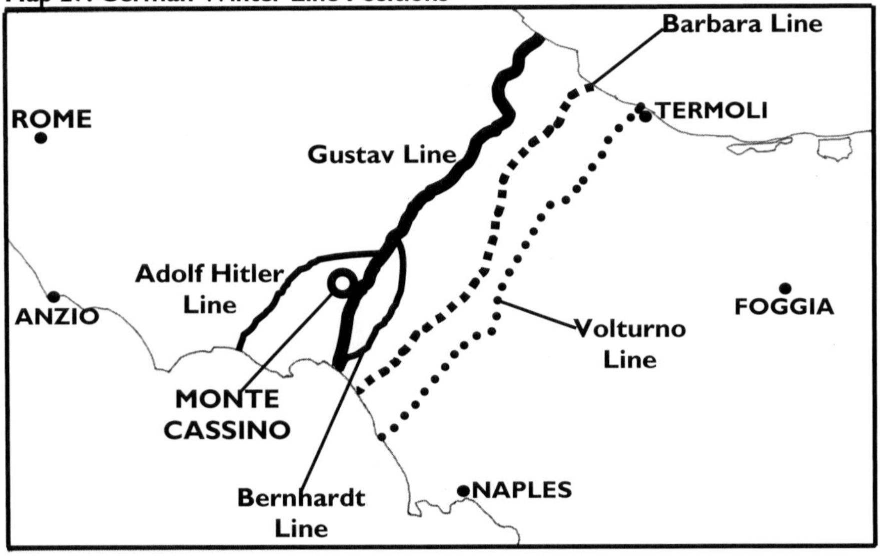

Not since Belisarius in the sixth century had a commander entered Italy from the south and advanced successfully to the north. Most had observed Napoleon's dictum that *'Italy is like a boot. You must... enter it from the top.'* As Allied forces settled into the hellish stalemate of an Italian winter, the cold and hungry troops on the ground experienced the bitter wisdom of this historical precedent.

---

[120] The Winter Line consisted of three defensive lines (Volturno, Barbara and Gustav) stretching from the Adriatic to the Tyrrhenian plus one line (Bernhardt) which offered extra protection to the Gustav Line south of Monte Cassino. These defensive lines were built *"to create an impregnable system of positions in depth, and so to save German blood."* They certainly conserved German blood, exacting a high toll on Allied forces in terms of casualties and resources required to overcome these obstacles (Alex Bowlby, *Countdown to Cassino: The Battle of Mignano Gap, 1943* (1995), p.8; Atkinson, *The Day of Battle*, p.254).

[121] Using these figures, Allied forces advanced 120 miles in eight months, averaging fifteen miles per month - so much for the 'soft underbelly'!

CHAPTER NINETEEN: OVERLORD SPELLED T-Y-R-A-N-T, September- November 1943

I will not allow the great and fruitful campaign in Italy to be cast away and end in a frightful disaster, for the sake of crossing the Channel in May. The battle must be nourished and fought out until it is won... Eisenhower and Alexander must have what they need to win the battle, no matter what effect is produced on subsequent operations. Stalin ought to be told bluntly that Overlord might have to be postponed.

Churchill to Lord Moran,
26th October 1943

To satisfy American shortsightedness we have been led into agreeing to the withdrawal of forces from the Mediterranean for a nebulous 2nd Front, and have emasculated our offensive strategy... I despair of ever getting our American friends to have any sort of strategic vision. Their drag on us has seriously affected our Mediterranean strategy and the whole conduct of the war.

General Brooke diary entries,
1st and 20th November 1943

Italy's surrender and the disintegration of its armed forces created a unique window in which Churchill's Mediterranean fantasies might yet be fulfilled. In Italy - for a fleeting moment - it conjured up the prospect of a stately progress up the peninsula, liberating historic towns and cities along the way. In the Balkans it created an opportunity to foment mass guerrilla activity and deprive Germany of vital raw materials. In the Aegean, it stimulated the possibility of Turkey entering the war to fulfil Churchill's deepest fantasies. The failure of these schemes by mid-October sparked a fierce backlash against Overlord in British circles which highlighted their profound opposition to Channel ventures and strong preference for Mediterranean initiatives.

I

With its extended Mediterranean coastline and land borders with Syria, Iraq, Iran and Russia, Turkey has always loomed large in imperial thinking. Britain and France supported the Ottomans against the Romanovs in the Crimean War and - a quarter of a century later - Britain supported Turkey in the Peace Conference following its 1877-78 conflict with Russia, gaining Cyprus as a reward. Churchill's early career ran aground at Gallipoli, while Lloyd George committed political suicide by threatening war with Turkey in 1922.[122]

Turkey remained significant in the era of the dictators. Britain guaranteed Turkey against Italy in May 1939 and - five months later - concluded a Treaty of Alliance with Turkey to defend its Mediterranean interests, consolidate its control of Middle Eastern oil and enhance its dominance over Suez.

Unfortunately, with Britain fighting for its life during 1940-42, the Anglo-Turkish Alliance proved to be something of a dead letter as Turkey found itself ringed by a trio of predators to the north, south and west. When Germany ripped into Russia during 1941/2, it gained control of the Black Sea and access to Turkey's exposed northern coastline, while Germany, Bulgaria and Italy devoured Greece in 1941. Germany claimed the territory adjacent to Turkey's European land border (Evros), while Bulgaria claimed Eastern Macedonia and the rest of Western Thrace (gaining an outlet to the Aegean)[123] and Italy occupied most of southern Greece and the Greek islands. Threatened on three fronts, Turkey upheld the neutrality it had hastily proclaimed in June 1940 and engaged in a vigorous commerce with Germany, exchanging raw materials for military-industrial hardware.

Allied victories at El Alamein and Stalingrad and the success of the Torch landings transformed the political landscape, with Churchill travelling to Adana directly after Casablanca to confer with Turkey's President Inönü. If Turkey joined the Allies, Germany would be forced to divert troops from other theatres to its south-eastern flank, while Allied bombers could range across the Balkans to threaten Romanian oil production. Gaining the Dardanelles would allow Britain and America to supply Russia via the Black Sea and Churchill even dreamed of joint Anglo-Soviet naval operations.

---

[122] The 'Chanak Crisis' erupted in September 1922 when the newly formed Turkish Republic demanded the withdrawal of all foreign forces based in Turkey, including the British garrison at Çannakale (Chanak) in the southern Dardanelles. Prime Minister Lloyd George refused and threatened war between Turkey and the British Empire. Appalled by his handling of the crisis, the Conservatives withdrew their support on 19th October and a General Election was called for 15th November. The Conservatives won an overall majority, Bonar Law became PM and Lloyd George never held high office again (Mark Clapson, *The Routledge Companion to Britain in the Twentieth Century* (2009), p.141; Rebecca Fraser, *A People's History Of Britain* (2004), p.680).

[123] Chapter 28 examines the significance of these two provinces in British plans to exclude Russia from the eastern Mediterranean.

Map 28: Turkey surrounded, 1941-44

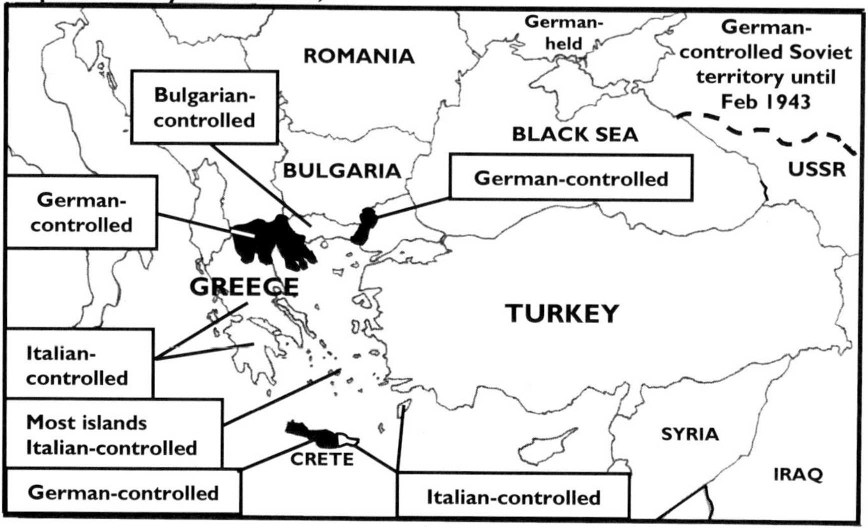

Unfortunately, these prospects held little appeal for Inönü. Germany's forward advance may have faltered but Luftwaffe bombers were still within thirty minutes of Istanbul, a city of largely wooden construction. Moreover, the prospect of expelling Germany from the Balkans only for it to be replaced by Russia - Turkey's traditional enemy - held little appeal for the Turks, and if Turkey's Army was mauled by the Wehrmacht in 1943, how could it resist post-war Soviet encroachment?

Adana ended in stalemate with Inönü submitting a lengthy 'shopping list' of items Turkey would need before entering any conflict, including 2,300 tanks, 2,600 artillery pieces, 1,200 aircraft and 120,000 tons of aviation fuel plus naval vessels, locomotives and rolling stock. The list's role as a stalling tactic is clear - Britain and America required these items for their own ventures, and submitting such a lengthy list allowed Inönü to express undying fealty to the Allied cause without having to translate words into action. At Adana, Inönü offered a master class in delay and prevarication comparable to Britain in its dilatory dealings with America.

Nevertheless, Britain was determined to lure Turkey into the conflict and provided £16m worth of aid during January-May, while Middle East Commander General Maitland Wilson visited Ankara for talks. These discussions produced Operation Hardihood, a plan to draw Turkey into belligerence by allaying its fear of German aggression. Air attacks on Istanbul were the Turks' biggest worry so Phase One of Hardihood proposed to base 25 RAF fighter squadrons plus anti-aircraft units and anti-tank regiments in Turkey. Phase Two would deliver 25 more RAF squadrons plus anti-aircraft units, Phase Three would provide two heavy anti-aircraft regiments, two light anti-aircraft regiments and two additional anti-tank regiments, while Phase Four would deliver two full armoured divisions. These supplies could only reach Turkey via İzmir - a port on Turkey's west coast - and Italy's control of the Dodecanese Islands blocked Allied access to İzmir. If Turkey was to enter the war, Britain would have to free the Dodecanese, and from this emerged Accolade, the shambolic Aegean venture of autumn 1943.

II

Earlier chapters in this book have charted Churchill's obsession with the eastern Mediterranean. He'd conceived the Gallipoli operation to eliminate Turkey from the war, support Russia via the Black Sea, assail the Central Powers by the 'back door' and avoid *"chewing barbed wire in Flanders."* General Ismay - Churchill's Chief of Staff - highlighted the continuity between Churchill's 1915 vision and his 1943 plans.

> *For some time past the Prime Minister had foreseen that an Italian collapse would give us a wonderful chance of seizing Rhodes and the other islands in the Dodecanese. Only relatively small forces would be required, and... with the Aegean in our hands, Turkey would probably come into the war, and convoys could then be sent to Russia via the Dardanelles and Black Sea, instead of through the hazardous Arctic Ocean. Churchill's underlying object was in fact much the same as that which had inspired him to press for the Gallipoli campaign in 1915.*

Churchill also believed that the Bulgarian armistice of 29th September 1918 had triggered Germany's November collapse and hoped to stimulate similar results by extending the war into the Balkans in 1943/44. A successful eastern Mediterranean campaign would expunge the trauma of Gallipoli and vindicate his original vision, while cultivating Turkey as an ally would threaten Germany's southern flank and develop a useful bulwark against Russian expansion into the Mediterranean. Extending the war into the Balkans might even render Overlord redundant,a prospect with huge appeal for British strategists.

The Dodecanese campaign of 1943 embodied the classic 'British way of warfare'. It was peripheral and indirect, shunning concentration of force and avoiding decisive engagement with sizeable enemy forces. Relatively few ground troops would be required - naval and air forces would predominate - and if successful, another power would fight Germany on Britain's behalf. The Red Army was ripping the guts from the Wehrmacht in Russia, America would underwrite the great northern European campaign and - if Churchill had his way - Turkey would 'bleed and burn' for Britain in the Balkans while Britain shored up its position in the Mediterranean. In every respect, Accolade presented the opportunity - as Churchill put it - to *"gain immense prizes at little cost"*[124] and perhaps even obviate Overlord.

It was also a highly opportunistic operation which relied heavily on exploiting the window of opportunity between Italy's surrender - expected in early September - and Germany's response to this defection. If Britain could infiltrate the islands - with Italian support - before Germany responded, great prizes might indeed be won but, if the Italians equivocated or German forces responded with their usual alacrity, the expense of the operation might exceed Britain's sparse resources.

Unfortunately, Accolade was doomed from the outset. The operation was to be largely conducted by 8th Indian Division but it was assigned to Italy on 26th August, while five landing ships, a headquarters ship and three cargo vessels which would have proved invaluable in the Aegean were allocated to South East Asia on 21st August. To remedy this deficit, Britain combed through its Mediterranean reserves to produce an assault force Max Hastings labelled

> *a hotchpotch of special forces, intelligence personnel, gunners, infantry and 'odds and sods', lacking mass, coherence and conviction. The main force, 234 Brigade, had spent the previous three years garrisoning Malta, where its soldiers gained much experience of bombing, hunger and boredom, and none of battle.*

As a result, Middle East Command warned on 31st August that it could only support small scale commando raids or unopposed landings but Churchill would have none of it. Early September was - in his view - *"the time to play high. Improvise and dare"* and on 13th, he invoked former imperial glories by informing General Wilson that

> *the capture of Rhodes by you... would be a fine contribution to the general war. Let me know what are your plans for this... This is a time to think of Clive and Peterborough and of Rooke's men taking Gibraltar.*

---

[124] Churchill employed this phrase in a 2nd August note to COS via Ismay.

Unfortunately, invoking past glories would prove a poor substitute for adequate troop numbers and enthusiastic allies.

Map 29: Dodecanese and Operation Accolade

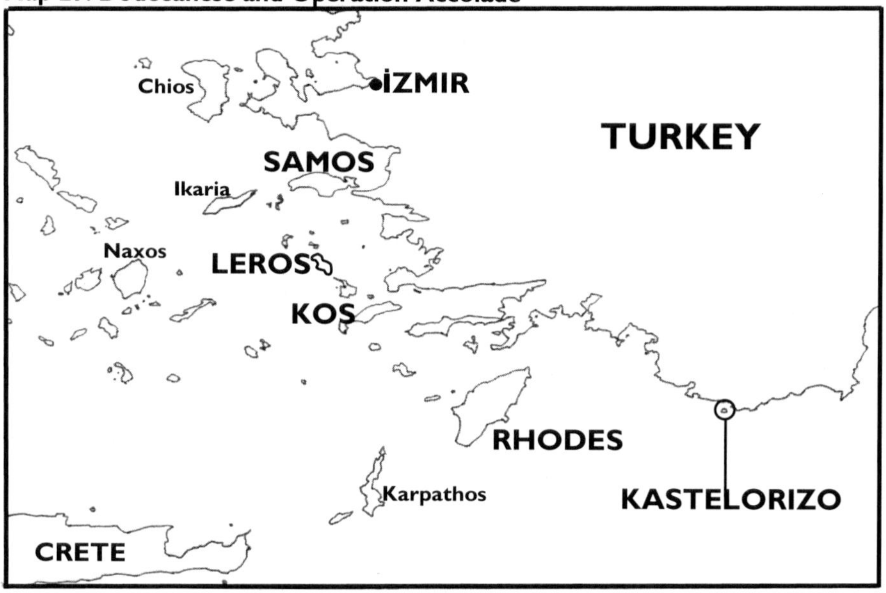

Accolade unravelled almost immediately. Rhodes is the largest island in the group and - by virtue of its three airfields - the most strategically significant and on 9th September, British agents parachuted onto the island to try to persuade Admiral Campioni's 40,000 Italian troops to overwhelm the smaller German garrison and surrender the island to Allied forces. Unfortunately, while the British and Italians parleyed, the Germans acted and - after a short but vicious fight - the island was under German control by 13th September. As a result, German Stukas and Me109s enjoyed regional air superiority and could harry British ships ferrying in reinforcements while the British had to rely on ungainly twin-engined Beaufighters flown in from Italy or Egypt - the air battle was unequal from the outset.

Having captured Rhodes, the Germans turned to Kos - the only other island with an airfield - and on 4th October, two thousand Germans wrested control of this island from 4,700 Allied and Italian soldiers. According to Brooke, this loss and the operation's impending collapse inspired Churchill to a frenzy:

> *Winston is becoming less and less balanced. I can control him no longer. He has worked himself into a frenzy of excitement about the Rhodes attack, has magnified its importance so that he can no longer see anything else and has set his heart on*

capturing this one island at the expense of endangering his relations with the President and with the Americans, and also the whole future of the Italian campaign.

With his pet project unravelling, Churchill appealed to Eisenhower for help but the Mediterranean Commander[125] was poised to launch his Volturno Offensive and declined to release troops or resources to the Middle East without explicit authorisation. Churchill then begged Roosevelt to release troops already assigned to Overlord, assuring him that their Mediterranean deployment would not impede Channel operations.

I beg you to consider this [request for a first class division] and not let it be brushed aside... Even if landing craft and assault ships on the scale of a division were withheld from the buildup of Overlord for a few weeks without altering the zero date it would be worthwhile. I feel we may easily throw away an immense but fleeting opportunity... I am sure that the omission to take Rhodes at this stage and the ignoring of the whole position in the Eastern Mediterranean would constitute a cardinal error in strategy.

Roosevelt's reply evidenced a disdain for dispersion and a determination to concentrate force for more significant operations.

I do not want to force on Eisenhower diversions which limit the prospects for the early successful development of the Italian operations to secure a line north of Rome. I am opposed to any diversion which will in Eisenhower's opinion jeopardize the security of his current situation in Italy, the build up of which is exceedingly slow... It is my opinion that no diversion of forces or equipment should prejudice Overlord as planned. The American Chiefs of Staff agree.

Snubbed by his American allies, Churchill then proposed a full Combined Chiefs of Staff meeting to undermine Trident and Quadrant in favour of Aegean activities.

---

[125] At this point, the Mediterranean basin was divided into Mediterranean Command (under Eisenhower) and Middle East Command (under Maitland Wilson) with the dividing line running through the Adriatic - the Aegean therefore fell within the British-controlled Middle East Command while Italy formed part of Eisenhower's Mediterranean Command, and Eisenhower was under no obligation to shift resources into Wilson's Command (Walter R. Roberts, *Tito, Mihailović, and the Allies, 1941-1945* (1973), p.148; Churchill, *Second World War*, Vol. V, pp.292-293).

We must find some means of resolving these difficulties, and making sure of what is the right thing to do. I am willing to proceed to Eisenhower's headquarters with the British Chiefs of staff immediately if you will send General Marshall, or your personal representative, to meet me there and we can then submit the results of a searching discussion to you and your Chiefs of Staff.

Roosevelt declined and - with Germany dominating the skies and America refusing to intervene - Accolade stumbled to its inevitable melancholy conclusion. Fewer than 3,000 Germans captured Leros from 8,500 British and Italian forces on 16th November and British forces abandoned Samos four days later. On 28th November, Britain yielded its final foothold in the region by relinquishing Kastelorizo, a tiny island two miles off the Turkish coast. British losses in the débâcle included four cruisers, ten destroyers, two submarines and five minesweepers sunk or badly damaged, 113 aircraft shot down and 4,800 men killed, wounded or captured. Thanks to Churchill's naïveté, Germany enjoyed its last strategic triumph of the war and Turkey remained neutral until February 1945 when it joined the Allies to secure entry to the nascent United Nations. Gallipoli's scars would not be healed in 1943.

III

The Dodecanese débâcle sparked a bitter backlash against Overlord in Britain's high command and the two developments are inter-linked. Accolade was part of a plan to lure Turkey into the war and extend the conflict into the Balkans and its failure removed one possible alternative to Overlord, ensuring that cross-Channel operations enjoyed priority. The news from Italy was equally dismal, eliminating another alternative to Overlord. In his 21st October appreciation, General Alexander noted the German intention to

hold a line south of Rome, where the country favours defence and allows no scope to the deployment of our superiority in armour or artillery. Coming bad weather will limit the employment of our air forces... It would therefore appear that we are committed to a long and costly advance to Rome, a 'slogging match', with our present slight superiority in formations on the battle-front offset by the enemy opportunity for relief [from northern Italy]... There is a danger that a successful conclusion of this 'slogging match' might leave us north of Rome in such a state of exhaustion and weakness as not to be able to hold what we have gained.

Far from being a 'soft underbelly', Italy now offered a debilitating 'slogging match' which might leave Allied forces too weak to exploit any victories they gained - the classic definition of a Pyrrhic victory. There would be no rapid advance to the Pisa-Rimini Line, far less to the Po Valley with the option of turning left into France or right into Austria and the Balkans.

Britain's response to these setbacks was paradoxical - instead of cutting its losses and advocating withdrawal from such sterile arenas, Churchill and his Chiefs argued for increased activity and additional resources. At a 19th October COS meeting, Churchill outlined the priorities the Allies would pursue *"if [Britain] were in a position to decide the future strategy of the war."*[126] These included commitments

> *(i) to reinforce the Italian theatre to the full*
> *(ii) to enter the Balkans*
> *(iii) to hold our position in the Aegean Islands*
> *(iv) to build-up our air forces and intensify our air attacks on Germany*
> *(v) to encourage the assembly in this country of United States troops... with a view to taking advantage of the softening in the enemy's resistance due to our operations in other theatres, though this might not occur until after the spring of 1944.*

Churchill's priorities are revealing. His top three ambitions were all Mediterranean/Balkan/Aegean while operations launched from the United Kingdom trailed in last and were liable to postponement. Significantly, Churchill's list did not refer directly to 'Overlord' or cross-Channel operations and his emphasis on *"taking advantage of the softening in the enemy's resistance due to our operations in other theatres"* echoed earlier British insistence on crossing the Channel only after Germany was debilitated by bombing, blockade and subversion. Where the Americans accepted the inevitability of facing unbroken German forces in France, Churchill nurtured the delusion that nibbling away at the enemy's periphery might allow small Allied contingents to waltz into Europe and advance rapidly to Berlin, pausing only to 'round up' stragglers and oddments. His second priority (*"to enter the Balkans"*) also reveals the fundamental dishonesty of his 31st May undertaking to General Marshall that *"he was not advocating sending an army into the*

---

[126] Leo Amery's 18th October diary entry further illuminates Churchillian thinking: *"In an expansive moment [in Cabinet] Winston told us his apprehensions about the 'Over-lord' policy which the Americans have forced upon us, involving a dangerous and time-wasting straddle of our transport and landing craft between two objectives when we might have gone on more effectively in Italy and the Balkans."* (Amery, *Empire At Bay,* p.947).

Balkans now or in the near future." His 19th October comments - only four and a half months later - reveal a clear desire to enter the Balkans and - in summer 1944 - Churchill championed the delusional Operation Armpit.[127]

Not everyone shared Churchill's unfettered Mediterranean enthusiasm and when Air Marshal Portal warned that any repudiation of Overlord might drive America towards the Pacific, Churchill responded by calmly stating that if the Americans

> *wished to transfer the bulk of their forces to the Pacific, he would be prepared to accept this providing they would leave the forces already in this country and would build-up their Air Force for operations against Germany as already promised.*

When Churchill made these remarks, only five American divisions were based in Britain[128] and United States forces were supposed to form the bulk of the Overlord assault and follow-up. If American troops stopped arriving in Britain in autumn 1943, Overlord could never proceed in any meaningful way and - with Britain driving Allied strategy - all energy would be directed towards the Mediterranean because that was Britain's preferred theatre and because the Allies would lack the manpower to do anything else. Churchill's blasé remarks in October 1943 reveal his extreme distaste for Overlord and his profound lack of interest in liberating Europe from fascism.

COS echoed Churchill's concerns but in a document so tortured and convoluted as to almost defy rational analysis. The 11th November aide memoire 'Overlord and the Mediterranean Operations' began by acknowledging British and American strategic differences, but quickly assured the Joint Chiefs (the document's intended audience) that their British counterparts did not *"in any way recoil from or wish to side track*

---

[127] A fanciful plan for Allied forces to enter southern Austria by pushing through the Ljubljana Gap (in present day Slovenia). By such means, the Allies would - it was hoped - gain a foothold in the northern Balkans which would both contribute to Germany's defeat and block Soviet penetration of south-central Europe. The plan had numerous pitfalls, not the least of which was the Gap's extremely rugged and easily defensible terrain. If the Allies did force their way through Gap, they would find themselves fighting alongside the Red Army, a situation fraught with potential difficulties, particularly as Stalin regarded central and eastern Europe as falling within his 'sphere of influence' (Jones, *Britain, the United States and the Mediterranean War,* pp.170-171 introduces Churchill's Ljubljana Gap/Operation Armpit strategies which are considered in detail in later chapters. Brooke vocally opposed the scheme).

[128] This would increase to 11 divisions by 31st December following the transfer of four divisions from the Mediterranean. By the end of 1943, 768,000 US service personnel were based in Britain (although the projections had originally called for 1.026m American soldiers by this date) and only one fully formed US division was present in Britain by 31st July 1943 (Matloff, *Strategic Planning for Coalition Warfare, 1943-44,* pp.391-392).

our agreed intention to attack the Germans across the Channel in the later spring or early summer of 1944." Having said that, a mere two sentences later they acknowledged that "*German strength in France next spring may... be something which makes Overlord completely impossible,*" suggesting a pronounced willingness to recoil from Channel operations. Having acknowledged the difficulties Overlord might face, COS then outlined a series of Balkan/Mediterranean/ Aegean operations the Allies could pursue to strengthen Overlord's prospects. These included

> *(i) unification of command*[129]
> *(ii) the offensive in Italy should be nourished and maintained until we have secured the Pisa-Rimini line.*
> *(iii) nourish partisans in Yugoslavia, Greece and Albania. If necessary, we might form a limited bridgehead on the Dalmatian or Albanian coasts*
> *(iv) bring Turkey into war this year*
> *(v) aim to open the Dardanelles as soon as possible*
> *(vi) do everything possible to promote a state of chaos and disruption in the satellite Balkan countries.*

While these ventures were intended to ease Overlord's path, COS proved to be remarkably coy in clarifying key features of the operation they were supposedly striving to promote. In their view, Overlord "*on a fixed date*" must not become "*the pivot of our whole strategy on which all else turns*" and they rather bizarrely insisted that they didn't "*attach vital importance to... any particular number of Divisions in the [Overlord] assault and follow-up.*" To appreciate the absurdity of this remark, one must recall that Overlord was proposed as an amphibious operation on a hostile shore against the most fearsome army in the world, yet COS opposed setting a target date for the venture and attached no "*vital importance*" to the number of divisions employed in the assault and follow-up! American scepticism over British commitment can be readily appreciated, particularly as Overlord was scheduled to launch in six months as "*the primary US-British ground and air effort against the Axis*" for 1944.

Behind all the palaver about wishing to support Overlord, the document's underlying thrust becomes clearer towards its conclusion when one drills down beyond the semantics and prevarication. In Section Five, COS confirmed that it did not want an Overlord target date "*to become our master, and to prevent us taking full advantage of all*

---

[129] This was achieved on 10th December 1943 with the creation of a unified Mediterranean Command (Matloff, *Strategic Planning for Coalition Warfare, 1943-44,* p.380).

opportunities that occur to us to follow what we believe to be the correct strategy" and finally offered some genuine insight into British motivations. COS wished to prioritise Mediterranean operations throughout early 1944 to assist Overlord, but if other *"opportunities"* came along which COS considered to be *"correct strategy"* they wanted to be able to exploit these opportunities without being tied to Overlord. As Britain favoured exclusively Mediterranean operations for early 1944, any 'opportunities' which emerged would be in the Mediterranean and Britain would seek to exploit these opportunities with full resources at Overlord's expense. Such had been Britain's *modus operandi* over the preceding eighteen months (from North Africa to Sicily then mainland Italy) and Churchill and his Chiefs would never have surrendered their 'soft underbelly' predilection if Mediterranean opportunities presented themselves in 1944 - Britain would press for action in this theatre at all costs in preference to the riskier yet potentially more rewarding Channel venture.

The document's eighth and final section delivers a further blow to Overlord in a manner that makes the tracts of the medieval schoolmen seem lucid and coherent. In section eight, COS expressed a desire *"to fight and bomb the Germans as hard as possible all through the winter and spring"* while forces in the United Kingdom were built up *"as rapidly as possible consistent with this."* Here lies the real threat to Overlord but pitched in terms so anodyne that it might be overlooked. Whereas Quadrant had confirmed Overlord as *"the primary US-British ground and air effort against the Axis in Europe (Target Date 1 May 1944),"* COS now sought to repudiate this by insisting that the build-up of forces in Britain for Overlord was to be *"consistent with"* (i.e. subordinate to) Mediterranean demands. If COS had its way, the Mediterranean would be the dominant theatre throughout 1944 while cross-Channel operations would be an optional add-on to be pursued only if German power suddenly and unexpectedly collapsed. And this reversal of priorities in section eight was reinforced by the hoary old British chestnut that the continent was to be invaded *"as soon as the German strength in France and the general war situation gives us a good prospect of success."* In other words, there was to be no clear-cut date or deadline for Overlord, only a subjective assessment of whether or not conditions were correct and, if the British assessment diverged from the American, the operation could not proceed from British-controlled ports. COS hoped to sabotage American strategy in the same way that it proposed to undermine German power in Europe - by avoiding direct conflict and nibbling away at the periphery. There would be no open rejection of Overlord, just endless hedging and delay and American frustrations with British prevarication are easy to understand. Churchill minuted *'I cordially agree'* on his copy of this tortuous, multi-layered document but both this paper and the record of the 19th October COS meeting (which also vehemently opposed Overlord) are absent from his otherwise meticulously researched multi-volume memoir *The Second World War* and one can only speculate on the reasons behind this omission.

Map 30: Turkey's (hoped for) advance to thwart Soviet moves

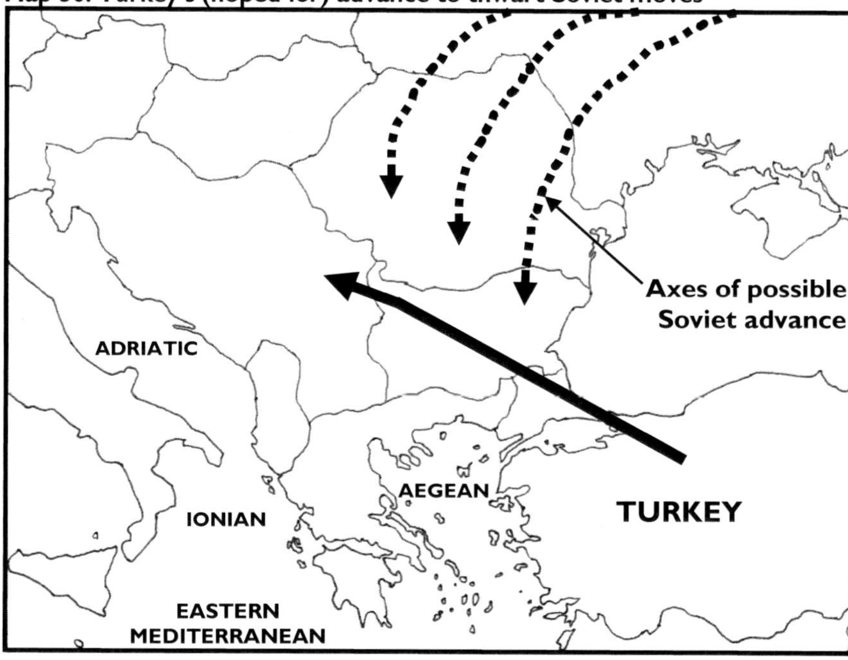

IV

The widening chasm in Anglo-American military strategy could only be resolved through further discussion and - by the end of October - Churchill and Roosevelt had agreed to convene in Cairo on 22nd November before meeting Stalin in Tehran on 28th November.[130]

Churchill and Roosevelt approached 'Sextant' with contrasting hopes. Churchill wanted to convert Roosevelt to a Mediterranean strategy which could then be presented to Stalin as a joint western vision but Roosevelt's motivations were more complex. He wanted to maintain good relations with the Prime Minister - Overlord could only proceed from British ports with full British support - but he had no desire to get bogged down in futile strategic debates when the British and American positions were starkly incompatible and with Britain

[130] Chapter 20 considers the Eureka Conference.

reluctant to honour its commitments.[131] Secondly, he wished to retain his freedom of action to develop a good rapport with Stalin to secure Soviet participation in the war against Japan following Germany's defeat, a goal which couldn't be achieved if Stalin believed America and Britain were conspiring against the Soviet Union. And finally, the Japanese war loomed large in American thinking and Roosevelt wanted more attention paid to this theatre.

These divergent goals could all be realised by inviting Chinese Nationalist leader Chiang Kai-shek to attend Sextant as a sort of 'geopolitical gooseberry'. Chiang's presence would satisfy multiple aspirations - it would limit opportunities for unhelpful discussions on Overlord versus the Mediterranean, reassure Stalin that the west wasn't conspiring against him and focus attention on Far Eastern affairs.[132] Roosevelt wanted China to detain Japanese forces in China and he also wanted China to become one of the 'Four Policemen' who would maintain post-war peace and inhibit Soviet and British imperialism in Asia. Roosevelt wanted to nurture China as a client, an ally and as a market and inviting the leader of Nationalist China to attend Sextant would fulfil these diverse ambitions.

Churchill was less than impressed to find Chiang and his wife already ensconced in Cairo when he arrived, with neither showing much interest in viewing the pyramids while the 'big boys' discussed politics. Churchill grumbled that Chinese affairs *"were lengthy, complicated and minor... with the result that Chinese business occupied first instead of last place at Cairo,"* which was precisely Roosevelt's plan. Denied opportunities for one to one sessions with the President, Churchill had to wait until 24th November before extolling the virtues of his Mediterranean strategy. After giving his customary reassurance that Overlord *"remained top of the bill,"*[133] Churchill - in line with the views expressed on 19th October and 11th November - nevertheless insisted that *"this operation should not be such a tyrant as to rule out every other activity in the Mediterranean"*[134] and listed his preferred priorities for 1944:

---

[131] Churchill and Brooke scathingly described the commitments given at Trident and Quadrant as *"lawyers' agreements"* which could be easily overturned (Moran, *Winston Churchill: The Struggle for Survival,* p.122; Alanbrooke, *War Diaries,* p.447).

[132] A principal Sextant outcome was the 27th November Cairo Declaration which insisted that Japan would be stripped of all territories acquired by force, that China would be reunited with Taiwan and Manchuria, and that Korea would gain independence (Alice Lyman Miller and Richard Wich, *Becoming Asia: Change and Continuity in Asian International Relations Since World War II* (2011), p.22. The Declaration was published on 1st December).

[133] It was bottom of the bill in his 19th October remarks.

[134] In his 24th November diary, Brooke wrote that *"The PM gave a masterly statement on his views concerning the European strategy and the best ways of maintaining the pressure on*

> *Rome in January, Rhodes in February, supplies to the Yugoslavs, a settlement of the Command arrangements and the opening of the Aegean, subject to the outcome of an approach to Turkey; all preparations for Overlord to go ahead full steam within the framework of the foregoing policy for the Mediterranean.*

Quadrant had confirmed Overlord as *"the primary US-British ground and air effort against the Axis in Europe"* for 1944 but Churchill now wished to relegate this landmark operation to secondary status and for it to proceed *"within the framework of the foregoing policy for the Mediterranean"* [i.e. subordinate to Mediterranean demands]. Yet at the same time, he also insisted that *"he had in no way relaxed his zeal for this operation"* - reconciling such contradictory statements with Churchill's alleged military genius is a challenge.

As the session ended, Churchill made one final attempt to convert General Marshall to an Aegean strategy, earning the sharp rebuke that *"God forbid if I should try to dictate but... not one American soldier is going to die on [that] goddamned beach."* Churchill never raised Rhodes again with Marshall but - to his credit - did not hold this uncharacteristically sharp retort against the US Army Chief in future meetings.[135]

Sextant must rank as one of Churchill's more dismal conferences. He'd been prevented from promoting his Mediterranean cause, denied one to one sessions with Roosevelt, prevented from developing joint strategy with the Americans, his health was poor[136] and he was about to meet the bogeyman from the Kremlin. All the portents for Eureka were unfavourable and - from Churchill's point of view - these gloomy omens would be fulfilled when the 'Big Three' convened in Tehran on 28th November.

Germany during the winter months, and the dangers of spelling Overlord... T-Y-R-A-N-T." (Alanbrooke, *War Diaries,* p.480).

135 Churchill had kept Marshall up to 2am the previous night extolling the virtues of Aegean operations and tiredness may have contributed to the General's testy response (Stanley Weintraub, *15 Stars: Eisenhower, MacArthur, Marshall: Three Generals Who Saved the American Century* (2007), p.205).

136 Churchill's health was poor throughout the last quarter of 1943, exacerbated by inoculations received before leaving for Cairo and Tehran and the strain of his responsibilities. Throughout October and November, he had sore throats and heavy colds, he had laryngitis in Tehran and missed the first dinner with Stalin and Roosevelt. He developed pneumonia in mid-December and suffered a mild heart attack on 15th December. His doctor thought he might die and summoned Clemmie to join him in Carthage (Gilbert, *Churchill, Vol. VII: Road to Victory, 1941-45,* p.552 and p.608; Geoffrey Best, *Churchill and War* (2006), p.194; Ponting, *Churchill,* pp.617-618).

CHAPTER TWENTY: THE BUFFALO, THE BEAR AND THE LITTLE ENGLISH DONKEY, November- December 1943

There I sat with the great Russian bear on one side of me, with paws outstretched, and on the other side, the great American buffalo, and between the two sat the poor little English donkey, who was the only one... who knew the right way home.

Churchill reflects on Eureka from
the perspective of August 1944

Sure, we are preparing for a battle at Tehran. You will find us lining up with the Russians.

Harry Hopkins to Lord Moran,
25th November 1943

Eureka (28th November - 1st December) was the war's defining conference, a four-day convocation which settled Allied strategy for securing victory. It was also the conference which confirmed Britain's weakness relative to its partners. By December 1943, Russia had eleven million men under arms and was relentlessly expelling German forces from its territory. America was the mighty 'arsenal of democracy' and - while sustaining a major Pacific campaign - could also deploy sixty divisions in Europe during 1944/45. At Eureka, Churchill conceded that the sixteen British-controlled divisions allocated to Overlord in summer 1944 would represent the sum total of Britain's commitment to north-western Europe and that, in manpower terms at least, Britain was at the end of its tether. By December 1943, the 'Big Three' had - in reality - become the 'Big Two and a Half' and with this, Britain's ability to influence strategy evaporated.

I

Churchill's observation that the *"little English donkey... was the only one who knew the right way home"* also applies to the strategic differences separating him from his allies. Twice denied a Second Front, Stalin would brook no further delay. America's Joint Chiefs had been pressing for cross-Channel operations since 1942, converted Roosevelt to their cause in 1943 and Quadrant had confirmed Overlord as the dominant Allied operation for 1944. Churchill - his frequent expressions of support for Overlord notwithstanding - was a devout Mediterraneanist and - as the British strategy papers of October-November reveal - hoped to prioritise Mediterranean over

Channel operations throughout early 1944. Such an arrangement would require Overlord's postponement by two to three months and - as Overlord could only proceed during the summer - any postponement beyond August would effectively cancel the operation for 1944 outright. Churchill could then blame tidal and meteorological conditions for the operation's postponement rather than his own Empire and oil obsessions.

The strategic differences separating Churchill from his colleagues came to the fore during the plenary sessions of 28th-29th November. Roosevelt repeatedly asserted that *"he was in favour of adhering to the original date for Overlord set at Quebec, namely, the first part of May"* and *"that nothing should be done to delay the carrying out of Overlord which might be necessary if any operations in the eastern Mediterranean were undertaken."* Stalin shared the President's Mediterranean antipathy, arguing that Italy was not

> *a suitable place from which to attempt to attack Germany proper; that the Alps constituted an almost insuperable barrier... the best method in the Soviet opinion was getting at the heart of Germany with an attack through northern or north-western France... [He] questioned the wisdom of dispersing Allied forces for the various operations mentioned such as Turkey, the Adriatic and Southern France since there would be no direct connection between these scattered forces.*

Stalin wanted the Allies to commit to Overlord in the early summer of 1944 and dangled an enticing carrot before his colleagues. If Overlord launched in the early summer, he would initiate simultaneous operations in the east to prevent German forces re-deploying to the west. The offer was first made on the 29th and repeated on the 30th:

> *In order to deny to the Germans the possibility of manoeuvring [Stalin] pledged that the Red Army would launch simultaneously with Overlord large scale offensives in a number of places for the purpose of pinning down German forces and preventing the transfer of German troops to the west.*

Such operations required a firm Overlord date and - apart from the relief the Soviet Union would enjoy by forcing Germany to fight on two fronts - further explains Stalin's insistence on securing a firm commitment.[137] And the eastern offensive wasn't Stalin's only Eureka

---

[137] The launching of simultaneous operations in the east would fulfil one of General Morgan's preconditions, namely that Germany would be limited in the divisions it could deploy in the

surprise. On 28th November, he informed Churchill and Roosevelt that the Soviet Union would join the struggle against Japan following victory in Europe, a move that would not only guarantee Japan's demise - by virtue of Russia's massive army and close proximity to Japan - but would also significantly influence operations in Europe for if Anglo-America could rely on Soviet aid to defeat Japan in 1944/45, it could prioritise European operations in 1943-44 and pursue a more aggressive German strategy.

Churchill's arguments appear weak and pusillanimous in the face of Stalinist generosity. He tried to justify Mediterranean operations in early 1944 on the grounds of assistance afforded to Russia but such arguments lost their force when their intended beneficiary expressed a willingness to forego this aid in exchange for Overlord confirmed for May or June.

Similarly, Churchill painted wonderful pictures of the benefits to be gained through an aggressive eastern Mediterranean strategy - the defection of Romania, Hungary and Bulgaria and aid to Russia via the Black Sea - but these benefits all depended on Turkey joining the Allies, an unlikely scenario following Britain's recent Aegean humiliation. Churchill's eastern Mediterranean castles were built on sand and Stalin's assertion that the Turks would remain neutral proved prophetic.

The Allies were still searching for strategic unity by the end of 29th November and time was running out. Stalin had to return to his *stavka* by 2nd December and stalemate would only comfort Hitler. Churchill couldn't be coerced into endorsing strategies he actively opposed so alternative means of bending the Prime Minister to combined Soviet-American will had to be found. The answer lay in the military men who'd accompanied their masters to Tehran and who'd attended the two plenaries. They knew the statesmen's priorities and preferences, which operations were non-negotiable and which might be considered 'optional extras'. At Roosevelt's urging, the US Joint Chiefs and British COS formed an Ad Hoc Committee of the Chiefs of Staff to resolve the strategic deadlock and - to speed their deliberations and ensure they identified the correct remedy - Roosevelt provided clear terms of reference:

---

west. When Operation Bagration launched on 22nd June (Barbarossa's third anniversary), 2.5m Soviet troops faced around 0.8m Germans (Douglas MacGregor, *Margin of Victory: Five Battles That Changed the Face of Modern War* (2016), p.87; Mitcham, *The German Defeat in the East*, p.9).

1. The Committee of the Chiefs of Staff will assume that Overlord is the dominating operation.

2. The Committee recommends that subsidiary operation(s) be included in the Mediterranean, taking into consideration that any delay should not affect Overlord.

With this, the Chiefs set to work at 9:30am to fashion a solution by lunchtime. Overlord in May/June 1944 was non-negotiable. Stalin and Roosevelt had endorsed this position during the plenaries, it had been endorsed by Quadrant and - though it may have been something of a smoke-screen - Churchill had repeatedly voiced support for the operation. The one area of debate was over timing. Quadrant had specified 1st May as D-Day and Roosevelt had expressed support for this date but - during Eureka - Stalin had indicated that any date in May was acceptable and the Chiefs worked to this formula. Scheduling the operation for an imprecise date in May would allow them to reconcile the operation with favourable lunar and tidal conditions and - as General Brooke observed - *"no Russian offensive had ever started before the end of May"* so launching Overlord in late May would more likely coincide with supporting Soviet operations.[138]

Aegean operations were excluded pending further advice from Churchill and Roosevelt and could not be confirmed while Turkey remained neutral, but Italy was a contender for ongoing operations given the sizeable Allied forces already present and Eisenhower's determination to smash the Cassino deadlock. Moreover, Churchill was a known Italian enthusiast and the prospect of Italian operations might console him for the loss of the Aegean and his acceptance of Overlord in May. This only left southern French operations (Anvil) which Stalin had championed at Eureka and which Quadrant had endorsed. At Eureka, Stalin had suggested that Anvil might precede Overlord by as much as two months but the Chiefs ruled this out as too risky. However, if sufficient shipping could be found, Anvil might run concurrently with Overlord or shortly after, giving the Allies access to two southern French ports - Marseille and Toulon - and providing an outlet for French colonial divisions based in North Africa.

The Chiefs placed their findings before Churchill and Roosevelt shortly before lunch and, in detail, they recommended:

---

[138] Bagration launched on 22nd June with an initial assault force of 124 divisions plus 42 follow-up divisions. By the time the operation concluded in mid-August, Soviet forces had regained most of Belarus, had a foothold in eastern Poland and were within striking distance of Berlin (William M. Connor, *Analysis of Deep Attack Operations: Operation Bagration, Belorussia, 22 June- 29 August 1944* (1987), p.14).

(a) that we should continue to advance in Italy to the Pisa-Rimini line (this means that the 68 LSTs which are due to be sent from the Mediterranean to the United Kingdom for Overlord must be kept in the Mediterranean until 15 January).

(b) that an operation shall be mounted against the South of France on as big a scale as landing craft permit. For planning purposes D-day to be the same as Overlord D-day.

(c) to recommend to the President and Prime Minister respectively that we should inform Marshal Stalin that we will launch Overlord during May, in conjunction with a supporting operation against the south of France on the largest scale that is permitted by the landing craft available at that time.

Roosevelt read these recommendations to Stalin at the start of lunch and the Soviet leader

> *expressed his great satisfaction with this decision. He added that the Red Army would at the same time undertake offensive operations, and would demonstrate by its actions the value it placed on this decision.*

The die for Overlord - supported by Anvil - was cast. The little English donkey must follow the bear and the buffalo and - given its relative weakness - no other outcome was possible. As a consolation, Churchill could anticipate Italian operations in the near future and an opportunity - along with Roosevelt - to meet President İnönü of Turkey directly after Eureka to urge Turkey to join the war. If İnönü could be persuaded to abandon Turkish neutrality, perhaps Churchill's Mediterranean ambitions might yet be realised?

II

Before considering the Sextant II debates, three other Eureka outcomes merit attention.

Firstly, it was at Eureka that Churchill, Roosevelt and Stalin agreed to shift Poland 150 miles to the west to accommodate Soviet territorial demands. Stalin wanted to reclaim territory Russia had gained under the Nazi-Soviet Pact and Poland was to be compensated with parts of Prussia and German territory up to the Oder-Neisse Line. The propriety of this decision falls beyond the scope of this book but

Chapter 23 analyses Anglo-Soviet enthusiasm for playing God with other European states (Greece, Bulgaria, Romania *et al*) in some detail.

While Churchill was busy adjusting other states' boundaries, he steadfastly defended Britain's Empire. During a discussion on the trusteeship of bases and strong points in the vicinity of Germany and Japan on 29th November, Churchill warned his colleagues that

> *as far as Britain was concerned, they do not desire to acquire any new territory or bases, but intended to hold on to what they had. He said that nothing would be taken away from England without a war. He mentioned specifically, Singapore and Hong Kong. He said a portion of the British Empire might eventually be released but that this would be done entirely by Great Britain herself, in accordance with her own moral precepts.*

Even in the midst of war, Churchill was doggedly defending the Empire to maintain his pledge that - on his watch at least - British imperial domains would never diminish.

Finally, the 'Declaration of the Three Powers' produced on 1st December offers a flavour of the resolve the three leaders brought to the task of defeating Germany. While the final sentence may have been concocted for the benefit of the press, every other line in this paragraph breathes fire and commitment.

> *[Britain, Russia and America] have concerted our plans for the destruction of the German forces. We have reached complete agreement as to the scope and timing of the operations which will be undertaken from the East, West and South... No power on earth can prevent our destroying the German armies by land, their U-boats by sea, and their war plants from the air. Our attack will be relentless and increasing. We came here with hope and determination. We leave here, friends in fact, in spirit and in purpose.*

The note sounded by the communiqué was, in Churchill's memorable phrase, *"[that of] brevity, mystery and a foretaste of impending doom for Germany."*

III

Sextant II in Cairo ran from 3rd - 7th December and considered two principal themes - Turkish entry into the war and America's determination to support China within Eureka's overall guidelines. The British and American representatives didn't always see eye to eye on these matters - particularly the latter - and tension occasionally flared during the meetings.

America placed a higher premium on China as an ally than did either Britain or Russia. As noted earlier, Roosevelt hoped to cultivate China as a market, a military partner and one of the 'four policemen' of the post-war world. He'd invited Chiang Kai-shek to Sextant I to frustrate Churchill and had promised him operations in the Bay of Bengal and northern Burma in spring 1944 to maintain morale and boost China's war effort. At the very least, active Chinse participation in the war would divert Japanese forces from the Pacific.

Churchill and Brooke didn't share Roosevelt's regard for China and - as long as the European war raged - regarded Southeast Asia as a distraction. This indifference was reinforced by Stalin's Eureka announcement that Russia would eventually join the war against Japan for - if the Allies could rely on Red Army support against Japan during 1944/45 - why invest significant resources in this theatre during 1943/44 which could be used more effectively in Europe? Churchill and his Chiefs had examined the Overlord and Anvil plans and concluded that the initial assault forces were too weak in both cases. Additional landing craft were required and cancelling the plan to capture the Andaman Islands in March 1944 (Buccaneer) would release landing craft for use in Europe.

Roosevelt disagreed. He had promised Chiang two operations for spring 1944 and believed the Allies *"had a moral obligation to do something for China and he would not be prepared to forego the amphibious operation [Buccaneer], except for some very great and readily apparent reason."* Churchill countered that *"this 'very good reason' might be provided by Overlord. At present the assault was only on a 3½ division basis, whereas we had put 9 divisions ashore in Sicily on the first day. The operation at present was on a very narrow margin."*

The discussion continued during 4th and 5th December with the military figures echoing their masters' views. General Marshall insisted that

> *if Buccaneer was cancelled, the Generalissimo would not allow Chinese forces to take part in Tarzan [the north Burma operation]... and this would have its repercussions on the operations in the Pacific. There would be a revulsion of feeling*

> *in China; the effect on Japan would be bad, and the line of communication between India and China would be at hazard.*

While appreciating the value of capturing the Andamans, Admiral Cunningham argued that this operation demanded

> *a very heavy commitment in maintenance. [The Andamans] were a thousand miles away from our nearest base. They were surrounded by Japanese air and it would be difficult to supply them to an extent which would make their use possible… [they were] not worth the candle, except as a stepping stone to a southward advance… [but] it had been agreed that the main effort should be made in the Pacific.*

Once more, time resolved the impasse. Roosevelt had been absent from Washington since 12th November and political issues were accumulating at home. With the British refusing to give ground and finally showing an interest in strengthening Overlord, Roosevelt gave way on 5th December, sending Churchill a curt note stating that "*Buccaneer is off.*" The Prime Minister was delighted and Chiang would have to make do with minor naval operations, commando raids and post-monsoon operations but, from December 1943 onwards, China's role within American thinking declined as resources increasingly shifted to the Pacific.

Having conceded ground in Asia, the Americans now sought to bind Britain to Overlord-Anvil and prevent any backsliding. On 5th December, CCS 423/2 'Operations in the European Theatre' clarified Allied commitments in Europe in a manner that eliminated all doubt. The first four points of this document insisted that:

> 1. Overlord and Anvil are the supreme operations for 1944. They must be carried out during May 1944. Nothing must be undertaken in any other part of the world which hazards the success of these two operations.[139]
>
> 2. Overlord as at present planned is on a narrow margin. Everything practicable should be done to increase its strength.
>
> 3. The examination of Anvil on the basis of not less than a two-division assault should be pressed forward as fast as possible… [and] consideration will have to be given to the provision of additional resources.

---

[139] At Churchill's prompting, Operation Shingle - the Anzio landing - was initiated on 22nd January, causing Anvil (later named Dragoon) to be delayed until 15th August (see Chapter 21).

4. Operations in the Aegean... are desirable, provided that they can be fitted in without detriment to Overlord and Anvil.

These recommendations reinforced the Eureka commitments in favour of Overlord-Anvil and were incorporated into CCS 426/1 'Report of the CCS to the President and Prime Minister,' endorsed by Churchill and Roosevelt on 6th December. For most people, this would have ended the debate on European strategy but Churchill was not 'most people' and neither he nor General Brooke felt bound by commitments they scathingly dismissed as 'lawyers' agreements'. The strategic debate rumbled on throughout 1944 with alternatives to Overlord and Anvil being proposed at various times and with varying degrees of success.

The discussions with İnönü over Turkish involvement in the war ran simultaneously with the Buccaneer debates with the PM taking the lead. Roosevelt was always keen to welcome new adherents to the Allied cause but was wary of Balkan entanglements, fearing they might jeopardise the carefully crafted consensus that had emerged around Overlord. For Churchill, undermining Overlord drove his engagement with İnönü. If Turkey could be persuaded to abandon its neutrality and join the Allies, major Balkan and Aegean operations might be feasible and the Allies could approach Germany via the Balkan back door instead of its well-defended French front. Churchill's preference was always to attack the crocodile via it's supposedly more vulnerable 'soft underbelly' and Turkey was his preferred pathway to this pressure point.

Churchill's great problem was that he had neither carrots nor sticks to employ against İnönü. If Turkey joined the Allies, Churchill could only offer Anglo-Soviet-American friendship and a seat at the victors' table but as Turkish and Soviet interests clashed in several important areas,[140] Churchill could offer Turkey nothing ahead of its larger and more influential neighbour.

And if Turkey remained neutral, all Churchill could threaten was loss of friendship and diplomatic isolation, Turkey would *"find herself alone, not on the bench but wandering about in Court. It would be dangerous if Turkey now missed the chance of joining the English speaking peoples."* However, İnönü was convinced that Russia would become the

[140] As an example of Soviet-Turkish tension, in June 1940 the Soviet Union demanded the return of Kars and Ardahan, two provinces ceded to the Ottoman Empire under the 1918 Brest-Litovsk Treaty (Yusuf Turan Çetiner, *Turkey and the West: From Neutrality to Commitment* (2014), p.46).

principal threat to European security following Germany's defeat and he believed the western powers would need Turkey as a bulwark against post-war Soviet expansion just as they hoped to use her as a stepping stone into south-eastern Europe in 1943-44. Any period of political *purdah* would be relatively brief and so it proved. Turkey declared war on Germany in February 1945 - when it was virtually meaningless - and was identified as a Truman Doctrine beneficiary in 1947.[141] In 1951, work commenced on a major air base at Incirlik in southern Turkey and in 1952, Turkey became a valued NATO partner, providing a *glacis* against Soviet expansion into the eastern Mediterranean.

At Cairo, İnönü used the tactics he'd employed so skilfully at Adana, pledging undying fealty to the Allied cause, stressing Germany's continuing threat to Turkey and emphasising his country's need for modern armaments. However, with three major operations pending for early-mid 1944, the Allies had nothing to spare - particularly for non-belligerents - and all they could offer was twelve RAF squadrons to be flown into Turkey once air facilities were prepared, accompanied by a Turkish promise to review its commitment to neutrality by 15th February. A British military mission arrived in Ankara in January but the Turks continued to demand additional resources and knowledge of Allied plans and it became clear that Turkey - despite Churchill's best efforts - would stonewall indefinitely. The British military mission departed on 3rd February amid accusations of bad faith and a once ardent courtship was replaced by a policy of "*not saying anything, generally sulking and taking negative action such as cutting off armament supplies.*" Churchill's great strategy for forcing entry into Europe via the back door finally ended in February 1944 but, by that stage, an Italian fiasco demanded his attention.

IV

The final piece of the Overlord pre-planning jigsaw fell into place with General Dwight Eisenhower's appointment as Overlord commander on 7th December. Roosevelt had made his decision on 5th December, informed Churchill on the 6th and casually updated Eisenhower on the 7th. Roosevelt had been swithering over this issue since Quadrant and was torn between Eisenhower (who had commanded volatile multi-national coalitions in North Africa, Sicily and Italy) and General Marshall (who had supervised US Army expansion from 190,000 men

---

141 In March 1947, President Truman confirmed that the United States would financially support Greece and Turkey and other democratic states threatened by 'authoritarian forces' (Fotios Moustakis, *The Greek-Turkish Relationship and NATO* (2003), p.32).

in 1939 to 7.5m by 1943). In the end, Roosevelt opted for Eisenhower because Marshall's colleagues on the US Joint Chiefs were reluctant to see him go. He'd formed a good working relationship with Navy chief Admiral King and it made no sense to break up a winning team with victory close at hand. Marshall had also made himself indispensable to Roosevelt who felt that *"I could not sleep at night with you [Marshall] out of the country"* and appointing Eisenhower in 1944 kept Roosevelt's options open for 1945. If Overlord failed in 1944, he could offer Marshall command of a revived operation, but it would be more difficult to offer Eisenhower Overlord in 1945 after passing him over in 1944.

Eisenhower's appointment and imminent departure from the Mediterranean created a vacancy which would have to be filled by a British officer as most forces in the region were British or British-imperial. On 8th January 1944, General Maitland Wilson - formerly in charge of the Middle East - was appointed Supreme Commander of an expanded Mediterranean theatre with General Alexander in charge of Allied Armies in Italy. In his 2nd September letter to Attlee, Churchill had observed that *"it will be a great advantage to us to have our own Commander [in the Mediterranean] and to be able to correspond directly and constantly with him."* Wilson's appointment gave Churchill the opportunity to actively influence Mediterranean strategy and - throughout December and January - he devised an Italian venture which he hoped would *"astonish the world [and] it will certainly frighten Kesselring."* Operation Shingle astonished the world but not in the manner Churchill intended and Chapter 21 considers this latest Mediterranean mishap.

CHAPTER TWENTY-ONE: THE ANZIO ABSCESS, December 1943- June 1944

Of course there is risk, but without risk there is no honour, no glory, no adventure.

Churchill's Anzio strategy,
7th January 1944

I felt like a lamb being led to the slaughter... this whole affair had a strong odour of Gallipoli and apparently the same amateur was still on the coach's bench... General Alexander... said in great glee that Overlord would be unnecessary [because of Shingle].

General Lucas ponders Operation
Shingle, 9th January 1944

By January 1944, a British officer exercised Supreme Command in the Mediterranean. Eureka had approved ongoing Italian operations and 68 Landing Ship Tanks (LSTs) had been retained in the theatre for that purpose. And as Churchill recovered from illness in North Africa, he was beyond the range of the professional planners who'd frustrated so many of his visionary schemes. Allied progress had stuttered to a halt on the Garigliano River by December 1943 and - in the PM's view - could be revived only through an amphibious landing between Cassino and Rome. With Shingle, Churchill hoped to 'hurl a wildcat' onto the shore to seize Rome by February; instead, he ended up with a 'stranded whale' and four months of trench warfare reminiscent of 1914-18.

I

Operation Shingle perfectly embodies Churchill's wishful Italian thinking - his perpetual anticipation of easy victories, his reluctance to countenance serious opposition and the baleful consequences flowing from such self-deception.[142] Superficially, Anzio represented an ideal spot to launch an amphibious venture to outflank Gustav[143] - it was 80 miles north of the Allied front, 35 miles south of Rome and within range of fighters operating from Naples. Its immediate hinterland was flat and - unlike Salerno - the nearest hills (the Colli Laziali/Alban Hills

---

[142] Churchill justified his opposition to Overlord on the grounds of Germany's rapid response, but the prospect of a swift enemy response to an Italian landing never troubled him, an unfortunate emphasis given the prolonged stasis which gripped Shingle following a successful landing.

[143] A defensive line stretching from the Adriatic to the Tyrrhenian and running south of Monte Cassino where it was augmented by the Bernhardt Line.

and Lepini Mountains) were a good twenty miles inland. If Allied forces could land at Anzio, capture the Alban Hills and adjacent roads (Highways 6 and 7), they could isolate German forces in the south, cut off their supplies and block any retreat to the north.

Map 31: Operation Shingle

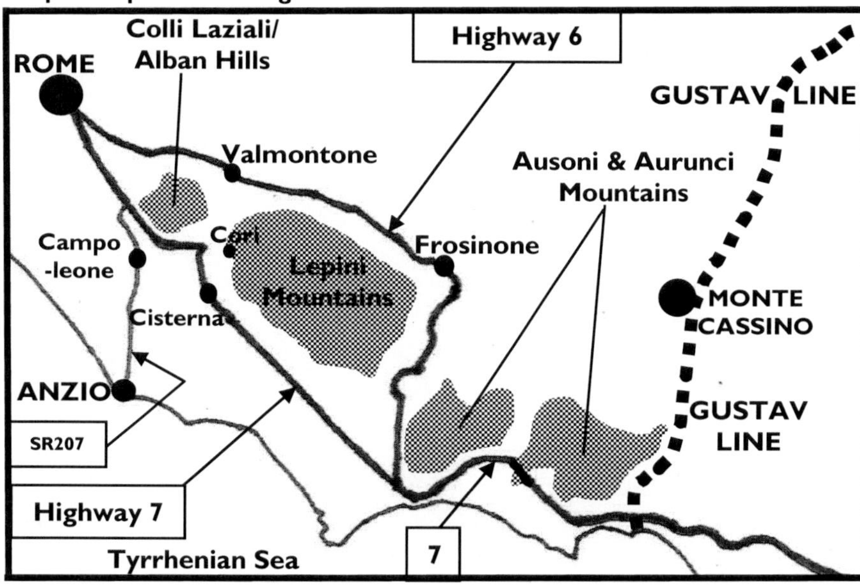

These prospects led to the development of Shingle I in November 1943 but Shingle I was considerably less ambitious than the operation launched in January 1944. In Shingle I, an Allied division would land at Anzio **after** Allied forces had broken through the Gustav Line and reached Frosinone, a town fifty miles north of Cassino and forty miles east of Anzio. In Shingle I, Anzio would supplement the main southern thrust, to be implemented **after** German forces had been forced into retreat. However, this operation was shelved on 18th December after hopes for a quick breakthrough on Gustav faded.

Enter Churchill. Over the preceding five weeks, he'd travelled thousands of miles to participate in high level military talks and his body finally succumbed to pneumonia in Carthage[144] on 11th December. Following his recovery, his doctor ordered an extended convalescence but Churchill's notion of recuperation was typically singular. While others might lie abed consuming fruit cordials, Churchill issued and received countless telegrams and listened to General Brooke's downbeat analysis of Italian operations. The

---

[144] A coastal suburb of modern day Tunis

"stagnation" on the Gustav Line, the Prime Minister thundered, *"is becoming scandalous"* and he wanted to know why *"can't I ever get any commanders who will fight? You don't care if we lose the war. You just want to draw your pay and eat your rations."* Churchill demanded the capture of Rome by February and the landing craft required for an amphibious assault were scheduled to leave Italy by 15th January - they had to be used now or be lost forever.

On Christmas Eve therefore, Churchill and two senior British commanders (Maitland Wilson and Alexander) conceived a more adventurous Shingle. In this new plan, two divisions would land at Anzio and drive inland to seize the Alban Hills and Highways 6 and 7. German forces - it was assumed - would be detached from the Gustav Line to counter this threat and Allied Fifth Army could then - it was hoped - puncture the weakened German line. Shingle II therefore reversed the original plan's thrust by identifying Anzio as the key to unlocking Gustav. Churchill's plan relied entirely on Tenth Army troops moving north to neutralise Anzio - the possibility that German forces might be re-deployed from other European locations to counter this threat wasn't seriously considered and was actively discouraged by Alexander's intelligence analysts who insisted that Germany's Tenth Army would *"make an attempt to seal off the beachhead, and [would] thereby be manoeuvred out of their strong defensive position at Cassino."*

Eisenhower - who'd spent the preceding week in Italy - learned of the plan on 25th December and while he refrained from voicing serious opposition,[145] quickly identified the operation's most serious defect:

> *The landing of two partially skeletonised divisions at Anzio... would not only be a risky affair but... the attack would not by itself compel the withdrawal of the German front... The Nazis had not instantly withdrawn from Africa or Sicily merely because of threats to their rear... a force of several strong divisions would have to be established in Anzio before significant results could be achieved.*

Churchill discounted these concerns and updated Roosevelt on 27th December, requesting permission for the LSTs assigned to Italy to remain in the theatre for three more weeks. Roosevelt consented and - to Churchill's great delight - Shingle was on!

---

[145] Eisenhower had already been appointed Overlord Commander and was on the verge of leaving Italy. General Maitland Wilson, a British officer, replaced him as Supreme Mediterranean Commander on 8th January 1944.

Shingle II was entirely British in origin, developed by Churchill and senior British commanders and presented to Ike as a *fait accompli*, secure in the knowledge that the departing Commander was unlikely to veto the venture. Wilson, Alexander and Cunningham[146] all endorsed Churchill's plan but the American commanders charged with delivering battlefield success - Clark (commanding Fifth Army) and Lucas (Shingle Force Commander) - remained sceptical, sharing Eisenhower's belief that two divisions would be annihilated if they advanced to the Alban Hills; Lucas, in fact, believed the operation required two Corps or even a full Army to guarantee success. Clark and Lucas requested additional time to prepare the operation (which was denied) and suggested that the initial assault force be drawn from one nation only - to simplify logistics - but this was also denied to ensure an even sharing of risk. Shingle would be a two-division assault because the available shipping could only handle two divisions and would launch in mid-January because the LSTs were scheduled to leave Italy by 5th February. Shingle was therefore determined by shipping availability rather than the prerequisites of success and the men on the beachhead paid the price.

Contrasting British and American expectations generated confused and contradictory operational orders. On 12th January, Alexander instructed Clark that Shingle Force's principal task was *"to cut the enemy's main communications in the Colli Laziali area southeast of Rome, and to threaten the rear of the 14th German Corps [at Cassino]... and to insure that the two forces operating [from the north and south] join hands at the earliest possible moment... [and] continue the advance North of Rome with the utmost possible speed."* However, Clark's misgivings about the operation led him to transmit vague and ambiguous orders, granting Lucas maximum flexibility to respond to conditions on the ground. Part One of Clark's orders instructed Lucas to *"seize and secure a beachhead in the vicinity of Anzio,"* but Part Two merely instructed him to *"advance* ***on*** *Colli Laziali,"* rather than **to** Colli Laziali, granting him maximum freedom to respond to local conditions. Clark further advised Lucas that he should only advance to the Alban Hills if the enemy proved supine and, as Lucas embarked on 21st January, Clark reminded him of the mauling he'd received four months earlier: *"Don't stick your neck out Johnny. I did at Salerno and got into trouble."*

Shingle Force therefore set sail on 21st January with a commander who felt *"like a lamb being led to the slaughter"* and whose operational orders contradicted those of his Army Group commander. As the

---

146 Admiral John Cunningham, Mediterranean Commander (Oct 1943- June 1946) - no relation to First Sea Lord Andrew Cunningham.

force sailed north, news arrived that an attempt to smash through Gustav had failed, reinforcing Lucas' innate caution.

Despite all these misgivings, the 22nd January landing was a great success. By the end of D-Day, 36,000 Allied troops and 3,200 vehicles were ashore for the loss of 13 dead and 97 wounded.[147] Much now depended on Lucas' exploitation of this advantage and the quality of the German response.

Lucas remained true to his pre-operational gloom. Anticipating attack at any moment, he insisted on building up his beachhead before advancing inland. By the end of January, 61,000 troops and 7,000 vehicles were crammed onto a beachhead fifteen miles wide by seven miles deep, and while Lucas may have been correct in not advancing to the Alban Hills, his failure to capture Campoleone or Cisterna - two important towns astride road junctions - constituted a serious error of judgment as these towns could be used as starting points for Allied advances going inland **or** for German offensives towards the sea. Lucas' failure to occupy these positions enabled the Germans to exploit them for their own purposes.

While Lucas consolidated his beachhead, Germans troops arrived from France, Yugoslavia and Germany to isolate Anzio while Gustav remained intact. Hitler wanted *"the abscess south of Rome lanced"* and - by the end of January - 70,000 men of General von Mackensen's Fourteenth Army were in position around Anzio, ready to hurl the Allies back into the sea. The Allies controlled the air and sea while the Germans had more troops and land-based communications and this rough parity engineered a stalemate that persisted through six weeks of bitter fighting and twelve weeks of tactical deadlock. The Germans lacked the strength to expel the Allies while - until the end of May - the Allies lacked the muscle to break out of the beachhead.

Consequently, the two sides' offensives simply cancelled each other out. Lucas attacked first on 30th January but - unfortunately - directed his assault towards an area where von Mackensen was massing 36 battalions for an attack planned for early February. The US 3rd Division

---

[147] By May 1944, a further 114,000 men would join the assault force in the beachhead, giving a total of 150,000 (five American and two British divisions). Maintaining a force of this size required vast quantities of shipping and - for a while - Anzio was the fourth largest port in the world. Ironically, Brooke and Churchill had always justified Mediterranean operations on the grounds of shipping savings but Shingle refutes this. Many of the LSTs assigned to Anzio in spring 1944 had originally been ticketed for Overlord (Morison, *Sicily-Salerno-Anzio,* p.374; Gregory Orfalea, *Messengers of the Lost Battalion: The Heroic 551st and the Turning of the Tide at the Battle of the Bulge* (1999), p.119; Clark, *Anzio,* p.231; Cray, *General of the Army*, p.446).

and British 1st Division reached Campoleone and Cisterna but were beaten back with heavy losses and regrouped inside the beachhead.

The Germans launched major attacks on 3rd, 16th and 29th February but were repulsed each time by a combination of well-entrenched forces plus massed tank, artillery, mortar and anti-aircraft fire augmented by naval bombardment and air support. General Lucian Truscott replaced Lucas - the failing operation's scapegoat - on 23rd February but the situation remained static. After six weeks of intense fighting, the two sides settled into a defensive stalemate, awaiting the return of warm weather and the outcome of fighting further south. Churchill had championed Italian operations to avoid a repeat of murderous trench warfare in France but - ironically - Anzio perfectly reproduced the misery and frustration of Flanders. According to one veteran,

> *we… had to form trenches, and Anzio then became an old fashioned World War One trench system and they were bombed and they were mortared and then we had to do trench patrols and occasionally keen generals used to send up people to try and find out who was opposite us and do a trench raid. It was right out of Journeys End.*[148]

In London, Foreign Office official Alexander Cadogan noted that "*we are bogged down in Cassino and, indeed, in Italy. It looks to me like a Passchendaele, beloved of Generals*". The Anzio abscess was raw and inflamed but had been contained and presented no immediate threat to Rome or Gustav while Churchill's dream of winning Rome by February turned to ash.

II

Anzio's unanticipated longevity affected other Allied plans, particularly Anvil, the southern French operation scheduled for May/June to draw German forces away from Normandy. Anvil was dependent on men and resources drawn from Italy but with twenty-three divisions engaged on the Gustav Line and Anzio in spring 1944, Anvil couldn't possibly proceed in tandem with Overlord and - in mid-April - it was deferred to 10th July. At this stage, the British wanted it cancelled altogether but General Marshall insisted on retaining it - albeit at a later date - to secure access to Marseille and Toulon, to provide an outlet for French colonial divisions in North Africa and to shift the

---

[148] A play by R.C. Sherriff set in the trenches near Saint-Quentin in spring 1918.

Allied centre of gravity towards France, the 'decisive theatre'. Anvil (subsequently renamed Dragoon) eventually launched on 15th August over strong objections from Churchill who - by this stage - favoured an advance up the so-called 'Ljubljana Gap' towards Vienna.

At the same time, the American Joint Chiefs finally - and reluctantly - embraced operations at Anzio and the Gustav Line as *de facto* alternatives to Anvil in terms of diverting German forces from Normandy. Although they had little enthusiasm for Italian operations, the Combined Chiefs instructed General Maitland Wilson on 19th April *"to give the greatest possible assistance to Overlord by destroying or containing the maximum number of German formations in the Mediterranean"* which would include *"launch[ing] as early as possible an all-out offensive in Italy."* Alexander then devised Diadem-Buffalo to destroy German power south of Rome and - by such means - materially assist Overlord.

III

Alexander's Diadem-Buffalo scheme re-worked the November 1943 Shingle I plan on a much larger scale. Under Diadem, Fifteenth Army Group was to puncture the Gustav Line in the south and, once this was accomplished, Shingle Force was to implement Buffalo by breaking out of Anzio and driving towards Highway 6 to trap Germany's Tenth Army at Valmontone, a small town in the Liri Valley. Alexander clearly and unambiguously identified Valmontone as Tenth Army's killing ground, instructing Shingle Force to

> *launch an attack from Anzio Bridgehead on the general axis Cori-Valmontone to cut Highway 6 in the Valmontone area, and there to prevent the supply and withdrawal of the troops of the German Tenth Army opposing the advance of Eighth and Fifth Armies.*

The first part of the plan worked admirably. Reinforced by British-imperial forces transferred from the Adriatic, Diadem launched on 11th May and - by 23rd May - German forces were in full retreat.[149] Alexander now instructed Clark and Truscott to implement Buffalo and by 25th May, lead units of Shingle Force were within 2-3 miles of Valmontone and - as it was guarded only by light units of the Hermann Göring Division - were confident of capturing it the following day. Had this been accomplished, Tenth Army would have been crushed in a giant pincer, redeeming much of the preceding four months' waste and sacrifice.

---

[149] A Polish flag flew over Cassino on 18th May (Buchanan, *American Grand Strategy,* p.151).

However, Clark now sabotaged Buffalo by ordering Truscott to direct the bulk of his force **away** from Valmontone and **towards** Rome. Clark's decision 'dumbfounded' Truscott but he duly complied, leaving only one division to advance towards Valmontone while three infantry divisions and one armoured division advanced towards Rome which was declared an 'open city' on 3rd June. American forces entered Rome on 4th June while - at the same time - seven German divisions escaped up Highway 6 towards the Gothic Line where they would block Allied progress over the winter.

Clark justified his decision by claiming that an exclusive focus on Valmontone wouldn't necessarily have trapped Tenth Army but his memoirs contradict this.

> *We [Fifth Army] not only wanted the honour of capturing Rome, but we felt that we more than deserved it… Not only did we intend to become the first army in fifteen centuries to seize Rome from the south, but we intended to see that the people at home knew that it was the Fifth Army that did the job... We Americans had slogged all the way up from Salerno and I was not going to have this great prize… denied to me and my GI's by anyone. We had earned it.*

Vanity and ego may have motivated Clark but historian Andrew Buchanan goes further by suggesting that - by prioritising Rome over Tenth Army's destruction - Clark was actively advancing American political interests. To support this, Buchanan draws attention to Clark's April 1944 visit to the United States where he had top level - but undisclosed - talks with Roosevelt and Marshall and where he may have been persuaded to consider the wider political picture. Britain and America had already clashed over control of the Allied Military Government in Sicily and they supported rival factions on the mainland; Churchill endorsed the conservative-monarchist faction centred on the former fascist Marshal Badoglio while the Americans favoured liberal anti-fascists such as Ivanoe Bonomi and Carlo Sforza. In the days following liberation, Clark prevented senior British officials - such as British Ambassador Sir Noel Charles - from entering Rome and on 9th June, Badoglio was manoeuvred into resigning as PM to be replaced by Bonomi. Roosevelt was clearly not displeased for the United States granted Italy's Government $100m of credit during November and December while the American military authorities spent $120m on Italian civilian relief. When Churchill griped about Bonomi's elevation, the President urged him to accept the *fait accompli,* suggesting that any interference in Italian politics would have serious repercussions *"to the detriment of the military situation and the profit of mischievous elements there."* Churchill could only splutter *"since when have we admitted the right of the Italians to form any government they please?"* but the truth is that his good friend Franklin - through the intermediary of US 5th Army - had unilaterally appointed Italy's new social democratic government. Significantly, Clark was never reprimanded for allowing Tenth Army to escape and, in December 1944, gained Command of Fifteenth Army Group following Alexander's elevation to Supreme Command in the Mediterranean.[150]

Clark enjoyed his moment in the sun and staged a highly public press conference on the Capitoline Hill on 5th June attended by photographers under strict instructions to capture only his favoured left side. However, his period of glory proved brief for on 6th June, Allied troops landed in Normandy, knocking Clark and Italy off the world's front pages.

---

[150] This followed Maitland Wilson's appointment to lead the British Joint Staff Mission in Washington following Field Marshal Dill's death on 4th November.

CHAPTER TWENTY-TWO: THIS BATTLE HAS BEEN FORCED UPON US, January- June 1944

> *I firmly believe that [Churchill and his chiefs] returned from Casablanca fully determined to repudiate the agreement that they had been forced to sign with the Americans [for an invasion of France]... Apart from a mere dislike of the project, the British authorities proceeded to make every possible step to impede progress in NW Europe by diverting their forces, as unobtrusively as possible, to other theatres of war.*
>
> Lt. General Frederick Morgan, interview with Forrest Pogue, 1947

> *Do you realise that by the time you wake up in the morning, 20,000 men may have been killed?*
>
> Winston to Clementine Churchill, 5th June 1944

Overlord was the defining western Allied operation of the war but - for eight months - it languished under the direction of a staff officer with minimal political clout, no recent experience of fighting Germans[151] and no Supreme Commander. This period of drift ended with the December 1943 appointment of Eisenhower and Montgomery as Supreme Commander and Ground Force Commander respectively and - in early 1944 - Montgomery 'gripped' Overlord as firmly as he'd once 'gripped' his famous desert campaigns. This chapter assesses Monty's impact on Overlord in spring 1944 and scrutinises Churchill's behaviour during the same period. In April 1942, the PM had expressed great enthusiasm for "*march[ing] forward into Europe... in a great crusade for the liberation of the tormented peoples*" but when the time came for liberation, his crusading zeal was strangely diminished.

I

Morgan and Montgomery approached Overlord in sharply contrasting styles reflecting their divergent personalities, status and experience. The Combined Chiefs told Morgan how many divisions he could deploy on D-Day - based on their May 1944 shipping estimates - and

---

151 Morgan had served as a Brigadier with 1st Armoured Division in France in 1940 but all his service thereafter was UK-based. At one point he was invited to develop plans for a Sardinian invasion which led to his COSSAC appointment (Zabecki, *World War II in Europe,* p.424; Morgan, *Overture to Overlord,* pp.13-20).

he planned accordingly. Consequently, his August 1943 plan envisaged a three-division assault over three beaches (Omaha, Gold and Juno) across a 25-mile front centred on Arromanches. This force would seize Caen - a major communications and transport hub - before splitting in two, one force driving towards Cherbourg, the other towards Paris.

Montgomery's approach was very different; instead of working within CCS-prescribed limits, he identified the resources essential for success and presumed the Chiefs would make good any shortfall between his estimate and theirs. This was the approach of a vainglorious general and an extremely conscientious soldier with a solid record of success who knew his views carried weight. The Allies had invaded Sicily with seven divisions - against two German and eleven Italian divisions - and Monty considered it absurd to land in France with a smaller force against fifty-plus German divisions lying in wait. As a first priority, Monty recommended expanding the initial assault from three to five divisions, supported by three parachute divisions dropped into France ahead of the main assault and two more divisions pre-loaded for delivery later on D-Day. Expanding the size of the assault force required a parallel expansion in the size of the invasion front (from twenty-five to fifty miles) and two new beaches (Utah and Sword) were added to Morgan's original three. Utah (to the west of the Douve River estuary) offered the prospect of quick access to Cherbourg and the Cotentin peninsula, while Sword (east of Juno) would exploit the natural defensive barrier of the Orne River and - it was hoped - offer swift access to Caen. General Bradley's US 1st Army would land on Utah and Omaha to capture Cherbourg and Cotentin, while General Dempsey's 2nd Anglo-Canadian Army would debouch onto Gold, Juno and Sword to seize Caen and shield the entire operation from the inevitable German counter-attack. Having seized Cherbourg and Cotentin, Bradley's force would drive south-west into Brittany and the Loire - capturing additional ports - before doubling back to join Second Army and destroy German forces west of the Seine. If all went well, Monty hoped to have seventeen divisions ashore by D+11 and for the Allies to reach Paris by D+90.

Monty therefore recommended a two-thirds expansion in the size of the initial assault force, a doubling of the invasion front and five invasion beaches instead of three. The two invading armies would perform contrasting but complementary tasks and Monty hoped this specialisation would allow Bradley and Dempsey to focus on completing their respective tasks without distraction. Normandy remained the focus for the operation as it was less well defended than the Pas de Calais (where Hitler anticipated the main assault), its broad beaches and firm sand were suitable for deploying armour and its lateral road and rail communications would support a swift breakout when the time came.

Map 32: Overlord

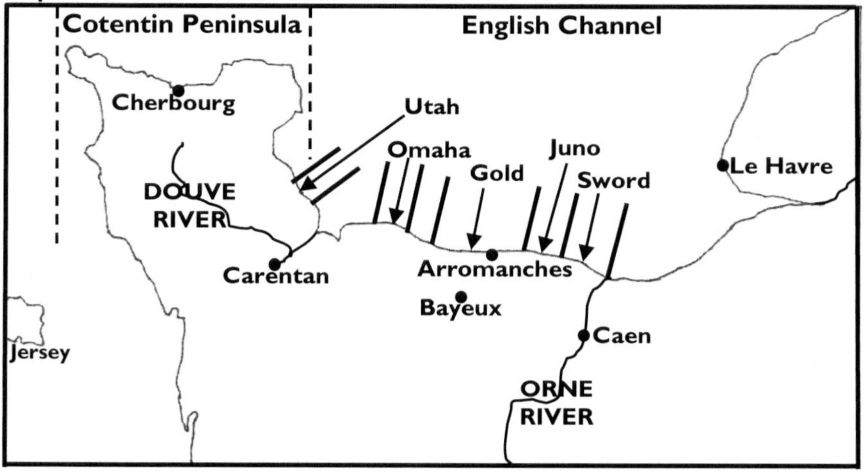

Monty presented his plans to Eisenhower and other Overlord commanders on 21st January, winning widespread approval. Indeed, Eisenhower had examined Morgan's draft plan in October 1943 and concluded that the initial attack lacked *"wallop"* so anything which enhanced Overlord's 'wallop' and boosted its initial punch was likely to win Ike's approval. Ike and Monty's sole difference was over the role of Anvil within Allied strategy. Monty regarded it as a wasteful distraction which would siphon resources away from Overlord while Ike knew that Marshall considered Anvil non-negotiable and was reluctant to contradict his mentor on this issue. He also knew that Monty's expanded Overlord plan would require additional resources which could only be provided by stripping other operations or by postponing Overlord - and possibly Anvil - an issue requiring extremely tactful exposition to his superiors.

Following a meeting with his senior commanders on 21st January, Ike drafted a two part 'bill' for Overlord which he submitted to the Combined Chiefs on 23rd January. In part one, he argued the case for Monty's expanded operation and the additional resources it required.[152]

---

[152] 271 extra landing craft and landing ships, 36 destroyers, five cruisers, four flotillas of minesweepers and eight fighter squadrons (Chandler (ed), *Papers of Dwight David Eisenhower,* Vol. 3, p.1674).

Ike also raised the possibility of a clash between Overlord and Anvil and - while acknowledging that *"Overlord and Anvil must be viewed as one whole"* - he also proposed reducing Anvil to a one division assault to release resources for Overlord. He also suggested postponing Overlord until the end of May, giving the Allies an extra month of Allied shipping production - from Britain alone he estimated this would yield an additional 96 Landing Craft Tanks (LCTs).

The Combined Chiefs responded on 31st January with a beguiling mix of clarity and equivocation. They approved Monty's expanded assault force and agreed to Overlord's postponement but failed to address Eisenhower's suggestion that Anvil might be delayed or his request (in part two of his bill) that SHAEF[153] exercise supreme control over UK-based bomber forces prior to D-Day.[154] The controversy over these two issues dragged on for months, generating considerable friction within the Allied camp. In the end, Eisenhower gained 'direction' but not 'command' over the Allied bombers while Anvil (subsequently renamed Dragoon) was postponed until 15th August and launched as a three-division assault.[155]

Delaying Overlord until late May effectively postponed the operation until early June for the airborne forces required a full moon for the parachute assault while the amphibious forces needed a low tide at dawn to avoid Rommel's beach obstacles and these two conditions would not converge again until 5th-6th June. Overlord was originally set for Monday 5th June but the forecast for that day was atrocious so the operation was postponed until Tuesday 6th. On 4th and 5th June, Group Captain Stagg - SHAEF's Chief Meteorological Officer - predicted a brief spell of good weather for Tuesday 6th so - following a brief consultation with his commanders - Eisenhower gave the go-ahead. Delaying until 19th June - the next suitable date - wouldn't necessarily guarantee better weather but would certainly incur the wrath of his superiors (and Stalin) but if Stagg's 6th June forecast proved wrong, the entire operation might be wrecked by bad weather, in which case the assault would be delayed until 1945 and proceed under a new commander.[156] Aware of these risks, Eisenhower drafted a short statement to be read out in the event of catastrophe but, fortunately,

---

153 Supreme Headquarters Allied Expeditionary Force - Eisenhower's HQ for the invasion of Europe.

154 Covered in Chapter 25.

155 Chapters 28 and 29 consider the Anvil/Dragoon and Armpit controversies.

156 Eisenhower's decision to proceed on 6th June proved prescient for severe storms lashed France during 19th-21st June, destroying the American Mulberry harbour and damaging the British one - proceeding on these dates may well have resulted in disaster (John Fuller, *Thor's Legions: Weather Support to the U.S. Air Force and Army, 1937-1987* (1990), pp. 99-100).

it was never needed - the most audacious amphibious operation in human history was also one of the most successful. By the end of D-Day, 156,000 men were ashore for the loss of 10,000 dead and wounded, a much lighter casualty rate than Churchill feared. Festung Europa had been breached and, in less than a year, Allied forces reached Berlin.

II

And what of Churchill during this period when Eisenhower and Montgomery were giving their all to Overlord?[157] Did the Prime Minister's commitment and resolution match those of his commanders or did his long-standing Mediterranean ardour compromise his crusading zeal? In 1940/41- when Britain faced its darkest hour - Churchill had given 'the roar to the lion' and roused the British people against Nazism but now in 1944, when Britain and its Allies faced an equally stern challenge, he was strangely silent - no ringing endorsements of Overlord, no rousing exhortations to the troops, no dynamic reworking of *Henry V*'s 'band of brothers' speech. Contrary to his post-war claims, Churchill remained profoundly pessimistic over Overlord, a negativity evident in numerous comments and statements.

Eisenhower received a full-throated blast of Churchillian pessimism shortly after his arrival in London which recalled Churchill's earlier conversation with Henry Stimson. In July 1943, Churchill had argued against Overlord on the grounds of *"the disastrous effects of having the Channel full of corpses of defeated allies"* and this premonition clearly haunted his remarks to Eisenhower when he conceded that

> *when I think of the beaches of Normandy choked with the flower of American and British youth, and when in my mind's eye I see the tides running red with their blood, I have my doubts. I have my doubts.*[158]

Similar sentiment surfaced in a 25th January note to Dominions Secretary Lord Cranborne.

---

[157] Ike's 23rd January Report to CCS conveyed this zeal by declaring that *"every obstacle must be overcome [in developing Overlord]. Every inconvenience suffered and every risk run to ensure our blow is decisive. We cannot afford to fail."* (Chandler (ed), *Papers of Dwight David Eisenhower,* Vol.3, p.1673)

[158] Churchill employed similar imagery in talks with Canadian PM Mackenzie King in May 1943 when he rejected a landing in France, stating *"that he did not want to see the beaches of Europe covered with slain bodies of Canadians and Americans. That there might easily be many Dieppes in a few days."* (Mackenzie King Diary, 18th May 1943: see Bibliography for reference). 'Dieppe' refers to the disastrous August 1942 Dieppe Raid which produced a 69% - mainly Canadian - casualty rate.

> *It is to my mind very unwise to make plans on the basis of Hitler being defeated in 1944. The possibility of his gaining a victory in France cannot be excluded. The hazards of battle are very great. The reserves of the enemy are capable of being thrown from point to point with great facility... In all our contacts with German troops, such as we see in Italy, their quality, discipline, and skill are apparent.*

Two themes emerge from the above. Firstly, Churchill's profound pessimism over Overlord and secondly, his unduly deferential attitude towards German military prowess. In July 1943, he'd counselled against Overlord on the grounds of the German army's *"extraordinary fighting efficiency"* and now, in 1944, he cited the *"quality, discipline, and skill"* of German arms to justify excessive caution. It's just as well that Overlord planning and execution were in the hands of men with unyielding faith in Allied arms - Eisenhower and Montgomery - rather than the timorous Minister of Defence.

In moments of stress, Churchill could always be relied on to dust down his favoured chestnut - an invasion of northern Norway (Jupiter) - and in February 1944 he informed COS that

> *I do not myself think it wise to rule out Jupiter finally from the operations of this war. We ought of course to have liberated Norway during the campaign of 1943, but... in the event of Overlord not being successful or Hitler accumulating forces there quite beyond our power to tackle it would perhaps be necessary to adopt the flanking movements both in Norway and from Turkey and the Aegean in the winter of 1944-45. In view of such contingencies I am reluctant to liquidate this force.*[159]

Again, this passage underlines Churchill's profound pessimism over Overlord and his preference for operations in Norway, Turkey and the Aegean as superior alternatives.

---

[159] Lord Annan recalls Churchill's idiosyncratic approach to liberating Europe in February 1944: *"One morning [Brooke] arrived to find that his brief for the first item of the War Cabinet agenda... was the Prime Minister's new proposal to substitute for Overlord... a landing at Lisbon and advance across the Pyrenees. Brooke, who had been brought up as a boy on the French side of the Pyrenees, told Churchill how ridiculous his plan was, adding that the time of his staff should not be wasted on such proposals."* (Annan, *How Wrong Was Churchill?* NY Review of Books, 8th April 1993). David Fraser's *Alanbrooke* biography (pp.369-70) provides further information on this bizarre episode. If Brooke rejected this strategy partly because of his familiarity with the Pyrenees, why did he endorse operations in Italy's equally rugged Apennine range?

Given his fervid distaste for Overlord, one should not be surprised to find Churchill attempting to review the need for D-Day with President Roosevelt in spring 1944. On 18th March, he invited the President to Bermuda to discuss Allied strategy, assuring him that *"it is not so much that there are new departures in policy to be taken but there is need after more than ninety days of separation for checking up and shaking together."* However, a draft note reveals his real reason for proposing a conference in which he hoped to ask:

> *What is the latest date on which a decision can be taken as to whether Overlord is or is not to be launched on the prescribed date?... if 20 to 25 mobile German divisions are already in France on the date in question, what are we going to do?*

By this stage, Overlord was less than three months away and Churchill was casting round for reasons to abandon it. It is perfectly understandable for a chief executive to experience doubt over a complex - and potentially very costly - operation prior to launch but to later masquerade as that operation's staunchest champion - as Churchill did - is extremely disingenuous.[160]

A new worm of doubt clearly entered the PM's mind during March for on 1st April he warned Foreign Secretary Anthony Eden that

> *once we [the western Allies] get on to the continent with a very large commitment, they [USSR] will have the means of blackmail, which they have not at present, by refusing to advance beyond a certain point, or even tipping the wink to the German that they can move more troops into the west.*

Churchill's comments are richly ironic - having duped Stalin for two years with phoney Second Front promises, he now questioned the Soviet leader's integrity. Again, he seems to be searching for reasons to abandon Overlord and, in this case, assumed the worst in his ally. In the end, Bagration - the Soviet summer offensive scheduled for June 1944 - went ahead as planned and materially assisted Britain and America by detaining German forces in the East and, throughout 1944/45, Red Army forces advanced steadily towards Berlin without either blackmailing the west or 'tipping the wink to the German'. Churchill's fears about Stalinist perfidy proved groundless and in January 1945, the Soviet Vistula-Oder offensive was brought forward

---

[160] Churchill apologists and supporters practise the same misrepresentation.

by one week at Churchill's request to help the Western allies mop up German forces following Hitler's Ardennes Offensive.[161]

Churchill expressed further distaste for Overlord in a 19th April note to Foreign Office official Alexander Cadogan, insisting that

> *this battle [Overlord] has been forced upon us by the Russians and by the United States military authorities. We have gone in wholeheartedly, and I would not raise a timorous cry before a decision in the field has been taken.*

This paragraph's opening sentence unambiguously confirms the central thesis of *Empire First* and it's significant that Churchill himself furnishes the evidence - perhaps he felt free to reveal his true feelings to a Whitehall insider? Churchill's confirmation that British participation in Overlord was 'forced' explains his refusal to publicly endorse the operation - he couldn't bring himself to fake enthusiasm for an operation he actively opposed.

Having confirmed that British participation in Overlord was 'forced', Churchill revealed his own strategic preferences to a group of Dominion Prime Ministers on 3rd May by informing them that - had he been directing Allied strategy - he

> *would have been in favour of rolling up Europe from the South-East, and joining hands with the Russians. However, it had proved impossible to persuade the United States to this view. They had been determined at every stage upon the invasion in North-West Europe, and had constantly wanted us to break off the Mediterranean operations.*[162]

These comments justify General Stanley Embick's suspicions outlined in his January 1943 Memo to Marshall in which he characterised Churchill's Balkan enthusiasms as evidence of a desire to exclude the Soviet Union from the Mediterranean rather than forming part of any coherent plan to defeat Germany.[163] Churchill's comments to the

---

[161] This also suited Stalin's purpose as it allowed Russian troops to attack before an anticipated thaw.

[162] Churchill made the same point to General Albert Wedemeyer in April 1944. In a 13th April note to General Handy, Wedemeyer described a conversation with Churchill in which the Prime Minister confirmed *"that if we had been able to persuade the Chiefs of Staff, the Allies would have gone through Turkey and the Balkans from the South and into Norway on the North, thus surrounding the enemy and further dispersing his forces"* (Albert N. Garland et al *United States Army in World War II: The Mediterranean Theater of Operations: Sicily and the Surrender of Italy* (2013), p.16).

[163] Eisenhower, *Eisenhower: At War, 1943-45,* p.21.

Dominion PMs confirm his preference for Balkan-Mediterranean operations and acknowledge that he relinquished these dreams only under combined Soviet-American pressure. As General Morgan observed, Churchill only supported Overlord once its success was proven.

Churchill's antipathy towards Overlord is further evident in his bizarre 15th May declaration to a 21st Army Group audience[164] that *"I am hardening to this enterprise [Overlord]. I repeat, I am now hardened toward this enterprise."* Churchill delivered these remarks **three weeks** before D-Day and, to a supporter such as General Ismay, the word 'hardening' simply indicated that *"the more you thought about it [Overlord] the more certain you were of success."* However, Dwight Eisenhower interpreted these remarks in a harsher light in a 1946 newspaper interview in which he confirmed that on 15th May he

> *realised for the first time that Mr. Churchill hadn't believed in [Overlord] all along and had no faith that it would succeed. It was quite a shocking discovery. Sir Alan Brooke had been extremely pessimistic at all times about our prospect of fighting through the bocage country and I believe the PM reflected Sir Alan's tactical views.*[165]

Churchill's 'hardening' towards Overlord a mere three weeks before launch suggests a certain 'softness' (i.e. lack of enthusiasm) in advance of the operation and - had senior Allied planners shared this distaste - Overlord would never have launched in summer 1944. A major amphibious assault such as Overlord requires extensive preparation and forward-thinking American attitudes rather than British parsimony and stochastic improvisation. Having come of age under Victoria, perhaps Churchill thought that Europe's liberation could proceed as easily as a nineteenth century punitive expedition against unruly tribes on the North West Frontier?

Weighing up the above - and evidence from earlier chapters - Churchill's antipathy towards Overlord prior to May 1944 is clear and unambiguous. He was excessively pessimistic towards the operation and its chances of success, unduly deferential towards German military power, he remained a convinced Mediterraneanist at heart and confirmed that Britain was forced to participate in Overlord while he strongly favoured Balkan and Mediterranean ventures. The Prime

---

[164] The audience included King George VI and senior Allied commanders.

[165] Eisenhower reiterated this point in a 1964 interview with Walter Cronkite *(Eisenhower's Return to Normandy,* 90 minute CBS documentary).

Minister appreciated that the Allies had to return to the continent at some point but hoped to do so **after** Germany had been pulverised by prolonged bombing, blockade and subversion - he consistently and resolutely opposed a contested landing in northern France along the lines considered necessary by the Americans. Left to Churchill, Allied resources would have been frittered away in imperially-driven pinprick operations in Turkey, Norway and the Aegean while the Red Army shouldered the burden of destroying German land forces. Success breeds many fathers but Churchill's paternity suit on Overlord can be dismissed out of hand.

Churchill remained weak and vacillating on Overlord throughout spring 1944 but there was one theatre where he was always virile and assertive and it is to this theatre - the eastern Mediterranean - that we now turn.

CHAPTER TWENTY-THREE: BRITAIN MUST BE THE LEADING MEDITERRANEAN POWER, April- December 1944

Our long term political and military objects are to retain Greece as a British sphere of influence and to prevent Russian domination of Greece, which would gravely prejudice our strategical position in the Eastern Mediterranean.

General Maitland Wilson, Middle East Commander-in-Chief, 6th May 1944

It seems to me that the collaborators in Greece in many cases did the best they could to shelter the Greek population from German oppression... The Communists are the main foe... there should be no question of increasing the severities against the collaborationists in order to win Communist approval.

Churchill to Sir Orme Sargent, 22nd April 1945

Strategists and statesmen have always been drawn to Greece and its extended Mediterranean coastline. Britain backed Greece in its struggles against the Ottoman Empire in the 1820s to discomfit its great rival and gain a new friend. The Allies supported Greece against Bulgaria in World War I, and Chamberlain guaranteed Greece against Italy two months after he'd guaranteed Poland against Germany. Churchill honoured this compact in spring 1941, despatching the cream of the Desert Army to Greece in a misguided attempt to staunch a German invasion and, as a result, squandered a golden opportunity to expel the Axis from Africa. In 1944, Greece once more assumed pole position in Winston Churchill's worldview.

I

Greece rose to the top of Britain's political agenda in spring 1944 as the Red Army advanced across southern Europe towards the Adriatic, threatening to isolate German forces in Greece. If Russia reached the Adriatic via Romania, Bulgaria and Yugoslavia, it could also - by forcing the German garrison to withdraw - gain control of Greece, a chilling prospect for Churchill and Eden who regarded the Mediterranean as a British lake[166] and were horrified by the thought of Soviet forces coming within striking distance of Suez and Alexandria.

[166] In November 1875, the *Daily Bristol Times and Mirror* declared *"the Mediterranean is an English lake and the Suez Canal is only another name for the Thames and the Mersey"* (Kyle, *Suez*, p.14).

Map 33: Dreaded Soviet Advance towards the Adriatic and/or Aegean

Consequently, in May 1944, Foreign Secretary Eden approached Ambassador Gusev with a business-like proposal - if Britain endorsed Russian control of Romania, would Russia accept British hegemony over Greece? Stalin - who hoped to erect a bulwark of protective client states on his western frontier - agreed on condition that America endorsed the agreement, a stipulation that generated some embarrassment for while Ambassador Halifax informed State Secretary Hull of these discussions, he failed to mention that the deal had already been agreed in principle. Churchill gave the game away in a telegram to Roosevelt, an oversight which drew a frosty rebuke from Washington. On 13th June, Roosevelt reluctantly endorsed the Anglo-Soviet *fait accompli* on condition that it (i) stood for no more than three months (ii) addressed military matters only, and (iii) set no precedent for territorial carve-ups without American involvement. Churchill expressed contrition to Roosevelt in correspondence but grizzled in private over Britain's declining autonomy.

Ongoing Allied successes in 1944 (principally Overlord and Operation Bagration) loosened Germany's grip on eastern Europe. Romania's pro-Axis regime was overthrown on 23rd August and - two days later - Romania declared war on Germany. Romania's defection profoundly influenced its Bulgarian neighbour, for while Bulgaria had never declared war on the Soviet Union, it had declared war on Britain and America.[167] On 25th August, Bulgaria restated its neutrality in the Nazi-Soviet conflict and ordered a German withdrawal from its territory. Russia declared war on Bulgaria on 5th September and - three days later - Red Army units crossed into Bulgaria; by the end of the day, Bulgaria was also at war with Germany.

The Bulgarian and Romanian defections completely altered the Balkan picture for there was now very little to prevent Russia from driving towards Yugoslavia or pushing south into Greece through Bulgaria. Britain and Russia had struck a deal over Greece and Romania but - in such rapidly changing circumstances - Churchill feared that Stalin might renege on this understanding in favour of easy Grecian pickings. Consequently, on 9th August, the British Cabinet agreed to despatch 10,000 British-imperial troops to Greece directly on Germany's departure, hoping that British 'boots on the ground' would force Stalin to stick to his agreement.

By early October, Britain's three-month deal with Russia over Greece was coming to an end[168] as was Germany's grip on the country. Churchill's deal with Stalin had to be formalised if Britain was to retain its Mediterranean hegemony so, on 9th October, Churchill flew to Moscow to carve up eastern Europe with the Soviet dictator. It was the perfect moment. Preoccupied with his fourth Presidential election, Roosevelt was unable to attend, leaving Churchill free to deal directly with Stalin. In the absence of his good friend Franklin, Churchill found Tolstoy a most liberating experience.

II

Churchill arrived in Moscow in the early afternoon of 9th October and met Stalin at 10pm. Having travelled to Moscow to resolve his anxieties over Greece, he wasted little time in getting down to business. After disparaging the leaders of Poland's Home Army - who had defied the Nazis for four weeks - he informed Stalin that

> *Britain must be the leading Mediterranean power and he hoped Marshal Stalin would let him have the first say about Greece in the same way as Marshal Stalin about Romania.*

---

[167] Germany coerced Bulgaria into declaring a 'symbolic' war on Britain and America on 13th December 1941 (Wojciech Roszkowski and Jan Kofman (eds), *Biographical Dictionary of Central and Eastern Europe in the Twentieth Century* (2015), p.258).

[168] Based on Churchill's 11th July telegram to Stalin on the subject.

Stalin agreed, acknowledging that it was a

> *serious matter for Britain... when the Mediterranean route was not in her hands... [he] agreed with the Prime Minister that Britain should have the first say in Greece.*

Having established a basic understanding, Churchill then suggested extending the Anglo-Soviet agreement over Greece and Romania to cover the whole of south-eastern Europe, an arrangement proposed without consulting any of the states in question or his Cabinet colleagues - Churchill unilaterally handed Stalin south-eastern Europe on a plate, such was his desperation to gain control of Greece.

In his so-called 'naughty document', Churchill awarded Britain 90% influence over Greece while the Soviet Union gained similar hegemony over Romania. Russia and the West would - in Churchill's scheme - jointly dominate Yugoslavia and Hungary while the Soviet Union acquired 75% dominance over Bulgaria. Churchill noted these figures on a piece of paper and handed the document to Stalin who added a large tick of approval. Feeling rather sheepish about the manner in which he'd happily surrendered millions of Europeans to Stalin, Churchill suggested burning the evidence but Stalin indicated he was happy for the PM to retain the document as a souvenir.

Through his 'naughty document', Churchill enthusiastically endorsed the division of Europe into two rival camps and Russian dominion over south-eastern Europe. Such a division would have occurred almost inevitably as Allied and Red Army forces advanced into Europe during 1944/45 but Churchill clearly condoned this arrangement and willingly surrendered Romania, Hungary and Bulgaria[169] to Stalin to gain control over Greece. Dominating the eastern Mediterranean was Churchill's prime objective and nothing - certainly not the rights and freedoms of small, inconveniently-located states - could be allowed to interfere.

Having resolved south-eastern Europe, Churchill and Stalin turned to Poland. At Tehran, the Big Three had decreed that Poland must shift 150 miles to the west to accommodate Soviet territorial demands but

---

[169] Eden and Molotov continued haggling, particularly over two Greek Aegean coastal provinces (Eastern Macedonia and Western Thrace) seized by Bulgaria in April 1941. Retention of both provinces by a Soviet client would afford Russia direct access to the Aegean, a prospect repugnant to Britain. Eden therefore reduced Britain's 'interest' in Bulgaria to 20% to secure the return of both provinces to Greece and re-establish a direct land link between Greece and Turkey, excluding Russia from the eastern Mediterranean. Britain's share in Hungary also declined to 20% during these talks while Yugoslavia pursued a 'non-aligned' stance after the war (Fenby, *Alliance*, p.323-324; Marietta Stankova, *Bulgaria in British Foreign Policy, 1943-49* (2014), pp.83-86).

had failed to inform the Polish government of this decision. With Russian troops now operating deep inside Polish territory, some sort of Polish endorsement was necessary and on 13th October, Prime Minister Mikolajczyk and two of his senior colleagues were summoned to Moscow to rubber-stamp the new borders. Aghast at the proposed mutilation of their country, Mikolajczyk and his colleagues rejected the proposals - accepting them would have placed four million Poles and the oil-producing region of Lviv under Russian control, undermined the morale of Polish forces fighting in Europe and compromised their own authority. Outspoken Polish opposition to these adjustments would only embarrass the Big Three so Churchill took it upon himself to bully the Poles into acquiescence; Stalin had just handed him Greece and Churchill was keen to repay the favour.

Churchill began with cajolery and appeals to 'reason' but quickly resorted to bullying and coercion as these extracts from his Polish conversations reveal:

> *Because of quarrels between Poles we are not going to wreck the peace of Europe. In your obstinacy you do not see what is at stake… We shall tell the world how unreasonable you are. You will start another war in which 25 million lives will be lost. But you don't care... You are absolutely crazy… unless you accept the frontier you are out of business forever. The Russians will sweep through your country and your people will be liquidated... We will be sick and tired of you if you go on arguing… you do not care about the future of Europe, you only have your own interests in mind... If you want to conquer Russia we shall leave you to do it. I feel as if I were in a lunatic asylum. I don't know whether the British government will continue to recognise you.*

The spectacle of a staunch anti-communist such as Churchill bullying an ally into ceding territory to Stalin verges on the grotesque but the Soviet leader had just obliged him over Greece and he wanted to repay the favour. Imperial boundaries were - in Churchill's view - sacrosanct but the jurisdictions of other states could be chopped and shaped at will to advance British interests. Six years earlier, Churchill had lambasted Chamberlain for coercing the Czechs into surrendering the Sudetenland to Hitler but - in 1944 - he helped Stalin grab the same slice of Poland offered to the USSR by the Fuhrer - hardly the 'Greatest Ever Briton's' finest hour.

Churchill's statesmanship failed to settle the Polish border at Tolstoy.

Buffeted by Churchill and Stalin, Mikolajczyk reluctantly agreed to present the proposed new borders to his colleagues in London but - away from Stalin's menace and Churchill's hectoring - they rejected the deal, forcing Mikolajczyk to resign. The Soviet occupation of Poland ultimately resolved the matter. In August 1945, a hand-picked Polish government accepted its new eastern border in exchange for parts of Prussia and 40,000 square miles of east German territory up to the Oder-Neisse Line. Russia gained territory from Poland, Germany was robbed to compensate the Poles and Stalin gained handsomely.

The Percentages Agreement granted Britain a free hand in Greece without fear of Russian intervention. German troops evacuated Athens on 12th October and British forces arrived two days later. On 18th October, Giorgios Papandreou's Government of National Unity arrived from Egypt to initiate a new chapter in Greek life. Churchill's chicanery had won Britain a free hand in Greece, it had an army on the ground and a friendly government in office but, unfortunately, things didn't turn out as Churchill hoped.

III

Greece proved to be more volatile than either Stalin or Churchill anticipated. The support given by the Greek King - George II - to the pre-war Metaxas dictatorship (1936-41) had converted many Greeks to republicanism; they were in no hurry to see their monarch return from exile and detested anyone who supported him. The country's two most vibrant resistance groups were both linked to the Greek Communist Party. EAM (*Ethniko Apeleftherotiko Metopo* - National Liberation Front) was a popular front of four centre-left parties with upwards of half a million members and a commitment to "*the full independence of our country … so that the sovereign people will decide on the form of its government.*" ELAS (*Ellinikós Laïkós Apeleftherotikós Stratós* - Greek People's Liberation Army) was EAM's military wing - it had 50,000 active members in October 1944 and controlled most of Greece apart from the big cities and a patch of territory around Epirus. Co-existing with EAM/ELAS were the Security Battalions, approximately 22,000 men who had collaborated with the Nazis to hunt down resistance fighters in the hills, while Organisation X comprised 2,500 rabid royalists in Athens. Even the Royal Hellenic Army (RHA) units fighting alongside Allied forces in Europe were heavily politicised. Following a purge of Republican and left-wing elements in April 1944, RHA units such as the 3rd Mountain (Rimini) Brigade and Sacred Band were staunchly Royalist and conservative in outlook. And finally there was Churchill, completely ignorant of Greek politics but determined to save Greece from communism and looking forward to a showdown with EAM/ELAS as his 7th November note to Anthony Eden indicates.

> *Having paid the price we have to Russia for freedom of action in Greece, we should not hesitate to use British troops to support the Royal Hellenic government under M. Papandreou... I fully expect a clash with EAM, and we must not shrink from it, provided the ground is well chosen.*

Despite these underlying tensions, all was sweetness and light at liberation. The Papandreou government contained six EAM members (one quarter of the total) and ELAS welcomed British troops to Greece. They made no attempt to exploit the power vacuum existing between Germany's departure and Papandreou's arrival, remaining in their rural strongholds as British forces occupied Athens.

The Greek honeymoon was shattered by disputes over the disarming and disbanding of resistance movements formed during the occupation. The German departure removed these groups' *raison d'être* but EAM/ELAS were reluctant to relinquish their weapons, fearing reprisals from conservative and monarchist elements re-asserting themselves within Greek society. Moreover, EAM/ELAS argued that the RHA units returning to Greece were equally politicised and should also disband. For a while, it looked as if Papandreou's government had fashioned a compromise by agreeing that ELAS and RHA units should merge equally within a new Greek army but General Scobie - British military governor of Greece since September - vetoed this solution, ordering ELAS to disarm by 10th December, while RHA units were to retain their guns and identity.

Churchill and Scobie's plans to precipitate a crisis by ordering ELAS to disarm worked perfectly for on 2nd December, the six EAM government ministers resigned and called a general strike for 4th December. On 3rd December, 200,000 people gathered in Athens' Constitution Square to vent their fury over British meddling in Greek affairs. The police opened fire, killing 28 and wounding 150.

The 3rd December massacre shattered the fragile peace that had prevailed since liberation. ELAS fighters poured into Athens to attack Greek government buildings and occupy 22 of the city's 25 police stations. Churchill responded in kind, reminding General Scobie that

> *you are responsible for maintaining order in Athens and for neutralising or destroying all EAM/ELAS bands approaching*

the city... do not hesitate to fire at any armed male in Athens who assails the British authority or Greek authority with which we are working... ***Do not hesitate to act as if you were in a conquered city where a local rebellion is in progress*** *[emphasis added]... We have to hold and dominate Athens. It would be a great thing for you to succeed in this without bloodshed if possible, but also with bloodshed if necessary.*

Churchill quickly boosted Britain's military presence in Greece. Two divisions, two infantry brigades, a tank regiment and supporting units were dispatched to Greece between 13th-16th December, increasing British troop numbers from 25,000 to 80,000. Bolstered by these extra forces, General Scobie assumed the offensive and on 22nd December, ELAS representatives first approached the British authorities to discuss armistice terms.

However gratifying this success, it also embarrassed the Allies whose moral authority rested on a promise to restore democracy to countries liberated from Nazi control without delay. Yet in Greece in December 1944, 80,000 British-imperial troops were actively suppressing a resistance movement which, only two months earlier, had been busy killing German soldiers. Churchill's 5th December instructions to Scobie also leaked into the public domain, generating a storm of protest in America and at home, where Churchill faced a Confidence Vote in the Commons on 8th December. Justifying Britain's sizeable military presence in Greece also became difficult after Hitler launched his 16th December Ardennes Offensive. As General Alexander indicated on 21st December, Greece needed a political solution and, on Christmas Eve, Churchill and Eden flew to Athens to search for that solution.

IV

Three considerations drew Churchill to Athens in December 1944:

- **imperialism:** Greece was vital to British imperial interests and Churchill flew to Athens to maintain British control over the eastern Mediterranean and exclude Soviet influence. The gateway to Suez and Middle Eastern oil had to be protected.

- **politics:** by late 1944, Britain was very much the junior partner in the Atlantic Alliance. Churchill had been forced to endorse Overlord, Dragoon and Eisenhower's broad front strategy, while his own Ljubljana

Gap strategy had been ruthlessly sidelined.[170] He resented this subordination and independent action in Greece would enable him to play the part of a big fish in a small pond.

- **excitement:** the man who'd attended the Sidney Street siege, who'd sought military command at Antwerp and who'd hoped to visit Normandy on D-Day derived a peculiar pleasure from proximity to gunfire and strife-torn Athens would certainly provide this.

The December unrest had completely undermined the Papandreou Government's credibility and Papandreou tendered his resignation on 4th December but Churchill refused to accept it, informing Sir Rex Leeper (British Ambassador) that *"you must force Papandreou to stand to his duty... should he resign, he should be locked up until he comes to his senses."* However, maintaining a lame duck Prime Minister suited no one - a new government was needed to drag Greece out of the mire. Unfortunately, the man with the power to appoint a new government - King George II - was unwelcome in Greece while most of the politicians capable of forming a new government were Athens-based. Leeper and MacMillan recommended a Regency and - in Archbishop Damaskinos - they believed they'd found their man. Damaskinos was a rare bird - a clergyman who'd acted with integrity during the occupation. He'd condemned the persecution of Greek Jews, opposed the deportation of Greek workers and questioned the collaborationist regime's authority. For all this, he'd been placed under house arrest and gained tremendous popularity without being tied to a political party.

Nevertheless - without having met him - Churchill formed a strong prejudice against the prelate, labelling him a "*quisling and a Communist*" and informing Roosevelt that *"there is suspicion that the Archbishop is ambitious of obtaining chief political power, and that, supported by EAM, he will use it ruthlessly against existing ministers."* Churchill's opposition to the Archbishop blocked any hope of forming a regency, but Leeper, MacMillan, General Alexander and senior American figures such as Edward Stettinius and Lincoln MacVeagh[171] endorsed the cleric and

---

[170] The Ljubljana Gap Strategy was a 'plan' for the Allies to force their way into southern Austria via a supposed 'gap' between the Julian and Dinaric Alps near Ljubljana in present-day Slovenia. Brooke rejected the plan on the grounds of terrain and weather, arguing that the campaign *"would not start till after September... [and] we should embark on a campaign through the Alps in winter... if we took the season of the year and the topography of the country in league against us, we should have three enemies instead of one."* (Howard, *The Mediterranean Strategy in the Second World War,* pp.62-66; Deakin et al, *British Political* and *Military Strategy in Central, Eastern and Southern Europe,* p.58; Ponting, *Churchill*, pp.625-626).

[171] Stettinius succeeded Cordell Hull as US Secretary of State (Foreign Secretary) on 1st December 1944 and MacVeagh was America's Ambassador to Greece.

finally, on 24th December, Churchill resolved *"to fly to Athens [to] see the situation on the spot, and especially make the acquaintance of the Archbishop, around whom so much was turning."*

Churchill and Damaskinos met for the first time on 25th December and - experiencing something of a Damascene conversion - the PM formed an entirely positive impression of the cleric. From having been his staunchest critic, Churchill became his fervent champion, a change of heart no doubt induced by the Archbishop's denunciation of EAM/ELAS during the recent crisis. As Churchill informed the President, *"I have seen the Archbishop several times, and he made a very good impression on me by the sense of power and decision which he conveyed as well as by his shrewd political judgements."*

Having favourably impressed the Prime Minister, Damaskinos became a key element in Churchill's three-pronged plan to dominate Greece. Between 26th-28th December, the Patriarch chaired a conference of all the leading players in the Greek drama sponsored by the PM. The conference failed to stop the fighting but overwhelmingly endorsed a Damaskinos Regency, prevailing upon Churchill to persuade the King to support such a move on his return to London.

While the conference was underway, General Scobie renewed his ground offensive and over-ran a key ELAS stronghold (13th Roumeli Division headquarters) on 29th December. ELAS morale crumbled and by the end of the month, ELAS units had been expelled from Piraeus and southern Athens. On 1st January, Communist representatives again approached General Scobie to discuss ceasefire terms.

Churchill returned to London on 29th December and immediately set about converting the King to a Regency. His Majesty balked at such a move, fearing it would dilute his own authority but Churchill had two formidable weapons at his disposal. Firstly, he informed the King that he would go ahead and acknowledge a Regency even if George refused to proclaim one and secondly, he simply tongue-lashed the hapless monarch into submission. Churchill saw George twice on 29th December, spending six hours in his company and finally - at 4:30am on 30th December - the supine sovereign succumbed to Churchill's verbal onslaught, proclaiming a Regency later that day.

Events moved quickly once the Archbishop was appointed Regent. Papandreou resigned on 1st January and General Nikolaos Plastiras was instructed to form a new government without EAM support on 3rd January. The Plastiras appointment was a master-stroke. A strident anti-communist, he reassured right-wing elements in Greece (and Churchill) that the struggle against EAM/ELAS would continue while his role in deposing George II's father in 1922 reassured those who feared a return of the Glücksburg monarchy.[172]

The military struggle ended around the same time. British troops launched their third and final offensive against ELAS on 3rd January and were in full control of Athens by the 6th. An armistice was agreed on the 11th and came into effect on 15th January. Under the ceasefire, ELAS forces were to withdraw one hundred miles to the north and west of Athens, give up Salonika and the Peloponnese and exchange prisoners of war captured in the recent fighting. Under the terms of the 12th February Varkiza Agreement, ELAS agreed to disband and surrender its weapons. The Greek Communist Party (KKE) was recognised as a legal political party with the right to participate in elections scheduled for 1946 and, for the time-being, the KKE renounced military action in favour of electoral politics. Churchill had won - Greece had been saved from Communism and Britain controlled the eastern Mediterranean - at least in the short term.

V

Three noteworthy points emerge from the above:

Firstly, Greece was entirely free of Germans by 1st November 1944 so the 80,000 British-imperial troops stationed in the country by December were not there to prosecute the war against Germany - their sole mission was to promote British imperial interests and many of these troops had been withdrawn from frontline duties in Italy, illustrating Churchill's obsessive commitment to maintaining control of the Mediterranean and his willingness to prioritise British oil and Empire interests over the defeat of fascism.

Secondly, concluding the Percentages Deal with Stalin illustrates Churchill's disinterest in democracy in states where no British interests were involved.[173] Greece benefited from British support because it possessed an extensive Mediterranean coastline but other states in the region were abandoned because they were either landlocked (Hungary) or bordered the Black Sea (Bulgaria and Romania). Churchill's enthusiasm for democracy was entirely self-serving and his famous Fulton, Missouri speech - in which he railed

---

[172] A Dano-German family which gained the Greek throne in 1863.

[173] Churchill said nothing about Franco's fascist assault on Spanish Republican democracy during 1936-39.

against Europe's division by an 'Iron Curtain' stretching from Stettin to Trieste - is a masterpiece in hypocrisy. If Europe was divided by an 'Iron Curtain', Churchill and Stalin jointly installed the rail from which this invidious curtain descended and to pretend otherwise is disingenuous. Churchill freely acknowledged his complicity in erecting Stalin's dominion over eastern Europe to colleagues and associates, reminding Anthony Eden on 11th December that

> *we really must not press our hand too far in Romania. Remember the percentages we wrote out on paper... It is an awful thing that one cannot have it both ways, but you and I took great responsibility and we cannot overplay our hand in Romania.*

Two months later he informed his doctor that

> *Stalin isn't going to butt in in Greece. In return, he expects a free hand in Bulgaria and Romania. The 50-50 plan arranged at Moscow is working out in his favour. He'll let his people be beaten up in Greece for the sake of his larger plans.*

Churchill sold the Bulgarians, Hungarians and Romanians down the river before shedding a few shameless crocodile tears to gloss over his role as Stalin's willing accomplice.

Finally, Churchill's Greek victory was short-lived. The Civil War resumed in March 1946 and continued until October 1949, killing 150,000 people and displacing 700,000. British forces remained in Greece until January 1950 but, in February 1947, Foreign Secretary Bevin reluctantly conceded that Britain could no longer afford to bankroll the Greek government. America stepped in with the Truman Doctrine,[174] announcing that it would defend Western interests in the eastern Mediterranean against any Soviet threat, a small but significant staging post on the path towards Britain's Suez humiliation.

---

[174] In March 1947, Truman confirmed that the United States would financially support Greece, Turkey and other democratic states threatened by 'authoritarian forces'.

CHAPTER TWENTY-FOUR: THE EMPIRE STRIKES BACK, 1942-45

The Mediterranean route to Egypt, India and the Far East is a strategic link of great importance in the overseas communications of the British Commonwealth.

Military Sub-Committee Report, November 1942

It will be the height of absurdity if one of the fruits of our victory is to be the abandonment of our predominant position in Egypt... it would be sheer madness to admit the French and the Russians to any degree of control over Egypt... [and] I should also be opposed to American participation... To agree to any weakening of our predominance here would… [be] 'losing the peace' with a vengeance.

Lord Killearn, Ambassador to Egypt, 16th May 1945

Chapter Twenty-three highlighted one example of Churchill's obsessive impulse to dominate the Mediterranean and to prioritise that goal above all others. In 1944, Allied troops were diverted from Italy - where they'd been fighting Germans - to Greece to crush an indigenous Communist movement: at that point, denying Russia access to the Mediterranean was more important than piercing Hitler's Italian defences. Chapter Twenty-four extends this analysis by considering the work of three wartime agencies charged with identifying post-war strategic priorities - the Military Sub-Committee, the Post-Hostilities Planning Committee and the Suez Canal Committee. Even in the midst of war, Britannia kept one eye fixed on the future and - as ever - that eye was trained firmly on the Mediterranean.[175]

I

Post-war planning started early. A War Aims Committee was established in August 1940 at Labour's request to consider issues such as housing and employment but a mechanism to identify Britain's long-term strategic goals didn't emerge until summer 1942. The Military Sub-Committee (MSC) was formed in June 1942 to work alongside the Ministerial Committee on Reconstruction Problems to

---

[175] Readers should compare Chapter 24 with Chapter 6 to note the continuity in proprietorial British attitudes towards the eastern Mediterranean.

> *ensure that the military issues which will affect our policy when hostilities cease receive due consideration... [and] to undertake a study of the military aspects of lessons that may be drawn from previous attempts to secure lasting peace.*

The MSC embraced the three services - Rear-Admiral Bellairs represented the Admiralty, Brigadier van Cutsem spoke for the War Office and Dr. J.M. Spaight (a senior civil servant) monitored Air Ministry interests. Bellairs chaired the Committee as the ranking officer.

Britain was locked into the Mediterranean and North Africa during 1942 and early MSC papers prioritised this region. In the second half of 1942, the MSC evaluated British 'Post-War Strategic Requirements in the Middle East' and identified multiple reasons to retain ongoing control of the region.

> *The Middle East is a focal point in our Imperial communications on the security of which our world strategy must be built. Our particular interests in the Middle East may be defined in general terms as communications and oil... its security is a paramount necessity.*[176]

Controlling the Middle East demanded control of the sea routes leading in and out of the region, and controlling the Nile Valley and Red Sea was vital

> *to safeguard communications between Egypt on the one hand, and West, South and East Africa on the other. The continued occupation of the Sudan, Aden and British Somaliland will be necessary for this control.*

Controlling the Persian Gulf permitted

> *the passage of tankers to India and the Red Sea. Such protection would remain of importance, even if... a pipeline were laid to connect Abadan [in southern Iran] with Haifa or Suez.*

Always essential for imperial communications, interest in the region was increasingly motivated by oil, a point acknowledged by the MSC:

---

[176] British interest in the region intensified following the 1938 discovery of oil in Kuwait and Saudi Arabia.

> *The importance of the oil supplies in the Middle East is likely to increase still further in the fairly near future for the following reasons:*
> *(a) the potential capacity of the Middle East oilfields is far above the present output.*
> *(b) the growth of Russia's internal requirements, which in the decade before the war was greater than the growth in production, so that by 1938 oil exports were negligible.*
> *(c) a similar condition to the above may well occur in the United States which may, within a relatively short period, become an oil importing country. This would limit the amount of oil available for export from South America to the eastern hemisphere... It is therefore clear that we shall continue to require oil concessions in Iraq, South Persia, the Persian Gulf and the Egyptian oil areas.*

The November 1942 draft of this paper identified additional reasons to justify ongoing British control:

> *The Middle East forms an important base from which we can exercise pressure against Southern Europe in the event of developments hostile to Anglo-American interests. It follows that we must not allow any developments in the Middle East which would threaten our... essential strategic and economic requirements and that we should have the necessary rights and facilities by treaties to permit the rapid development of effective aid in order to meet any such threat.*

The MSC's evaluation of 'Post-War Strategic Requirements in the Mediterranean Basin' reproduced many of the arguments advanced in the Middle East paper. For example,

> *the Mediterranean route from Great Britain and North America... to Egypt, Iraq and the Persian Gulf (with their essential oil supplies), East Africa, India, the Far East, Australia and New Zealand... is a strategic link of great importance in our imperial communications... [it is also] the highway for our immense trade with our Dominions and Colonies, India and Burma, and all the countries East of Suez.*

The MSC could not *"forecast what the European situation will be and how it will affect the Mediterranean… in 10 or 15 years' time"* but insisted that

> *the Mediterranean will retain for us all its importance strategically, as a main highway and as an area from which*

> *we can exercise influence on Southern Europe, including the Balkans.* ***All our war experience present and past goes to prove the importance to us of controlling this sea, for when we have temporarily lost control we have suffered, and have then found it necessary to take drastic steps to regain that control*** *[emphasis added].*

The final draft of the 'Mediterranean Basin' document (June 1943) justified British control of the region on various grounds.

> ***The security of the Middle East with its existing and prospective oil resources is a vital interest of the British Empire*** *[emphasis added]. The ability to exercise superior sea and air power in the Eastern Mediterranean is essential if the security of the Middle East is to be assured, and furthermore if a European aggressor coming down through the Balkans is to be prevented from... threatening our Indian Ocean Communications... The Mediterranean is also important because it is the highway for the immense trade between the British Isles and the Dominions, Colonies, India, Burma and all countries east of Suez... The security of our sea and air communications in the Mediterranean is therefore a primary requirement which we should take steps to ensure under post-war conditions.*

Such arguments readily explain Churchill's repeated attempts to divert resources away from Overlord and into the Mediterranean and his obsession with dominating Greece.

II

Much improved military conditions inspired the formation of the Post-Hostilities Planning Committee [PHPC] in August 1943 to ensure that the

> *military issues which will affect the policy of His Majesty's Government in the United Kingdom when hostilities cease are given due consideration... [The PHPC] will be collectively responsible for representing the Joint Service viewpoint in regard to post hostilities strategic questions, and you will also act as a channel through which the Service Departments can exchange views with the Foreign Office and with other interested Departments of State.*

Gladwyn Jebb - a Foreign Office Counsellor and former Head of its

Economic and Reconstruction Department - chaired the Committee to prioritise Foreign Office interests and minimise inter-service rivalries.

In December 1943, the PHPC generated a paper on 'British Strategic Needs in the Levant States' (i.e. those bordering the eastern Mediterranean) which reproduced arguments advanced in earlier MSC papers. The PHPC identified British strategic needs in the Levant as:

> *(a) the security of Imperial communications*
> *(b) the security of oil supplies*
> *(c) the availability of this area as a base from which to exert pressure in case of developments threatening British vital interest.*

Map 34: Principal Middle East Oilfields

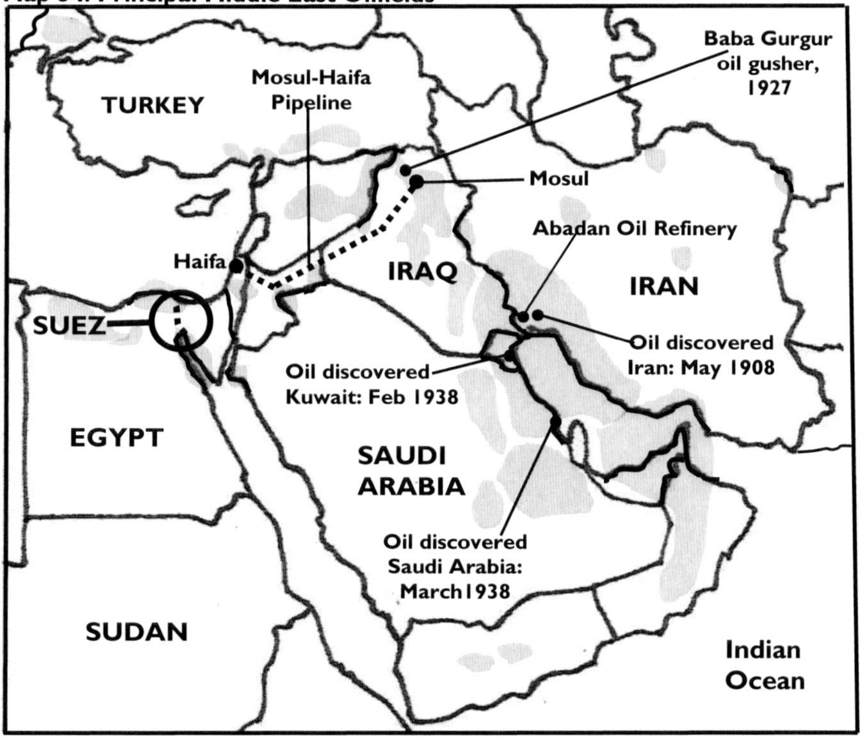

Oil increasingly inspired British interest in the region. According to the PHPC,

> *the security of the existing and future pipelines and refineries and of the oil-producing areas themselves is, and will remain, a major British interest. For this purpose we shall need at all times to enjoy the full use of the lines of communication*

> *passing through Lebanon, Greater Syria, Jewish and Jerusalem states including the railway from Kantara to Haifa and Tripoli and the road from Haifa to Baghdad.*

The eastern Mediterranean and Middle East also formed

> *the nodal point of our imperial communications. Any threat to the canal and its sea approaches can be met by forces stationed in or near the Canal Zone. Any threat against any part of the east-west route, or against any British territories in Asia, Africa or the Pacific, can be met by quick transport of the armed forces stationed at or near the nodal point of the Suez Canal to the scene of the threat.*

The paper concluded by noting that

> *whatever security system emerges, the importance to the British Empire and Commonwealth of the oilfields of the Middle East, the capacity of which is believed to be many times the present output, cannot be over-stressed. Moreover, the extent of the fields already discovered is very great, both in Iraq and Persia, and on the Arabian Littoral.*

III

The Suez Canal was variously dubbed the Empire's 'jugular vein' or 'main artery' and Suez Canal Company headquarters were transferred from Paris to London in 1940 to avoid complications arising from the Occupation. However, liberation saw control return to Paris and the Suez Canal Committee was formed on 25th September 1944 to advance British interests in the artery. Two issues concerned the Government at this time - excluding collaborators from all future Company business and increasing the number of British directors. The Company's curious voting structure ensured that only 31% of its directors were British while the British government and private investors owned 49% of Company stock, and the Committee wanted at least five more British directors (15 out of 32) to reflect British share ownership and the Canal's vital significance to Empire.

The Suez Canal Committee met regularly throughout 1944/45 and identified its principal objectives as:

> *(a) responsibility for the defence of the Canal should be vested in His Majesty's Government in perpetuity.*
> *(b) Canal dues should be fixed at the lowest rate compatible with efficient administration and with a reasonable return to the shareholders, including the Treasury.*
> *(c) the Canal should be so administered as to facilitate the exercise of His Majesty's Government's defence responsibilities. It is further desirable that the British Empire should have a share in the management and control of the administration consistent with its predominant position in the area and as the greatest user of the Canal.*

Of course, the Suez Canal runs through Egypt and Britain had recognised Egypt as a sovereign state in 1922.[177] Fearing Italian aggression in 1936,[178] Egypt signed a Treaty with Britain regulating Canal usage up to 1956 but - with the Italian threat entirely removed by 1945 - Egypt demanded immediate renegotiation of the 1936 Treaty and an early withdrawal of British troops from the Canal Zone. Mounting tension over these issues eventually toppled the Eden government in 1957.

IV

Having introduced Churchill's heir apparent, this chapter closes by revisiting Anthony Eden's views on the imperial significance of Suez and the Middle East. A backbencher in 1929, he'd dubbed Suez *"the swing-door... [and] jugular vein of the British Empire"* and his views on this artery remained constant over the next sixteen years. His April 1945 War Cabinet memo 'Defence of the Middle East' boldly asserted that

> *the Middle Eastern area... with Egypt and the Suez Canal as its core, is the meeting place of two continents and, if Turkey be added, of three. It is thus one of the most important strategic areas in the world, and* ***it is an area the defence of which is a matter of life and death to the British Empire since... it is there that the Empire can be cut in half. Consequently we are bound to give the***

---

[177] This did not prevent Britain from forcing a change in Egypt's government considered vital to the war effort in February 1942. It simply surrounded the Abdin Palace (Egypt's governmental headquarters) with tanks and troops and coerced King Farouk into appointing a new Prime Minister who would clamp down on Axis sympathisers. This naked display of British power - and Farouk's craven submission - later inspired the nationalist coup of 1952 (Roger Hardy, *The Poisoned Well: Empire and Its Legacy in the Middle East* (2018), p.134).

[178] Italy invaded Ethiopia (Abyssinia) with maximum ferocity in October 1935 and controlled Egypt's Libyan neighbour.

> ***Middle East an extremely high priority when allotting our available resources to the areas where we have responsibilities*** *[emphasis added]. For this reason alone, we cannot afford to resign our special position in the area.*

Britain needed oil and, according to Eden,

> *the Middle East is the sole really large source of oil outside America which is available to us. Recent studies indicate that in ten years' time neither the British Empire nor even the United States will be able to exert their full war effort... without the oil supplies of the Iraq-Persian Gulf area.*

Dominating Suez and the Mediterranean was vital to Britain before 1939 and considered essential to maintaining Britain's Great Power status after 1945 - the notion that this grand obsession simply evaporated during the war without informing Churchill's counsels with Roosevelt and Stalin is utterly implausible. Dominating Suez was embedded in the psyche of all imperial statesmen who came of age during 1880-1940 - it was engrained deep within their DNA and formed their 'default position' on all matters of strategy. Chapter 29 collates and analyses the evidence presented in the preceding chapters but before proceeding to this final Conclusion, four further issues merit investigation - Britain's bomber offensive against Germany, the Battle of the Atlantic, Britain's war against Japan during 1944-45 and Anglo-Indian wartime relations. No analysis of the global conflict could be considered complete without detailed scrutiny of these topics, both for their illumination of Churchill's strategic competence and on Britain's grand obsession with Oil, Empire and the Mediterranean.

CHAPTER TWENTY-FIVE: REAPING THE WHIRLWIND, Bombing Germany, 1939-45

Continuous reflection leaves me with the conclusion that, upon the whole, our best chance of winning the war is with the big Bombers. It certainly will be several years before British and American land forces will be capable of beating the Germans on even terms in the open field.

Winston Churchill to Clement Attlee,
29th July 1942

The moral effect of [high explosive] is vast. People can escape from fires, and the casualties on a solely fire-raising raid would be as nothing. What we want to do in addition to the horrors of fire is to bring the masonry crashing down on top of the Boche, to kill Boche and to terrify Boche.

Air Marshal Harris outlines his
strategic philosophy

To its supporters, the bomber was the wonder weapon of the twentieth century. It could brutalise 'uncivilised tribes' into submission and Basil Liddell Hart argued that air power would render large scale ground combat obsolete. Churchill and his Chiefs insisted that Germany could be reduced through a combination of bombing, blockade and subversion, while 'Bomber' Harris believed that Britain could triumph through air power alone. However, three years of bombing failed to break the will of the German people as it had once traumatised defenceless Iraqi peasants.

I

Despite the above, the bomber weapon was largely sheathed throughout the 'Phoney War'. Chamberlain and Hitler had initially hoped to resolve their differences through negotiation, a process that would have been hindered by initiating mutually destructive bombing campaigns. This changed on 10th May when Hitler launched his blitzkrieg on the west and Churchill became Prime Minister. Bombing was integral to blitzkrieg so there was little point in further restraint. On 15th May, Churchill authorised RAF attacks on land targets east of the Rhine.

The RAF initiated its attack on Germany with daylight precision raids on military-industrial targets. Conventional wisdom decreed that civilians would crack under prolonged aerial bombardment and Britain had no wish to provoke retaliatory raids from the larger Luftwaffe fleet. However, contrary to Stanley Baldwin's prediction, the bomber didn't always get through and - even when it did - often inflicted only minor damage. The Whitleys, Hampdens and Wellingtons[179] that comprised Britain's bomber force during 1939-41 were slow, lightly armed and under-powered - easy prey for German fighters and anti-aircraft fire so, in the second half of 1940, the RAF abandoned daylight bombing for precision night attacks. However, the bomber crews hadn't been trained for night attacks, they lacked target-finding equipment and the Mark 7 bombsight was useless on bombers trying to weave through flak. The August 1941 Butt Report confirmed the suspicion that night bombing yielded nothing productive by revealing that, of the planes which actually entered German airspace, only 33% dropped their bombs within five miles of the intended target while, over the smoky, well-defended Ruhr, this number slumped to one in ten.[180]

This dismal assessment placed Churchill and his Chiefs in a quandary for by autumn 1941, Britain had been ejected from Europe and the Libyan Battleaxe Offensive had ground to a halt.[181] The Soviet Union was demanding a Second Front but Churchill had no appetite for an early return to the continent. The Prime Minister had promised Stalin that Britain would "*bomb Germany by day as well as by night in ever-increasing measure*" but the RAF could hardly send its highly trained young men and expensive machines to crater the German countryside so, in the winter of 1941/42, the RAF abandoned night precision bombing in favour of general area bombing of German cities, largely because it could do little else. Britain had invested heavily in its bomber force - which had to be gainfully employed - and Churchill was under pressure to take offensive action, so the switch from precision to area bombing was implemented in early 1942. While area bombing is forever associated with the name of 'Bomber' Harris, the concept was fully articulated within RAF policy long before he assumed command. In September 1941, the suave and urbane Sir Charles Portal (Chief of the Air Staff) rationalised the new strategy by observing that

> *the weakest point in the German war machine is the morale of the civil population and in particular of the industrial*

---

[179] Although not suited to heavy bombing, the Wellington proved to be a remarkably effective aircraft, remaining in production until 1945. Its geodesic structure could absorb heavy punishment from fighters and flak while remaining airborne.

[180] Only two-thirds of the bombers which set out to attack Germany entered German air space and - if this attrition is factored into the equation - only 20% of bombers dropped their bombs within 5 miles of their intended target. Over the Ruhr, this figure slumped to 6-7%.

[181] See Chapter 10.

> *workers ... [the] attack on morale is not a matter of pure killing... It is rather the general dislocation of industrial and social life arising from damage to industrial plant, dwelling houses, shops, utility and transportation services, from the resultant absenteeism and, in fact, from interference with all that goes to make up the general activity of a community... It is in the thickly populated towns that the moral effect of bombing will be chiefly felt... it is an adaptation, though on a greatly magnified scale, of Air Control.*

The 'Air Control' reference confirms the continuity between the RAF's bludgeoning of defenceless tribes between 1918 and 1939 and the tactics employed against German cities during 1942-45. Directive 22 of 14th February 1942 confirmed the new strategy by stating that "*the primary object of operations should now be focused on the morale of the enemy civil population and, in particular, of the industrial workers.*" To avoid any uncertainty, Portal confirmed the following day that "*the aiming points are to be the built-up areas, not, for instance, the dockyards or aircraft factories.*" Britain was now committed to a policy of killing German workers without explicitly saying so, stating that it merely wished to 'de-house' them although the means by which workers' houses were to be destroyed without also killing large numbers of their inhabitants was never fully explained. Directive 22 also identified eighteen German cities as targets for the new strategy - seven primary targets (within 350 miles range of RAF Mildenhall and the Gee navigational system) and eleven secondary targets (further afield). The list expanded as Britain's bomber force gained in accuracy and range until it contained every German city with a population greater than 100,000 (58 in total) and Bomber Harris methodically worked his way through this list over the next three years.

Lord Cherwell's De-Housing Paper of 30th March 1942 also endorsed the new strategy, although it rests on dubious data and questionable analysis. Cherwell[182] calculated that, in its fourteen-mission lifetime,

---

[182] Lord Cherwell (Prof. Frederick Lindemann) was Churchill's chief scientific advisor and Paymaster General, 1942-45. A leading advocate of area bombing, he strongly opposed Coastal Command requests for Very Long Range (VLR) aircraft to protect convoys from u-boats and as a result, Allied shipping suffered huge losses during the winter of 1942/43. To remedy these losses, Cherwell recommended a 60% cut in Indian Ocean shipping in January 1943, which Churchill approved. Consequently, there was a serious shortage of ships to carry food to India when Bengal experienced major famine in the second half of 1943 which contributed to mass starvation in 1943/44. Area bombing therefore not only handicapped Allied efforts to win the Battle of the Atlantic but also contributed to the death of 3m Indians. Chapter 26 considers the consequences of Churchill's steadfast denial of VLR aircraft to Coastal Command throughout 1942 while Chapter 28 examines the 1943-44 Bengal Famine (Chris Wrigley, *Winston Churchill: A Biographical Companion* (2002), p.242).

each RAF bomber could de-house between 4,000-8,000 German civilians and if Bomber Command could deploy 5,000 bombers to their fullest extent against Germany's 58 largest cities during 1942/43[183] it would de-house 20-40 million Germans (one third of the German population) and - because losing one's house is a uniquely depressing experience - this would *"break the spirit of the [German] people"* and end the war.

Cherwell's superficially plausible analysis crumbles under even casual scrutiny. Firstly, at its February 1945 peak, Bomber Command operated no more than 1,600 frontline bombers so the notion of deploying 5,000 bombers against Germany during 1942/43 is nonsensical.[184] Cherwell also claimed that his research was based on a survey of the impact of German bombing on Hull and Birmingham during 1940/41, but whereas Cherwell insisted that civilian morale had buckled under these raids, the authors of the Hull/Birmingham survey - which appeared ten days after Cherwell's report - stated that

> *in neither town was there any evidence of panic resulting either from a series of raids or from a single raid... In both towns actual raids were... associated with a degree of alarm and anxiety... which in no instance was sufficient to provoke mass anti-social behaviour. There was no measurable effect [from the bombing] on the health of either town.*

Based on such dubious analysis, it's hardly surprising that area bombing failed to deliver the results advocated by its adherents.

Finally, on 22nd February 1942, Sir Arthur Harris was appointed Air Officer Commanding, Bomber Command and charged with delivering victory through area bombing. As Harris had developed 'Air Control' as a squadron leader in Iraq,[185] it was entirely appropriate that he should direct Bomber Command efforts to apply the same tactics on a much larger scale over Germany.

---

[183] Cherwell anticipated construction of around 10,000 heavy bombers (including Wellingtons) between March 1942 and summer 1943 and speculated that Germany's will to resist would crumble if *"half the total load of 10,000 bombers were dropped on the built-up areas of these fifty-eight German towns."* For simplicity, the notion of 10,000 bombers dropping **half** their total load on Germany's largest towns has been condensed to 5,000 bombers dropping **full** loads on these targets.

[184] Britain produced 2,515 four-engined bombers during 1940-42 and 2,182 in the first six months of 1943 (4,697 in total), falling well short of Cherwell's mythical target of 10,000 heavy bombers, particularly as not all the aircraft which entered service during 1940/41 were available for use during 1942/43 (Postan, *British War Production*, pp.484-485).

[185] See Chapter 4.

Like Churchill and many other senior British figures, Harris virulently opposed a Channel assault, viewing it as a costly and unnecessary 'diversion'. If Britain was to win the war, he argued *"it is imperative... [that we] abandon the disastrous policy of military intervention in the land campaigns of Europe, and... concentrate our air power against the enemy's weakest spots."* If Britain entered the continent on anything other than *"a mopping up police basis"* (i.e. a 'round up') it would *"play right into Germany's hands; [by inviting] her... to take best advantage of the one superior asset remaining to her, a vast and efficient army."* This would probably *"lead to the easily avoidable immolation of the flower of the youth of this under-populated country in the mud of Flanders and France"* and perhaps even a second Dunkirk. Like Churchill, Harris dreaded the prospect of a return to attritional trench warfare or - even worse - a major military setback. The Air Marshal believed that Britain could win the war through bombing alone and three months into post gruffly asserted *"give me 20,000 bombers and I will finish Germany in a week"* while in December 1943 he boldly declared that *"the Lancaster force alone should be sufficient... to produce in Germany by April 1st 1944, a state of devastation in which surrender is inevitable."* Harris shared Churchill's profound aversion to Overlord and the two men formed a strong working relationship over the next three years - reinforcing each other's fears and prejudices - until they diverged over Dresden.[186]

Harris's fierce commitment to area bombing - and his abrasive personality - drew him into conflict with anyone or anything inimical to this policy, particularly Coastal Command, his direct competitor for resources. On 17th June, he denounced Coastal Command - then engaged in a bitter life or death struggle with Dönitz's u-boats - as *"merely an obstacle to victory,"* demanding that Bomber Command have first call on all the new heavy bombers and target-finding aids (particularly centimetric radar) entering service.[187] At that time,

---

[186] Following a heavy raid on Dresden in February 1945 (which killed 25,000 - 30,000 people), Churchill drafted a memo stating that *"it seems to me that the moment has come when the question of bombing of German cities simply for the sake of increasing the terror, though under other pretexts, should be reviewed."* Harris was incensed, arguing that Bomber Command was merely implementing the strategy agreed by the Government and Air Staff. As a result, Churchill redrafted his memo but relations between the two men soured. Harris retired in 1946 and was aggrieved that Bomber Command crews were denied a WWII campaign medal. He was also omitted from the Berlin victory parade and Bomber Command was excluded from Churchill's victory-in-Europe speech (Grant, *1001 Battles That Changed the Course of History*, p.885; CAB 120/303, PM's Personal Telegram, Serial No. D83/5, General Ismay for COS Committee, 28th March 1945; Neil James Mitchell, *Democracy's Blameless Leaders: From Dresden to Abu Ghraib, How Leaders Evade Accountability for Abuse, Atrocity, and Killing* (2012), p.83).

[187] After the war, Harris' Director of Bomber Operations (Air Vice Marshal Sidney Bufton) offered the following thoughts on his old boss: *"He misused the bomber force in pursuit of his own policy which had no validity, no authority and no future. He played to a gallery of Buckingham Palace*

Coastal Command badly needed Very Long Range (VLR) aircraft to close the Mid-Atlantic Gap and centimetric radar to detect submarines but on every occasion when Bomber Command and Coastal Command clashed, Churchill backed the bombers with disastrous consequences for Britain's control of its sea-lanes. Chapter 26 considers the lamentable consequences of Churchill's support for Harris' 'offensive' bomber strategy over Coastal Command's more 'defensive' role.

II

Having been elevated to Bomber Command Chief, Harris was under pressure *"to regard the operations of the next few months [spring 1942] as a commercial traveller's samples which I could show to the war cabinet"* and his first two samples were Lübeck and Rostock, bombed on 28th March and 23rd-27th April respectively. Neither were major industrial targets but they were coastal towns (easy to locate) and largely built of wood (highly flammable) and suited Harris' purpose perfectly - he wanted *"his crews to be well-blooded... to have a taste of success"* and the Hanseatic ports served admirably. For the loss of only sixteen aircraft, Harris' force destroyed 3,200 buildings and flattened 320 acres in a series of raids on the two towns.

Map 35: Key German targets

---

and Chequers, and hoped to emerge as some sort of Duke of Wellington who won the war on his own." (Orange, *Slessor*, p.86).

However, the centrepiece of Harris' new strategy was the 30th May Thousand Bomber Raid on Cologne. By this stage, Britain had lost its Far Eastern Empire, Japan was on India's border, Tobruk would fall on 21st June and Churchill faced a confidence vote in the Commons on 2nd July. However, Britain's ability to put 1,000 bombers into the air over Germany fostered the impression of a belligerent Empire fighting back, and the raid's destructive impact was impressive - 600 acres flattened, 13,000 homes destroyed and 45,000 people rendered homeless for the loss of 43 aircraft. Even more gratifying was Churchill's response, recalled by Harris in his memoirs.

> *I always knew from the tone and quality of Churchill's voice... whether or no he was satisfied. I knew at once that he was satisfied then. At a time when there was no other conceivable offensive weapon we could use against the Germans, and when on every front and theatre of war we were confined to purely defensive action, Churchill now knew that we had an immensely powerful weapon which would give us that initiative that only comes from taking the offensive.*

Summer 1942 was full of promise for Harris. Area Bombing was enshrined as official RAF policy and new navigational aids (Gee, Oboe, H2S) and heavy bombers - particularly the Lancaster - were entering service in increasing numbers.[188] And the USAAF entered the fray in the summer. The first units of 8th Air Force arrived in May and conducted their first operation - against Rouen's rail marshalling yards - on 17th August. The Americans practised daylight precision bombing which complemented Harris's night attack strategy without ever compromising it. And as his bomber force gradually expanded, Harris could look forward to scourging the Reich in 1943 with three great air battles - over the Ruhr, over Hamburg and over Berlin itself.

III

Harris' first great battle of 1943 targeted Germany's Ruhr heartland, a focus that satisfied both Bomber Command objectives and the January 1943 Casablanca Directive[189] which encouraged *"the progressive*

---

188 Britain produced 1,956 four-engined bombers during 1942, of which 688 (35%) were Lancasters.

189 The 21st January 1943 Casablanca Directive advocated *"the progressive destruction and dislocation of the German military, industrial and economic system"* and identified five main targets for air attacks including (i) Germany's submarine construction yards (ii) aircraft industry (iii) transport system (iv) oil plants and (v) other targets in enemy war industry. The June 1943 Pointblank Directive prioritised destruction of German fighter strength as the key focus for Allied air activity (Garrett, *Ethics and Airpower in World War II,* p.53).

destruction and dislocation of the German military, industrial and economic system, and undermining of morale of the German people to a point where their capacity for armed resistance is fatally weakened." Between March-July 1943, the steel works and armaments factories of Essen, Dortmund and Duisburg experienced 43 major raids in which 34,000 tons of bombs were dropped. Steel production dropped by 8% with knock-on effects on the manufacture of aero engines, flak guns and steel plates for U-boats. Essen - home to the Krupp armaments complex - was a particular target for RAF raids and by the end of June, 100,000 people had been de-housed while 39% of the city lay in ruins.

The iconic raid by 617 Squadron's Lancasters on the Eder, Möhne and Sorpe dams on 16th-17th May was the centrepiece of the Ruhr Battle, a rare example of precision bombing among the general mayhem. The Sorpe was the most important of the three dams but it was an earthworks dam and not suited to attack by Barnes Wallis' 'bouncing bomb'. The Möhne and Eder dams were breached but the Sorpe remained intact, severely limiting flood damage.[190] Several small coal mines, factories and power plants were knocked out but water output and the electricity grid were fully operational again by the end of June. However, this partial success should not detract from the skill, bravery and ingenuity displayed by all involved in the raid.

As the Ruhr Battle ended, Hamburg endured a week of torment at the hands of 8th Air Force and Bomber Command, culminating in a massive firestorm which ravaged eight square miles of the city and killed 42,000. Many died when they were pulled into the raging inferno or when oxygen was stolen from their lungs as they sheltered in cellars. Coming directly after Kursk, Hamburg was the first time many senior Nazis entertained doubts over the prospect of final victory, as Field Marshal Keitel revealed in a letter to his wife.

> *Hamburg has been a catastrophe for us, and... [the] same must be expected for Berlin as soon as the nights are long enough for the longer flying time involved. That is why I want you to leave Berlin as soon as possible in view of the enormous danger there now is of fires breaking out... I am afraid of vast conflagrations consuming whole districts, streams of burning oil flowing into the basements and shelters, phosphorus, and the like. It will be difficult to escape from the*

---

[190] The planes attacking the Sorpe also experienced extreme bad luck - four were shot down, two were forced home, one lost its bomb and two hit the dam (with minimal effect) (Peter Jacobs, *Daring Raids of World War Two: Heroic Land, Sea and Air Attacks* (2015), p.167).

> *shelters then, and there is the danger of tremendous heat being generated. This will not be cowardice, but the sheer realization that in face of phenomena like these one is completely powerless; in the heart of the city you will be quite powerless.*

By the time Harris was preparing his next big battle (Berlin), the Allies held the upper hand in Europe. They controlled North Africa and the Mediterranean, and Mussolini's fascist regime had collapsed with the landing in Sicily; in the east, Germany had experienced major reverses at Stalingrad and Kursk, the latter being the Red Army's first warm weather triumph over German arms. More ominously for Harris, General Morgan delivered his Overlord draft plan on 15th July and the Quadrant Conference identified Overlord as *"the primary US-British ground and air effort against the Axis in Europe"* with a 1st May 1944 deadline. If Harris was to bring Germany to its knees before the Allies landed in Europe, he would have to move quickly and on 3rd November he addressed Churchill, summarising RAF achievements to date and outlining his plans for the coming year. In his letter, Harris noted that nineteen German cities had been *"virtually destroyed"*, nineteen had been *"seriously damaged"* and nine were *"damaged"*. From this, he informed the Prime Minister, *"that the Ruhr is largely 'out', and that much progress has been made towards the elimination of the remaining essentials of German war power."* Given the damage inflicted on Germany in 1943, Harris felt *"certain that Germany must collapse before this programme [of destroying Germany's largest cities]... has proceeded much further. We have not got far to go."* To end the war quickly and administer a *coup de grace*, Harris advocated a major offensive against Berlin to ravage it as Hamburg had been pulverised. Harris evinced a staunch belief that

> *we can wreck Berlin from end to end... It will cost us between 400-500 aircraft. It will cost Germany the war.*[191]

Only two weeks earlier, Churchill and his Chiefs had articulated strong objections to Overlord and a strong desire to remain focused on the Mediterranean [see Chapter 19] so Harris' confident assertion that he could defeat Germany by bombing Berlin *"until the heart of*

---

[191] Harris' original note stressed the importance of USAAF involvement in securing Berlin's destruction but 8th Air Force was forced to suspend air operations over Germany in autumn 1943 following catastrophic losses in the Schweinfurt-Regensburg raids of August and October, and their aircraft were also unsuited to night operations. The RAF would therefore have to attack Berlin on its own but in December 1943, Harris confidently asserted that *"the Lancaster force alone"* could force a German surrender (Tucker, *Battles that Changed History*, p.507; Grant, *1001 Battles That Changed the Course of History*, p.857).

Nazi Germany ceases to beat" reinforced these preferences. Other senior RAF and Air Ministry figures were starting to doubt Harris' area bombing strategy but as long as he enjoyed Churchill's support, he could ignore the Combined Chiefs' specific instructions and continue his area bombing offensive. Churchill endorsed Harris' intention to attack Berlin, believing that *"if this great industrial centre [Berlin] could have been paralysed like Hamburg, German war production as well as morale might have been given a mortal blow."* With Churchill's support, the Battle of Berlin commenced on 18th November.

Perhaps because it had been conceived as a means of pre-empting Overlord - rather than as a sound military operation in its own right - Bomber Command suffered a severe setback over Berlin. Berlin was located in the heart of Germany, forcing Allied bombers to fly over several hundred miles of enemy-held territory, clearly advertising their intended target. As the Reich capital, Berlin was ringed by powerful searchlights and ferocious anti-aircraft batteries and the Nazis had learned from the previous nine months' depredations, introducing numerous counter-measures. Lichtenstein SN-2 radar could differentiate between 'window'[192] and real targets, Naxos could detect and locate H2S emissions (turning this target-finding device into a homing beacon for German night fighters) while *schräge musik* comprised a battery of upward-firing cannons mounted on German fighters, allowing them to rip into Allied bombers' unprotected underbellies. The RAF lost 1,050 aircraft over Germany between November 1943 and March 1944 - 500 over Berlin alone - and 3,500 RAF aircrew were killed or captured in attacks on the German capital. By early March it was clear that losses on this level could not be sustained and that, far from defeating Germany, Bomber Command had suffered a serious setback. Even worse, Harris was now ordered to suspend area bombing and divert his aircraft to operations in support of Overlord. Instead of pre-empting Overlord, Bomber Command would now have to support an operation Harris considered wasteful and unnecessary - it was a directive he intended to resist with every fibre of his being.

IV

Nothing better illustrates the bomber barons' dogged obsession with strategic bombing than their vocal opposition to the Transport Plan during January-March 1944. According to Montgomery's draft plan, five Allied divisions were to land in Normandy on D-Day with a

---

[192] Small aluminium strips dropped *en masse* from aircraft to confuse and overwhelm radar defences.

further twelve arriving by D+11 while fifty or sixty German divisions skulked in eastern France and western Germany, ready to drive the liberators back into the sea. Should this occur, Europe's liberation would be delayed until at least 1945, Hitler's empire would be revived and he could focus his hubris on the east with predictable consequences for Anglo-Soviet-US relations. This grim scenario could be avoided by denying German forces speedy access to Normandy and this could be achieved by smashing the Franco-German rail network. If the Germans were forced off the rails and onto the roads - a slower and more vulnerable form of transport - their numerical superiority would be nullified and Overlord's prospects for success greatly enhanced.

To this end, SHAEF[193] devised a Transport Plan in early 1944 to dislocate the French rail network. The plan would undergo multiple revisions before receiving final approval but one constant in the planning was the expectation that RAF and USAAF heavy bombers would undertake this mission. In Prof. Zuckerman's[194] mid-January draft, Allied bombers would undertake a ninety-day mission to destroy 72 rail centres (marshalling yards, repair facilities etc) in France, Belgium and Germany to reduce rail traffic to 33% of its normal capacity. In the run-up to D-Day, this would be enhanced by a short-term strategy of interdicting bridges, gun emplacements and airfields in the immediate vicinity of the landing zones, with every attack in Normandy matched by two in the Pas de Calais to conceal the Allies' true intention.

The bomber barons opposed Zuckerman's Plan from the outset and Harris' outlined his objections in a 13th January letter to Portal.

> *Overlord must now presumably be regarded as an inescapable commitment... It is clear that the best and indeed the only efficient support which Bomber Command can give to Overlord is the intensification of attacks on suitable industrial centres in Germany. If we attempt to substitute for this process attacks on gun emplacements, beach defences, communications or dumps in occupied territories, we shall commit the irremediable error of diverting our best weapon from the military function for which it has been equipped and*

---

[193] SHAEF - Supreme Headquarters Allied Expeditionary Force.

[194] An academic zoologist, Prof. Solly Zuckerman assessed the impact of bombing on buildings and people in the early stages of the war before developing plans for the aerial bombardment of Pantelleria and Sicily. These operations proved successful and he developed and refined the original Transport Plan to disrupt the Franco-German-Belgian rail network in the run-up to D-Day (Eisenhower, *Eisenhower*, p.114; Orange, *Tedder*, p.223).

> *trained to tasks which it cannot effectively carry out. Though this might give a specious appearance of 'supporting' the army, in reality it would be the greatest disservice we could do them. It would lead directly to disaster.*

Harris and Spaatz's[195] opposition intensified when the plan was formally presented to them on 15th February by Air Marshal Leigh-Mallory, designated commander of the Allied Expeditionary Air Force (AEAF). Harris and Spaatz wanted to continue with Pointblank but for very different reasons. Spaatz knew that Overlord required air supremacy and wanted to continue his attacks on aircraft factories to shatter German fighter production and tempt the Luftwaffe into aerial combat where it could be destroyed.[196] He simply didn't believe the Luftwaffe would come out and fight to defend French rail targets.

Harris also wanted to stick with Pointblank but mainly because it allowed him to continue his area attacks on German cities. Despite the disappointing results from the Battle of Berlin, Harris believed that Germany was on the verge of collapse and switching to a 'panacea target'[197] at this critical juncture would give Germany "*a breathing-space in which to effect a general industrial recovery.*" Petty prejudice may also have influenced Harris and Spaatz's opposition to Zuckerman's Plan - Spaatz and Harris were bomber men through and through while Leigh-Mallory was an ex-fighter commander and the notion of a former fighter chief exercising command over bomber forces was anathema to both men. When Leigh-Mallory announced his intention to take control of all British-based bombers by 1st March, Spaatz simply said "*That's all I want to know; I've nothing further to say,*" and took no further part in the discussion. Two days later, Harris wrote to AEAF insisting that the demands placed on his Command "*cannot be fulfilled, and I am compelled to disavow any responsibility for the consequences which their non-fulfilment would entail.*"

---

[195] Carl A. Spaatz, Commander of US Strategic Air Forces in Europe from January 1944 onwards. This included US 8th Air Force in Britain and 15th Air Force in Italy.

[196] By spring 1944, the P51 Mustang - equipped with disposable fuel tanks - was accompanying American bombers on raids deep inside Germany. It outclassed contemporary German fighters and inflicted heavy damage on Germany's remaining fighter strength. Between January 1944 and D-Day, the Luftwaffe lost 6,259 planes in combat and roughly half that number in non-combat accidents. As a result, Allied bombers faced minimal fighter opposition during the last year of the war and could bomb Germany virtually at will. Similarly, German fighters were largely absent from the skies over Normandy, flying 319 sorties on D-Day against 14,500 Allied sorties (Boog et al, *Germany and the Second World War*: Vol. 7, pp.86-87).

[197] A 'panacea target' was Harris' dismissive term for anything other than area bombing of German cities and included attacks on German oil production facilities and rail centres. The possibility that his own manic obsession with area bombing might constitute something of a 'panacea' in itself never troubled him.

The Transport Plan therefore faced great hostility from senior Allied air commanders from the start but Eisenhower and his SHAEF team were equally adamant that - without the Transport Plan - Overlord would fail. This generated deadlock and all the time the clock was ticking towards Overlord in late May/early June - the stakes couldn't have been higher.

While Harris and Spaatz opposed the Plan for largely military reasons, other figures expressed political and diplomatic reservations, for not only did Eisenhower want the bombers to focus on rail targets in the run-up to D-Day, he also wanted the bombers to come under SHAEF control during this critical period. This reflected his Mediterranean experiences where - at critical moments such as Salerno - he'd been forced to beg for air support and was determined not to repeat this demeaning necessity in the larger and more decisive Overlord venture. So strongly did Eisenhower feel on this issue that on at least two occasions - once during a meeting with Churchill - he threatened resignation if his request was rebuffed.

Churchill queried Eisenhower's demands on both pragmatic and political grounds. Overlord was setting off from the United Kingdom with - at the outset at least - a majority of British-imperial forces but would do so under an American commander and if this same commander also controlled the RAF, Britain's great power status would be seriously compromised. Furthermore, if Britain came under renewed attack - through a revived u-boat threat or Hitler's vengeance weapons - while the RAF was under Eisenhower's command, it would be unable to offer a prompt and independent response, a state of affairs that could both compromise British security and embarrass Churchill politically.

Churchill and Eden also worried about the scale of French casualties likely to arise from the Transport Plan for - no matter how accurate the bombing was - French civilians would die if French targets were attacked. Looking ahead to the post-war world, Britain would need France to balance out the Soviet presence in Europe and restrain Germany, but Anglo-French relations had been soured by Mers-el-Kébir[198] and would deteriorate further if the RAF killed large numbers

[198] Following the June 1940 armistice, Churchill was worried lest the French Navy fell into German hands and - to prevent this - ordered a pre-emptive strike against the French naval base of Mers-el-Kébir in Algeria on 3rd July. Royal Navy forces sank one battleship, damaged five other vessels and killed 1,297 French sailors. The French admirals had assured Churchill that they would scuttle their ships rather than let them fall into German hands and were outraged by what they considered a prime example of 'perfidious Albion' (Robert O'Neill and Paul Collier, *World War II: The Mediterranean 1940-1945* (2010), pp.24-25).

of French civilians in the run-up to D-Day. The War Cabinet discussed the issue on 3rd April and expressed *"a grave and on the whole an adverse view of the proposal."* They agreed to discuss it at future meetings and Churchill informed Eisenhower that he would raise the matter with Roosevelt while the Foreign Office contacted the State Department.

The Transport Plan therefore had to overcome several major obstacles before it could be implemented and its eventual adoption is a tribute to the persistence and diplomacy of the men who championed this vital Plan. Chief among these was Sir Charles Portal, Chief of the Air Staff and Sir Arthur Harris' commanding officer. A former Bomber Command Chief (and therefore entitled to Harris' and Spaatz's respect), he was a member of the British Chiefs of Staff and also the Combined Chiefs' representative with responsibility for air operations originating in the UK. He enjoyed a close working relationship with Eisenhower's deputy (Air Marshal Tedder) and the two men worked together to secure the Plan's acceptance. As Harris' main objection was Bomber Command's supposed inability to bomb precision targets, Portal decided to test this theory by ordering a series of raids on French railway targets throughout March. If the raids failed, Harris' concerns would be vindicated and a valuable lesson learned but - if they succeeded - Harris' concerns would be invalidated and the Transport Plan could proceed.

The raids commenced on 6th March with an attack on the rail marshalling yards at Trappes - just outside Paris - and concluded with an attack on Laon on 24th March, with the Trappes attack setting a standard of excellence for the other five raids. The rail yard was attacked by 261 bombers and 699 tons of bombs, with 190 bombs falling directly onto the tracks, destroying a large quantity of rolling stock, engines, engine sheds, footbridges and electric lines. The marshalling yards were out of action for a month and French civilian casualties were relatively light. Moreover, only six of the 1206 bombers despatched on these six raids were lost, producing a loss rate of 0.5% which compared favourably with a 3.6% loss rate in raids over Germany. Even Harris was forced to concede that

> *the new means and tactics of precision bombing were so rapidly mastered (I myself did not anticipate that we should be able to bomb the French railways with anything like the precision that was achieved)... [and] not even the most hopeful of the allied leaders had thought that the casualties would be so light or the setbacks so few.*

With Harris acknowledging the raids' success, it was difficult to maintain objections on the grounds of Bomber Command's supposed inaccuracy, and Spaatz finally conceded on 25th March when he accepted that his other preferred plan - attacking synthetic oil plants - would not directly assist Allied forces on D-Day.

The controversy over who would control the bombers rumbled on through March and April as French rail targets were attacked. Portal drafted a paper on 9th March to try to resolve the matter with Tedder nominated to coordinate operations in execution of the Transport Plan and Leigh-Mallory coordinating the Tactical Plan. Eisenhower, who endorsed the paper, agreed to accept direction from the British Chiefs of Staff on any occasion when British home security was threatened and he also agreed to accept the Combined Chiefs' direction on any occasion when they wished to impose additional tasks on the bomber force. This arrangement would continue until Allied troops were safely lodged on the continent.

The draft was submitted to the US Joint Chiefs on 17th March who rejected it because it did not explicitly award Eisenhower 'command' over the bomber forces. The paper was then returned to the British Chiefs who finally agreed on 22nd March to give Eisenhower 'direction' over the bomber forces, a form of wording acceptable to all. Eisenhower gained 'direction' (but not 'command') over the bomber forces on 14th April and issued his first directive three days later, instructing the bombers to:

> *(a) deplete the German Air Force, particularly the German fighter forces, and to destroy and disorganise the facilities supporting them; and*
>
> *(b) destroy and disrupt the enemy's rail communications, particularly those affecting the enemy's movement towards the Overlord lodgement area.*

As in all Allied agreements, the final arrangement was a blend of compromise and negotiation. The bombers could continue attacking German fighter targets as long as they also punished the rail network - Harris and Spaatz's mulish resistance had gained some significant concessions.

The debate over French civilian casualties raged on throughout March and April, inspired by inflated statistics furnished by Bomber Command (who predicted 80,000 - 160,000 casualties (25% fatal)) and Lord Cherwell (who anticipated 160,000 casualties (25% fatal)). At the same time, Churchill and Eden were concerned by the prospect of excessive French casualties. Churchill believed that a high death rate "*will smear the good name of the Royal Air Force across the world*" while Eden worried that significant French and Belgian casualties might drive the two states towards the Soviet Union *"in a Europe that was already looking more to Russia than we would wish."*

Three things resolved the debate in favour of the Transport Plan. Firstly, the bombing of Trappes *et al* clearly demonstrated the bombers' ability to obliterate rail targets while avoiding heavy civilian casualties. Secondly, Free France endorsed the Plan for the sake of the greater good. General Bedell Smith - Eisenhower's Chief of Staff - interviewed General Marie-Pierre Koenig, Commander of Free French Forces in Britain, who observed that "*this is war and it must be expected that people will be killed... we would take twice the anticipated loss to be rid of the Germans.*" Koenig's pragmatic response undercut Churchill's misguided objections.

And finally, Prof. Zuckerman unpicked the Bomber Command statistics to reveal their flaws. He discovered that in devising their estimates, Bomber Command had used his own formulae from the 1940-41 Hull and Birmingham research to calculate casualties per ton of bombs dropped and applied it to a very different context; in Hull and Birmingham, the Luftwaffe had launched surprise attacks on built-up areas to maximise loss of life while, in the Transport Plan, the Allies proposed to launch precision raids on non-residential areas using sophisticated target-finding equipment and giving the local population advance warning of the attack. He also noted Bomber Command's tendency to distort statistics by applying mysterious and unexplained 'operational factors' in inconsistent and inappropriate ways. Zuckerman's calculations suggested a maximum of 12,000 French civilian fatalities - a significantly lower rate than the one feared by Cherwell and Bomber Command - and he submitted this information to Tedder who duly presented it to the Defence Committee on 3rd May. Finally, after much swithering, the Defence Committee cautiously endorsed the Transport Plan as long as civilian fatalities did not exceed 10,000.[199]

Even now - with the Transport Plan securing a cautious endorsement - Churchill launched his final attack on the Plan in a manner which casts doubt on both his military judgment and overall commitment to Overlord.

---

[199] Approximately 10-12,000 French and Belgian civilians died in Transport Plan attacks (Hastings, *Bomber Command,* p.274).

At various points during 1943-44, Churchill had expressed confidence in the Allies' ability to land in France while at the same time expressing grave concern over Germany's ability to reinforce its bridgehead positions faster by land than the Allies could ferry in reinforcements by sea. As he informed Stalin at Tehran, *"I was not afraid of going on shore, but of what would happen on the thirtieth, fortieth, or fiftieth day"* and he raised this anxiety again on 19th October 1943 by declaring that - as far as Overlord was concerned - *"he was not afraid of the Channel crossing or of the landing on the enemy coast"* but the later stages of the campaign were deeply worrying.

> *He felt that by landing in Northwest Europe we might be giving the enemy the opportunity to concentrate, by reason of his excellent roads and rail communications, an overwhelming force against us and to inflict on us a military disaster greater than that of Dunkirk. Such a disaster would result in the resuscitation of Hitler and the Nazi regime.*

Churchill was right to be concerned about Germany's fast and ferocious response but the Transport Plan was designed to neutralise this concern. On 7th May - four days after the Defence Committee had cautiously approved the Plan - Churchill wrote to Roosevelt expressing grave concern over excessive *"French slaughters"*[200] and proposing the Plan's cancellation. As he explained to the President,

> *the War Cabinet have been much concerned during the last three weeks about the number of Frenchmen killed in the raids on the railway centres in France... I am personally by no means convinced that this is the best way to use our air forces in the preliminary period, and still think that the German air force should be the main target... The war cabinet share my apprehensions of the bad effect which will be produced upon the French civilian population by these slaughters... They may easily bring about a great revulsion in French feeling towards their approaching United States and British liberators... The Cabinet ask me to invite you to consider the matter from the highest political standpoint and to give us your opinion as a matter between Governments... The war cabinet is unanimous in its anxiety about these French slaughters... and also in its doubts as to whether almost as good military results could not be produced by other methods.*

---

[200] Churchill was making these points after the RAF had demonstrated a clear ability to successfully interdict French rail targets - at least Harris accepted the evidence that his bombers could take out French rail targets with minimal civilian casualties.

Given his well-founded fears over German reinforcement capacity, why did Churchill attempt to undermine the Transport Plan one month before Overlord? Had he simply forgotten his reservations of autumn 1943? Is it just another example of his famed inconsistency? Did he wish to implicate the United States as an accessory in excessive *"French slaughters"* or - given that he'd never really supported Overlord - did he simply find it impossible to give the project his full backing even at this late date?

Whatever his motives, Roosevelt responded with clarity and purpose, advising Churchill on 11th May that

> *I share fully with you your distress at the loss of life among the French population. However regrettable the attendant loss of civilian lives is, I am not prepared to impose from this distance any restriction on military action by the responsible commanders that in their opinion might militate against the success of Overlord or cause additional loss of life to our Allied forces of invasion.*

It was Number Ten's last throw of the dice. With Roosevelt's support, the Transport Plan was fully implemented despite Churchill's last-minute efforts to derail it.

V

The Transport Plan climaxed in the last five weeks before Overlord. A total of 76,200 tons of bombs were dropped under the Plan (71,000 on rail centres) and by 19th May, French railway traffic was reduced to 69% of its January level; by 9th June it was down to 38% and by mid-July had shrunk to 23%. The Transport Plan had clearly dislocated the French railway network but did it inhibit the rapid deployment of German forces to Normandy? German sources answer this question best. On 13th June, Germany's Air Ministry acknowledged that

> *the raids carried out in recent weeks have caused the breakdown of all main lines; the coastal defences have been cut off from the supply bases in the interior, thus producing a situation which threatens to have serious consequences... large scale strategic movement of German troops by rail is practically impossible… and must remain so while attacks are maintained at their present intensity.*

Three weeks later, Rommel advised Field Marshal von Kluge that

> *supply conditions, especially in Normandy, were already becoming difficult... due to the heavy bombing of railway installations... All the reserves that came up arrived far too late to smash the enemy landing by counter-attacks. By the time they arrived the enemy had disembarked considerably stronger forces and himself gone over to the attack under cover of powerful air and artillery support.*

Field Marshal von Rundstedt - senior Commander in the West - endorsed Rommel's assessment.

> *The Allied air force paralysed all movement by day, and made it very difficult even at night. They had smashed the bridges over the Loire as well as over the Seine, shutting off the whole area. These factors greatly delayed the concentration of reserves there - they took 3 or 4 times longer to reach the front than we had reckoned.*

The Transport Plan was a resounding success. Along with Operation Fortitude,[201] it kept the Germans away from Normandy and gave Allied forces a fighting chance of getting ashore on D-Day and staying there. It reduced Allied casualties in Normandy and contributed materially to victory in the west. We owe much to the men who championed this project, often in the face of powerful and ill-informed opposition.

---

[201] Operation Fortitude was a series of deception operations undertaken to confuse the Germans over the location of Allied landings in summer 1944. Of these, the most notable was Operation Quicksilver in which the completely fictitious US 1st Army Group under General Patton was created to convince the Germans that Allied forces would land in the Pas de Calais. This reinforced Hitler's expectations and - as a result - the nineteen divisions of Germany's Fifteenth Army remained in the Pas de Calais until early August, giving Allied forces in Normandy ample time to secure a lodgement and initiate a breakout. Throughout this period, Hitler remained convinced that Normandy was merely a diversion (Mary Barbier, *D-Day Deception: Operation Fortitude and the Normandy Invasion* (2007), pp.63-65; Milan Vego, *Operational Warfare at Sea: Theory and Practice* (2009), p.154).

CHAPTER TWENTY-SIX: THE ONLY THING THAT EVER REALLY FRIGHTENED ME,
The Battle of the Atlantic, 1940-43

The country is now more concerned with the Prime Minister winning the war than with his winning a debate in the House of Commons. The Prime Minister wins debate after debate and loses battle after battle. The country is beginning to say that he fights debates like a war and the war like a debate.

Aneurin Bevan, House of Commons,
2nd July 1942

Our fight with the Air Ministry becomes more and more fierce as the war proceeds. It is a much more savage one than our war with the Huns, which is very unsatisfactory and such a waste of effort.

Admiral Whitworth, Second Sea Lord,
15th December 1942

Control of the Atlantic underpinned every facet of western Allied strategy. Without it, Britain would be driven from the war and without Britain, there could be no Overlord - Hitler would be confirmed in his European majesty, free to fasten his malevolent fury on the east. Both sides appreciated the centrality of the Atlantic and - for six years - the men of the Kriegsmarine and Allied air and naval forces contested control of this crucial theatre. The Atlantic was truly decisive but - at critical moments - Churchill and Hitler both spurned opportunities to gain mastery over this vital arena.

I

There would be no great clash of capital ships in World War II. Britain and France enjoyed a 7:1 superiority over Germany in battleships and a 10:1 superiority in cruisers, and while German commerce raiders might menace Allied shipping, there could be no great toe to toe encounter to determine mastery of the oceans. If Germany was to triumph at sea, it would be through its u-boats and in Admiral Karl Dönitz, the Kriegsmarine possessed a ruthless and calculating commander. A submarine captain in the Great War, Dönitz believed his u-boats could win the war for Germany and he presented his prospectus to his Fuhrer in September 1939.

> *After a careful examination of the whole question of u-boat warfare, I am convinced that in the u-boat we have... a weapon capable of dealing Britain a mortal blow at her most vulnerable spot. The u-boat war... can only be successfully waged if we have sufficient numbers... The minimum requisite total is 300 u-boats... Given this number of boats, I am convinced that the u-boat arm could achieve decisive success.*

Hitler was indifferent. A *mitteleuropean* with a tendency to seasickness, he knew little of naval affairs and didn't even see the sea till he reached his 'forties. His dreams were of landmass and *lebensraum,* prizes his army and air force would surely grasp. Constructing u-boats would compromise tank and aircraft production so there would be no crash-building programme to furnish Dönitz with 300 submarines - he would have to make do with the 22 ocean-going and 34 coastal vessels he commanded at the start of the conflict.

Nevertheless, the u-boat arm benefited greatly from the conquest of western Europe. Germany acquired the Channel ports, forcing Britain to retain a large part of its fleet in home waters as insurance against invasion. France - Britain's great ally and fourth largest navy in the world - was out of the conflict, replaced by Italy, a fascist power with 115 submarines and a burning desire to master the Mediterranean. Germany also gained the French western seaboard, granting direct access to the Atlantic and effectively doubling the size and range of Dönitz's flotilla.

As a result, the u-boat crews viewed the nine months following victory in France as *die Glückliche Zeit* ('Happy Time'). Britain was stretched to breaking point and lacked the resources to meet its obligations in the Channel, the Mediterranean, the North Sea and the Atlantic while also maintaining a watchful eye over Japan in the east. In the first twelve months of conflict, German u-boats sank 1.6m tons of Allied shipping, reducing British food imports by almost 50% and in spring 1941, u-boats destroyed 792,000 tons of merchant shipping in the Atlantic alone. German successes were also attributable to Dönitz's innovative *rudeltaktik* (pack tactic). Submarines had formerly hunted as lone wolves but they now predated in packs, directed by radio to areas rich in convoys. Once in position, the submarines formed a line and fell upon their prey, overwhelming any escort. If an escort vessel broke off to hunt a submarine, this merely enhanced the convoy's overall vulnerability. In the spring of 1941, 99 u-boats and 5,000 submariners[202] came close to sinking the British Empire.

---

[202] Dönitz's u-boat fleet on 1st March 1941. Each boat carried a crew of 45-50 men (Boog et al, *Germany and the Second World War*: Vol. 6, p.348).

Britain and its allies introduced a series of counter-measures throughout the first half of 1941. In February, Coastal Command came under Admiralty control to maximise cooperation between the two agencies charged with defeating the u-boats. In September 1940, Britain gained fifty destroyers from the United States in exchange for American leases on Canadian and Caribbean bases and these ships came into service in spring 1941 - along with the new Flower-class corvettes, they could protect convoys across the full length of the Atlantic. The retrieval of a working Enigma machine from U-110 enabled Bletchley Park cryptanalysts to crack the reserve German hand cipher in June, turning an asset - Dönitz's central direction of the u-boats - into a liability; if the Admiralty knew where the packs were lurking, they could direct convoys away from those areas and despatch corvettes, destroyers and patrol aircraft to hunt the predators.

The United States became a combatant in all but name during 1941. Congress passed the Lend-Lease Act in March 1941 and undertook to safeguard its shipments across the western half of the Atlantic. In April, Roosevelt extended the Pan-American Security Zone to cover most of the western Atlantic, reporting German ships found in this sector directly to the Admiralty. In August, Britain and America divided the Atlantic in two, with Britain guarding convoys in the east and America and Canada protecting those in the west. After a u-boat attacked USS *Greer* in September, Roosevelt authorised a 'shoot on sight' policy against Axis ships found within America's security zone. By autumn 1941, America was effectively fighting an undeclared war against Germany in the North Atlantic.

Hitler finally declared war on the United States on 11th December - four days after Pearl Harbor - convinced that America would be pre-occupied with Japan in the Pacific and unable to support its British ally in the Atlantic. Dönitz re-deployed his long-range Type IX submarines to American waters and although Germany and America were now at war, American ships continued to sail in nice straight lines, showing lights and generating radio chatter, silhouetted against brightly lit coastal cities. Fully stretched in the Pacific, the US Navy couldn't escort ships across the Atlantic, ordering them to sail independently in the hope that this would prove safer than sailing in unescorted convoys. As a result, the u-boats enjoyed a second *Glückliche Zeit* in the first half of 1942, sinking 3m tons of Allied shipping in American waters, the Gulf of Mexico and the Caribbean. The 'American shooting season' finally ended in July when convoys and escorts started operating and American aircraft instituted regular patrols of US coastal waters. Britain also despatched a flotilla of armed trawlers to assist its ally in the Caribbean, while 53 Squadron Coastal Command was for a time - based on Rhode Island to protect New York harbour. As u-boat sinkings increased,[203] Dönitz looked for a place where his packs could predate with impunity, directing them to a section of the Atlantic known as the Mid-Atlantic Gap or 'Black Pit'.

II

As its name suggests, the 'Mid-Atlantic Gap' was a sector of the central Atlantic beyond the range of most Allied aircraft, an important consideration given u-boat limitations in 1942/43. Most u-boats spent the bulk of their time on the surface, sailing at 18 knots on diesel power[204] and while this allowed them to manoeuvre into strong attacking positions, it also rendered them supremely vulnerable to aircraft which could appear suddenly and were faster and more manoeuvrable than surface warships. Equipped with ASV radar,[205] they could detect u-boats on or below the surface and shatter their hulls with powerful torpex depth charges.[206] U-boats usually disengaged on sighting a plane so aircraft didn't necessarily have to sink u-boats to safeguard shipping, a concept Air Marshal Harris experienced singular difficulty in grasping.

In June 1942, Britain had one solitary squadron of Very Long Range (VLR) aircraft patrolling the Mid Atlantic Gap - 120 Squadron of Coastal Command equipped with B-24 Mark I Liberators[207] operating out of Iceland and Northern Ireland. The squadron had received a dozen Liberators in July 1941 but normal wear and tear and lack of replacements had reduced it to between 5-8 operational aircraft by August 1942, a completely inadequate number to patrol 180,000 square miles of ocean lying between Greenland, Iceland and the Azores.

---

[203] US forces sank 1 u-boat in April, 1 in May, 2 in June and 5 in July (Robert J. Cressman, *The Official Chronology of the U.S. Navy in World War II* (2000), pp.88-110).

[204] Diesel engines require ventilation for cooling and emission of exhaust gases and can only be used on the surface. Electric motors were used when u-boats were submerged - they had limited range, required regular re-charging and offered a top speed of only 7 knots.

[205] Air to Surface Vessel radar. Throughout 1942, Allied aircraft used ASVII radar which operated on a 1.5 metre frequency but from spring 1943 onwards, employed ASVIII radar which operated on a 9.1cm frequency and was more effective in identifying targets and almost impossible for u-boats to detect. The Bomber Command version of centimetric radar was known as H2S (Sebastian Cox and Peter Gray (eds), *Air Power History: Turning Points from Kitty Hawk to Kosovo* (2002), p.131; David Fairbank White, *Bitter Ocean: The Battle of the Atlantic, 1939-1945* (2007), p.243; Guy Hartcup, *The Effect of Science on the Second World War* (2000), p.30).

[206] Torpex was 50% more powerful than TNT, entering operational use in mid-1942.

[207] Mark I Liberators had a 2,500 mile range, compared to 1,680 miles (for the Mark II) and 1,800 miles (Mark III) - both later versions required substantial modification before serving in a VLR capacity (Richard Goette, *Britain and the Delay in Closing the Mid-Atlantic 'Air Gap'*, Northern Mariner/Le Marin du Nord, XV, No 4, Oct 2005, p.30).

Map 36: Mid-Atlantic Gap or 'Black Pit'

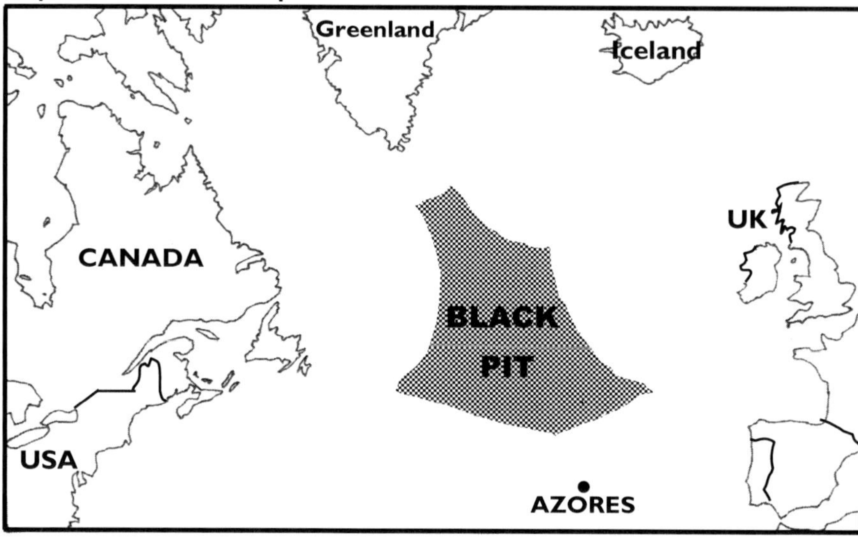

Admiralty figures highlighted these shortcomings in multiple memoranda throughout 1942. On the same day that Bomber Command embraced area bombing, First Lord of the Admiralty Alexander requested six and a half Bomber Command squadrons and 81 four-engined bombers from the United States to provide continuous land-based cover for convoys crossing the Atlantic, and five days later, Air Marshal Joubert de la Ferté of Coastal Command summarised the essence of the problem in a memo which noted that

> *the prospect of Coastal Command being able to work at reasonable efficiency appeared to be becoming more and more remote. The promise of centimetric ASV fitted Liberators had come to nothing [and] the one Liberator squadron was being allowed to die out... While fully aware of the importance of the sustained bomber offensive, it appeared to him that, if England was to survive this year... some part of the bomber offensive would have to be sacrificed and a long-range type such as the Lancaster diverted to the immediate threat on our sea communications.*

Two weeks later, First Sea Lord Admiral Pound warned the Defence Committee that *"if we lose the war at sea, we lose the war... [and we] lose the war at sea when we can no longer maintain those communications which are essential to us."* To avert disaster, Pound recommended major increases in Coastal Command strength to enable it to protect shipping and naval forces around the world. Pound returned to the fray with a 16th June memo warning that u-boats were sinking ships faster than Allied yards could build them and, left unchecked, this deficit would compromise Britain's island security. Referring to the recently published Singleton Report,[208] Pound argued that as Bomber Command's area bombing strategy could only generate long term results, Coastal Command should receive an immediate allocation of four-engined aircraft to deal with the "*supreme urgency*" of the u-boat threat.

While Pound and Alexander penned thoughtful memoranda, 'Bomber' Harris blasted pungent broadsides, branding Coastal Command as 'the enemy'. His 17th June note to Churchill described Coastal Command and its request for additional aircraft as "*merely an obstacle to victory*". Arguing that Bomber Command could win the war unaided, Harris insisted that his Command should enjoy exclusive access to Britain's entire bomber output and all the 'planes provided by America. Dismissing the deterrent impact of aircraft on u-boats, Harris insisted that

> *the purely defensive use of air power is grossly wasteful. The naval employment of aircraft consists of picking at the fringes of enemy power, of waiting for opportunities that may never occur, and indeed probably never will occur, of looking for needles in a haystack. They attempt to sever each capillary vein, one by one, when they could, with much less effort, cut the artery. Bomber Command attacks the sources of all Naval power, rather than the fringes of one type of enemy Naval operation which obviously menaces us - the submarine.*

The principal protagonists had outlined their competing arguments by June 1942. In one corner Harris, Air Chief Marshal Portal and Air Secretary Archibald Sinclair argued that Bomber Command should receive all the heavy bombers produced in Britain and America to win the war through bombing alone. In the opposite corner, Pound, Alexander and Joubert warned that - without additional VLR aircraft - the Admiralty and Coastal Command would lose the war at sea and the Allies would therefore lose the war, presenting a straight choice

---

[208] Lord Cherwell's March 1942 De-Housing Paper generated significant controversy and was heavily criticised by Sir Henry Tizard and Prof. Patrick Blackett. Mr. Justice Singleton - a High Court Judge - was invited to adjudicate on these claims but his May 1942 Report proved equivocal. On the one hand, he noted that *"I do not think it (the bombing offensive) ought to be regarded as of itself sufficient to win the war or to produce decisive results; the area is too vast for the effort we can put forth"* while at the same time observing that *"if Russia can hold Germany on land I doubt whether Germany will stand 12 or 18 months' continuous, intensified and increased bombing, affecting, as it must, her war production, her power of resistance, her industries and her will to resist."* (Terry Copp, *A Nation at War, 1939-1945: Essays from Legion Magazine* (2004), p.40; Overy, *Why The Allies Won*, p.104).

between Coastal Command's defensive strategy and Bomber Command's more aggressive posture. Locked in stalemate, the argument was referred to Churchill for adjudication but before considering the PM's response, a quick summary of the political and military pressures he faced in mid-1942 is essential. In North Africa, Eighth Army was defeated at Gazala by 17th June and retreated in disorder to El Alamein while Tobruk surrendered on 21st June.[209] Japan had penetrated eastern India and only the combination of unfavourable terrain, monsoon and over-stretched supply lines inhibited further incursion. In spring 1942, Labour politician Sir Stafford Cripps emerged as a potential replacement for Churchill while the Prime Minister faced a confidence vote on 3rd July which inspired Nye Bevan's caustic retort. And all the while, the Americans, Russians and large parts of the home audience were clamouring for a Second Front which Churchill was determined to resist. Indeed, on 12th August he flew to Moscow to personally inform Stalin that the Second Front was cancelled for 1942. Under such circumstances and given his own inclination towards offensive action at all costs, Churchill invariably supported the Bomber barons over the Coastal chiefs in every debate concerning resources. This was the strategy that would play best in Washington and Moscow, and the Thousand Bomber Raid had generated screeds of positive publicity. Throughout the summer and autumn of 1942, Churchill repeatedly rebuffed Coastal Command requests for additional resources to shut down the Mid-Atlantic Gap while lending his full weight to Bomber Command's area bombing strategy. When the First Lord of the Admiralty requested Bomber Command squadrons to plug the Air Gap in early May, Churchill advised "*I cannot agree to this further inroad upon the only offensive against Germany now in progress.*" When Admiral Pound requested additional VLR aircraft to attack u-boats passing through the Bay of Biscay, Churchill warned "*you must not trench so heavily upon the resources of the RAF.*" Churchill outlined his view of the Admiralty in a 28th August memo by insisting that

> *there can be no question of taking machines which will be used in action by the RAF in order to build up inordinate reserves for the Admiralty. The Admiralty always want not only to win the game, but to go to bed with the ace. This tendency must be strongly resisted.*[210]

Although Churchill expressed occasional doubts over Bomber

---

[209] See Chapter 12

[210] Churchill was referring to the allocation of fighters to the Fleet Air Arm in this note but it summarises his overall attitude towards the Admiralty.

Command's grandiose folly, on 17th September he instructed the Air Ministry to submit plans to increase Bomber Command from 32 to 50 operational squadrons by December, even suggesting that two of these squadrons be drawn from Coastal Command's meagre resources.

Churchill's enthusiasm for area bombing directly reflected the political and military pressures he faced but, given the Allies' prodigious aircraft production at this time, it was an extremely facile response. By mid-1942, Britain was producing 160 four-engined bombers per month[211] while Ford's Willow Run plant near Detroit produced 107 B-24s in December 1942 and 2,184 throughout 1943. Even a small portion of this output - two weeks' worth - would have enabled Coastal Command to close the Air Gap without compromising Bomber Command's long term strategy, and Churchill's refusal to accede to this relatively modest request represents a catastrophic error of judgment on his part which wreaked havoc on Allied shipping later in the year. In supporting Bomber Command over Coastal Command, Churchill also appears to have been swayed by the Bomber barons' dogged insistence that Bomber Command and Coastal Command demands were mutually exclusive.[212] In March 1942, Lord Cherwell - Churchill's confidant and crony - submitted his De-housing Paper which claimed that Germany could be defeated in 1943 if its major cities were obliterated by 5,000 heavy bombers[213] and, in the summer of 1942, Bomber Command was some way off this target. Indeed, it had only been able to mount the Thousand Bomber Raid by utilising its Heavy Conversion and Operational Training Units and three-quarters of the participating 'planes were

---

[211] Britain produced 1,956 four-engined bombers during 1942, equivalent to 163 per month. Coastal Command didn't want these bombers for their bombing capability but for use as VLR aircraft - any four-engined bomber could serve in a VLR capacity once suitably modified (Gavin J. Bailey, *Arsenal of Democracy* (2013), p.253).

[212] In a 28th June letter to Churchill, Harris warned that *"those who advocate the breaking-up of Bomber Command for the purpose of adding strength to Coastal and Army Co-operation Commands and overseas requirements are like the amateur politician who imagines that the millennium will arrive through the simple process of dividing available cash equally between all... the outcome would be to give every individual £50 once at the cost of wrecking the entire industrial organisation and income of the country. Similarly, if the Medium and Heavy Bomber Operational Squadrons of Bomber Command were distributed between the many claimants for favour... none of these claimants would receive anything more than a mere morsel... [while] our only offensive weapon against Germany would be destroyed."* Following his return from Moscow in August 1942, Churchill circulated this absurd letter (and an equally strident note from ex-RAF Chief Viscount Trenchard) to War Cabinet members with the comment that they *"serve as a considerable answer to those who attack the usefulness of our Bombing policy."* (CAB 66/28/35 WP (42) 374, 24th August 1942, Note by Air Marshal Sir Arthur Harris on the Role and Work of Bomber Command (28 June 1942); CAB 66/28/35 WP (42) 399, 5th September 1942, Note by Lord Trenchard on our War Policy - August 1942 (29th August, 1942); CAB 66/28/35 WP (42) 405, 9th September 1942, Air Policy: Note by the Prime Minister (9th September, 1942); Bell, *Churchill and Sea Power,* p.267).

[213] See Chapter 25.

twin-engined mediums rather than four-engined heavies.[214] This explains Harris, Portal and Sinclair's ferocious resistance to Coastal Command claims - every plane lost to Coastal Command moved Bomber Command away from the talismanic figure of 5,000 aircraft which, in their view, would win the war.[215] Unfortunately, just as the ex-First Lord of the Admiralty was turning his back on the Atlantic, the formerly hydrophobic Fuhrer was converting to Dönitz's gospel of aggressive submarine warfare, and this blend of Churchillian indifference and Hitler's new-found enthusiasm for u-boat operations precipitated an Allied shipping crisis by the end of the year.

III

The Fuhrer's limited interest in naval affairs declined further following the *Bismarck's* sinking in May 1941. *Bismarck* was more than just a ship - it was the pride of the Kriegsmarine, a symbol of German power and its loss refuted Nazi claims of invincibility. Following this incident, Germany withdrew its remaining capital ships (*Tirpitz*, *Scharnhorst* et al) to the safety of the Norwegian fjords where they could threaten Arctic convoys and discourage Allied designs on Norway. Thereafter, these leviathans lived a curious half-life - too powerful to be left idle but too prestigious and vulnerable to be risked in conventional operations. Hitler's disenchantment with his surface fleet peaked on 31st December 1942 when a small force of British destroyers embarrassed two German heavy cruisers in the Battle of the Barents Sea off the Norway coast. Admiral Raeder tendered his resignation on 6th January[216] and the Fuhrer threatened to scrap his remaining capital ships and convert their guns to coastal batteries.

But the u-boats were different. These small, stealthy and relatively inexpensive craft inflicted major losses on Allied shipping throughout 1940-42. In 1940, they sank 2.19m tons (471 ships) worldwide and a further 2.17m tons (432 ships) in 1941 but in the first half of 1942 alone, they sank 3.28m tons of Allied shipping in all theatres (585 ships). In June 1942, Rommel was rampaging across North Africa and Case Blue was about to devastate the Soviet Union - could the u-boats complete the Nazi triptych of success by dominating the

---

[214] Of the 1,047 aircraft participating in the Cologne raid, 755 were twin-engined Wellingtons, Manchesters, Hampdens or Whitleys, while only 292 were four-engined Lancasters, Stirlings or Halifaxes (Alan F. Wilt, *War from the Top: German and British Military Decision Making during World War II* (1990), p.233; Zabecki (ed), *World War II in Europe*, p.1427).

[215] Chief of the Air Staff Portal was much more reasonable in his demands - he believed that Bomber Command could defeat Germany in six months with only 4,000 aircraft (Hastings, *Bomber Command,* p.120).

[216] Dönitz replaced Raeder as Kriegsmarine chief on 30th January 1943.

Atlantic? Hitler's enthusiasm for u-boat operations peaked during a series of naval conferences in the spring and early summer of 1942 and - as a mark of the Fuhrer's growing favour - Dönitz attended the 14th May conference, assuring Hitler of his u-boats' war-winning potential. Indifferent in 1939, Hitler now displayed a convert's zeal, declaring that

> *victory depends on destroying the greatest amount of Allied tonnage possible. Thus all offensive operations of the enemy can be slowed down or even stopped entirely... The submarine war will in the end decide the outcome of the war.*

To achieve these goals, u-boat production was increased from seventeen boats per month *"to the very limit,"* shipwrights were exempted from conscription and scarce metals required for submarine construction (such as copper) were obtained from French and Belgian sources. And the Fuhrer was as good as his word. Throughout 1942, Dönitz gained 240 new u-boats, expanding his fleet to 400 by the end of the year, enough to sustain wolf packs at either end of the Mid-Atlantic Gap.

Dönitz benefited from more than just his Fuhrer's enthusiasm and an enlarged fleet. Throughout 1942, his wolf packs were supported by a flotilla of *milch cow* supply submarines which would rendezvous with his Type VII's and Type IX's in the middle of the Atlantic to re-provision them with food, fuel and ammunition and extend the duration of their patrols. The addition of a fourth Enigma rotor in February 1942 concealed German signals traffic from Bletchley Park for the next ten months, while B-Dienst (the Kriegsmarine's decoding service) cracked the British cipher used to schedule transatlantic convoys in December 1941 and could read British naval signals for a full year. During the most crucial year in the Battle of the Atlantic, the Kriegsmarine knew where to find Allied shipping while the Admiralty remained in the dark over wolf pack locations, greatly assisting the German submariners.

German vigour blended with British under-provision to produce a 'perfect storm' in the North Atlantic by late 1942. Monthly tonnage losses fluttered around the half-million mark in the late summer but climbed to 619,000 tons in October and 729,000 tons in November,[217] a hugely significant figure for Dönitz who believed that

---

[217] The October and November figures reflect losses from u-boat action across all theatres. A further 18,000 tons was lost to other causes (mines, e-boats, aircraft etc) in October and an additional 79,000 tons to other causes in November (Roskill, *The War at Sea, 1939-45,* Vol. II, p.485).

Germany could win the war if his u-boats destroyed 700,000 tons of Allied shipping every month.

Losses on this scale generated the Admiralty's predicted 'imports crisis'. Britain imported 61m tons of food, fuel, munitions and raw materials in 1940 but this slumped to 39m tons in 1942 and, based on the volume of imports during November 1942 - January 1943, imports for 1943 would decline to 17m tons. In July 1942, the War Cabinet had identified 27m tons as Britain's minimum import requirement for 1943, vividly illustrating the scale of the crisis. During this same period, 50% of the raw materials consumed in British factories were drawn from stocks - rather than imports - and the Royal Navy was down to two months of oil supplies. Churchill had anticipated a certain level of loss and setback when he supported Bomber Command over Coastal Command in mid-1942,[218] but presumably not on a scale which threatened Britain's survival. In July 1942, he had observed that *"it might be true to say that the issue of the war depends on whether Hitler's u-boat attack on Allied tonnage, or the increase and application of Allied air power, reach their full fruition first"* and, by the end of 1942, it was clear that Germany's u-boats were closer to their target than Britain's bombers.

As late as 24th October, Churchill was still insisting that *"in spite of u-boat losses, the Bomber Offensive should have the first place in our air effort"* but the October shipping figures forced him to execute a hasty u-turn and reconvene the former Battle of the Atlantic Committee[219] in its new guise as the Anti-U-Boat Warfare Committee. Chaired by Churchill himself, the Committee comprised all the key figures with responsibility for the Atlantic - Joubert, Pound, Portal, Alexander and Sinclair - plus scientists from Coastal Command's operational research section. As a Cabinet-level committee, its directives were binding on all other Ministries and headquarters.

The Committee's first session on 4th November acknowledged the

---

[218] Churchill's 'A Review of the War Position' on 21st July indicated that Britain could survive 1942 only *"by running down our stocks heavily"* and he considered the possibility of saving 1m tons by *"tightening the belt"* [i.e. introducing further rationing]. Any problems with shipping or supplies would - he hoped - be resolved by America allocating additional ships to Britain during 1943/44 (Churchill, *The Second World War*, Vol. IV, pp.781-784; Bell, *Churchill and Sea Power*, pp.264-265).

[219] In his post-war memoirs, Churchill described the 'u-boat peril' as *"the only thing that ever really frightened me,"* but he still allowed the Battle of the Atlantic Committee (formed in March 1941) to lapse in October 1941, long before the u-boat peril was defeated. Churchill's post-war reminisce should never be confused with actual wartime deeds (Richard Goette, *Britain and the Delay in Closing the Mid-Atlantic 'Air Gap'*, Northern Mariner/Le Marin du Nord, XV, No 4, Oct 2005, p.41; Dennis Haslop, *Britain, Germany and the Battle of the Atlantic: A Comparative Study* (2013), p.35).

scope and scale of the crisis and identified solutions. First Lord of the Admiralty Alexander noted that

> *the air had been of great help in meeting the U-boat menace; but there was a blind spot in the centre of the North Atlantic where no air cover was provided and it was here that our heaviest losses occurred. Aircraft with an overall range of 2,500 miles would be needed to cover this area.*

Air Marshal Joubert confirmed that Coastal Command needed no more than 40 VLR aircraft to plug the Mid-Atlantic Gap, a risibly small figure given the scale of Allied bomber production. The very modesty of this request underlines Churchill's folly in denying Coastal Command a reasonable VLR provision earlier in the year.

The next two meetings on 12th and 18th November authorised action to resolve the crisis. On 18th November, the Committee elevated the defence of trade (i.e. closing the Mid-Atlantic Gap) over both the Bomber Offensive and the Bay of Biscay Offensive,[220] ordering that 33 Mk 3A Liberators currently employed in the Bay of Biscay be converted to VLR status for deployment in the Atlantic. Churchill, Roosevelt and the Combined Chiefs considered the shipping crisis at Casablanca, confirming that *"the defeat of the u-boat must remain a first charge on the resources of the United Nations."* To give teeth to this commitment, the Combined Chiefs agreed to speed up the delivery of Liberators to Britain in early 1943, ordering that twenty Liberators per month be fitted with centimetric radar before leaving America to accelerate their conversion to VLR status on arrival.

By January 1943, both the supreme Allied war council and the Anti-U-Boat Warfare Committee had identified elimination of the Mid-Atlantic Gap as the leading Allied priority and had earmarked resources to meet this goal. Unfortunately, translating theory into practice proved problematic. Converting the Mk 3A Liberators to VLR status required removal of their gun turrets, surplus armour and engine superchargers, the installation of 335-gallon fuel tanks and centimetric radar, and the company charged with converting the

---

[220] Coastal Command received 33 Mk3A Liberators during the late summer of 1942 and - because of their limited 1680-mile range - deployed them in the Bay of Biscay in an attempt to destroy u-boats passing in and out of their French bases. This initiative produced only limited results and - with hindsight - it would have been better to convert these aircraft to full VLR status immediately on receipt. Although Coastal Command was correct in its efforts to try to destroy the u-boat menace at a critical location, it must carry some responsibility for the persistence of the Mid-Atlantic Gap through to 1943 (Barnett, *Engage The Enemy More Closely*, p.476).

'planes - Scottish Aviation in Prestwick - had a full order book and limited capacity. As a result, it took 53 and 25 days respectively to convert the first two Liberators, ensuring that they didn't enter service until February 1943. Even by late March, Coastal Command still only had 20 operational VLR Liberators operating in the Atlantic from a total force of 34. The Air Gap was shrinking but not fast enough and the Kriegsmarine and the Allies were now engaged in a brutal race - would the Allies flood the Air Gap with Liberators to purge it of u-boats before Dönitz's force inflicted a decisive knockout blow, or would Dönitz's u-boats gain victory in this crucial arena before the deadly Liberators were deployed? The Battle of the Atlantic entered its grimmest and most decisive phase in spring 1943.

IV

Allied shipping losses dipped during December and January as a result of bad weather - which hampered u-boat attacks - but spiked again during February and March. Early March must be considered the most critical period in the battle for in the first ten days, German forces sank 41 Allied ships (230,000 tons) and despatched a further 56 (282,000 tons) over the next ten days. In a mere three weeks they had accounted for 97 Allied ships and 512,000 tons, and if this success continued till the end of the month, the 700,000 ton mark would again be breached. The mood of elation in Berlin and in Dönitz's Paris headquarters can be readily appreciated.

However, victory slipped through Dönitz's fingers just as it appeared to be within his grasp. Allied shipping losses in the last third of March totalled 181,000 tons, bringing the overall figure to 693,000 tons - severe but still below the 700,000 ton mark. Even more alarming for the Nazis, Allied shipping losses fell to 345,000 tons in April and slumped to 299,000 tons in May while a full quarter of Dönitz's operational submarine force (41 vessels) was destroyed during May. On 22nd May, Dönitz scolded his commanders, declaring that

> *if there is anyone who thinks that combating convoys is no longer possible, he is a weakling and no true u-boat captain. The Battle of the Atlantic is getting harder but it is the determining element in the waging of the war.*

This admonition failed to produce the desired results and - two days later - Dönitz withdrew his u-boats from the North Atlantic on the grounds that *"the situation in the North Atlantic now forces a temporary shift in operations to areas* ***less endangered by aircraft*** *[emphasis* *added].*" The withdrawal was only temporary and the predators returned in September equipped with acoustic torpedoes, improved radar and powerful anti-aircraft guns but the results were equally conclusive. In the last quarter of 1943, u-boats sank 25 Allied vessels (127,284 tons) in the North Atlantic but lost 53 of their own, an unsustainable loss rate which demanded a second and final withdrawal from the theatre. By summer 1943, the Allies were masters of the Atlantic and could proceed with Overlord planning, secure in the knowledge that the u-boat scourge had been vanquished.[221]

Many factors contributed to Allied victory in the Battle of the Atlantic and the deployment of VLR Liberators equipped with ASVIII radar certainly played a part, a point Dönitz acknowledged in his 24th May remarks and in his post-war memoirs which confirmed that the *"enemy air force... [was] the greatest problem for the u-boat command and it was* ***therefore surprising that it was only later that the enemy recognised and used this weapon as being the most effective means against the u-boat*** *[emphasis added]."* In November 1942, Air Marshal Joubert had predicted that 40 VLR aircraft could close the Mid-Atlantic Gap and - by May 1943 - 41 long-range Liberators were operating in the central Atlantic.

Other developments were equally influential. Another stricken u-boat yielded a working Enigma machine in October 1942 and Bletchley Park analysts cracked the German Triton cipher in December, giving the Admiralty valuable knowledge of u-boat locations throughout 1943. The successful completion of Torch in November 1942 allowed the Allies to re-deploy naval resources to the Atlantic which would eventually overwhelm the u-boats, and two developments are significant in this regard. Firstly, the Allies developed Support Groups (six by May 1943) with the express purpose of hunting and harrying u-boats to destruction. Whereas escort vessels performed a primarily defensive function, Support Groups (usually 6-7 destroyers, sloops or corvettes) were free to attack u-boats wherever they were found and pursue them until a result was obtained. On one occasion, Captain Frederic Walker of 2nd Support Group hunted a u-boat for 38 hours before lack of oxygen forced it to surface. Alongside the Support Groups, three Escort Carriers were operating in the Atlantic by May 1943. An Escort Carrier is basically an improvised aircraft carrier - a merchant hull with a flight deck bolted on top - and each Escort Carrier carried 15-25 single-engined aircraft (Swordfish, Martlets, Sea Hurricanes etc) equipped with rockets, torpedoes, depth charges and

---

[221] 105 convoys of 3,360 merchant vessels crossed the Atlantic during January-March 1944 with only three ships lost (Orange, *Slessor,* p.122).

20mm cannon. Ships such as USS *Bogue* might not win any design awards but they delivered Allied air power to the heart of the Mid-Atlantic Gap and - working in tandem with the Support Groups and VLR aircraft - eliminated the u-boats' final hunting ground. Victory is also attributable to superb teamwork among British, Canadian and American air and naval forces, and the ingenuity of Allied scientists, shipbuilders and technologists who designed the weapons which gave Allied forces the edge. Victory in the Atlantic is also a tribute to the superb seamanship of the men of the Merchant Navy, civilian non-combatants who kept the convoys sailing through good times and bad - thirty thousand seamen sacrificed their lives during the conflict, laying the basis for ultimate Allied victory.

CHAPTER TWENTY-SEVEN: A GRIEVOUS AND SHAMEFUL BLOW TO BRITISH PRESTIGE, War Against Japan, 1944-45

> *Singapore must be redeemed and Malaya freed... We had to regain on the field of battle our rightful possessions in the Far East, and not have them handed back to us at the peace table.*
>
> Winston Churchill, *The Second World War: Triumph and Tragedy*

> *The [politicians'] attitude of mind… is astonishing. They are obviously afraid of the Americans laying down the law as to what is to happen when Japan is defeated to the various islands, ports and other territories… But they will not lift a finger to get a force into the Pacific; they prefer to hang about outside and recapture our own rubber trees*
>
> First Sea Lord Admiral Cunningham, 14th July 1944

Britain's war with Japan regained prominence as Hitler's domain crumbled. By spring 1944, Leningrad (Saint Petersburg), Crimea and much of the Ukraine had been freed and Allied forces dominated the Mediterranean. The u-boats had been beaten, the Luftwaffe was being purged from Europe's skies and Overlord planning was up and running. The noose around Germany was tightening but, paradoxically, these happy circumstances inspired a major breach between Churchill and his Chiefs which directly threatened D-Day.

I

British strategy against Japan in early 1944 resolved into two principal options - a 'Bay of Bengal Strategy' to reclaim lost Empire territory in Malaya and Singapore or a 'Pacific Strategy' directed at Japan in partnership with America to end the war as quickly as possible. COS endorsed the Pacific Strategy and hoped to send a British fleet - released from the Mediterranean by Italy's surrender - to the Pacific in 1944, to be supported by land and air forces following victory in Europe. Brooke outlined his thinking to Dill on 30th March:

> *I am quite clear... that strategically it is right for us to use all our forces in close co-operation from Australia across the Pacific in the general direction of Formosa [Taiwan]. By operating our forces alongside of MacArthur, we can pool resources at sea and in the air for various closely connected*

steps. Whereas retaining our forces in the Indian Ocean we operate independently... with the result that operations will be more protracted.

COS wanted to focus on Japan to end the war promptly but - true to form - Churchill prioritised the Empire over all other considerations. In his mind, the shame of 1941/42 could be expunged only by evicting Japan from Malaya and Singapore, as he informed COS on 13th March.

The effect in India and, indeed, in England, of strong operations against Malaya to recapture Singapore, would be very much greater than the effect of operations through New Guinea towards the Philippines... It was in Malaya, Borneo, and the Netherlands East Indies that our reputation had suffered.

General Ismay received similar wisdom.

The political importance of our making some effort to recover British territory must not be underrated. Rangoon [Yangon] and Singapore are great names in the British eastern world, and it will be an ill day for Britain if the war ends without our having made a stroke to regain these places… A major attack on Singapore... is the supreme British objective in the whole of the Indian and Far Eastern theatres. It is the only prize that will restore British prestige in this region.[222]

Imperial resurrection off the back of American victories was simply unacceptable.

A decision to act as a subsidiary force under the Americans in the Pacific raises difficult political questions about the future of our Malayan possessions. If the Japanese should withdraw from them or make peace as the result of the main American thrust, the United States Government would after the victory feel greatly strengthened in its view that all possessions in the East Indian Archipelago should be placed under some international body upon which the United States would exercise a decisive concern. They would feel with conviction: 'We won the victory and liberated these places and we must

---

[222] Eden echoed Churchill's imperial obsession. In February 1944, he insisted *"that we must have a part of our own to play in the Far Eastern war. If we are merely dragged along at the tail of the Americans, we shall get no credit whatsoever... We want to make it plain to the world that we have played our part in regaining our Far Eastern Empire."* (Andrew J. Whitfield, *Hong Kong, Empire and the Anglo-American Alliance at War, 1941-45* (2001), p. 137).

> *have the dominating say in their future and derive full profit from their products, especially oil.*

Churchill's European and Asian strategies were two sides of the same imperially-obsessed coin. In Europe, imperially-inspired operations in the Mediterranean were prioritised over efforts to defeat Germany directly via north-western Europe; in Asia, defeating Japan came second to rebuilding the Empire in Malaya and Singapore. Italy and the Balkans were on the outskirts of Hitler's empire while Singapore lies three thousand miles south of Tokyo. Russia bore the brunt of crushing the Axis in Europe and - if Churchill had his way - America would perform the same function against Japan. Young men were being sacrificed in Italy to advance British interests in a strategic *cul de sac* while similar sacrifices would be made in Malaya and Singapore if Prime Ministerial preference prevailed. Britain sought mastery over Suez to secure access to its eastern Empire and Singapore and Malaya - with their tin mines and rubber plantations - was that Empire; Britain required colonies such as Malaya to maintain its 'Great Power' status and ignoble, selfish considerations inspired Churchillian strategy at all times, prioritising imperial interests over efforts to smash fascism and restore peace to the world. However, whereas COS supported Churchill in Europe, it rejected his Asian strategy, inspiring a major cleft within Britain's high command in the run-up to D-Day.

Conflict between Churchill and his Chiefs climaxed in spring 1944. Churchill first became aware of COS opposition to his strategy as he plotted the Anzio fiasco in Carthage and he convened a Defence Committee meeting shortly after his return. On 24th January, he submitted a note to COS arguing for an *"outlet in 1944-45... for the very large air and military forces we have standing in India and around the Bay of Bengal"* and championed Culverin, an operation to land British-imperial forces on northern Sumatra as a prelude to invading Malaya, only twenty miles across the Malacca Straits.

The arrival of a Japanese fleet in Singapore in late February[223] - to re-group following clashes with US forces - crystallised the cleavage between Churchill and his Chiefs. Churchill viewed the Japanese fleet as a threat to India which would have to be countered by operations in south-east Asia which, in turn, would assist America by keeping Japanese forces out of the Pacific. The Chiefs, in contrast, argued that existing air and naval forces were sufficient to deter any Japanese advance on India and that Japan's sizeable naval presence in Singapore invalidated Culverin.

---

[223] The Japanese force included seven battleships, two aircraft carriers and eight cruisers.

Map 37: Bay of Bengal vs. Pacific Strategy

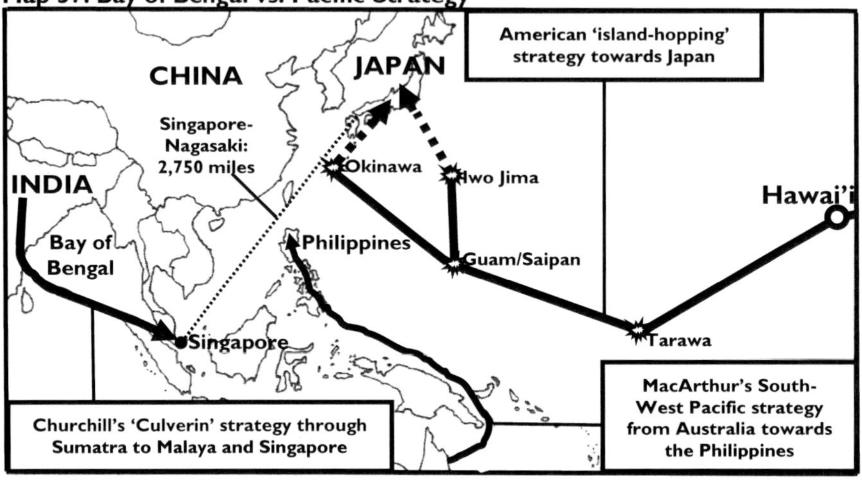

Acknowledging his Chiefs' opposition, Churchill drafted a paper on 29th February to win them over, summarising the principal options open to Britain and listing the Pacific Strategy's main defects which included

> *a division of our forces... between the Indian and Australian theatres. It throws out of offensive action permanently all the very large forces which must... be left in the Indian theatre... It overlooks the diversionary and wearing-down value upon the Japanese Air and military forces which would be entailed by amphibious operations across the Bay of Bengal. It vastly lengthens our line of communication. It throws out of action all our bases in the Indian Ocean... as well as those more distant bases in the Suez Canal and Red Sea.*

Having enumerated the Pacific Strategy's flaws, Churchill insisted that

> *we should certainly be rendering a great service to the United States by keeping up the [Culverin] threat and holding the Japanese fleet at Singapore as long as possible, thus leaving the United States with no hostile naval forces worth speaking of before them in the Pacific.*

Churchill was determined to enforce his will and submitted his paper to the Defence Committee on 3rd March in an effort to mobilise support against the Chiefs, a tactic he employed occasionally in an effort to get his way[224] but which usually backfired when used against

[224] On 25th February, Brooke noted in his diary that "*[Churchill] had packed the house against us, and was accompanied by Anthony Eden, Oliver Lyttleton [Minister of Production], and Attlee, in*

strong characters such as Brooke, Portal and Cunningham.[225] Brooke particularly detested political meddling, observing in his diary that *"the PM is trying at present to frame up the War Cabinet against the Chiefs of Staff Committee... it looks very serious and* ***may well lead to the resignation of the Chiefs of Staff Committee*** *[emphasis added]."*

Churchill's Chief of Staff - General Ismay - was alert to the dangers of a major rupture and warned Churchill the next day of the *"clear-cut divergence of opinion"* between COS and the PM, advising him that *"the possibility of resignation on the part of the [COS Committee members]"* could not be excluded. To avert this, Ismay suggested a series of meetings in which *"both cases can be fully ventilated and argued,"* urging Churchill to justify his strategy on political grounds, arguing that *"the Chiefs of Staff would accept this decision with complete loyalty and would set to work... to make the best possible plans for implementing it."*

Before Churchill could implement this advice, COS produced a 6th March paper which repudiated his 29th February arguments *in toto*. Chiding him for failing to accept that the Pacific Strategy's first object is *"to obtain a footing in Japan's inner zone at the earliest possible moment,"* the Chiefs reminded him that - as land and air forces were required - his Bay of Bengal strategy could only be implemented **six months after victory in Europe**, and while Churchill sought to manoeuvre Roosevelt into rejecting the offer of a British fleet in the Pacific, COS insisted that

> *the right approach is to consider what strategy is best calculated to bring about the early overthrow of Japan and what contributions we can make to that strategy, and then go to the Americans and put forward our case.*

COS further insisted that both strategies - a Pacific 'military' strategy and a Bay of Bengal 'imperial' strategy - would require large fleet trains and an expansion of military and naval bases, while ships for the Pacific would be furnished through *"the diminution of sinkings [by u-boats and] the very high rate of building."* Faced with such determined opposition, Churchill ramped up the pressure by writing to the Chiefs individually - rather than as COS Committee members - in an effort

---

addition the whole of Dickie Mountbatten's party consisting of Wedemeyer, Binney, Macleod, Dewing, Naval and Air Officers. The whole party were against the Chiefs of Staff." (Alanbrooke, *War Diaries, 1939- 1945*, p.525).

[225] Sir Andrew Cunningham replaced Dudley Pound as First Sea Lord on 15th October 1943, and Pound died of a brain tumour six days later. Brooke greatly appreciated Cunningham's robust, assertive personality (Roskill, *Churchill and the Admirals*, p.328; Robin Brodhurst, *Churchill's Anchor: The Biography of Admiral Sir Dudley Pound* (2000), p.284).

to undermine their collective authority. Reminding them of his role as their civilian master, Churchill informed each Chief that:

> *(a) unless unforeseen events occur, the Indian theatre and the Bay of Bengal will remain, until the summer of 1945, the centre of gravity for the British and Imperial war effort against Japan.*
>
> *(b) all preparations will be made for amphibious action across the Bay of Bengal against the Malay peninsula... the ultimate objective being the reconquest of Singapore.*
>
> *(c) a powerful British fleet will be built up, based on Ceylon, Addu Atoll, and East Indian ports under the shield of our strong shore-based aircraft.*
>
> *(d) the plans of South-East Asia Command for amphibious action across the Bay of Bengal will be examined, corrected, and improved, with the desire of engaging the enemy as closely and as soon as possible.*

Churchill presented these rulings as final, insisting that *"the difference on long-term plans is now settled"* and offered to meet COS to discuss joint approaches to the Americans.

Churchill's obstinacy sparked a crisis. As senior military experts, the Chiefs proffered professional advice on operational matters and - if this advice was consistently rejected - resignation was the only option open to them. This was certainly considered during their 21st March meeting, Brooke later diarising that *"we discussed... how best to deal with Winston's last impossible document. It is full of false statements, false deductions and defective strategy. We cannot accept it as it stands, and* ***it would be better if we all three resigned sooner than accept his solution*** *[emphasis added]."*

By 21st March, Overlord was ten weeks away and *en masse* resignation by COS would wreck the most decisive Anglo-American venture of the war and shatter Britain's international credibility. Cancelling Overlord in spring 1944 would destroy the war-winning Anglo-American-Soviet Alliance and give fresh heart to fascists in Berlin and Tokyo. Britain had survived multiple military disasters during 1940-42 but now - with victory so close - Churchill was willing to sacrifice everything by promoting imperial concerns over sound military objectives. His insistence on a Mediterranean strategy in Europe - had it been implemented - would have prolonged the war against Germany and facilitated Soviet domination of north-western

Europe,[226] and prioritising the Empire in Asia carried the potential to wreck the Grand Alliance, undermine Overlord and revive German and Japanese power at a time when it was visibly waning. Such would have been the consequences of Churchill's imperial obsession and commitment to defective strategy.

Fortunately, the American Chiefs - like the cavalry - rode to the rescue, for while COS was considering resignation in London, the Joint Chiefs were contemplating Asian strategy in Washington and fully supported their British colleagues. Just as COS was pondering resignation on 21st March, Washington informed London that

> *in our opinion, once US forces have a strangle-hold on enemy communications in [the China-Formosa-Luzon] area, the strategic value of operations in Malaya, and the Netherlands East Indies will be considerably reduced. Furthermore, the requirements for a major amphibious operation in the South East Asia Theatre this year are not in sight. We cannot, therefore, at this time agree to support Operation 'Culverin' or any similar operation involving large amphibious commitments in the South East Asia Command.*

With backing from the Joint Chiefs and Roosevelt, COS merely had to remain in office to win the argument. Churchill might be able to overwhelm his Chiefs at home but he couldn't overcome a coalition containing both sets of military advisers plus the President. British reliance on American aid precluded any maverick action.

In the end, the British gift for compromise averted disaster for even as COS was pondering resignation, it indicated a need for additional information before finally evaluating the merits of the two strategies. The Chiefs spent a full week drafting a response to Churchill's 20th March memo, with General Ismay advising at every turn. The 28th March COS response tactfully suggested that the PM might have misinterpreted their proposals and welcomed opportunities for further discussion. COS indicated that additional data was required on the merits of Indian and Australian bases and *"it is not until these have been cleared up... that it will be possible for us to make a final recommendation as to which of the two policies offers the greater military advantages."* Churchill sagely declined to press the Chiefs as they drafted their compromise.

In the long run, Allied successes finally reconciled the PM and his

---

[226] discussed in Chapter 28

mutinous Chiefs. American forces smashed Japan's carrier fleet in the Battle of the Philippine Sea (19-20th June) to gain control of the Central Pacific and seize the Marshall, Mariana and Caroline Islands. With Japan increasingly isolated from its southern conquests, any rationale for 'liberating' Malaya and Singapore simply evaporated - it would serve no purpose and, to use one of Churchill's phrases, Japan's southern possessions simply became 'cut flowers in a vase',[227] making it more sensible to bypass them than to incur heavy losses in 'liberating' them. With America controlling the Philippines,[228] operations in Malaya and Singapore could be justified only on imperial grounds and America would never release the resources such operations required.

Myanmar (Burma) also increasingly entered the picture in summer 1944. Churchill had earlier declared that *"going into [the] swampy jungles [of Myanmar] to fight the Japanese is like going into the water to fight a shark,"* but the collapse of Japan's summer 1944 U-Go offensive and the crumbling of its position in Myanmar forced Churchill to rethink his strategy. Forces that might have been deployed in Malaya were increasingly despatched to Myanmar and on 3rd June, Mountbatten was ordered *"to develop, maintain, broaden and protect the air link to China"* which necessarily demanded a heavy commitment of troops and resources to Myanmar. Under the inspired leadership of General Slim, British-imperial forces scored notable successes in Myanmar in late 1944 and early 1945 and the prospect of major action in Sumatra, Malaya or Singapore evaporated.[229]

Allied successes in Myanmar and the Central Pacific informed the decisions of the 12th-16th September Octagon Conference in Quebec. Mountbatten was ordered to *"recapture… all [of] Burma at the earliest date"* through Capital (an advance into north-eastern Myanmar towards Mandalay) and Dracula (a combined amphibious and airborne assault on Yangon/Rangoon). Adjusting to the new realities, Churchill finally accepted that Britain could only contribute to Japan's defeat by acting in concert with American forces and offered the use of Britain's fleet on that basis. Roosevelt accepted - to Admiral King's great chagrin[230] - and Royal Navy warships participated

---

[227] See Chapter 7.

[228] American forces landed on Leyte in the eastern Philippines on 20th October and gained control over the archipelago by February 1945. (Sean Sheehan, *War in the Pacific* (2009), pp.26-29).

[229] Mandalay was liberated on 20th March 1945 and Yangon [Rangoon] fell on 3rd May. (Kaushik Roy, *Sepoys Against the Rising Sun: The Indian Army in Far East and South-East Asia, 1941-45* (2016), pp.379- 381).

[230] King hoped to defeat Japan's fleet without British assistance.

in joint operations against Japan's home islands throughout the first half of 1945. The Pacific Strategy had finally triumphed though - thanks to its much larger fleet - America reigned supreme on the high seas.[231]

On the evening of 29th July 1945, Britain's most modern battleship - *King George V* - participated in the bombardment of Hamamatsu, a city on Japan's main Honshu Island. In a barrage lasting 37 minutes, it fired 265 fourteen-inch shells at a musical instrument factory latterly converted to manufacturing aircraft propellers. This was the last occasion on which a British battleship fired its guns in anger and one of the war's final operations. One week later, a form of hell visited Hiroshima when a solitary bomb dropped from a single aircraft obliterated 70,000 people in an instant. Three days later, a similar horror scourged Nagasaki when 40,000 people were expunged from the earth in a blinding second.[232] Bowing to the inevitable, Japan surrendered on 15th August and - after six years of brutal, bloody and senseless violence - a fragile peace returned to a shattered world.

---

[231] The British Pacific Fleet was one of the largest British fleets ever assembled but was still dwarfed by its US ally - where Britain provided four aircraft carriers, the US provided 79, the two British battleships were over-shadowed by 23 American, there were 15 US cruisers for every one deployed by the Royal Navy, and while the Royal Navy provided ten destroyers, the US Navy allocated 296 (Ponting, *Churchill,* pp.635-636).

[232] The ultimate death toll in Hiroshima and Nagasaki exceeded those killed on 6th and 9th August and may have reached 200,000-250,000 overall (Dawn Rothe and Christopher Mullins (eds), *State Crime: Current Perspectives* (2011), p.74).

CHAPTER TWENTY-EIGHT: COOLIES DIE BY THE WAYSIDE, Churchill, Cripps, India and the Bengal Famine, 1942-44

Mindful of our difficulties about food I told him [Bengal Chief Minister Fazlul Huq] that he simply must produce more rice out of Bengal for Ceylon even if Bengal itself went short!

Viceroy Linlithgow to Indian Secretary Amery, 26th January 1943

A dull Cabinet, but it brought home to me the very different attitude towards feeding a starving population when the starvation is in Europe. In this case it is Holland which needs food, and ships will of course be available, quite a different answer to the one we get whenever we ask for ships to bring food to India.

Field Marshal Wavell's Diary, 9th April 1945

Churchill was a man of contradiction and nowhere was this more evident than in his dealings with India. He loved India - as imperial property - but hated the Indian people, particularly the Hindu majority. Indians - as a whole - were *"a beastly people with a beastly religion"* while *"Hindus were a foul race protected by their mere pullulation [rapid breeding] from the doom that is their due."*[233] And then in 1942 - with Japan pressing at India's gates - Indian nationalists refused to rally behind the flag unless India gained self-government. Even more galling, his good friend President Roosevelt and Labour Cabinet colleagues endorsed this outrageous proposal! Unusual times call for unorthodox measures and in March 1942, a radical socialist MP and Indian independence enthusiast was despatched to India to persuade Congress to suspend its agitation and rally to the cause. War produces some strange bedfellows but none stranger than Winston Churchill's 'brief encounter' with Sir Stafford Cripps.

I

Only the extreme conditions of spring 1942 could have induced Churchill to negotiate with Indian nationalism. By this stage, he'd presided over two years of defeat in which Britain had been evicted from Europe and lost its Far Eastern Empire (Hong Kong, Malaya, Singapore and Myanmar (Burma)). Churchill's stock was low and he

[233] The comments attributed to Churchill were recorded by Leo Amery (Sept 1942) and Jock Colville (Feb 1945) (Mukerjee, *Churchill's Secret War*, p.78; Ponting, *Churchill*, p.700).

faced a Confidence Vote in the Commons on 29th January. On 19th February - four days after Singapore fell - he reshuffled his War Cabinet to placate his critics. Labour's position was strengthened as Clement Attlee was promoted to Deputy PM, and Sir Stafford Cripps[234] - recently returned from the Soviet Union - was appointed Lord Privy Seal and Leader of the House. Cripps, Attlee and Bevin (who remained as Minister of Labour) all favoured Indian self-government, arguing that concessions were necessary to boost India's martial ardour. Reliant on Labour support to survive, Churchill reluctantly conceded.

America also favoured *rapprochement.* Roosevelt was determined to keep China fighting - to divert Japanese resources from the Pacific - and this involved ferrying supplies into southern China from a stable and supportive north-east India. American strategy demanded active Indian support for the war and - as Britain's principal benefactor - Uncle Sam couldn't be ignored. On 11th March, Roosevelt appointed Col. Louis Johnson - his former Assistant Secretary of War - to act as his Personal Representative and participate in parleys between British and Indian representatives.

American strategy, Labour anti-colonialism and harsh military reality forced Churchill's government to produce a Draft Declaration on Indian self-government on 11th March 1942. Largely authored by Cripps and Attlee, the Declaration was written to appeal to Indian nationalists, convince the Americans that Britain was willing to negotiate and secure Prime Ministerial support. Drafted to satisfy multiple constituencies, the document was bound to disappoint some.

It certainly highlighted the gulf between Britain's vision for India and Indian National Congress[235] aspirations. The Declaration proposed *"to lay down in precise and clear terms the steps which [HM Government] propose shall be taken for the earliest possible realisation of self-government in India"* but it didn't go far or fast enough to satisfy nationalist sentiment. Where Congress called for immediate self-government, Britain proposed to introduce this *"immediately upon the cessation of hostilities."* India demanded full, unfettered independence while Britain offered *"a new Indian Union which shall constitute a Dominion, associated with the United Kingdom and the other Dominions by a common allegiance*

---

[234] Cripps was expelled from the Labour Party in 1939 for advocating a Popular Front against Germany and didn't re-join the party until February 1945. He held several posts in the Attlee Government, including Chancellor of the Exchequer, 1947-50.

[235] The Indian National Congress was founded in 1885 to campaign for a bigger governmental role for educated Indians and to promote dialogue between Indians and the Raj. Congress adopted a *swaraj* (self-rule) policy in December 1920 following the Amritsar Massacre – see Chapter 4 (John R. McLane, *Indian Nationalism and the Early Congress* (1977), p.3).

to the Crown." And where Congress aspired to a unitary state embracing the entire sub-continent, the Declaration affirmed *"the right of any province of British India that is not prepared to accept the new Constitution to retain... its present constitutional position [with the United Kingdom]."* The Muslim League had already demanded an independent Pakistan, so an unrevised Declaration would kill Gandhi and Nehru's dream of a united, non-sectarian India. Only the final clause - Clause (e) - opened a path towards active and immediate involvement by Indians in their country's government. Britain would bear full responsibility for Indian defence in the current crisis but His Majesty's Government desired and invited

> *the immediate and effective participation of the leaders of the principal sections of the Indian people in the counsels of their country, to give their active and constructive help in the discharge of a task so vital and essential for the future freedom of India.*

This vague and imprecise formula would generate considerable wrangling in the coming weeks.

Having drafted the Declaration, it now had to be sold to India and Sir Stafford Cripps was the man for the job. Having just completed a successful stint as Britain's Ambassador to Russia, his stock was sky-high and he was even mentioned as a possible replacement for Churchill. He'd been corresponding with Nehru since 1936, the Indian leader had stayed with Cripps when he visited Britain in 1938 and reciprocated during Cripps' 1939 visit to India. Cripps supported Indian self-government and had good relations with senior Congress figures - if anyone could sell the Declaration to Congress, it was Cripps. His absence from Britain would temporarily strengthen Churchill's position and - if the Cripps Mission failed - his prestige would be punctured. Needless to say, if Cripps succeeded, his stock would soar and calls for him to replace Churchill would intensify.

Cripps landed in Delhi on 23rd March and - after spending two days with Viceroy Linlithgow[236] and his Executive Council - spent five days conferring with representatives of India's political organisations (e.g. Congress, Muslim League, Mahasabha, Sikhs, Depressed Classes, Liberals etc). The immediate outcome of this process was the re-wording of Clause (e) in a manner likely to boost Indian participation

---

[236] Victor Hope (2nd Marquess of Linlithgow) served as India's Viceroy between April 1936 and September 1943.

in India's wartime government. While Britain would retain full responsibility for India's defence, Clause (e) now confirmed that

> *the task of organising to the full the military, moral and material resources of India must be the responsibility of the Government of India with the co-operation of the peoples of India... [through] the immediate and effective participation of the leaders of the principal sections of the Indian people in the counsels of their country, of the Commonwealth and of the United Nations.*

Emphasising *"the co-operation of the people in the counsels of their country"* could pave the way towards greater participation by Indians in Indian government but the precise form of this involvement demanded clarity.

The revised Declaration was published on 29th March and - as it still contained objectionable elements - was rejected by Congress, but this was merely a prelude to five days of intense negotiation between Cripps and Johnson (who arrived in Delhi on 3rd April) and Nehru and Abdul Kalam Azad (representing Congress). By 8th April, the outlines of a provisional agreement which would enable Congress to endorse the Declaration, support the war and enter India's Government had been agreed.

Under the Cripps-Johnson formula, India's war effort would be shared between a War Ministry (led by General Wavell, British Commander-in-Chief) and a Defence Ministry (controlled by an Indian). The War Ministry would direct the military prosecution of the war while the Defence Ministry would prioritise munitions production, recruitment, internal security and procurement of supplies, the two Ministries working collaboratively.

The Executive Council would also be transformed. At this point, the Executive Council consisted of ten Indian and four British members and - while each held responsibility for a specific portfolio - the Council's role was essentially advisory. All Council appointments were endorsed by London and Delhi, and the Viceroy retained a veto over Council decisions which, in his opinion, affected "the *safety, tranquillity* and *interests of British India*", enabling him to over-rule Council decisions at will.

Under the Cripps-Johnson-Congress formula, the current Council incumbents would be replaced by representatives of Indian political organisations as the first step towards the Council becoming India's *de facto* National Government. As the Executive Council gained legitimacy, the Viceroy's power would be pared back to that of a 'constitutional monarch', obliged to follow his 'Cabinet's' collective advice and stripped of his veto. Real power would therefore shift from an autocratic Viceroy answerable to London to an Executive Council representing Indian political aspirations. These changes, if implemented, would transform India's relationship with Britain and satisfy the expectations of the United States, Labour anti-colonialists and Indian nationalists – but how would Churchill and the Viceroy respond? Two factors militated against the scheme's success.

Firstly, these profound changes would be underpinned by nothing more than 'conventions' and 'understandings' rather than formal written agreements. The crisis conditions of spring 1942 were judged unsuitable for extended constitutional debate and Cripps intimated as much in his 29th March press conference when he said "*you cannot change the constitution. All you can do is to change the conventions of the constitution.*" Cripps was relaxed about this scenario, believing the Viceroy would never contradict an 'Indianised' Council which fully backed the war effort. He also hinted that a new Viceroy might be appointed after Congress entered the Council, but not before.

Where Cripps was bullish and optimistic, Congress was wary. To enter a political arrangement on the basis of unwritten conventions would expose it to risk and - if the conventions were later repudiated - shatter its political credibility. The whole system appeared to rest on trusting a Viceroy who had shown little interest in working with Congress in the past - was the Cripps Offer simply a scam to prop up a declining Empire?

Congress was right to be wary for while Congress, Cripps and Johnson were busy imagineering India's political future, the Viceroy, Churchill and Amery were actively plotting to maintain the status quo and thwart all reform. Linlithgow had no intention of renouncing any of his powers and was furious when Cripps appeared to be striking deals behind his back. Linlithgow had extended his term in office twice at London's request, he had already threatened to resign over the Draft Declaration and - with the enemy at the door - knew that London couldn't afford to lose him. He therefore asked Churchill and Amery to reassert his traditional authority and Amery obliged in a 6th April telegram to Cripps, reminding the Minister that

> *the constitutional position of the Viceroy's Council... cannot be altered in present circumstances. The position is and*

> *must remain that the Viceroy in Council acts as a collective body responsible to the Secretary of State and subject to the Viceroy's special powers and duties...There should be no misunderstanding between you and Indian political leaders on this point.*

Events over the next few days confirmed the full significance of this communication. Following a hard day's discussion on 8th April, Cripps cabled Churchill at 1am on 9th April in a positive mood, declaring that *"largely owing to very efficient and wholehearted help of Col. Johnson... I have hopes scheme may now succeed,"* and asking the Prime Minister to thank the President for Johnson's assistance.

However, in the early afternoon of 9th April - just before Cripps was due to see Nehru and Azad - Linlithgow sent Cripps a pointed reminder of Amery's 6th April telegram, advising him that

> *before your interview with Congress leaders this afternoon, I think I should draw your attention to... the Secretary of State's note... stipulating that the constitutional position of the Viceroy's Council cannot be altered, and the emphasis laid by the War Cabinet on the necessity of avoiding misunderstanding between yourself and Indian political leaders on this point... I trust you will be able to make the position clear.*

Only this intervention can explain Cripps' cold and unimaginative response to Nehru and Azad's concerns during their evening meeting. The Congress negotiators sought reassurances over the working of the new system, requesting confirmation that it would operate in the manner Cripps proposed and expressing concern over the Viceroy's willingness to work with them. Cripps should have responded with clear and unambiguous reassurances but - with Linlithgow's note fresh in his mind - limply stated that

> *it was a matter for them to discuss with the Viceroy. They should take the power and make the most of it, aware as they were how difficult it would be for the Viceroy to over-ride them... the operation of the government was for the Viceroy to decide and that there could be no major change in the constitution.*

Nehru and Azad were unconvinced and communicated their concerns to their colleagues. Congress finally rejected the Cripps Offer at 7pm on Friday 10th April, attributing its repudiation to the previous day's disappointing discussions.

> *The new picture that you placed before us was really not very different from the old, the difference being one of degree and not of kind. The new government could neither be called... nor could it function as a National Government. It would just be the Viceroy and his Executive Council with the Viceroy having all his old powers... we did ask for definite assurances and conventions which would indicate that the new government would function as a free government... [but] were informed that nothing could be said at this stage even vaguely and generally about the conventions that should govern the new government and the Viceroy. This was a matter in the Viceroy's sole discretion.*

And just as Congress was repudiating Cripps, London was also pulling the rug away.

At 10:30am on Thursday 9th April, Churchill met Harry Hopkins - Roosevelt's chief advisor - who was in London to discuss proposals for a Second Front. Churchill quizzed Hopkins over Johnson's role in the Delhi talks and Hopkins unhelpfully - and incorrectly - suggested that Johnson didn't enjoy the President's full support, and that Cripps was exploiting the 'Roosevelt connection' for his own ends.[237]

This was what Churchill had been looking for - for five days, he'd tolerated Johnson's imperial meddling because he believed he carried the Presidential *imprimatur* but now, with this seemingly withdrawn, he immediately advised Cripps that

> *Colonel Johnson is not President Roosevelt's personal representative in any matter outside the specific mission dealing with Indian munitions and kindred topics on which he was sent. I feel sure President would be vexed if he... [was] drawn into the Indian constitutional issue. His*

---

[237] Hopkins formed the impression during his 10:30am meeting with Churchill that the War Cabinet was about to repudiate Cripps' negotiations in the afternoon and didn't want Roosevelt dragged into anything which might jeopardise the Anglo-American alliance. He therefore sought to distance Roosevelt from Johnson, even though Johnson enjoyed Roosevelt's full support (R.J. Moore, *Churchill, Cripps, and India, 1939-1945* (1979), p.116; Ponting, *Churchill*, p.697; Auriol Weigold, *Churchill, Roosevelt and India: Propaganda During World War II* (2008), p.88).

> *message to me*[238]*... was entirely opposed to anything like US intervention or mediation.*

That same afternoon, the War Cabinet advised Cripps that *"it is essential to bring the whole matter back to Cabinet's plan which you went out to urge, with only such amplifications as are agreed to be put forward."* Next day, Churchill informed Cripps that

> *we are concerned about the Viceroy's position. You agreed with the definition of his powers... (including retention of powers of overriding the Executive Council) and we must definitely reject suggestion of a convention which would restrict them.*

Repudiated by Congress and his own government, Cripps folded and he exited India on 12th April. Congress and the Raj abjured further dialogue and - when Congress launched its Quit India campaign in August 1942 - the Raj simply locked up 90,000 Congress activists (including Gandhi, Nehru and Azad) until the war was safely won.

In spring 1942, adverse circumstance compelled Churchill to parley with Indian nationalists and countenance American interference in imperial affairs but - following his game-changing victory at El Alamein - he crowed that he had *"not become the King's First Minister in order to preside over the liquidation of the British Empire."* However, just as Churchill was enjoying his moment in the sun, the dark shadow of famine was darkening Bengal to reveal why, for the Indian people, independence was never just a minor constitutional conundrum - it was a matter of life or death.

II

The summer months of 1943 seduced Churchill with bright Mediterranean promise. North Africa was cleared, Sicily liberated and Mussolini toppled. Italy concluded a secret armistice with the Allies on 3rd Sept and the PM was busy hatching schemes to convert Turkey to belligerence by liberating the Dodecanese.[239] A successful Turkish offensive would confirm the primacy of the Mediterranean over Overlord and exclude the Soviets from this strategically sensitive arena.

---

[238] Churchill is disingenuous here - he implies that Roosevelt had recently communicated with him but no such message has ever been found.

[239] See Chapter 19

Unfortunately, a devastating famine in Bengal - India's worst since 1900 - coincided with the prospect of winning *"immense [Mediterranean] prizes at little cost."* Britain had accumulated large food reserves in the Middle East to feed soon-to-be liberated Greeks and Italians but - as summer turned to autumn - Churchill would have to choose between nurturing the descendants of Caesar and Alexander or saving *"gross, dirty and corrupt"* Indians from starvation.[240]

Britain had been exploiting India for almost two centuries by 1943. The sub-continent absorbed a large part of Britain's industrial output, it exported cheap raw materials and imported expensive finished goods. India was the perfect imperial possession - *"an English barrack in the oriental seas from which we may draw any number of troops without paying for them,"* subsidising its own occupation and underwriting the conquest of others.

The exploitation intensified during 1939-45. On 3rd September, Viceroy Linlithgow declared war on Germany without consulting a single Indian voice, and India provided Britain with history's largest volunteer army - 2.5m men fighting for a 'democracy' denied to India. Indian factories, farms and mines worked overtime churning out £1.5bn of boots, uniforms, goods and services for the Allied cause, funded by inflationary increases in the money supply. As a result, the General Index of Wholesale Prices rose by 154% between August 1939 and March 1946, placing many goods beyond the reach of ordinary Indians.

The Raj was even more reckless with India's food. British rule - and the substitution of cash crops for food crops - had remorselessly stripped India of the ability to feed itself. Before the war, India had imported 1.1m tons of grain yearly,[241] with 15% of its rice (1.5m tons) also coming from Myanmar. This system collapsed with Japan's spring 1942 occupation, depriving India of a major food source and driving half a million hungry refugees across the border. Fearing a further Japanese advance, Britain enforced a 'denial policy' along the Bengal coast, stripping the region of food supplies and destroying 46,000 small boats, which both deterred a Japanese invasion and ensured that these boats were unavailable for fishing or food transportation, intensifying pressure on local supplies.

---

[240] Education Minister R.A. Butler records Churchill describing 'baboos' - a dismissive term for western-educated Indians - as *"gross, dirty and corrupt"* in March 1943 (Warren Dockter, *Churchill and the Islamic World: Orientalism, Empire and Diplomacy in the Middle East* (2015), p.246).
[241] An average for the six years between 1935 and 1941.

Map 38: Indian Famine Locations

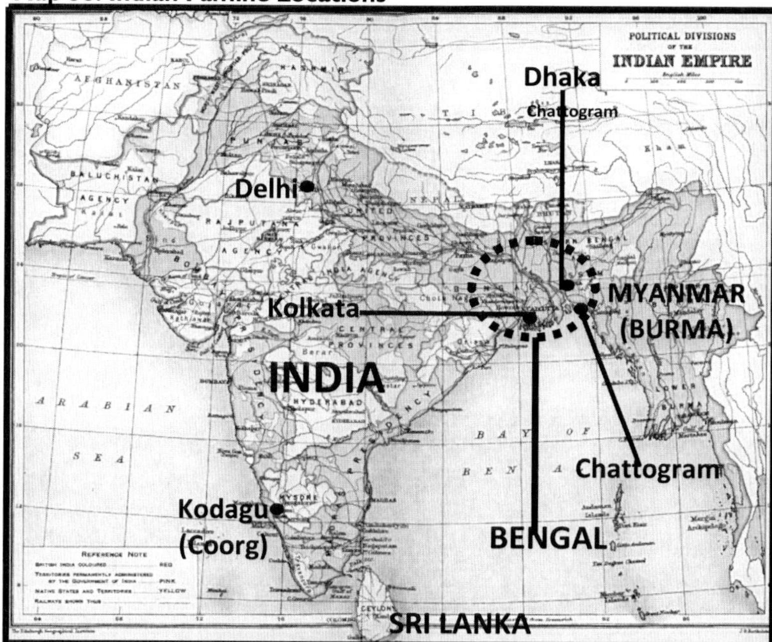

(This work - originally created by the UK Government - is in the public domain, with HMSO declaring that the expiry of Crown Copyright applies worldwide. Source: *Imperial Gazetteer of India,* 1909.)

Having scorched Bengal's earth and absorbed an extra half million mouths, the Raj now decided that India would take on the responsibility of feeding two other countries which has also relied on Myanmarese rice - Sri Lanka and Arabia. In 1940/41, India had imported 431,000 tons of grain but it was forced to export 361,00 tons in 1941/42 and the simple mathematics of forcing a country which couldn't feed itself to start feeding other countries nurtured disaster. In the 1930s, 61% of all Indians and 78% of all Bengalis were either 'poorly nourished' or 'very badly nourished' and reducing the calorific intake of malnourished people would quickly convert normal 'everyday' hunger to outright starvation.

Even nature appeared to turn against India when powerful cyclones ripped through eastern Bengal in October 1942, forcing farmers to eat rice that should have been planted in the winter and reducing the size of the following summer's rice crop. Already ravaged by inflation, rice prices rose by 400% in cities such as Dhaka between March and October 1943, with clear signs of hunger and want by June.

The contrast between glittering Mediterranean prospects and the grotesque human tragedy unfolding in Bengal was pronounced. Operations Accolade (in the Aegean) and Avalanche (Salerno) launched on 9th September, with Churchill anticipating quick victories followed by food deliveries to the local population to nurture pro-British sentiment. Meanwhile, in Kolkata,

> *scores of persons collapsing from under-nourishment are daily picked up from the streets... 155 dead bodies... [were] removed from public thoroughfares by the authorities' new Corpse Disposal Squad during the ten days ending on August 24; during the week ending August 21 mortality was 1,129 as against an average of 574 in the corresponding weeks of the previous five years. Cholera... is again on the increase... typhoid spreads; dysentery is exceptionally prevalent.*

As General Wolfe observed, *"war is an option of difficulties"* and autumn 1943 would force Churchill to choose between his ambitious Mediterranean fantasies and the harsh realities facing India.

Having largely authored the crisis, the Raj now pleaded for help. Anticipating a 1.29m ton grain shortfall for 1943/44 - plus additional rice shortages - Viceroy Linlithgow asked Britain to provide 500,000 tons of grain to help India through the difficult months between September 1943 and February 1944, with Indian Secretary Leo Amery underlining this plea through a strongly worded memo to the War Cabinet. Churchill and his colleagues convened on 4th August to discuss the matter.

Amery opened the meeting by warning that *"the Indian economy was being strained almost to breaking-point by the enormous demands made upon it, as a source of supplies and men for the Army, and as a base for military operations."* Conceding that *"the present shortage of grain was connected with the inflationary position,"* he insisted that *"no further anti-inflationary measures instituted at this date could have any effect in extracting grain from the producers to meet the immediate situation"* and urged the War Cabinet to *"treat this [crisis] as a very serious situation which, unless it was met, would seriously impair India's war effort."*

The War Cabinet rejected Amery's pleas, insisting that the grain shortage *"was not the result of physical deficiency but of hoarding, due to inflationary conditions. There was general agreement that the situation could not be dealt with simply by the importation of grain."* Instead of shipping grain to a region where hundreds - if not thousands - were dying every day, the Cabinet proposed the classic Whitehall solution - formation of a Standing Committee on Indian Financial Questions to consider steps to combat inflation and *"examine the growing indebtedness of the United Kingdom to India."* At a time when Bengalis were starving in their thousands, the Cabinet was more concerned with curbing expenditure on a war it had forced India to join. The Cabinet also hoped the Raj could 'spin' its way out of crisis by employing *"good propaganda... [and] effective advertising of whatever supplies we could manage to send,"* with glossy PR taking the place of putting food in people's bellies. Almost as an afterthought, the Cabinet *"thought that it might be possible... to make available up to 100,000 tons of barley from Iraq"* plus 50,000 tons of Australian wheat to help India overcome its crisis. However, this wheat should not proceed directly to India but ship to Sri Lanka *"to await instructions there."* Presumably it could be disbursed to India if the death toll reached a suitably high level or be shipped elsewhere if mortality rates remained acceptable.

Growing misery and a mounting death toll exposed the futility of these pathetic gestures. Describing a scene in west Bengal in mid-September, a Friends' Ambulance Unit worker observed that

> *during the last fortnight there has not been a morning on which I have not seen... dead bodies by the roadside. A fight between vultures and dogs is not a rare sight... In the villages the affairs are worse; people are dying in large numbers of malaria and starvation. There are not enough able-bodied men to burn the dead, which often are just pushed into the nearest canal. If you go down the canal from Contai to Panipia, you will feel sick; for the bloated dead bodies you will see will be numerous.*

With a massive military presence in India, Britain's Chiefs of Staff were fully aware of India's suffering and shared an intelligence assessment[242] with the War Cabinet on 17th September, confirming that

> *in Chittagong [Chattogram], A.R.P. personnel have had to take over the daily removal of corpses from streets and houses. In Dacca [Dhaka], the poor are living on what rice water they can get, since even the rich are unable to obtain rice. Cholera, small-pox and starvation are causing hundreds of deaths daily in the surrounding villages. Similar conditions prevail over a large area of East Bengal, and have given rise to a widespread incidence of thefts and dacoities [banditry]. Suicides and child-selling have been reported... In planting districts in Coorg coolies die by the wayside of starvation.*[243]

---

[242] The intelligence assessment was dated 20th August.

Clearly, the Standing Committee on Indian Financial Questions wasn't producing the desired result and on 22nd September - five days after COS shared its assessment - Amery renewed his request for 500,000 tons of grain between September 1943 and February 1944 and the *"importation of one million tons of grain annually till normal conditions are re-established… to help us through the dangers which must be faced this present autumn."* Stung by COS and Amery's concerns, the War Cabinet re-considered the catastrophe on 24th September.

The second Cabinet opened with Amery insisting that India's problems *"could only be met by the early despatch of additional supplies of food grains to India, and he urged the War Cabinet… to give a firm assurance that 500,000 tons of cereals would be shipped to India before March 1944."* Viceroy-Designate Wavell supported Amery, confirming that *"there was a grave risk that military operations would be jeopardised if sufficient food were not made available, not only for the Army but also for the industrial populations on whose efforts our military operations depended."*

War Transport Minister Frederick Leathers responded for the Government, decrying the prospect of shipping 500,000 tons of grain to India because even reduced shipping losses following victory over the u-boats *"did not make it easier to relieve India's immediate needs; for it would not be possible to work additional ships into positions from which they could lift grain for delivery in India before the next Indian harvest."* Leathers reminded his colleagues that 150,000 tons of Iraqi barley and Australian wheat had already been allocated to India but conceded that - despite the child-selling, suicides and *"hundreds of deaths daily"* - this barley hadn't even been purchased and could only ship to India once a price was agreed. Food Minister Lord Woolton hurriedly confirmed that this issue would be settled *"within the course of the next few days."* The government's failure to despatch even this minimal aid to India almost two months after it had been agreed perfectly illustrates Cabinet indifference to Indian suffering.

Leathers also confirmed that a further 60,000 tons of grain might be available for India but reminded his colleagues that

> *the only means by which he could make additional supplies available was to ship a further 30,000 tons of barley from the stocks which were being built up in the Middle East with a view to supplying the irregular forces operating against the enemy in the Balkans and to divert another*

---

[243] Coorg (now known as Kodagu) is in Karnataka in southwest India, revealing the spread of famine misery by August 1943.

> *30,000 tons of wheat and flour which was now being sent to the Middle East to augment those stocks. If these additional measures were authorised, he would be able to ship a total of 210,000 tons of food grains to India by the end of the year. The result would be, however, to reduce substantially the stocks which we had been trying to accumulate in the Middle East for the supply of the Balkans.*

In Leathers' mind, feeding Balkan irregulars and accumulating stockpiles in the Middle East to feed Italians and Greeks who **might** become British responsibilities in the future enjoyed full parity with efforts to save Bengalis from imminent starvation. Perhaps embarrassed by their paltry response, the Cabinet agreed that 50,000 of the 60,000 tons identified by Leathers might be allocated to India but refused to consider provision for 1944, insisting that *"the position should be reviewed again at the end of the year in the light of the Indian harvests."* Amery's request for the *"importation of 1m tons grain annually till normal conditions are re-established"* was *"out of the question"* with the Cabinet declaring that "*every effort must… be made to remedy the long-term situation by internal measures in India.*" Removing British rule might enable Indians to resolve matters by 'internal measures' but the Cabinet did not consider this option.

The official minutes portray a meeting which might have been discussing paper clip shortages but the diaries of Leo Amery and Archibald Wavell - both present on 24th September - offer sharper insight into Cabinet conversations.

Leo Amery was Churchill's Harrow contemporary and the PM had appointed his old chum Secretary of State for India on 13th May 1940. Equally committed to the imperial project, Amery nevertheless doubted whether mass starvation would advance British interests, recording that

> *I fought my battle for Indian food as hard as I could. Winston was prepared to admit that something should be done but very strong on the point that Indians are not the only people who are starving in this war and that... it is just as important to get food to Greece...* ***Winston may be right in saying that the starvation of anyhow under-fed Bengalis is less serious than sturdy Greeks****... but he makes no sufficient allowance for the sense of Empire responsibility in this country [emphasis added].*

Field Marshal Wavell also attended as Viceroy-Designate, scheduled to replace Linlithgow in October. He would inherit Linlithgow's outstanding problems and so - apart from any humanitarian considerations - had a strong vested interest in resolving India's food difficulties. Immune to Churchillian blather, Wavell recorded that the

> *PM spoke scathingly of India's economic inefficiency which made it necessary to supply it with food which otherwise might not be needed.*[244] *100,000 tons of barley from Iraq had been arranged and 50,000 tons of wheat from Mediterranean, but more could not be provided without taking it from Egypt and the Middle East where reserve was being accumulated for Greece and Balkans.* ***Apparently it is more important to save the Greeks and liberated countries from starvation than the Indians*** *and there is reluctance either to provide shipping or to reduce stocks in this country [emphasis added].*

Wavell and Amery's diaries highlight Churchill's role in the 24th September discussions and the issues which motivated him.

Greece and Greeks feature prominently in both entries - and the Balkans in Wavell's record - confirming the PM's profound Mediterranean obsession and his wildly unrealistic hopes for Operation Accolade. If Wavell's transcript is true, Churchill was anticipating a time when Britain would be responsible for feeding liberated Greeks but - in September 1943 - Greece was German-occupied, it would remain German-occupied until October 1944, and Accolade was already unravelling.[245] A rational man might have considered his first duty to save imperial subjects from starvation, but Churchill was not a rational man, he detested Indians and his Mediterranean obsession coloured everything. Two weeks later - on 8th October - General Brooke lamented that

> *Winston is becoming less and less balanced. I can control him no longer. He has worked himself into a frenzy of excitement about the Rhodes attack, has magnified its importance so that he can no longer see anything else and has set his heart on capturing this one island.*

---

[244] Britain survived on imports so Churchill's criticism of Indian requests for food is richly ironic, particularly as India's import-reliance resulted from the Raj-imposed policy of substituting cash crops (jute, cotton etc) for food crops.

[245] German forces captured Rhodes - the most strategically significant Dodecanese island - on 13th September and Cos fell on 4th October.

Perhaps 'Mediterranean mania' already gripped the PM on 24th September when he prioritised feeding Greeks - who might become British responsibilities - over saving Bengalis from imminent starvation?

The reference to *"anyhow under-fed Bengalis"* also contradicts Churchill's fanciful depiction of India as a paradise on earth in which *"famine had been gripped and controlled,"*[246] and his suggestion that the Bengalis' malnourished condition might disqualify them from prompt attention - rather than place them at the front of the queue - may also disturb modern readers. Lastly, the comparison between 'sturdy Greeks' and 'anyhow under-fed Bengalis' simply reflects white supremacist values in which everything white and European was considered superior to anything brown-skinned or Asian. In Churchill's mind, Greeks were superior to Indians and his reflexive racism undoubtedly influenced Britain's shoddy and inadequate response to Bengali suffering.

Churchill clearly saw the matter as a zero-sum game between India and the Mediterranean and - as always - Mediterranean obligations (retaining food to feed Greeks) trumped anything Indian (preventing mass starvation). The 24th September War Cabinet granted India an extra 50,000 tons of grain and Churchill did *"admit that something should be done"* but - given the anticipated 1.29m ton grain shortfall - British support for India in its hour of need was pitifully parsimonious. By February 1944, Amery calculated that Britain had provided India with 320,000 tons of grain out of the 500,000 tons he had requested,[247] and the famine continued into 1944, claiming between two and three million lives[248] through a malignant blend of starvation and disease.

To contextualise Britain's indifferent response to Bengali suffering, it may be useful to contrast the cornucopia of food and raw materials entering the UK while India starved. Britain had experienced an 'imports crisis' in early 1943 but - with the u-boats beaten and US shipyards performing prodigiously - the situation was entirely reversed

---

[246] See Chapter 6.

[247] Based on Amery's figures to the 28th January War Cabinet, including 130,000 tons of Iraqi barley, 180,000 tons of Australian wheat and 10,000 tons of Canadian grain (Nicholas Mansergh, *The Transfer of Power 1942-47,* vol. 4, *The Bengal Famine and the New Viceroyalty,* 15 June 1943 - 31 August 1944 (1973), Document 347, p.678).

[248] It's impossible to accurately estimate the final death toll, but the figure of 2-3 million lies in the mid-range of estimates provided by the Famine Inquiry Commission, Chattopadhyaya and Mukerjea, Amartya Sen and P.R. Greenough (Arnold P. Kaminsky and Roger D. Long (Eds) *Nationalism and Imperialism in South and Southeast Asia: Essays Presented to Damodar R. SarDesai* (2017), p.91).

by the end of the year. Throughout 1943, Britain - with its significantly smaller population[249] - imported 4m tons of wheat, grain and flour, 1.6m tons of meat, 1.4m tons of sugar, 409,000 live cattle and 131,000 tons of rice and - by December - had accumulated a 7.6m ton food stockpile over and above its immediate requirements (i.e. 7.6m tons of food in reserve).[250] India had requested 500,000 tons of grain and sharing even a small portion of the British surplus might have relieved Bengal's suffering, but Britain's Government retained this food to enjoy freedom of action in deploying its merchant fleet and as insurance against post-war price fluctuations - this surplus food would not be consumed in 1943/44 but would sit in sheds, warehouses and, in the case of the oilseeds and sugar, under tarpaulins while countless Bengalis slowly starved. Retaining food for white Europeans who **might** benefit from it at some point - rather than sharing it with Asians facing imminent starvation - was always Britain's way, a selfish and morally questionable stance.

Nor - despite Lord Leathers' protestations - was Britain short of ships to ferry food to India. Firstly, Churchill had reduced Indian Ocean sailings by 60% in January 1943 to compensate for losses incurred as a result of his refusal to furnish Coastal Command with VLR aircraft, but these ships were simply employed in augmenting Britain's already massive food and raw material reserves.[251] Secondly, just as British food stocks bounced back following the u-boats' defeat, so too did Allied shipping. Almost seventeen million tons of new shipping entered the Allied fleet during 1943 - 11.5m tons from America alone - to produce a shipping 'glut' by the end of the year and so - contrary to Leathers' assertions - the Allies had plenty of ships to transport food to India had they the will to use them so, but they were all either sailing the Atlantic - augmenting already massive British food stockpiles - or servicing imperially-inspired follies in the Mediterranean such as Operation Shingle. Churchill and Brooke had continually urged Mediterranean operations on the grounds of prospective shipping savings but any gains made were squandered in ongoing Italian operations such as Anzio which - for a time - became the 'fourth busiest port in the world', absorbing ships from both India and Overlord. Within this context, the Cabinet's rejection of a

---

[249] Britain's wartime population was around 47.7m against 60.3m for Bengal.

[250] British food stocks rose from 6.2m tons in July 1943 to 7.6m tons by December and - by the end of the year - Britain also held a 10.9m ton raw materials reserve. The shipping removed from India was therefore ferrying food to Britain which wasn't urgently needed (C.B.A. Behrens, *Merchant Shipping and the Demands of the War,* (1955) p.325).

[251] See Chapter 26 for full details. It's estimated that Indian Ocean shipping re-deployed to the Atlantic carried 2m tons of food and raw materials to Britain between January and June 1943, more than enough to end India's food misery (Mukerjee, *Churchill's Secret War*, p.119).

Canadian offer of 100,000 tons of wheat and a 10,000-ton ship to carry this food to India on 10th November as *"uneconomical from the shipping point of view"* is perplexing given the resources available to the Allies at this time. Perhaps the gentlemen of the War Cabinet simply had no interest in the saving rickety babies and emaciated skeletons entering relief centres in Chattogram and Dhaka in autumn 1943?

Comparing the aid allocated to imperial India and liberated Italy during 1943-45 is also instructive as both countries endured miserable harvests, the consequences of 'scorched earth' policies and widespread malnutrition throughout this period.[252] However, while India suffered malign neglect, Italy - a former enemy - was generously inundated with assistance. While Britain reluctantly gave India 320,000 tons of grain between September 1943 and February 1944, liberated Italy - with its much smaller population[253] - received 492,000 tons of grain and flour from Britain and America between July 1943 and September 1944. Throughout the period July 1943 to September 1945, Allied sources provided Italy with 2.42m tons of grain and flour (valued at $490m), with Britain providing 632,000 tons of this total (worth $95m). Britain, Canada and America also provided Italy with more than 30,000 tons of seed potatoes in spring 1944, nutrition officers were attached to the Allied Control Commission to ensure efficient deployment of aid and a Typhus Control Board was formed to eradicate the disease among Italian civilians. Britain - along with America - experienced no great problem in shipping massive quantities of aid to white, Mediterranean Italians so why did it prove so difficult to despatch aid to brown-skinned Bengalis?

And finally we come to the United Nations Relief and Rehabilitation Administration (UNRRA), formed in November 1943 to *"operate in these areas of food shortages... to assume a fair distribution of the available supplies among all of the liberated peoples, and second to ward off death by starvation or exposure among these peoples."* UNRRA was established to alleviate suffering **in liberated territories** and Italy - which cannily switched sides in September 1943 - was UNRRA's second largest beneficiary during 1944-47, receiving $418m in

---

[252] In September 1944, the Allied Control Commission reported that Italy's general mortality rate had doubled in twelve months, infant mortality was four times its pre-war level and Italian adults had - on average - lost five to ten pounds in weight (Edward R. Flint, *The Development of British Civil Affairs and its Employment in the British Sector of Allied Military Operations during the Battle of Normandy, June to August 1944* (Doctoral thesis, Cranfield University, 2008, p.153).

[253] Around 15-20m Italians lived in liberated territory south of Rome by 1944, with a further 25-30m living under German control in the north. Between July 1943 and September 1945, Italy received 93,000 tons of grain and flour per month from Anglo-American sources while India's larger population received 53,300 tons of grain per month from British-imperial sources between September 1943 and February 1944, giving a clear sense of Allied and imperial priorities.

commodity aid in the form of food, clothing, textiles, medical supplies and industrial and agricultural equipment. By spring 1945, Allied forces and UNRRA were feeding 24m Italian civilians, with UNRRA shipping in 15,000 tons of relief every month to supplement the diets of 2m Italian mothers and children. UNRRA - with its 4,000 staff - remained Italy's principal import agency until spring 1947 when Italy's government assumed the role.

Aid provided by UNRRA helped Italy avoid mass starvation during 1943-45 but some - such as Rep. Karl Mundt of South Dakota - wondered why former enemies - such as Italy - enjoyed generous UNRRA support while faithful allies enduring grave hardship - such as India - received nothing? Mundt tabled an amendment to the UNRRA Appropriations Bill before Congress in December 1943 to try to qualify India for UNRRA support and - after an initial setback - his Amendment was adopted on 25th January to ensure that *"any area important to United Nations military operations which may be stricken by famine or disease may be included in the benefits available through the UNRRA."* As UNRRA's largest benefactor, anything endorsed by the United States would inevitably be adopted by UNRRA itself.[254]

From spring 1944 onwards, India qualified for UNRRA support but India requested no assistance. Viceroy Wavell was keen to explore this option - and also solicit direct aid from America - but the 19th February War Cabinet quashed the notion by reminding members that *"the policy of His Majesty's Government has hitherto been that the British Empire should not come within the sphere of UNRRA activities"* and that this policy would continue. India was an UNRRA founding signatory, it provided $30m of support to UNRRA[255] and UNRRA rules were specifically amended to assist India in its hour of need but Churchill's government steadfastly refused to request UNRRA support to relieve Indian suffering. Such a policy would have compromised British authority and, to an arch-imperialist such as Churchill, was completely unacceptable - from his twisted perspective, it was better for Indians to die under the Union Jack than prosper under UNRRA. In the long run, such a stance could only sharpen India's clamour for independence.

---

[254] The Senate approved the UNRRA Bill in February and UNRRA's Council adopted the 'India Clause' in May. (Manish Sinha, *The United Nations Relief and Rehabilitation Administration (UNRRA) and the Question of Food Aid during the Bengal Famine of 1943*, Proceedings of the Indian History Congress, vol. 73, 2012, pp.1048-9).

[255] Britain donated $30m of India's wartime earnings to the UNRRA fund, making India UNRRA's sixth largest contributor (Mukerjee, *Churchill's Secret War*, p.208).

CHAPTER TWENTY-NINE: MR. CHURCHILL'S BALKAN TRIANGLE

British policy... is essentially today what it has always been... it is directed primarily at the preservation of the Empire connections and the sea route to India... to finding where Britain can secure the firmest vantage ground for the preservation of a stake in the Balkans - obviating total control of Southeastern Europe by any other great power. It is very far from a policy aimed at the reconstruction of the occupied countries as free and independent states.

US Ambassador Lincoln MacVeagh to President Roosevelt, 17th February 1944

I asked him how he really felt about it [Overlord] now and he said that if he had been responsible for the planning, he would have done it on a broader front and he would have liked to have had Turkey on our side and the Danube under threat as well as Norway cleaned up ***before*** *we undertook it [emphasis added].*

John J. McCloy, US Assistant Secretary of War, summarises a conversation with Churchill, 26th April 1944

This book was written to answer one question and one question only - did Churchill and COS prioritise British oil and empire interests in the Mediterranean over efforts to liberate Europe from fascism, a question which cuts to the very core of British identity. The evidence presented throughout *Empire First* is overwhelmingly affirmative but - before offering a final summing up - two further factors which diluted enthusiasm for Overlord merit scrutiny.

I

Churchill's support for Overlord was hobbled by his low opinion of British military capability. This ineffectuality was the result of two decades of "*niggling, cheeseparing [and] parsimony*" - to which Churchill himself had contributed - which undermined the Army, leaving it ill-prepared to meet the challenges of 1939-42.[256] The successive humiliations of Norway, Dunkirk, Greece, Crete and Dieppe sapped

[256] Readers will recall General Morgan's Chapter 12 comments: *"Americans knew at first hand of the immense power and resources that the United States could throw into the battle. We British had... to overcome the effects of a lifetime of niggling, cheeseparing, parsimony and making do... We had been brought up to advocate the answer that was least costly. An answer that cost nothing but appeared good enough had always been a winner."*

faith in the Army's ability to impose its will on opponents endowed with *"extraordinary fighting efficiency."*[257] The Singapore surrender formed a keystone in this arch of negativity by posing a

> *crucial question to which the Prime Minister had no answer. How came 100,000 men (half of them of our own race) to hold up their hands to inferior numbers of Japanese? The surrender of the fortress stunned him... One evening, months later, when he was sitting in his bathroom… he stopped drying himself and gloomily surveyed the floor: 'I cannot get over Singapore,' he said sadly.*[258]

Tobruk's capitulation four months later- *"one of the heaviest blows I can recall during the war"* - shattered Prime Ministerial confidence in the British-imperial army.

> *In Tobruk, a garrison of seasoned soldiers had laid down their arms to perhaps one half of their number… I did not attempt to hide from the President the shock I had received. It was a bitter moment. Defeat is one thing: disgrace is another.*[259]

The surrender of British-imperial troops to smaller enemy forces in both cases reinforced the impression of an army incapable of imposing its will on determined opponents. Chief of the Imperial General Staff General Brooke was well-placed to observe the Army's frailties, attributing them to a

> *lack of good military commanders. Half of our Corps and Divisional Commanders are totally unfit for their appointments, and yet if I were to sack them I could find no better! They lack character, imagination, drive and power of leadership.*

This was the product of a moral decline ensuring

---

[257] Churchill's July 1943 assessment of German martial capabilities.

[258] Harold Nicolson's record of a conversation between Churchill and Violet Bonham Carter on 11th February 1942 further illustrates Prime Ministerial - and more general - pessimism: *"She had been to see Winston yesterday, and for the first time in their long friendship she had found him depressed... underneath it all was a dreadful fear... that our soldiers are not as good fighters as their fathers were. 'In 1915', said Winston, 'our men fought on even when they had only one shell left and were under a fierce barrage. Now they cannot resist dive-bombers. We have so many men in Singapore, so many men - they should have done better.' It is the same, of course, in Libya. Our men cannot stand up to punishment... There is something deeply wrong with the whole morale of our Army."* (Nicolson, *Diaries and Letters, 1939-45,* p.211).

[259] Churchill also disparaged American troops. At the November 1943 Cairo Conference he informed General Marshall that, in his view, one German division was equal to two and a half American divisions. Marshall thundered back *"I never want to hear this again"* and Churchill dropped the subject (Cray, *General of the Army*, p.424).

> *that we are not anything like as tough as we were in the last war. There has been far too much luxury, safety first, red triangle etc in this country. Our one idea is to look after our comforts and avoid being hurt in any way.*

It also resulted from

> *the cream of the manhood having been lost in the First World War. It was the real leaders, in the shape of platoon, company and battalion commanders, who were killed off. These were the men we were short of now. I found this shortage of leaders of quality applied to all three fighting services.*[260]

Readers can decide if Brooke's analysis is correct or if pre-1914 officer recruitment practices[261] also contributed to the malaise but the result was the same - an incompetent officer class and a profound aversion to decisive engagement with sizeable German forces. Brooke's views enjoyed widespread currency among his colleagues. General Pownall castigated career officers who regarded war *"as an upsetting, rather exhausting and distinctly dangerous interlude in the happier, more comfortable and more desirable days of peace-soldiering,"* while Sir Alexander Cadogan argued that

> *our soldiers are the most pathetic amateurs, pitted against professionals... The Germans are magnificent fighters and their Staff are veritable Masters of Warfare. Wavell and suchlike are no good against them. It's like putting me up to play Bobby Jones*[262] *over 36 holes.*

Sir James Grigg was even more scathing.

> *The Army is <u>LISTLESS</u> and <u>LAZY</u>... <u>all BLAME, SHAME lies on every individual</u>; that they didn't want conscription in peacetime, that they allowed Baldwin to do nix - and liked it; that they enjoyed and enjoy a high standard of living; that they are soft; they have been found wanting. They must bow their heads in shame until their exertion wins the war* [emphases in original].

Grigg's role as Churchill's War Secretary (1942-45) merely underlines the depth of this pessimism and, under such circumstance, it was

---

[260] This is one of Brooke's post-war reflections, commenting on his 8th October 1941 diary entry.
[261] See Chapter 1.
[262] The Tiger Woods of his day.

considered prudent to shield the Army from risky operations such as Overlord which would only expose its frailty. Air Marshal Portal confirmed the Chiefs' desire to protect the Army from humiliation by admitting that COS

> *never had the same confidence in our troops [as the Americans had in theirs]. It was clear to us that they had been very badly shaken by the early defeats and* ***we were very much afraid of setting them a task beyond their capacity*** [emphasis added].

Churchill, Brooke and COS considered Overlord beyond the Army's capacity and did everything they could to stall the operation. In their view, the Army should stick to secondary operations in theatres such as Italy which straddled vital Mediterranean sea-routes and which - because of the relatively small numbers involved - minimised opportunities for failure and embarrassment.[263]

II

Britain's Great War losses also stifled support for Overlord. The Empire had lost 960,000 men, mainly in France and Flanders, a savage toll which diminished desire for repeat engagements in the same theatre. The shadows of Ypres, Passchendaele - and more recent reverses - stalked 'Bomber' Harris' jeremiads against continental operations.

> *To enter upon a Continental land campaign, other than on a mopping up police basis, is to play right into Germany's hands... such a course must lead to the easily avoidably immolation of the flower of the youth of this under-populated country in the mud of Flanders and France... The moral effect of another Dunkirk on the people of this country and on the world, would be disastrous... Let us all well remember that*

---

[263] Britain's extremely limited manpower resources further inhibited support for Overlord. With 11 British and 8 Canadian divisions operating in north-western Europe by spring 1945 (against 60 US divisions and 11m Soviet soldiers under arms) and 10% of all British conscripts being drafted into coalmining as 'Bevin Boys', Britain simply couldn't afford casualties on the same scale as its allies - any major bloodletting would have crippled Britain in the war's closing months and weakened its post-war power. Concentrating in Italy - with its limited capacity to absorb troops - minimised the risk of mass casualties and fostered the semblance of parity with America. If both powers had roughly the same number of divisions operating in Italy, Britain could masquerade as America's equal, a deceit which would be exposed once Channel operations commenced. Operating on Italy's east coast, British-imperial troops were also well-placed to cross the Adriatic and block Russian access to Yugoslavia if required.

> *we have yet to meet on land the German army on the defensive, and all that implies.*

They also informed the deception practised by Churchill *et al* during Marshall and Hopkins' April 1942 visit to London. This was America's first attempt to sell Channel operations to its hesitant ally and Churchill, Brooke and Ismay paid lip service to the ideal, ensuring that *"our American friends went happily homeward under the mistaken impression that we had committed ourselves to both Roundup and Sledgehammer."* Ismay conceded the deception after the war by admitting that

> *we should have come clean, much cleaner than we did, and said. 'We are frankly horrified because of what we have been through in our lifetime - 60,000 in a day, the 1st of July 1916, 60,000.... We, who survived [WWI] had got that into our minds: 'Never again'. We are not going into this [invading Europe] until it is a cast-iron certainty'.*

Churchill's Great War experiences also undermined his enthusiasm for Overlord. His description of *"a large casualty clearing station in the height of a battle"* in 1915 evokes Bosch at his most apocalyptic.

> *More than 1,000 men suffering from every form of horrible injury, seared, torn, pierced, choking, dying, were being sorted according to their miseries into the different parts of the Convent... At the entrance the arrival and departure of the motor ambulances, each with its four or five shattered and tortured beings, was incessant: from the back door, corpses were being carried out at brief intervals to a burying party constantly at work. One room was filled to overflowing with cases not worth sending any farther, cases whose hopelessness excluded them from priority in operations... Everywhere was blood and bloody rags.*

Such experience informed his later aversion to cross-Channel operations.

> *I was not convinced that [a direct assault across the Channel] was the only way of winning the war, and I knew that it would be a very heavy and hazardous venture. The fearful price we had had to pay in human life and blood for the great offensives of the First World War was graven in my mind. Memories of the Somme and Passchendaele and many lesser frontal attacks upon the Germans were not blotted out by time or reflection.*

When American Assistant Secretary of War John J. McCloy visited London in April 1944, Churchill confirmed that if America felt he was *"using all his efforts to avoid such another slaughter as had taken place in World War I due to inadequately equipped men,"* these suspicions were well-founded. The previous July, McCloy's superior - Henry Stimson - had formed the impression that Churchill opposed Overlord because *"the shadows of Passchendaele and Dunkerque still hang too heavily over… his government"* - a perceptive and damning assessment.[264]

III

Fears of opening up a new 'Western Front' and doubts over Allied military capability are frequently trotted out to justify British opposition to D-Day, but imperial obsession is routinely excluded as acknowledging such an impulse would taint Britain's moral stature, impugn the integrity of its great war leader and contradict the mythology of 'Brave Little Britain Battling Alone'. One cannot be both 'Brave Little Britain Battling Alone' **and** 'The Greatest Empire The World Has Ever Seen' so - as a result - the Empire is excluded from most conventional histories, a sleight of hand which approaches its absurd apogee in Andrew Roberts' bizarre contention that *"control of the Mediterranean had not really been a British policy objective since Nelson's day."* The evidence presented throughout *Empire First* - particularly in Chapters 6 and 24 - starkly refutes such bunkum.

Analysing British strategic preferences after 12th July 1943 clarifies matters. Allied power was clearly ascendant by summer 1943 – the Axis was expelled from Africa, Mussolini de-throned and the Nazis bested at Kursk. The Americans urged *"decisive military operations* ***conducted at times and places of our choosing - not the enemy's****"* (i.e. north-western Europe) while Britain favoured ongoing peripheral operations in the Mediterranean, championing Sicily and Italy as venues following victory in Africa. The Mediterranean emphasis is evident in Churchill's 19th July[265] note to COS urging Italian operations in preference to Overlord and in his 'Roundhammer' denunciations to Stimson later that day. It is present in the 20th July COS 'stand-still' order and in the 6th August COS aide memoire advocating an advance to Milan and Turin while fighting in Sicily was

---

[264] According to General Hollis, *"Churchill… was determined that this war should not repeat the incredible folly of 1914-18, when tens of thousands would die in a single action, and for no tangible result. The shadow of that lost generation… continually darkened our counsels."* (James Leasor, *War at the Top* (2001), p.234).

[265] Is it purely coincidental that Churchill's Overlord vituperations commenced one week after Russia's great victory at Kursk and four days after Morgan submitted his draft Overlord plan? Readers, draw your own conclusions.

still underway. It is evident in the 19th October COS meeting in which Churchill prioritised Italian, Balkan and Aegean operations over the build-up of American forces in Britain and it informed the 11th November COS memo which rejected Overlord *"on a fixed date... [as] the pivot of our whole strategy on which all else turns."* It is also present in the autumn 1943 Dodecanese Campaign and informed the Shingle shambles and naïve hopes of capturing Rome by February 1944.

A cursory glance at a relief map of Europe illustrates the absurdity of such ambitions. Unlike northern Europe's 2,000 miles of perfectly flat tank country joining the Urals to the Channel, the entirety of German-occupied southern Europe - with one exception[266] - is vertiginously mountained.

Map 39: Southern European Mountains vs. North European Plain

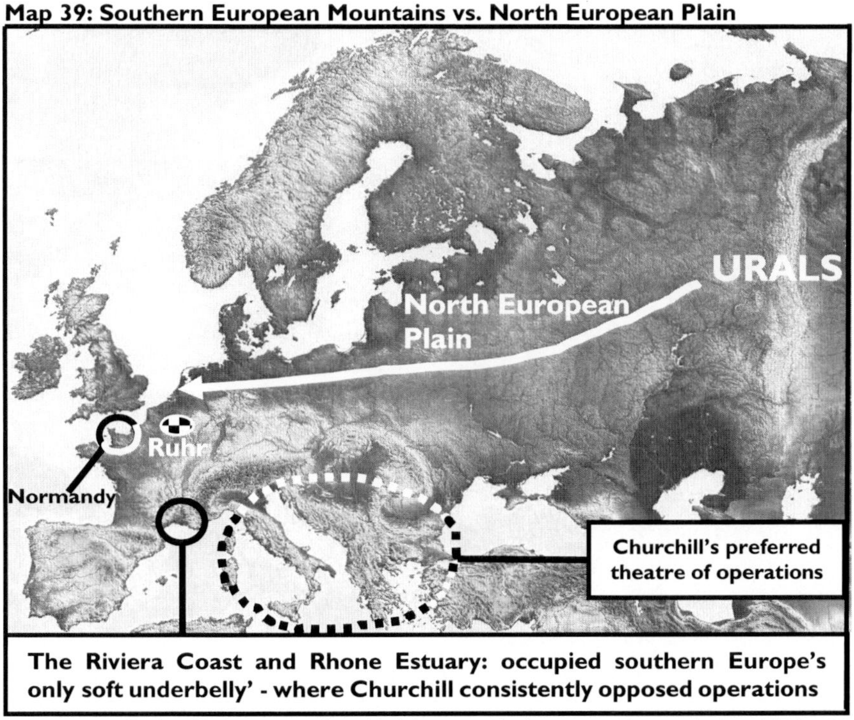

(map courtesy of Pixabay: all Pixabay content can be used freely for commercial and non-commercial purposes in print and digital media)

Italy is dominated by the Apennines and topped by the Alps. Former Yugoslavia is covered by the Julian and Dinaric Alps, seventy percent

[266] The terrain around the Riviera and Rhone estuary is flat and was the location for the successful August 1944 Dragoon landing. Churchill, however, opposed this operation (which confirmed France as the 'decisive theatre') and advocated Operation Armpit and the Ljubljana Gap strategy - in heavily mountained areas – as alternatives. Chapter 29 and further footnotes in this chapter explore this controversy.

of Albania is mountainous and the Balkan Mountains link Serbia to the Black Sea. This is appalling terrain in which to fight German forces as Monty - who was relieved to leave the region in December 1943 - appreciated:

> *The 'leg' of Italy is essentially ideal defensive country... The Adriatic winter is severe... on land progress would become impossible off the main roads owing to snow and mud; mountain torrents subject to violent fluctuations would create great bridging difficulties... The country generally was ideal for delay by the action of small units co-ordinated with skilfully sited demolitions... The Germans took the fullest advantage of this fact and our advance throughout was barred and delayed by demolitions on the widest possible scale.*

Brooke visited Italy in December and lamented:

> *The terrain defies description. It's like the North-West Frontier; a single destroyed culvert can hold up an army for a day.*

Why would any sane person wish to fight Germany in such terrible terrain so far from Hitler's heartland?

The shifting balance of power in the East explains this quixotic preference. Germany's pummelling of Russia concluded with Kursk - a bittersweet victory from a western perspective which both assured Allied victory **and** a Soviet advance into regions Britain identified as *"the nodal point in our imperial communications... [and] the highway for the immense trade between the British Isles and the Dominions, Colonies, India, Burma and all countries east of Suez."* The prospect of Soviet forces gaining direct access to the Mediterranean through the Balkans horrified Churchill and drove him to conclude the Percentages Agreement with Stalin in October 1944 (see Chapter 23). In 1943-44, it prompted him to champion multiple operations in the greater Mediterranean region which had nothing to do with defeating Germany but everything to do with maintaining British hegemony over its Mediterranean 'lake'.[267] Churchill's three preferred operations for 1943-44 form a single unitary plan - his Balkan Triangle Strategy.

Accolade (Sept - Nov 1943) formed the first part of this plan and was

---

[267] As noted earlier, the *Daily Bristol Times and Mirror* described the Mediterranean as *"an English lake and the Suez Canal is only another name for the Thames and the Mersey"* (Kyle, *Suez*, p.14).

designed to draw Turkey into the war by providing it with vital war *matériel* via İzmir following the liberation of the Dodecanese.[268] In Churchill's fevered imagination, a Turkey liberated from fear of Germany would drive west into Bulgaria to discomfit Germany and coincidentally exclude Russia from all territory below that axis of advance.

Map 40: Axis of Turkey's proposed post-Accolade Balkan offensive

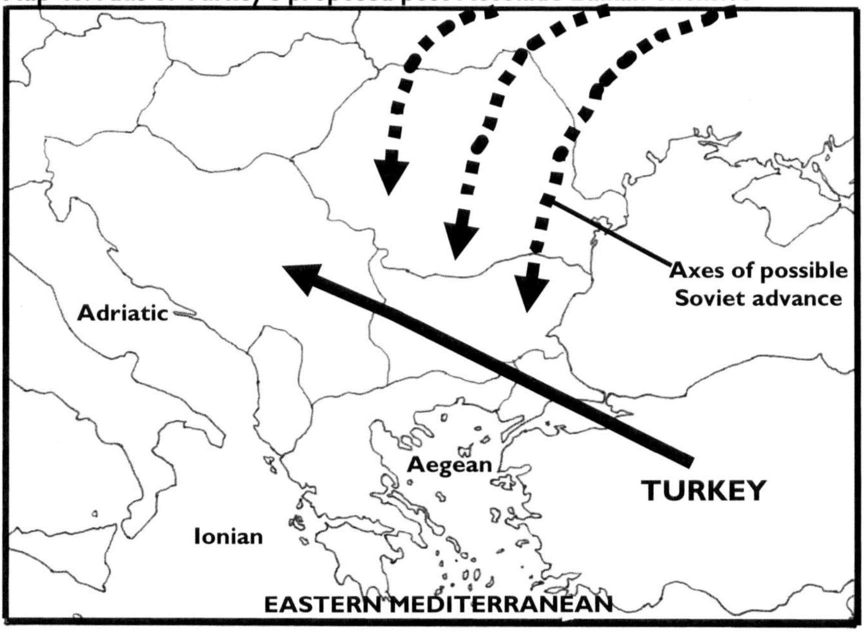

A successful Turkish Balkan Offensive might even draw resources away from Overlord - how could America fail to back a successful Allied offensive via the 'soft underbelly' - and by threatening to isolate its garrison, might even force Germany to relinquish Greece in 1943 or early 1944, conferring on Britain all the advantages of the Percentages Agreement without any obligation to accommodate Stalin. The Anglo-Turkish partnership - which had excluded Russia from the Mediterranean in the past - would be revived and Turkish soldiers would 'bleed and burn' for Britain's Empire.[269] Churchill hoped to *"gain immense prizes at little cost"* from this operation, *"becoming less and less balanced… [and working] himself into a frenzy of excitement"*

[268] Operation Hardihood aimed to provide Turkey with two armoured divisions, fifty RAF squadrons, four anti-aircraft regiments and numerous anti-tank regiments in phased deliveries.

[269] Ownership of the Dodecanese was uncertain (Italy had seized the islands in 1912) and, following a successful operation, Britain could use the islands as bargaining chips to reward Turkey (for entering the war) or thank Greece (for accepting British tutelage). Britain could also build bases on Rhodes or Kos to dominate the Aegean. In 1947, the islands were given to Greece.

when it failed. Accolade, the aborted Hardihood and the stillborn Turkish offensive form Part One of Churchill's Great Balkan Triangle.

Shingle and Armpit form Part Two of this fanciful conceit, conceived to seal off the Triangle's western vertex and access to the Adriatic. As Chapter 22 indicated, Shingle was intended to destroy German forces in central Italy and project Allied power into northern Italy in spring 1944. Once there, Allied forces would launch an amphibious assault on the Istrian Peninsula at the top of the Adriatic (Operation Armpit) and - by means of an enchanted forest path known as the

Map 41: Churchill's Shingle/Armpit fantasy

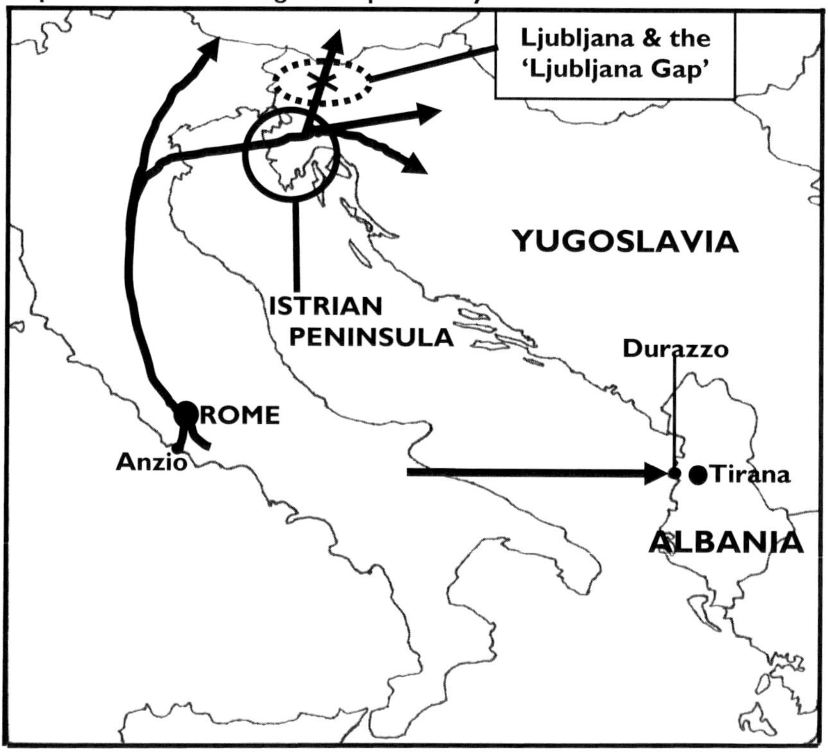

'Ljubljana Gap'[270] - drive into central Austria and Yugoslavia to exclude Russia from those regions. We know this was Churchill's dream because he enthusiastically evangelised for Armpit following the

---

270 Chapters 19 and 21 introduced the 'Ljubljana Gap' and Churchill's faith in Operation Armpit rested on the notion that a 'Gap' between the Julian and Dinaric Alps would permit easy access into Austria. However, Field Marshal Brooke and historians such as Michael Howard, Samuel E. Morison and Eric Larrabee have all queried the Gap's easy traversibility. Eric Larrabee describes it as *"not a gap at all but a heavily forested, narrow, ascending defile nearly two hundred miles long wound through by a double-track railroad and a single, poorly surfaced road twenty feet wide, with many tunnels, steep gradients, and two mountain passes at about two thousand feet dominated by higher mountains on either side. Room for manoeuvre is there none... it would be*

fall of Rome in June 1944 and an Allied presence in Yugoslavia would exclude Russia from the Adriatic and Mediterranean.

Manna, Britain's action in Greece during 1944-45, formed the third part of the Balkan Triangle and was the only operation to succeed, largely because German forces had already evacuated by the time British troops arrived and because Churchill had purchased Stalin's willing acquiescence with Bulgaria, Romania and Hungary.

Map 42: Greece - southern vertex of the Balkan Triangle

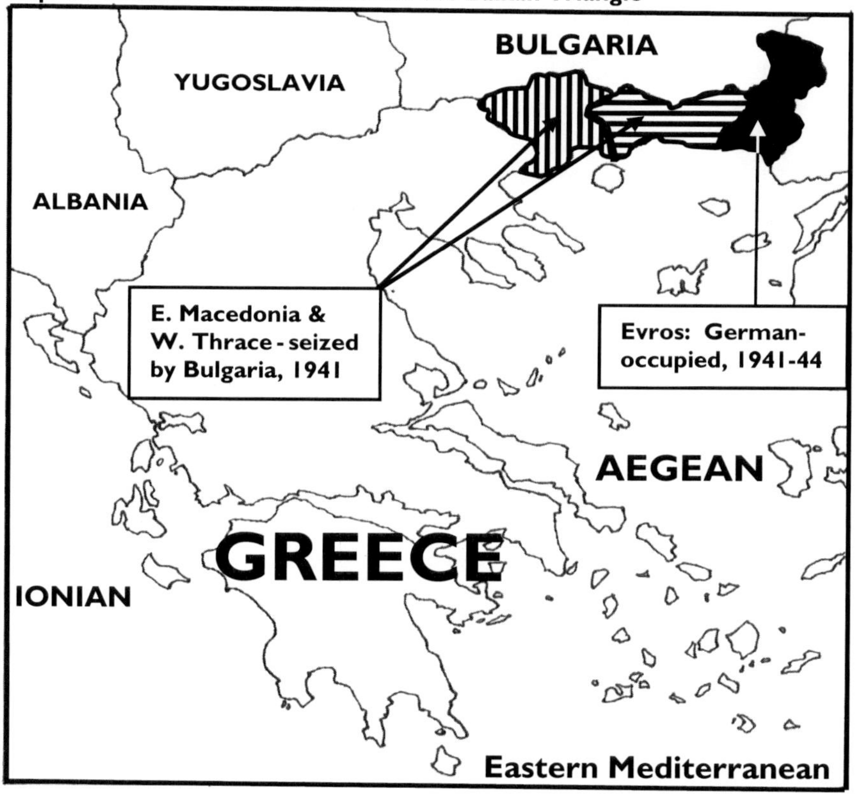

Manna confirmed Greece within Britain's sphere of influence and sealed off the triangle's southern vertex and access to the Aegean and Ionian Seas. All Britain had to do was crush a motley assortment of amateur resistance fighters who - only weeks earlier - had been busy killing Germans and secure the return of two Aegean coastal provinces seized by Bulgaria in 1941.

---

difficult to imagine a battleground more made to order for those masters of demolition and defence, the Germans." (Larrabee, *Commander-in-Chief,* p.497). Any attempt to enter Austria via the Ljubljana Gap would therefore simply transpose the stasis of Italy to northern Yugoslavia, enmiring Allied troops in protracted alpine operations easily resisted by German forces.

Aggregating these three thrusts into a single entity reveals Churchill's Mediterranean Master-Plan - his Great Balkan Triangle Strategy.

Map 43: The Balkan Triangle Strategy aggregated

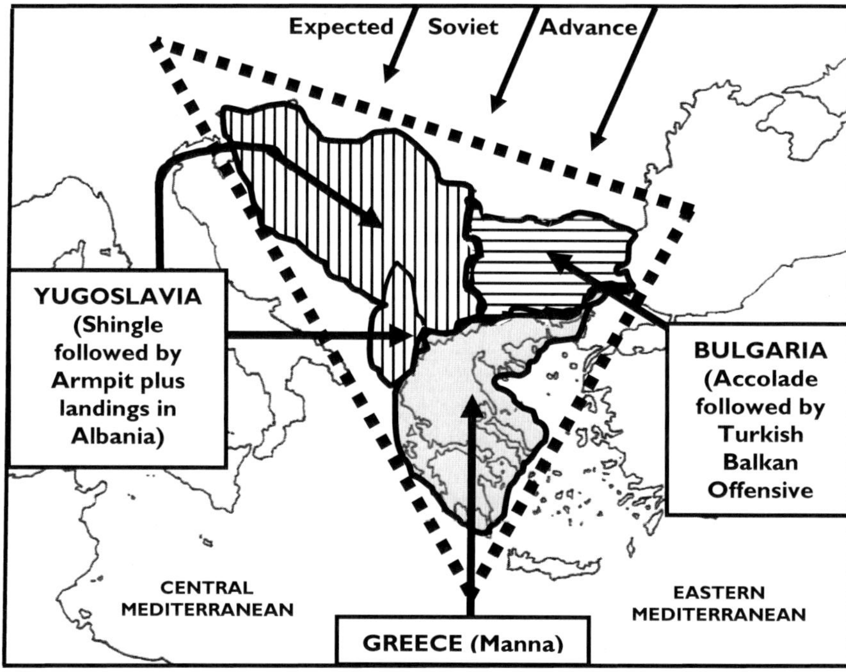

Accolade and the phantom Turkish offensive would secure the Triangle's eastern corner and the Aegean, Shingle/Armpit would seal off the western sector and the Adriatic, while Manna[271] secured Greece and the entire southern vertex.

These were not random, disconnected operations but three parts of a single plan to exclude Russia from the Mediterranean and consolidate British control over its oil and Empire highway. Accolade and Shingle/Armpit failed abysmally but fortune smiled on Britain in two other regards. Firstly, Tito's highly independent Yugoslavia practised a form of socialism **outwith** the Soviet bloc after the war, denying Russia easy access to the Adriatic and, secondly, repatriating Eastern Macedonia and Western Thrace to Greece from Bulgaria in 1944 sealed off the Aegean from pernicious Russian influence. Bulgaria had occupied both provinces in April 1941 but - at German prompting – it had foolishly declared war on Britain and America in December 1941,

[271] Britain's October 1944 Greek intervention was dubbed Operation Manna to conceal its true intention (projecting power) by pretending that it was driven by humanitarian considerations (delivering bread to starving Greeks).

granting the western Allies considerable leverage over Bulgarian armistice terms in 1944.[272]

Map 44: Eastern Macedonia and Western Thrace

Eden lobbied hard for the return of both provinces to Greece in his October 1944 talks with Molotov and agreed to reduce Britain's Percentages Agreement 'share' of Bulgaria from twenty-five to twenty percent to seal the deal. The return of these provinces to Greece in October 1944 consolidated Anglo-Greek friendship and - by re-establishing a Greek land border with Turkey - formed a narrow but effective *cordon sanitaire* to exclude Russia from the Aegean and eastern Mediterranean.[273] Ingress was still possible via the Bosporus

---

[272] Russia gained similar leverage by declaring war on Bulgaria on 5th September.

[273] Germany occupied Evros - adjacent to Turkey - during 1941-44 but this formed part of Western Thrace and reverted to Greece with the rest of the province as a condition of Bulgaria's October 1944 armistice.

and Dardanelles but - as Churchill knew to his cost - such transit was often problematic.

The Balkans lie 1200 miles from the Ruhr[274] and are heavily mountained. Normandy sits 350 miles from Germany's industrial heartland on the western edge of the extremely flat, tank-friendly North European Plain. There was no military rationale for engaging Germany in Italy or the Balkans in 1943-44 but every rationale for Britain to secure its Mediterranean imperial lifeline by excluding its age-old adversary from a theatre considered *"a matter of life and death to the British Empire."* Oil and Empire considerations inspired British enthusiasm for Balkan-Mediterranean operations in 1943-45 and vindicate the assessments of men such as War Secretary Stimson and his deputy McCloy, Admirals King and Leahy, Ambassador MacVeagh and General Stanley Embick[275] who correctly perceived that

> *since April 1942 America had been led down the "primrose path" by Britain's "agreements in principle" to Overlord... the British... pursued a traditional balance-of-power strategy aimed solely at preserving the Empire and British interests in a postwar world.* ***British designs in the Balkans and the Mediterranean... were not war measures against Germany, but aimed at checking the Soviet advance into these regions*** [emphasis added].

This analysis – endorsed by *Empire First* - matters because it strips Britain of much of the moral virtue acquired through participation in Overlord. Many young British and Commonwealth men gave their lives to liberate western Europe in 1944/45 - and generals such as Montgomery fully backed the venture - but the foregoing analysis reveals Churchill and Brooke as extremely reluctant participants in Overlord, corralled into a venture they actively opposed through joint Soviet-American pressure.[276] Churchill enthusiastically advocated Balkan and Mediterranean ventures at a time when circumstance merited more assertive strategies aimed directly at Hitler's heartland. Churchill hoped to sabotage Overlord for 1944 (and promote British

---

[274] The distance between Sofia and Dortmund. Dortmund and Ljubljana are 630 miles apart (but separated by major mountain ranges).

[275] Co-author of a January 1943 memo warning Marshall against British imperial designs in the eastern Mediterranean and Balkans.

[276] As a reminder, Churchill informed Sir Alec Cadogan in April 1944 that Overlord *"has been forced upon us by the Russians and by the United States military authorities"* and he assured Dominion PMs in May that - had he been directing strategy - he *"would have been in favour of rolling up Europe from the South-East, and joining hands with the Russians."* (see Chapter 22).

oil and Empire interests) by diverting Allied resources into the Balkans over the winter of 1943-44 just as Torch - over the winter of 1942-43 - had undermined Roundup for 1943. Too weak to openly challenge or confront American strategic preferences, Churchill hoped to undermine his ally's war plans by subtle and insidious means - through endless cavilling and prevarication - just as he disingenuously proposed to break German power in Europe through indirect (and ineffectual) peripheral operations. Post-war claims to the contrary, Churchill fervently opposed Overlord until May 1944 and all inconvenient evidence (e.g. the 19th October COS meeting in which he prioritised Italian, Balkan and Aegean operations over America's build-up in Britain) was excluded from his otherwise meticulously researched memoirs to foster an entirely false impression of his strategic agenda.

Churchill's efforts to prioritise British oil and empire interests over the liberation of Europe also invalidate his much vaunted reputation as a champion of liberty and freedom.[277] History confirms June 1944 as the optimal moment to assault Festung Europa but Churchill campaigned to divert Allied energies into the eastern Mediterranean **as alternatives to Overlord** to pursue operations which - because of the distance and terrain involved - would have contributed nothing to defeating Hitler while blatantly reinforcing British influence over the region. Churchill was quite happy for western Europe to remain under Nazi control as long as British oil and empire interests were advanced and any German casualty figures resulting from his Balkan follies would have been cited to justify these operations while concealing his true motives. Stalin is rightly castigated for failing to liberate Warsaw in August 1944 but - had Churchill had his way - Western Europe would have languished under Nazi control throughout 1944/45 and beyond, with millions more dying in the death camps, on Europe's battlefields, in Germany's ruined cities and even in bucolic southern England as a result.[278] Of course, if Churchill believed his Mediterranean fantasy possessed genuine military merit, his reputation for strategic genius cannot stand - only a fool would choose to fight German forces across endless mountain ranges in southern Europe.

A Balkan-Mediterranean focus in 1944-45[279] would have precipitated

---

[277] His enthusiasm for Britain's Empire - an institution based on denying freedom and liberty to subject peoples - rather contradicts this reputation.

[278] German V1 and V2 'vengeance' weapons killed or injured 33,500 Britons between June 1944 and March 1945, and the death toll would have been higher had Allied forces not overrun their northern French launch sites in autumn 1944. After two years of relatively safety, these attacks generated considerable anxiety.

[279] In addition to the proposed Istrian landing, Britain also considered ferrying troops across the Adriatic into Albania or southern Yugoslavia. Eden gave the game away on 31st May 1943 when

disaster for all concerned - apart from Hitler. As Italian events reveal, fighting through mountains is slow and arduous work[280] and investing Allied resources in south-eastern Europe would have projected the stasis of the Italian campaign across the whole of southern Europe to the Fuhrer's considerable delight. Carefully constructed defensive fortifications would have enmired Anglo-America in sterile, unproductive operations for years, extending the war and prolonging Nazi barbarism for no good reason. Such would have been the dismal consequences of implementing Churchill's toxic Balkan Triangle Strategy.

And while Anglo-America was bogged down in the Balkans, an entirely different war might have prevailed in northern Europe as the Red Army exploited the region's flat and favourable terrain - and any weakening of German resistance - to storm through Germany, Denmark, Holland, Belgium, Luxembourg and northern France to reach the Channel.[281] In one of history's great ironies, Anglo-America might have become entrenched in southern Europe's impoverished underbelly while the Soviet Union established itself in rich and prosperous north-western Europe, dividing the continent along an east-west axis to generate an affluent Communist 'north' and a backward capitalist 'south'[282] - how different the Cold War might

---

he informed Churchill, Marshall and Eisenhower that Turkey would become more amenable to Allied interests *"when our troops had reached the Balkan area"* (Chapter 16). Churchill consistently advocated aid to partisans and commando raids across the Adriatic and on 19th October 1943, instructed COS to study the Mediterranean situation ***"in a most secret manner and on the assumption that commitments into which we have already entered with the Americans, particularly as regards 'Overlord', could be modified by agreement to meet the exigencies of a changing situation*** *[emphasis added]."* On 8th November, the Joint Planners produced the 'Relation of Mediterranean to Overlord' paper which recommended establishing a bridgehead at Durazzo Bay in Albania capable of handling 2,000 tons of shipping per day. This would demand forces from Britain and ***"require the postponement of Overlord for one month, to 1 June 1944, and would also mean that Operation Anvil in the south of France would have to be abandoned*** *unless it became clear that enemy resistance in that area would be slight [emphasis added]."* This was Britain's preferred means of undermining Overlord - slow, steady attrition rather than outright opposition. COS *"accepted these proposals as the basis of the argument they would develop"* at the November and December Cairo Conferences where they were rejected. (Hinsley et al, *British Intelligence,* Vol.III, part 1, pp. 15-16). Alexander revived Operation Armpit as Operation Gelignite in October 1944. Under this scheme, Allied forces would land at Trieste and Rijeka to the north and south of Istria before linking up with Allied forces in northern Italy and driving towards Vienna. Brooke opposed the scheme and it was finally dropped on 2nd December in favour of ongoing concentration in northern Italy (John R. Lampe, *Yugoslavia as History: Twice There Was a Country* (2000), p.441).

280 Allied forces required 22 months to travel 850 miles from Sicily to Milan and eleven months to travel 750 miles from Normandy to Torgau (80 miles south of Berlin).

281 I'm aware I'm entering the realms of speculation here which I hope the reader can forgive on the grounds of the extensive foregoing empirical analysis.

282 As a foretaste of what might have happened, Denmark was only retained within the western sphere because British troops entered Lübeck on 2nd May **twelve hours ahead** of Red Army forces, excluding them from the Jutland Peninsula. Soviet forces occupied Bornholm Island (a

have been under such circumstances.

Map 45: Strategic developments without Overlord

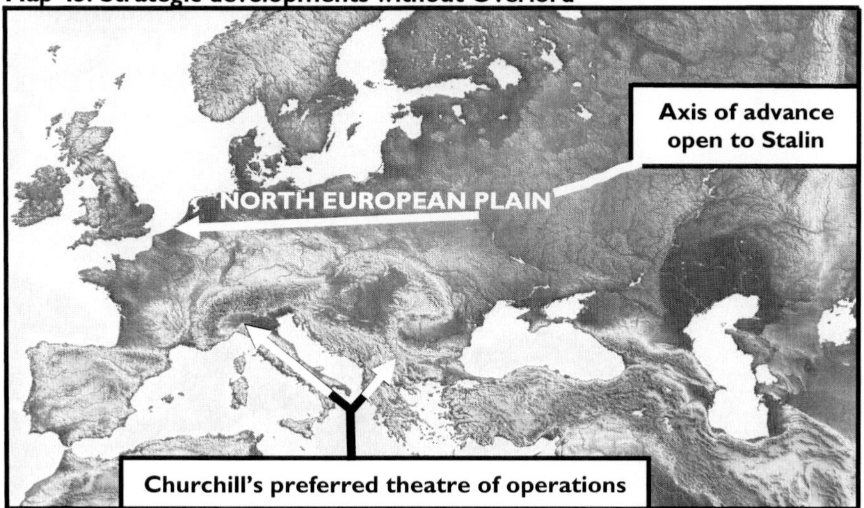

(map courtesy of Pixabay: all Pixabay content can be used freely for commercial and non-commercial purposes in print and digital media)

A Balkan-Mediterranean emphasis along Churchill's preferred lines might have secured Britain's imperial lifeline in the Mediterranean while Stalin's T-34's surged forward to replace Hitler's panzers at Calais - a remarkably poor return to the British people after six years of blood, sweat and tears - and the emerging Cold War would have been conducted on terms entirely favourable to Stalin. We should be eternally grateful to men such as George Marshall and Franklin Roosevelt - even to Stalin himself - who compelled Britain's timid and imperially-obsessed military hierarchy to support and endorse an operation in north-western Europe it actively opposed. Without such intervention, Churchill's attempts to sabotage Overlord - had they succeeded - would have tarnished his reputation as the man who defied Hitler in 1940 beyond repair, reducing him from a celebrated icon to damaged goods. Ironically, his Allies' intervention saved the 'Great Bloviator' from his own worst tendencies.

The conflicts currently convulsing Britain are also clearly evident in the great strategic debates of 1942-44. Some Britons wish to turn their backs on Europe and embrace a globally freebooting role, forging new partnerships with some old and familiar faces, including many former colonies and dominions - Empire 2.0 if you like. The same impulse inspired Churchill in 1943-45, driving him to prioritise

---

Danish territory in the Baltic) for a full year after the war (May 1945 - April 1946). (Parker, *The Second World War,* p.223; Tony Insall and Patrick Salmon (eds), *Documents on British Policy Overseas, Series I, Vol. IX: The Nordic Countries, From War to Cold War, 1944-51* (2011), p. xiii).

Britain's **global** oil and empire interests over the liberation of **western Europe** from Nazism. The consequences of such a policy, had it been implemented, are too grotesque to contemplate - a longer war, an inflated death toll and Stalinist hegemony over rich and prosperous north-western Europe, undermining British home security while supposedly 'bolstering' an Empire which would start collapsing within two years of the war's end. Those advocating an anti-Europe policy today are liable to inflict similar damage on Britain, impoverishing its people, detaching them from their European friends and strengthening the hand of those who wish us ill. Such will be the toxic legacy of Churchill's utterly misguided Brexit military strategy of 1943-45.

CHAPTER THIRTY: CAPTAIN MAINWARING IN DOWNING STREET

He knows no details, has only got half the picture in his mind, talks absurdities and makes my blood boil to listen to his nonsense. I find it hard to remain civil. And the wonderful thing is that three-quarters of the population of the world imagine that Winston Churchill is one of the Strategists of History, a second Marlborough, and the other quarter have no conception what a public menace he is and has been throughout this war!

Field Marshal Brooke on Winston Churchill, 10th September 1944

Churchill is the greatest military genius in history. He can use one division on three fronts at the same time.

General Ismay to Averell Harriman, 1943

Empire First begins and ends with Churchill but - given the tremendous volume of extant material - what new or original insights can this book offer? Watching *Dads Army* recently, I was struck by the similarities between Britain's wartime Premier and Captain Mainwaring of the Home Guard.[283] While the comparison might seem facetious at first, the similarities emerge on a moment's reflection. Both men were physically brave, willing to fight and die for their country. Both were patriots, proud Britons conscious of their country's role in the world. Neither lacked self-esteem, believing their opinions merited full attention and both were dynamic and purposive, catalysing less decisive characters into action. Mainwaring animated his Home Guard unit while Churchill attached 'Action This Day' stickers to reports demanding immediate implementation. Both were chippy outsiders - Churchill the 'half breed American' who only won his party's love after 1940, Mainwaring the upwardly mobile grammar school boy forever discomfited by his aristocratic Sergeant's effortless *élan*.

However, when it came to military planning - an area in which both considered themselves uniquely gifted - they were impetuous, impractical and - to use a Mainwaring phrase - liable to 'enter the realms of fantasy'. While Sergeant Wilson's suavely diffident 'Do you think that's wise, sir?' punctured many of Mainwaring's eccentric schemes, Roosevelt, Stalin and Brooke performed the same role with Churchill throughout the war, albeit less deferentially. Without such

---

[283] Significantly, Toby Jones' Mainwaring dresses as Churchill at one point in the 2016 *Dad's Army* film.

checking and restraining, the Allies would undoubtedly have lost the struggle.

I

Churchill's many admirable qualities included:

- his ability to marshal the English language in defence of Britain, a skill far beyond Mainwaring's rhetorical panache.

- his enthusiasm for America - inherited from his mother - was immensely helpful in a war in which Britain required American support.

- his determination to overcome his mental health issues, live life to the full and achieve his human potential is genuinely inspiring.

- his playfulness and sense of humour is constantly refreshing and, in the midst of war, offered an invaluable safety valve.

- his rich diet, lack of exercise and excessive tobacco and alcohol consumption notwithstanding, his indefatigable energy and perpetual motion remain sources of wonder. [284]

- his refusal to yield in 1940 saved the world from fascism and paved the way for victory, but if Churchill was solely and exclusively responsible for Britain's survival in 1940 - as so many proclaim - what does this tell us about the rest of Britain's spineless ruling class in that fateful year?[285]

Churchill - Britain's self-nominated Minister of Defence - saw himself in a line of military titans stretching from Alexander the Great through to Marlborough and Bonaparte. The analysis in the preceding chapters shatters this delusion while this chapter's compilation of Churchill's 'Top Ten Military Blunders' eviscerates this fantasy forever. Having already analysed these episodes in detail, we re-visit them now in summary form.

I: Norway, 1940

Churchill cannot be faulted for Britain's tardy involvement in Norway nor for the country's antiquated command structure but he committed multiple gaffes throughout the campaign which nurtured

[284] Churchill's constant activity may also have helped him master his 'demons'.

[285] Churchill, of course, was not the only Briton who refused to yield in 1940 but it suits some to inflate his role while downplaying the contributions of other patriots.

failure. Firstly, he wrongly identified the German invasion force as a purely naval force heading for the Atlantic and ordered Allied troops to disembark from their ships to allow Royal Navy cruisers to give chase; by the time the error was discovered, German forces were well established in Norway.

Admiral Evans had been planning the Narvik operation in partnership with General Mackesy since early March but on 10th April, Churchill replaced him with Admiral Boyle, an old friend and fellow 'fire-eater'. As a result, Boyle and Mackesy never met before they sailed for Norway (on separate ships), Churchill offered Boyle no written instructions and Boyle was unable to review General Mackesy's orders from the Chief of the Imperial General Staff - all this in an operation requiring exemplary army-navy cooperation!

Churchill also attempted to micro-manage the campaign from a distance of 1,300 miles with predictable results. When several German destroyers were sunk at Narvik, he wrongly assumed the port to be in Allied hands and divided the force bound for Narvik in two, one half continuing on its original course, the other sailing to Trondheim. Neither force possessed the power to complete its original mission and operational logistics were thrown into chaos. Churchill changed his mind on Allied objectives fourteen times over a three-week period[286] and was relieved as Chair of the Military Coordination Committee - yet it was Norway which propelled him into power! After the war, he conceded that *"I certainly bore an exceptional measure of responsibility for the brief and disastrous Norwegian campaign - if campaign it can be called."*

2: Greece, 1941

By February 1941, General O'Connor's desert army had defeated an Italian force five times its size, conquered eastern Libya and captured 130,000 prisoners. The whole of Libya lay within Britain's grasp and had this opportunity been seized, Britain could have gained possession of North Africa in spring 1941. Yet on 12th February, Churchill instructed Wavell to halt O'Connor's advance and send three divisions to Greece in a futile attempt to staunch an anticipated German attack. And on the very day that Churchill ordered this diversion, Rommel and the first Afrika Korps units landed in Tripoli. Rommel had been assigned a purely defensive role but appreciated the weakness of the forces confronting him and attacked on 24th March, driving British-imperial troops back into Egypt. And so began two

---

[286] The estimate is Clive Ponting's.

years of seesaw struggle until the Allies finally triumphed in May 1943. Without this misguided dispersion to Greece, Britain could have gained control of North Africa in 1941, enabling American forces to proceed directly to Britain in 1942 in preparation for a Channel crossing in 1943.[287] The Greek diversion is one of Churchill's least known yet most prodigious military blunders.

3: Japan, Singapore and Malaya

British forces suffered severe setbacks in their fight against Japan as a consequence of complacency, arrogance and inadequate resourcing with Churchill implicated in all of these miscalculations. In December 1924 he informed Prime Minister Baldwin that *"I do not believe there is the slightest chance of [war with Japan] in our lifetime... Japan is at the other end of the world. She cannot menace our vital security in any way,"* and dismissed the prospect of a Japanese assault on Australia during *"any period... which we or our children need foresee."*

Churchill's 1939 Memorandum on Sea Power repeated the same blinkered thinking by insisting that Singapore was safe because a land assault was unthinkable and Japan would never attack by sea. According to Churchill, *"Japan would have to send the bulk of her fleet... and begin a siege which would end only in disaster if the Japanese sea-communications were cut at any stage. One can take it as quite certain that Japan would not run such a risk. They are an extremely sensible people."*

Unfortunately, the *"extremely sensible"* Japanese attacked Singapore overland through Malaya. As Japanese forces approached, Churchill clung onto the absurd delusion of 'Fortress Singapore' even though only the narrow Johor Straits separated Singapore Island from mainland Malaya, its northern perimeter was entirely unfortified, it housed a large civilian population and lacked significant fresh water supplies. And the impossibility of a land-based assault was so deeply engrained in British thinking that the island's gun batteries lacked high explosive ordnance for use against infantry. The result of this negligence was the largest surrender in British history as 80,000 British-imperial troops surrendered to 35,000 soldiers dismissed by Churchill as the 'Wops of the Pacific'.

4: Bombing Germany

Compressing an operation as complex and multi-faceted as the strategic bombing of Germany into a few paragraphs is an invidious exercise so readers should simply consider the following:

---

[287] The Allies may or may not have launched a cross-Channel assault in 1943 but would - at least - have enjoyed the option.

- A.J.P. Taylor and Max Hastings estimate that Britain invested between 25% - 33% of its total war production in strategic bombing,[288] a staggering level of investment which restricted opportunities to attack Germany by other means.

- the attempt to bomb an advanced industrial economy such as Germany into submission was unprecedented and no-one knew if the strategy would succeed. Harris acknowledged the experimental nature of his project by observing that *"a lot of people... are in the habit of repeating the silly phrase 'Bombing can never win a war'. We shall see. It hasn't been tried yet, and* ***Germany... will make a most interesting subject for the initial experiment*** *[emphasis added]."*

- the RAF had no means of accurately assessing the impact of its raids. It could provide countless pictures of bombed-out buildings and gutted factories but it had no reliable means of gauging fluctuations in civilian morale or industrial output.[289] There was no means of accurately assessing if the bomber offensive was succeeding - the bomber crews simply had to deliver their payloads and hope for the best.

- although Churchill entertained significant doubts over the efficacy of the bomber campaign[290], he made no effort to challenge Harris and Portal's strategy or to direct their efforts into other avenues until the war's final months, and actively campaigned against the Transport Plan in the run-up to D-Day.

Based on the above, it's difficult to endorse strategic bombing as representing an efficient use of resources. The campaign certainly curtailed German war production and forced Germany to divert resources to air defence but whether this justified Britain's heavy

---

[288] AJP Taylor suggests that around 25% of British war production was devoted to strategic bombing while Max Hastings and Stephen Garrett venture one-third. Garrett estimates that Bomber Command absorbed resources equivalent to those given to British land forces and, at its peak, the Ministry of Aircraft Production employed 1.7m people (not all working on bombers). Webster and Frankland suggest that the bomber offensive employed 7% of the nation's manpower. (Taylor, *English History 1914-1945,* p.571; Hastings, *Finest Years,* p.425; Garrett, *Ethics and Airpower in World War II*, p.49 and p.184; Hastings, *Bomber Command*, p.349).

[289] The British believed that Germany's economy was so close to collapse in 1940/41 that even minor disruption might push it over the edge. Germany's industrial resilience during 1943/44 exposed this fallacy, and German production remained robust until the war's final months.

[290] In September 1941, Churchill advised Air Marshal Portal that *"it is very disputable whether bombing by itself will be a decisive factor in the present war... all that we have learnt since the war began shows that its effects, both moral and physical, are greatly exaggerated."* However, this co-existed with numerous strong endorsements of strategic bombing (Blake and Louis (eds), *Churchill,* p.368).

investment in the project is debatable.[291] The bombing campaign fulfilled mainly political goals - illustrating Britain's determination to carry the war to Germany at a time when it rejected cross-Channel operations - and Churchill hoped that Germany might crack under 'trial by fire' but - at the end of the day - it didn't deliver its declared objective (i.e. forcing a German surrender). If Churchill and Harris wished to pursue experimental air warfare over Germany, a force of 2,00-3,000 twin-engined Mosquito bombers[292] might have produced better results at a reduced cost and with fewer casualties but - throughout the conflict - the bludgeon trumped the rapier.

5: The Battle of the Atlantic

In *The Second World War*, Churchill described the Battle of the Atlantic as *"the only thing that ever really frightened me"* but his actions suggest otherwise. In October 1941, the Battle of the Atlantic Committee (formed March 1941) was allowed to lapse long before the u-boats had been defeated and throughout 1942, Churchill deprived Coastal Command of the resources it needed to close the Mid-Atlantic Gap, enabling Dönitz's u-boats to inflict terrible damage on Allied shipping and generate an 'imports crisis' which pushed Britain to the brink by early 1943. In November 1942, the Battle of the Atlantic Committee (now called the Anti-U-Boat Warfare Committee) was reconvened and the issue was debated at Casablanca where *"the defeat of the u-boat... [was identified as] a first charge on the resources of the United Nations."* Coastal Command finally received the resources it needed to close the 'Black Pit' in spring 1943 and the North Atlantic was safe for Allied shipping by May. However, this victory could have been achieved 6-9 months earlier had Churchill allocated 40-60 VLR Liberators to Coastal Command to cover the mid-Atlantic. Unfortunately, he continually backed Harris' politically expedient - but largely wasteful - bombing 'experiment'.

6: The Dodecanese Debacle

Accolade was Churchill's second attempt at fabricating a 'Balkan Front'. In 1941, he'd attempted to 'magic' a fifty division-strong Balkan Front into existence by despatching three British-imperial divisions to

---

[291] One German died for every 3.4 tons of Allied bombs dropped (Claudia Baldoli and Andrew Knapp, *Forgotten Blitzes: France and Italy Under Allied Air Attack, 1940-1945* (2012), p.16).

[292] The De Havilland Mosquito was one of the war's most versatile 'planes, possessing a top speed of 415mph (Mk XVI) and serving as a tactical and night bomber, pathfinder, day/night fighter, fighter-bomber, maritime strike aircraft and photo-reconnaissance aircraft. It could outrun most single-engined fighters and carried a 4,000 lbs bomb-load. Its manoeuvrability and speed made it suitable for precision raids such as the February 1944 Amiens Prison attack and it was the mainstay of the Pathfinder force. Made of wood, it was cheap to build and required a two-man crew against the Lancaster's seven (Thomas Newdick, *The World's Most Powerful Military Aircraft* (2017), pp.70-73).

Greece[293] and he now hoped to induce Turkey to enter the war by seizing control of the Dodecanese coincidentally with Italy's surrender. Churchill was informed that Britain lacked the troops to implement Accolade but - such was his desperation to activate a Balkan Front - he authorised the operation with predictably dismal results. The small German garrisons reacted more swiftly than either the British or Italians and - after a two-month tussle - the islands remained in German hands until the end of the war. Accolade was not a catastrophic defeat - though it handed Hitler his last victory of the conflict - but it illustrates Churchill's willingness to initiate operations he knew to be militarily unsound and his almost pathological desire to promote his Balkan Triangle Strategy ahead of Overlord.

7: Anzio

By December 1943, Italy's 'soft underbelly' had been exposed as a 'hard and bristling spine'[294] and Churchill needed a major success to maintain the Mediterranean as a counterweight to Overlord. Unfortunately, his preferred scheme was Shingle II, an operation which rested on the highly questionable premise that Germany's Tenth Army would detach forces from the Gustav Line to seal off a threat to its rear, enabling Allied Fifth Army to break through the weakened Cassino front. Unfortunately, Hitler worked to a different script, drawing in forces from Yugoslavia, France and Germany to seal the Anzio beachhead while Fifth Army remained stuck south of Rome. As a result, 150,000 men were trapped in Anzio for four months and - as Anzio became the fourth busiest port in the world - Operation Anvil/Dragoon (designed to save Allied lives by drawing enemy forces away from Normandy in June 1944) was delayed until August.

8: Opposing Anvil/Dragoon

Originally devised to divert German forces from Normandy, Anvil/Dragoon was delayed when Montgomery expanded the Overlord assault force and Anzio trapped Allied forces in Italy. However, Marshall and Eisenhower revived Anvil directly after Overlord to accelerate the delivery of supplies and reinforcements into France - by capturing Marseille and Toulon - and seven divisions from Italy were earmarked as Anvil's assault force. Southern France also offered an ideal location to employ US-equipped French colonial forces and, following the capture of Marseille, Allied troops could advance rapidly up the Rhone Valley to threaten German supply lines into Normandy.

---

[293] Churchill hoped to form Turkey, Yugoslavia and Greece into a Balkan Front in spring 1941 *"at the wave of our wand."* (see Chapter10).

[294] The description is General Albert Wedemeyer's, a senior member of the US War Plans Division.

Despite the operation's great potential, Churchill opposed the transfer of troops from Italy to France to furnish Anvil's strike force. Allied forces had just triumphed at Cassino and Rome and Generals Alexander and Maitland Wilson were full of heady dreams of smashing Kesselring's forces in the Po Valley before advancing to Vienna through the Ljubljana Gap. This was more to Churchill's liking and throughout June-August, he campaigned to undermine Anvil and retain Allied forces in Italy, informing Roosevelt that

> *there is no doubt that an advance up the Rhone Valley… could easily be blocked and stemmed by a smaller number of German troops... The country is most formidable*[295]*… I doubt whether you will find that [Anvil] will have any important strategic effect on the tremendous battle which Montgomery and Eisenhower are fighting... It seems more likely to prove a cul-de-sac into which increasing numbers of United States troops will be drawn.*

Churchill also argued that Allied forces would need 6-12 weeks to prepare for Anvil and that Allied forces would need three months to capture Lyon and influence events in Normandy.

Anglo-American strategic struggles dragged on interminably during 1943 but America was all powerful by mid-1944 and the US Joint Chiefs simply used their greater clout to insist on Anvil (subsequently renamed Dragoon) by 15th August. Churchill was outraged by this naked display of American power and vented his spleen in a series of draft notes to Roosevelt and Hopkins in which he threatened "*to devise some other machinery for conducting the war, including the separation of the commands in the Mediterranean,*" even "*break[ing] the Allied Command in the Mediterranean and have it settled with the American sphere playing the fool at Anvil and the British sphere doing the best it can towards Trieste.*"[296] Churchill's Mediterranean mania shines through once more and his willingness to consider breaking up the Allied command structure at a critical moment reveals both the depth of his Mediterranean obsession and his resentment at playing Roosevelt's understudy. Britain had ceded Overlord command to an

---

[295] As always, Churchill exaggerated terrain difficulties in areas where he opposed operations (Rhone Valley, Normandy) and diminished them in regions where he favoured initiatives (Italy, the Balkans). Samuel Eliot Morison described *"the route north from Marseilles... [as] an open speedway compared with the Ljubljana route to Vienna"* and General Patch's 7th Army advanced 400 miles up the Rhone Valley in less than a month, reaching Strasbourg - on the Franco-German border - on 23rd November 1944, three months and a week after Dragoon launched (Morison, *Invasion of France and Germany,* p.228; Zabecki (ed), *Germany at War,* pp.38-39).

[296] Trieste is Italy's easternmost city, located directly above the Istrian Peninsula.

American and Churchill argued that *"we have to have command in the Mediterranean."*[297]

Map 46: Operation Dragoon

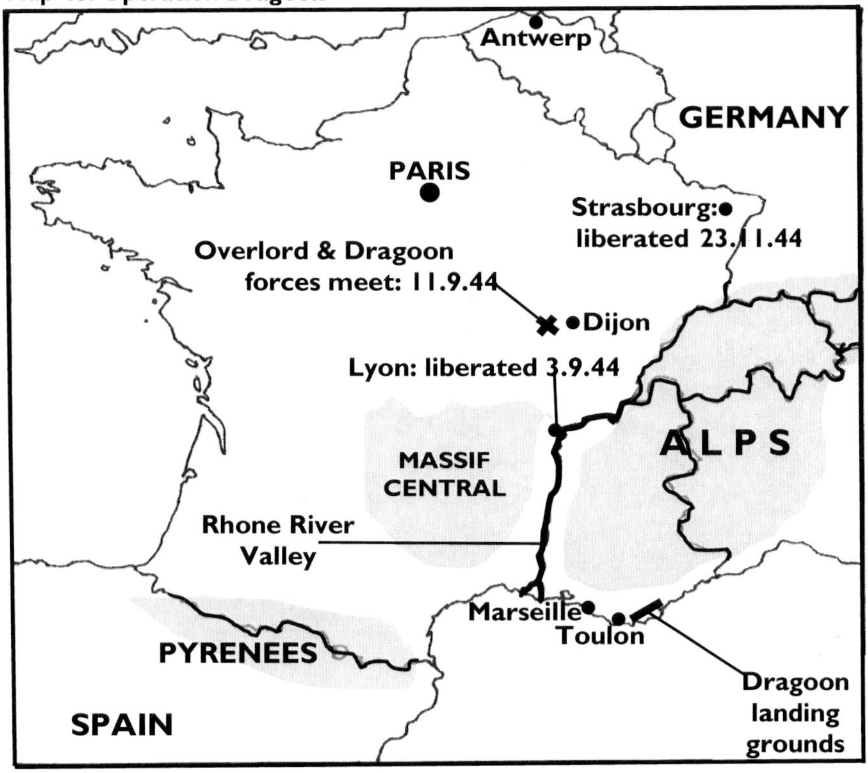

Dragoon succeeded admirably after launching on 15th August. Marseille and Toulon were liberated by the end of the month and the first Liberty Ships docked on 15th September. Over the next four months - until Antwerp was operational[298] - 40% of all Allied supplies and reinforcements entering France came through Marseille and Toulon.[299] Similarly, the advance up the Rhone Valley defied Churchill's gloomy predictions. Allied troops entered Lyon on 3rd September - two and a half months ahead of Churchill's gloomy estimate - and Dragoon forces linked up with units from Normandy near Dijon on 11th September, giving the Allies a solid wall of force

[297] Churchill twice threatened resignation over Anvil/Dragoon - once in a draft telegram to Roosevelt and once in conversation with Eisenhower six days before the operation's launch (Kimball, *Churchill and Roosevelt:* Complete Correspondence, Vol.3, p.225; D'Este, *Eisenhower,* p.566).

[298] Antwerp was liberated on 4th September but could not be used until the Scheldt Estuary was cleared and the harbour de-mined. The first Allied ships docked on 29th November 1944, almost three months after the port was liberated.

[299] The supplies could also move north on a rail system untouched by Allied bombing.

stretching from Antwerp to the Swiss border and penning the Fuhrer's legions into their fetid lair behind the Siegfried Line.

Why did Churchill oppose Anvil/Dragoon? Did he genuinely believe it to be flawed or did he consider it a threat to his addled Balkan-Mediterranean dream? If the former is true, Churchill is revealed as a hapless and incompetent strategist; if the latter is accurate, Churchill came close to aiding and comforting the enemy by prioritising narrow British interests over sound Allied plans to secure victory.

9: The 'Soft Underbelly'

Churchillian oratory is masterful and inspiring, rivalling the greatest works of Burns, Shakespeare and Dickens in power and imagination but - beyond the realms of hucksterism - ideas must always master words and words should never dominate ideas - a distinction Churchill often overlooked to his colleagues' dismay. Charles Masterman - his Home Office deputy - dubbed Churchill a

> *slave of the words which his mind forms about ideas. He sets ideas to Rhetoric as musicians set theirs to music. And he can convince himself of every truth if it is once allowed thus to start on its wild career through his rhetorical machinery.*

Robert Menzies - the Australian PM who attended War Cabinet meetings in spring 1941 - identified Churchill's "*real tyrant [as] the glittering phrase - so attractive to his mind that awkward facts have to give way*" while South African PM Jan Smuts praised Churchill's imagination which "*expressed itself... in an ornate phraseology which soon soared above the sober and often intransigent facts of reality.*" Churchill diagnosed his own tendency towards verbal diarrhoea early in his career, conceding that he wrote "*for the impression my words produce & the reputation they give me...* ***I v[er]y often yield to the temptation of adapting my facts to my phrases*** *[emphasis added].*"

Churchill's attempt to depict southern Europe as a 'soft underbelly' - an easy point of entry into Hitler's Empire - is the most pernicious example of this failing. Southern Europe is blessed with a balmy climate and is a pleasant holiday destination but - as previous chapters revealed - its interior is characterised by mountains, gorges, gullies and fast flowing rivers. It is entirely unsuited to mobile offensive warfare and, unlike Normandy, geographically distant from Germany's industrial heartland. American soldiers displayed a surer grasp of the region's topography by labelling it a "*tough old gut,*" and a "*hard and bristling spine"* with *"chrome-steel baseboards."* [300] For reasons already noted, Churchill vehemently opposed operations in the only part of southern Europe which truly presented a 'soft underbelly' - the Riviera and Rhone Estuary.

Why did Churchill spout such claptrap? Did he genuinely believe this specious nonsense? Was it the product of defective reasoning or a fevered imagination?[301] Or a dodgy salesman's attempt to divert Allied resources into an area vital to British interests? Whatever Churchill's motives, Russia and America rejected his toxic rationale and blocked the transfer of troops to theatres beneficial to Britain's Empire and the Third Reich.

10: Opposing Overlord

Opposing Overlord - and championing a peripheral Mediterranean Strategy in its place - was Churchill's most egregious failing and - had this nonsense prevailed - the conflict would have continued beyond 1945 and the early Cold War would have been conducted on terms favourable to Stalin. Overlord destroyed German power in the west and - while the operation's inherent risks merited a degree of caution - history vindicates American insistence on D-Day in 1944. The reasons advanced to justify British hesitation over this operation were entirely selfish as confirmed by a quick comparison with Churchill's Pacific priorities. In that theatre, Churchill championed imperial objectives (regaining Singapore and Malaya) while America - had the PM's nonsense prevailed - would have been left to prosecute the war against Japan. Churchill's European strategy was identical - America championed a strategy aimed directly at Germany's heart while Churchill advocated secondary operations in the Mediterranean which would have contributed nothing to crushing Germany. Russia and America insisted on Overlord and it was a resounding success whereas Churchill's preferred options would have prolonged the war, magnified the death toll and altered the contours of the early Cold War. A 'southern' strategy might have secured British access to Suez but Stalin would have gained north-western Europe as far as the Channel, an arrangement hardly conducive to British home security. We should be eternally grateful that America - keen to focus on the Pacific - wanted a speedy end to the European war and that Stalin

---

[300] One American soldier compared Italian combat to *"climbing a ladder with an opponent stamping on his hands at every rung."* (Atkinson, *Day of Battle*, p.258).

[301] His excitability at key moments (e.g. selling Gallipoli, Norway in 1940, obsessing over Accolade, opposing Anvil/Dragoon etc) coupled with his 'down' moments suggest cyclothymia, a rapid cycling form of bipolar disorder.

didn't share Hitler's insatiable lust for *lebensraum*.[302] Materially exhausted, Russia wanted a quick end to the war through Overlord, forcing the little English donkey to follow the bear and the buffalo who - in reality - knew the way home far better than he.

Map 47: Post-war Europe without Overlord

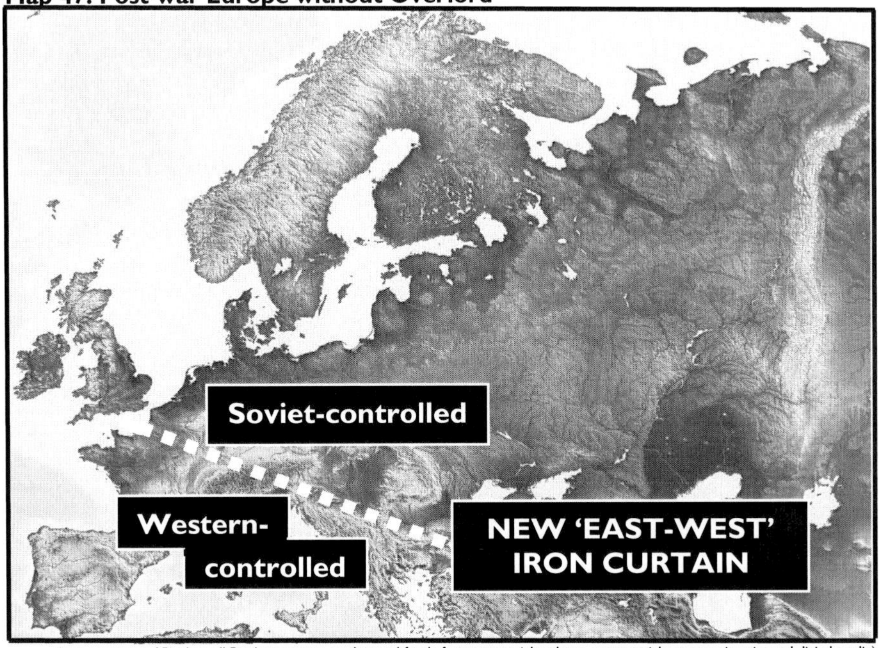

(map courtesy of Pixabay: all Pixabay content can be used freely for commercial and non-commercial purposes in print and digital media)

****

We live in a technologically advanced era yet remain emotionally primitive. We can communicate with anyone anywhere in the world while retaining a deep-seated need to transform fallible human beings into iconic heroes. Churchill is one such totem but - like everyone else - he lived with frailty. If the *Empire First* portrait appears unfamiliar, it's because it acknowledges blemishes normally concealed by the court artists and hagiographers, but one can never truly know a man by scrutinising only one side of his face.[303]

I knew relatively little about Churchill when I started this book but grew up in a world saturated by *"the War"*. My early adolescence was spent constructing 1:72 scale models of World War Two aircraft. I devoured *Victor, Hotspur* and *Warlord* comics and *Commando War*

[302] This does not deny Stalin's desire to control a belt of defensive satellites on Russia's western border.

[303] Marlon Brando's only directorial outing - *One-Eyed Jacks* (1961) - is interesting in this regard.

Stories for boys. I pillaged my local library for World War Two books and still watch repeats of *The World At War* on TV. I possessed an army of 1:32 scale model soldiers plus supporting tanks, jeeps and artillery and cheered on John Mills, Jack Hawkins and Kenneth More in their monochrome matinees. I was - and remain - Generation Airfix made flesh.

After researching this book, I feel that Churchill has been greatly over-rated by individuals and an industry with a vested interest in perpetuating toxic and delusional myths for their own profit and the stupefaction of others. A Churchill industry has developed - a secular church with its own priests, rituals and scriptures - but if his achievements and failures are tallied in a critical ledger, we must acknowledge that he was wrong on Gallipoli, he was wrong on the Gold Standard, his views on Gandhi and Indian nationalism are frankly embarrassing and he was a major architect of the military austerity which crippled Britain at the outset of the war. He was right on Hitler's threat in the 'thirties and advocated resistance in 1940 but he should have stood down and let others take over after Casablanca. A once proud symbol of bulldog defiance, he was increasingly a tired and querulous old man[304] more intent on preserving the Empire than in winning the war - with the Allies in the ascendant, Attlee or Eden would have done better though both may have been seduced by Mediterranean sirens. If anyone is to be lionised, I - as a Scot - would prefer to see Robert the Bruce portrayed as an all-conquering hero but, as the anarchists say, *'no leaders, no heroes, no gods: only people'* and we'll all gain by implementing this simple maxim.

[304] pp. 618-20 of Clive Ponting's biography offers numerous accounts of a dysfunctional Churchill during 1943-45. In March 1944, Brooke *"found him in a desperately tired mood. I am afraid he is losing ground rapidly. He seems quite incapable of concentrating for a few moments on end and keeps wandering continuously."* Attlee raised similar concerns with Churchill in January 1945: *"I consider the present position... injurious to the war effort... More and more often you have not read even the note prepared [by Committee] for your guidance. Often half an hour or more is wasted in explaining what could have been grasped by two or three minutes of reading the document. Not infrequently, a phrase catches your eye which gives rise to a disquisition on an interesting point only slightly connected to the subject matter."* (David Dilks, *Churchill and Company: Allies and Rivals in War and Peace* (2015), p.64; Lehrman, *Lincoln and Churchill*, p.304).

CODA

For centuries, the naval command of the Mediterranean had been a fundamental principle of British policy. Indeed, without the unimpeded passage of British ships through the Mediterranean, the maintenance of the British Empire would have been impossible. Gibraltar, Malta, and the Suez Canal had... become the outward and visible signs of our control of the great inland sea. Even in the critical days... when we were hard put to withstand the German onslaught, we had been able to keep our unshaken grip on all the important military positions that guarded the narrow waterways between Great Britain, India, China and our Pacific Empire.

Sir Samuel Hoare[305] in his memoir,
Ambassador on Special Mission

There are always earnest spinsters in Pennsylvania, Utah, Edinburgh or Dublin persistently writing letters and signing petitions and ardently giving their advice to the British Government, urging that India be given back to the Indians and South Africa back to the Zulu or Boers, but as long as I am called by his Majesty the King to be his First Minister, I shall not assist at the dismemberment of the British Empire. And, just as I am sure that, if at this moment someone came over the garden wall to attack us... that Marine guard would willingly give his life to protect us; so I shall, with the last drop of energy I have in me, defend His Majesty's Empire.

Winston Churchill to Kenneth Whittemore
Pendar, Marrakech, 25th January 1943

---

[305] Hoare had served as Indian Secretary (1931-35), Foreign Secretary (June-December 1935), First Lord of the Admiralty (1936-37), Home Secretary (1937-39) and Ambassador to Spain (1940-44). Co-author - with French Premier Pierre Laval - of the December 1935 Hoare-Laval Plan which proposed to buy Italian friendship by sacrificing Ethiopian (Abyssinian) independence. The plan leaked, forcing Hoare's resignation. He was elevated to Viscount Templewood in 1944.

Eleven years after the War ended, Britain again tried to secure control of Suez, using an Israeli incursion into Egypt as its pretext. However, Britain, France and Israel had agreed the attack in secret conference twelve days before Anglo-French forces entered the Canal Zone. The justification for Eden's 1956 adventure was every bit as bogus as Churchill's claim that Allied operations in Italy, Greece and the Balkans offered a better means of defeating Germany than landing in Normandy. The continuity between these two shabby 'Oil and Empire' episodes is striking.

APPENDIX A: PEOPLE

ALEXANDER, Albert Victor 'A.V.' (Labour)
First Lord of the Admiralty 1929-31 and 1940-45

ALEXANDER, General Harold
General Officer Commanding, Burma Feb-July 1942
Middle East Commander-in-Chief, Aug 1942-Feb 1943
Commander, 8th Army Group and Eisenhower's Mediterranean Deputy, 1943
Commander, 15th Army Group, Sicily, 1943
Allied Armies in Italy Commander, 1944
Supreme Allied Commander, Mediterranean, 1944-1945

AMERY, Leo (Conservative)
Churchill's Harrow school friend
Secretary of State for India, 1940-45

ARNOLD, General Henry 'Hap'
Commander, USAAF 1941-45
Air Force representative on the US Joint Chiefs of Staff

ASQUITH, Herbert (Liberal)
Prime Minister, 1908-16

ATTLEE, Clement (Labour)
Labour leader and member of Churchill's first War Cabinet
Lord Privy Seal, 1940-42
Deputy Prime Minister, 1942-45
Lord President of Council, 1943-45

AUCHINLECK, General Claude
Middle East Commander-in-Chief, 1941-42
Assumed direct command of Eighth Army following General Ritchie's dismissal, June-Aug 1942
Commander-in-Chief, India, 1941 and 1943-47

AZAD, Abdul Kalam (Maulana)
Senior Indian National Congress figure.
Represented Congress (with Nehru) in Cripps Mission talks, April 1942

BALDWIN, Stanley (Conservative)
Prime Minister, 1923-24, 1924-29 and 1935-37

BEAVERBROOK, Lord (Conservative)
Churchill friend and confidant
Minister of Aircraft Production, 1940-41
Minister of Supply, 1941-42
Minister of War Production, 1942
Lord Privy Seal, 1943-45

BEVAN, Aneurin 'Nye' (Labour)
Ebbw Vale MP, 1929-60 and leading Churchill critic

BEVIN, Ernie (Labour)
Transport and General Workers Union Gen. Secretary, 1922-45
Minister of Labour and National Service, 1940-45

BRADLEY, General Omar
Deputy Commander, US II Corps, 1942-43
Succeeded Patton as II Corps Commander, March 1943
Commander, US 1st Army in Overlord
Commander, 12th Army Group 1944-45

BROOKE, General Alan
'Second BEF' Commander, 1940
British Home Forces Commander, 1940-41
Chief of the Imperial General Staff, 1941-1946
Chair of Chiefs of Staff Committee, 1942-46

CADOGAN, Sir Alexander
Permanent Under-Secretary of State for Foreign Affairs, 1938-48

CHAMBERLAIN, Neville (Conservative)
Health Minister, 1923, 1924-29 and 1931
Chancellor of the Exchequer, 1923-24, 1931-37
Prime Minister 1937-40
War Cabinet Member and Lord President of Council, May-Oct 1940

CHERWELL, Lord (Prof. Frederick Lindemann) (Conservative)
Churchill confidant and scientific advisor
Paymaster General, 1942-45
Author of De-Housing Paper and Area Bombing enthusiast

CHURCHILL, Clementine
Winston Churchill's spouse, companion and champion, 1908-65

CHURCHILL, Winston
Colonial Under-Secretary, 1905-08 (Liberal)
President of Board of Trade, 1908-10 (Liberal)
Home Secretary, 1910-11 (Liberal)
First Lord of the Admiralty, 1911-15 (Liberal)
Munitions Minister, 1917-19 (Liberal)
Secretary of War and Air 1919-21 (Liberal)
Colonial Secretary, 1921-22 (Liberal)
Chancellor of the Exchequer, 1924-29 (Conservative)
First Lord of the Admiralty, 1939-40 (Conservative)
Prime Minister and Minister of Defence 1940-45 (Conservative)
Prime Minister, 1951-55 (Conservative)

CLARK, General Mark
Commander, US 5th Army, Jan 1943-Dec 1944
Commander, 15th Army Group, Dec 1944-July 1945

CRIPPS, Sir Stafford (Labour)
Bristol East MP, 1931-50
Ambassador to USSR, 1940-42
British representative in negotiations with Indian National Congress, April 1942
Leader of the House of Commons and Lord Privy Seal, Feb-Nov 1942
Minister of Aircraft Production, 1942-45

CUNNINGHAM, General Alan
East India Force Commander, 1940-41
Eighth Army Commander, Aug-Nov 1941 (replaced by General Ritchie)

CUNNINGHAM, Admiral Andrew
Commander-in-Chief, Mediterranean Fleet, Feb-Oct 1943
First Sea Lord, 1943-46 (replaced Dudley Pound)
Admiralty representative on Chiefs of Staff Committee

CURTIN, John
Australian Prime Minister, Oct 1941-July 1945

DALTON, Hugh (Labour)
Minister of Economic Warfare, 1940-42
President of Board of Trade, 1942-45

DAMASKINOS, Archbishop
Archbishop of Athens and Greece, 1941-49
King George II's Regent, 1944-46

DARLAN, Admiral Francois
Minister of Marine, June 1940-Feb 1941
French Prime Minister, Feb 1941-April 1942
High Commissioner of French North Africa, Nov-Dec 1942

DE GAULLE, General Charles
Commander, 4th Armoured Division, 1940
Free French leader, 1940-44
Head of French Republic Provisional Government, 1944-46

DILL, Field Marshal John
Chief of Imperial General Staff, 1940-41
Chief of British Joint Staff Mission in Washington, 1941-44

DÖNITZ, Admiral Karl
German U-boat Chief, October 1939- January 1943
Kriegsmarine Chief, January 1943 - May 1945
German Head of State, 30th April - 23rd May 1945

EDEN, Anthony (Conservative)
Foreign Secretary, 1935-38 and 1940-45
Secretary of State for War, May-Dec 1940
Prime Minister, 1955-57

EISENHOWER, General Dwight 'Ike'
US War Plans Division, Deputy and Chief, 1941-42
Commander-in-Chief, Allied Forces in North Africa, 1942-43
Allied Supreme Commander, Mediterranean, 1943
Supreme Commander, Allied Expeditionary Force in Europe, 1943-45

FISHER, Admiral John 'Jackie'
First Sea Lord, 1904-10 and 1914-15

GANDHI, Mohandas K. (Mahatma)
Inspirational Indian independence and civil rights leader. Initially active in South Africa, he returned to India in 1915 and championed Indian independence as an individual and as a senior Indian National Congress figure until his death in 1948

GEORGE, David Lloyd (Liberal)
President of the Board of Trade, 1905-08
Chancellor of the Exchequer, 1908-15
Munitions Minister, 1915-16
War Secretary, 1916
Prime Minister, 1916-22

GEORGE II, King
King of Greece, 1922-24 and 1935-47 (in exile, 1941-46)

GREENWOOD, Arthur (Labour)
Member of Churchill's first War Cabinet
Minister without Portfolio, 1940-42

GRIGG, Sir Percy James 'PJ' (National)
Former civil servant and War Secretary, 1942-45

GUSEV, Fedor
Soviet Ambassador to Britain, 1943-46

HALIFAX, Viscount (Lord Irwin) (Conservative)
Viceroy and Governor General of India, 1926-31
Secretary of State for War, 1935
Foreign Secretary, 1938-40
British Ambassador to the United States, 1940-46

HANKEY, Sir Maurice
Secretary, Committee of Imperial Defence, 1912-38
Cabinet Secretary, 1916-38
Chancellor of Duchy of Lancaster, 1940-41

HARRIMAN, Averell
Roosevelt's Special Envoy to Europe and Lend Lease Coordinator, 1941-43
US Ambassador to the Soviet Union, 1943-46

HARRIS, Air Chief Marshal Arthur
Commander, 45 Squadron, Iraq, 1922-24
Air Officer Commanding, Bomber Command, 1942-45

HART, Basil Liddell
Military theorist and historian, active 1925-70

HITLER, Adolf
Nazi Party Leader, 1921-45
German Chancellor 1933-45 and Fuhrer 1934-45

HOPKINS, Harry
New Deal executive
Roosevelt's principal confidant and adviser, 1941-45

ISMAY, General Hastings
Chief of Staff to the Minister of Defence (Churchill) and Deputy Secretary to the War Cabinet, 1940-45

JEBB, Gladwyn
Post-Hostilities Planning Committee Chair, 1943-45

JOHNSON, Col. Louis
US Assistant Secretary of War, 1937-40
Roosevelt's representative in April 1942 Cripps Mission talks

JOUBERT DE LA FERTÉ, Air Marshal Philip
Commander-in-Chief, Coastal Command, 1941-43

KEITEL, Field Marshal Wilhelm
Chief of Oberkommando der Wehrmacht (OKW)
Germany's de facto War Minister, 1939-45

KENNEDY, General John
Director of Military Operations and Plans, War Office, 1940-43
Assistant Chief of the Imperial General Staff, 1943-45

KEYNES, John Maynard
British economist and critic of Churchill's decision to return to the Gold Standard

KILLEARN, Lord (Sir Miles Lampson)
British Ambassador to Egypt and Sudan, 1936-46

KING, Admiral Ernest
Commander-in-Chief, US Fleet & Chief of Naval Operations, 1941-45
Navy representative on US Joint Chiefs of Staff

KOENIG, General Marie-Pierre
Commander, Free French Forces in Britain
Commander of French Forces of the Interior, June 1944 onwards

LEAHY, Admiral William
US Ambassador to Vichy France, 1941-42
Joint Chiefs of Staff Chair, 1942-45
Roosevelt's Chief of Staff, 1942-45

LEATHERS, Lord (Conservative)
Industrialist and shipping magnate
Adviser to Ministry of Shipping, 1914-18 and 1940-41
Minister of War Transport, 1941-45

LEIGH-MALLORY, Air Marshal Trafford
Fighter Command Commander-in-Chief, 1942-43
Commander-in-Chief, Allied Expeditionary Air Force, 1943-44

LINLITHGOW, Viscount
Victor Hope, 2nd Marquess of Linlithgow
Indian Viceroy, 1936 - 1943

LUCAS, General John
Commander, US VI Corps during Operation Shingle (Anzio)
Replaced by General Truscott, 23rd February 1944

MacARTHUR, General Douglas
Supreme Commander Allied Forces, South West Pacific, 1942-45

MacDONALD, Ramsay (Labour)
Foreign Secretary, 1924
Prime Minister 1924 and 1929-35
Lord President of Council, 1935-37

MARSHALL, General George
US Army Chief of Staff, 1939-45
Army representative on Joint Chiefs of Staff

MENZIES, Robert
Australian Prime Minister, 1939-41
Attended War Cabinet meetings, spring 1941

MIKOLAJCZYK, Stanislav
Prime Minister of Polish Government-in-Exile, 1943-44

MOLOTOV, Vyacheslav
Soviet Minister of Foreign Affairs, 1939-49

MONTGOMERY, Field Marshal Bernard 'Monty'
Commander, 8th Army, August 1942- December 1943
Principal Overlord planner 1943-44
Overlord Ground Force Commander, Dec 1943- Aug 1944
Commander, 21st Army Group, 1944-45

MORAN, Lord (Sir Charles Wilson)
Churchill's personal physician, 1940-65

MORGAN, General Frederick
Chief of Staff, Supreme Allied Commander (COSSAC) April-Dec 1943
Overlord draft plan author

MOUNTBATTEN, Admiral Louis
Combined Operations Chief, 1941-43
Commander, South East Asia Command, 1943-46

MUNDT, Karl
US Congressman (South Dakota), 1939-48

MUSSOLINI, Benito
Italian Prime Minister, 1922-43 and Fascist Duce, 1919-43
Duce, Italian Social Republic, 1943-45

NEHRU, Jawaharlal
Senior Indian National Congress figure and independence activist, 1912-64
Represented Congress (with Azad) in Cripps Mission talks, April 1942.

O'CONNOR, General Richard
Commander, Western Desert Force and Field Commander, Operation Compass 1940-41
Prisoner of War, April 1941- Dec 1943
VIII Corps Commander, North-Western Europe, 1944-45

PAPANDREOU, Giorgios
Prime Minister of Greek Government-in-Exile and immediately after liberation, April 1944- January 1945

PORTAL, Air Chief Marshal Charles
Commander-in-Chief Bomber Command, 1940
Chief of the Air Staff, 1940-45 and RAF representative on COS Committee

POUND, Admiral Dudley
First Sea Lord, June 1939-Oct 1943 (replaced by Admiral Cunningham)
Admiralty representative on COS Committee

RAEDER, Grand Admiral Erich
Kriegsmarine Chief, 1939-43 (replaced by Dönitz)

RITCHIE, General Neil
Commander, Eighth Army, Nov 1941-June 1942
Commander, XII Corps in North-Western Europe, 1944-45

ROMMEL, General Erwin
Commander, 7th Panzer Division, 1940-41
Field Commander, Axis forces in Africa 1941-43
Commander, Army Group B in northern Italy, 1943
Transferred to France to implement Directive 51, Nov 1943
Army Group B commander (France) until wounded, 17th July 1944

ROOSEVELT, Franklin
Assistant Secretary of the Navy, 1913-20
US President and Commander-in-Chief, 1933-45

SCOBIE, General Ronald
British Military Governor of Greece
Commander, British-Imperial forces in Greece, 1944-46

SINCLAIR, Sir Archibald (Liberal)
Churchill's second-in-command, 6th Battalion, Royal Scots Fusiliers
Secretary of State for Air, 1940-45

SLIM, General William
Commander, 14th Army in Burma (Myanmar), 1943-45

SMITH, General Walter Bedell
Eisenhower's Chief of Staff, 1942-45

SPAATZ, General Carl
Commander, US Strategic Air Force in Europe, Jan 1944- June 1945
(comprising 8th USAAF in Britain and 15th USAAF in Italy)

STAGG, Group Captain James
Overlord Chief Meteorological Officer, 1943-45

STALIN, Josef
De facto Soviet leader, 1929-53
Soviet Communist Party General Secretary, 1922-52

STIMSON, Henry
US Secretary of War, 1911-13 and 1940-45

TRUMAN, Harry S.
Roosevelt's Vice President, 1945
American President and Commander-in-Chief, 1945-53

TRUSCOTT, General Lucian
Commander, 3rd Infantry Division in Tunisia and Sicily, 1943
Replaced General Lucas as VI Corps and Shingle Force Commander, 23rd February 1944
Commander, VI Corps, Dragoon landings, August 1944

WAVELL, General Archibald
Commander-in-Chief, Middle East, 1940- June 1941 (replaced by Auchinleck)
Commander, American - British - Dutch - Australian Command, Dec 1941- Feb 1942
Commander-in-Chief, India, 1941-43
Viceroy and Governor-General of India, 1943-47

WEDEMEYER, General Albert
Senior US Planning Officer and author of 1941 Victory Programme
Mountbatten's Chief of Staff in SEAC, 1943-44
Commander, US Forces in China, 1944-46

WILSON, General Henry Maitland
Commander, Expeditionary Force to Greece, 1941
Commander, Iran-Iraq Command, 1942-43
Commander in Chief, Middle East 1943-44
Supreme Allied Commander, Mediterranean 1944
Chief of British Joint Staff Mission (succeeded Dill), 1944-45

ZUCKERMAN, Prof. Solly
Academic zoologist
Assessed impact of bombing on buildings and people early in war
Developed plans for bombardment of Pantelleria and Sicily, 1943
Developed Transport Plan to disrupt Franco-German railways before Overlord.

APPENDIX B: CONFERENCES

1941

RIVIERA, 9 - 12 August (Placentia Bay): Churchill and Roosevelt meet to draft the Atlantic Charter. Dill and Marshall form the basis of their later working relationship.

ARCADIA, 22 December - 14 January 1942 (Washington): First Anglo-American conference with both states as combatants. Confirms 'Germany First' and forms the Combined Chiefs of Staff.

1942

ARGONAUT, 18 - 25 June (Washington): Anglo-American conference to settle strategy for 1942-43. Loss of Tobruk precludes cross-Channel operations for 1942-43, confining Allied forces to North Africa.

BRACELET, 12 - 16 August (Moscow): First Churchill-Stalin meeting. Churchill informs Stalin there will be no Channel assault in 1942 but confirms major operations for 1943.

1943

SYMBOL, 14 - 24 January (Casablanca): Anglo-American conference which confirms Sicily as the target following liberation of North Africa. Identifies defeat of the u-boats as the *"first charge on the resources of the United Nations"* and approves *"the heaviest possible bomber offensive against the German war effort."*

TRIDENT, 12 - 25 May (Washington): Anglo-American conference to confirm western Allied operations for 1943-44. Confirms that *"forces and equipment should be established in the United Kingdom with the object of mounting an operation with target date of 1 May 1944 to secure a lodgement on the continent."* Seven Allied divisions to be withdrawn from the Mediterranean to prepare for cross-Channel operations.

QUADRANT, 14 - 24 August (Quebec): Anglo-American conference which confirms Overlord as *"the primary US-British ground and air effort against the Axis in Europe,"* target date 1st May, 1944.

SEXTANT I, 22 - 26 November (Cairo): Anglo-American-Chinese conference before Eureka. Churchill hopes to forge a united front with Roosevelt before meeting Stalin but Chiang Kai-shek's presence prevents this.

EUREKA, 28 November - 1 December (Tehran): Roosevelt, Stalin and Churchill confirm Overlord for May 1944. Stalin confirms that Russia will launch a supporting operation in the east to assist Overlord and declare war on Japan following Germany's defeat.

SEXTANT II, 3 - 7 December (Cairo): Churchill tries and fails to convince Turkey to join the war against Germany. Roosevelt cancels operations in the Bay of Bengal to strengthen the assault on Europe.

1944

OCTAGON, 12 - 16 September 1944 (Quebec): Anglo-American conference at which Churchill confirms the Royal Navy will support the United States in operations against Japan's home islands.

TOLSTOY, 9 - 19 October (Moscow): Churchill and Stalin approve the Percentages Agreement, giving Britain control over Greece while Russia gains Bulgaria, Romania and Hungary.

APPENDIX C: OPERATIONS

ACCOLADE: failed autumn 1943 operation to liberate Dodecanese Islands. Intended to encourage Turkey to join the Allies and open a Balkan Front against Germany.

ANVIL: original codename for Operation Dragoon, August 1944 landing in southern France.

ARMPIT: proposal for Allied forces to enter the Balkans and access Austria via the 'Ljubljana Gap'. Favoured by Churchill as an alternative to Dragoon.

AVALANCHE: September 1943 Salerno landings - part of invasion of Italy (see also Baytown and Slapstick). Concocted in haste following Mussolini's downfall, this amphibious operation almost ended in failure.

BATTLEAXE: British-imperial effort in June 1941 to clear Axis forces from eastern Libya and relieve Tobruk. It failed and British forces sustained heavy tank losses. Auchinleck replaces Wavell as Middle East Commander in the aftermath.

BAYTOWN: Allied landing at Reggio Calabria on 3rd September 1943 - part of invasion of Italy (see Avalanche and Slapstick).

BOLERO: movement of US troops and resources to Britain during 1942-43 to prepare for cross-Channel operations in 1943.

BREVITY: Operation launched on 15th May 1941 to capture Halfaya on the Egypt-Libya border. Enjoyed initial success but Axis forces regained Halfaya in late May.

BUFFALO: Operation launched 23rd May 1944 to break out of the Anzio beachhead and block German forces retreating north up Highway 6 following Diadem. Undermined by General Clark who ordered Shingle Force to prioritise taking Rome over Valmontone (see Diadem).

CASABLANCA DIRECTIVE: advocated an Allied bomber offensive to ensure *"the progressive destruction and dislocation of the German military, industrial and economic system, and undermining of morale of the German people to a point where their capacity for armed resistance is fatally weakened"* (21st January, 1943). The Directive's principal targets included submarine yards, aircraft plants, enemy transport, oil facilities and other German war industries. Replaced by June 1943 Pointblank Directive.

COMPASS: successful British-imperial operation against Italian positions in Egypt and eastern Libya, 9th Dec 1940-12th Feb 1941. Expelled Italian forces from Cyrenaica and captured 130,000 prisoners but the operation was halted on 12th February and three divisions despatched to Greece.

CRUSADER: series of British-Axis engagements in eastern Libya between 18th Nov 1941 - 6th Jan 1942. Tobruk relieved on 10th December and Axis forces pushed back to El Agheila but British tank losses prevented exploitation of this success. Auchinleck sacked Cunningham on 26th November, assuming direct command of Eighth Army and Rommel returned to the offensive on 21st January 1942.

CULVERIN: Churchill's scheme to re-take Malaya and Singapore in 1945 as an alternative to joining American forces in direct attacks on Japan.

DIADEM: Operation launched 11th May 1944 to pierce the Gustav Line and force German troops to retreat north where they would be intercepted by Allied forces breaking out of Anzio. The plan failed when Clark ordered Shingle Force to prioritise taking Rome over Valmontone (see Buffalo).

DRAGOON (formerly Anvil): Anglo-American landings in southern France in August 1944 to capture Marseille and Toulon and support Overlord.

FORTITUDE: series of deception operations undertaken in spring/summer 1944 to confuse Germany over proposed location of Allied landings. Operation Quicksilver manufactured a fictitious Army Group (US 1st Army Group under General Patton) to convince Germany that Allied forces would land in the Pas de Calais.

GYMNAST: original code name for Operation Torch (North African landings).

HARDIHOOD: plan to deliver fighter squadrons, armoured divisions, anti-tank regiments and anti-aircraft units to Turkey following liberation of Dodecanese Islands (Accolade) - abandoned due to Accolade's failure.

HUSKY: Allied liberation of Sicily, 10th July-15th Aug 1943.

JUPITER: Churchill's pet scheme to land Allied forces in northern Norway to assist the passage of Arctic convoys to Russia - championed as an alternative to Roundup and Overlord.

LIGHTFOOT: Part One of the Second Battle of El Alamein. Launched 23rd October, Lightfoot encountered severe difficulties, forcing Montgomery to launch Supercharge on 2nd November.

MANNA: British-Greek operation to land forces in Greece in October 1944 coincidentally with German withdrawal.

OVERLORD: successful Allied landing in Normandy on 6th June 1944. After securing a lodgement, Allied forces staged a breakout on 25th July leading to the liberation of Paris and encirclement of German forces in the Falaise Gap.

PIKE (aka Western Air Plan 106): fanciful Anglo-French project to attack Soviet oil facilities in the Caucasus in spring 1940. Abandoned when Hitler attacked western Europe on 10th May 1940.

POINTBLANK DIRECTIVE: identified destruction of German fighter strength as principal focus for Allied air activity in Europe. Issued on 14th June 1943 to replace January 1943 Casablanca Directive.

RAF DIRECTIVE 22: committed RAF to area bombing of German cities and confirmed that "*the primary object of operations should now be focused on the morale of the enemy civil population and, in particular, of the industrial workers.*" Directive issued 14th February 1942 and Sir Arthur Harris became Bomber Command Chief eight days later.

RANKIN: provisional plans to exploit a rapid collapse in German military power in 1943 through rapid deployment of Allied forces to western Europe.

ROUNDUP I: December 1941 British plan for a return to northern France following German collapse. Unlike the later American Roundup, this would be an unopposed landing with British forces 'rounding up' disorganised enemy forces.

ROUNDUP II (1942): American plan for an opposed landing in northern France in summer 1943. Abandoned after Allied forces were diverted to North Africa and the Pacific during 1942-43.

SHINGLE: British plan for Allied units to outflank German forces on the Gustav Line by landing at Anzio in January 1944. Hitler rushed divisions from Yugoslavia, France and Germany to contain Allied forces and the Gustav Line held until May 1944.

SLAPSTICK: landing by British 1st Airborne Division at Taranto on 9th September 1943 - part of Allied invasion of Italy (also see Baytown and Avalanche).

SLEDGEHAMMER: American plan for an 'emergency landing' in northern France in autumn 1942 following either a Soviet or German collapse.

SUPERCHARGE: Part Two of second Battle of El Alamein, launched 2nd November 1942 following failure of Operation Lightfoot. This operation proved successful, forcing Axis forces to retreat by 4th November.

TORCH (formerly Gymnast): Anglo-American landings in Oran, Algiers and Casablanca on 8th November 1943 to liberate French North West Africa and support 8th Army's drive to Tunisia following El Alamein.

TRANSPORT PLAN: scheme developed by Prof. Solly Zuckerman to disrupt Franco-German rail network and inhibit deployment of German forces to Normandy during Overlord.

WATCHTOWER: first US offensive against Japanese forces in the Pacific at Guadalcanal. Launched on 7th August 1942, it had forced a Japanese withdrawal by February 1943.

BIBLIOGRAPHY

PRIMARY SOURCES

PARLIAMENTARY PAPERS: HANSARD

House of Commons Debates: 21 February 1876 (vol. 227), 13 May 1901 (vol. 93), 8 July 1920 (vol. 131), 23 December 1929 (vol. 233), 16 March 1939 (vol. 345) and 9 September 1941 (vol. 374)

House of Lords Debate: 3 August 1965 (vol. 269)

OFFICIAL BRITISH DOCUMENTS AND ARCHIVES

CAB 37/123/43, 'The Future of Palestine', Herbert Samuel Memorandum to Cabinet, 21 January 1915

CAB 80/13, COS (40) 469 JP, Military Implications of the Withdrawal of the Eastern Mediterranean Fleet: Note by the Joint Planning Sub-Committee submitting a Draft Report to the Chiefs of Staff, 17 June 1940

CAB 69/2, D.O. (41) 8th Meeting, War Cabinet Defence Committee (Operations), Minutes of Meeting at 6pm on 11/2/41, Annex: Prime Minister to General Wavell, 11 February 1941

CAB 79/12, JP (41) 444, Joint Planning Staff, Future Strategy: Review, 14 June 1941

CAB 80/59, COS (41) 155 (c), Chiefs of Staff Committee, General Strategy, Review by the Chiefs of Staff, 31 July 1941

CAB 69/4/8, DO (42) (23), Air Requirements for the Successful Prosecution of the War at Sea, Memorandum by the First Sea Lord, 5 March 1942

CAB 79/21/30, DO (42) 47, The Bombing of Germany, 16 June 1942

CAB 80/63, COS (42) 171 (0), The Bombing of Germany. Memorandum by First Sea Lord (DO (42) 47), 16 June 1942

AIR 14/3507, Harris to Churchill, 17 June 1942

CAB 79/56, COS (42) 73rd Meeting (0), War Cabinet, Chiefs of Staff Committee, Effect of Gymnast on Roundup, 16 July 1942

D137/2, Prime Minister Directive of 23 July 1942

CAB 65/31/7, WM (42) 95th Conclusion, Minute 3. War Cabinet meeting at 5pm on 24 July 1942

CAB 66/28/35, WP (42) 374, Note by Air Marshal Sir Arthur Harris on the Role and Work of Bomber Command originating 28 June 1942, 24 August 1942

CAB 119/65 MSC (42), Post-War Strategic Requirements - Middle East, Second Draft, 3 September 1942

CAB 66/28/35, WP (42) 399, Note by Lord Trenchard on our War Policy - August 1942 (dated: 29 August 1942), 5 September 1942

CAB 66/28/35, WP (42) 405, Air Policy: Note by the Prime Minister (dated: 9 September 1942), 9 September 1942

CAB 79/57, COS (42) 119th Meeting (0), part of COS 263rd Meeting, Minute 10 held at 10:30am on 15 September 1942

CAB 79/58, COS (42), 156th Meeting (0) COS Committee, Part of COS (42) 296th Meeting at 10:30am on 22 October 1942

CAB 66/30, WP (42) 483, Policy for the Conduct of the War. Memorandum by the Minister of Defence, 24 October 1942

CAB 80/65, COS (42,) 345 (0) (Final) COS Committee. American-British Strategy Report, 30 October 1942

CAB 119/65, MSC (42) 3 (Third Revise), Post-War Strategic Requirements in the Middle East, November 1942 [specific date not indicated]

CAB 80/65, COS (42) 399 (0), Strategy in 1943. Minute by the Prime Minister, 18 November 1942

CAB 80/66, COS (42) 421 (0), Future Strategy. Minute by Prime Minister [D208/2], 29 November 1942

CAB 80/66, COS (42) 432 (0), COS Committee. Future Strategy. Reply to PM, 3 December 1942

CAB 80/66, COS (42) 452 (0), (Final) COS Committee. Future Strategy Memorandum, 13 December 1942

CAB 119/65, JP (42) 1025, Post-War Strategic Requirements in the Mediterranean Basin (4th Draft), 20 December 1942

CAB 80/66, COS (42) 466 (0) (Final), COS Committee. American-British Strategy in 1943. Report, 31 December 1942

CAB 119/65, MSC/53 (Final), Post-War Strategic Requirements in the Mediterranean Basin, 25 June 1943

CAB 66/39 WP (43) 349 India's Requirements of Imported Food Grains, 31 July 1943

CAB 80/73, COS (Q) 3 Revise, Chiefs of Staff Committee, Operations in the European Theatre of War, Aide-Memoire, 6 August 1943

CAB 80/73, COS (Q) 8 (Revise) Chiefs of Staff Committee, Operation Overlord: Outline Plan. Covering Note by British Chiefs of Staff, 10 August 1943

CAB 65/35 WM (43) 131 Conclusions of War Cabinet meeting held in PM's Room in House of Commons, 3pm on 24 September 1943

CAB 79/66, COS (43) 254th Meeting (0) COS Committee, Minutes of a Staff Conference held at 10:30pm on 19 October 1943

PREM 3/14/1, Harris to Churchill, 3 November 1943

CAB 65/36 WM (43) 152 Conclusions of War Cabinet meeting at 10 Downing St, 6pm, 10 November 1943

CAB 81/41, PHP (43) 41 (Final), British Strategic Needs in the Levant States, inc. Appendix B 'Oil in the Middle East', 13 December 1943

CAB 69/6/3, DO (44) 9th Meeting, Defence Committee (Operations), Minutes of the Meeting held in the Defence Map Room at 10:30pm on 3 May 1944

CAB 65/43, WM (44) 127th Conclusions, Conclusions of War Cabinet Meeting at 5:30pm on 25 September 1944, plus WP (44) 556, Suez Canal Committee Note by Secretary of the War Cabinet, 4 October 1944

CAB 95/18, SC (M) (44) 1st Meeting, Suez Canal Committee, Minutes of Meeting in Conference Room B, Great George St at 5:15pm on 11 October 1944

CAB 120/303, PM's Personal Telegram, Serial No. D83/5, General Ismay for COS Committee, 28 March 1945

OFFICIAL AMERICAN DOCUMENTS AND ARCHIVES

United States Department of State. Foreign Relations of the United States.

Conferences at Washington, 1941-1942, and Casablanca, 1943, I. The First Washington Conference (Dec 22 1941- Jan 14 1942) Memorandum by the United States and British Chiefs of Staff, America-British Grand Strategy, December 31, 1941

Conferences at Washington, 1941-1942, and Casablanca, 1943 II. The Second Washington Conference. Churchill to Roosevelt (Hyde Park) June 20, 1942

Conferences at Washington, 1941-1942, and Casablanca, 1943 (1941-1943) CCS 135 Basic Strategic Concept for 1943, December 26, 1942.

Conferences at Washington, 1941-1942, and Casablanca, 1943 (1941-1943) CCS 155/1 Conduct of the War in 1943, January 19, 1943

Conferences at Washington, 1941-1942, and Casablanca, 1943 (1941-1943) CCS 169, Note by the Combined Staff Planners, January 22, 1943

Conferences at Washington, 1941-1942, and Casablanca, 1943 (1941-1943) CCS 171/2/D, Directive to the Commander in Chief, Allied Expeditionary Force in North Africa (Eisenhower), January 23, 1943

Conferences at Washington and Quebec, 1943. Meeting of the Combined Chiefs of Staff (CCS) with Roosevelt and Churchill, White House at 2:30pm, May 12, 1943.

Conferences at Washington and Quebec, 1943. Meeting of the CCS, Federal Reserve Building at 10:30am, May 13, 1943

Conferences at Washington and Quebec, 1943. Meeting of the CCS, Federal Reserve Building at 10:30am, May 19, 1943

Conferences at Washington and Quebec, 1943. Meeting of the CCS, Federal Reserve Building at 4:30pm, May 19, 1943

Conferences at Washington and Quebec, 1943. Meeting of the CCS with Roosevelt and Churchill, White House at 4:45pm, May 24, 1943

United States Department of State. Foreign Relations of the United States. Diplomatic Papers. Conferences at Cairo and Tehran, 1943.

First Plenary Meeting, Conference Room, Soviet Embassy, 4pm, November 28, 1943

Second Plenary Meeting, Conference Room, Soviet Embassy, 4pm, November 29, 1943

CCS Meeting, British Legation, 9:30am, November 30, 1943

Roosevelt-Churchill-Stalin Luncheon Meeting, Roosevelt's Quarters, Soviet Embassy, 1:30pm, November 30, 1943

Third Plenary Meeting, Conference Room, Soviet Embassy, 4pm, November 30, 1943

CCS Meeting with Roosevelt and Churchill, Roosevelt's Villa, 11am, December 4, 1943

First Tripartite Meeting of Heads of Government, President's Villa, 5pm, December 4, 1943

CCS Meeting, Mena House, 10:30am, December 5, 1943

CCS 423/2 Report by the CCS. Operations in the European Theater, Cairo, December 5, 1943

CCS 426/1 Report of the CCS to the President and Prime Minister, Cairo, December 6, 1943

World War Two Inter-Allied Conferences. Quadrant Conference, 1943. Papers and Minutes of Meetings (Joint History Office, Washington DC, 2003)

Annex B Operation Overlord, COSSAC (43) 8, and COSSAC (43) 32 (Final), July 15, 1943

COSSAC (43) 32 (Final), Annex B, Digest of Operation Overlord, July 27, 1943

1st Meeting of the President and Prime Minister with the Combined Chiefs of Staff at 5:30pm, August 19, 1943

2nd Meeting of the President and Prime Minister with the Combined Chiefs of Staff at 5:30pm, August 23, 1943

Miscellaneous

Trident Conference, May 1943, Papers and Minutes of Meetings Edited and Published by the Office, US Secretary, Office of the Combined Chiefs of Staff, 1943 (Digitised 2001)

The Impact of Allied Air Interdiction on German Strategy for Normandy. Saber Measures (Bravo). United States Air Force, Assistant Chief of Staff, Studies and Analysis, August 1969
(available at www.dtic.mil/dtic/tr/fulltext/u2/859421.pdf)

Allied Command Structures in the New NATO. National Defense University, Institute for National Strategic Studies, Fort McNair, Washington, 1997/ January 2002
(available at http://www.dtic.mil/dtic/tr/fulltext/u2/a422953.pdf)

SECONDARY SOURCES

HISTORY OF THE SECOND WORLD WAR: UNITED KINGDOM MILITARY SERIES

John Ehrman, *Grand Strategy*, vol. V, August 1943 - September 1944 (1956)

F. H. Hinsley et al, *British Intelligence in the Second World War,* vol.III, part I (1984)

F. H. Hinsley et al, *British Intelligence in the Second World War,* vol.III, part II (1988)

Michael Howard, *Grand Strategy, Vol. IV, August 1942 - September 1943* (1972)

C.J.C. Molony, *The Mediterranean and Middle East: Vol. V: The Campaign in Sicily 1943, and the Campaign in Italy, 3rd September 1943 to 31st March 1944* (1973)

I.S.O. Playfair et al, *The Mediterranean and Middle East, Vol. I: The Early Successes Against Italy, to May 1941 (1974)*

Stephen Roskill, *The War at Sea, 1939-45, Vol. I: The Defensive* (1954)

Stephen Roskill, *The War at Sea, 1939-45, Vol. II: The Period of Balance* (1956)

Charles Webster and Noble Frankland, *The Strategic Air Offensive Against Germany, 1939-45, Vol. II Endeavour, Part 4* (1961)

HISTORY OF THE SECOND WORLD WAR: UNITED KINGDOM CIVIL SERIES

C.B.A. Behrens, *Merchant Shipping and the Demands of War* (1955)

Michael M. Postan, *British War Production* (1952)

THE TRANSFER OF POWER, 1942-47

Nicholas Mansergh, *The Transfer of Power 1942-47,* vol. 1, *The Cripps Mission* January–April 1942 (1970)

Nicholas Mansergh, *The Transfer of Power 1942-47,* vol. 4, *The Bengal Famine and the New Viceroyalty,* 15 June 1943 - 31 August 1944 (1973)

JOURNAL ARTICLES

8th Air Force News, Journal of the Eighth Air Force History Society, vol. 20, 1994, p.20

Correlli Barnett, *The Partnership Between Canada and Britain in Winning the Battle of the Atlantic,* Canadian Military History, vol.13, no. 4, Autumn 2004, pp.5-18

Richard Goette, *Britain and the Delay in Closing the Mid-Atlantic 'Air Gap' during the Battle of the Atlantic,* The Northern Mariner/Le Marin du Nord, vol. 15, no. 4, Oct 2005, pp.19-41

Christina Goulter-Zervoudakis, *The Politicization of Intelligence: The British Experience in Greece, 1941-1944*, Intelligence and National Security, vol. 13, no.1, Spring 1998, pp.165-94

Manish Sinha, *The United Nations Relief and Rehabilitation Administration (UNRRA) and the Question of Food Aid during the Bengal Famine of 1943*, Proceedings of the Indian History Congress, vol. 73 (2012), pp.1042-1052

UNPUBLISHED DISSERTATIONS

Lieutenant Colonel Michael J. Finnegan, *General Eisenhower's Battle for Control of the Strategic Bombers in Support of Operation Overlord*, U.S. Army War College, Carlisle Barracks, Pennsylvania, 1999
(available at www.dtic.mil/get-tr-doc/pdf?AD=ADA364514)

Edward R. Flint, *The Development of British Civil Affairs and its Employment in the British Sector of Allied Military Operations during the Battle of Normandy, June to August 1944* (Doctoral thesis, Cranfield University, 2008)

NEWSPAPER ARTICLES

Herbert Mitgang, *Eisenhower Manuscript Used By Son For A Book,* New York Times, 29 May 1982

Noel Annan, *How Wrong Was Churchill?* New York Review of Books, 8 April 1993

Jenny Nolan, *Willow Run and the Arsenal of Democracy*, Detroit News, 28 January 1997

Jonathan Glancey, *Our Last Occupation,* Guardian, 19 April 2003

MISCELLANEOUS

Eisenhower's Return to Normandy, 90-minute CBS documentary commemorating Overlord's 20th Anniversary presented by Walter Cronkite (1964). A 60min version of the original programme is available at www.youtube.com/watch?v=R_dj2aba1hE

Tough Old Gut: Italy, November 1942 - June 1944, Episode 13 of Thames TV series, *The World At War* (1973)

William Lyon Mackenzie King Diary. Record of a Conversation with Churchill in the White House, 6pm, 18th May 1943. The full Diary is available online at
https://www.bac-lac.gc.ca/eng/discover/politics-government/prime-ministers/william-lyon-mackenzie-king/Pages/diaries-william-lyon-mackenzie-king.aspx

BOOKS: DIARIES AND MEMOIRS

Field Marshal Lord Alanbrooke, *War Diaries, 1939- 1945* (2001)

Leo S. Amery, *The Empire At Bay: The Leo Amery Diaries, 1929-1945* (1988)

Lord Boothby, *My Yesterday, Your Tomorrow* (1962)

Sir Austen Chamberlain, *The Austen Chamberlain Diary Letters: The Correspondence of Sir Austen Chamberlain with His Sister Hilda and Ida, 1916-37* (1995)

Winston S. Churchill, *India, Speeches and an Introduction* (1931)

Winston S. Churchill, *My Early Life* (1941)

Winston S. Churchill, *The Second World War, Vol. II, Their Finest Hour* (1949)

Winston S. Churchill, *The Second World War, Vol. III, The Grand Alliance* (1950)

Winston S. Churchill, *The Second World War, Vol. IV, The Hinge of Fate* (1951)

Winston S. Churchill, *The Second World War, Vol. V, Closing the Ring* (1952)

Winston S. Churchill, *The Second World War, Vol. VI, Triumph and Tragedy* (1954)

Winston S. Churchill, *The World Crisis, 1911-1918: Abridged and Revised Edition* (2005)

Winston S. Churchill, *The World Crisis, 1916-18,* Vol. III, Part 2 (1927)

Mark Clark, *Calculated Risk* (1951)

John Colville, *The Fringes of Power: Downing Street Diaries 1939-1955* (1985)

Hugh Dalton, *The Fateful Years: Memoirs, 1931-45* (1957)

Karl Dönitz, *Memoirs: Ten Years and Twenty Days* (2012)

General Dwight Eisenhower, *Crusade in Europe* (1948)

W. Averell Harriman, *Special Envoy to Churchill and Stalin, 1941- 1946* (1976)

Sir Arthur Harris, *Bomber Offensive* (1947)
Oliver Harvey, *The War Diaries of Oliver Harvey* (1978)

Brian Horrocks, *A Full Life* (1974)

General Lord Ismay, *The Memoirs of General the Lord Ismay* (1960)

Wilhelm Keitel, *The Memoirs of Field-Marshal Wilhelm Keitel* (2000)

General Sir John Kennedy, *The Business of War* (1957)

Admiral William D. Leahy, *I Was There* (1950)

Field Marshal Bernard Montgomery, *El Alamein To The River Sangro* (1948)

Field Marshal Bernard Montgomery, *Memoirs of Field Marshal Montgomery* (1958)

Lord Moran, *Winston Churchill: The Struggle for Survival, 1940-65* (1966)

Gen. Sir Frederick Morgan, *Overture to Overlord* (1962)

Harold Nicolson, *Diaries and Letters, 1939-1945* (1967)

Kenneth W. Pendar, *Adventure in Diplomacy: Our French Dilemma* (1945)

Elliott Roosevelt, *As He Saw It* (1946)

Henry L. Stimson and McGeorge Bundy, *On Active Service in Peace and War* (1948)

Viscount Templewood (Sir Samuel Hoare), *Ambassador on Special Mission* (1946)

Lord Wavell, *Wavell: The Viceroy's Journal* (1973)

General Albert C. Wedemeyer, *Wedemeyer Reports!* (1958)

Solly, Baron Zuckerman, *From Apes to Warlords* (1978)

BOOKS: GENERAL WORKS

Paul Addison, *Churchill on the Home Front, 1900-1955* (1993)

Paul Addison, *Churchill: The Unexpected Hero* (2005)

Stephen E. Ambrose, *Eisenhower: Soldier and President* (1990)

Stephen E. Ambrose, *The Supreme Commander: The War Years of General Dwight D. Eisenhower* (2012)

Rick Atkinson, *An Army at Dawn: The War in North Africa, 1942-1943* (2003)

Rick Atkinson, *The Day of Battle: The War in Sicily and Italy, 1943-1944* (2007)

Elisabeth Barker, *British Policy in South East Europe in the Second World War* (1978)

Elisabeth Barker, *Churchill and Eden at War* (1978)

Correlli Barnett, *Engage The Enemy More Closely* (1991)

Correlli Barnett, *The Desert Generals* (1999)

Christopher M. Bell, *Churchill and the Dardanelles* (2017)

Christopher M. Bell, *Churchill and Sea Power* (2013)

Christopher M. Bell, *The Royal Navy, Seapower and Strategy between the Wars* (2000)

Tuvia Ben-Moshe, *Churchill: Strategy and History* (1992)

Robert Blake and Wm. Roger Louis (eds), *Churchill* (2002)

Martin Blumenson, *Anzio: The Gamble that Failed* (2001)

Martin Blumenson, *United States Army in World War 2, Mediterranean Theater of Operations: Salerno to Cassino* (1993)

Horst Boog et al (eds), *Germany and the Second World War: Vol. 6: The Global War* (2001)

Horst Boog et al (eds), *Germany and the Second World War: Vol. 7: The Strategic Air War in Europe and the War in the West and East Asia, 1943-44/5* (2006)

Piers Brendon, *Decline and Fall of the British Empire* (2008)

Stephen Brooks (ed), *Montgomery and the Battle of Normandy: a selection from the diaries, correspondence and other papers of Field Marshal the Viscount Montgomery of Alamein, January to August 1944* (2008)

Arthur Bryant, *Triumph in the West 1943-1946: Based on the Diaries and Autobiographical Notes of Field Marshal, the Viscount Alanbrooke* (1959)

Andrew Buchanan, *American Grand Strategy in the Mediterranean during World War II* (2014)

David Cannadine, *In Churchill's Shadow: Confronting the Past in Modern Britain* (2003)

Alfred D. Chandler (ed), *The Papers of Dwight David Eisenhower*, vol.3 (1970)

John Charmley, *Churchill: The End of Glory* (1993)

Lloyd Clark, *Anzio: The Friction of War, Italy and the Battle for Rome, 1944* (2006)

Robert W. Coakley and Richard M. Leighton, *Global Logistics and Strategy: 1940-43* (1995)

Ed Cray, *General of the Army: George C. Marshall, Soldier and Statesman* (1990)

William Deakin et al, *British Political and Military Strategy in Central, Eastern and Southern Europe in 1944* (1988)

Carlo D'Este, *Bitter Victory: The Battle for Sicily, 1943* (1991)

Carlo D'Este, *Eisenhower: Allied Supreme Commander* (2004)

Carlo D'Este, *Warlord: A Life of Churchill at War 1874-1945* (2009)

Carlo D'Este, *World War II in the Mediterranean, 1942-1945* (1990)

David Edgerton, *Britain's War Machine* (2012)

David Edgerton, *Warfare State: Britain, 1920-1970* (2006)

David Eisenhower, *Eisenhower: At War, 1943-45* (1986)

John S.D. Eisenhower, *Allies: Pearl Harbor to D-Day* (2000)

John S. D. Eisenhower, *They Fought at Anzio* (2007)

Jonathan Fenby, *Alliance: The Inside Story of How Roosevelt, Stalin and Churchill Won One War and Began Another* (2006)

David Fraser, *Alanbrooke* (1997)

David French, *Raising Churchill's Army: The British Army and the War against Germany 1919-1945* (2000)

David French, *The British Way in Warfare, 1688-2000* (1990)

Stephen A. Garrett, *Ethics and Airpower in World War II: The British Bombing of German Cities* (1993)

Martin Gilbert, *Churchill: A Life* (1991)

Martin Gilbert, *Churchill and America* (2005)

Martin Gilbert, *D-Day* (2004)

Martin Gilbert, *The Churchill War Papers: The Ever Widening War, Vol. III 1941* (2000)

Martin Gilbert, *Winston S. Churchill, Vol.III: Companion, Part I, Documents, July 1914 - April 1915* (1972)

Martin Gilbert, *Winston S. Churchill, Vol. IV: World in Torment, 1916-22* (1975)

Martin Gilbert, *Winston S. Churchill, Vol. IV,* Companion, Part 2, Documents, July 1919-March 1921 (1977)

Martin Gilbert, *Winston S. Churchill, Vol. V: The Prophet of Truth, 1922-39* (1976)

Martin Gilbert, *Winston S. Churchill, Vol. V: Companion, Part 3, Documents, The Coming of War, 1936-39* (1982)

Martin Gilbert, *Winston S. Churchill, Vol. VI: Finest Hour, 1939-41* (1983)

Martin Gilbert, *Winston S. Churchill, Vol.VII: Road to Victory, 1941-45* (1986)

John Glendevon, *The Viceroy at Bay: Lord Linlithgow in India, 1936-1943* (1971)

Emily Goldman, *Power in Uncertain Times: Strategy in the Fog of Peace* (2011)

R. G. Grant, *1001 Battles That Changed the Course of History* (2017)

A. C. Grayling, *Among the Dead Cities: Is the Targeting of Civilians in War Ever Justified?* (2014)

Kent Roberts Greenfield (ed), *Command Decisions* (1960)

Nigel Hamilton, *Monty: Master of the Battlefield, 1942-1944* (1983)

Gordon A. Harrison, *Cross-Channel Attack* (1993)

Basil H. Liddell Hart, *A History of the Second World War (2014)*

Max Hastings, *Bomber Command* (1979)

Max Hastings, *Finest Years* (2009)

Arthur Herman, *Gandhi and Churchill: The Rivalry That Destroyed an Empire and Forged Our Age* (2009)

Trumbull Higgins, *Soft Underbelly: The Anglo-American Controversy over the Italian Campaign, 1943-45* (1968)

Michael Howard, *The Continental Commitment: The Dilemma of British Defence Policy in Two World Wars* (1972)

Michael Howard, *The Mediterranean Strategy in the Second World War* (1993)

Ronald Hyam, *Understanding the British Empire* (2010)

Ashley Jackson, *Churchill* (2012)

Ashley Jackson, *The British Empire and the Second World War* (2006)

Robert Rhodes James, *Churchill: A Study in Failure, 1900-1939* (1973)

Robert Rhodes James, *Winston S. Churchill: His Complete Speeches, 1897-1963, Vol.1, Vol.5 & Vol.6* (1974)

Keith Jeffery, *The British Army and the Crisis of Empire, 1918-22* (1984)

Roy Jenkins, *Churchill* (2001)

Matthew Jones, *Britain, the United States and the Mediterranean War, 1942-44* (1996)

John Kent, *British Imperial Strategy and the Origins of the Cold War, 1944-49* (1993)

John Kent, *Egypt and the Defence of the Middle East, Part I 1945-49* (1998)

John Maynard Keynes, *Essays in Persuasion* (2010)

Warren F. Kimball, *Churchill and Roosevelt: The Complete Correspondence, Vol.1 Alliance Emerging, October 1933- November 1942* (1984)

Warren F. Kimball, *Churchill and Roosevelt: The Complete Correspondence, Vol.2 Alliance Forged, Nov 1942- Feb 1944* (1984)

Warren F. Kimball, *Churchill and Roosevelt: The Complete Correspondence, Vol.3 Alliance Declining, Feb 1944- April 1945* (1984)

Nigel Knight, *Churchill: The Greatest Briton Unmasked* (2009)

Keith Kyle, *Suez: Britain's End of Empire in the Middle East* (2011)

Eric Larrabee, *Commander in Chief: Franklin Delano Roosevelt, His Lieutenants, and their War* (1987)

Lewis E. Lehrman, *Churchill, Roosevelt & Company: Studies in Character and Statecraft* (2017)

Lewis E. Lehrman, *Lincoln & Churchill: Statesmen at War* (2018)

Ronald Lewin, *Churchill As Warlord* (1974)

Julian Lewis, *Changing Direction: British Military Planning for Post-war Strategic Defence, 1942-47* (2003)

Jack London, *People of the Abyss* (2004)

William Roger Louis, *British Strategy in the Far East, 1919-1939* (1971)

William Roger Louis, *Ends of British Imperialism: The Scramble for Empire, Suez, and Decolonization* (2006)

John Lukacs, *Five Days in London: May 1940* (1999)

Maurice Matloff and Edwin M. Snell, *Strategic Planning for Coalition Warfare, 1941-1942* (1999)

Maurice Matloff, *Strategic Planning for Coalition Warfare, 1943-44* (1994)

Samuel W. Mitcham, *The German Defeat in the East, 1944-45* (2007)

Samuel W. Mitcham, *Rommel's Desert Commanders: The Men Who Served The Desert Fox, North Africa, 1941-42* (2007)

Samuel W. Mitcham, *Rommel's Desert War: The Life and Death of the Afrika Korps* (2007)

Steve Morewood, *The British Defence of Egypt, 1935-40: Conflict and Crisis in the Eastern Mediterranean* (2005)

Samuel Eliot Morison, *History of United States Naval Operations in World War II: Sicily - Salerno - Anzio, January 1943-June 1944* (2002)

Samuel Eliot Morison, *History of United States Naval Operations in World War II: The Atlantic Battle Won, May 1943- May 1945* (2002)

Samuel Eliot Morison, *History of United States Naval Operations in World War II: The Invasion of France and Germany: 1944-1945* (2002)

Madhusree Mukerjee, *Churchill's Secret War: The British Empire and the Ravaging of India During World War II* (2010)

Janam Mukherjee, *Hungry Bengal: War, Famine and the End of Empire* (2015)

Nigel Nicolson, *Alex: The Life of Field Marshal Earl Alexander of Tunis* (1973)

Joseph A. Obieta, *The International Status of the Suez Canal* (1960)

Patrick K. O'Donnell, *Beyond Valor: World War II's Ranger and Airborne Veterans Reveal the Heart of Combat* (2001)

Vincent Orange, *Slessor: Bomber Champion: The Life of Marshal of the Royal Air Force, Sir John Slessor* (2006)

Vincent Orange, *Tedder: Quietly in Command* (2006)

Richard Overy (ed), *The Oxford Illustrated History of World War Two* (2015)

Richard Overy, *The Origins of the Second World War* (2017)

Richard Overy, *Why The Allies Won* (1996)

Devendra Panigrahi, *India's Partition: The Story of Imperialism in Retreat* (2004)

R.A.C. Parker, *The Second World War: A Short History* (2001)

Roger Parkinson, *A Day's March Nearer Home: The War History from Alamein to VE Day Based on the War Cabinet papers of 1942 to 1945* (1974)

Roger Parkinson, *The War in the Desert* (1976)

G. C. Peden, *Arms, Economics and British Strategy: From Dreadnoughts to Hydrogen Bombs* (2007)

Forrest C. Pogue, *George C. Marshall, Ordeal and Hope, 1939-42* (1966)

Forrest C. Pogue, *United States Army in World War II: European Theater of Operations: The Supreme Command* (1954)

Clive Ponting, *Churchill* (1994)

Douglas Porch, *Hitler's Mediterranean Gamble: The North African and the Mediterranean Campaigns in World War II* (2004)

Anita Prażmowska, *Poland: A Modern History* (2010)

Harold E. Raugh, *The Victorians at War: An Encyclopedia of British Military History* (2004)

Harold E. Raugh, *Wavell in the Middle East, 1939-1941: A Study in Generalship* (2013)

David Reynolds, *Britannia Over-Ruled: British Policy and World Power in the Twentieth Century* (1991)

David Reynolds, *From World War to Cold War: Churchill, Roosevelt, and the International History of the 1940s* (2006)

David Reynolds, *In Command of History: Churchill Fighting and Writing the Second World War* (2004)

Gowher Rizvi, *Linlithgow and India: A Study of British Policy and the Political Impasse in India (1978)*

Andrew Roberts, *Masters and Commanders* (2008)

Norman Rose, *Churchill: An Unruly Life* (2010)

Stephen Roskill, *Churchill and the Admirals* (2004)

Trevor Royle, *Montgomery: Lessons in Leadership from the Soldier's General* (2010)

Robert E. Sherwood, *Roosevelt and Hopkins: An Intimate History* (1948)

Robert E. Sherwood, *The White House Papers of Harry L. Hopkins, Vol. I, September 1939 - January 1942* (1948)

Charles R. Shrader, *The Withered Vine: Logistics and the Communist Insurgency in Greece, 1945-1949* (1999)

Zara S. Steiner, *The Lights that Failed: European International History, 1919-1933* (2005)

Mark A. Stoler, *Allies and Adversaries* (2000)

Mark A. Stoler, *Allies in War* (2005)

Nicholas Tamkin, *Britain, Turkey and the Soviet Union, 1940-45: Strategy, Diplomacy and the Soviet Union, 1940-45* (2009)

A.J.P. Taylor, *Churchill Revised: A Critical Assessment* (1969)

A.J.P. Taylor, *English History 1914-1945* (1965)

John Terraine, *Business in Great Waters* (1989)

John Terraine, *The Right of the Line: The Role of the RAF in World War Two* (1985)

Richard Toye, *Churchill's Empire* (2010)

Richard Toye, *Lloyd George and Churchill: Rivals for Greatness* (2008)

Richard Toye (ed), *Winston Churchill: Politics, Strategy and Statecraft* (2017)

Haris Vlavianos, *Greece, 1941-49: From Resistance to Civil War: The Strategy of the Greek Communist Party* (1992)

Weinberg, Gerhard L, *A World At Arms: A Global History of World War II* (1994)

David T. Zabecki (ed), *Germany At War: 400 Years of Military History* (2014)

David T. Zabecki (ed), *World War II In Europe: An Encyclopaedia,* Vols. 1 and 2 (1999, 2015)

REFERENCES

EPIGRAPHS

[Overlord] has been forced... United States military authorities. Gilbert, *Winston S. Churchill, vol.VII*, p.745

All our war experience... regain that control. CAB 119/65 JP (42) 1025, 20th December 1942, Post-War Strategic Requirements in the Mediterranean Basin (4th Draft)

Had we had our way... done in 1944. Kennedy, *The Business of War*, p.305

PREFACE

Stimson argued that... *after the war is over."* Jones, *Britain, the United States and the Mediterranean War, 1942-44*, p.84

Admiral King... informed newsmen... *lower priority."* Stoler, *Allies And Adversaries*, p.116

Admiral Leahy... perceived a *"British desire... how the war may end."* Roberts, Masters and Commanders, p.359

Eisenhower... insisted that *"Britishers... the viewpoint of the Empire."* Jones, *Britain, the United States and the Mediterranean War, 1942-44*, p.27

General John Kennedy... conceded that *"had we had our way... would not have been done in 1944."* Kennedy, *The Business of War*, p.305

General Frederick Morgan... observed that *"the British authorities... conviction it could not succeed."* Hastings, *Finest Years*, p.385 and p.478

CHAPTER ONE

When you learn... equal to the white man. Moran, *Churchill*, p.370

Whatever happens... and they have not. D'Este, *Warlord*, p.104

His mother's alleged and confirmed lovers included: List compiled from numerous print and online sources, although the term 'lover' has carried different definitions at different times.

While other officers pickled... familiarity with modern politics. D'Este, *Warlord*, pp. 64-65; Toye, *Churchill's Empire*, p. 27

Reade despised the *"sickly... is a crime."* Toye, *Churchill's Empire*, pp. 27-30

As Churchill recorded... *punitive devastation.* Churchill, *My Early Life*, p.162

Churchill observed British... burn him alive. Toye, *Churchill's Empire*, p.39

Churchill labelled the Pashtuns *"little savages... cannot be alluded to.* D'Este, Warlord, p.79; David Spurr, *The Rhetoric of Empire: Colonial Discourse in Journalism, Travel and Imperial Administration* (1996), p.82

It was Churchill's belief that *in proportion... progress of mankind accelerated.* David Spurr, *The Rhetoric of Empire: Colonial Discourse in Journalism, Travel and Imperial Administration* (1996), p.82

Wounded Sudanese soldiers... *Kitchener was responsible for this."* Warren Dockter, *Churchill and the Islamic World* (2015), p.36

Their first attempt on 11th December... claiming he couldn't re-enter. Toye, *Churchill's Empire*, pp. 71-2; D'Este, *Warlord*, pp. 144-45

Churchill employed libel law... exonerating him. D'Este, *Warlord*, p. 167

Salisbury's description of India... is apposite. Carl Cavanagh Hodge (ed), *Encyclopedia of the Age of Imperialism, 1800-1914, vo.1* (2008), p.550

According to Indian Viceroy... *third rate power.* Gisela Hermann-Brenneke and Wolf Kindermann (eds), *Anglo-American Awareness: Arpeggios in Aesthetics* (2005), p.136

He warned that *our continued existence... could be no recovery.* Brendon, *Decline and Fall of the British Empire*, p. 384

Disraeli described the purchase... *the wisdom of [this] step.* Hansard, HoC debate, 21 February 1876 vol. 227, 562-661

Disraeli's Lord Chancellor summarised the symbiosis... *the unit that makes these ciphers valuable.* A.N. Wilson, *The Victorians* (2003), p.390

Britain's Empire covered 12.7 million ... under French rule. Raugh, *The Victorians at War*, p. xvi. The French Empire ruled 70m subjects in 1812 and 110m in 1939

In 1914, British overseas investments... and America £700m. A.G. Kenwood & A.L. Lougheed, *The Growth of the International Economy, 1820-2000* (1999), p.28

In 1854, Britain had £260m invested... and only 5% in Europe. ibid, p.30

80% of all City of London capital issues in 1913 were for foreign ventures. M.W. Kirby, *The Decline of British Economic Power Since 1870* (1981), p.14

Between 1870-1913, Germany and America invested... Britain invested 7%. Rondo Cameron (ed), *International Banking, 1870- 1914* (1991), p.25

During this same period, 21.7% of American GNP... and Britain 8.7% Michael Edelstein, *Overseas Investment in the Age of High Imperialism: The United Kingdom, 1850- 1914* (1982), p.200. The German figure is an average of the 11.4% invested in domestic capital formation between 1870-1890, and the 14.2% invested 1890-1910.

Between 1870 and 1913, German industrial efficiency... stumbled along at 0.6%. Derek H. Aldcroft (ed), *The Development of British Industry and Foreign Competition, 1875-1914* (1968), p.13

As M.W. Kirby noted, *"no country before or since... such a sustained period."* M.W. Kirby, *The Decline of British Economic Power Since 1870* (1981), p.14

In 1913, 9% of British GNP was invested overseas. A.G. Kenwood & A.L. Lougheed, *The Growth of the International Economy, 1820- 2000* (1999), p.28

It produced 33%... £200 million per annum. Kenneth D. Brown, *Britain and Japan: A Comparative Economic and Social History since 1900* (1998), p.11; Norman McCord et al, *British History, 1815-1906* (1991), p.437

India remained a vast dumping ground... 8.5% of British GDP. Rondo Cameron (ed), *International Banking, 1870- 1914* (1991), p.25

When Churchill joined... Churchill family funds. D'Este, *Warlord,* p.45

Montgomery... was *astonished to find... success in the competitive entrance examination.* Montgomery, *Memoirs*, p.23

Horrocks entered Sandhurst... *military career.* Horrocks, *A Full Life*, p. 14

In *My Early Life... into the army."* Churchill, *My Early Life,* p. 42

Lt. Gen. Henry Pownall... *to suit meal-times.* Hastings, *Finest Years*, p. 263

London railed against... *edge of starvation.* London, *People of the Abyss*, p.242

There was *"little glory... flush its sewers."* Toye, *Churchill's Empire*, p.95

CHAPTER TWO

We are not a young people... to others than to us. Ponting, *Churchill*, p.132

We do require your assistance... us to support it. Greg Kennedy (ed), *Imperial Defence: The Old World Order, 1856-1956* (2008), p.268

There are not wanting those... uttermost ends of the earth. Rhodes James, Churchill: Complete Speeches, vol.1, p. 28

Imperial enthusiasm informed... *progress of the English people.* David Jablonsky, *Churchill, The Great Game and Total War* (2006), p.16

In October 1940, he reassured… *our island life.* Rose, *Churchill*, p.268

He famously endorsed… *else would have to be found.* Rhodes James, Churchill: Complete Speeches, vol.6, 1935-42, pp.6692-6695

Churchill offered to swap Morocco… *dismemberment of the British Empire.* Pendar, *Adventure in Diplomacy*, pp.156-157

In the 1903 Alaskan boundary dispute… two Canadian representatives. Stephen R. Rock, *Appeasement in International Politics (*2000), p.29

First Lord of the Admiralty Selborne… *Germany and France and Russia.* Shawn T. Grimes, *Strategy and War Planning in the British Navy, 1887-1918* (2012), p.52

First Lord of the Admiralty Winston Churchill… every Germany warship completed. Bell, *Churchill and Sea Power*, p.18

Britain should remain… *petty expeditions.*" Herman, *Gandhi and Churchill*, p. 99

He condemned Brodrick's plans… *security of any.* Addison, *Churchill on the Home Front,* p.13; Hansard, HoC debate, 13 May 1901 vol. 93, 1572-1575

To ensure that "*the first and main... military to marine.*" Jackson, *Churchill*, p. 89

In October 1903 he wrote… *& their methods."* Gilbert, *Churchill: A Life*, p.158

His constituency organisation… next to Lloyd George. Ponting, *Churchill*, pp.52- 54; Alfred F. Havighurst, *Radical Journalist: H. W. Massingham,* 1860-1924 (1974), p.132; Leonard Dudley, *Information Revolutions in the History of the West* (2008), p.241

In autumn 1908, First Lord of the Admiralty… construction of six new dreadnoughts. Amelia Hadfield-Amkhan, *British Foreign Policy, National Identity, and Neoclassical Realism* (2010), p.114; David Stevenson, *Armaments and the Coming of War: Europe, 1904-1914* (2002), p.169

Churchill and Lloyd George argued for four… naval retrenchment and economy. Barry Gough, *Churchill and Fisher: The Titans at the Admiralty Who Fought the First World War* (2017), p.131; Phillips Payson O'Brien, *British and American Naval Power: Politics and Policy, 1900-1936* (1998), p.93

The impasse was resolved… if required later. John Brooks, *The Battle of Jutland* (2016), p.14

First Lord of the Admiralty Churchill reversed his position… threatening resignation if they were rejected. Ponting, *Churchill*, pp.131-132

Churchill urged the sterilisation… *year has passed.* Ponting, *Churchill*, p.102

Naval spending increased... £44.4m by 1913/14. Peden, *Arms, Economics and British Strategy,* p.38 (Peden's table is from Mitchell, *British Historical Statistics,* pp.589-591)

As he later explained, *to commit... the prize of the venture.* William Hopkinson and Julian Lindley-French, *The New Geopolitics of Terror: Demons and Dragons* (2017), p.17

CHAPTER THREE

I think a curse... every second of it. Toye, *Lloyd George and Churchill,* p.127

I am absolutely unable... danger than the Germans. Bell, *Churchill and the Dardanelles,* p.177; Ernest Sanger, *Letters from Two World Wars* (1993), p.44

The eve of war found Churchill... *moods of levity.* Jackson, *Churchill,* p.136

Churchill was supremely... *matter in me.* Jenkins, *Churchill,* p.203

His mouth waters... in military routine'. Rhodes James, Churchill, pp.76-77

On 30th July, he instructed Admiral Milne... *in combination with the French"* Roskill, *Churchill and the Admirals,* pp.32-33

Churchill was desperate to grapple... *rats in a hole."* Ponting, *Churchill,* p.146

Churchill can be exonerated... *any services they can render."* Bell, *Churchill and the Dardanelles,* p.31

The message sent to his Cabinet colleagues... *prospects of a victorious result.* Geoffrey Best, *Churchill: A Study in Greatness* (2006), p.55

Churchill was equally enthusiastic... *enable the Russians to do so too?* Gilbert (ed), *Winston S. Churchill: Companion,* vol.III, Part I, p.344

Admiral Scott... *always out-argues me."* Rhodes James, Churchill, p.86

Clementine Churchill poignantly summarised... *die of grief.* Mary Soames, *Winston and Clementine: The Personal Letters of the Churchills* (2001), p.107

Churchill depicted his predicament... *a front seat.* John B. Severance, *Winston Churchill: Soldier, Statesman, Artist* (1996), p.51

In later years, a brother... *our friend.* Andrew Dewar Gibb, *With Winston Churchill at the Front: Winston in the Trenches, 1916* (2016), pp. 176-177

Churchill recommended postponing... *decisive effort in a later year.* Excerpt from a WSC speech in the House of Commons secret session, 10th May 1917, quoted in Gilbert, *Winston S. Churchill, vol. IV,* p.17

The situation was even worse… *every gun, every resource.* WSC, 5/3/18 memo to the War Cabinet, 'Munitions Programme, 1919' available in Churchill, The World Crisis, 1916-18, vol. III, part 2, pp. 394-403

Churchill always believed… *result would be decisive.* WSC, 5/3/18 memo to the War Cabinet, 'Munitions Programme, 1919'. ibid, pp. 394-403

Churchill neatly merged the two principal themes… *everything else is swept away.* Gilbert, *Churchill: A Life*, p.378

Sir Maurice Hankey clarified… *first class British war aim.* Liam Anderson and Gareth Stansfield, *Crisis in Kirkuk: The Ethnopolitics of Conflict and Compromise* (2009), p.22

Balfour echoed Hankey's views… *oil should be available."* Timothy C. Winegard, *The First World Oil War* (2016), p.113

In his July 1918 memorandum… Admiral Edmond Slade… *territory can be conserved to war.* Liam Anderson and Gareth Stansfield, *Crisis in Kirkuk: The Ethnopolitics of conflict and Compromise* (2009), p.22

Chaim Weizmann summarised… *effective guard for the Suez Canal.* John Quigley, *The International Diplomacy of Israel's Founders: Deception at the United Nations in the Quest for Palestine* (2016), p.13

Herbert Samuel… *the British Empire.* CAB 37/123/43, 'The Future of Palestine', Herbert Samuel Memorandum to Cabinet, 21 January 1915

On 14th November… surged forward to occupy Mosul. Spencer C. Tucker, *The Great War, 1914-1918* (1998), p.190

CHAPTER FOUR

Winston Churchill: *What is the use of being… wouldn't appoint you War Secretary.* Knight, *Churchill*, p.23

In August 1919, the Cabinet… *required for this purpose.* R. Boyce, *The Great Interwar Crisis and the Collapse of Globalization* (2009), p.89

Defence spending slumped… Navy gained 50% and the RAF 13%. Ian J. Cawood, *Britain in the Twentieth Century* (2004), p.151; Robert Johnson, *British Imperialism* (2003), p.164; Goldman, *Power in Uncertain Times*, p.85

The 1916 Naval Expansion Act… *what we please."* Michael Lindberg and Daniel Todd, *Anglo-American Shipbuilding in World War II: A Geographical Perspective* (2004), p.58; George C. Herring, *Years of Peril and Ambition: U.S. Foreign Relations, 1776-1921* (2017), p. 395; Godfrey Hodgson, *Woodrow Wilson's Right Hand: The Life of Colonel Edward M. House* (2006), p.123

Lloyd George outlined Britain's dilemma… *greatest resources of the world.* Roger Louis, *British Strategy in the Far East*, pp.52-53

At the Nov 1921-Feb 1922 Washington Naval Conference… not exceed 35,000 tons. Howard Jones, *Crucible of Power: A History of American Foreign Relations from 1897* (2008), pp.128-129; Will Kaufman and Heidi Slettedahl Macpherson (eds), *Britain and the Americas: Culture, Politics, and History*, vol. I (2005), p.387

On 13th April 1919, fifteen thousand people… escape the shooting. Harish Jain (ed), *The Making of Punjab* (2003), p.226; Stephen Knapp, *Crimes Against India And The Need To Protect Its Ancient Vedic Tradition* (2009), pp.109-110

When asked why… *fool of myself.* Richard L. Johnson (ed), *Gandhi's Experiments with Truth: Essential Writings by and about Mahatma Gandhi* (2006), p.233

Churchill denounced the slaughter… *singular and sinister isolation."* Hansard, HoC debate, 8 July 1920 vol. 131, 1725

Britain formalised its relationship with Egypt… (iv) Sudan (which controlled Egypt's water supply). A. Adu Boahen (ed), *General History of Africa, Vol. 7, Africa Under Colonial Domination, 1880-1935* (1990), p.252; Obieta, *The International Status of the Suez Canal*, pp.14-15

Britain's High Commissioner… *but a fraud.* Kyle, *Suez*, p.17

Throughout 1920, the RAF flew 4,000 hours… servicemen killed or wounded. Jonathan Glancey, *Our Last Occupation*, *Guardian* article, *19 April 2003;* David Brown et al, *The Guinness History of Air Warfare* (1976), p.64

J.A. Chamier described the harsh reality… *lesson is once properly learnt.* James S. Corum and Wray R. Johnson, *Airpower in Small Wars: Fighting Insurgents and Terrorists* (2003), p.58

45 Squadron's Commanding Officer… *effective means of escape.* Imbesat Daudi, *Civilization & Violence: Islam, the West, and the Rest* (2014), p.282

In 1922 he signed… air bases at Basra and Habbaniya. Shyam Radhey Shyam Chaurasia, *History of Middle East* (2005), pp.44-45; Leon M. Jeffries (ed), *Iraq: Issues, Historical Background, Bibliography* (2003), pp.145-146

The cost of garrisoning Iraq… troops remained in the country. Peter Sluglett, *Britain in Iraq: Contriving King and Country, 1914-32* (2007), p.182

Churchill outlined Britain's… *of the British Empire.* Addison, *Churchill*, p.99

The Mosul-Haifa pipeline started pumping oil… British-controlled territory at all times. Robert Byron, *The Road to Oxiana* (2016), p.175

CHAPTER FIVE

I wish they were admirals… a great misfortune for this country. Hansard, HoL debate, 3 August 1965, vol. 269, 164

The true defence… upon the Rhine. Chamberlain, *The Austen Chamberlain Diary Letters,* p.266

The Economic Consequences of Mr Churchill… beaten to the ground. Maynard Keynes, *Essays in Persuasion,* p.211

Table 1: British Defence Expenditure, 1920-1930 Goldman, *Power in Uncertain Times,* pp.85-86

First Sea Lord Beatty… *a quite unnecessary luxury.* Knight, *Churchill,* p.50

Whatever funds were available… *result in a Socialist victory.* ibid, p.47

Asked Prime Minister Baldwin: *Why should... security in any way.* ibid, p.49

When the Admiralty submitted its 1925/26… *next twenty years.* ibid, p.49

In Beatty's opinion, *an eight-inch [gun] ship… 7.5" gunships out of date.* Donald J. Lisio, *British Naval Supremacy and Anglo-American Antagonisms, 1914-1930* (2014), p.70

In 1924/25, the Admiralty estimated… if left unchecked. Bell, *Churchill and Sea Power,* pp. 103-107

Churchill invited Foreign Secretary Austen Chamberlain… *a contingency to be seriously apprehended".* ibid, pp.107-8; Knight, *Churchill,* p.49

Churchill responded by delaying… was still underway. Bell, *Churchill and Sea Power,* pp. 111-112

He convinced the Committee of Imperial Defence… than it had been in 1925. Greg Kennedy (ed), *Imperial Defence: The Old World Order, 1856-1956* (2008), p.78; John H. Maurer (ed), *Churchill and Strategic Dilemmas Before the World Wars* (2013), p.93; Rhodes James, Churchill, p.215; Bell, *Churchill and Sea Power,* pp.120-125; Toye (ed), *Winston Churchill: Politics, Strategy and Statecraft,* p.40

In 1923, Prime Minister Baldwin… the one advocated in 1923. Peden, *Arms, Economics and British Strategy,* p.145; Ponting, *Churchill, p.318;* Colin Sinnott, *The RAF and Aircraft Design, 1923-1939: Air Staff Operational Requirements* (2001), pp.6-7; Short History of the Royal Air Force, Chapter 2, *The Inter-War Years,* pp.49-90

The army's budget was progressively reduced… overseas on imperial duties. Goldman, *Power in Uncertain Times,* pp.85-86; D.G. Williamson, *The British in Interwar Germany: The Reluctant Occupiers, 1918-30* (2017), p.37

The Chiefs of Staff highlighted... *take note of them."* Frank McDonough (ed), *The Origins of the Second World War: An International Perspective* (2011), p.39

This view was reiterated in 1930... *France and Belgium in 1914.* Steiner, *The Lights that Failed,* p.578

The General Staff made ... *would be fatal strategically.* R. Boyce, *The Great Interwar Crisis and the Collapse of Globalization* (2009), p.133

Having exacerbated unemployment... discourage this alleged dependency. Ponting, *Churchill,* pp.304-5; Gilbert, *Winston S. Churchill, Vol. V,* p.117

He knew his policies... unsuccessful strategies. Addison, *Churchill,* pp.114-115

In September 1945, he finally confided... *return to the Gold Standard."* Geoffrey Best, *Churchill: A Study in Greatness* (2006), p.111

Churchill blithely predicted... *better in design."* Gilbert, *Winston S. Churchill, Vol. V,* p.250

He also informed Sir Douglas... *will be out-matched."* Donald J. Lisio, *British Naval Supremacy and Anglo-American Antagonisms, 1914-1930* (2014), p.301

Historian Paul Kennedy noted that *the long years of virtually... Admiralty's rearmament schemes.* David Edgerton, *Warfare State,* p.17

M.M. Postan... *quantity production.* Edgerton, *Warfare State,* p.17

Sir Warren Fisher summarised the impact... *model for subsequent governments.* Taylor, *Churchill Revised,* p.103

CHAPTER SIX

The loss of India will be the death-blow... hideous signal hoisted. Rhodes James, Churchill: Complete Speeches, vol.5, p.5015

He is really... subject of India. Roger Louis, *Ends of British Imperialism,* p.386

Churchill thundered... *mischievous in its effects.* Rhodes James, Churchill, p.252

Churchill vituperated with gusto... *representative of the King-Emperor.* Rhodes James, Churchill: Complete Speeches, vol.5, p.4985

He did *not agree that the dog... taken their place.* Arundhati Roy, *War Talk* (2003), p.58

[Churchill] presented a vision... *by scores of millions.* Churchill, *India,* p.30

If that authority is injured… duty on the part of Great Britain. Rhodes James, Churchill: Complete Speeches, vol.5, pp.5006-5007

If you took the antagonisms of France… will dispute this. ibid, p.5007

The Indian congress and other… for a very few Indians. ibid, p.4986

There are 450,000 villages... discuss their common affairs. ibid, p.5187

The great enterprises… struggle for more power. ibid, p.5012 & p.5271

As twentieth century liberalism… *of commercial rights.* Jenkins, *Churchill,* p.457

The Act was framed by imperial policy-makers… areas of 'special responsibility'. L. J. Butler, *Britain and Empire: Adjusting to a Post-Imperial World* (2002), pp.12-13: Stanley A. Kochanek and Robert L. Hardgrave, *India: Government and Politics in a Developing Nation* (2008), p.52

Andrew Roberts' bizarre notion… *since Nelson's day."* Roberts, *Masters and Commanders*, p.359

At the 1921 Imperial Conference, Massey dubbed Egypt … *of the main artery.* Jeffery, *The British Army and the Crisis of Empire,* p.38

Austen Chamberlain observed that *the relationship between… those vital interests.* Hansard, HoC debate, 23 December 1929, vol.233, 1956-1957

[Eden] dubbed Suez *"a link in our chain… people of Egypt.* Hansard, HoC debate, 23 December 1929, vol.233, 2046-2048

Ramsay MacDonald insisted that… *vital link in British communications.* Obieta, *The International Status of the Suez Canal,* p.15

MacDonald retorted *"that the whole of the British imperial strategy… position to protect it."* Morewood, *The British Defence of Egypt,* p.86

In 1938, Sir Maurice Hankey… *passage of the Suez Canal.* ibid, p.180

The Chiefs of Staff noted that *the first commitment… interests in the Middle East.* Howard, *The Continental Commitment,* pp.137-138

Future Prime Minister Winston Churchill drafted… should be *"England's first battlefield."* Gilbert, *Winston S. Churchill, Vol. V,* Companion, part 3, *The Coming of War, 1936-39,* pp.1414-1417

CHAPTER SEVEN

We are in the remarkable… taking it away from us. Larry Pratt, *East of Malta, West of Suez: Britain's Mediterranean Crisis, 1936-1939* (1975), p.3

It is beyond… theatres of war. Reynolds, *Britannia Over-Ruled,* p.124

Neville Chamberlain… viewed economic stability… *of no avail."* Larry Pratt, *East of Malta, West of Suez: Britain's Mediterranean Crisis, 1936-1939* (1975), pp.102-103

When the Cabinet repudiated… *financial and economic situation."* Bell, *The Royal Navy, Seapower and Strategy between the Wars,* p.99

Table 1 British Defence Expenditure, 1928/29 - 1939/40 (£m) Peden, *Arms, Economics and British Strategy,* p.151

Table 2 British Defence Expenditure, 1929/30 - 1939/40 (£m) ibid, p.151

Table 3 Comparative Defence Expenditure (% GNP) Overy, *The Origins of the Second World War,* p.53

While Britain was spending… New Zealand 0.8%. Reynolds, *Britannia Over-Ruled,* p.123

Prompting Michael Howard to compare the Empire… *to protect, direct or control."* Howard, *The Continental Commitment,* p.75

The Chiefs of Staff warned... *of potential allies.* Ponting, *Churchill,* p. 392

In April 1939, the Chiefs of Staff again warned… *geographical combination of enemies.* Barnett, *Engage The Enemy More Closely,* p.34

Should Italy prove hostile, *"England's [sic] first… decisive victory there."* Gilbert, *Winston S. Churchill, Vol. V,* Companion, part 3, *The Coming of War, 1936-39,* pp.1414-1417

He made the same point in his 16th March… *the prime objective."* Rhodes James, Winston S. Churchill: Complete Speeches, vol.6, p.6088

Churchill held Italy's fighting… *if not starved.* Gilbert, *Winston S. Churchill, Vol. V,* Companion, part 3, *The Coming of War, 1936-39,* pp.1414-1417

Writing for the New York Herald Tribune… *Italy's overseas ventures.* New York Herald Tribune article, April 4th 1939 quoted in Ronald S. Kain, *Europe: Versailles to Warsaw* (1939), p.154

His 'Memorandum on Sea Power' declared… *between us and these results.* Gilbert, *Winston S. Churchill, Vol. V,* Companion, part 3, *The Coming of War, 1936-39,* pp.1414-1417

As always, the Empire influenced Churchill's priorities… *cannot tolerate this on any account.* ibid, pp.1414-1417

Churchill invited the reader to *consider how vain... are an extremely sensible people.* ibid, pp.1414-1417

Ironside... identified Italy... *our offensive.* Reynolds Salerno, *Vital Crossroads: Mediterranean Origins of the Second World War, 1935-1940* (2002), p.137

General Wavell concurred... *the winning of the war.* ibid, p.137

Admiral Cunningham.... endorsed an Italy/Mediterranean ... *Italians to lose heart.* ibid, p.137

The French endorsed this Mediterranean emphasis... *naval action from the outset.* John B. Hattendorf (ed), *Naval Strategy and Policy in the Mediterranean: Past, Present and Future* (2000), p.59

First Sea Lord Dudley Pound... *abandoned the eastern Mediterranean.* Reynolds Salerno, *Vital Crossroads: Mediterranean Origins of the Second World War, 1935-1940* (2002), p.138

CHAPTER EIGHT

Early misfortunes... prepare for it. Edgerton, *Britain's War Machine,* pp.45-46

The British have planned... scientific warfare. Colville, The Fringes of Power, p.116

Chamberlain informed his sister... *won the war by the spring.* Talbot C. Imlay, *Facing the Second World War: Strategy, Politics, and Economics in Britain and France, 1938-40* (2003), p.105; French, *The British Way in Warfare,* p.195

Churchill shared this view. In March 1939, he informed... *melted down for scrap.* Hansard, HoC debate, 16 March 1939, vol.345, 680

Six months later, he informed cabinet... *German military machine."* Ponting, *Churchill*, p.410

French assessment stated... *systems of Russia.* Agayev et al, *World War II and Azerbaijan*, Azerbaijan International, Summer 1995 (3.2), pp. 50-55 and 78

The plans were proposed... operational by mid-May. *Patrick Osborn, Operation Pike: Britain versus the Soviet Union, 1939-1941* (2000), *pp.145-155*

Churchill... [informed] Admiral Pound... *excluded the offensive principle.* Barnett, *Engage The Enemy More Closely*, p.92

Operation Catherine was a plan... Allied orbit. Markku Ruotsila, *Churchill and Finland: A Study in Anti-communism and Geopolitics* (2005), pp.73-74

Operation Royal Marine... their waters. Ponting, *Churchill,* pp.419-420

Churchill advocated such action… *indeed be immediately decisive.* Knight, *Churchill*, p.96; Bell, *Churchill and Sea Power*, p.174

Churchill cared nothing for Norway's territorial integrity… *protection and enforcement.* Gilbert, *Winston S. Churchill, vol.VI*, p.106

When German ships were spotted… a considerable time advantage. Richard Lamb, *Churchill As War Leader: Right or Wrong* (1991), p.35

The Ironside Diaries describe Churchill's… *He was overruled.* ibid, pp.36-37

Clive Ponting describes… *maps of Namsos.* Ponting, *Churchill*, p.423

Ponting estimates… three week period. Ponting, *Churchill*, p.426

He aggravated matters… Chiefs of Staff or Military Coordination Committee. Knight, *Churchill*, p.103; Charmley, *Churchill*, p. 386

General Ismay… describes the administrative confusion… *confusion worse confounded.* Henrik O. Lunde, *Hitler's Pre-Emptive War: The Battle for Norway, 1940* (2010), p.245

[Churchill] was relieved as Chairman… refused to work with him. Gilbert, *Winston S. Churchill, vol.VI*, p.245

According to Neville Chamberlain… *position in a war.* Robert Self, *Neville Chamberlain: A Biography* (2006), p.417; Charmley, *Churchill*, p. 385

Admiral John Godfrey… Churchill's working methods… *quite trivial questions.* Ponting, *Churchill*, p.411

General Ironside described Churchill… *extraordinary how mercurial he is.* Raugh, *Wavell in the Middle East*, p.58

Writing to General Ismay… *campaign it can be called."* Ponting, *Churchill*, p.421

The Prime Minister called the two principal… as his replacement. Ponting, *Churchill*, pp.429-430

When Churchill finally became Prime Minister... *I should not fail.* Sebastian Haffner, *Churchill* (2005), p.102

CHAPTER NINE

The good clean tradition… but talkative people. Rose, *Churchill*, p.261

We have no continental… German military power. Colville, The Fringes of Power, p.186

According to General Ismay… *of a War Staff in Commission'.* Ismay, *The Memoirs of General the Lord Ismay*, p.159

There could be no hiding… *the military side."* Taylor, *English History*, p.479

When Halifax suggested seeking terms… *portion of the force.* Jenkins, *Churchill*, p.603

Churchill replied that he *would be thankful… cession of territory.* Ponting, *Churchill*, p.444

Chamberlain recorded Churchill's alleged willingness… *he couldn't beat us."* Lukacs, *Five Days in London*, p.120

Churchill replied that he *would not join… to consider them.* ibid, p.151

Churchill again advocated delay… *offered to us now.* Mitchell, *Democracy's Blameless Leaders*, p.82; Gilbert, *Winston S. Churchill, vol.VI*, p.418

According to Hugh Dalton… *own blood upon the ground.* Dalton, *The Fateful Years*, pp.335-336

[Churchill] returned to the War Cabinet… *express themselves so emphatically.* Lukacs, *Five Days in London*, p.185

While appreciating the Admiral's logic… *attack our Far Eastern possessions.* CAB 80/13 *Military Implications of the Withdrawal of the Eastern Mediterranean Fleet: Note by the Joint Planning Sub-Committee submitting a Draft Report to the Chiefs of Staff*, COS (40) 469 JP, 17/6/40, pp.132-133

Long term imperial considerations… *not be easily forgotten.* ibid, p.133

On 23rd June, he vetoed Pound's proposal… Alexandria to contest the Mediterranean. Barnett, *Engage The Enemy More Closely*, p.212

As the PM observed… *military power."* Colville, The Fringes of Power, p.186

CHAPTER TEN

The Cabinet is deplorable… colleagues fear him. Maria Hill, *Diggers and Greeks: The Australian Campaigns in Greece and Crete* (2010), p.65

The loss of Egypt… successful defence of Egypt. Gilbert, *The Churchill War Papers*, vol. III 1941, p.556

Graziani… advising Count Ciano… *rapid and total disaster."* Churchill, *The Second World War*, vol. II, p.415

The 154 tanks sanctioned… between August and December. George Forty, *Desert Rats at War: North Africa, Italy, Northwest Europe* (2014), p.8; Playfair et al, The Mediterranean and Middle East Vol. I, p.246

Operation Compass launched... 25,000 further prisoners. Barnett, *The Desert Generals*, pp.37-60; James C. Bradford (ed), *International Encyclopedia of Military History* (2006), p.364; Zabecki (ed), *World War II in Europe*, p.437

O'Connor wired back... *despatched without delay.* Raugh, *Wavell in the Middle East, 1939-1941*, p.124; Barnett, *Engage The Enemy More Closely*, p.326

On that same day, Rommel landed... Axis from Africa was lost forever. Ian Baxter, *Afrika Korps* (2014), p.40

Churchill immediately informed the Greek Prime Minister... *share a united victory."* Churchill, *The Second World War*, vol. II, p.472

Greece requested British assistance... support on 22nd-23rd February. Ralph Bennett, *Intelligence Investigations: How Ultra Changed History* (2005), p.95; Maria Hill, *Diggers and Greeks: The Australian Campaigns in Greece and Crete* (2010), p.39

Kennedy summarised... *sound military proposition.* Kennedy, *The Business of War*, pp.82-83

Churchill rejected this advice... *be swallowed up."* Ponting, *Churchill*, p.484

Churchill described the Greek request... *combine Yugoslavia, Greece and Turkey.* Churchill, *The Second World War*, vol. III, pp.83-84

Churchill defended his decision... *nut for the Germans to crack.* Boothby, *My Yesterday, Your Tomorrow*, p.209

Wavell was ordered to *make yourself... men and material.* CAB 69/2 War Cabinet Defence Committee (Operations) D.O. (41) 8th Meeting Minutes of 11/2/41 Meeting 6pm, Annex Prime Minister to General Wavell, 11/2/41

By early April, 58,000 troops had been moved to Greece. Jackson, *The British Empire and the Second World War*, p.106

The Royal Navy was forced to evacuate... better employed in Africa. David Brown, *The Royal Navy and the Mediterranean: Vol. II: November 1940-December 1941* (2001), p.84, p.115; Ponting, *Churchill*, p.520; Peter Antill, *Crete 1941: Germany's Lightning Airborne Assault* (2005), p.13

The Navy had to rescue... killed, wounded or captured. Norman Polmar and Thomas B. Allen, *World War II: The Encyclopedia of the War Years, 1941-1945* (2012), p.228; John Strawson, *The Battle for North Africa* (2004), p.60

[Churchill]... demanded a desert victory... 53 fighters to Wavell Barnett, *Engage The Enemy More Closely*, p.367

The convoy arrived on 12th May...initiated Battleaxe on 15th June. ibid, p.367; David Alvarez (ed), *Allied and Axis Signals Intelligence in World War II* (2013), p.91

On 21st June, he was ordered to swap... Wavell's North African command. Knight, *Churchill,* p.175

On 11th January, he informed... *fate of allies.* Ponting, *Churchill*, p.516

On 12th February, he again instructed Wavell... *Turks and Yugoslavs.* Churchill, *The Second World War*, vol. III, pp.56-59

On 10th January, Hopkins informed Washington... *the British public for it.* Sherwood, *The White House Papers of Harry L. Hopkins, vol. I,* p.240

As soon as Greece was lost ... *thrown out of Cyrenaica.* Gilbert, *The Churchill War Papers,* vol. III 1941, p.556

Lord Hankey... described Churchill's management... *the position of 'Joint Planners'.* Charmley, *Churchill,* p.446

General John Kennedy described... *point of danger.* Kennedy, *The Business of War*, pp.114-115

John Colville... detected worrying trends... *labour and production.* Lehrman, *Lincoln & Churchill,* p.334

Churchill accepted responsibility... *if I had been convinced.* Churchill, *The Second World War*, vol. III, p.90

CHAPTER ELEVEN

Roosevelt: *After the war, one of the preconditions...* Churchill: *England does not propose... foundation of our greatness.* Roosevelt, *As He Saw It*, pp.35-37

An ideology that was *not a policy... with extraordinary rapidity.* Hansard, HoC debate, 29 May 1919, vol. 116, 1526

[Churchill] cheerfully informed his Private Secretary, *"if Hitler invaded... in the House of Commons."* Churchill, *The Second World War*, vol. III, p.331

Churchill advised the British people that *any man... of service to them.* ibid, p.332-333

Churchill promised that Britain would *bomb Germany... showered upon mankind.* Martin Bowman, *Bomber Command: Reflections of War - Live to Die Another Day, June 1942- summer 1943,* vol.2 (2012), p.79

Churchill listed the reasons... *far more harm than good.* Gilbert, *Winston S. Churchill, vol.VI*, p.1139

The 1936 Anglo-Egyptian Treaty... enter Egypt in time of war. Spencer C. Tucker and Priscilla Roberts (eds), *The Encyclopaedia of the Arab-Israeli Conflict: A Political, Social, and Military History*, Vol.1 (A-H) (2008), p.107

In September 1940, America exchanged fifty... the western hemisphere (e.g. Jamaica, Trinidad, Antigua). Zabecki (ed), *World War II in Europe*, p.60

The March 1941 Lend Lease Act was formally titled... house had caught fire. Benjamin D. Rhodes, *United States Foreign Policy in the Interwar Period, 1918-1941* (2001), p.175; Ronald E. Powaski, *Toward an Entangling Alliance: American Isolationism, Internationalism, and Europe, 1901-1950* (1991), p.95

Churchill dubbed Lend Lease *"the most unsordid...* until December 2006. David Jablonsky, *Churchill, The Great Game and Total War* (2006), p.113; Neil A. Wynn, *The A to Z of the Roosevelt-Truman Era* (2008), p.247

Churchill set off... *some further forward step."* Ponting, *Churchill*, p.534

The final draft of Article Four... *needed for their economic prosperity.* Martin McCauley, *Origins of the Cold War 1941-1949* (2016), pp.165-166

The final wording of Article Three... *deprived of them.* ibid, pp.165-166

Churchill informed Parliament... *owe allegiance to the British Crown.* Hansard, HoC debate, 9 September 1941, vol.374, 68-69

Operation Crusader launched... forcing a retreat. Bernd Hartmann, *Panzers in the Sand: The History of Panzer-Regiment 5, 1935-1941* (2010), pp.244-246; Ian F. Beckett, *Rommel: A Reappraisal* (2013), pp.75-76; Pier Paolo Battistelli, *Rommel's Afrika Korps: Tobruk to El Alamein* (2013), pp.45-47; Mitcham, *Rommel's Desert Commanders*, pp.56-57

Cunningham requested permission... assumed direct command of 8th Army. Daniel Todman, *Britain's War: Into Battle, 1937-1941* (2016), p.709

CHAPTER TWELVE

It was... blessing that Japan attacked... the British Empire. Rose, *Churchill*, p.290

The U.S. has been seeking... its empire in the Middle East. Jones, *Britain, the United States and the Mediterranean War, 1942-44*, p.21

Arcadia's principal strategy document confirmed... *operations against Germany."* US Dept of State. FRUS. *The Conferences at Washington, 1941-1942, and Casablanca, 1943*, I. The First Washington Conference (Dec 22 1941- Jan 14 1942) Memorandum by the United States and British Chiefs of Staff, America-British Grand Strategy, December 31, 1941, pp.214-217

No land offensives... *countries of Northwestern Europe.* ibid, pp.214-217

In 'The Atlantic Front'... Churchill identified... *Suez Canal.* Winston S. Churchill for the Chiefs of Staff Committee (Cabinet Papers 69/4) Memorandum on the Conduct of the War, Part I - The Atlantic Front, 16 December 1941. Available in Gilbert, *The Churchill War Papers,* vol. III, pp.1633-1637

The British Chiefs of Staff (COS) and American Joint Chiefs of Staff (JCS) formed... the implementation of Allied strategy. Barnett, *Engage The Enemy More Closely,* p.435

CCS sat in Washington... bond with General Marshall. Ian Blackwell, *The Battle for Sicily: Stepping Stone to Victory* (2008), p.14; Anne Sharp Wells, *The A to Z of World War II: The War Against Japan* (2009), p.86

Japan bombed Darwin... killing 243 people. Kate Darian-Smith, *On the Home Front* (2009), p.32

The Australian government... United States as its keystone. Alan Watt, *The Evolution of Australian Foreign Policy 1938-1965* (1968), p.55

In a late February memo, Eisenhower identified... occupation was merely 'desirable'. Ambrose, *The Supreme Commander,* pp.32-33

Eisenhower clarified his thinking... *a land attack as soon as possible.* Howard, *The Mediterranean Strategy in the Second World War,* p.22

Eisenhower's completed Review... offensive at the earliest practicable time. Stoler, *Allies and Adversaries,* p.75; Ray S. Cline, *Washington Command Post: The Operations Division* (1990), p.152

By spring 1943 - it was assumed that... in Britain ready for action. Wesley Frank Craven and James Lea Cate (eds), *The Army Air Forces in World War II, Vol. I: Plans and Early Operations, January 1939- August 1942* (1948), p.652

The northern French landings scheduled... Antwerp as its main goal. Howard, *The Mediterranean Strategy in the Second World War,* p.26; Hastings, *Finest Years,* p.283; Cray, *General of the Army,* p.306

If Germany or the Soviet Union showed... codenamed SLEDGEHAMMER Howard, *The Mediterranean Strategy in the Second World War,* p.26; Hastings, *Finest Years,* p.283; Cray, *General of the Army,* p.306

Roosevelt, Marshall and Stimson... proposals to the British. Williamson Murray et al (eds), *The Shaping of Grand Strategy: Policy, Diplomacy, and War* (2011), p.192; Richard G. Davis, *Carl A. Spaatz and the Air War in Europe* (1993), p.70

According to Morgan, the *Americans knew... always been a winner.* Morgan, *Overture to Overlord,* p.137

According to Churchill, *there can be no question... the defeat of the enemy.* Churchill, *The Second World War*, vol. III, pp.706-707

The Joint Planners shared this gloomy... *road to Germany and victory.* CAB 79/12, JP (41) 444, June 14, 1941, Joint Planning Staff, Future Strategy. Review

British planners could only envisage... *Palestine in 1936."* ibid

According to the Joint Planners... *within is the basic conception."* ibid

Churchill maintained that *"the uprising... corpus of the liberating offensive."* Winston S. Churchill for the Chiefs of Staff Committee, Memorandum on the Future Conduct of the War, 18 December 1941, available in Gilbert, *The Churchill War Papers,* vol. III, pp.1644

Churchill estimated that *"an amphibious striking force... envisaged in the west."* Churchill, *The Second World War*, vol. III, p.706

COS *"[did] not foresee vast armies of infantry as in 1914-18."* CAB 80/59, COS (41) 155 (c) Chiefs of Staff Committee, General Strategy, Review by the Chiefs of Staff, July 31, 1941

In this new struggle *there would be no... prevented from crossing.* CAB 79/12, JP (41) 444, June 14, 1941, Joint Planning Staff, Future Strategy. Review

According to COS, *the loss of our... whole Moslem world.* CAB 80/59, COS (41) 155 (c) Chiefs of Staff Committee, General Strategy, Review by the Chiefs of Staff, July 31, 1941

Britain's own survival... *defence might be vitally affected.* CAB 79/12, JP (41) 444, June 14, 1941, Joint Planning Staff, Future Strategy. Review

According to the Joint Planners, *"the loss of Egypt... order to avoid it."* ibid

On 12th April, he cabled Roosevelt... *in all the history of the war.* Gilbert, *Winston S. Churchill, vol.VII,* p.88

Two days later, he again enthused... *concentration against the main enemy.* Churchill, *The Second World War*, vol. IV, p.283

He also solemnly informed Marshall and Hopkins... *liberation of the tormented peoples.* Larrabee, *Commander-in-Chief*, p.135

While trumpeting his desire to march... *object proposed by General Marshall.* Churchill, *The Second World War*, vol. IV, 1986, p.283

Rommel struck first... Tobruk to the east. James Lucas, *Hitler's Commanders: German Action in the Field 1939-1945* (2014), p.211; Adrian Stewart, *Early Battles of the Eighth Army: Crusader to the Alamein Line, 1941-42* (2010), pp.70-72

Churchill also warned Molotov... *at our discomfiture.* Kimball, *Churchill and Roosevelt:* The Complete Correspondence, vol. 1, pp.495-498

His second telegram advised Roosevelt... *need be towards that."* ibid, p.494

Mountbatten dined with Roosevelt... landing in French North West Africa. Keith Sainsbury, *The North African Landings, 1942: A Strategic Decision* (1976), p.108; Boog et al (eds), *Germany and the Second World War: Volume 6*, p.75; George Bruce, *Second Front Now! The Road to D-Day* (1979), p.66

Ritchie responded by ordering a hasty withdrawal... transmitted to London in January. Barnett, *The Desert Generals*, pp.161-169

On 14th June, Auchinleck was ordered to hold Tobruk. ibid, pp.158-161

Churchill, Ismay and Brooke landed... intimate conversations. Roberts, *Masters and Commanders*, pp.187-188; Ponting, *Churchill*, pp.572-573

During the meeting, Brooke and Marshall agreed... *resources and weaken our effort."* Roberts, *Masters and Commanders,* p.193

The Combined Chiefs' conference... *possible speed and energy"* ibid, p.193

After stating that Sledgehammer *"was certain to lead... operation Gymnast should be studied."* Churchill to Roosevelt (Hyde Park) 20th June 1942, US Dept of State. FRUS. *The Conferences at Washington, 1941-1942, and Casablanca, 1943,* II. The Second Washington Conference, p.461

On 21st June, Churchill received... seven thousand tons of fuel and supplies. Asa Briggs and Patricia Clavin, *Modern Europe, 1789-Present* (1997), p.353; Lawrence Paterson, *Schnellboote: A Complete Operational History* (2015), p.186

Churchill was devastated... crumbling position in the desert. Rose, *Churchill*, p.286; Frank Costigliola, *Roosevelt's Lost Alliances: How Personal Politics Helped Start the Cold War* (2012), p.173; Fenby, *Alliance*, p.130

Ismay's Memorandum opened... *must be ready with an alternative.* Wedemeyer, *Wedemeyer Reports!* pp.156-157

Point Three identified the alternative... *the United States.* ibid, pp.156-157

Auchinleck sacked Ritchie... north of the Qattara Depression. Pradeep Barua, *The State at War in South Asia* (2005), p.147; N.S. Nash, *Strafer Desert General: The Life and Killing of Lieutenant General William Gott* (2013), p.192

The First Battle of El Alamein began... early July was simply 'The Flap'. Bernd Hartmann, *Panzers in the Sand: The History of Panzer-Regiment 5, 1942-45* (2011), p.34; Nicholas Rankin, *A Genius for Deception: How Cunning Helped the British Win Two World Wars* (2008), p.362

On 2nd July, COS advised... *should be mounted."* Greenfield, *Command Decisions*, p.182

On 7th July, the War Cabinet... proceeding with Sledgehammer. Roberts, *Masters and Commanders*, p.226; Gilbert, *Winston S. Churchill, vol.VII*, p.143

Churchill relayed this information... *large scale action in 1943.* Kimball, *Churchill and Roosevelt: The Complete Correspondence*, Vol.1, p.520

Churchill nudged the President... *be delivered this autumn.* ibid, p.520

On 10th July, they informed Roosevelt... *acting decisively against the enemy.* Barnett, *Engage The Enemy More Closely*, p.534

Marshall and his colleagues... *the Pacific.* Cray, *General of the Army*, p.328

Roosevelt called Marshall's bluff... within one week of arriving. Lehrman, *Churchill, Roosevelt & Company*, p.78; Stoler, *Allies and Adversaries*, pp.86-87; Parker, *The Second World War*, p.122

His one attempt to lure the British... the discussions were locked in stalemate. Barnett, *Engage The Enemy More Closely*, pp.534-535

Roosevelt responded by identifying five operations... (v) the reinforcement of Iran. Greenfield, *Command Decisions*, p.186

He selected the activity he considered... the next best option. Pogue, *George C. Marshall, Ordeal and Hope, 1939-42*, pp.346-347; Greenfield, *Command Decisions*, p.186; George Bruce, *Second Front Now! The Road to D-Day* (1979), p.81

Marshall warned that *a commitment to this... air operations and blockade.* Barnett, *Engage The Enemy More Closely*, p.535

When it was transmitted to Roosevelt... political advantage in the 3rd November US mid-term elections. Stoler, *Allies and Adversaries*, p.90

[Churchill] was not about to carp... *plans I cherished were adopted.* Churchill, *The Second World War*, vol. IV, 1986, p.404

CHAPTER THIRTEEN

A man who... afraid of the Germans? Gilbert, *Winston S. Churchill, vol.VII*, p.177

There is one thing I would like to make... soil of England itself. ibid, p.216

Roosevelt... approved a joint communiqué... *second front in Europe in 1942."* Steven Casey, *Cautious Crusade: Franklin D. Roosevelt, American Public Opinion, and the War Against Nazi Germany* (2001), p.91

Auchinleck's removal coincided… under General Harold Alexander. Peter Calvocoressi and Guy Wint, *Total War: Causes and Courses of the Second World War*, vol.2 (1973), p.360; Parkinson, *The War in the Desert*, p.123

Churchill met Stalin… Front during 1942. Eisenhower, *Allies*, pp.116-117

Stalin looked 'glum'… *Mr. Churchill's arguments."* Gilbert, *Winston S. Churchill, vol.VII*, p.176 and p.178

Churchill then informed Stalin… *persevere and try."* ibid, p.175-178

The Chiefs discussed the Joint Planners report… *not as a supplement to Roundup."* CAB 79/56, War Cabinet, Chiefs of Staff Committee, COS (42) 73rd Meeting (0) 16th July 1942, Effect of Gymnast on Roundup

The issue was explored… *Torch therefore had the field.* CAB 65/31/7, WM (42) 95th Conclusion, Minute 3. War Cabinet meeting, 24th July 1942, 5pm. This document doesn't directly attribute the above remarks to Churchill but his 23rd July Minute to COS maintained that *"it should not be admitted that Gymnast, though it impinges temporarily on Bolero, is at the expense of Roundup."* (D137/2, Prime Minister Directive of 23/7/42, quoted in Howard, *History of the Second World War*, vol.4, p. xxiv). The same source identifies Brooke as COS spokesman on the day, as does Roberts, *Masters and Commanders*, pp.256-257.

Churchill explained that Britain and America… *attacked its hard snout [northern France]."* Sherwood, *Roosevelt and Hopkins*, p.617; Addison, *Churchill*, p.193

The second meeting opened… *and these of inferior quality."* Gilbert, *Winston S. Churchill, vol.VII*, p.184

Stalin accused the British of being *afraid of fighting… win a war without fighting.* Gilbert, *Winston S. Churchill, vol.VII*, p.185

The British Prime Minister was all for leaving… meet Stalin at 7pm. Donald Gillies, *Radical Diplomat: The Life of Archibald Clark Kerr Lord Inverchapel, 1882-1951* (1999), pp.132-136

Stalin invited Churchill to his private… *look at the matter more optimistically."* Frank Costigliola, *Roosevelt's Lost Alliances: How Personal Politics Helped Start the Cold War* (2012), p.176; Blake and Louis (eds), *Churchill*, pp.316-317

The two leaders agreed a joint communiqué… *Great Britain and the United States of America."* Churchill, *The Second World War*, vol. IV, 1986, p.449

Detecting a new mood of optimism in Eighth Army… *regrouped in solid units."* Gilbert, *Winston S. Churchill, vol.VII*, p.215

Montgomery fought an entirely… give chase. A.J. Smithers, *Rude Mechanicals: An Account of Tank Maturity During the Second World War* (1987), pp.131-132

CHAPTER FOURTEEN

Let me... make this clear in case… would have to be found. Rhodes James, Churchill: Complete Speeches, vol.6, pp.6692-6695

I think the best way... for the next twenty-five years. Stoler, *Allies at War*, p.78

Act One of the Second Battle… clearing paths for Montgomery's armour. Spencer C. Tucker (ed), *A Global Chronology of Conflict: From the Ancient World to the Modern Middle East* (2010), p.1982; Philip Kaplan, *Rolling Thunder: A Century of Tank Warfare* (2012), p.133

The *teufelsgarten's* depth… dogfight by Day Six. Patrick Delaforce, *Monty's Marauders: The 4th and 8th Armoured Brigades in the Second World War* (2008), pp.49-50; Niall Barr, *Pendulum Of War: Three Battles at El Alamein* (2005), pp.272-283; Barnett, *The Desert Generals*, pp.272-283

Churchill unleashed a *flow of abuse… one single battle?* Niall Barr, *Pendulum Of War: Three Battles at El Alamein* (2005), pp.366

General Alexander informed Churchill… *in the enemy's rear areas.* Churchill, *The Second World War*, vol. IV, 1986, p.537

Rommel withdrew to Mersa… Egypt into Libya. Andrea Molinari, *Desert Raiders: Axis and Allied Special Forces 1940-43* (2013), p.91; Adrian Stewart, *Eighth Army's Greatest Victories: Alam Halfa to Tunis, 1942-1943* (1999), p.127

The British were extremely bullish… operating from Sicily. Buchanan, *American Grand Strategy in the Mediterranean during World War II*, p.68; Kevin Smith, *Conflict Over Convoys: Anglo-American Logistics Diplomacy in the Second World War* (2002), p.78; Coakley and Leighton, *Global Logistics and Strategy, 1940-43*, pp.417-419

Vichy resistance ceased… transport shortages allowed. P. M. H Bell, *France and Britain, 1940-1994: The Long Separation* (2014), p.45; D'Este, *World War II in the Mediterranean*, pp.9-10; Barnett, *Engage The Enemy More Closely*, p.570

By the end of November, 7,000 Axis troops … battalion of Tiger tanks. Holger Afflerbach and Hew Strachan (eds), *How Fighting Ends: A History of Surrender* (2012), p.352; Mitcham, *Rommel's Desert War*, p.186

Churchill had discussed this idea... *Round-up in late 1943.* CAB 79/57 COS (42) 119th Meeting (0) COS 263rd Meeting, 15th September 1942

Churchill contradicted himself… *no Roundup till 1944."* Churchill, *The Second World War*, vol. IV, 1986, p.512

Churchill anticipated a time… *the French Riviera or... the Balkans".* Gilbert, *Winston S. Churchill, vol. VII*, p.242

On 24th October, Churchill... *Mediterranean theatre."* CAB 66/30 WP (42) 483, Policy for the Conduct of the War. Memorandum by the Minister of Defence, 24th October 1942

On 18th November… *prove physical impossibility.* CAB 80/65 COS (42) 399 (0) Strategy in 1943. Minute by the PM, 18th November 1942

On 29th November, he repudiated… *east to the west.* CAB 80/66 COS (42) 421 (0) Future Strategy. Minute by PM [D208/2], 29th November 1942

COS outlined its preferences… *defeat would be a disaster.* CAB 80/65 COS (42) 345 (0) (Final) COS Committee. American-British Strategy Report, 30th October 1942

General Brooke estimated... operations became feasible. CAB 79/58 COS (42) 156th Meeting (0) COS Committee, Part of COS (42) 296th Meeting on 22nd October 1942

COS proposed that *the successful conclusion… liability for Germany.* CAB 80/65 COS (42) 345 (0) (Final) COS Committee. American-British Strategy Report, 30th October 1942

COS argued that *our main amphibious… amphibious campaign abroad.* CAB 80/65 COS (42) 345 (0) (Final) COS Committee. American-British Strategy Report, 30th October 1942

When Oliver Harvey… learned of the COS strategy… *the exhausted animal.* Harvey, *The War Diaries of Oliver Harvey,* p.183

Blade Force… encountering resolute opposition. Brian Lane Herder, *Operation Torch 1942: The Invasion of French North Africa* (2017), pp.80-82

By early December 1942, only 170,000 American… those in the UK (123,000). Matloff and Snell, *Strategic Planning for Coalition Warfare, 1941-1942* (vol.3), pp.354-355

American planners were equally gloomy… *eight divisions with supporting troops.* Fraser, *Alanbrooke*, p.279

Marshall made a similar point later… *crack in German morale.* Ben-Moshe, *Churchill: Strategy and History,* p.204

America initiated its first Pacific offensive… until February 1943. Kev Darling, *U.S. Carrier War: Design, Development and Operations* (2011), p.99
By the end of 1942, more American troops… UK combined (378,000). Stoler, *Allies at War*, p.85

In Prof. David Reynolds' words… *in the observance."* Reynolds, *From World War to Cold War*, p.42

On 18th November, he'd declared he'd... *prove physical impossibility."* CAB 80/65 COS (42) 399 (0) Strategy in 1943. Minute by the Prime Minister, 18 Nov 1942

COS provided this evidence... forty well-equipped German divisions. CAB 80/66 COS (42) 452 (0) (Final) COS Committee Future Strategy Memorandum, 13th December 1942. The document confirming that the Allies would face 40 German divisions was CAB 80/66 COS (42) 432 (0) COS Committee. Future Strategy. 3rd December 1942

Churchill finally surrendered... *convince first, and then Stalin.* Alanbrooke, *War Diaries, 1939- 1945,* p.349, entry for 16th December 1942

Churchill's abrupt capitulation... *discussions with the President.* Kennedy, *The Business of War,* p.277

British strategy was articulated... *position in the Mediterranean."* CAB 80/66 COS (42) 466 (0) (Final) COS Committee. American-British Strategy in 1943. Report, December 31, 1942.

The US Joint Chiefs renounced Boxing Day... *Western Europe in 1943."* United States Department of State/*Foreign relations of the United States. The Conferences at Washington, 1941-1942, and Casablanca, 1943* (1941-1943) CCS 135 Basic Strategic Concept for 1943, December 26th, 1942.

CHAPTER FIFTEEN

They swarmed... practically all the time. Wedemeyer, *Wedemeyer Reports!* p.192

If I had written... favourable to our ideas. D'Este, *Bitter Victory,* p.51; Stoler, *Allies at War,* p.103

Roosevelt and his Chiefs... *among the planners."* Stoler, *Allies and Adversaries,* p.100; Stoler, *Allies at War,* p.87

Wedemeyer.... described American preparations... *resources on indecisive, limited operations.* Wedemeyer, *Wedemeyer Reports!* p.185

Dwight Eisenhower identified the maturity... *in defeating the real enemy.* Jones, *Britain, the United States and the Mediterranean War, 1942-44,* p.27

Dill assured Brooke that he was closer... *mess they would make of it."* Atkinson, *An Army at Dawn,* p.289; Hastings, *Finest Years,* p.358

In Slessor's words... *Germany in 1943.* Larrabee, *Commander-in-Chief,* p.186

Slessor recalled the tense few moments... *notes on it in pencil.* ibid, p.186

While CCS 170/2 'Final Report of the Combined Chiefs of Staff... Japanese base in eastern New Britain) had been neutralised. US Dept of State. FRUS.

The Conferences at Washington, 1941-1942, and Casablanca, 1943 (1941-1943) CCS 155/1 Conduct of the War in 1943, January 19th, 1943, pp.774-775

Wedemeyer's mordant confession... *and we were conquered."* Wedemeyer, *Wedemeyer Reports!* p.192; Jones, *Britain, the United States and the Mediterranean War, 1942-44, p.44*

CCS169 considered the *"organisation of command, control... his combined staff in London.* US Dept of State. FRUS. *The Conferences at Washington, 1941-1942, and Casablanca, 1943* (1941-1943) CCS 169, Note by the Combined Staff Planners, 22nd January 1943, pp.789-791

This led to the appointment of General Frederick Morgan... detain German forces in France. Zabecki (ed), *World War II in Europe,* p.424; Harrison, *Cross-Channel Attack,* p.49; Thaddeus Holt, *The Deceivers: Allied Military Deception in the Second World War* (2004), pp.477-478

The document... Tedder in charge of air. US Dept of State. FRUS. *The Conferences at Washington, 1941-1942, and Casablanca, 1943* (1941-1943) CCS 171/2/D, Directive to the Commander in Chief, Allied Expeditionary Force in North Africa (Eisenhower), 23rd January 1943, pp.799-800

Brooke... lambasted Eisenhower... *military matters.* Atkinson, *An Army at Dawn*, P.282

Brooke clarified this... *so seriously lacking.* D'Este, *Bitter Victory*, p.50; Michael R. Matheny, *Carrying the War to the Enemy: American Operational Art to 1945* (2011), p.177

Eisenhower reassured Marshall that... *'committee' system of command.* Larrabee, *Commander-in-Chief*, p.430

He also took... *British Empire.* Pendar, *Adventure in Diplomacy*, pp.156-157

Rommel knew the Tunisian game... from Africa, never to return. Anthony Livesey, *Battles of the Great Commanders* (1990), p.159

Patton's II Corps shattered 10th Panzer Army... to avoid encirclement. D. A. Lande, *I Was with Patton: First Person Accounts of WWII in George S. Patton's Command* (2002), p.50; Edward Grace, *The Perilous Road to Rome and Beyond* (2007), p.37

CHAPTER SIXTEEN

At this [Trident] meeting... as quickly as possible. Leahy, *I Was There*, p.9

In private conversation... Brooke told me... sustain in Italy. Eisenhower, *Crusade in Europe*, pp.167-168

Marshall and Secretary of War Henry Stimson… *after the war is over."* Jones, *Britain, the United States and the Mediterranean War, 1942-44,* p.84

America had nine divisions in North Africa… thirteen in the Pacific. Ponting, *Churchill*, pp.599-600; Waldo Heinrichs and Marc Gallicchio, *Implacable Foes: War in the Pacific, 1944-1945* (2017), p.16

Marshall instructed his planners… championing Channel operations. Stoler, *Allies and Adversaries*, pp.119-121; Atkinson, *The Day of Battle*, pp.11-12

Brig. Albert Wedemeyer was delighted... *both naval and air.* Wedemeyer, *Wedemeyer Reports!* p.215

Marshall and Leahy would champion Pacific… *not be ready until tomorrow."* Stoler, *Allies and Adversaries*, pp.119-121

For Churchill, "*the first objective… of their doom.*" US Dept of State. FRUS. *Conferences at Washington and Quebec, 1943. Meeting of the Combined Chiefs of Staff with Roosevelt and Churchill, May 12, 1943. 2:30pm, White House, pp.25-26.*

Churchill enumerated the hurdles... *be under-rated."* US Dept of State. FRUS. *Conferences at Washington and Quebec, 1943. Meeting of the Combined Chiefs of Staff with Roosevelt and Churchill, May 12, 1943. 2:30pm, White House, p.27*

Churchill nevertheless assured his hosts… *could be made."* ibid, p.27

Roosevelt adopted the opposite… *play into Germany's hand."* ibid, p.30

Roosevelt insisted that *if one or other… the spring of 1944.* ibid, p.30

Brooke… sturdily advanced Mediterranean operations… *not an unlimited commitment.* US Dept of State. *FRUS. Conferences at Washington and Quebec, 1943. Meeting of the Combined Chiefs of Staff, May 13, 1943, 10:30am, Federal Reserve Building, p.43 and p.46*

Brooke still argued that *only by… not even then be possible.* ibid, p.46

Brooke still felt moved… *British divisions available in England.* ibid, p.44

Brooke advanced the startling thesis that… *available on our side.* ibid, p.45

Marshall drily observed that *"it appeared… the European war?"* ibid, p.45

General Brooke opened the session… *must be eliminated.* United States Dept of State. *Foreign relations of the United States. Conferences at Washington and Quebec, 1943. Meeting of the Combined Chiefs of Staff, May 19, 1943, 10:30am, Federal Reserve Building,* p.112

Marshall went further, maintaining that… *the logistic problem.* ibid, p.116

Marshall also rejected… Allied troops following invasion. ibid, p.115

The debating chamber was cleared… their masters. ibid, p.116

By the time the Chiefs… military-industrial muscle. US Dept of State. FRUS. *Conferences at Washington and Quebec, 1943. Meeting of the Combined Chiefs of Staff, May 19, 1943, 4:30pm, Federal Reserve Building,* pp.117-118

CCS 237/1 'Resolutions by the Combined Chiefs of Staff (20th May)… *operations from the United Kingdom.* Trident Conference, May 1943, Papers and Minutes of Meetings Edited and Published by the Office, US Secretary, Office of the Combined Chiefs of Staff, 1943 (Digitised 2001), pp.122-123

The Combined Chiefs spent the next five days… in North Africa etc). Trident Conference, May 1943, Papers and Minutes of Meetings Edited and Published by the Office, US Secretary, Office of the Combined Chiefs of Staff, 1943 (Digitised 2001), pp.415-466

The paper presented to Churchill… a finely calibrated compromise. US Dept of State. FRUS. *Conferences at Washington and Quebec, 1943. Meeting of the Combined Chiefs of Staff with Roosevelt and Churchill, May 24, 1943, 4:45pm, White House,* p.189

The failure to nominate … *insurgents of the Balkan countries.* ibid, pp.193-194

Revealing the depth… *our possession a desirable island.* ibid, pp.194-195

Roosevelt, Marshall, King… *amendments for consideration."* ibid, pp.195

CCS 242/3 was finally approved… President and Prime Minister.' Trident Conference, May 1943, Papers and Minutes of Meetings Edited and Published by the Office, US Secretary, Office of the Combined Chiefs of Staff, 1943 (Digitised 2001), pp.169-181

Such was Churchill's… *great success.* Churchill, *The Second World War*, vol. IV, p.738

Eden attended the 31st May session… *reached the Balkan area."* ibid, p.739

Churchill moved to squelch… *now or in the near future."* ibid, p.739

This quote features… misremembered him. D'Este, *Bitter Victory*, p.143

According to Eisenhower… *the Soviet task easier.* ibid, p.143

CHAPTER SEVENTEEN

It is true… the Americans consider… grateful they should be. Higgins, *Soft Underbelly*, p.61

We cannot now rationally ... hearts are not in it. Stimson and Bundy, On Active Service in Peace and War, pp.228-229

Eden explained the matter thus... *force in this point of view.* Jones, *Britain, the United States and the Mediterranean War, 1942-44,* p.85

Ike strongly endorsed a *"policy of joint... under the Allied commander."* Jones, *Britain, the United States and the Mediterranean War, 1942-44*, p.85

The suave Etonian... *operations of the Emperor Claudius."* ibid, p.80

He therefore advised Eden... *British administration' goes too far.* ibid, p.85

Churchill exploded... *country's rights and the British Empire.* ibid, p.86

Chastened, the urbane classicist... *anything but the shadow.* ibid, p.86

When Churchill learned in March 1943... *decisions on the spot.* ibid, pp.89-90

Roosevelt insisted that... *no 'senior partner'."* ibid, p.90

Roosevelt affirmed that the military... *proportion of Americans.* ibid, p.90

The same P.M who had once... *hope I have given satisfaction.* ibid, p.90

One of MacMillan's... Eisenhower's Allied Forces HQ. ibid, pp.91-92

MacMillan reassured Churchill... *protection to British interests."* ibid, p.92

By 17th July, it was clear... had been captured. Barbara Tomblin, *G.I. Nightingales: The Army Nurse Corps in World War II* (1996), p.95

Churchill informed General Smuts... *act by ourselves.* Jones, *Britain, the United States and the Mediterranean War, 1942-44*, p.148

Further clarified his strategic preferences... *the landing were successfully accomplished.* Howard, *History of the Second World War*, vol.4, pp.564-565

In this note he declared that *"the forces available... open in the west."* Gilbert, *Winston S. Churchill, vol.VII,* p.444

Stimson had travelled to Britain to review... *altered my trip accordingly.* Stimson and Bundy, *On Active Service in Peace and War,* pp.223-224

Churchill *at once broke out... the ROUNDHAMMER operation.* ibid, pp.225-226

Churchill expressed his views... *against Mediterranean diversions.* ibid, p.226

After flying to Algiers... *will tend to neutralise each other.* ibid, p.227

Stimson drafted a further memo... *any British commander* ibid, pp.228-229

Stimson therefore urged the President... *this great operation.* ibid, pp.229-230

Stimson recorded his impressions... *delighted at his definiteness.* ibid, p.230

Only five days after General Morgan submitted... Mediterranean theatre until further notice. Molony, *History of the Second World War,* vol. V, pp.200-201

CHAPTER EIGHTEEN

If we once set foot... go the whole hog. Hastings, *Finest Years,* p. 389

I was ordered to invade... typically British. Jones, *Britain, the United States and the Mediterranean War, 1942-44,* p.150

Roundup had anticipated an assault force ... two divisions later in the day. World War Two Inter-Allied Conferences. Quadrant Conference, 1943. Papers and Minutes of Meetings (Joint History Office, Washington DC, 2003). COSSAC (43) 32 (Final), Annex B, Digest of Operation Overlord, July 27, 1943, p.98; Harrison, *Cross-Channel Attack,* p.74

Morgan also advocated: (i) a major reduction... Overlord's first two months. CAB 80/73 COS (Q) 8 (Revise) Chiefs of Staff Committee, Operation Overlord - Outline Plan. Covering Note by the British Chiefs of Staff, SS Queen Mary, 10th August 1943

German fighter strength could be reduced... *enemy's front line units."* World War Two Inter-Allied Conferences. Quadrant Conference, 1943. Papers and Minutes of Meetings (Joint History Office, Washington DC, 2003). COSSAC (43) 32 (Final), Annex B, Digest of Operation Overlord, p.101; Harrison, *Cross-Channel Attack,* p.77

Morgan admonished... *our own preparations."* World War Two Inter-Allied Conferences. Quadrant Conference, 1943. Papers and Minutes of Meetings (Joint History Office, Washington DC, 2003). Annex B Operation Overlord, COSSAC (43) 8, 15 July 1943 (p.96) and COSSAC (43) 32 (Final), p.106

COS responded to Morgan's plan... *General Morgan's first condition.* CAB 80/73, COS (Q) 3 Revise, Chiefs of Staff Committee, Operations in the European Theatre of War Aide-Memoire, 6th August 1943

The aide memoire further... *throughout the winter [of 1943-44].* ibid

The Chiefs urged the Allies *"to exploit... Milan-Turin area as our objective."* ibid

The Chiefs' 10th August Overlord... *to be slow."* CAB 80/73 COS (Q) 8 (Revise) Chiefs of Staff Committee, Operation Overlord - Outline Plan. Covering Note by the British Chiefs of Staff, SS Queen Mary, 10th August 1943

The only issue of substance confirmed… Eisenhower's departure for Overlord. Stoler, *Allies in War,* p.125, Gilbert, *Churchill and America*, p.281

As Churchill acknowledged… *constantly with him."* Reynolds, *In Command of History,* p.386

General Brooke opened… *the desired result.* World War Two Inter-Allied Conferences. Quadrant Conference, 1943. Papers and Minutes of Meetings (Joint History Office, Washington DC, 2003), pp.434-435

Admiral King who observed that… *accomplishing Overlord."* ibid p.435

It was General Marshall who deftly dissected… *air bombing alone.* ibid p.436

In such a case, Marshall warned… *towards the Pacific.* ibid, p.436

General Brooke's diary offers a flavour… *cross-Channel and Italian operations.* Howard, *History of the Second World War*, vol.4, p.569

The compromise document of 17th August… they later repudiated it. World War Two Inter-Allied Conferences. Quadrant Conference, 1943. Papers and Minutes of Meetings (Joint History Office, Washington DC, 2003), pp.87-89

Churchill re-emphasised General Morgan's preconditions... speedily endorsed by Marshall. World War Two Inter-Allied Conferences. Quadrant Conference, 1943. Papers and Minutes of Meetings (Joint History Office, Washington DC, 2003), 1st Meeting of the President and Prime Minister with the Combined Chiefs of Staff, 19th August 1943, 5:30pm, pp.395-404

Churchill advised that *"he was not… the kind suggested."* ibid, pp.395-404

On 23rd August, Churchill revived… *have to be abandoned.* World War Two Inter-Allied Conferences. Quadrant Conference, 1943. Papers and Minutes of Meetings (Joint History Office, Washington DC, 2003), 2nd Meeting of the President and Prime Minister with the Combined Chiefs of Staff, 23rd August 1943, 5:30pm, pp.405-413

The Final Report to the President and Prime Minister… *decision of the Combined Chiefs of Staff.* World War Two Inter-Allied Conferences. Quadrant Conference, 1943. Papers and Minutes of Meetings (Joint History Office, Washington DC, 2003), pp.249-263

Morgan's draft plan… *with Overlord"* was endorsed. ibid, pp.249-263

The 20th July COS 'stand-still' order was revoked on 19th August. Playfair et al, *The Mediterranean and Middle East:* Vol. 5, p.201

Operation Avalanche… defeat it in detail. Walter J. Eldredge, *Finding My Father's War: A Baby Boomer And The 2nd Chemical Mortar Battalion In World War II* (2004), p.95; Eric Linklater, *The Campaign in Italy* (1977), p.72

Kesselring ignored… secure the beachhead. Zabecki (ed), *World War II in Europe,* pp.1665-1666; Barbara Tomblin, *With Utmost Spirit: Allied Naval Operations in the Mediterranean* (2004), pp.282-283; Kenneth V. Smith, *Naples - Foggia* (1994), pp.8-14

German forces withdrew… Volturno and Biferno Rivers. Zabecki (ed), *World War II in Europe,* p.1666; Higgins, *Soft Underbelly,* p.120; Blumenson, *United States Army in World War 2, Mediterranean Theater of Operations,* p.172

Most had observed Napoleon's… *from the top.'* O'Donnell, *Beyond Valor,* p.57

CHAPTER NINETEEN

I will not allow… to be postponed. Moran, *Churchill,* p.122

To satisfy American shortsightedness… whole conduct of the war. Alanbrooke, *War Diaries,* p.465 and p.475

Germany claimed the territory… southern Greece and the Greek islands. Raphael Lemkin, *Axis Rule in Occupied Europe: Laws of Occupation, Analysis of Government, Proposals for Redress* (2005), p.185

A lengthy 'shopping list'… locomotives and rolling stock. Howard, *History of the Second World War,* vol.4, p.380

Britain was determined… Ankara for talks. Ehrman, *History of the Second World War,* Volume V, p.89; Selim Deringil, *Turkish Foreign Policy During the Second World War: An 'Active' Neutrality* (2004), p.148

Phase One of Hardihood proposed… two full armoured divisions. Ehrman, *History of the Second World War,* Volume V, p.90

General Ismay… highlighted the continuity… *Gallipoli campaign in 1915.* Ismay, *The Memoirs of General the Lord Ismay,* p.322

Accolade presented… *prizes at little cost."* Ponting, *Churchill,* p.608

The operation was to be largely conducted… South East Asia on 21st August. Ehrman, *History of the Second World War,* Volume V, p.92

Britain combed through… *and none of battle.* Hastings, *Finest Years,* p.408

Middle East Command warned… *Rooke's men taking Gibraltar.* Ehrman, *History of the Second World War,* Volume V, pp.92-93; Ponting, *Churchill,* p.608

On 9th September, British agents… German control by 13th September. Ehrman, *History of the Second World War,* Volume V, p.93; Nicholas Rankin, *Ian Fleming's Commandos: The Story of the Legendary 30 Assault Unit* (2011), p.207; Richard Lamb, *Churchill As War Leader: Right or Wrong* (1991), p.239

This loss and the operation's impending… *future of the Italian campaign.* Alanbrooke, *War Diaries, 1939- 1945,* p.458-459

Churchill then begged Roosevelt... *a cardinal error in strategy.* Churchill, *The Second World War*, vol. V, pp.188-189

Roosevelt's reply evidenced... *American Chiefs of Staff agree.* Kimball, *Churchill and Roosevelt:* The Complete Correspondence, vol2, p.501

Churchill then proposed... *you and your Chiefs of Staff.* Churchill, *The Second World War*, vol. V, 2010, p.189

British losses in the débâcle... 4,800 men killed, wounded or captured. Barnett, *Engage The Enemy More Closely*, p.684; Spencer C. Tucker, *The Great War, 1914-1918* (1998), p.536

In his 21st October appreciation... *to hold what we have gained.* Churchill, *The Second World War*, vol. V, 2010, pp.219

At a 19th October COS meeting... *spring of 1944.* CAB 79/66 COS (43) 254th Meeting (0) COS Committee, Minutes of a Staff Conference held on 19th October 1943 at 10:30pm

Churchill responded by calmly stating... *Germany as already promised.* ibid

When Churchill made these remarks, only five American divisions were based in Britain. This refers to the one US division present in the UK by July 1943 and the Trident-Quadrant agreement to transfer four US divisions from the Mediterranean to the UK by November 1943. Matloff, *Strategic Planning for Coalition Warfare, 1943-44*, pp.391-392

The 11th November aide memoire... *the satellite Balkan countries.* Ehrman, *History of the Second World War,* Volume V, pp.109-111

While these ventures were intended... *in the [Overlord] assault and follow-up.*" Ehrman, *History of the Second World War,* Volume V, pp.109-111

In Section Five, COS confirmed... *the correct strategy.*" ibid, pp.109-111

In section eight, COS expressed... *consistent with this.*" ibid, pp.109-111

This reversal of priorities... *a good prospect of success.*" ibid, pp.109-111

Churchill minuted '*I cordially...* multi-layered document. ibid, pp.109-111

Churchill grumbled that Chinese affairs... *last place at Cairo.*" Aron Shai, *Britain And China, 1941-47: Imperial Momentum* (1984), p.24

After giving his customary... *policy for the Mediterranean.* Blake and Louis (eds), *Churchill*, p.349; Barnett, *Engage The Enemy More Closely*, p.685

Churchill made one final... *goddamned beach.*" Hastings, *Finest Years*, p.421

CHAPTER TWENTY

There I sat... knew the right way home. Lehrman, *Lincoln & Churchill,* p.251

Sure, we are preparing...lining up with the Russians. Moran, *Churchill,* p.132

Roosevelt repeatedly asserted... *eastern Mediterranean were undertaken."* US Dept of State. FRUS. *Diplomatic Papers. The Conferences at Cairo and Tehran, 1943. First Plenary Meeting, November 28, 1943, 4pm, Conference Room, Soviet Embassy, p.495 & Second Plenary Meeting, November 29, 1943, 4pm, Conference Room, Soviet Embassy,* p.538

Stalin shared the President's Mediterranean antipathy ... *these scattered forces.* US Dept of State. FRUS. Diplomatic Papers. *The Conferences at Cairo and Tehran, 1943. First Plenary Meeting, November 28, 1943, 4pm, Conference Room, Soviet Embassy,* p.490 and p.494

The offer was first made on the 29th... *transfer of German troops to the west.* US Dept of State. FRUS. Diplomatic Papers. *The Conferences at Cairo and Tehran, 1943. Second Plenary Meeting, November 29, 1943, 4pm, Conference Room, Soviet Embassy, p.537;* US Dept of State. FRUS. Diplomatic Papers. *The Conferences at Cairo and Tehran, 1943. Third Plenary Meeting, November 30, 1943, 4pm, Conference Room, Soviet Embassy,* p.577

On 28th November, he informed Churchill... victory in Europe. US Dept of State. FRUS. Diplomatic Papers. *The Conferences at Cairo and Tehran, 1943. First Plenary Meeting, November 28, 1943, 4pm, Conference Room, Soviet Embassy,* p.489

At Roosevelt's urging, the US Joint Chiefs... should not affect Overlord. US Dept of State. FRUS. Diplomatic Papers. *The Conferences at Cairo and Tehran, 1943. Second Plenary Meeting, November 29, 1943, 4pm, Conference Room, Soviet Embassy,* p.539 *and* pp.550-552

The Chiefs set to work at 9:30am... a solution by lunchtime. US Dept of State. FRUS. Diplomatic Papers. *The Conferences at Cairo and Tehran, 1943. Meeting of the Combined Chiefs of Staff, November 30, 1943, 9:30am, British Legation,* p.555

General Brooke observed *"no Russian offensive... end of May."* ibid, p.561

The Chiefs placed their findings... at that time. ibid, pp.563-564

The Soviet leader... *placed on this decision.* US Dept of State. FRUS. Diplomatic Papers. *The Conferences at Cairo and Tehran, 1943. Roosevelt-Churchill-Stalin Luncheon Meeting, November 30, 1943, 1:30pm, Roosevelt's Quarters, Soviet Embassy,* p.565

On 29th November, Churchill warned... *moral precepts.* Toye, *Churchill's Empire,* p.245

[Roosevelt] had promised Chiang two operations… *readily apparent reason."* US Dept of State. FRUS. Diplomatic Papers. *The Conferences at Cairo and Tehran, 1943. Meeting of the Combined Chiefs of Staff with Roosevelt and Churchill, December 4, 1943, 11am Roosevelt's Villa, p.680*

Churchill countered that *"this 'very good… narrow margin."* ibid, *p.680*

General Marshall insisted that *if Buccaneer… would be at hazard.* ibid, *p.681*

Cunningham argued… *in the Pacific.* US Dept of State. FRUS. Diplomatic Papers. *The Conferences at Cairo and Tehran, 1943. Meeting of the Combined Chiefs of Staff, December 5, 1943, 10:30am, Mena House, p.702*

Roosevelt gave way on 5th December… *"Buccaneer is off."* Eisenhower, *Allies,* pp.421-422

On 5th December, CCS 423/2 'Operations in the European… to Overlord and Anvil. US Dept of State. FRUS. Diplomatic Papers. *The Conferences at Cairo and Tehran, 1943. CCS 423/2 Report by the Combined Chiefs of Staff. Operations in the European Theater, Cairo, 5 December 1943, p.796*

These recommendations… incorporated into CCS 426/1… Churchill and Roosevelt on 6th December. US Dept of State. FRUS. Diplomatic Papers. *The Conferences at Cairo and Tehran, 1943. CCS 426/1 Report of the Combined Chiefs of Staff to the President and Prime Minister, Cairo, 6 December 1943.*

If Turkey remained neutral …*English speaking peoples."* US Dept of State. FRUS. Diplomatic Papers. *The Conferences at Cairo and Tehran, 1943. First Tripartite Meeting of Heads of Government, December 4, 1943, 5pm, President's Villa, p.691*

The Allies had nothing… *cutting off armament supplies."* William M. Hale, *Turkish Foreign Policy Since 1774* (2013), p.72; Tamkin, *Britain, Turkey and the Soviet Union, 1940-45,* pp.137-142

On 8th January 1944, General Maitland… Allied Armies in Italy. Blumenson, *United States Army in World War 2, Mediterranean Theater of Operations*, p.294; Institute for National Strategic Studies: National Defense University, *Allied Command Structures in the New NATO,* p.49

Throughout December and January… *will certainly frighten Kesselring."* D'Este, *World War II in the Mediterranean, 1942-1945,* p.130

CHAPTER TWENTY-ONE

Of course there is risk… no glory, no adventure. Daniel K. R. Crosswell, *Beetle: The Life of General Walter Bedell Smith* (2010), p.559

I felt like… unnecessary [because of Shingle]. Dominick Graham and Shelford Bidwell, *Tug of War: The Battle for Italy, 1943-45* (2004), *p.139*

Eureka had approved... theatre for that purpose. Blumenson, *Anzio,* p.42

In Shingle I... shelved on 18th December. Eisenhower, Eisenhower, p.52; Parker, The Second World War, p.188. Eisenhower suggests that Frosinone is twenty miles south of Anzio but this author's research reveals this to be incorrect.

The *"stagnation"* on the Gustav... *eat your rations."* James Scott Wheeler, *Jacob L. Devers: A General's Life* (2015), p.250; Atkinson, *The Day of Battle,* p.322. The latter comments are from early January 1944 but reflect Churchill's frustration over the Italian campaign in December 1943.

On Christmas Eve... weakened German Line. Clark, Anzio, pp.64-65; Steven Ross, *American War Plans, 1941-1945: The Test of Battle* (2007), p.87; Thomas E. Griess (ed), *The Second World War: Europe and the Mediterranean* (2002), p.239. Churchill had already agreed the essence of the scheme with Brooke on 18th December, Gilbert, *Winston S. Churchill, vol.VII,* p.611

The possibility that German... *position at Cassino."* Atkinson, *The Day of Battle,* pp.323-326

Eisenhower... quickly identified... *could be achieved.* Eisenhower, *Crusade in Europe,* pp.212-213

Churchill discounted these concerns... Shingle was on! Atkinson, *The Day of Battle,* pp.323-28; Clark, Anzio, pp.67-68

The American commanders charged... Italy by 5th February. Clark, Anzio, p.76; D'Este, *World War II in the Mediterranean, 1942-1945,* p.132; Eisenhower, They Fought At Anzio, pp.91-95; Atkinson, *The Day of Battle,* pp.324-325

On 12th January, Alexander... *utmost possible speed."* Greenfield (ed), *Command Decisions,* pp.329-330

Part One of Clark's orders... than **to** Colli Laziali. Clark, Anzio, p.77

Clark further advised... *got into trouble."* Atkinson, *The Day of Battle,* p.355

By the end of January, 61,000 troops... towards the sea. Atkinson, *The Day of Battle,* pp.371-380; Barbara Tomblin, *G.I. Nightingales: The Army Nurse Corps in World War II* (1996), p.107; Horace Edward Henderson, *The Greatest Blunders of World War II: How Errors Mistakes and Blunders Determined Victory or Defeat* (2001), p.326; Blumenson, *Anzio,* pp.86-89

German troops arrived from... position around Anzio. Atkinson, *The Day of Battle,* p.380; O'Donnell, *Beyond Valor,* p.82; Mark Zuehlke, *The Liri Valley: Canada's World War II Breakthrough to Rome* (2004), p.17

Lucas attacked first... inside the beachhead. O'Donnell, *Beyond Valor,* p.82; Zabecki (ed), *World War II in Europe,* p.1360; Horace Edward Henderson, *The Greatest Blunders of World War II: How Errors Mistakes and Blunders Determined Victory or Defeat* (2001), p.326

The Germans launched... naval bombardment and air support. Stephen Badsey (ed), *The Hutchinson Atlas of World War II Battle Plans: Before and After (2016),* p.64; Steven J. Zaloga, *US Armored Units in the North African and Italian Campaigns 1942-45* (2013), p.76

General Lucian Truscott... on 23rd February. Clark, Anzio, p.199

According to one veteran... *right out of Journeys End.* *Tough Old Gut: Italy, November 1942 - June 1944,* Episode 13 of Thames TV series, *World At War* (1973) (approx 36 mins into the programme, transcribed by author)

Alexander Cadogan noted... *beloved of Generals".* Jones, *Britain, the United States and the Mediterranean War, 1942-44,* p.159

The Combined Chiefs... *offensive in Italy."* Thomas E. Griess (ed), *The Second World War: Europe and the Mediterranean* (2002), p.243; Ehrman, *History of the Second World War,* Vol. V, p.259; Clark, Anzio, pp.267-268

Under Diadem, Fifteenth Army... *Eighth and Fifth Armies.* Wilson A. Heefner, *Dogface Soldier: The Life of General Lucian K. Truscott, Jr.* (2010), p.170; Rudolf Bohmler, *Monte Cassino: A German View* (2015), p.255; Eisenhower, *They Fought at Anzio,* p.227-228; Nicolson, *Alex,* pp.248-249; John Gooch (ed), *Decisive Campaigns of the Second World War* (2004), p.149

Reinforced by British-imperial forces... the following day. Buchanan, *American Grand Strategy in the Mediterranean during World War II,* p.151; Philip A. St. John, *History of the Third Infantry Division* (1994), p.17; James Holland, *Italy's Sorrow: A Year of War, 1944-45* (2008), p.163; Wilson A. Heefner, *Dogface Soldier: The Life of General Lucian K. Truscott, Jr.* (2010), p.175

Clark now sabotaged... 'open city' on 3rd June. Atkinson, *The Day of Battle,* p.546; Zabecki (ed), *World War II in Europe,* p.1361; Bryn Evans, *The Decisive Campaigns of the Desert Air Force, 1942-45* (2014), p.170

American forces entered Rome... towards the Gothic Line. Buchanan, *American Grand Strategy in the Mediterranean during World War II,* p.151; Clark, Anzio, pp.303-304

[Clark's] memoirs... *had earned it.* Clark, *Calculated Risk,* p.332; Brian Harpur, *The Impossible Victory: A Personal Account of the Battle for the River Po* (1980), p.110

Buchanan draws attention... wider political picture. Buchanan, *American Grand Strategy in the Mediterranean during World War II,* pp.152-153

Churchill endorsed… from entering Rome. Kimball, Churchill and Roosevelt: The Complete Correspondence, vol3, p.176; John Patrick Diggins, *Mussolini and Fascism: The View from America* (1975), pp.380-381; Buchanan, *American Grand Strategy in the Mediterranean during World War II,* p.154

On 9th June, Badoglio… replaced by Bonomi. Buchanan, *American Grand Strategy in the Mediterranean during World War II,* pp.153-154

The United States granted… Italian civilian relief. Patrick J. Hearden, *Architects of Globalism: Building a New World Order During World War II* (2002), p.80

The President… *mischievous elements there."* Kimball, *Churchill and Roosevelt:* The Complete Correspondence, vol3, p.189; Patrick J. Hearden, *Architects of Globalism: Building a New World Order During World War II* (2002), p.80

Churchill could only splutter… *government they please?"* Buchanan, *American Grand Strategy in the Mediterranean during World War II,* p.154

CHAPTER TWENTY-TWO

I firmly believe that… theatres of war. Hastings, *Finest Years,* p.385

Do you realise… have been killed? Richard M. Langworth, *Winston Churchill, Myth and Reality: What He Actually Did and Said* (2017), p.137

The Allies had invaded Sicily… reach Paris by D+90. Brooks (ed), *Montgomery and the Battle of Normandy,* pp.34-36 provides Montgomery's own critique of Morgan's plan and his revised Overlord plan; overviews of the Overlord planning process are available in Hamilton, *Monty,* pp.511-516; Joseph Balkoski, *Utah Beach: The Amphibious Landing and Airborne Operations on D-Day* (2006), pp.4-13; Royle, *Montgomery,* pp.108-112

Normandy remained the focus… when the time came. Terry Crowdy, *Deceiving Hitler: Double-Cross and Deception in World War II* (2008), p.234; Eisenhower, *Eisenhower,* p.107

On 21st January, Ike drafted… 96 landing craft tanks (LCTs). Chandler (ed), The Papers of Dwight David Eisenhower, vol. 3, pp.1672-1675; Eisenhower, *Eisenhower,* pp.123-124; Hamilton, Monty, p.517

The Combined Chiefs… three division assault. Eisenhower, *Eisenhower,* pp.124-125; Zabecki (ed), *World War II in Europe,* p.1495; Chapter 25 considers Eisenhower's relationship with the allied bomber force.

[Churchill] conceded that… *I have my doubts.* Ambrose, *The Supreme Commander,* p.400

Similar sentiment surfaced… *skill are apparent.* Churchill, *The Second World War,* vol. V, p.602

Churchill could always be relied upon… *liquidate this force.* ibid, p.608

On 18th March… *shaking together.*" Gilbert, *Churchill and America,* p.295

However, a draft note… *what are we going to do?* Ponting, *Churchill,* p.613

On 1st April he warned… *into the west.* Gilbert, *Winston S. Churchill, vol.VII,* p.725

Churchill expressed further distaste… *has been taken.* ibid, p.745

Churchill revealed his own… *off the Mediterranean operations.* ibid, p.767

Churchill's antipathy… three weeks before D-Day. Daniel K. R. Crosswell, *Beetle: The Life of General Walter Bedell Smith* (2010), p.609

To a supporter… *were of success*" Gilbert, *Winston S. Churchill, vol.VII,* p.771

Dwight Eisenhower… *Sir Alan's tactical views.* D'Este, *Eisenhower,* p.502

CHAPTER TWENTY-THREE

Our long term… Eastern Mediterranean. Christina Goulter-Zervoudakis, *The Politicization of Intelligence: The British Experience in Greece, 1941-1944,* Intelligence and National Security, vol. 13, no.1 (Spring 1998), p.183

It seems to me… win Communist approval. Lars Bærentzen et al (eds), *Studies in the History of the Greek Civil War, 1945-1949* (1987), p.43

In May 1944, Foreign Secretary Eden… America endorsed the agreement. Jones, *Britain, the United States and the Mediterranean War, 1942-44,* p.190; Barker, *British Policy in South East Europe in the Second World War,* p.140

While Ambassador Halifax… without American involvement. Barker, *Churchill and Eden at War,* pp.279-281; Jones, *Britain, the United States and the Mediterranean War, 1942-44,* pp.190-191; Kent, *British Imperial Strategy and the Origins of the Cold War, 1944-49,* pp.26-27; John O. Iatrides, *Revolt in Athens: The Greek Communist 'Second Round', 1944-1945* (1972), p.80

On 9th August, the British Cabinet… Germany's departure. Ponting, *Churchill,* p.671

On 9th October, Churchill flew… with the Soviet dictator. Gilbert, *Churchill and America,* p.315

After disparaging the leaders… *Stalin about Romania.* Jones, *Britain, the United States and the Mediterranean War, 1942-44,* p.216

Stalin agreed... *first say in Greece.* Gilbert, *Winston S. Churchill, vol.VII,* p.991

In his so-called 'naughty document'… a souvenir. Reynolds, *In Command of History,* pp.458-459; Ponting, *Churchill,* pp.661-662; Fenby, *Alliance,* p.322-323

On 13th October, Prime Minister Mikolajczyk… their own authority. Prażmowska, *Poland,* p.155; Jan Karski, *The Great Powers and Poland: From Versailles to Yalta* (2014), pp.429-434

Churchill began with cajolery… *continue to recognise you.* Halik Kochanski, *The Eagle Unbowed: Poland and the Poles in the Second World War* (2012), p.455; David Dilks, *Churchill and Company: Allies and Rivals in War and Peace* (2015), p.195; Jenkins, *Churchill,* p.762

Buffeted by Churchill… Mikolajczyk to resign. Arnold A. Offner, *Another Such Victory: President Truman and the Cold War, 1945-1953* (2002), p.28

EAM… was a popular front… *the form of its government."* John O. Iatrides, *Revolt in Athens: The Greek Communist 'Second Round', 1944-1945* (1972), p.22; John O. Iatrides and Linda Wrigley (eds), *Greece at the Crossroads: The Civil War and Its Legacy* (1995), pp.54-55

ELAS… EAM's military wing… territory around Epirus. Richard C. Hall (ed), *War in the Balkans: An Encyclopedic History from the Fall of the Ottoman to the Breakup of Yugoslavia* (2014), p.100

Following a purge… conservative in outlook. Buchanan, *American Grand Strategy in the Mediterranean during World War II,* p.259; André Gerolymatos, *An International Civil War: Greece, 1943-1949* (2016), p.97

[Churchill was] looking forward to… *ground is well chosen.* Churchill, *The Second World War*, vol. VI, p.250

The Greek honeymoon… guns and identity. Tim Jones, *SAS: The First Secret Wars: The Unknown Years of Combat and Counter-Insurgency* (2005), p.36; Walter L. Hixson (ed), *The American Experience in World War II, Vol.5: The United States in the European Theater* (2003), p.143; Kimball, Churchill and Roosevelt: The Complete Correspondence, vol3, pp.466-7 and pp.486-7

On 2nd December, the six EAM… wounding 150. Shrader, *The Withered Vine,* p.39; Neni Panourgiá, *Dangerous Citizens: The Greek Left and the Terror of the State* (2009), p.68

ELAS fighters poured into Athens… the city's 25 police stations. Efraim Inbar (ed), *Democracies and Small Wars* (2005), p.125; John Koliopoulos and Thanos Veremis, *Greece: The Modern Sequel, from 1831 to the Present* (2002), pp.77-80

Churchill responded… *bloodshed if necessary.* Knight, *Churchill,* pp.206-207

Two divisions, two infantry brigades… discuss armistice terms. Vlavianos, *Greece, 1941-49,* p.51; Higgins, *Soft Underbelly,* p.198; Nicolson, *Alex,* p.269-70; Shrader, *The Withered Vine,* pp.41-42; Jonathan M. House, *A Military History of the Cold War, 1944-1962* (2012), pp.13-14

As General Alexander indicated… needed a political solution. Nicolson, *Alex*, p.272; Herbert Feis, *Churchill-Roosevelt-Stalin: The War They Waged and the Peace They Sought* (1957), p.541

Papandreou tendered… *comes to his senses."* Walter L. Hixson (ed), *The American Experience in World War II, Vol.5: The United States in the European Theater* (2003), p.143; Vlavianos, *Greece, 1941-49*, p.50

Churchill formed a strong prejudice… *against existing ministers."* Robert Frazier, *Anglo-American Relations With Greece: The Coming Of The Cold War 1942-47* (1991), p.64; Gilbert, *Winston S. Churchill, vol.VII*, p.1103

Leeper, MacMillan, General Alexander… *much was turning."* Vlavianos, *Greece, 1941-49*, p.51; Churchill, *The Second World War*, vol. VI, p.270

Churchill and Damaskinos met… *shrewd political judgements."* Gilbert, *Winston S. Churchill, vol.VII*, pp.1119-1132

Between 26th-28th December… return to London. Jonathan M. House, *A Military History of the Cold War, 1944-1962* (2012), p.15; Fenby, *Alliance*, pp.339-340

General Scobie renewed… ceasefire terms. Shrader, *The Withered Vine*, p.41; Christopher M. Woodhouse, *The Struggle for Greece, 1941-1949* (2002), p.133

Churchill returned to London… later that day. Hastings, *Finest Years*, p.539; Fenby, *Alliance*, p.340; Churchill, *The Second World War*, vol. VI, pp.279-280

Under the terms… scheduled for 1946. Shrader, *The Withered Vine*, p.43

On 11th December… *in Romania.* Gilbert, *Winston S. Churchill, vol.VII*, p.1095

Two months later… *for the sake of his larger plans.* Moran, *Churchill*, p.233

CHAPTER TWENTY-FOUR

The Mediterranean route… of the British Commonwealth CAB 119/65 MSC (42) 3 (Third Revise), November 1942, Post-War Strategic Requirements in the Middle East

It will be the height of absurdity… 'losing the peace' with a vengeance. FO 141/1043, no.1 Anglo-Egyptian Treaty Revision at San Francisco: inward telegram no.1092 from Lord Killearn to Foreign Office on the need to retain a predominant position in Egypt, reproduced in Kent, *Egypt and the Defence of the Middle East, vol1*, pp.15-16

The Military Sub-Committee (MSC)… *secure lasting peace.* Chris Madsen, The Royal Navy and German Naval Disarmament, 1942-1947 (1998), p.1; Lewis, *Changing Direction*, p.345

The MSC embraced… ranking officer. Lewis, *Changing Direction*, pp.19-22

In the second half of 1942… *paramount necessity.* CAB 119/65 MSC (42) 3, Sept 1942 Post-War Strategic Requirements - Middle East, Second Draft

Controlling the Middle East demanded… *necessary for this control.* ibid

Controlling the Persian Gulf permitted… *with Haifa or Suez.* ibid

Interest in the region was… *Persian Gulf and the Egyptian oil areas.* ibid

The November 1942 draft… *meet any such threat.* CAB 119/65 MSC (42) 3 (Third Revise), November 1942, Post-War Strategic Requirements in the Middle East

The MSC's evaluation... *countries East of Suez.* CAB 119/65 JP (42) 1025, 20th December 1942, Post-War Strategic Requirements in the Mediterranean Basin (4th Draft)

The MSC could not *"forecast what… steps to regain that control.* ibid

The final draft of the 'Mediterranean Basin'… *post-war conditions.* CAB 119/65 MSC/53 (Final), Post-War Strategic Requirements in the Mediterranean Basin, 25th June 1943

Much improved military conditions… *interested Departments of State.* Lewis, *Changing Direction*, p.346

In December 1943… *British vital interest.* CAB 81/41 PHP (43) 41 (Final), 13th December 1943, British Strategic Needs in the Levant States, inc. Appendix B 'Oil in the Middle East'

According to the PHPC, *the security… road from Haifa to Baghdad.* ibid

The eastern Mediterranean and Middle East… *scene of the threat.* ibid

The paper concluded by noting that… *the Arabian Littoral* ibid

Suez Canal Company headquarters… British interests in the artery. Simon C. Smith (ed), *Reassessing Suez 1956: New Perspectives on the Crisis and Its Aftermath* (2008), p.24; CAB 65/43, WM (44) 127th Conclusions, Conclusions of War Cabinet Meeting at 10 Downing St, 25th September 1944 at 5:30pm (plus WP (44) 556, Suez Canal Committee Note by Secretary of the War Cabinet, 4th October 1944)

Two issues concerned... vital significance to Empire. CAB 95/18, SC (M) (44) 1st Meeting, Suez Canal Committee, Minutes of Meeting in Conference Room B, Great George St, 11th October 1944, 5:15pm

The Suez Canal Committee met regularly… *user of the Canal.* ibid

Fearing Italian aggression in 1936… British troops from the Canal Zone. Obieta, *The International Status of the Suez Canal*, pp.15-17; Derek Hopwood, *Egypt 1945-1990: Politics and Society* (1993), pp.23-26

His April 1945 War Cabinet memo... *special position in the area.* CAB 66/65, WP (45) 256 'Defence of the Middle East': War Cabinet Memorandum by Mr. Eden, 13 April 1945, reproduced in Kent, *Egypt and the Defence of the Middle East, vol.1,* pp. 6-9

According to Eden… *of the Iraq-Persian Gulf area.* ibid, pp. 6-9

CHAPTER TWENTY-FIVE

Continuous reflection leaves… even terms in the open field. Michael L. Dockrill and Brian J. C. McKercher (eds), *Diplomacy and World Power: Studies in British Foreign Policy, 1890-1951* (2002), p.217

The moral effect… to terrify Boche. Grayling, *Among the Dead Cities,* p.103

The August 1941 Butt Report… slumped to one in ten. Hastings, *Bomber Command,* p.108; Frederick Fooy, *One of Thousands: A Navigator in the European Air War* (2015), p.158

In September 1941, the suave… *scale, of Air Control.* Ponting, *Churchill, p.539;* Hastings, *Bomber Command,* p.132

Directive 22… *of the industrial workers."* David H. N. Johnson, *Rights in Air Space* (1965), p.49

To avoid any uncertainty… *aircraft factories."* Alan J. Levine, *The Strategic Bombing of Germany, 1940-1945* (1992), p.37

Directive 22 also identified… secondary targets (further afield). Tony Joel, *The Dresden Firebombing: Memory and the Politics of Commemorating Destruction* (2013), p.49

Lord Cherwell's De-Housing… end the war. Zuckerman, *From Apes to Warlords,* p.142

At its February 1945 peak… 1,600 frontline bombers. Hastings, *Bomber Command,* p.136

The authors of the Hull/ Birmingham… *health of either town.* Zuckerman, *From Apes to Warlords,* p.143

If Britain was to win the war… even a second Dunkirk. AIR 14/3507, Harris to Churchill, 17th June 1942

The Air Marshal believed that… *surrender is inevitable."* Garrett, *Ethics and Airpower in World War II,* p.171; Larrabee, *Commander-in-Chief, p.588*

On 17th June, he denounced… entering service. AIR 14/3507, Harris to Churchill, 17th June 1942

Harris was under pressure… *the war cabinet."* Garrett, *Ethics and Airpower in World War II,* p.15

Even more gratifying… *the offensive.* Harris, *Bomber Offensive,* pp.112-113

Between March-July 1943, the steel works… 39% of the city lay in ruins. Zabecki (ed), *World War II in Europe,* p.1267; Alan J. Levine, *The Strategic Bombing of Germany, 1940-1945* (1992), p.115; Vera Brittain, *One Voice: Pacifist Writings from the Second World War* (2005), p.148; Webster and Frankland, *The Strategic Air Offensive Against Germany, 1939-45,* vol. II Endeavour, Part 4, p.48

Hamburg was the first time… *quite powerless.* Keitel, *The Memoirs of Field-Marshal Wilhelm Keitel,* p.187

General Morgan delivered… 1st May 1944 deadline. See Chapters 17 and 18

On 3rd November, he addressed… *not got far to go.* PREM 3/14/1, Harris to Churchill, 3rd November 1943

Harris evinced a staunch belief… *cost Germany the war.* ibid

Harris' confident assertion… reinforced these preferences. Phillips Payson O'Brien, *How the War Was Won: Air-Sea Power and Allied Victory in World War II* (2015), p.283

Churchill endorsed Harris' intention… *a mortal blow."* Churchill, *The Second World War,* vol. V, p.460

The RAF lost 1,050 aircraft… attacks on the German capital. Grant, *1001 Battles That Changed the Course of History,* p.859; Spencer C. Tucker, *Battles that Changed History: An Encyclopedia of World Conflict* (2011), p.550

According to Montgomery's draft… back into the sea. See Chapter 22

In Prof. Zuckerman's mid-January… Allies' true intention. Eisenhower, *Eisenhower,* p.114; Mary Barbier, *D-Day Deception: Operation Fortitude and the Normandy Invasion* (2007), p.144; John F. Kreis (ed), *Piercing the Fog: Intelligence and Army Air Forces Operations in World War II* (1996), p.226

Harris outlined his objections… *directly to disaster.* Hastings, *Bomber Command,* p.275

Harris and Spaatz's opposition... defend French rail targets. Stephen Darlow, *D-Day Bombers: The Veterans' Story* (2004), pp.50-54; Oliver Clutton-Brock, *Footprints on the Sands of Time: RAF Bomber Command Prisoners-of-War in Germany, 1939-45* (2003), pp.123-124

Harris believed... *general industrial recovery*." Finnegan, *General Eisenhower's Battle for Control of the Strategic Bombers in Support of Operation Overlord*, p.28
Two days later... *non-fulfilment would entail*." Stephen Darlow, *D-Day Bombers: The Veterans' Story* (2004), p.54

Not only did Eisenhower... request was rebuffed. Ambrose, *Eisenhower*, p.126; Overy, *Why The Allies Won*, pp.148-149; Eisenhower, *Allies*, p.447

The War Cabinet... contacted the State Department. Churchill, *The Second World War*, vol. V, p.466

Even Harris was forced... *setbacks so few*. Harris, *Bomber Offensive*, p.266

Spaatz finally conceded... Allied forces on D-Day. John Buckley (ed), *The Normandy Campaign 1944: Sixty Years On* (2006), p.150

Portal drafted a paper... additional tasks on the bomber force. Pogue, *United States Army in World War II*, p.124; Orange, *Tedder*, p.255

The draft was submitted... *the Overlord lodgement area*. Pogue, *United States Army in World War II*, pp.124-125; Peter Gray, *The Leadership, Direction and Legitimacy of the RAF Bomber Offensive from Inception to 1945* (2012), p.219; Adrian R. Lewis, *Omaha Beach: A Flawed Victory* (2001), p.216; Zuckerman, *From Apes to Warlords*, p.245

The debate over French civilian... 160,000 casualties (25% fatal)). Allen Andrews, *The Air Marshals: The Air War in Western Europe* (1970), p.264; Levine, *The Strategic Bombing of Germany, 1940-1945*, p.131; Boog et al (eds), *Germany and the Second World War: Volume 7*, p.136

Churchill believed... *more to Russia than we would wish*." Gilbert, *D-Day*, p.86; Claudia Baldoli and Andrew Knapp, *Forgotten Blitzes: France and Italy Under Allied Air Attack, 1940-45* (2012), p.36

Koenig... observed that "*this is war... to be rid of the Germans*." Daniel K. R. Crosswell, *Beetle: The Life of General Walter Bedell Smith* (2010), p.602

Prof. Zuckerman unpicked... civilian fatalities did not exceed 10,000. Zuckerman, *From Apes to Warlords*, pp.248-247 and p.252; CAB 69/6/3 DO (44) 9th Meeting, Minutes of the Meeting held in the Defence Map Room on 3rd May 1944 at 10:30pm

As he informed Stalin... *fortieth, or fiftieth day*." David M. Kennedy, *The American People in World War II: Freedom from Fear, Part Two* (1999), p.269

He raised this anxiety again... *Hitler and the Nazi regime.* Gilbert, *Winston S. Churchill,* vol. VII, pp.533-534

On 7th May... Churchill wrote... *not be produced by other methods...* Roosevelt responded... *Allied forces of invasion.* Churchill, *The Second World War*, vol. V, pp.466-468

A total of 76,200 tons... had shrunk to 23%. Olivier Wieviorka, *Normandy: The Landings to the Liberation of Paris* (2008), p.128; Ambrose, *Eisenhower*, p.127; Alan J. Levine, *From the Normandy Beaches to the Baltic Sea: The Northwest Europe Campaign, 1944-45* (2000), p.46; Pogue, *United States Army in World War II*, p.132

On 13th June, Germany's Air Ministry... *present intensity.* Hinsley et al, *British Intelligence in the Second World War,* vol.3, part 2, p.115

Three weeks later, Rommel... *air and artillery support.* The Impact of Allied Air Interdiction on German Strategy for Normandy. Sabre Measures (Bravo). United States Air Force, Assistant Chief of Staff, Studies and Analysis, August 1969, pp. 15-16 (available at www.dtic.mil/dtic/tr/fulltext/u2/859421.pdf)

Field Marshal von Rundstedt.... *than we had reckoned.* ibid, p.14

CHAPTER TWENTY-SIX

The country is now more concerned... the war like a debate. Hansard, HoC debate, 2 July 1942, vol.381, 528

Our fight with the Air Ministry... a waste of effort. Goette, Britain and the Delay in Closing the Mid-Atlantic 'Air Gap' during the Battle of the Atlantic, The Northern Mariner/Le Marin du Nord, XV, No 4, Oct 2005, p.33

Dönitz believed his u-boats... *achieve decisive success.* Adrian Fort, *Prof: The Life of Frederick Lindemann* (2003), p.273

In the first twelve months... in the Atlantic alone. Roskill, *The War at Sea, 1939-45,* Vol. I, pp.615-616; Boog et al (eds), *Germany and the Second World War: Volume 6*, p.368

In June 1942, Britain had... operational aircraft by August 1942. *Goette, Britain and the Delay in Closing the Mid-Atlantic 'Air Gap' during the Battle of the Atlantic,* The Northern Mariner/Le Marin du Nord, XV, No. 4, Oct 2005, p.26; Barnett, *Engage The Enemy More Closely,* p.481; David Owen, *Anti-Submarine Warfare: An Illustrated History* (2007), p.92; Martin Bowman, *Battlefield Bombers: Deep Sea Attack* (2014), p.71

On the same day... crossing the Atlantic. Bell, *Churchill and Sea Power,* p.258

Air Marshal Joubert... *sea communications.* Terraine, *The Right of the Line*, p.418

First Sea Lord Admiral Pound… *essential to us."* CAB 69/4/8 DO (42) (23), Air Requirements for the Successful Prosecution of the War at Sea, Memorandum by the First Sea Lord, 5th March 1942

Pound returned to the fray… Britain's island security. Bell, *Churchill and Sea Power,* p.263

Pound argued that… *"supreme urgency"* of the u-boat threat. CAB 79/21/30 DO (42) 47, The Bombing of Germany, 16th June 1942; CAB 80/63 COS (42) 171 (0), *The Bombing of Germany.* Memorandum by the First Sea Lord, 16th June 1942; Bell, *Churchill and Sea Power,* p.263

His 17th June note to Churchill… provided by America. See Chapter 25

Harris insisted that *the purely… menaces us - the submarine.* Hastings, *Bomber Command,* p.179; Bell, *Churchill and Sea Power,* p.263

When the First Lord… *now in progress."* Bell, *Churchill and Sea Power,* p.267

When Admiral Pound… *resources of the RAF."* ibid, p.267

Churchill outlined his view… *be strongly resisted.* ibid, p.268

On 17th September… Coastal Command's meagre resources. ibid, p.268

By mid-1942, Britain was producing… 2,184 throughout 1943. Gavin J. Bailey, *Arsenal of Democracy* (2013), p.253; Nolan, *Willow Run and the Arsenal of Democracy,* Detroit News, 28th January 1997; 8th Air Force News, Journal of the Eighth Air Force History Society, vol.20, 1994, p.20

In 1940, they sank 2.19m tons… in all theatres (585 ships). Roskill, *The War at Sea, 1939-45,* Vol. I, p.616 and Vol. II, p.485

Dönitz attended the 14th May conference… *decide the outcome of the war.* Clay Blair, *Hitler's U-Boat War: The Hunters 1939-1942* (2000), p.564

To achieve these goals… French and Belgian sources. ibid, p.564

Throughout 1942… signals for a full year. *Goette, Britain and the Delay in Closing the Mid-Atlantic 'Air Gap' during the Battle of the Atlantic,* The Northern Mariner/Le Marin du Nord, XV, No. 4, Oct 2005, p.36; Edwin P. Hoyt, *The U-Boat Wars* (2002), p.208; Phillips Payson O'Brien, *How the War Was Won: Air-Sea Power and Allied Victory in World War II* (2015), p.252

Monthly tonnage losses… 729,000 tons in November. Roskill, *The War at Sea, 1939-45,* Vol. II, p.485

Dönitz who believed that… Allied shipping every month. Stoler, *Allies in War,* p.106

Britain imported 61m tons… decline to 17m tons. Orange, Slessor: Bomber Champion, p.104; Bell, *Churchill and Sea Power*, p.275

In July 1942, the War Cabinet… import requirement for 1943. *Barnett, The Partnership Between Canada and Britain in Winning the Battle of the Atlantic,* Canadian Military History, vol.13, No. 4, Autumn 2004, p.5

50% of the raw materials… than imports. Barnett, *Engage The Enemy More Closely*, p.476

The Royal Navy… two months of oil supplies. Daniel Yergin, *The Prize: The Epic Quest for Oil, Money & Power* (2008), p.358

In July 1942… *their full fruition first.*" Bell, *Churchill and Sea Power*, p.265

As late as 24th October… *first place in our air effort.*" *Goette, Britain and the Delay in Closing the Mid-Atlantic 'Air Gap' during the Battle of the Atlantic,* The Northern Mariner/Le Marin du Nord, XV, No 4, Oct 2005, p.32

The October shipping figures… Ministries and headquarters. ibid, pp.32-33

First Lord of the Admiralty… *needed to cover this area.* ibid, p.33

Air Marshal Joubert confirmed… plug the Mid-Atlantic Gap. ibid, p.33

The next two meetings… for deployment in the Atlantic. ibid, pp.33-34

Churchill, Roosevelt and the Combined Chiefs… VLR status on arrival. See Chapter 15; ibid, p.36

Converting the Mk3A Liberators… until February 1943. ibid, pp.35-36

Coastal Command still only had 20… a total force of 34. ibid, p.37

Early March must be considered… would again be breached. *Barnett, The Partnership Between Canada and Britain in Winning the Battle of the Atlantic,* Canadian Military History, vol.13, No. 4, Autumn 2004, p.37; Dönitz, *Memoirs Ten Years and Twenty Days,* p.329; Jurgen Rohwer, *Critical Convoy Battles of WWII: Crisis in the North Atlantic, March 1943* (2015), p.206

Allied shipping losses... destroyed during May. Terraine, *Business in Great Waters*, p.768

On 22nd May, Dönitz scolded… *waging of the war. Barnett, The Partnership Between Canada and Britain in Winning the Battle of the Atlantic,* Canadian Military History, vol.13, No. 4, Autumn 2004, p.18

Two days later - Dönitz… *endangered by aircraft.*" Morison, *History of United States Naval Operations in World War II*, p.108

The predators returned… withdrawal from the theatre. Barnett, *Engage the Enemy More Closely*, p. 802; Terraine, *Business in Great Waters*, p.768

The deployment of VLR Liberators… *against the u-boat." Goette, Britain and the Delay in Closing the Mid-Atlantic 'Air Gap' during the Battle of the Atlantic,* The Northern Mariner/Le Marin du Nord, XV, No 4, Oct 2005, pp.40-41

In November 1942, Air Marshal Joubert… operating in the central Atlantic. *Goette, Britain and the Delay in Closing the Mid-Atlantic 'Air Gap' during the Battle of the Atlantic,* The Northern Mariner/Le Marin du Nord, XV, No. 4, Oct 2005, p.33; *Barnett, The Partnership Between Canada and Britain in Winning the Battle of the Atlantic,* Canadian Military History, vol.13, No. 4, Autumn 2004, p.41

Another stricken u-boat… cipher in December. Ian Hawkins (ed), *Destroyer: An Anthology of First-hand Accounts of the War at Sea, 1939-1945* (2006), p.524

CHAPTER TWENTY-SEVEN

Singapore must be redeemed... the peace table. Churchill, *The Second World War*, vol. VI, pp.129-130

The [politicians'] attitude… rubber trees. Bell, *Churchill and Sea Power*, p.299

Brooke outlined his thinking... *more protracted.* Barnett, *Engage The Enemy More Closely*, p.874

The shame of 1941/42… *reputation had suffered.* Parkinson, *A Day's March Nearer Home*, p.272

General Ismay… *prestige in this region.* Gilbert, *Winston S. Churchill, vol.VII*, p.834; Churchill, *The Second World War*, vol. VI, p.146. The above quote is a composite of two minutes for COS via Ismay on 24th June and 12th September 1944.

Imperial resurrection off the back… *especially oil.* Ehrman, *History of the Second World War*, vol. V, p.442

Churchill first became… after his return. Ehrman, *History of the Second World War*, vol. V, pp.426-427; Churchill, *The Second World War*, vol. V, pp.504-505

On 24th January… across the Malacca Straits. Churchill, *The Second World War*, vol. V, pp.505

Churchill drafted a paper... *Suez Canal and Red Sea."…* Having enumerated the Pacific… *before them in the Pacific…* Churchill was determined… against the Chiefs. Ehrman, *History of the Second World War*, vol. V, pp.441-444

Brooke particularly detested… *the Chiefs of Staff Committee."* Alanbrooke, *War Diaries, 1939-1945*, p.528

Churchill's Chief of Staff was alert... *for implementing it."* Ehrman, *History of the Second World War*, vol. V, p.448-449

COS produced a 6th March paper... *put forward our case.* ibid, pp.445-446

COS further insisted that both... *high rate of building."* ibid, p.447

Churchill ramped up the pressure... *as soon as possible.* Churchill, *The Second World War*, vol. V, pp.511-512; Ismay, *The Memoirs of General the Lord Ismay*, p.400; Fraser, *Alanbrooke*, p.385

Churchill presented these rulings... joint approaches to the Americans. Churchill, *The Second World War*, vol. V, p.512

Brooke later diarising... *accept his solution."* Alanbrooke, *War Diaries, 1939-1945*, p.533

While COS was considering... *South East Asia Command.* Ehrman, *History of the Second World War. Grand Strategy*, vol. V Aug 1943-Sept 1944, p.452

Even as COS was pondering resignation... *greater military advantages."* Bryant, Triumph in the West 1943-1946, pp.169-171

Churchill had earlier declared... *air link to China."* Churchill, *The Second World War*, vol. IV, p.702; Tim Moreman, *The Jungle, Japanese and the British Commonwealth Armies at War, 1941-45* (2005), p.141; Graham Dunlop, *Military Economics, Culture and Logistics in the Burma Campaign, 1942-1945* (2016), p.159

Mountbatten was ordered... assault on Yangon/Rangoon). Ehrman, *History of the Second World War*, vol. V, p.517; Frank McLynn, *The Burma Campaign: Disaster into Triumph 1942-45* (2011), p.366

Churchill finally accepted... the first half of 1945. Ponting, *Churchill*, p.635; Barnett, *Engage The Enemy More Closely*, p.876

CHAPTER TWENTY-EIGHT

Mindful of our difficulties... if Bengal itself went short. Mukherjee, *Hungry Bengal*, p. 93

A dull Cabinet.... ships to bring food to India. Wavell, *Wavell: The Viceroy's Journal*, p.123

Churchill's stock was low... Commons on 29th January. Knight, *Churchill: The Greatest Briton Unmasked*, p.161

On 19th February... and Leader of the House. Chris Wrigley, *Winston Churchill: A Biographical Companion* (2002), p.143; Devendra Panigrahi, *India's Partition*, p.191

On 11th March, Roosevelt… British and Indian representatives. Bhim Sen Singh, *The Cripps Mission: A Handiwork of British Imperialism* (1979), p.65

American strategy, Labour anti-colonialism… on 11th March 1942. Ishita Banerjee-Dube, *A History Of Modern India* (2015), p.391

The Declaration proposed *"to lay... future freedom of India.* Panigrahi, *India's Partition,* pp.198-199

He'd been corresponding with… Cripps' 1939 visit to India. Auriol Weigold, *Churchill, Roosevelt and India: Propaganda During World War II* (2008), p.43; Benjamin Zachariah, *Nehru* (2005), p.95; Peter Clarke, *The Cripps Version: The Life of Sir Stafford Cripps, 1889-1952* (2003) p.133

Cripps landed in Delhi on 23rd March… Mahasabha, Sikhs, Depressed Classes, Liberals etc). G.S. Chhabra, *Advance Study in the History of Modern India, Vol. 3 1920-1947* (2005), p.138; Glendevon, *The Viceroy at Bay,* p.229; Rizvi, *Linlithgow and India,* p.185

The immediate outcome… *and of the United Nations.* Mansergh, *The Transfer of Power 1942-47,* vol. 1, Document 456, pp.565-566

By 8th April, the outlines of… India's Government had been agreed. Rizvi, *Linlithgow and India, p.194;* Peter Clarke, *The Cripps Version: The Life of Sir Stafford Cripps, 1889-1952 (*2003), pp.314-315

Under the Cripps-Johnson formula… the two Ministries working collaboratively. Rizvi, *Linlithgow and India, p.194;* B.N. Pandey (ed), *The Indian Nationalist Movement 1885-1947: Select Documents* (1979), pp.140-141

At this point, the Executive Council… Council decisions at will. Glendevon, *The Viceroy at Bay,* p.16; Wavell, *Wavell: The Viceroy's Journal*, p.30; Rizvi, *Linlithgow and India, p.169.* Wavell suggests that the Executive Council consisted of ten Indian and four British members, Rizvi suggests eight Indian and four British.

Under the Cripps-Johnson-Congress formula… Indian political aspirations. Glendevon, *The Viceroy at Bay,* pp.231-232; Gowher Rizvi, *Linlithgow and India,* pp.198-201

The crisis conditions of spring 1942… *change the conventions of the constitution.*" Panigrahi, *India's Partition,* p.207

He therefore asked Churchill… *Indian political leaders on this point.* Mansergh, *The Transfer of Power 1942-47,* vol. 1, Document 538, p.663

Following a hard day's discussion… President for Johnson's assistance. Mansergh, *The Transfer of Power 1942-47,* vol. 1, Document 556, p.697

However, in the early afternoon… *make the position clear.* Mansergh, *The Transfer of Power 1942-47,* vol. 1, Document 570, p.709

Cripps should have responded… *no major change in the constitution.* R.J. Moore, *Churchill, Cripps, and India, 1939-1945* (1979), p.115

Congress finally rejected the Cripps Offer… *the Viceroy's sole discretion.* Mansergh, *The Transfer of Power 1942-47,* vol. 1, Document 587, pp.726-730

At 10:30am on Thursday 9th April… 'Roosevelt connection' for his own ends. R.J. Moore, *Churchill, Cripps, and India, 1939-1945* (1979), p.116; Ponting, *Churchill,* p.697; Auriol Weigold, *Churchill Roosevelt and India: Propaganda During World War II* (2008), p.88

[Churchill] immediately advised Cripps… *US intervention or mediation.* Mansergh, *The Transfer of Power 1942-47,* vol. 1, Document 564, p.704

That same afternoon, the War Cabinet… *as are agreed to be put forward."* Mansergh, *The Transfer of Power 1942-47,* vol. 1, Document 567, pp.707-708

Churchill informed Cripps… *a convention which would restrict them.* Mansergh, *The Transfer of Power 1942-47,* vol. 1, Document 582, pp.721-722

Repudiated by Congress… he exited India on 12th April. Panigrahi, *India's Partition,* p.215

When Congress launched… the war was safely won. Anya Schiffrin (Ed), *Global Muckraking: 100 Years of Investigative Journalism from Around the World* (2014), p.82

On 3rd September, Viceroy Linlithgow declared… consulting a single Indian voice. Daniel Todman, *Britain's War: Into Battle, 1937-1941* (2016) p.231

India provided Britain with… 'democracy' denied to India. Francis Pike, *Hirohito's War: The Pacific War, 1941-1945* (2017), p.712

The General Index of Wholesale… and March 1946. Rajkumar A. Waingade, *A Historical Analysis of Inflation in India 1935 to 2005* (PhD thesis, Shivaji University, 2010), p.72

Before the war, India had imported… coming from Myanmar. Mansergh, *The Transfer of Power 1942-47,* vol. 4, Document 367, pp.709-710; Jackson, *The British Empire and the Second World War,* p.360

Britain enforced a 'denial policy'… 46,000 small boats. Michael Schwartz et al (eds), *Ethics in the Global South* (2017), pp.43-44; Asok Mitra, *Towards Independence, 1940-1947: Memoirs of an Indian Civil Servant* (1991), p.105

The Raj now decided that India… Sri Lanka and Arabia. Mukerjee, *Churchill's Secret War*, p.106

In 1940/41, India had imported… 361,00 tons in 1941/42. Mansergh, *The Transfer of Power 1942-47,* vol. 4, Document 367, pp.709-710

In the 1930s, 61% of all Indians… or 'very badly nourished'. Mukerjee, *Churchill's Secret War*, p.53

Even nature appeared to… want by June. Herman, *Gandhi & Churchill,* p.512; Suresh G. Borkar, *History of Plant Pathology* (2017), pp.141-143

Meanwhile, in Kolkata… *is exceptionally prevalent.* Mukherjee, *Hungry Bengal*, p.126

Anticipating a 1.29m ton grain… memo to the War Cabinet. Mansergh, *The Transfer of Power 1942-47,* vol. 4, Document 38, pp.75-77; CAB 66/39 WP (43) 349 India's Requirements of Imported Food Grains, 31 July 1943

Amery opened the meeting… *would seriously impair India's war effort."* Mansergh, *The Transfer of Power 1942-47,* vol. 4, Document 71, pp.155-158

The War Cabinet rejected Amery's pleas… Sri Lanka *"to await instructions there."* ibid, pp.155-158

Describing a scene in west Bengal… *dead bodies you will see will be numerous.* Mukherjee, *Hungry Bengal*, p.131

The Chiefs of Staff were fully aware… *by the wayside of starvation.* Mansergh, *The Transfer of Power 1942-47,* vol. 4, Document 119, pp.270-273

On 22nd September… *faced this present autumn."* Mansergh, *The Transfer of Power 1942-47,* vol. 4, Document 132, pp.303-306

The second Cabinet opened with Amery insisting… *remedy the long-term situation by internal measures in India."* CAB 65/35 WM (43) 131 Conclusions of War Cabinet meeting held in PM's Room in House of Commons, 3pm on 24 September 1943

Amery nevertheless doubted… *responsibility in this country [emphasis added].* Amery, *The Empire at Bay*, p.943

Wavell recorded that the PM… *reduce stocks in this country [emphasis added].* Wavell, *Wavell: The Viceroy's Journal,* p.19

Two weeks later… *capturing this one island.* Alanbrooke, War Diaries, 1939-1945, pp.458-459

The 24th September War Cabinet… *should be done"* CAB 65/35 WM (43) 131 Conclusions of War Cabinet meeting held in PM's Room in House of Commons, 3pm on 24 September 1943; Amery, *The Empire at Bay*, p.943

Throughout 1943, Britain… its immediate requirements. Mukerjee, *Churchill's Secret War*, p.209

Britain's Government retained this food… sugar, under tarpaulins ibid, p.209

Almost seventeen million tons… 'glut' by the end of the year. Lance E. Davis and Stanley L. Engerman, *Naval Blockades in Peace and War: An Economic History since 1750* (2006), p.311; Overy (Ed), *The Oxford Illustrated History of World War Two*, p.151

Within this context, the Cabinet's rejection… is perplexing. CAB 65/36 WM (43) 152 Conclusions of War Cabinet meeting at 10 Downing St, 6pm, 10th November 1943

Liberated Italy - with its smaller… eradicate the disease among Italian civilians. Flint, *The Development of British Civil Affairs* (Cranfield University Doctoral Thesis, 2008), pp.154 -155

The United Nations Relief and Rehabilitation… *exposure among these peoples."* M. Srinivas Chary, *The Eagle and the Peacock: U.S. Foreign Policy Toward India Since Independence* (1995), p.23

Italy - which cannily switched sides… industrial and agricultural equipment. William I. Hitchcock, *The Bitter Road to Freedom: A New History of the Liberation of Europe* (2008), p.234

By spring 1945, Allied forces… 2m Italian mothers and children. Flint, *The Development of British Civil Affairs* (Cranfield University Doctoral Thesis, 2008), p.154

UNRRA - with its 4,000 staff… Italy's government assumed the role. William I. Hitchcock, *The Bitter Road to Freedom: A New History of the Liberation of Europe* (2008), p.234

Mundt tabled an amendment… *available through the UNRRA* M. Srinivas Chary, *The Eagle and the Peacock: U.S. Foreign Policy Toward India Since Independence* (1995), pp.24-25

The 19th February War Cabinet… this policy would continue. Mansergh, *The Transfer of Power 1942-47*, vol. 4, Document 391, p.744

[India] provided $30m support to UNRRA. Mukerjee, *Churchill's Secret War*, p.208

CHAPTER TWENTY-NINE

British policy... is essentially today... free and independent states. Jones, *Britain, the United States and the Mediterranean War, 1942-44,* P.123

I asked him... we undertook it. Russell Frank Weigley, *The American Way of War: A History of United States Military Strategy and Policy* (1973), p.333

The Singapore surrender formed... *he said sadly.* Moran, *Churchill,* p.27

Tobruk's capitulation... *disgrace is another.* Conrad Black, *Franklin Delano Roosevelt: Champion of Freedom* (2003), p.747

General Brooke was well-placed... *power of leadership.* Alanbrooke, *War Diaries, 1939- 1945,* p.243

This was the product... *in any way.* Alan Allport, *Browned Off and Bloody-minded: The British Soldier Goes to War, 1939-1945* (2015), pp.102-103

It also resulted... *three fighting services.* Alanbrooke, *War Diaries, 1939-1945,* pp.188-89

Sir Alexander Cadogan... *Bobby Jones over 36 holes.* ibid, p.259

Sir James Grigg was even more... *wins the war.* Alan Allport, *Browned Off and Bloody-minded: The British Soldier Goes to War, 1939-1945* (2015), p.102

Portal confirmed... *their capacity.* Roberts, *Masters and Commanders,* p.149

The shadows of Ypres... *all that implies.* AIR 14/3507, Harris to Churchill, 17th June 1942

Churchill, Brooke and Ismay... *a cast-iron certainty."* Ismay, *The Memoirs of General the Lord Ismay,* p.250; Roberts, *Masters and Commanders,* p.158

[Churchill's] description... *bloody rags.* Churchill, *The World Crisis, 1911-1918,* pp.446-47

Such experience informed... *time or reflection.* Churchill, *The Second World War,* vol. V, p.514

Churchill confirmed... suspicions were well-founded. Gilbert, *Churchill and America,* p.299

Andrew Roberts' bizarre contention... *since Nelson's day."* Roberts, *Masters and Commanders,* p.359

The Americans urged *"decisive military operations... not the enemy's"* World War Two Inter-Allied Conferences. Quadrant Conference, 1943. Papers and Minutes of Meetings (Joint History Office, Washington DC, 2003), pp.72-83.

This is appalling terrain… *demolitions on the widest possible scale.* Montgomery, *The Memoirs of Field Marshal Montgomery, pp.*175-177; Montgomery, *El Alamein To The River Sangro,* pp.103-104 and p.113

Brooke visited Italy in December… *hold up an army for a day.* Roberts, *Masters and Commanders*, p.463

A Soviet advance into regions… *India, Burma and all countries east of Suez."* CAB 81/41 PHP (43) 41 (Final), 13th December 1943, British Strategic Needs in the Levant States, inc. Appendix B 'Oil in the Middle East'; CAB 119/65 JP (42) 1025, 20th December 1942, Post-War Strategic Requirements in the Mediterranean Basin (4th Draft)

Eden lobbied hard… twenty percent to seal the deal. Marietta Stankova, *Bulgaria in British Foreign Policy, 1943-49* (2014), pp.83-86.

Men such as War Secretary Stimson… *Soviet advance into these regions.* Eisenhower, *Eisenhower: At War, 1943-45,* p.21 This is David Eisenhower's summary of a 4th Jan 1943 paper drafted by Gen. Stanley Embick for Gen. Marshall analysing British strategy ahead of the Casablanca Conference. The original document has been requested from US National Archives.

CHAPTER THIRTY

He knows no details… throughout this war! Alanbrooke, *War Diaries, 1939-1945,* p.590

Churchill is the greatest… the same time. Harriman, *Special Envoy to Churchill and Stalin, 1941- 1946,* p.216

Harris acknowledged… *initial experiment."* Andrew Knapp and Hilary Footitt (eds), *Liberal Democracies at War: Conflict and Representation* (2013), p.56

Throughout June-August… *United States troops will be drawn.* Kimball, Churchill and Roosevelt: The Complete Correspondence, vol.3, p.228

Churchill also argued… influence events in Normandy. Eisenhower, *Eisenhower,* p.317; Eisenhower, *Crusade in Europe,* p.283; Conrad Black, *Franklin Delano Roosevelt: Champion of Freedom* (2003), p.953-955

Churchill was outraged… *towards Trieste."* Jones, *Britain, the United States and the Mediterranean War, 1942-44,* pp.182-184

Britain had ceded… *command in the Mediterranean."* ibid, p.179

Marseille and Toulon were liberated… 40% of all Allied supplies… Marseille and Toulon. Steven J. Zaloga, *Atlas of the European Campaign: 1944-45* (2018), p.130; Norman Polmar and Thomas B. Allen, *World War II: The*

Encyclopedia of the War Years, 1941-1945 (2012), p.40; Porch, *Hitler's Mediterranean Gamble*, p.664; Hastings, *Finest Years*, p.482

Allied troops entered… Dijon on 11th September. Reynolds, From World War to Cold War, p.130; O'Neill and Collier, *World War II*, p.58

Charles Masterman… *rhetorical machinery.* Blake and Louis (eds), *Churchill*, p.508

Menzies… Churchill's "*real tyrant… facts have to give way.*" Gilbert, *Winston S. Churchill, vol. VI*, p.1018;

Jan Smuts praised Churchill's imagination… *intransigent facts of reality."* Cannadine, *In Churchill's Shadow*, p.94

Churchill diagnosed… *my facts to my phrases."* D'Este, *Warlord*, p.83

CODA

For centuries… Pacific Empire. Templewood, *Ambassador on Special Mission*, p.27

There are always… His Majesty's Empire. Pendar, *Adventure in Diplomacy*, p.157

INDEX